THE ROUGH GUIDE TO

Southwest USA

written and researched by

Greg Ward

roughguides.com

Contents

INTRODUCTION 4

Where to go	4	Things not to miss	14
When to go	10	Itineraries	24

BASICS 26

Getting there	27	Festivals and events	35
Getting around	29	The great outdoors	36
Health	31	Travelling in Indian country	38
Accommodation	33	Travel essentials	40
Food and drink	34		

THE GUIDE 44

1 The Four Corners	44	5 Flagstaff and central Arizona	250
2 Santa Fe and northern New Mexico	102	6 The Grand Canyon	292
3 Albuquerque and southern New Mexico	162	7 Southern Utah	338
4 Phoenix and southern Arizona	200	8 Las Vegas	436

CONTEXTS 458

History	459	Books	486
The Hopi	476	Glossary	489
The Navajo and the Apache	480		

SMALL PRINT & INDEX 490

OPPOSITE HIKER AT TOROWEAP OVERLOOK **PREVIOUS PAGE** COUPLE MOUNTAIN BIKING ON MOAB SLICK ROCK TRAIL, UTAH

Introduction to

Southwest USA

The Southwest is the most extraordinary and spectacular region of the United States. The splendour and scale of its scenery consistently defies belief – a glorious panoply of cliffs and canyons, buttes and mesas, carved from rocks of every imaginable colour, and enriched here by groves of shimmering cottonwoods and aspens, there by cactuses and agaves. In addition, the Southwest is unique in being the only part of the United States whose original inhabitants remain in residence. Though century after century has brought fresh waves of intruders, none has entirely succeeded in displacing its predecessors, leaving the various groups to coexist in an intriguing blend of cultures and traditions.

The area covered by this book roughly corresponds to the former Spanish colony of **New Mexico**, which has only belonged to the US since 1847, and is now divided between the modern states of New Mexico, Arizona, Utah, Colorado and Nevada. Though rainfall is scarce everywhere, it's not all **desert**; indeed, the popular image of the Southwest as consisting of scrubby hillsides studded with many-armed saguaro cactuses is true only of the Sonoran Desert of southern Arizona. Towering snow-capped **mountains** rise not only in southern Colorado and northern New Mexico, at the tail-end of the Rockies, but are scattered across Utah and Arizona as well, while dense **pine forests** cloak much of northern Arizona.

Where to go

The most dramatic landscapes lie on the **Colorado Plateau**, an arid mile-high tableland, roughly the size of California, which extends across the **Four Corners** region of Arizona, Utah, Colorado and New Mexico. Atop the main body of the plateau, further layers of rock are piled level upon level, creating a "**Grand Staircase**" of successive cliffs and

ABOVE TAOS PUEBLO POW WOW **OPPOSITE** ANTELOPE CANYON

plateaus. During the last dozen or so million years, the entire complex has been pushed steadily upwards by subterranean forces. As it has risen, the earth has cracked, warped, buckled and split, and endless quantities of crumbling sandstone have been washed away by the Colorado River and its tributaries. The **Grand Canyon** is simply the most famous of hundreds of dramatic **canyons**, and can seem too vast for the human mind to comprehend. No one, however, could fail to be overwhelmed by the sheer weirdness of **southern Utah** – the red rocks of **Monument Valley**, the fiery sandstone pinnacles of **Bryce Canyon**, the endless expanses of **Canyonlands**.

Reminders of the Southwest's remarkable **history** are everywhere you look. Ancient archeological sites abound, ranging from the free-standing pueblos of Chaco Canyon and the cliff dwellings of Mesa Verde to the hollowed-out caves of Bandelier and the haunting rock art of Horseshoe Canyon. The region now holds fifty distinct Native American reservations, ranging from tiny **pueblo** villages in New Mexico to the huge "**Navajo Nation**", the largest reservation in the country, which covers 27,000 square miles and takes up much of the Colorado Plateau. Unlike elsewhere in the US, where Native Americans were forcibly displaced onto poorer lands with which they lack any spiritual connection, most Southwestern tribes continue to occupy the homelands of their ancestors.

The **Spanish** too have been in the region for almost five hundred years; exquisite eighteenth-century missions survive at San Xavier and Tumacácori in southern Arizona, while northern New Mexico holds stunning adobe churches such as San Francisco de Asis at Taos, and the humbler but still ravishing shrine at Chimayó. Next to arrive after the Spaniards were the **Mormons**, who through utter determination and communal effort colonized Utah in the nineteenth century. **American** settlers arrived soon after, and swiftly outnumbered everyone else.

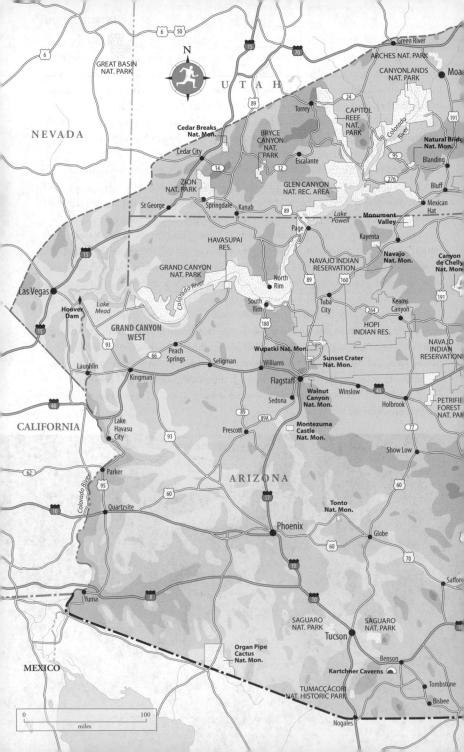

FACT FILE

• New Mexico – the fifth largest state – covers 121,355 square miles and holds a population of 2,085,538, ten percent of whom are of Native American descent. The state has 22 reservations, comprising 19 separate pueblos plus the Jicarilla and Mescalero Apache lands and part of the Navajo Nation. New Mexico became the 47th state on January 6, 1912; its capital is Santa Fe.

• Arizona, with an area of 113,635 square miles, is the sixth largest state. Around five percent of its 6,553,255 population are of native American descent. Its 21 Indian reservations include the homelands of the Navajo, the Hopi, the Havasupai, the Hualapai, the O'odham, and the San Carlos, Tonto, and White Mountain Apache. With Phoenix as its capital, it achieved statehood in 1912, as the last of the "lower 48."

• Although Utah as a whole comprises 82,144 square miles – 65 percent of which is owned by the federal government – and has a population of 2,855,287 (of which over 60 percent are Mormons), this guide only covers the desert areas in the south of the state, where around 175,000 people are spread across 27,000 square miles. It became the 45th state in 1896.

• The portion of southwest Colorado described in this guide represents about 5000 of the state's 103,730 square miles, and holds around two percent of its total population of 5,187,582. Colorado was the 38th state to join the Union in 1876.

In the early years of US rule, the Southwest was very much the **Wild West**. A sense of that era survives in towns like **Lincoln**, New Mexico, where Billy the Kid blazed his way out of jail, and **Tombstone**, Arizona, where the Earps and the Clantons fought it out at the OK Corral. The century since Utah, Arizona and New Mexico achieved statehood has seen the landscape transformed on an unprecedented – not to say unnatural, let alone unsustainable – scale. Monumental **water** projects, including the construction of the **Hoover Dam**, the damming of Utah's Glen Canyon to form **Lake Powell**, and the creation of a network of canals across hundreds of miles of the Arizona desert, have brought the region prosperity as the **Sunbelt**.

While the wilderness remains the supreme attraction for most visitors, certain Southwestern **cities** make worthwhile destinations. **Santa Fe** is the best example, with its four-hundred-year history, top-quality museums and galleries, and superb hotels and restaurants; **Tucson** holds an enjoyable combination of desert parks, Hispanic history, restaurants and ranch resorts; and **Las Vegas**, entirely and quintessentially a product of the modern era – it was only founded in 1905 – is far too amazing to miss. **Phoenix**, on the other hand, is one to avoid; it's possible to have a good time there, but you'd have to have a *very* long vacation before there'd be much point including it on your itinerary.

Though most of the region's **smaller towns** are best treated as overnight pit stops, some have blossomed into appealing bases for a few days' stay. **Moab** and **Springdale** make welcome exceptions to the typical monotony of southern Utah farming communities; the college town of **Flagstaff** is a lively enclave within easy reach of the Grand Canyon; and **Taos** still has the feel of the artists' colony that attracted Georgia O'Keeffe and D.H. Lawrence.

The only practicable way to explore the Southwest in any detail is to **drive** yourself around; public transport options are very limited (see p.29).

CLOCKWISE FROM TOP LEFT COW SKULLS, TUCSON; NAVAJO WOMAN, MONUMENT VALLEY; RISTRAS, ALBUQUERQUE; ADOBE FACADE, SANTA FE

ROUTE 66

If you do ever plan to motor west, there's still one definitive highway that's the best. Eighty-five years since it was first completed, seventy-five since John Steinbeck called it **"the mother road, the road of flight"** in *The Grapes of Wrath*, and sixty-six since songwriter Bobby Troup set it all down in rhyme, what better reason to visit the Southwest could there be than to get hip to this timely tip, and get your kicks on **Route 66**?

The heyday of Route 66 as the nation's premier cross-country route – winding from Chicago to LA – lasted barely twenty years, from its being paved in 1937 until it began to be superseded by freeways in 1957. It was officially rendered defunct in 1984, when Williams, Arizona, became the last town to be bypassed. Nonetheless, substantial stretches of the original Route 66 survive, complete with the motels and drive-ins that became icons of vernacular American architecture. Restored 1950s roadsters and the latest Harley-Davidsons alike flock to cruise along the atmospheric, neon-lit frontages of towns such as Albuquerque and Flagstaff, or through such empty desertscapes as those between Grants and Gallup in New Mexico, or Seligman and Kingman in Arizona.

When to go

Summer is the peak tourist season for most of the Southwest, even though temperatures in excess of 100°F render cities such as Phoenix and Tucson all but unbearable, and make it an ordeal even to get out of your car in many of the national parks. Hikers, bikers and rafters do better to come either between mid-September and late October, when the crowds are gone and dazzling autumn colours brighten the canyons, or in April and May, when wildflowers bloom in the desert.

RIGHT FROM TOP HUBBELL TRADING POST; HIKERS ON MESA ARCH, CANYONLANDS; STRATER HOTEL, DURANGO

Author picks

As well as the Four Corners, and plenty of other corners besides, our author has been exploring the highways, byways, nooks and crannies of the Southwest for the past 25 years. Here are some of his favourite experiences:

Hiking it easy You don't always have to tackle the longest and hardest trails; sometimes the shortest and most obvious ones are the best, as with the trail to Shoshone Point in the Grand Canyon (see p.306), or the Mesa Arch Trail in Canyonlands (see p.407).

Trading posts Here and there, the outposts where Yankee storekeepers traded with tribes like the Navajo during the nineteenth century have survived into the twenty-first, and make great places to buy crafts and souvenirs; prime specimens include Cameron Trading Post (see p.328) and Hubbell Trading Post (see p.64).

Slot canyons Ethereal, almost translucent, and often downright dangerous, these delicate hidden canyons attract daredevil devotees – try to see at least one, like Antelope Canyon (see p.394) or Peek-A-Boo Gulch (see p.379).

Long-lost ruins Far from the big-name national parks, the Southwest abounds in lesser-known and all the more atmospheric ancient sites, like Butler Wash Ruins in Utah (see p.430) and Puye Cliff Dwellings in New Mexico (see p.140).

Historic hotels Wild West relics that make memorable overnight halts include the *Strater* in Durango (see p.81), *La Fonda* in Santa Fe (see p.120) and Mary Jane Colter's extraordinary *La Posada* at Winslow (see p.261).

> Our author recommendations don't end here. We've flagged up our favourite places – a perfectly sited hotel, an atmospheric café, a special restaurant – throughout the guide, highlighted with the ★ symbol.

If your timings aren't flexible, however, don't worry. It's always possible to escape the heat – the thermometer drops by 3°F for every thousand feet above sea level, so Santa Fe, for example, is always relatively cool – and the summer is also peak period for the region's festivals (see p.35).

Winters can be seriously cold, and snowfalls close down certain areas altogether – don't reckon on seeing high-altitude destinations like Mesa Verde, for example, or the North Rim of the Grand Canyon, between October and April. Those parks that remain open are often at their most beautiful when frosted with snow, however – Bryce Canyon is quite magical – while ski resorts like Telluride and Taos are in full swing, and Tucson and Phoenix fill up with sun-seeking "snowbirds" from colder states. The major disadvantage of visiting in winter is that with significantly fewer hours of daylight, it's much harder to drive from your overnight base into a national park, do any great amount of touring or hiking, and then drive on to your next stop.

ROCK ART

The deserts of the Southwest abound in both **petroglyphs**, images scratched or chipped onto stone surfaces, and painted **pictographs**. At the single most remarkable site, Utah's **Great Gallery**, Archaic shamans daubed enigmatic, ghost-like figures onto remote canyon walls. Other locations include the "Newspaper Rocks" in Utah and Arizona, carvings in Monument Valley, and painted panels in Capitol Reef. The best-known motif in Ancestral Puebloan rock art, found throughout the Four Corners, is the "hunchback" flute-player **Kokopelli** (see p.114).

The rock art tradition continued into very recent times. Thus the Navajo depicted nineteenth-century Spanish raids on the sandstone walls of the Canyon de Chelly, while the Spaniards themselves added their own carvings to the remarkable Inscription Rock at El Morro.

AVERAGE TEMPERATURES AND RAINFALL

	Jan	Feb	Mar	Apr	May	Jun	Jul	Aug	Sep	Oct	Nov	Dec
GRAND CANYON (SOUTH RIM)												
Av high °F	41	45	51	60	70	81	84	82	76	65	52	43
Av low °F	18	21	25	32	39	47	54	53	47	36	27	20
Rainfall (in)	1.3	1.5	1.4	0.9	0.7	0.4	1.8	2.3	1.6	1.1	0.9	1.6
LAS VEGAS, NV												
Av high °F	56	67	68	77	87	98	104	101	94	81	66	57
Av low °F	33	37	42	49	59	68	75	73	65	53	41	33
Rainfall (in)	0.5	0.5	0.4	0.2	0.2	0.1	0.5	0.5	0.3	0.3	0.4	0.3
PHOENIX, AZ												
Av high °F	65	69	75	84	93	102	105	102	98	88	75	66
Av low °F	38	41	45	52	60	68	78	76	69	57	45	39
Rainfall (in)	0.8	0.8	0.8	0.5	0.3	0.3	0.7	0.9	0.6	0.6	0.6	0.8
SANTA FE, NM												
Av high °F	40	44	51	60	69	79	82	80	74	63	50	41
Av low °F	19	22	28	35	43	52	57	56	49	38	27	20
Rainfall (in)	0.6	0.8	0.8	0.9	1.2	1.1	2.4	2.3	1.7	1.1	0.7	0.7
ZION NATIONAL PARK, UT												
Av high °F	52	57	63	73	83	93	100	97	91	78	63	53
Av low °F	29	31	36	43	52	60	68	66	60	49	37	30
Rainfall (in)	1.6	1.6	1.7	1.3	0.7	0.6	0.8	1.6	0.8	1.0	1.2	1.5

ABOVE WOODPECKER ON A SAGUARO CACTUS

things not to miss

It's not possible to see everything that the Southwest has to offer in one trip – and we don't suggest you try. What follows is a selective taste of the region's highlights: spectacular national parks, unforgettable outdoor activities, Wild West towns and Las Vegas glitz. All entries have a page reference to take you straight into the Guide, where you can find out more.

1

1 CANYON DE CHELLY

Page 58
Perhaps the most beautiful canyon in the Southwest, rendered all the more magical by its magnificent Ancestral Puebloan ruins.

2 NATIVE AMERICAN CRAFTS

Page 38
From silver and turquoise jewellery to Hopi *kachinas* or fine Pueblo ceramics, the Southwest is renowned for its locally produced craft works and souvenirs.

3 LA FONDA DE SANTA FE

Page 120
Historic Western hotels don't come any more atmospheric than this beauty at the end of the Santa Fe Trail.

4 RIDE THE DURANGO & SILVERTON RAILROAD

Page 80
Taking a steam train up to the old Colorado mining town of Silverton is the perfect way to spend a day in the Rockies.

5 ÁCOMA PUEBLO
Page 99

The Acoma still occupy the mesa where Spaniards attacked them five centuries ago.

6 LAS VEGAS BUFFETS
Page 451

Las Vegas' all-you-can-eat buffets are great value; at some, the food itself is good too.

7 TOROWEAP POINT
Page 337

This unique Grand Canyon overlook, above a 3000-foot drop to the river, has an immediate visceral impact.

8 TOMBSTONE
Page 237

Tombstone loves to ham up its past, and it's great fun to visit.

9 SAGUARO NATIONAL PARK
Page 225

Saguaro cactuses spread in majestic abundance across the deserts of southern Arizona.

10 WHITE SANDS NATIONAL MONUMENT
Page 184

These knife-edge snow-white dunes are hidden away in lonely southern New Mexico.

11 MONUMENT VALLEY
Page 54

Your first real-life glimpse of the silhouetted buttes of Monument Valley is a guaranteed heart-stopping moment.

12 A MULE RIDE TO PHANTOM RANCH
Page 300

Generations of Grand Canyon visitors have entrusted their lives to these sure-footed beasts; the reward, a night beside the river.

13 LA POSADA
Page 261

This rambling, lovingly restored railroad hotel is an unexpected highlight on Route 66.

14 MESA VERDE
Page 74

If you've never understood all the fuss about "cliff dwellings", the ancient remains hidden in these Colorado canyons should make their appeal abundantly clear.

15 LINCOLN
Page 179

The scene of Billy the Kid's legendary exploits remains a lonesome frontier outpost.

16 TAOS PUEBLO
Page 151

The most famous modern pueblo is a dramatic sight beneath the Sangre de Cristo mountains.

17 ALBUQUERQUE INTERNATIONAL BALLOON FIESTA
Page 167

The early-morning mass ascents of hundreds of colourful hot-air balloons are an utterly breathtaking sight.

12

13

14

15

16

17

18 **SAN XAVIER DEL BAC MISSION**
Page 230

Churches throughout the Southwest bear witness to the region's Hispanic heritage, but none is more exquisite than the "White Dove of the Desert".

19 **LAS VEGAS AT NIGHT**
Page 442

The blazing neon along the Strip, with its volcanoes and pyramids, is an all-out assault on the senses.

20 **BRYCE CANYON**
Page 367

An unforgettable landscape, where the earth peels back to reveal a rainbow-hued forest of towering sandstone pinnacles.

21 **THE GREAT GALLERY**
Page 410

The most fascinating and mysterious ancient rock art in the Southwest, only accessible via a long desert hike.

22 **DELICATE ARCH**
Page 418

The trail up to Utah's symbol, an extraordinary free-standing natural arch, epitomizes the wonder of the state's wilderness parks.

23 **HAVASU FALLS**
Page 324

These lush turquoise waterfalls turn the Havasupai Reservation into an amazing Grand Canyon oasis.

24 **THE INTER-TRIBAL INDIAN CEREMONIAL**
Page 95
The classic Route 66 town of Gallup, New Mexico, comes alive in August for this annual Navajo fair.

25 **CIRQUE DU SOLEIL**
Page 455
Staging several of the finest shows the city has to offer, the Canadian circus troupe dominates Las Vegas' entertainment scene.

26 **ZION CANYON**
Page 350
Carved by the Virgin River into the red-rock hills of southern Utah, Zion makes the ideal escape from the mayhem of Las Vegas.

27 **CALF CREEK FALLS**
Page 381
Not far off the highway in the heart of southern Utah, this glorious two-part waterfall is the highlight of Grand Staircase-Escalante National Monument.

28 **RAFTING IN CANYONLANDS**
Page 424
Whether you choose a gentle float or a multi-day whitewater epic, Canyonlands National Park makes a fabulous destination for a raft trip.

29 **HIKING IN THE GRAND CANYON**
Page 309
Explore the innermost secrets of the Grand Canyon on one of its many superb hiking trails.

24

25

Itineraries

The Southwest is not really a place for quick visits. A week only gives time for a brief circuit, looping perhaps to Grand Canyon and Zion national parks from Las Vegas; through all Utah's national parks from Salt Lake City; or up to Santa Fe and Taos from Albuquerque. With two weeks, try to take in more of the Four Corners region and/or southern Utah. Only with three weeks or more is it really worth venturing into southern New Mexico and southern Arizona as well.

WESTERN WONDERS

Allow ten days or more to complete this grand route around the dramatic desertscape of the Colorado Plateau.

① Las Vegas Fly into Sin City to spend your first two nights – not a weekend, to avoid high room rates – savouring the sights, sounds and assorted flavours of the Strip. **See p.438**

② Zion Utah's most beautiful national park, a little over two hours' drive from Las Vegas, is a tranquil idyll, with superb hiking. **See p.350**

③ Bryce Canyon Quite the weirdest array of top-heavy, multi-coloured rock formations you're ever likely to see. **See p.367**

④ Capitol Reef Driving through the remote wilderness at the heart of southern Utah, a fresh bizarre desertscape unfolds at every turn in the road. This gorgeous oasis makes the perfect overnight base. **See p.384**

⑤ Moab A dynamic former mining town that's abuzz with adventurous types setting off each morning for yet more hiking and biking in Arches and Canyonlands parks. **See p.421**

⑥ Monument Valley Immense, glowing buttes and mesas, silhouetted against the desert sun, and familiar from a thousand Western movies. **See p.54**

⑦ South Rim, Grand Canyon Be sure to allow at least one full day on the South Rim, from sunrise to sunset, to appreciate the full majesty of this vast and varied chasm. **See p.299**

INDIAN COUNTRY

This loop through millennia of Southwest history takes a (very) good two weeks, heading beyond New Mexico into the deserts of the Four Corners, once the Ancestral Puebloan heartland and now home to the Navajo and Hopi.

① Albuquerque As well as its Route 66 frontage, New Mexico's largest city is home to the Pueblo Indian Cultural Center. **See p.164**

② Santa Fe After more than four centuries as a meeting place for different cultures, Santa Fe remains as fascinating as it is beautiful, with superb museums and galleries. **See p.104**

③ Taos A thriving arts centre, Taos is also renowned as the home of a spectacular, thousand-year-old pueblo. **See p.146**

④ Durango Take a day to venture into the snow-capped peaks of the Rockies, perhaps taking the steam train up to tiny, time-forgotten Silverton as well. **See p.80**

⑤ Mesa Verde Tucked into clifftop recesses, the Ancestral Puebloan "palaces" of Mesa Verde provide an extraordinary glimpse of life in North

ABOVE WUPATKI NATIONAL MONUMENT

America long before the Europeans knew the continent was there. **See p.74**

❻ Navajo National Monument Ranger-led hikes can take you up to, and into, a golden ancient community cradled beneath a colossal natural alcove. **See p.52**

❼ Hopi Mesas Descendants of the Ancestral Puebloans, the Hopi still live atop isolated mesas, far removed from modern Arizona. **See p.66**

❽ Canyon de Chelly Now home to a handful of Navajo sheep farmers, unsullied by paved roads, this glorious canyon holds magnificent rock formations as well as countless Ancestral Puebloan sites. **See p.58**

❾ Ácoma Pueblo The people of Ácoma fought off Spanish *conquistadores* in the sixteenth century, and remain in proud possession of "Sky City", a mesa-top settlement that also features a monumental mission church. **See p.99**

THE WILD WEST AND ROUTE 66

Take ten days to tour the cowboy-haunted frontier towns of southern Arizona and New Mexico, then motor west along Route 66 – or combine with the other itineraries here to make a three-week trip of a lifetime.

❶ Phoenix This sunbaked megalopolis of the New West is a convenient springboard for venturing into the region's past. **See p.202**

❷ Tucson With its saguaro cactuses and whitewashed mission churches, Tucson is a very likeable desert city. **See p.220**

❸ Tombstone Sawdust-floored saloons and daily gunfights at the OK Corral; what more could any Western fan want? **See p.237**

❹ Silver City Childhood home of the Kid himself, this mining town retains a nineteenth-century charm. **See p.196**

❺ White Sands Dazzling white dunes, hundreds of miles from the ocean. **See p.184**

❻ Lincoln The town where Billy the Kid blazed his way to fame has barely changed in a hundred years. **See p.179**

❼ Carlsbad Caverns Detour south to take in this eerie subterranean world – served with a side-order of Fifties' kitsch. **See p.188**

❽ Fort Sumner Billy the Kid lies buried where Pat Garrett gunned him down. **See p.177**

❾ Albuquerque Follow Route 66 west into the Albuquerque sunset; and you'll be rewarded with the glowing neon signs of its vintage motels and diners. **See p.164**

❿ Gallup Long a rendezvous for New Mexico's cowboys and Indians, Gallup oozes old-West atmosphere. **See p.94**

⓫ Winslow Stop off in this quintessential Route 66 town to stay in the splendid *La Posada* hotel – or simply stand on the corner. **See p.261**

⓬ Flagstaff As lively a Wild West town as you'll find anywhere on Route 66 – and a great base for the Grand Canyon, just north. **See p.262**

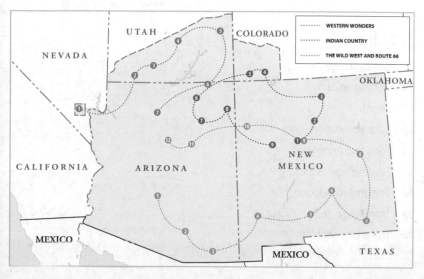

VINTAGE HOTEL SIGNS, LAS VEGAS

Basics

27 Getting there

29 Getting around

31 Health

33 Accommodation

34 Food and drink

35 Festivals and events

36 The great outdoors

38 Travelling in Indian country

40 Travel essentials

Getting there

For US and Canadian travellers who live too far from the Southwest simply to drive there, and for international travellers, the most cost-effective way to visit Southwest USA is to fly to one of three major cities covered in this book, rent a car, make a loop tour, and fly home from the same airport.

Las Vegas, Nevada, is probably the best bet, as it offers low air fares and rental-car rates, welcomes more direct flights from overseas than its rivals, and makes an exhilarating starting point for tours to the Grand Canyon and the national parks of southern Utah. **Phoenix**, Arizona, is equally well served by the major domestic carriers, and although Phoenix itself is a less appealing destination it's convenient for both the Grand Canyon and the deserts of southern Arizona. New Mexico's principal airport, in **Albuquerque**, receives fewer long-distance flights, but it's the obvious point of arrival if you want to see Santa Fe and Taos, and it's also the closest airport to the Four Corners region.

If Utah is your prime destination, you could also fly to Salt Lake City. Although the state capital lies in Utah's mountainous northwest corner, outside the area covered in this guide, it's little more than half a day's drive from lively Moab and national parks such as Canyonlands and Arches.

Flights from North America

Flights to the Southwest are at their most expensive in summer, which despite soaring temperatures is the peak season for travel. Prices drop from September to shortly before Christmas, and from March through May, and are cheapest from January to February. Flying on weekends, to Las Vegas in particular, can add a hefty premium to fares; price ranges quoted below assume midweek travel.

In general, the best bargains tend to be on flights to **Las Vegas**. It's usually possible to find round-trip fares to Las Vegas for little more than $100 from Los Angeles, $200 from Seattle, $350 from New York, and CAN$500 from Toronto. A round-trip from New York to **Phoenix** should cost from $300; the equivalent figure for Chicago might be $275, and for Los Angeles, less than $150. Sample fares from Montréal or Vancouver to Phoenix start from CAN$450. Fares to **Albuquerque** are similar, with a round-trip from New York costing upwards from $250; a round-trip to **Salt Lake City** may cost from $300 from New York, or from CAN$650 from Toronto. A good first

call is to contact **Southwest Airlines** (Ⓦsouthwest.com), which flies to Phoenix, Las Vegas, Tucson, Salt Lake City, and Albuquerque from around fifty other US cities. **JetBlue** (Ⓦjetblue.com) serves Phoenix, Las Vegas, and Salt Lake City, while **Westjet** (Ⓦwestjet.com) connects Albuquerque, Las Vegas, Phoenix and Tucson with various cities in Canada.

Commuter airlines like Skywest (Ⓦskywest.com), Great Lakes Airlines (Ⓦflygreatlakes.com), and Frontier Airlines (Ⓦflyfrontier.com) connect the Southwest's major airports with smaller communities in the region. Thus Phoenix has links with towns such as Durango, Farmington, Flagstaff, Page, Show Low, Tucson, and Yuma; Denver with several towns in the Four Corners region and beyond; and Salt Lake City is connected with airports in southern Utah such as St George. Las Vegas also has good connections, including direct flights to – and over – the Grand Canyon (see p.328).

Few of these flights are particularly suited to the needs of tourists, however. The cheapest fares tend to be on the scale of $75–150 for a one-way trip, and it's far easier to drive from place to place than to have to rent another car every few days. If you absolutely have to fly somewhere that only has a minor airport, your best bet is to fly to the Southwest with a specialist regional carrier that will also provide a connecting service to your ultimate destination for a small additional cost.

Flights from the UK and Ireland

Only two airlines offer direct, nonstop flights from Britain or Ireland to any of the cities covered in this book. **British Airways** (Ⓦba.com) flies from both London Gatwick and London Heathrow to Las Vegas, and to Phoenix from London Heathrow only. Virgin Atlantic (Ⓦvirgin-atlantic.com) flies to Las Vegas daily from London Gatwick, and once weekly from Manchester. Typical round-trip fares range from around £600 in winter up to £900 in summer.

Most other transatlantic carriers can get you to Phoenix, Las Vegas, or Albuquerque, with at least one stop en route, for significantly lower fares. From the UK, you can either fly nonstop to the West Coast and then double back toward the Southwest, or touch down on the East Coast and then fly west; time-wise, it makes little difference. If you'd rather keep your flying time to a minimum, it's also worth considering flying nonstop to California and driving to the Southwest from there, taking advantage of the state's low rental-car rates.

From Ireland, Aer Lingus (Ⓦaerlingus.com) flies from Dublin or Shannon to Boston, Chicago, New

York, and Orlando, and Delta (Ⓦdelta.com) from Dublin to Atlanta and New York, and Shannon to New York. Alternatively, you can fly to London and take your pick of transatlantic routes.

Packages

Packages can work out cheaper than arranging the same trip yourself, especially for a short-term stay. **Fly-drive** deals, which include cut-rate (sometimes free) car rental when you buy a transatlantic ticket from an airline or tour operator, are likely to be cheaper than renting on the spot, and give great value if you intend to do a lot of driving.

Several operators go one stage further and book accommodation for **self-drive tours**; some travellers consider having their itineraries planned and booked by experts to be a real boon. Schemes under which you buy pre-paid hotel vouchers in advance, and then have to seek out hotels that will accept them, tend to be more bother than they're worth, and seldom save any money.

Companies such as TrekAmerica (Ⓦtrekamerica .com) organize **camping tours** of the Southwest, usually starting in California or Las Vegas and circling through Utah's national parks and the Grand Canyon. Typical trips range in price – excluding flights – from £620 for a week in low season up to around £700 in mid-summer. TrekAmerica also offers some trips that use hotel accommodation, like the eighteen-night version of their "Westerner" tour, which starts at £1749.

Flights from Australia, New Zealand, and South Africa

There are no direct flights from Australia, New Zealand or South Africa to any of the Southwestern cities, so you'll have to fly to one of the main US gateway airports and pick up onward connections – or a rental car – from there.

The cheapest route from Australia and New Zealand, and the one with the most frequent services, is to Los Angeles, which also has plenty of onward flights to Albuquerque, Las Vegas, and Phoenix. Air New Zealand (Ⓦairnewzealand.com) and Qantas/American (Ⓦqantas.com.au) fly to LA at least twice daily, while United (Ⓦunited.com) flies once a day. From South Africa, by far the cheapest route is usually to fly with Virgin Atlantic (Ⓦvirgin -atlantic.com) from Johannesburg to London, and then from London to Las Vegas, which costs in the region of 13,000SAR.

Packages and tours

Package deals available to travellers in Australia and New Zealand range from fly-drive options to fully escorted bus tours and camping treks, and can work out significantly cheaper than making the same arrangements yourself; no-frills flight and car-rental packages, for example, can cost less than a flight alone. You can also add on whatever extra tours you choose; by way of example, Adventure World (Ⓦadventureworld.com.au) offers trips from LA like the two-week "Western Values" that starts at A\$1246, or the one-week "Western Trails" jaunt to the Grand Canyon, Zion, and Las Vegas for A\$876.

By train

Amtrak rail service to and within the Southwest is restricted to three completely separate east–west routes. Two pass through Arizona and New Mexico on the way to and from Los Angeles, while the other crosses northern Utah.

The daily **Southwest Chief** originates in Chicago and crosses from Colorado into northern New Mexico near Raton, passing close to Santa Fe (connected by a bus service from tiny Lamy) and through Albuquerque before heading west via Gallup, Flagstaff – where connecting buses run north to the Grand Canyon – and Williams, the home of the entirely distinct Grand Canyon Railway (see p.315). The thrice-weekly **Sunset Limited** from New Orleans reaches southern New Mexico via El Paso, Texas, then calls at Deming and Lordsburg, before hitting the Arizona towns of Benson, Tucson, Maricopa and Yuma. En route between Chicago and San Francisco, the daily **California Zephyr** calls at Green River in Utah, as well as Denver and Salt Lake City.

There is no rail service to Phoenix – the closest station is Maricopa, 35 miles south – or to Las Vegas, which is linked by bus with Barstow, California, on the Southwest Chief route.

For fares and schedules, visit Ⓦ amtrak.com.

By bus

If you're happy to sit on a bus for days on end, you can reach the Southwest using Greyhound, though these days it's no cheaper than flying. A one-way trip to Albuquerque from Los Angeles takes around nineteen hours and costs $99 if booked at least two weeks in advance, or $112.50 on the day of travel; the ride from Milwaukee to Phoenix takes up to 44 hours and costs $129 or $218, respectively; and the cross-country trek from New York to Las Vegas takes almost three days and costs $149 or $245.

For full details of routes, fares, and potential discounts, and to make reservations, visit Ⓦ grey hound.com.

AGENTS AND OPERATORS

North South Travel UK ☎ 01245 608291, Ⓦ northsouthtravel .co.uk. Friendly, competitive flight agency, offering discounted fares. Profits are used to support projects in the developing world.

STA Travel US ☎ 1800 781 4040, Ⓦ statravel.com; UK ☎ 0871 230 0040, Ⓦ statravel.co.uk; Australia ☎ 134 782, Ⓦ statravel.com.au; New Zealand ☎ 0800 474 400, Ⓦ statravel.co.nz; South Africa ☎ 0861 781 781, Ⓦ statravel.co.za. Worldwide specialists in low-cost flights for students and under-26s; other customers also welcome.

Trailfinders UK ☎ 020 7368 1200, Ⓦ trailfinders.com; Ireland ☎ 01 677 7888, Ⓦ trailfinders.ie. One of the best-informed and most efficient agents for independent travellers.

SOUTHWEST USA TOUR OPERATORS

Backroads ☎ 800 462 2848, Ⓦ backroads.com. Hiking and/or biking tours covering New Mexico, Arizona, and southern Utah. A five-night cycling trip to Zion and Bryce, staying in motels, costs around $2400; five nights' walking in New Mexico, again staying in motels, from $2800.

Canyonlands Field Institute ☎ 435 259 7750 or ☎ 800 860 5262, Ⓦ cfimoab.org. NPS-authorized adult and family wilderness expeditions, not exclusively in Canyonlands; from around $1800 for a five-night hike to remote Rainbow Bridge, $860 for a four-night rafting and hiking trip along the San Juan River. Also one-day tours near Moab.

Delta Vacations Ⓦ deltavacations.com. Flight and hotel packages, especially to Las Vegas.

Grand Canyon Field Institute ☎ 928 638 2481 or ☎ 800 858 2808, Ⓦ grandcanyon.org/learn/grand-canyon-field-institute. Highly recommended, park-sponsored programme of hikes and educational expeditions in the Grand Canyon. Typical prices range from around $560 for a three-night hike down into the canyon to $770 for a four-night rim-to-rim backpacking trip.

Green Tortoise ☎ 800 867 8647, Ⓦ greentortoise.com. California-based, youth-oriented bus tours. The nine-day "Canyons of the West" tour from Los Angeles costs around $890 including food kitty.

MNA Ventures ☎ 928 774 5211, Ⓦ mnaventures.org. Flagstaff's prestigious Museum of Northern Arizona runs an extensive programme of tours and excursions in the Four Corners region, camping and/or staying in hotels.

REI Adventures ☎ 800 622 2236, Ⓦ rei.com/travel. Small-group hiking trips in Utah and Arizona; a six-night trip, with accommodation, typically costs around $2800.

Sierra Club Outings ☎ 415 977 5522, Ⓦ sierraclub.org/outings. The environmental group offers some fabulous opportunities to come to grips with the landscapes and resources of the Southwest, such as a week in Utah's Dark Canyon or Arizona's Rainbow Plateau for $945.

Southwest Ed-ventures ☎ 800 525 4456, Ⓦ fourcornersschool .org. Hiking, backpacking and rafting trips for all ages on the Colorado Plateau, with a strong educational element.

TrekAmerica/Grand American Adventures US ☎ 800 221 0596, UK ☎ 0844 576 1370; Ⓦ trekamerica.com or Ⓦ grandamericanadventures.com. A wide array of tantalizing Southwest expeditions, including ten-day national-park hiking trips, costing from £1099 if you camp, £1379 staying in hotels; rates exclude flights. The TrekAmerica tours are targeted at ages 18–38.

Getting around

Attempting to tour the Southwest by public transport is an extremely bad idea. While buses and planes – and, to a much lesser extent, trains – connect the major urban areas, the national parks and wide-open landscapes that are the region's greatest attractions simply cannot be explored without your own vehicle. Even public transport within the cities is minimal. Unless you're an extremely energetic cyclist, therefore, you'll need a motorbike or car.

If you can't drive, the only itinerary that makes much sense is to cross northern Arizona and northern New Mexico by bus or train, flying in or out of Albuquerque in the east or Las Vegas in the west. Obvious stops would include Flagstaff, with a side-trip by bus to the Grand Canyon, and Santa Fe, the only city small enough to be seen on foot. Phoenix and Tucson are no fun at all without a car, while what little public transport exists in southern Utah is no use for seeing the parks. Hitchhiking is not recommended under any circumstances.

By car

To rent a car, you need to have held your licence for at least one year; drivers under 25 may encounter problems and have to pay higher than normal insurance premiums.

All the major rental companies have outlets at the main regional airports. Reservations are handled centrally rather than locally, so the best way to shop around for rates is online. Potential variations are endless; certain cities and states are consistently cheaper than others, while individual travellers may be eligible for corporate, frequent-flier, or AAA discounts. In low season, you might find a tiny car (a "subcompact") for as little as $120 per week, but a typical budget rate would be more like $40 per day, and $175 per week. A car rented in Las Vegas can easily cost $100 less per week than one rented in Colorado, and prices in Arizona, New Mexico, and Utah range between the two.

Don't automatically go for the cheapest rate. Little-known local rental companies may offer appealing prices, but if you break down several hundred miles from their offices it may be hard to get assistance. Even between the major operators, there can be a big difference in the quality of cars. Always be sure to get free unlimited mileage, and remember that leaving the car in a different city from the one where you rent it can incur a drop-off charge of as much as $200.

When you rent a car, read the small print carefully for details on Collision Damage Waiver (CDW), sometimes called Liability Damage Waiver (LDW), a form of insurance that often isn't included in the initial rental charge but is well worth considering. This specifically covers the car that you are driving yourself; you are in any case insured for damage to other vehicles. At $15–25 a day extra, it can add substantially to the total cost, but without it you're liable for every scratch to the car – even those that aren't your fault. Some credit card companies offer automatic CDW coverage to anyone using their card; contact your issuing company for details. Your rental papers should include an emergency number to call in case of breakdown or accident; contact the rental company before you arrange, or pay, for any repairs.

The American Automobile Association, or AAA (☎800 222 4357, ⓦaaa.com), provides free maps and assistance to its members and to members of affiliated associations overseas, such as the British AA and RAC.

Renting an RV

Recreational vehicles – RVs – can be rented at prices starting at around $750 per week (plus mileage charges) for a basic camper on the back of a pickup truck, with sleeping room for two adults. If you're looking for one of those huge juggernauts that rumble down the highway complete with multiple bedrooms, bathrooms, and kitchens, you'll have to pay significantly more. Though good for groups or

> ## TOP 5 SCENIC DRIVES
> **The High Road** Northern NM. See p.142
> **Hwy-12** Southern UT. See p.376
> **Road between the Rims** Northern AZ.
>   See p.328
> **Route 66** Northern NM and AZ. See p.10
> **San Juan Skyway** Southwest CO.
>   See p.83

families travelling together, RVs can be unwieldy on the road, and as people tend to own their own, rental outlets are not as common as you might expect. On top of rental fees, you'll also have to take into account the cost of gas (some RVs do twelve miles to the gallon or less) and any drop-off charges. It's rarely legal simply to pull up in an RV and spend the night at the roadside; you are expected to stay in designated parks that cost $20–30 per night.

The Recreational Vehicle Rental Association (ⓦwww.rvra.org) maintains a searchable online directory of rental firms. Large companies offering RV rentals include Cruise America (ⓦcruiseamerica .com) and Moturis (ⓦwww.moturis.com).

Advice for drivers from overseas

Foreign nationals from English-speaking countries can drive in the US using their full domestic driving licences. (International Driving Permits are not always regarded as sufficient.) Not having your licence with you while driving is an arrestable offence.

Fly-drive deals are good value if you want to rent a car, though you can save up to sixty percent simply by booking in advance with a major firm. If you choose not to pay until you arrive, be sure you take a written confirmation of the price with you. Remember that most standard rental cars have automatic transmissions, and that it's safer not to drive immediately after a long transatlantic flight.

It's easier and cheaper to book RVs in advance from Britain. Most travel agents who specialize in the US can arrange RV rental, and usually do it cheaper if you book a flight through them as well. A price of £1500 for a five-berth van for two weeks is fairly typical.

Desert driving

Whenever you drive in the desert, be sure to have two gallons of water per person in the car. You should also carry flares, matches, a first-aid kit, and a compass, plus a shovel, air pump, and extra gas. If the car's engine overheats, don't turn it off; instead, try to cool the engine quickly by turning the front end toward the wind. Carefully pour some water on the front of the radiator, and turn the air-conditioning off and heating up full blast. In an emergency, never panic and leave the car; you'll be harder to find wandering around alone.

By bus

Greyhound buses link all major cities and many smaller towns in the Southwest; for fares, schedules, and reservations, visit ⓦgreyhound.com. Routes that are particularly useful for tourists – as well as services offered by other operators – are detailed at the relevant points in this book.

While scheduled buses can get you from city to city, they're of no use when it comes to enjoying the great outdoors. Tour buses, however, do set off into the wilderness from most major towns; they, too, are detailed throughout this book.

By train

Details of the very limited Amtrak rail service to and across the Southwest appear on p.28. The region also holds a number of historic and scenic railroads – some steam-powered or running along narrow-gauge mining tracks – including the Cumbres & Toltec line in northern New Mexico (ⓦcumbres toltec.com); the Grand Canyon Railway between Williams and the Grand Canyon in northern Arizona (ⓦthetrain.com); the Verde Canyon Railroad in northern Arizona (ⓦverdecanyonrr.com); and the Durango & Silverton Narrow Gauge Railroad in Colorado (ⓦdurangotrain.com).

By bike

Although cycling in the Southwest can be absolutely exhilarating, long-distance riders face a fearsome challenge, above all in the heat of summer. Neighbouring towns can be as much as a hundred miles apart, along desert highways that offer no food, water, or shade. Quite apart from the high mountains and deep canyons, most areas covered in this book are a mile or more above sea level, so the altitude alone can be a real problem. The only road from A to B may well turn out to be a major interstate; when there's no alternative, cyclists are generally allowed to ride on interstate shoulders, but they have to battle the slipstream of mighty trucks.

If you have a good bike and know how to maintain it, however, and time your trip for the cooler months, it is feasible to explore the Southwest by bike. Specific regions that lend themselves to cycle touring are north-central New Mexico, where countless routes radiate from Santa

Fe; the vicinity of Flagstaff and Sedona in Arizona; and southwest Utah, around Zion National Park. Areas hugely popular with mountain-bikers include Moab, Utah – home of the gruelling Slickrock Bike Trail (see p.424) – and Durango, Colorado.

For general information and advice, contact the New Mexico Touring Society (ⓦnmts.org), the Arizona Bicycle Club (ⓦazbikeclub.com), or Bicycle Utah (ⓦbicycleutah.com). The national, nonprofit Adventure Cycling Association (formerly Bike centennial; ⓦadventurecycling.org) publishes maps (downloadable for $14.75 each) of several 400-mile routes, including the *Grand Canyon Connector*, detailing campgrounds, motels, restaurants, bike shops, and sites of interest. Backroads Bicycle Tours (☎800 462 2848, ⓦbackroads.com) arranges group tours.

Greyhound, Amtrak, and major airlines all carry passengers' bicycles – dismantled and packed into a box – for a small additional fee.

Health

The major health and safety issues facing Southwest travellers centre on coping with desert conditions. For anyone unused to dealing with extremes of heat and cold, and the sheer inhospitality of this kind of terrain, it's essential to take precautions.

Desert survival

If you plan to hike in the desert, it's crucial to plan ahead. Don't expect mobile (cell) phones to provide coverage in all the remote regions described in this book; tell somebody where you are going and write down all pertinent information, including your expected time of return. Carry an extra two days' food and water, and never go anywhere without a map. Try to cover most of your ground in early morning: the midday heat is too debilitating.

Stick to official trails in the national parks and you shouldn't face any serious technical difficulties. Many trails are marked only by occasional stone cairns, however, and if your concentration starts to wander your feet may do so too. If you do get lost, try your utmost to retrace your steps; if that fails, find some shade and wait. As long as you've registered, the rangers will eventually come and fetch you.

There are two more good reasons not to try to blaze your own trail. The first is the risk of becoming rim-rocked; picking your way across even a shallow gully, it's much easier to climb up than down, and you may well find yourself stuck above a drop that you're unable to negotiate. The other is the **crypto-biotic crust** – what looks like a faint coating of dead moss on the sand is the building block on which all desert life depends, and merely treading on it has serious ecological consequences.

Whatever experience you may have had anywhere else, hiking in **canyons** is different. Most hikers are far more familiar with walking up hills and mountains, where it's the initial climb that's most demanding, and when your energy levels flag you can simply turn around and walk back to base. Canyon hiking is deceptively seductive. The descent seems easy, and your progress quick. Eventually, however, you have to pay: start the climb back out when you're already tired and the midday heat has set in, and you're in for a murderously long haul. Turn back after a third of your allotted time; if you plan a six-hour hike, reckon on two hours hiking down and four hours to hike up.

To stay cool during the day, wear full-length sleeves and trousers. Shorts and a T-shirt will expose you to far too much sun – something you won't be aware of until it's too late. A wide-brimmed hat and good sunglasses will spare you the blinding headaches that can result from the desert light.

You may also have to contend with **flash floods**, which can appear from nowhere. One innocent-looking dark cloud can turn a dry wash into a raging river, and rain elsewhere can cause a flood even when the sky above is clear. Never camp in a dry wash, and don't attempt to cross flooded areas until the water has receded.

Much of the Southwest is more than a mile above sea level, and the **altitude** alone can impose severe demands on even the fittest of athletes. Be prepared for below-freezing temperatures at high elevations at night.

Water

It's essential to carry – and **drink** – large quantities of liquid in the desert. An eight-hour hike in typical summer temperatures of more than 100°F would require you to drink a phenomenal **thirty pints** of water. Loss of appetite and thirst are early symptoms of heat exhaustion, so it's possible to become seriously dehydrated without feeling thirsty. Watch out for dizziness or nausea; if you feel weak and stop sweating, it's time to get to the doctor. You should always know whether water will be available on your chosen trail – ask park rangers – and carry at least two pints per person even if you expect to be able to pick up more en route. Just to confuse things, there's also the risk of **hyponatremia**, or water intoxication,

which in its first stages closely resembles heat exhaustion, and happens if you drink too much without eating. As hikers can burn up to a thousand calories per hour, expect to eat at least twice as much **food** as normal, both during your hike and also, ideally, before it. Salty snacks such as cookies, crackers, and trail mix are recommended, as well as jerky or salami and dried ready-made meals. Finally, it's easy to forget that at the end of a long hike there may be no facilities at the trailhead. Don't forget to leave some food and water in your vehicle as well.

Backpackers should never drink from rivers and streams, however clear and inviting they may look; you never know what unspeakable acts people – or animals – have performed further upstream. **Giardia** – a water-borne bacteria that causes an intestinal disease, characterized by chronic diarrhoea, abdominal cramps, fatigue, and weight loss – is a serious problem. Water that doesn't come from a tap should be boiled for at least five minutes or cleansed with an iodine-based purifier, or a giardia-rated filter, available from any outdoor store.

Insects and allergies

Mosquitoes and biting insects are rarely a problem in the Southwest, though in springtime you may encounter them near rivers in parks such as Zion. Anything containing DEET is a fairly reliable repellent. **Ticks** – tiny beetles that plunge their heads into your skin and swell up with your blood – can be a hazard. If you pluck them off you can sometimes leave their heads inside, causing blood clots or infections, so get advice from a park ranger if you've been bitten.

Beware, too, of **poison oak**, an allergenic shrub that grows all over the western states, usually among oak trees. Its leaves come in groups of three and are distinguished by prominent veins and shiny surfaces. If you come into contact, wash your skin (with soap and cold water) and clothes as soon as possible – and don't scratch. In serious cases, hospital emergency rooms can give antihistamine or adrenaline jabs.

Snakes and creepy-crawlies

Though the Southwestern deserts are home to **poisonous creatures** that include snakes, scorpions, and spiders, these are rarely aggressive toward humans. By observing obvious precautions, you should be able to avoid trouble. Don't attempt to handle wildlife; keep your eyes open as you walk, and watch where you put your hands when scrambling over obstacles; shake out shoes, clothing, and bedding before use; and back off if you do spot a creature, to give it room to escape.

If you are **bitten** or stung – whatever creature is responsible – apply a cold compress to the wound, constrict the area with a tourniquet to prevent the spread of venom, drink lots of water, and bring your temperature down by resting in a shady area. Stay as calm as possible and seek medical help immediately.

Medical resources for travellers

CDC ☎ 800 232 4636, ⓦ cdc.gov/travel. Official US government travel health site.

International Society for Travel Medicine ⓦ istm.org. An extensive list of travel health clinics, including many in the Southwest.

Accommodation

Accommodation in the Southwest is relatively inexpensive. Most travellers simply want a bed for the night before moving on the next day, so motels everywhere provide clean, no-frills places to sleep without bothering to offer additional amenities.

Basic room rates in rural areas start as low as $40 per night, while prices along the principal highways and interstates tend to start at around $65. Only in the most popular summer destinations – cities such as Santa Fe, or "gateway" towns near the major national parks – will you find it hard to get a room for under $80. If you prefer a bit more comfort, it's almost always available; in most areas covered by this book you can get a room in a top-class hotel for under $150.

Many motel rooms hold two double beds, and will accommodate three or four guests for slightly over the normal two-person rate. On the other hand, the lone traveller has a hard time of it: a "single" room is just a double at a fractionally reduced rate.

Wherever you stay, you'll be expected to pay in advance, at least for the first night and perhaps for further nights too. Most places ask for a credit card imprint when you arrive, but they'll also accept cash or dollar travellers' cheques. Reservations – essential in busy areas in summer – are only held until 5pm or 6pm unless you've warned the hotel you'll be arriving late.

Hotels and motels

It's easy to find a basic **motel room** in the Southwest. Drivers approaching any significant town pass lines

of motels along the highway, while the choice along major cross-country routes is phenomenal. Most of the towns mentioned in this book hold more motels than there's room to review; the very few that have none at all are clearly indicated.

Hotels and **motels** are essentially the same thing, although motels tend to be beside main roads away from city centres, and thus much more accessible to drivers. The budget ones are pretty basic, but in general there's a uniform standard of comfort – each room comes with a double bed, a TV, a phone, and an attached bathroom – and you don't get a much better deal by paying, say, $100 instead of $70. Over $90 or so, the room and its fittings simply get bigger and more luxurious, and there'll probably be a swimming pool which guests can use for free. Almost all hotels and motels (except in Las Vegas) offer free **wi-fi**.

The cheapest properties tend to be family-run, independent motels, but there's a lot to be said for paying a few dollars more to stay in the national **chains**. Most travellers find that a particular chain consistently suits their requirements and budget. Few budget hotels or motels offer breakfast, although many provide free self-service coffee and pastries.

Travellers who belong to the AAA can usually get a discount of around ten percent, as can members of equivalent foreign organizations such as Britain's AA. Look out for **discount coupons**, especially in the free brochures available at state and local visitor centres. These can offer excellent value – $50 for a double room in a mid-range chain – but rates are often limited to midweek.

Many towns throughout the Southwest still hold **historic hotels**, whether dating back to the arrival of the railroads or to the heyday of Route 66 in the 1940s and 1950s. Not all have up-to-date facilities to match their period charm, but they can make wonderfully characterful places to spend a night or two. Those that are exceptionally well preserved or restored may charge $200 or more per room, but a more typical rate for a not overly luxurious but atmospheric, antique-furnished room would be more like $120. Occasionally, venerable Western hotels have been refitted to serve as budget-oriented accommodation options, as with Tucson's *Hotel Congress* (p.227) and Flagstaff's *Monte Vista* and *Weatherford* (p.265).

Several **national parks** feature long-established and architecturally distinguished hotels, traditionally known as **lodges**, that can be real bargains thanks to their federally controlled rates. The only drawback is that all rooms tend to be reserved far in advance. Among the best are *El Tovar* and *Grand Canyon Lodge* on the south and north rims, respectively, of the Grand Canyon, and *Zion Lodge* in Zion Canyon.

Bed and breakfasts

Bed and breakfast has become ever more popular, often as luxurious – if not necessarily more expensive – alternatives to conventional hotels.

The price you pay for a B&B – which typically varies from around $80 to $175 – always includes a huge and wholesome breakfast. The crucial determining factor in price is whether each room has an en-suite bathroom, even though providing private bath facilities can damage the authenticity of a fine old house.

In many areas, B&Bs have grouped together to form central booking agencies, making it much easier to find a room at short notice; we've given addresses and numbers for these where appropriate. Statewide organizations include the Arizona Association of B&B Inns (W arizona-bed-breakfast .com); B&B Inns of Utah (W bbiu.org); B&B Innkeepers of Colorado (W innsofcolorado.org); and the New Mexico B&B Association (W nmbba.org). Almost every B&B has its own website; simple searches throw up myriad possibilities.

Hostels

Around a dozen **hostels** provide accommodation for backpackers and budget travellers in the Southwest. Most work out little cheaper than motels for two people travelling together, so there's not much point staying in hostels unless you prefer

---

their youthful ambience and sociability. Many are not accessible on public transport, or particularly convenient for sightseeing in the towns and cities, let alone in rural areas.

These days, most hostels are independent, with no affiliation to HI-AYH (Hostelling International–American Youth Hostels) network. Many are no more than converted motels, where the "dorms" consist of a couple of sets of bunkbeds in a musty room that's also let out as a private unit on demand; others may be purpose-built rural properties, or at least modernized to a high standard. Most expect guests to bring sheets or sleeping bags. Rates range from $18 to about $27 for a dorm bed, from perhaps $35 for a double room. Those few hostels that do belong to HI-AYH tend to impose curfews and limit daytime access hours, and segregate dormitories by sex.

Especially in high season, it's advisable to reserve ahead. The maximum stay is often restricted to three days, though this rule tends to be ignored if there's space. Few hostels provide meals, but most have cooking facilities.

Food and drink

The short-lived international craze for contemporary Southwestern cuisine did little to turn the Southwest itself into a gourmet's paradise. However, Santa Fe still holds dozens of top-class restaurants, while the upscale resorts of Phoenix, Tucson, Taos and Sedona – as well, of course, as Las Vegas – all offer opportunities for fine dining.

Out on the road, the great American diner still holds sway. Southern Utah, for example, is the last place to go if lingering over an exquisite meal in atmospheric surroundings ranks high on your vacation wish list. With typical prices for a diner meal starting below $10, however, travellers happy to eat the same old steak or chicken, with baked potato and salad bar, can get excellent value for money.

The Hispanic regions of New Mexico and southern Arizona have their own indigenous cuisine, broadly similar to Mexican food but influenced by the Pueblo Indians. The essential ingredient is the chile, technically the "fruit" of the pepper plant. (New Mexicans insist it should never be spelled *chili* or *chilli*, which indicates the Texas-style stew made with ground beef and tomato sauce.) Bright-red *ristras* – strings of dried

---

TOP 5 HISTORIC HOTELS

Andaluz Albuquerque, NM. See p.173
Historic Taos Inn Taos, NM. See p.154
Strater Hotel Durango, CO. See p.81
La Fonda Santa Fe, NM. See p.120
La Posada Winslow, AZ. See p.261

peppers – adorn the region's doorways and restaurant entrances, celebrating the fiery delights that lie within. In principle the red pepper is the mature version of the green, but confronted with a plateful there's no guarantee which will be hotter. Both are used to make spicy salsa, which usually contains tomato and onion, cilantro (coriander) and other herbs, oil and lemon juice, plus other secret ingredients. If it's too hot for you, the best remedy is to drink milk.

A basic meal in a New Mexican café or diner is broadly similar to what you'd eat south of the border, though it may make more use of fresh meats and vegetables. The essentials are: lots of rice and pinto beans, often served refried as *frijoles* (ie boiled, mashed, and fried), with variations on the tortilla, a very thin cornmeal or flour pancake that can be wrapped around the food and eaten by hand (a *burrito*); folded, fried, and filled (a *taco*); rolled, filled, and baked in sauce (an *enchilada*); or fried flat and topped with a stack of filling (a tostada). Meals are usually served with complimentary *nachos* (chips) and salsa dip, or with *sopaipillas*, deep-fried air-filled pastry "pillows," often sweetened with honey. The *chile relleno* is a good vegetarian option – a green pepper stuffed with cheese, dipped in egg batter and fried.

You'll also find Native American restaurants, both on and off the reservations. The most ubiquitous dish, generally known as a Navajo taco, consists of a piece of fry bread – a puffy deep-fried slab of bread – smothered with beans, lettuce, and cheese. A Hopi taco, an Apache taco, and a Pueblo taco are all surprisingly similar. Corn or maize, the first crop cultivated in the Americas, comes in some amazing multicoloured varieties. Blue corn chips have spread beyond the Southwest, but you may also encounter blue cornflakes and wafer-thin *piki* or *piiki* bread made with blue cornflour.

Drinking

To buy and consume alcohol in the US, you must be aged 21 or over; you may be asked for ID even if you look much older. In New Mexico and Arizona, most restaurants have liquor licences, and it's always easy to find a drink. In Mormon-dominated Utah things are a bit more complicated, though it's not quite the "dry" state of popular legend. Most small towns have at least one restaurant licensed to sell beer or wine to diners. Alcohol is prohibited altogether on Indian reservations; you can't have beer in your car, let alone in your motel room.

Festivals and events

The Southwest's major annual festivals are listed below. Specific events are described in the relevant town accounts, and you'll also find a full calendar of events in the pueblos of New Mexico on p.138. Also, tourist offices for each state (see p.43) can provide full lists. As a rule, only the Indian Market in Santa Fe and the Balloon Festival in Albuquerque attract large enough crowds to place a serious strain on accommodation and other facilities.

Early Feb Festival of the Arts, Tubac, AZ ⓦ tubacaz.com

Late May Iron Horse Bicycle Classic, Durango, CO ⓦ ironhorsebicycleclassic.com

Late May Zuni Festival of Arts & Culture, Museum of Northern Arizona, Flagstaff, AZ ⓦ musnaz.org

Late May to mid-July World Series of Poker, Las Vegas, NV ⓦ wsop.com

Mid-June Bluegrass Festival, Telluride, CO ⓦ bluegrass.com

Late June New Mexico Arts & Crafts Fair, Albuquerque, NM ⓦ nmartsandcraftsfair.org

Late June to Oct Utah Shakespeare Festival, Cedar City, UT ⓦ bard.org

Late June to Aug Santa Fe Opera, Santa Fe, NM ⓦ santafeopera.org

Late June Hopi Festival of Arts & Culture, Museum of Northern Arizona, Flagstaff, AZ ⓦ musnaz.org

July 4 Nambe Falls Celebration, Nambe Pueblo, NM ⓦ nambepueblo.org

July (second week) Taos Pueblo Powwow, Taos Pueblo, NM ⓦ taospueblopowwow.com

July (last week) Spanish Market, Santa Fe, NM ⓦ spanishcolonialblog.org

Early Aug Navajo Festival of Arts & Culture, Museum of Northern Arizona, Flagstaff, AZ ⓦ musnaz.org

Early Aug Jazz Celebration, Telluride, CO ⓦ telluridejazz.com

Aug (first week) Old Lincoln Days and Billy the Kid Pageant, Lincoln, NM ⓦ billythekidpageant.org

Aug (second week) Inter-Tribal Indian Ceremonial, Gallup, NM ⓦ theceremonial.org

Aug (third week) Indian Market, Santa Fe, NM ⓦ swaia.org

Late Aug Central Navajo Fair, Chinle, AZ

Sept 2 San Esteban Feast Day, Ácoma Pueblo, NM ⓦ sccc .acomaskycity.org

Labor Day (first Mon in Sept) All-American Futurity (horse race), Ruidoso, NM ⓦ raceruidoso.com

Early Sept Hatch Chile Festival, Hatch, NM ⓦ hatchchilefest.com

Early Sept Film Festival, Telluride, CO ⓦ telluridefilmfestival.org

Early Sept Fiestas de Santa Fe, Santa Fe, NM ⓦ santafesta.org

Sept (second week) Navajo Nation Fair, Window Rock, AZ ⓦ navajonationfair.com

Mid-Sept New Mexico State Fair, Albuquerque, NM 🖤 exponm.com

Early Oct International Balloon Fiesta, Albuquerque, NM
🖤 balloonfiesta.com

Mid-Oct Western Navajo Fair, Tuba City, AZ
🖤 westernnavajonationfair.org

Late Oct Arizona State Fair, Phoenix, AZ 🖤 azstatefair.com

Oct (third week) Helldorado Days, Tombstone, AZ
🖤 helldoradodays.com

Early Dec National Finals Rodeo, Las Vegas, NV 🖤 prorodeo.com

Early Dec Shalako ceremony, Zuni Pueblo, NM 🖤 zunitourism.com

The great outdoors

Cut by deep canyons, coated by dense forests, and capped by great mountains, the Southwest glories in some of the most fabulous wilderness areas in the United States.

The easiest way for visitors to enjoy this natural wonderland is to plot an itinerary that samples the countless national, state, and county parks. Although these are not invariably the most beautiful places of all – some are simply lands that pioneer farmers, Indian tribes, and mining corporations never bothered or managed to grab – they do offer the campgrounds and hiking trails that make backcountry exploration possible even for the least experienced tourists.

National parks and monuments

The National Park Service administers both national parks and national monuments. Park rangers do a superb job of providing information and advice to visitors, maintaining trails, and organizing such activities as free guided hikes and campfire talks.

In principle, a **national park** preserves an area of outstanding natural beauty, encompassing a wide range of terrain as well as sites of historic interest, while a **national monument** is much smaller, focusing perhaps on a single archeological site or geological phenomenon and thus holding a narrower appeal for tourists. In practice, however, that distinction is somewhat blurred in the Southwest. Most **parks** cover desert regions that have barely known human occupation, and thus boast little historic significance, and although the **Grand Canyon** and **Zion** are huge and very varied, parks such as **Bryce Canyon** and **Carlsbad Caverns** are essentially one-trick wonders. And while many **monuments** do consist of a single Indian ruin or nineteenth-century fort, several more are as diverse and spectacular as the parks –

Arizona's **Canyon de Chelly**, for example, would surely be a national park were it not on the Navajo reservation. In addition, vast national monuments have been created in areas that need extra federal protection but are not intended to become major tourist destinations. **Grand Staircase-Escalante** monument in Utah, the best-known example, is larger than any of the national parks in this book.

Other public lands

National parks and monuments are often surrounded by tracts of **national forest**, also federally administered but much less protected. While these too tend to hold appealing rural campgrounds, most allow limited logging or other land-based industry – ski resorts more often than strip mines, fortunately.

Further government departments administer wildlife refuges, national scenic rivers, recreation areas, and the like by basically leaving the natural landscape alone. The **Bureau of Land Management** (BLM) has the largest holdings of all, most of it open rangeland, such as in Utah, but also including some enticingly out-of-the-way reaches.

State parks and state monuments are a mirror-image of the national system, preserving sites of more limited, local significance. Many are explicitly designed for recreational use and thus hold better campgrounds than their federal equivalents.

Fees and passes

Most national parks and monuments charge an admission fee of between $5 and $25, which covers a vehicle and all its occupants for up to a week. For anyone on a touring vacation, it will almost certainly make more sense to buy one of various **passes**. The annual **National Parks Pass**, officially known as the "America the Beautiful – National Parks and Federal Recreational Lands Pass – Annual Pass", costs $80, and can be bought at all national parks and monuments, or online at 🖤 store.usgs .gov/pass. It grants unrestricted access for a year from the date of purchase to the bearer, and any accompanying passengers, to all national parks and monuments, as well as sites managed by such agencies as the US Fish and Wildlife Service, the Forest Service, and the BLM. It does not however cover or reduce additional fees like camping charges or permits for backcountry hiking or rafting.

Two further passes, obtainable at any park but not online, grant **free access** for life to all national parks and monuments, again to the holder and any accompanying passengers, and also provide a fifty

TOP 5 HIKING TRAILS
Mesa Arch Trail Canyonlands; 1hr.
See p.407
Delicate Arch Trail Arches; 2hr. See p.418
White House Trail Canyon de Chelly; 2hr
30min. See p.62
Horseshoe Canyon Canyonlands; 5hr.
See p.409
West Rim Trail Zion; 1 day. See p.355

percent discount on camping fees. The **Senior Pass** is available to any US citizen or permanent resident aged 62 or older for a one-time fee of $10, while the **Access Pass** is issued free to blind or permanently disabled US citizens or permanent residents.

Information resources

For information on the National Park Service, access Ⓦnps.gov. Websites for individual parks appear throughout this book. For general maps and camping information, Ⓦpubliclands.org, the **Public Lands Information Center** website, has details on BLM and forest-service lands, or visit the **state parks** offices for **Arizona** (Ⓦpr.state.az.us); Colorado (Ⓦparks.state.co.us); **New Mexico** (Ⓦwww.emnrd.state.nm.us); or **Utah** (Ⓦstateparks.utah.gov).

Camping and backpacking

The ideal way to see the Southwest – especially if you're on a low budget – is to tour the region by car and **camp** at night in state and federal campgrounds. These may lack the amenities of the many commercially run campgrounds near the larger towns, but they tend to be far more peaceful, scenic, and better positioned for days of hiking and canyoneering. Typical public campgrounds range in price from free (usually when there's no water available, which may be seasonal) to around $15 per night; commercial fees are more like $15–30, for sites that can be more like open-air hotels, with shops and restaurants.

There may be plenty of campgrounds, but plenty of people want to use them: if you're camping during public holidays or the high season, reserve in advance or avoid the most popular areas. By contrast, basic campgrounds in isolated areas may well be completely empty whatever time you go.

Backcountry camping in the national parks is usually by permit and may be free or cost a few dollars per night. Before you set off on anything more than a half-day hike, and whenever you're headed for anywhere at all isolated, be sure to inform a ranger of

your plans and ask about weather conditions and specific local tips. Carry sufficient food and drink to cover emergencies, as well as all the necessary equipment and maps. In summer, you have to carry so much water that you'll need to lighten your load as much as possible, perhaps by sleeping in a lightweight sack rather than a sleeping bag.

When camping rough, check whether **fires** are permitted. Even if they are, try to use a camp stove instead of local materials – in some places firewood is scarce, although you may be allowed to use deadwood. In wilderness areas, try to camp on previously used sites. Where there are no toilets, bury human waste at least six inches into the ground and a hundred feet from the nearest water supply and campground. Burn what trash you can and take the rest away.

Finally, you may remember reports of the "mystery illness" that killed around fifty people in the Four Corners region in 1993. It was eventually traced to a hantavirus spread by the droppings of deer mice. Such viruses remain present in the region, so backpackers should take care to avoid camping near rodent nests.

Flora and fauna

Though the Southwest is commonly imagined as an arid wasteland, it holds a broad spectrum of plant and animal life. Scientists divide the earth, according to climate and distance from the equator, into "**life zones**" that hold different groups of species. In the Southwest, altitude substitutes for latitude; the higher you are, the cooler it gets. Within the Grand Canyon alone, the range of habitat is equivalent to a trip from the deserts of Mexico to the forests of the Canadian mountains.

It's the lowest, hottest level, the **Lower Sonoran** zone, that's home to the rattlesnakes and cacti you're probably expecting. Southern Arizona is the obvious example, with its dramatic saguaro and organ-pipe cacti.

By the time you reach a mile above sea level – the height of most of Utah's national parks – you're in the **Upper Sonoran** zone. This is characterized by smaller prickly pear cacti and sagebrush, animals such as rabbits and prairie dogs, and predators like coyotes and mountain lions (not that tourists are at all likely to encounter lions). Low rainfall results in a "pygmy forest" where gnarled, long-lived trees such as the piñon (or pinyon) pine and Utah juniper grow to a maximum height of little over twenty feet.

Around ten thousand feet up in the mountains of southern Colorado, northern New Mexico, and

ADVENTURE TRAVEL

The Southwest offers vast opportunities for active travelling. In its major base for adventure travel of all kinds, the former mining town of **Moab**, Utah, mountain biking is the speciality, with rafting and four-wheel-driving (4WD) as close rivals; full listings can be found on p.424. Other towns popular with energetic visitors include **Durango**, Colorado (see p.80), and **Sedona**, Arizona (see p.271); guides, outfitters, and local tour operators are recommended throughout this book.

central-southern Utah, the **Canadian** zone is even more densely forested, with Douglas firs joining the aspen and ponderosa, and bighorn sheep making an appearance in remoter areas. The Colorado Rockies and Utah's Henry and La Sal ranges rise higher still into the **Hudsonian** zone, between eleven and twelve thousand feet. Before the tree cover gives out altogether, ultra-resilient species such as the bristlecone pine, which can live for literally thousands of years, cling to the slopes.

The highest summits in the Southwest – like the San Francisco Peaks (12,633ft) near Flagstaff, Arizona, and Uncompahgre Peak (14,309ft) near Ouray, Colorado – belong to the **Arctic** or **Alpine** zone, where the occasional tiny mammal scuttles through the tundra-like grasses and mosses.

Wherever and whenever **water** is abundant, however, the picture changes. Southwestern riverbeds are lined with magnificent **cottonwood** and **aspen** trees, so many a canyon buried deep in the desert still manages a superb display of autumn colours, while spring snowmelts help bring the mountain hillsides and the meadows of Zion alive with wild flowers.

Travelling in Indian country

The Southwest holds around fifty separate Indian reservations, ranging in size from the vast "Navajo Nation", which extends across three states in the Four Corners region, to the nineteen autono-mous pueblos of New Mexico, many of which consist of a single village.

Some reservations make no effort to attract or inform visitors; some do the bare minimum to sate tourists' curiosity; some eagerly encourage paying guests to stay in tribal-run motels and campgrounds. Among the most compelling attractions on Native American soil are **Monument Valley** and Canyon de Chelly and Navajo national monuments, all on the Navajo reservation; the stupendous waterfalls of the **Havasupai reservation**, deep in the Grand Canyon; the **Skywalk** on the Hualapai reservation, in the so-called "Grand Canyon West"; and the adobe pueblos of **Taos** and **Ácoma** in New Mexico.

Many outsiders – Americans and non-Americans alike – feel uncomfortable about entering Native American land, but so long as you behave with due **cultural sensitivity** you will almost always be made welcome. In particular, travellers in "Indian Country" should respect the laws that bar the sale, possession, and consumption of **alcohol** on the reservations. Always request permission before **photographing** (or even drawing) people or personal property, and accept that you may be asked for a fee. As well as obeying explicit signs that ask you not to enter specific areas, such as shrines or *kivas*, remember that off-road driving and off-trail hiking or climbing is forbidden. If you have to drive up to someone's home or *hogan*, stay in your car and wait to be approached, rather than blundering in.

On a more general note, attempts to make friends may run contrary to what Native Americans regard as **good manners**. In the words of a leaflet issued by the Navajo, "the general exuberance many cultures define as friendliness is not considered such by the American Indians." Most Southwestern Indians regard **eye contact** as rude and will avoid meeting your eye; they may also prefer not to shake hands. Your clothing may also be an issue; the Hopi, for example, request that visitors not wear shorts or hats, or use umbrellas. Persistent, intrusive questioning is obviously liable to offend. In Pueblo communities especially, don't ask about religious matters when children are present, as children are only initiated into religious secrets at the appropriate age.

Buying Indian crafts

For many tourists, the quest to buy **Indian crafts** becomes a major focus of their visit to the Southwest. Museums and galleries throughout the region display beautiful Pueblo pots, Navajo rugs, Apache baskets, and silver and turquoise jewellery of all kinds, stimulating a desire for affordable gifts and souvenirs with which stores can barely keep up.

Much of what's widely regarded as traditional Indian craftwork has in fact only developed recently. The collapse of traditional tribal economies coincided with the nineteenth-century arrival of the railroads, and with them the Southwest's first wave of tourists. Enterprising traders encouraged Indians to adapt or learn craft techniques to make souvenirs; as one anthropologist put it, the resultant hybrid was "the Indian's idea of the trader's idea of what the white man thought was Indian design."

To ensure good prices and good quality, you should ideally buy specific Indian crafts as near as possible to where they're made. On the Navajo reservation, head for the **Hubbell Trading Post** (see p.64); on the Hopi reservation, try the **Hopi Cultural Center** and the nearby stores; Ácoma, Taos, and San Ildefonso pueblos are also good bets. More accessibly, the Indian traders in front of the Palace of the Governors in **Santa Fe** are a reliable source, while that city's summer **Indian Market** is a showcase for the entire region. In addition, the Museum of Northern Arizona in Flagstaff, the Heard museum in Phoenix, and the Millicent Rogers museum in Taos all have excellent stores.

If you want to be sure that whatever you're buying was individually crafted by a Southwestern Indian, you're entitled to ask the vendor for a written certificate of authenticity. Only the phrase "Authentic Indian handmade" has any legal force. "Indian handmade" means that the object was designed and assembled by American Indians; "Indian crafted" means that American Indians had a hand in the process; and words such as "real" and "genuine" mean nothing. The website of the **Indian Arts & Crafts Association** (Ⓦ iaca.com) holds a directory of recommended crafts workers and retail outlets.

Jewellery

Jewellery is perhaps the oldest Southwestern craft of all. The Ancestral Puebloans made necklaces of disks cut from seashells; a single specimen unearthed near Kayenta was 36 feet long and held over fifteen thousand beads. Such necklaces are now known as *heishi* and are the speciality of New Mexico's Santo Domingo Pueblo.

Turquoise has always been prized by Southwestern Indians; the prehistoric city at Chaco Canyon was probably founded on the turquoise trade, while the Navajo see the greenish-blue, semiprecious stone as symbolizing the state of harmony and beauty known as *hozho*. Necklaces of raw and polished turquoise beads are widely available; the stone also adds colour and character to the **silver** jewellery made by the Hopi, Zuni and Navajo in particular.

Silversmithing is a relatively recent tradition, probably introduced from Mexico in the mid-nineteenth century. For many years, acquiring chunky silver bracelets or belts studded with solid-silver conches was the standard Navajo way to accumulate wealth. Such items could be pawned for cash at trading posts and then redeemed when times got easier; now known as pawn jewellery, they count as valuable collectors' pieces. Casual buyers tend to prefer – and to be more able to afford – the more delicate **overlay** style, in which a stencilled design is cut from a thin sheet of silver, then soldered onto a backing sheet. This technique originated in 1947, when returning Hopi servicemen were trained in the technique, and the Hopi remain its finest exponents. Overlay designs can be seen on earrings, belt buckles, rings and, especially, the clasps of *bola*, or bootlace, ties.

Weaving

The finest **weavers** in the Southwest are generally acknowledged to be the Navajo. In legend, they acquired the craft from Spider Woman, who lives atop Spider Rock in the Canyon de Chelly; in fact, they were probably taught by the Pueblo peoples after the Pueblo Revolt of 1680. That was also when they began to raise sheep, which were introduced by the Spanish a century earlier.

Originally, the Navajo wove blankets and clothing; **Navajo rugs** were the brainchild of nineteenth-century traders, who also suggested that using "earth" colours such as brown would appeal to tourists expecting a "natural" look. Many individual Navajo communities or families weave designs named for their own area, such as Teec Nos Pos, Ganado, or Two Gray Hills. As a rule, the patterns have no religious significance, but most include an "escape route" or "spirit line," which runs to the edge of the rug and ensures that the weaver's spirit is not trapped within it. Traditional rugs also have a hole in the centre, as in a spider's web.

Authentic Navajo rugs take months to create and sell for thousands of dollars; anything you see cheaper is probably a mass-produced Mexican imitation. The Navajo Rug Auction at Crownpoint in New Mexico (Ⓦ crownpointrugauction.com) is the best opportunity to pick up a genuine bargain.

Pottery

Spanish explorers in 1540 spoke of Pueblo women as making "jars of extraordinary labour and workmanship, which were worth seeing." The ceramic tradition of northern New Mexico's pueblos remains as strong as ever, having been revitalized in the twentieth century by the San Ildefonso potter Maria Martinez. Although she consciously modelled her earlier work on ancient designs, the black-on-black museum pieces for which she became famous are a far cry from the popular conception of Native American crafts. Many tourists prefer either the straightforward pots and jars, painted with rectilinear "pueblo motifs," created at Ácoma Pueblo, or the "storyteller" figures, showing a mother surrounded by children, that were first created at Cochiti Pueblo.

Travel essentials

Costs and money

This book contains detailed price information for lodging and eating throughout the Southwest. Accommodation rates, explained on p.33, exclude any local taxes that may apply, while restaurant prices include food only and not drinks or tip. For museums and similar attractions, the entrance fees quoted are for adults; unless specified otherwise, assume children get in half-price.

North American travellers find **prices** in the Southwest broadly similar to the rest of the US, with food and lodging generally cheaper than in major US cities and tourist regions, and gas and groceries, especially in out-of-the-way places, a little more expensive. Most visitors from Europe and Australasia feel that their money goes further in the US than it does at home. However, if you're used to travelling in the less expensive countries of Europe, let alone in the rest of the world, you can't expect to scrape by on the same minuscule budget in the US.

As explained on p.29, the only way to reach most places in this book is to drive. If you can't bring your own vehicle, your least avoidable major expense will be **car rental**, at around $150 per week. What you spend on **accommodation** is more flexible. For most of the year, in most places, you should have no problem getting a motel room for under $75, though even the cheapest peak-season rates in or near certain national parks, or in downtown Santa Fe, are more like $100. Although **hostels** offering dorm beds – usually for $15 to $25 – are reasonably common, they're by no means everywhere, and in any case save little money for two or more travelling together. **Camping** is not only cheap, with park campgrounds ranging from free to perhaps $18 per night, but in many wilderness areas it's the only option.

As for food, $25 per day is enough to get an adequate life-support diet, consisting of perhaps one full-scale diner meal plus a stash of groceries,

TIPPING

You shouldn't depart a bar or restaurant without leaving a **tip** of at least 15–20 percent (unless the service is utterly disgusting). About the same amount should be added to taxi fares – and round them up to the nearest 50¢ or dollar. Tip hotel porters roughly $1 per item for carrying your baggage to your room. When paying by credit or charge card, you're expected to add the tip to the total bill before filling in the amount and signing

while for a daily total of around $40 you can eat pretty well. If you're visiting national parks and monuments, buy an annual pass (see p.36); the $80 fee covers all passengers in your vehicle. You'll probably also spend $5 to $12 a day on admissions to state parks, museums, and the like.

Sales tax is added to virtually everything you buy in a shop, but isn't included in the marked price. In the states covered in this book it ranges between around five and seven percent – except on Indian reservations, which do not levy sales tax. Most towns also charge lodging taxes of between five and fifteen percent.

Expect to pay most of your major expenses by **credit** or **debit card**; hotels and car rental agencies usually demand a card imprint as security, even if you intend to settle the bill in cash, and you'll be at a serious disadvantage if you don't have one.

You'll also need to carry a certain amount of **cash**. If you have a Mastercard or Visa, or a cash-dispensing card linked to an international network such as Cirrus or Plus, you can withdraw cash from appropriate automated teller machines (ATMs). Also consider carrying US dollar **travellers' cheques**, which offer the security of knowing that lost or stolen cheques will be replaced. Cheques issued by American Express, Visa, and Thomas Cook are universally accepted as cash in shops, restaurants, and gas stations, and change from your transactions will be rendered in hard currency.

Crime and personal safety

No one could pretend that America is crime-free, although away from the urban centres crime is often remarkably low. All the major tourist areas and the main nightlife zones in cities are invariably brightly lit and well policed. By planning carefully and taking good care of your possessions, you should, generally speaking, have few problems.

When parking in the wilderness, in national or state parks for example, leave your belongings out of sight, and carry any valuables with you.

Electricity

The US **electricity** supply is 110 volts AC. Plugs are standard two-pins – foreign visitors will need an adapter and voltage converter for their own electrical appliances.

Entry requirements

Under the **visa waiver scheme**, passport-holders from Britain, Ireland, Australia, New Zealand and most European countries do not require visas for trips to the US, so long as they stay less than ninety days and have an onward or return ticket. However, anyone planning to use the visa waiver scheme is required to apply for **travel authorization** in advance, a quick and straightforward process via ⓦesta.cbp.dhs.gov /esta/. Fail to do so, and you may well be denied entry. Once you have authorization, which costs $14, you can simply fill in the visa waiver form that's handed out on incoming planes. Immigration control takes place at your point of arrival on US soil.

In addition, your passport must be machine-readable, with a barcode-style number. All children need to have their own individual passports. Holders of older non-readable passports should either obtain new ones, or apply for visas prior to travel.

Prospective visitors from parts of the world not mentioned above need a valid passport and a non-immigrant visitor's visa. How to obtain a visa depends on what country you're in and your status when you apply, so call the nearest US embassy or consulate. For full details visit ⓦtravel.state.gov.

Gay and lesbian travellers

Websites catering to gay and lesbian visitors to, and residents of, Arizona include ⓦgayarizona.com and Wingspan in Tucson (ⓦwingspan.org); Albuquerque Pride (ⓦabqpride.com) is an equivalent for New Mexico, and the Gay and Lesbian Community Center of Southern Nevada is based at 953 E Sahara Ave, Las Vegas (ⓦthecenterlv.com). The Gay Las Vegas website, ⓦgayvegas.com, can tell you all you need to know about Sin City.

Insurance

Because medical care in the US is expensive, all travellers visiting from overseas should be sure to buy some form of **travel insurance**. American and Canadian citizens should check they're not already covered by their homeowners, renters, or – in some cases – credit card policies. Most Canadians are covered for medical mishaps overseas by their provincial health plans.

Internet access

Almost every hostel, motel and hotel listed in this book, as well as most cafés, offers free **wi-fi access**; Las Vegas, where most casinos charge high access fees, is the main exception. Guests usually also have the option of using a computer in the lobby area of many hotels. On the streets, however, **public internet access** is not as widely available as you might expect; public and university libraries, and internet cafés in larger towns, are your best bet.

Mail

Post offices in the Southwest are usually open Monday to Friday from 9am until 5pm, and Saturday from 9am to noon, and there are blue mailboxes on many street corners. Ordinary mail within the US costs 46¢ for a letter weighing up to an ounce. Airmail between the US and Europe or Australia costs $1.10 for postcards, and generally takes about a week.

ROUGH GUIDES TRAVEL INSURANCE

Rough Guides has teamed up with WorldNomads.com to offer great **travel insurance** deals. Policies are available to residents of over 150 countries, with cover for a wide range of **adventure sports**, 24hr emergency assistance, high levels of medical and evacuation cover and a stream of **travel safety information**. Roughguides.com users can take advantage of their policies online 24/7, from anywhere in the world – even if you're already travelling. And since plans often change when you're on the road, you can extend your policy and even claim online. Roughguides.com users who buy travel insurance with WorldNomads.com can also leave a positive footprint and donate to a community development project. For more information go to ⓦ**roughguides.com/travel-insurance**.

Maps

The best general-purpose **road map** for the principal areas covered in this book is the *Indian Country Guide Map*, available free to members of the AAA and sold throughout the Southwest for $4.95. It focuses on the Four Corners region, however, and does not extend into southern Arizona, southern New Mexico, or Nevada, and furthermore it's not reliable for dirt roads and backcountry routes. Each individual state also issues a free **highway map**, which is fine for general route planning and can be obtained from local visitor centres. In addition, Rand McNally produces good regional and state maps, while free town maps are generally available at local visitor centres.

All national parks, and most state parks, national forests, and the like provide reasonable maps. Both these, and the maps throughout this book, are adequate for day-hikes on the most popular trails. Serious hikers and backpackers, however, should equip themselves with detailed **topographical maps**. Among the best are the waterproof and tearproof national-park maps published by National Geographic–Trails Illustrated.

Opening hours and public holidays

On national **public holidays**, shops, banks, and offices are liable to be closed all day. The traditional summer season for tourism runs from Memorial Day, in late May, to Labor Day, in early September; some tourist attractions are only open during that period. Normal **banking hours** are from 9am or 10am until 3pm or 4pm Monday to Thursday, and slightly longer on Friday.

Jan 1 New Year's Day
Jan 15 Martin Luther King Jr's Birthday
3rd Mon in Feb Presidents' Day
Last Mon in May Memorial Day
July 4 Independence Day
1st Mon in Sept Labor Day
2nd Mon in Oct Columbus Day
Nov 11 Veterans' Day
Last Thurs in Nov Thanksgiving Day
Dec 25 Christmas Day

Phones

Foreign visitors can generally assume that their **mobile phones** (cell phones) will work in the US. Check with your phone provider that your existing payment scheme will cover you, and what charges you may incur. Many providers offer short-term packages that make phone usage on the road more affordable. If you plan to go online via your phone, make sure you know the relevant roaming charges, which may can be hugely expensive.

Making an international call from a motel-room phone will almost certainly be very expensive. The cheapest way to communicate is to use **Skype**, or a similar programme, to make free wi-fi calls from your phone or laptop. Alternatively, prepaid **phone cards** are widely available from gas stations, supermarkets and other outlets.

Senior travellers

For **older travellers**, the Southwest makes a wonderful vacation destination. So long as you're driving rather than using public transport, everywhere is easily accessible, with motels and hotels of a high standard available almost everywhere. All the national parks hold overlooks and short trails suitable for older travellers.

Anyone over the age of 62 can enjoy certain discounts. Amtrak and Greyhound, for example, offer (smallish) percentage reductions on fares to older passengers. US residents aged 50 or over can join the American Association of Retired Persons (W aarp.org), which organizes group travel for senior citizens and can provide discounts on accommodation and vehicle rental. Road Scholar (W roadscholar .org) runs educational and activity programmes in the Southwest for persons aged 60 and over. Senior Passes allow free national-parks admission for US citizens or residents aged 62 or older (see p.36).

Spectator sports

The most popular spectator sports in the Southwest are baseball and football. Phoenix is home to renowned pro and college teams.

Study and work programmes

AFS Intercultural Programs W afs.org. Intercultural exchange organization with programmes in over 50 countries.
American Institute for Foreign Study W aifs.com. Language study and cultural immersion, as well as au pair and Camp America programmes.
BTCV (British Trust for Conservation Volunteers) W tcv.org.uk. One of the largest environmental charities in Britain. Offers working holidays (as a paying volunteer) in Nevada.
BUNAC W bunac.org. Working holidays in a range of destinations for students, including 8- to 12-week programmes in Western national parks.
Camp America W campamerica.co.uk. Nine-week stints on summer camps in the US.

Time

New Mexico, Utah, Colorado and Arizona all operate on **Mountain Standard Time**, which is two hours behind Eastern Standard Time, and seven hours behind Greenwich Mean Time, so 2pm in Santa Fe is 4pm in New York City and 9pm in London. Nevada and California are on Pacific Standard Time, another hour behind. Between the second Sunday in March and the first Sunday in November, New Mexico, Utah, Colorado and Nevada adopt **Daylight Savings Time** and advance their clocks by one hour. Arizona, however, does not, so in summer it joins Nevada in being an hour behind New Mexico and Utah. That said, confusingly, the Navajo Nation in northeast Arizona does shift to Daylight Savings Time, making it one hour later than the rest of Arizona in summer, while the Hopi reservation, entirely surrounded by the Navajo Nation, stays put.

Tourist information

There's no single perfect source for information on the entire Southwest; that's the point of this book, after all. Each state covered here has its own tourist office. In addition, the region includes ten national parks, as well as dozens of federally managed national monuments, national forests and the like, and fifty or so Indian reservations, each of which attempts to meet the needs of visitors in its own way.

Local information

Most towns **run their own visitor centres**, often known as the "Convention and Visitors Bureau," or CVB. In cities such as Las Vegas, Phoenix and Santa Fe, **free newspapers** carry dining and entertainment listings. In addition, you're likely to come across the useful **Welcome Centers** along the interstates close to the state borders, which dispense maps and information on the entire state.

STATE TOURIST OFFICES

Arizona Office of Tourism Ⓦ arizonaguide.com.
Colorado Tourism Office Ⓦ colorado.com.
Nevada Commission on Tourism Ⓦ travelnevada.com.
New Mexico Tourism Department Ⓦ newmexico.org.
Utah Travel Industry Ⓦ utah.com.

SOUTHWEST USA WEBSITES

Websites for regional and local tourism information, activity operators, hotels and accommodation options, parklands and other attractions are listed throughout this book. In addition, the following more general sites may be of interest.
The AmericanSouthwest Ⓦ americansouthwest.net. Fan site devoted to the national parks and wilderness areas of the desert Southwest, featuring great photos, masses of links, and a copious section on slot canyons.
Discover Navajo Ⓦ discovernavajo.com. The official tourism website of the Navajo Nation is packed with useful information for Four Corners travellers.
High Country News Ⓦ hcn.org. Newspaper devoted to environmental issues in the West as a whole, with special reference to national parks and public lands, and a useful online archive.
Inside Outside Southwest Ⓦ insideoutsidemag.com. The website of this now-defunct Durango-based magazine holds a useful archive of every edition ever published, and remains a valuable resource of all aspects of Southwest life.
Las Vegas Review-Journal Ⓦ lvrj.com. The online version of Las Vegas's daily newspaper provides news on the West as well as up-to-date listings of what's happening in the city.
National Park Service Ⓦ nps.gov. This invaluable website covers every component of the national park system, with full practical details for the whole gamut of monuments and recreation areas as well as for the parks themselves. For big names, such as the Grand Canyon, the range of information is breathtaking, covering camping, hiking, wildlife and lodging, with links to accommodation options and activity operators in the vicinity.
National Scenic Byways Online Ⓦ byways.org. Sponsored by the Federal Highway Administration, this luscious site honours America's most beautiful driving routes.
Sierra Club Ⓦ sierraclub.org. The veteran environmental organization uses its website to promote awareness of issues and events throughout the US, with links to "chapters" in each individual state for coverage of local activities. For travellers, however, its most useful feature is the "Outings" section, which details not only fully-fledged adventure-travel expeditions, but also weekly activities for local volunteers.

Travellers with disabilities

For information on specific states, contact the tourism departments listed above. Useful independent sources of information include SATH (Ⓦ sath.org), Mobility International USA (Ⓦ miusa.org) and MossRehab Resource Net (Ⓦ mossresourcenet.org). The Access Pass, issued without charge to permanently disabled US citizens, gives free lifetime admission to all national parks.

Travelling with children

Although children travelling in the Southwest are likely to be enthralled by the spectacular Western-movie landscapes and the cowboys-and-Indians atmosphere of many frontier towns, parents planning a road trip in the region need to be realistic about quite how much time they'll have to spend in the car. If your kids don't like hours of driving, you're potentially letting yourself in for a miserable time.

The Four Corners

50 Northeast Arizona: the Navajo Nation

66 The Hopi Indian reservation

70 Southwest Colorado

86 Northwest New Mexico

94 Western New Mexico

FULL MOON OVER MONUMENT VALLEY

1

The Four Corners

The Four Corners region is the heartland of the Southwest, not because the states of Arizona, Utah, Colorado and New Mexico happen to meet here, but because it remains dominated by Native American cultures to an extent that's unique in the modern United States. The region centres on the Colorado Plateau, said to be the highest inhabited plateau in the world, bar Tibet. These dramatic and hauntingly beautiful uplands may have held a larger population a thousand years ago, when the people now known as the Ancestral Puebloans occupied settlements scattered throughout the deserts. Although they're chiefly remembered for their fabulous "cliff dwellings," which cling like eagles' nests to the walls of soaring red-rock canyons, in fact the Ancestral Puebloans lived everywhere, from the valley floors to the mesa tops.

Seven centuries ago, the Ancestral Puebloans left the plateau, to be replaced at some point thereafter by the nomadic Navajo. Now over 300,000 strong, the Navajo are the largest single Native American group in the United States, and their reservation occupies the bulk of the Four Corners area. Contrary to popular legend, however, the Ancestral Puebloans did not vanish completely. Some of their descendants still live nearby, in the **Hopi** villages of Arizona and the pueblos of **Zuni** and **Ácoma**, across the border in New Mexico. Still more migrated further west, to the valley of the Rio Grande.

The ruins left by the Ancestral Puebloans have become the Four Corners' prime visitor destinations. Among the most significant are those at **Mesa Verde National Park** in southwest Colorado, where dozens of graceful pueblo complexes are tucked into high rocky alcoves, and the fully fledged cities of New Mexico's remote **Chaco Canyon**, where Ancestral Puebloan civilization reached its peak. For sheer beauty, however, **Canyon de Chelly National Monument** in Arizona, where Navajo farmers live alongside the ancient remains, far surpasses both. Elsewhere, the main appeal is the scenery, which ranges from the Western-movie deserts epitomized by **Monument Valley**, via lone outcrops such as **Shiprock**, to the snow-capped peaks of southwest Colorado.

Planning a Four Corners itinerary can be hard work. The major attractions tend to be widely separated, while the towns in between are nothing special. Apart from a handful of expensive motels near Canyon de Chelly and Monument Valley, **accommodation** tends to be concentrated around the fringes. "Edge-of-the-res" towns like Gallup and Farmington may no longer be the alcohol-fuelled hell-holes of yesteryear, but they're basically characterless concrete conglomerations, and you'd do better to stay slightly further afield, in places like **Durango**, Colorado, or **Flagstaff**, Arizona (covered in Chapter 5).

Navajo Fairs p.50
Hard times at Black Mesa p.54
Valley Tours p.55
Monument Valley and the mythic West p.57
Canyon de Chelly tours p.59
The Navajo hogan p.62
Hopi religion: The Kachinas p.67
Mesa Verde tours and tickets p.76
Mesa Verde: a human history p.78

The Durango & Silverton Railroad p.80
Skiing and snowboarding in Telluride p.85
The Beast Is Dead p.88
The Pueblitos of Dinétah p.90
The Chaco phenomenon p.92
First contact with the Zuni p.96
Zuni Tribal Fair and the Shalako Dance p.96
A history of Ácoma Pueblo p.99

CLIFF PALACE, MESA VERDE NATIONAL PARK

Highlights

❶ Hiking to Betatakin Beautiful ranger-led hike to one of the Southwest's most spectacular ancient ruins, in Navajo National Monument. See p.53

❷ Monument Valley Where the West was won, in the movies at any rate; nowhere in the world can match it. See p.54

❸ White House Trail Everything about the Canyon de Chelly is magnificent, but the one free-access trail down into it is absolutely unmissable. See p.62

❹ The Hopi Mesas These unbelievably remote and isolated desert fastnesses hold the oldest communities in North America. See p.66

❺ Mesa Verde Perhaps the most photogenic of all the Southwest's ancient cliff dwellings, tucked into the hillsides of southwestern Colorado. See p.74

❻ Durango & Silverton Railroad Ride a steam train through the majestic Colorado Rockies. See p.80

❼ Silverton Former mining town, high in the Rockies, that oozes Wild West romance from its every dirt-packed street. See p.83

❽ Ácoma Pueblo With the most dramatic setting of any Pueblo community, "Sky City" has occupied a sheer-sided butte for almost a thousand years. See p.99

HIGHLIGHTS ARE MARKED ON THE MAP ON PP.48–49

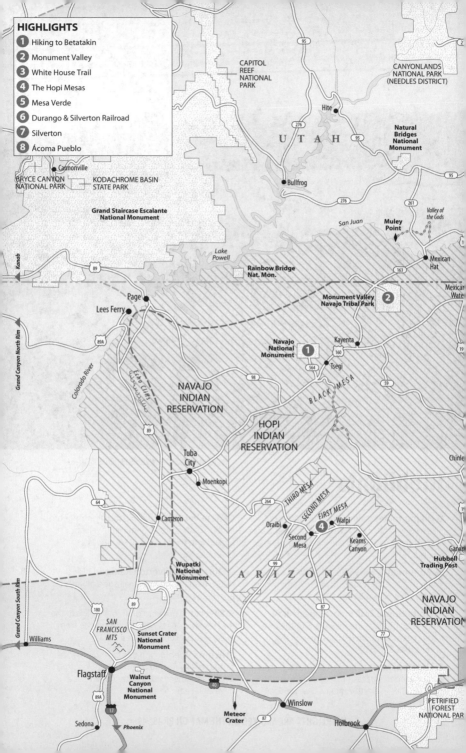

HIGHLIGHTS

1. Hiking to Betatakin
2. Monument Valley
3. White House Trail
4. The Hopi Mesas
5. Mesa Verde
6. Durango & Silverton Railroad
7. Silverton
8. Ácoma Pueblo

BRYCE CANYON
NATIONAL PARK

Cannonville

KODACHROME BASIN
STATE PARK

Grand Staircase Escalante
National Monument

Kanab

CAPITOL
REEF
NATIONAL
PARK

U T A H

95

276

Hite

Bullfrog

276

CANYONLANDS
NATIONAL PARK
(NEEDLES DISTRICT)

2

Natural
Bridges
National
Monument

95

95

261

Valley of
the Gods

San Juan

Muley
Point

163

Mexican
Hat

Mexican
Wate

Lake
Powell

Rainbow Bridge
Nat. Mon.

89

Page

Lees Ferry

89A

Monument Valley
Navajo Tribal Park

2

Kayenta

160

19

Navajo
National
Monument

1

564

Tsegi

Grand Canyon North Rim

Colorado River

Echo Cliffs

89

NAVAJO
INDIAN
RESERVATION

98

BLACK MESA

59

HOPI
INDIAN
RESERVATION

Chinle

Tuba
City

Moenkopi

264

THIRD MESA

SECOND MESA

FIRST MESA

Oraibi

4

Walpi

Cameron

64

Second
Mesa

Keams
Canyon

Ganado

Hubbell
Trading Post

Grand Canyon South Rim

Wupatki
National
Monument

A R I Z O N A

99

NAVAJO
INDIAN
RESERVATION

180

89

SAN
FRANCISCO
MTS

Sunset Crater
National
Monument

87

77

Williams

Flagstaff

89A

17

Walnut
Canyon
National
Monument

40

PETRIFIED
FOREST
NATIONAL PAR

Sedona

Phoenix

Meteor
Crater

87

Winslow

Holbrook

THE FOUR CORNERS

LA SAL JUNCTION
46
90
62
Ridgway
550
Ouray
Telluride
550
Monticello
191
7 Silverton
491
550
Dolores
C O L O R A D O
Blanding
262
Purgatory Ski area
Canyons of the Ancients National Monument
Dolores
145
6
Hovenweep National Monument
Cortez
145
Mancos
Durango & Silverton Railroad
Durango
160
Dulce
262
MESA VERDE NATIONAL PARK
Towaoc
5
140
ruff
Four Corners Monument
160
UTE MOUNTAIN TRIBAL PARK
160
Teec Nos Pos
574
Aztec
64
Shiprock
Farmington
173
Gobernador Canyon
64
64
Bloomfield
64
N E W
537
Los Alamos
Lukachukai
Tsaile
550
Largo Canyon
371
NAVAJO INDIAN RESERVATION
3
Nageezi
Cuba
Canyon de Chelly National Monument
491
M E X I C O
CHACO CULTURE NATIONAL HISTORICAL PARK
197
264
Window Rock
St Michaels
Crownpoint
509
Gallup
40
537
191
602
Thoreau
Grants
Zuni Pueblo
El Malpais National Monument
Laguna Pueblo
53
El Morro National Monument
117
8 Ácoma Pueblo (Sky City)
Ojo Caliente
191
Albuquerque

0 — 25 miles

⊡⊡⊡⊡⊡ Dirt road

N

Northeast Arizona: the Navajo Nation

The **Navajo Indian Reservation** – or, as it prefers to style itself, the **Navajo Nation** – is the largest of all Native American reservations. Extending for 27,000 square miles across northeast Arizona, northwest New Mexico, and southern Utah, it's larger than ten of the fifty US states. Its population approaches 350,000, of whom two-thirds are under 21 and between a quarter and a half are Christians.

Although tourist facilities on the reservation are minimal – only half a dozen widely scattered towns offer even a single motel – the region holds a trio of top-class attractions. The stunning sandscape of **Monument Valley** presents the definitive image of the Southwest, and is now home to a superb Navajo-run hotel; the beautiful **Canyon de Chelly** is home both to magnificent Ancestral Puebloan remains and traditional Navajo *hogans*; and **Navajo National Monument** preserves further awe-inspiring ancient cliff dwellings.

The Navajo Nation has minimal water resources – the **San Juan River** and **Colorado River** simply skirt its borders to the north and west respectively. Monument Valley in the north and the Painted Desert region in the south technically count as desert, but most of the rest of the terrain is **steppe**, where the land is too poor to grow crops but can just about support livestock. It used to be covered with native grasses, but having evolved in tandem with the Southwest's indigenous fauna, these could not survive being gnawed to the roots by imported animals. The sagebrush that now dominates the region looks appropriately Western to most visitors, but is, like the tumbleweed or Russian thistle, just another interloper.

While a declining proportion of Navajo are now farmers or shepherds, their nomadic origins remain evident. Most Navajo choose not to live in urbanized areas, so what few towns there are on the reservation tend to be ugly modern accretions, consisting of trailer homes gathered around a few dishevelled lots.

Spend a day or two driving across the Navajo Nation, and you'll swiftly sense you're in another land. Whether in diners, stores or on the radio, you're sure to hear spoken Navajo, a language of such complexity that it was adapted during World War II as an uncrackable military code. You'll also get a chance to try the ubiquitous **Navajo taco**, a piece of open-topped fry bread smothered with chile and/or refried beans.

Note that between early April and late October, when the Navajo Nation joins Utah and New Mexico on Daylight Savings Time, it's one hour later than the rest of Arizona, including the Hopi Reservation.

For more information on the nation as a whole, check out the official websites ⓦ discovernavajo.com, ⓦ explorenavajo.com; and ⓦ navajo-nsn.gov.

Brief history

The Navajo, who call themselves the **Diné** ("the People"), are relative newcomers to the Four Corners region. Having drifted down from the far Northwest less than a thousand years ago, they occupied their present territory within the last three or four centuries. They have always been great assimilators, quick to adapt to new environments and acquire skills from their neighbours. Navajo religion and social organization draw

---

NAVAJO FAIRS

The ideal time to visit the Navajo Nation is to coincide with one of its various annual fairs. The five-day **Navajo Nation Fair** takes place in Window Rock in early September (ⓦ navajonationfair .com), while the **Central Navajo Fair** is in Chinle in late August, and Tuba City welcomes the **Western Navajo Fair** in mid-October (ⓦ westernnavajofair.org). Largely secular occasions, characterized much like county or state fairs throughout the West by country music, rodeos and other livestock-related events, these also double as pow wows, and attract Native Americans from far and wide.

heavily on Pueblo examples, while many "traditional" crafts, now sold in roadside stalls and trading posts, were learned from outsiders and adapted in response to tourist demand. Above all, contemporary Navajo culture was shaped by the acquisition of the horses and sheep brought by the Spanish, which were originally seized in raids on settlements along the Rio Grande.

Tuba City

Though it's the largest community on the western side of the Navajo Nation, there's no great reason to stop at **TUBA CITY** unless you need a place to spend the night. Straddling US-160 ten miles northeast of US-89, just under eighty miles north of Flagstaff and as far east of the Grand Canyon's South Rim, it's also an important crossroads, marking the point where Hwy 164 begins its fifty-mile journey east to the Hopi Mesas (see p.69). If you're feeling weary, incidentally, spare a thought for the Hopi runner reported as having *run* to Flagstaff and back from Tuba City in under 24 hours.

The town's unusual name is a corruption of "Tuuvi," a Hopi from nearby Moenkopi who converted to Mormonism in 1877 and invited a group of Mormon families to settle here. Soon, however, the Mormons were monopolizing the site's precious springs, fed by an aquifer that reaches to Monument Valley. They were forced to move out when the area was added to Navajo lands in 1903.

Tuba City has two unusual claims to fame. The first is a set of petrified **dinosaur tracks**, near the highway five miles southwest of town. These widely spaced 65-million-year-old sandstone imprints were left by a ten-foot creature known as a Dilophosaurus. It's hard to spot the tracks on your own – in truth, they're not all that riveting – but waiting Navajo guides can lead you to them for a small donation. Secondly, Tuba City straddles two separate **time zones**. Most businesses along the highway, such as Basha's supermarket, operate on Mountain Standard Time, while clocks in the town proper, a block or two uphill to the north, are set in summer to Daylight Savings Time, an hour later.

ACCOMMODATION AND EATING   TUBA CITY

Diné Inn Motel 322 US-160 ☎ 928 283 6107. Head just east from Tuba City's central intersection to find this cheap motel, offering clean but very basic en-suite rooms with uncomfortable beds. $81

Grey Hills Inn Turn left off US-160, half a mile northeast of town ☎ 928 283 6271. This bare-bones hostel is attached to the high school, and only open during the summer holiday period. Staffed by students training for tourism jobs, it offers utterly plain grey-brick rooms with shared bathrooms. $50

Hogan Restaurant 10 N Main St ☎ 928 283 5260. Part of the same complex that includes the *Quality Inn*, this local family restaurant is in no way remarkable, but it's the most conventional option in town. The lunch buffet is atrocious, but if you order from the long, inexpensive Mexican–American menu, the food is OK. There's also an espresso cafe alongside. Daily 7am–9pm.

★ **Moenkopi Legacy** US-160 ☎ 928 283 4500, ⓦ experiencehopi.com. Tuba City's fanciest hotel by far, right by the crossroads that provides access to the Hopi Reservation, this impressive hundred-room structure was opened in 2010 as a business venture by the nearby Hopi community of Moenkopi. Beyond its attractive facade, designed to evoke traditional Pueblo architecture, and the huge lobby adorned with historic photos, the actual rooms could be in any generic high-end motel, but they have whirlpool baths, there are some larger suites, and there's also a decent pool. $145

Quality Inn 10 N Main St ☎ 928 283 4545 or ☎ 800 644 8383, ⓦ qualityinntubacity.com. Standing alongside the *hogan*-shaped Tuba City Trading Post, a mile north of Tuba City's central intersection, this large, attractively maintained motel offers pricey but acceptable rooms, with RV spaces also available. $122

Tuuvi Cafe US-160 ☎ 928 283 4374, ⓦ experiencehopi .com. Part of a Hopi-run roadside complex that also includes a gas station, this all-day diner serves all-American egg, ham and pancake breakfasts, and then a largely uninspiring menu which as well as $8 burgers and sandwiches includes Hopi tacos (much the same as Navajo tacos), and a different Hopi stew each day. Daily 6am–9pm.

1

Navajo National Monument

50 miles northeast of Tuba City, 20 miles southwest of Kayenta, reached via a ten-mile spur road that runs north from US-160 • Free •
☎ 928 672 2700, ⓦ nps.gov/nava

Despite its name, **NAVAJO NATIONAL MONUMENT** has little to do with the Navajo. Instead, it's among the most beautiful Ancestral Puebloan sites in the Southwest.

Each of the monument's three separate parcels preserves a long-lost Ancestral Puebloan **cliff dwelling**, a ravishing, centuries-old pueblo of interlocking, adobe-walled homes, plazas, and kivas. Set in an enormous rocky alcove, **Betatakin** can be admired from an overlook near the visitor centre, or accessed via a six-hour, ranger-led hike. The even larger **Keet Seel** is a seventeen-mile round-trip hike from the road, and so is only seen by a dedicated few. Finally, fragile **Inscription House** has been closed to visitors for fifty years.

Brief history

Archeologists divide the Ancestral Puebloans of the Four Corners into three subgroups. One is centred on Mesa Verde (see p.74) and another on Chaco Canyon (see p.91); the focus in Navajo National Monument, **Tsegi Canyon**, is the definitive **Kayenta** site. Though its inhabitants were still living in pithouses long after the people of Chaco and Mesa Verde were constructing sophisticated pueblos, they were fine potters, and Kayenta ceramics are now much-prized museum pieces. Tree-ring dating pinpoints their move into the alcoves of Tsegi Canyon to around 1250 AD. Within fifty years, intensive irrigation had lowered the water table and rendered farming impossible, and the canyon had been abandoned.

What became of the Kayenta people is no mystery. According to the Navajo, Keet Seel was built by settlers from Navajo Mountain, and Betatakin by a group from Chaco. That dovetails with the **Hopi** legend that eight of their clans lived here shortly before their migrations ended at the Hopi Mesas, fifty miles south. A pictograph at Betatakin – a bird-like figure within a large white circle – shows Masaw, the symbol of the Hopi Fire Clan, and Hopis regularly return for ceremonies.

Navajo National Monument was established in 1909, after Navajo guides led members of the Wetherill family of Mesa Verde fame (see p.78) to Keet Seel. Betatakin was "discovered" a year or two later, by chance already within the monument boundaries.

Visitor Centre

10 miles north of US-160, along Hwy-564 • Daily: summer 8am–5.30pm; winter 8am–5pm • Free • ☎ 928 672 2700, ⓦ nps.gov/nava

It takes at least half an hour to drive to the **visitor centre** there and back from the main road, and even once you're there you have to hike a mile (round-trip) to see the actual ruins. The visitor centre does holds some interesting displays, including a mock-up of three rooms from Betatakin, and a reconstruction of a Navajo *hogan*. Hwy-564 continues beyond the monument, but is not paved; ordinary vehicles should not drive any further.

The Sandal Trail

If you only have time for a brief visit to Navajo National Monument, all you can do is gaze across the canyon to **Betatakin** from the end of the **Sandal Trail**, an easy, paved, one-mile round-trip hike from the visitor centre. The view from Betatakin Overlook at the end, where a sumptuous orange recess in the canyon wall arches above the 135-room cluster of dwellings, is especially amazing in late afternoon, when direct sunlight penetrates the alcove. Their straight walls rise in tiers from a ledge above the canyon floor; hence the Navajo name Betatakin, or "house on ledges." It's all in such good condition – everything you see is original, except for the ladders and a few of the roof beams – that it's hard to believe the 120 or so inhabitants left not seven years but seven centuries ago.

Hiking to Betatakin

Accessible on guided hikes only; precise schedules vary year to year, but typically Memorial Day to Labor Day daily 8.15am & 10am, Labor Day to Memorial Day occasional tours only • Free • ☎ 928 672 2700, ⓦ nps.gov/nava

It's worth visiting Navajo National Monument for the long-distance views from the end of the Sandal Trail. However, if you plan ahead and can spare the time, you can enjoy an even more rewarding experience, and learn more about the land and its history, by joining one of the **free ranger-guided hikes** that go all the way to **Betatakin** itself. Numbers are limited, so call a day or two in advance to reserve a place. Remember the time difference if you're hurrying here from beyond the Navajo Nation; the monument is an hour ahead of other Arizona locations, like the Grand Canyon or Flagstaff, during Daylight Savings Time.

All hikers must bring enough food and water (at least half a gallon) to last the five-hour round-trip. Although you rendezvous for a briefing at the visitor centre, the hike starts a mile or two's drive away, along a trail that drops steeply into spectacular **Tsegi Canyon** from the top of Skeleton Mesa. Betatakin itself only comes into sight right at the end, as you head up a steadily narrowing side canyon, filled with delicate aspens that turn a gorgeous yellow in the fall. The closer you approach, the more overwhelming the awesome dimensions of the alcove become; it's 452ft high, 370ft wide, and 135ft deep. Rangers normally lead visitors right into the ruin itself; you can't enter individual dwellings, but sitting in the plaza of the ancient pueblo is an extraordinarily evocative experience. Its remarkable echo was no doubt exploited to the full in ceremonies.

Keet Seel

Getting all the way to **Keet Seel** – Arizona's largest cliff dwelling – is a major undertaking. The gruelling seventeen-mile, self-guided round-trip **hike**, which branches into Tsegi Canyon off the Betatakin trail, is generally considered too much to attempt in a single day, so most hikers spend the night at the primitive campground near the ruin. There's no drinkable water en route.

All hikers *must* make reservations through the visitor centre, anywhere from one day to five months in advance. The trail is only open in summer, when up to twenty (free) permits per day are issued, on condition that you attend a briefing session, held daily at 8.15am and 4pm. You won't have time to do it as a day-hike unless you attend the briefing the day before.

Visitors to Keet Seel can only enter the ruins with the ranger stationed nearby. The village reaches deep back into the hillside, so well sheltered that its 150-plus rooms have barely deteriorated. No more than half a dozen are *kivas* – the Kayenta were not such relentless builders of these ceremonial chambers as their neighbours at Mesa Verde. Keet Seel was a longer-lasting and more dynamic settlement than Betatakin; its cliff dwellings date from the same era, but people lived in the vicinity from around 950 AD, and migrating groups came and went for the next few hundred years. Little now survives of the large free-standing pueblo that stood on the valley floor not far away.

ACCOMMODATION AND EATING   **NAVAJO NATIONAL MONUMENT**

Anasazi Inn Tsegi, on US-160, 8 miles northeast of the intersection with Hwy-564 ☎ 928 697 3793. This sprawling, low-slung and frankly rundown 57-room motel offers the closest accommodation to the monument, but it's still 20 miles from the visitor centre, and is only of value as a fallback when everything in Kayenta, another 13 miles northeast, is booked up. Some of the accommodation is in rudimentary trailers with poor plumbing. Its desert setting is dramatic, though, and it does at least have a small, if unremarkable, restaurant (open noon–2.30pm & 5.30–8pm). **$95**

★ **Sunset View Campground** Near the visitor centre ☎ 928 672 2700, ⓦ nps.gov/nava. This lovely little campground remains open year-round, and all its first-come first-served sites are free; there are no hook-ups for RVs. In summer, visitors who arrive after the campground is full are accommodated in the more primitive *Canyon View Campground* a mile north. **Free**

1

HARD TIMES AT BLACK MESA

Immediately opposite the Navajo National Monument turn-off, a broad but poorly surfaced road sets off south to climb **Black Mesa**. Only 4WD vehicles can get more than a mile or two along here, so few tourists see the gaping **strip mines** where for many years the Peabody Western Coal Company extracted the prodigious coal deposits for which the mesa is named.

The future of these mines is uncertain and surrounded by controversy. **Black Mesa Mine** itself, which supplied coal to the Mohave Power Plant in Laughlin, Nevada, closed down at the end of 2005. Amazingly enough, the coal was crushed and slurried on its 265-mile, three-day trip around the Grand Canyon by pipeline. That process, the only such operation in the US, used an extravagant 1.3 billion gallons of pure water per year. When springs and water sources, many of which were considered sacred, started to run dry across the Hopi and Navajo reservations, many tribal members called for Peabody's leases to be discontinued, or at least renegotiated. Black Mesa Mine closed not because of local activism, however, but because the Mohave Power Plant could not afford to reduce its sulfur dioxide emissions to meet air pollution standards. Peabody has been fighting in the courts ever since to be allowed to reopen the mine, potentially in conjunction with the still-operational **Kayenta Mine** nearby, but thanks largely to Hopi opposition permission has not been granted.

Kayenta

KAYENTA, where US-160 meets US-163 twenty miles northeast of Navajo National Monument, is not in any sense an historic town. Having begun life in the 1950s as a dormitory community for workers in the uranium mines to the north, it later became the main base for the miners of Black Mesa. Just twenty miles south of **Monument Valley**, it now also caters to ever-increasing numbers of tourists, but remains little more than a conglomeration of trailer homes, with barely a two-storey building to its name.

ACCOMMODATION AND EATING   KAYENTA

As well as some unenthralling diners and fast-food places, Kayenta is home to three upscale **motels**, two of which hold restaurants. With Monument Valley so close at hand, room rates are very high, and between May and September it's essential to reserve in advance – ideally online, where you may be able to find better rates. As everywhere on the reservation, alcohol is not permitted.

★ **Hampton Inn Kayenta** On US-160 just west of the central intersection ☎928 697 3170, ⓦhamptoninn.com. Kayenta's smartest and best-value motel, with 73 comfortable rooms plus an open-air terrace and a pool. Rates include a free hot breakfast, and the on-site *Reuben Heflin* restaurant is recommended. **$179**

Kayenta Monument Valley Inn Junction of US-160 and US-163 ☎928 697 3221 or ☎866 306 3458, ⓦkayentamonumentvalleyinn.com. Large motel complex, immediately south of the highway intersection, facing drivers arriving from Monument Valley. Its 164 rooms are plain but perfectly adequate, and there's a small outdoor pool, heated in low season, and tiny fitness centre. The *Wagon Wheel* restaurant isn't bad. **$209**

Reuben Heflin Hampton Inn Kayenta. The pick of the motel restaurants, named after its original owner, this surprisingly good option serves tasty $18 dinner specials such as lamb shanks or beef chimichangas in an appealing environment. Daily: mid-March to mid-Oct 11.30am–10pm; mid-Oct to mid-March 5–9pm.

Wetherill Inn 1000 Main St ☎928 697 3231, ⓦwetherill-inn.com. This very standard chain motel, a mile north of the highway intersection towards Monument Valley, offers two storeys of dark but acceptable rooms at the lowest rates in town. There's an indoor swimming pool, and while they don't have a restaurant, they provide free continental breakfast. **$136**

Monument Valley

The classic Wild West landscape of stark sandstone buttes and forbidding pinnacles of rock, poking from an endless expanse of drifting red sands, has become an archetypal image. Only when you arrive at **MONUMENT VALLEY** do you realize how much your perception of the West has in fact been shaped by this one spot. Such scenery does exist

1

elsewhere, but nowhere is it so perfectly concentrated and distilled. While movie-makers have flocked here since the early days of Hollywood, the sheer majesty of the place still takes your breath away. Add the fact that it remains a stronghold of **Navajo** culture, and Monument Valley may well prove to be the absolute highlight of your trip to the Southwest.

Although you can see the buttes for free – whether silhouetted on the skyline from anything up to fifty miles away, or towering alongside US-163 – the four-mile detour to enter **Monument Valley Navajo Tribal Park** rewards with much closer views, while the tours beyond the end of the road are unforgettable.

Brief history

Monument Valley is not really a valley. There's no permanent stream, nor higher ground to either side, and no valley has buttes along its floor. This whole region was once a flat plain, concealing the top of what are now the tallest "monuments." In the past ten million years, the Monument Uplift – part of the general upthrust of the Colorado Plateau – has pushed that plain up from below, bulging to create cracks that have since eroded to leave only isolated nuggets of harder rock.

On the surface, thanks to annual rainfall of under ten inches, this looks like an unpromising region in which to live. However, sand dunes are surprisingly efficient at conserving moisture, and a huge aquifer deeper down stretches all the way to Tuba City. Beneath the small **cliff dwellings** that burrow into the rocks, the slopes are littered with ancient potsherds; the Ancestral Puebloans were here until around 1300 AD. After that, the area may have remained unoccupied until a band of Navajo retreated here to avoid Kit Carson's round-up in 1864 (see p.471). Their leader, **Hoskinnini**, discovered silver nearby. Two white prospectors sneaked some of the metal away in 1880, but were killed when they returned, at the bases of **Mitchell Mesa** and **Merrick Butte** respectively.

The Navajo, who named Monument Valley *Tse Tbübndisgaün*, or "there is a treeless area amid the rocks," see the whole place as a *hogan*, with its "door" facing east from the visitor centre, and the butte behind *Goulding's Lodge* (see p.58) its central hearth.

Monument Valley Navajo Tribal Park

Straddling the Arizona–Utah state line, 24 miles north of Kayenta and 25 miles southwest of Mexican Hat • **Car park** daily 24hr, **visitor centre** daily: May–Sept 6am–8pm; Oct–April 8am–5pm • $5 • ☎ 435 727 5870, ⓦ navajonationparks.org

The approach road to **Monument Valley Navajo Tribal Park** ends at a large car park, four miles east of US-163, just beyond a booth where the park admission fee is collected. Every new arrival rushes to the walled terrace that lines the car park's upper edge, for the first close-up view of the valley's signature buttes.

VALLEY TOURS

Taking a **guided tour** in and around Monument Valley is very highly recommended, though prices have risen considerably in recent years.

Several Navajo-run outfits offer **jeep tours** and **guided hikes** of varying lengths. It's usually easy to get on a tour if you simply ask around the kiosks at the tribal park's parking area. Shop around, as prices can vary enormously for what's essentially the same experience. Broadly speaking, though, jeep tours cost upwards from $50 for 1hr and $175 for a full day, while hiking tours tend to start from $100. All can be booked in advance, via the operators listed on ⓦ navajonationparks.org, while the *View Hotel* and *Lodge* can also arrange tours.

Horseback tours generally work out cheaper if you book in advance rather than arranging them with the outfitters waiting in the parking lot. Typical prices, through operators such as Roy Black (☎ 928 429 1959, ⓦ blacksmonumentvalleytours.com), range from $79 for 1hr 30min up to $195 for a full day. In addition, if you drive down to the stables at John Ford's Point on the valley floor, it's often possible to saddle up on the spur of the moment for a good price, and you don't have to pay for the extra riding time to and from the valley proper.

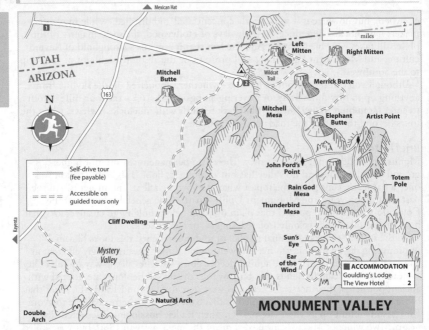

The most prominent buttes visible from here are the pair known as **The Mittens**, which consist logically enough of the Left or West Mitten and the Right or East Mitten. Rising a thousand feet from the desert floor, each has a distinct "thumb" that splinters off from its bulkier central section. Alongside them stands **Merrick Butte**, completing a trio that's illuminated a glowing red at sunset.

The complex of buildings that sprawls beside the car park includes the *View Hotel and Restaurant* (see p.58), and a gift store, as well as the park's **visitor centre**, which holds displays on Navajo culture and history, including the story of the wartime Code Talkers, as well as on the valley itself.

The road through the valley

Daily: summer 8am–6pm; winter 8am–4.30pm

A rough, **unpaved road** drops from the western end of the tribal park's parking area, to run through Monument Valley. While taking a guided tour is preferable, the 17-mile loop marked as the **self-drive** route makes a bearable, if bumpy, hour-plus ride in an ordinary vehicle. You're allowed to stop en route to stretch your legs, but not to hike for any distance.

At the main halt, **John Ford's Point**, you can enjoy the classic wide-screen valley panorama and also browse a few jewellery stalls. A Navajo man normally poses on horseback at the tip of the nearby promontory, while closer at hand, children in traditional dress invite you to photograph them for a dollar or two. The road goes on to pass near the **Totem Pole** before heading back via **Artist Point** to the visitor centre.

Guided tours follow the same route, but they also take visitors "behind the scenes", beyond the main road, and offer a fascinating Navajo perspective. Likely stops on longer tours include the **Sun's Eye** – a high natural arch, with petroglyphs of bighorn sheep at its base – and the similar, even more dramatic **Ear of the Wind**, as well as an obligatory visit to a *hogan* for a weaving demonstration. The most striking **Ancestral Puebloan remains** are in adjacent **Mystery Valley**, which you'll probably only visit if you take a full-day tour.

Wildcat Trail

The one opportunity to hike without a Navajo guide in Monument Valley is along the **Wildcat Trail** (allow 2hr to complete the full 3.2-mile loop). Starting beside the park's primitive campground, just under half a mile down the unpaved road towards the valley floor from the visitor centre, this takes just over three miles to circle the Left Mitten butte. It's an utterly exhilarating hike, though the pitiless lack of shade means it's best undertaken early or late in the day, and for that matter early or late in the year as well. Only the brief uphill trudge back to the trailhead at the end is at all physically demanding.

MONUMENT VALLEY AND THE MYTHIC WEST

The real star of my Westerns has always been the land … My favorite location is Monument Valley. It has rivers, mountains, plains, desert, everything that land can offer … I consider this the most complete, beautiful, and peaceful place on earth. John Ford, Cosmopolitan, *March 1964*

In 1937, Harry Goulding, of *Goulding's Lodge*, heard that Hollywood producers were planning to shoot Western-themed movies in the Southwest. Although Monument Valley had featured in a 1925 silent, *The Vanishing American*, its splendours remained largely unknown. Goulding set off for California with a portfolio of photographs. Within a year, **John Ford** brought a crew to Goulding's remote desert outpost and was filming *Stagecoach*.

From their first moment on screen, Monument Valley's emblematic buttes served as a visual shorthand for the **Wild West**. The geographical reality was irrelevant. While *Stagecoach* supposedly followed a coach through Apache territory from Tonto in southern Arizona to Lordsburg in New Mexico, it did no more than duck in and out of Monument Valley; as John Wayne put it, "there's some things a man just can't run away from." Similarly, in *The Searchers* (1956), Wayne spent five years scouring Texas for Scar's band of Comanche, although in reality both he and they remained within the same five-mile radius of the Mittens. In *My Darling Clementine* (1946), Henry Fonda as Wyatt Earp drove his cattle across Monument Valley and into Tombstone, somehow transplanted from southern Arizona complete with saguaro cacti; the OK Corral perched on a mesa nearby. Monument Valley consistently symbolized the untamed wilderness that lay beyond the ramshackle towns, beleaguered forts, isolated cabins, or crude fences of the West's earliest white pioneers.

In total, John Ford made seven movies in Monument Valley, including his "cavalry trilogy" of *Fort Apache* (1948), *She Wore A Yellow Ribbon* (1949), and *Rio Grande* (1950). Ford worked closely with the Navajo, who featured as all-purpose Indians, camping out in wigwams in *The Searchers*, for example, at what's now known as John Ford's Point. Medicine man Hosteen Tso, kept on hand to control the weather, is credited with producing a snowstorm and a sandstorm to order for *Stagecoach*. The construction of Monument Valley's first road, in the 1950s, spoiled Ford's hitherto pristine landscape, but he carried on filming here until *Cheyenne Autumn* (1963). He died shortly after announcing plans to make *Appointment at Precedence* in the valley, in 1972.

The spectacle of Henry Fonda's son smoking marijuana in Monument Valley, in *Easy Rider* (1969), may have marked an end to the days of the classic Western, but the valley itself has remained in demand. Clint Eastwood had some perilous moments atop the Totem Pole in *The Eiger Sanction* (1975), and Michael J. Fox's souped-up DeLorean outgunned pursuing Indian warriors in *Back to the Future III* (1989). Other visitors have included Tom Hanks in *Forrest Gump* (1994), while in Mario van Peebles' hip-hop *Western Posse* (1993), Monument Valley was bursting with Sioux Indians, gold mines, railroads, and buffalo soldiers.

Monument Valley's starring role as the setting for many **Roadrunner** cartoons probably stems from its appearances in the popular *Krazy Kat* comic strip of the 1920s and 1930s. Learned critics such as e e cummings, who referred to the strip's "strictly irrational landscape," and Umberto Eco, who spoke of "surrealistic inventions, especially in the improbable lunar landscapes," were clearly oblivious that artist **George Herriman** was a regular visitor to *Goulding's Lodge*. The adventures of Krazy Kat and Ignatz Mouse – set in Coconino County – were played out against realistic depictions of Monument Valley formations.

1

Assorted plants used by the Navajo are labelled along the way, but the real glory of the trail is the chance to be alone in this overwhelming landscape, dwarfed beneath the mighty rock formations. Stretches of broad, rutted sandy roads are interspersed with narrow, scrubby tracks; watch out for the cairns that mark the route.

ACCOMMODATION AND EATING   **MONUMENT VALLEY**

Goulding's Lodge Two miles west of US-163, across from the park approach road ☎435 727 3231, ⓦgouldings.com. Having begun life as a trading post in the 1920s, *Goulding's Lodge* now incorporates an upscale motel with dramatic, long-range valley views, an indoor pool, a general store, a gas station, a museum of movie memorabilia, and a campground. Since the Navajo built the *View Hotel*, it has been rather eclipsed. Still, it makes a good if pricey overnight stop, oozing old-West atmosphere, but there's no reason to go out of your way to visit, or to dine at its *Stagecoach Dining Room*, open for all meals daily. Tents $26, RV spaces $45, rooms $209

Mitten View Campground Monument Valley Tribal Park ☎435 727 5870, ⓦnavajonationparks.org. The park's exposed campground, half a mile down the unpaved road that leads from the visitor centre to the valley itself, is first-come, first-served. It was being updated as this book went to press, so facilities may well have improved, and rates increased. As things stand, however, water is available in summer only, and rates are charged per person, for anyone aged over 6. $5

★ **The View Hotel** Monument Valley Tribal Park ☎928 727 3470, ⓦmonumentvalleyview.com. All of the luxurious rooms in this stunning Navajo-owned hotel, alongside the tribal park visitor centre, have private balconies that command a magnificent panorama of Monument Valley; the best, and most expensive, are up on the second floor. Casual visitors can enjoy the same view from the adjoining terrace. $209

The View Restaurant Monument Valley Tribal Park ☎928 727 3470, ⓦmonumentvalleyview.com. The only eating option in the tribal park enjoys prime position overlooking the valley, with some irresistible outdoor tables. The food is good but not exceptional, and they make a point of serving authentic Navajo dishes such as mutton stew or pork with red chile posole (both $14) and blue-corn fry bread ($5), alongside more conventional burgers and salads, and Western-style steaks and other meats – there's even Clint Eastwood fried chicken ($17). They also operate a little espresso stand by the main entrance. Daily 7am–2pm & 5pm until late.

From Monument Valley to Canyon de Chelly

The most direct – and most scenic – route between the Navajo Nation's two major tourist attractions, Monument Valley and Canyon de Chelly, is **Arrowhead Hwy-59**. This gorgeous drive heads south off US-160 eight miles east of Kayenta, and then spends almost fifty miles skirting the northern flanks of Black Mesa.

For most of the way, it runs across flat desert grasslands, like a slightly more fertile version of Monument Valley, with cracks in the plains to either side hinting at unfathomable canyons. Occasionally, off to the south, villages such as **Chilchinbito** and **Rough Rock** nestle against the mesa, but the road ignores them. When it finally drops down **Carson Mesa** to reach Chinle Valley, you're confronted by the unlikely waters of **Many Farms Lake**. The road meets US-191 at the community of **Many Rivers**, fourteen miles north of Chinle.

Canyon de Chelly National Monument

2 miles east of Chinle, Arizona; 87 miles southeast of Monument Valley, 85 miles north of the I-40 town of Chambers, Arizona • 24hr access, but to rim drives only, not valley floor • Free • ☎928 674 5500, ⓦnps.gov/cach

A short way east of **Chinle**, twin sandstone walls emerge abruptly from the desert floor, then climb with phenomenal speed to become the thousand-foot cliffs of **CANYON DE CHELLY NATIONAL MONUMENT**. Between these sheer sides, the cottonwood-fringed Chinle Wash meanders through an idyllic oasis of meadows and planted fields. Here and there, a *hogan* stands in a grove of fruit trees, a straggle of sheep is penned in by a crude wooden fence, or ponies drink at the water's edge. And everywhere, perched above the valley on ledges in the canyon walls and dwarfed by the towering cliffs, are the long-abandoned dwellings left by the **Ancestral Puebloans**.

1

The monument in fact holds two main canyons, which branch apart a few miles upstream: **Canyon de Chelly** to the south and **Canyon del Muerto** to the north. Each twists and turns in all directions, scattered with immense rock monoliths, while several smaller canyons break away. The whole labyrinth threads its way upwards for thirty miles into the Chuska Mountains.

Canyon de Chelly is a magnificent place, easily on a par with any of the Southwest's national parks. Its relative lack of fame owes much to the presence of the **Navajo**, for whom the canyon retains enormous symbolic significance, despite the fact that they did not themselves construct its cliff dwellings. Casual visitors are restricted to peering into the canyon from above, from overlooks along the two "rim drives." There's no road in, and apart from one short but superb hike, the **White House Trail**, you can only enter the canyons with a Navajo guide. Incidentally, "de Chelly" is pronounced "de shay;" it's a corruption of the Navajo *tségi*, meaning "rock canyon."

CANYON DE CHELLY TOURS

With the exception of the White House Trail (see p.62), the only way to get a close-up view of Canyon de Chelly's amazing Ancestral Puebloan remains, or to see the rock art that lines its walls, is to take a **guided tour** with a Navajo guide. The glorious, glowing cliffs tower far above you; and tranquil Navajo farms spread out to either side. The best-known operators are listed below, but you can find more extensive listings on the park website.

JEEP TOURS

Only sturdy 4WD vehicles could hope to negotiate the rutted riverbed and deep sandy drifts inside the Canyon de Chelly. If you have your own, you can hire a Navajo guide to accompany you, for around $16.50 per hour. Otherwise, you'll have to join a tour with one of several local companies. A typical half-day trip will get you to and from White House Ruin; continuing beyond to see Spider Rock takes a full day.

Canyon de Chelly Tours ☎928 674 5433, ⓦcanyondechellytours.com. Jeep tours with Navajo guides. Scheduled 3hr tours to White House Ruin, starting from *Chinle Holiday Inn*, March–Oct daily 9am, 1pm & 4pm; $75, under-13s $50. Also customised tours, costing from around $220 for a 3hr jaunt for 1–3 passengers, plus $77 for each additional hour, and overnight trips.

Thunderbird Lodge ☎928 674 5841, ⓦtbirdlodge .com. For most of the year, these popular "shake'n'bake" tours zigzag into either or both canyons in open-top flatbed trucks; in winter they carry on in glass-roofed army vehicles with caterpillar tracks. Half-day trips daily: summer 9am & 2pm; winter 9am & 1pm; adults $51.50, under-13s $40. Full-day tours late spring to late fall only: daily 9am; $83, no reductions.

GUIDED HIKES

National Monument Visitor Center ☎928 674 5500, ⓦnps.gov/cach. In season, the National Park Service organizes highly recommended Navajo-led group hikes into the canyon, for a charge of $15. Precise schedules and destinations vary year to year, but most recently there have been hikes on Fri, Sat & Sun only, with a 3hr walk departing at 8.30am in April, May & Sept, and a 4hr 30min walk setting off at 7am

June–Aug. They also offer occasional 2hr night hikes. **Footpath Journeys** ☎928 724 3366, ⓦfootpath journeys.com. This Navajo-owned company offers a fuller but much more expensive hiking experience of the canyon than the park service. During their five-day, four-night trips, usually to coincide with the full moon, you camp on family land close to the canyon at night and take different hikes each day, starting from $800.

HORSEBACK TOURS

Totsonii Ranch 1.5 miles along a dirt road beyond the end of the South Rim Drive ☎928 551 0109, ⓦtotsoniiranch.com. This remote Navajo ranch, 16.5 miles from the visitor centre, organizes horseback trips

both along the rim and into the canyon. 2hr rim ride $62.50, 4hr Spider Rock ride $125, 6hr to White House ruin $187.50, overnight camping $350.

1

Brief history

Ancestral Puebloan Basketmakers first occupied Canyon de Chelly around 200 AD, digging primitive pithouses into the valley floor. Over the next thousand years, their descendants moved first into free-standing "pueblo" apartment-style blocks, and then into elegant cliff dwellings. Virtually all these canyon-wall complexes face south to catch the sun, with cooler storage chambers set in deep recesses. Many now look more inaccessible than they actually were, thanks to rock falls and the erosion of toe- and hand-holds in the soft sandstone. The valley's population peaked at roughly one thousand, shortly before drought drove the Ancestral Puebloans out around 1300 AD.

For the next few centuries, **Hopis** from the west farmed the canyon floor in summer, but no permanent inhabitants returned before the Pueblo Revolt of 1680 (see p.467). As the Spanish reasserted control over New Mexico, the first **Navajo** arrived in the region, quite possibly accompanied by Pueblo refugees. From then on, the Navajo and Spanish were locked in a bloody cycle of armed clashes and slave raids. As the "stronghold of the Navajo," Canyon de Chelly became the target of punitive Spanish expeditions. In 1805, Lieutenant Narbona's party gunned down over a hundred Navajo in the Canyon del Muerto.

After the Yankees took over in Santa Fe, the US Army in turn set about dislodging the Navajo. The process culminated in 1864, when General Carleton's men despatched all the Navajo they could round up on the "**Long Walk**" to Fort Sumner (see p.481). In Canyon de Chelly, **Kit Carson** starved the last Navajo warriors down from the natural Navajo Fortress and destroyed their homes, livestock, and beloved peach orchards. Within a few years, however, Congress allowed the Navajo to return from their barbaric imprisonment. To this day, 25 Navajo families still farm the Canyon de Chelly in summer, the land having passed down from mother to daughter from the women between whom it was reapportioned in the 1870s.

Visitor centre

2 miles east of Chinle • Daily 8am–5pm • Free • ☎ 928 674 5500, ⍟ nps.gov/cach

The **visitor centre** for Canyon de Chelly National Monument, an essential first stop to pick up details of current conditions and activities, is located immediately west of the mouth of the canyon itself. Perched on the low mound where Kit Carson signed the "treaty" that ended his siege of the canyon in 1864, it holds useful displays and is the place to arrange hiking or motorized expeditions.

The rim drives

Each of the monument's two rim drives is equally superb. The dead-end **South Rim Drive** traces the south rim of the Canyon de Chelly, while the **North Rim Drive** follows the north rim of the Canyon del Muerto and then heads off to the northeast. Each involves a round-trip drive of up to forty miles from the visitor centre, punctuated by overlooks where short walks across the mesa-top lead to views of natural or archeological wonders. Even if you don't stop at every overlook, each drive takes around half a day; for the best **photographs**, tour the North Rim in the morning and the South Rim in the afternoon. Thefts from cars are a major problem, so be careful.

The South Rim Drive

The first stop along the South Rim Drive – **Tunnel Overlook**, two miles from the visitor centre – is a trailhead for guided hikes; unaccompanied travellers have no reason to stop. **Tsegi Overlook**, just beyond, stands high above a sweeping curve in the canyon. Though the wash itself is seldom more than a trickle, its broad sandy floor clears a wide gap between the fringe of cottonwoods. Behind the *hogan* near the stream, fields and paddocks reach to the cliffs.

Two miles further, **Junction Overlook** marks the meeting of the two main canyons. Canyon de Chelly narrows off to the right, behind a large monolith, while Canyon del

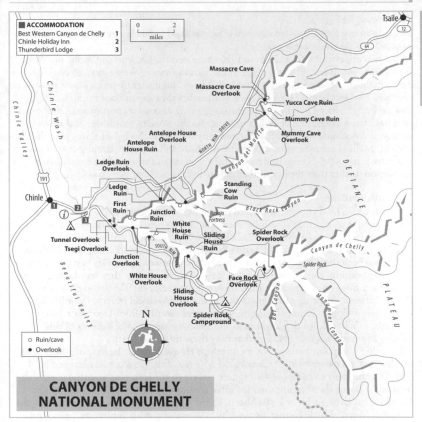

**CANYON DE CHELLY
NATIONAL MONUMENT**

Muerto to the left is much less conspicuous. Two tiny ruins indent the base of the canyon walls opposite.

By **White House Overlook**, six miles from the visitor centre, Canyon de Chelly is 550ft deep, its rim topped by strange whorls of slickrock. Pale and majestic, the cliff that drops on the far side of the wash forms a stupendous backdrop for the photogenic **White House Ruin**. Squeezed into a tiny recess, well above the fields, this cluster of rooms originally stood above a larger pueblo on the valley floor, half of which has now eroded away; it was probably reached by ladders on the roofs of the topmost towers.

From **Sliding House Overlook** – twelve miles along, and reached first by following a spur road off the main road, and then walking across a couple of hundred yards of cairned slickrock – the **Sliding House Ruin** appears to be tucked into the slenderest of crevices in the cliff face. It's now steadily slipping down toward the ploughed Navajo fields below.

South Rim Drive ends fifteen miles from the visitor centre – twenty if you take the detour to Sliding House en route – at the astonishing double monolith of **Spider Rock**, where Monument and Bat canyons split away from Canyon de Chelly. A short walk from the parking area leads to a railed, 200-yard cement path overlooking the abyss; keep going right to the end for the best views. Soaring to within two hundred feet of the canyon rim, the eight-hundred-foot twin pinnacles of rock are said by the Navajo to be home to Spider Woman. She taught them the art of weaving, but also steals misbehaving children; their bleached, gnawed bones lie strewn across the top.

1

White House Trail

Trailhead at White House Overlook, 6 miles from visitor centre on South Rim Drive • 2.5-mile round-trip; it takes 30–45min to get down to the ruin, and 1hr to climb up again, so allow at least 2hr

As the sole opportunity for visitors to hike alone into the Canyon de Chelly, the **White House Trail**, which sets off to the right of the viewing area at White House Overlook, is a major highlight of any Southwest itinerary. A beautiful if slightly precarious walk – some of it along ledges chiselled into the rock – it reaches the canyon floor through a tunnel that perfectly frames a Navajo *hogan* and its glowing attendant cottonwood. Thus far the ruin has been hidden from view, but once across the wooden footbridge that spans the wash you can admire it close up, separated only by a fence. Sixty feet above you, the ancient dwelling seems in almost perfect condition, still with the dazzling coat of plaster that gave it its name. Navajo traders nearby sell sodas and trinkets and ensure hikers wander no further than the permitted hundred yards in either direction.

The North Rim Drive

Hwy-64, which heads northeast beyond the monument, doubles as the **North Rim Drive**. It runs parallel to, but roughly a mile from, the canyon rim, so there no views from the road itself. Instead, successive spur roads run south to reach the various overlooks.

You'll miss little by skipping the **Ledge Ruin Overlook**, five miles along the North Rim Drive, but both the viewpoints at **Antelope House Overlook**, five miles beyond that and an utterly beautiful spot in its own right, are well worth seeing. They stand five minutes' walk apart, along an unpaved, cairned trail over the slickrock. The first faces across to **Navajo Fortress**, at the tip of the mesa that divides Canyon del Muerto from Black Rock Canyon. It took Kit Carson's besieging forces three months, from December 1863 onwards, to starve down defiant Navajo warriors who reached the summit of this solitary tower of rock using ladders that they drew up behind them.

The other viewpoint looks down on **Antelope House Ruin**, at the base of a huge white overhang in a separate twist of Canyon del Muerto. This site was first occupied in 693 AD, and grew to comprise two square towers to the rear, plus a central plaza that held half a dozen dwellings. It's named after an antelope pictograph painted by the Navajo artist Dibé Yazhi, or Little Sheep, in the 1830s. He was also responsible for the "Spanish Mural" a little further along, which shows a Spanish lieutenant, priest and

---

THE NAVAJO HOGAN

The traditional dwelling known as a *hogan* (pronounced *ho-wun*), as seen throughout Canyon de Chelly, is the focus of Navajo life. Each is built as the home for a family, but can also be transformed to become the venue for sacred ceremonies. Few Navajo now live in a *hogan* year-round, but every family owns at least one, and those who still farm and raise sheep in the backcountry often have several.

The earliest *hogans*, first described in the sixteenth century and still widely used until the 1940s, were "**male**" *hogans*. They consisted of three vertical forked sticks propped against each other, aligned to the north, south, and west, covered with logs, brush, and mud, and with a door that faced east to greet the rising sun.

Virtually all *hogans* today are "**female**," larger six- or eight-sided structures made of cribbed horizontal cedar logs and once again covered with mud. These became more popular at the end of the nineteenth century, with the advent of steel saws to cut the timber and wagons to haul it; in fact many were made from salvaged railroad ties. The doorway still faces east, with a floor of hard-packed dirt to provide contact with the earth and a smoke hole in the domed roof for access to the sky. Each area of the *hogan* has a particular significance; the south side "belongs" to the women and the north to the men, while the male head of the household sits to the west. Food is prepared and stored on the northeast side; the southwest is the sleeping area.

Since the 1970s, more and more Navajo have chosen to live in trailers rather than face the labour of constantly renewing a *hogan*'s protective mud coating. Navajo custom dictates that a dwelling place in which a death has occurred must be abandoned.

troops advancing through the canyon. Across the wash, in the **Tomb of the Weaver**, the embalmed body of an old man was found wrapped in golden eagle feathers.

The next, final spur road off the North Rim Drive splits to reach two separate overlooks, well over a mile apart. To the south, **Mummy Cave Overlook** offers a clear view of the single most striking ruin in the monument – **Mummy Cave Ruin**, which the Navajo call **House Under The Rock**. Inhabited for over a thousand years, it consists of two pueblo complexes deep in the shade of adjacent alcoves, with a prominent **Central Tower** on the spur in between. The sophisticated masonry of the tower has been dated to 1284, so archeologists speculate it was built by migrants from Mesa Verde.

In the "cave" visible from **Massacre Cave Overlook**, to the north, Narbona's expeditionary forces killed more than a hundred Navajo in 1805 (see p.60). It's less of a cave than a pitifully exposed ledge, far above the canyon floor, on which the huddled group were easily picked off by the Spanish, using ricochets off the overhang above. The cement path curves onwards from here to reach another railed overlook, facing down the canyon. Continue over the rocks to the protective wall around the tip of the outcrop, lower down to your right, to see **Yucca Cave Ruin**, which is unusually close to the mesa-top. It's an amazing location, set in a hollow in the rock above a sheer drop, with no conceivable way down to the valley floor, but almost none of the buildings survive.

Hwy-64 continues for another fifteen miles to meet Arrowhead Hwy-12 in little **TSAILE**. The upper floors of Diné College here hold the stimulating **Ned Hatathli Museum** of Navajo history (Mon–Fri 8.30am–4.30pm; free), which also sells craft items. It's possible to hike into Canyon del Muerto from this end, with a guide hired in Chinle.

ACCOMMODATION AND EATING   CANYON DE CHELLY

Although Canyon de Chelly remains remarkably unspoiled, nearby facilities are overstretched in summer, so it's essential to book **accommodation** well in advance. No **camping** is permitted in the actual canyons. In addition to the **restaurants** in the hotels, there is also a handful of fast-food places in Chinle, which is otherwise a brief nondescript straggle on the highway.

HOTELS

Best Western Canyon de Chelly 100 Main St, Chinle ☎928 674 5875 or ☎800 327 0354, ⓦcanyondechelly .com. This low-slung motel, immediately east of the US-191 intersection in Chinle, makes an adequate but somewhat characterless spot to spend the night, and has its own restaurant, the *Junction* (open daily for all meals), as well as heated indoor pool. **$108**

Chinle Holiday Inn Route 7, Chinle ☎928 674 5000, ⓦholiday-inn.com/chinle-garcia. Smart, adobe-fied motel, on the site of the former *Garcia Trading Post*, half a mile short of the monument entrance, with a hundred comfortable, well equipped rooms. *Garcia's Restaurant*, the cosy, colourful on-site dining room, serves a breakfast buffet, full lunches (Mon–Fri only) and dinner until 10pm. The food itself, and the drab salad bar in particular, is nothing exceptional, but it's the best you'll find in Chinle, with $14 specials such as glazed pork chops. **$154**

Thunderbird Lodge At the start of South Rim Drive ☎928 674 5841 or ☎800 679 2473, ⓦtbirdlodge.com. The closest accommodation to the canyon, reached by turning right just past the visitor centre. Conventional, clean if somewhat faded motel rooms surround a century-old trading post, which houses a large and reasonably priced self-service cafeteria (daily 6.30am–9pm) that most visitors find interesting only because it's often busy with Navajo from

surrounding communities. The consistently boring food is made no better by the prohibition of alcohol. The dining room is festooned with rugs from the giftshop next door (daily 7.30am–9pm). If you take a *Thunderbird* sightseeing tour on the day you leave, check out of your room first; they charge you for another day after 11am. **$122**

CAMPGROUNDS

Cottonwood Campground At the start of South Rim Drive ☎928 674 2106, ⓦnavajonationparks.org. The first-come first-served *Cottonwood Campground* spreads among the trees beside *Thunderbird Lodge*; each of the ninety sites accommodates up to four for no additional fee. There's a five-day maximum stay, but there are no showers, and when the water is cut off, as it often is between November and March, no restrooms either. No RVs. Cash only. **$10**

Spider Rock RV & Campground 12 miles along South Rim Drive ☎928 674 8261, ⓦspiderrockcampground .com. This primitive Navajo-owned campground, on private land beside South Rim Drive beyond Sliding House Overlook, offers a chance to escape the crowds. As well as tent and RV sites, it also holds a couple of forked-stick *hogans* that provide welcome shelter in winter especially; one holds two campers, the other four. Canyon tours also available. Cash only. Tent **$10**, RV **$15**, small *hogan* **$29**, large *hogan* **$39**

1

Hubbell Trading Post

1 mile west of Ganado, 30 miles west of Window Rock • Daily: mid-May to Sept 8am–6pm; Oct to mid-May 8am–5pm • Free, home tours $2 • ☎ 928 755 3475, ⓦ nps.gov/hutr

After the Navajo returned from New Mexico, white entrepreneurs set up trading posts at the edge of the reservation, supplying goods from the world beyond in return for craft items such as blankets and jewellery. One such merchant, John Hubbell (1853–1930), established more than thirty trading posts during his long career. His original base, founded in the 1870s, stands near the village of **GANADO**, halfway between Chinle and I-40 to the south, which was named after Chief Ganado Mucho ("Won a lot"), a signatory of the 1868 treaty that ended the Navajo's imprisonment at Fort Sumner.

Set beside the Pueblo Colorado Wash, at the end of a tree-lined avenue, the **Hubbell Trading Post** is now a fascinating living museum, run by the Park Service. Visitors can watch Navajo weavers at work and wander out to the old stables, piled with hay and filled with venerable wooden wagons. Serious collectors pay premium prices for the best rugs and silverwork, but the groceries in the general store – pretty historic themselves – make less expensive souvenirs. Regular tours explore the fascinating Hubbell family home, behind the store.

To the east, Hwy-264 climbs onto the thickly wooded Defiance Plateau and heads for Window Rock, while US-191 undulates for forty miles due south, through more forests, to Chambers on I-40.

Window Rock

The capital of the Navajo Nation, **WINDOW ROCK** sits on the Arizona–New Mexico border 25 miles northwest of Gallup. An administrative headquarters rather than a lively town, it only became the capital in the 1930s. Technically, if you simply pass through on Hwy-264 like most casual visitors, you're not in Window Rock at all; you also won't see the rock itself.

Both "town" and rock are a mile or two north on Arrowhead Hwy-12. The **Window Rock**, an impressive, almost circular hole in a golden sandstone cliff, used to surmount a spring where water was collected for the Water Way ceremony. With the spring now dry, it's the focus of a picnic area, where a statue of a crouching Navajo soldier, complete with walkie-talkie, commemorates the work of the Code Talkers during World War II. Nearby, the **Navajo Tribal Council** meets at least four times yearly in the octagonal **Council Chamber**.

Window Rock also hosts the annual five-day **Navajo Nation Fair** (ⓦnavajonationfair .com), which starts on the Wednesday after Labor Day.

Navajo Nation Museum and zoo

Hwy-264 • Museum Summer Mon 8am–5pm, Tues–Fri 8am–6pm, Sat 9am–5pm; winter Mon–Fri 8am–5pm • Donation • ☎ 928 871 7941, ⓦ navajonationmuseum.org • Zoo Mon–Sat 10am–4.30pm • Free • ☎ 928 871 6574, ⓦ navajozoo.org

On Hwy-264, the large **Navajo Nation Museum** is a good spot to pick up tourist information and ask questions. Surprisingly, it doesn't hold permanent displays covering Navajo history and culture, but there are often interesting temporary exhibitions. Tucked among the rocky outcrops across the parking lot, a small **zoo** holds specimens of local wildlife. All were rescued at a time when they would not otherwise have survived; they include a bald eagle and a growling cougar that endlessly eyes the neighbouring elk. The captions are in Navajo, so visits double as language lessons.

Navajoland Inn St Michaels ☎928 871 5690, ⓦnavajoland-innsuites.com. Smart motel, on the brow of a hill two miles west of Window Rock, with spacious rooms, wi-fi and a good-sized indoor pool. **$70**

Quality Inn Window Rock 48 W Hwy-264 ☎928 871 4108 or ☎800 662 6189, ⓦqualityinnwindowrock.com. Much of the Navajo's day-to-day business is conducted in

the *Diné* restaurant and coffee shop of this showpiece motel, which is open for all meals daily, with Navajo tacos or mutton stew for around $10. Ask for details of their local tours, which can incorporate pretty much anything you're interested in doing, but start at an expensive $100 per day. The rooms are good value, but can be hard to come by in summer. **$89**

The Hopi Indian reservation

A remote desert enclave, dwarfed and entirely surrounded by the huge Navajo reservation, the **Hopi Indian reservation** extends over 1.5 million acres in northeast Arizona. Its ten thousand inhabitants live in twelve villages, set atop the **Hopi mesas** roughly fifty miles north of I-40, fifty miles east of Tuba City, and ninety miles southwest of Canyon de Chelly. All can be accessed along a 25-mile stretch of

HOPI RELIGION: THE KACHINAS

The Hopi do not feel the urge, let alone the obligation, to divulge details of their **religious beliefs** and practices to outsiders. While anthropologists and missionaries have gleaned what they can, well-known accounts of Hopi spirituality, such as Frank Waters' *Book of the Hopi*, are based on the reports of informants not initiated into its innermost secrets. Inevitably, Hopi spirituality has been repeatedly misrepresented, whether as barbarous devil-worship or New Age guff.

There is in any case no single Hopi religion; ceremonials vary from clan to clan and village to village. The basic common element is the role of the *kachina* (often spelled *katsina*, with the plural *katsinum*). These "spirit messengers," which may represent the spirits of the dead, live in the San Francisco peaks north of Flagstaff, and return to the mesas in the form of rain-bearing clouds.

There are over three hundred different *kachinas*. At one time, they visited the mesas in person; now they come in the form of masked dancers. Not every village follows the same **ceremonial calendar**, but in general the *kachinas* arrive in early February for the *Powamuya* ceremony, or **Bean Dance**. Each matriarch receives fresh bean sprouts to plant for the coming year, and the *so'so'yoktu* ogres that threaten to eat disobedient (*ka-hopi*) children are placated by gifts of food. The *kachinas* continue to visit throughout the growing season, then return home after the *Niman* ceremony or **Home Dance** in July.

The Hopi do not worship the *kachinas*; they are primarily teaching tools for children. A Hopi baby receives a *tihu* – what outsiders call a **kachina doll** – at its first *Niman* ceremony, and the girls receive further dolls at each *Powamuya* and *Niman* ceremony thereafter. Most boys and girls alike are initiated into a **kachina society** at around the age of 10.

All the Southwestern pueblos had some form of *kachina* cult, which is thought to have developed in **Mexico**, and spread north to the Hopi mesas and Zuni Pueblo via the **Mimbres** culture to the south. It then moved east to the Rio Grande, where it was subsequently almost entirely stamped out by the Spanish colonists.

The role and iconography of specific Hopi *kachinas* strongly echo **Aztec** deities such as **Tlaloc**, the god of rain, and **Quetzalcoatl**, the plumed serpent who also brought rain and corn. For the Aztec preoccupation with death, blood and human sacrifice, however, the Hopi and other Southwestern peoples substituted an obsessive focus on **rain**.

ATTENDING HOPI CEREMONIES

The Hopi used to promote their ceremonies as tourist attractions. Even after cameras were banned in 1916, the **Snake Dance**, when members of the Snake clan dance with live snakes between their teeth, would draw as many as 2500 observers. These days, however, the Hopi **exclude** non-Indians. Second Mesa closed all its ceremonies to outsiders by 1989, and was joined by all the First Mesa villages in 1992 after a *Marvel* comic characterized the *kachinas* as violent avengers.

Hwy-264, where three distinct spurs, numbered from east to west as **First**, **Second**, and **Third** mesas, poke from the southern flanks of **Black Mesa**.

The Hopi trace their ancestry back well over a thousand years, to the **Ancestral Puebloan** people who formerly dominated the entire Four Corners region. What's more, they have occupied this same spot for at least eight hundred years. To outsiders, it's not immediately obvious why, with the whole Southwest to pick from, they chose to live on these barren and unprepossessing fingers of rock. The answer lies within Black Mesa itself: although it has no perennial streams, its subterranean rocks are tilted at just the correct angle to deliver a tiny but dependable trickle of water, while the "black" in its name comes from the coal that gives the Hopi limitless reserves of fuel. In addition, the Hopi used to farm and hunt across a much wider area, only to be restricted to their mesa-top villages by the steady encroachment of their Navajo neighbours. Although the Hopi are celebrated for their skill at "**dry farming**," preserving enough precious liquid to grow corn, beans and squash on hand-tilled terraces laid out beneath the villages, this precarious way of life was forced upon them.

The Hopi **language**, Hopic, belongs to the Uto-Aztecan group of languages, and different dialects are spoken on each mesa. Although it bears similarities to Ute and

While spectators are now unlikely to be allowed at any *kachina* dances, some **social dances**, held between August and January when the *kachinas* are away from the mesas, may still be "open." Held in the village plazas, these usually take place at the weekend. Specific timings tend not to be announced until a few days in advance; for information, ask at the Cultural Center (see p.69) or call ☎ 928 734 2401. If you do get the chance to attend a ceremony, wear clothing that fully covers your body, keep your distance, and do not photograph, sketch, or question either dancers or audience.

KACHINA DOLLS

Kachina **masks**, as worn by ceremonial dancers, are sacred objects; the Hopi have successfully petitioned to remove them from museum displays. However, a "*kachina* doll" or *tihu* (the plural is *ti'tihu*) is simply an instructional tool, and can therefore be sold to outsiders as a collector's item.

The *ti'tihu* given to Hopi children were originally flat dolls to be hung within the home. Made from white kaolin clay, the basic shape was painted to show a head, plus a pair of arms folded over a kilt that represented rain. Trading posts stocked these simple dolls in the 1890s, and by 1900 they were being made specifically for sale.

Since then, they have become much more complex in form and colour, and acquired feet. Most are carved from cottonwood roots; the carving is seen as a prayer for water, symbolizing the roots' own search for water. Thanks to the art market's desire for signed pieces, the artists themselves are no longer anonymous. Strictly speaking, only men should carve *ti'tihu*, but some women make them now as well.

Not all *ti'tihu* represent *kachinas*. Some depict the **clowns** who also appear during ceremonies, such as the black-and-white-striped *koshares*, and the knobbed "mudheads" or *koyemsi*. Just as the clowns may devise costumes to mock tourists, for example, certain *ti'tihu* caricature figures like basketball players or anthropologists.

The Hopi do, however, draw the line at attempts by others to cash in on the commercial success of the *kachina*-doll business, though the tribal council has been unable to copyright the word "*kachina*" to stop Navajo and other non-Indian copyists using the name. Genuine hand-carved dolls are both exquisite and expensive, and a top-class carver will produce fewer than fifty per year, while fake *kachinas* are mass-produced in New Mexico. Good places to buy a *kachina* doll include the Hopi Cultural Center on Second Mesa, the Museum of Northern Arizona in Flagstaff, and Albuquerque's Indian Pueblo Cultural Center, though it's hard to find a reasonable-sized piece for under $300. Prices on the reservation itself tend to be cheaper; carvers show their work to visitors on tours of Walpi or at the entrance to Oraibi, and there are also several crafts stores, including Tsakurshovi on Second Mesa (☎ 928 734 24/8) and the Monongya Gallery at Oraibi (☎ 928 734 2344).

1

Paiute, the Hopi have little in common with either tribe. Their culture and beliefs are instead closely related to those of the Pueblo peoples of New Mexico. The Hopi are a matriarchal society, with homes, land, and clan affiliation passing down the female line. They are not a united people; each village is an independent entity, and only four currently recognize the Hopi Tribal Council.

By their very survival, and the persistence of their ancient beliefs and ceremonies, the Hopi have long fascinated outsiders. Visitors are welcomed, but the Hopi have no desire to turn themselves into a tourist attraction. A motel makes it possible to stay on the reservation, and stores and galleries sell prized **crafts** such as pottery, basketwork, silver overlay jewellery, and hand-carved **kachina dolls**. However, tourists who arrive in the hope of extensive sightseeing – let alone spiritual revelations – are likely to leave disappointed, and quite possibly dismayed by what they perceive as conspicuous poverty.

Since 1986, when increased mining revenues finally placed the tribal economy on a relatively secure footing, non-Indians have been barred from almost all Hopi ceremonies. These days, the easiest way for visitors to get a sense of traditional life is to join a guided tour of either the magnificently situated village of **Walpi** on First Mesa, or **Sipaulovi** on Second Mesa.

Touring the Hopi mesas

Each of the mesa-top Hopi villages centres around a **plaza**, where successive generations have built new houses on top of the old ones as they crumble into sand. Often the main entrance is via the roof, itself reached by a wooden ladder. Though a few buildings are now constructed of grey concrete blocks, they still blend almost imperceptibly into the ruins that trail away down the slopes. Several villages stand on open seams of coal, and large chunks of coal lie scattered around. Outhouses are dotted across the hillsides; all waste was traditionally thrown over the edge of the mesa to tumble down and fertilize the terraces, a policy that works less well now that refrigerators and old bedsteads are thrown over too.

As you tour the reservation, signs beside the highway point out shops and stalls selling Hopi handicrafts. At some point down any side road you choose to follow, as you approach a village, a large notice will forbid you to drive any further, but may allow you to walk within a specified area.

First Mesa

Walpi tours set off daily 9am–3pm • $13 • ☎ 928 737 2670

First Mesa, 75 miles southwest of the Canyon de Chelly, is home to the most impressive of the two Hopi villages that offer guided tours. To reach **WALPI**, take Hwy-264 to modern **POLACCA**, at the foot of the mesa, then drive a mile up the twisting paved road until it ends in **SICHOMOVI**. Although you can't tell where one village stops and the next begins, you've just passed through **HANO**. Its inhabitants arrived during the Pueblo Revolt to offer their services as the defenders of First Mesa, and still speak the Tewa language.

Tours assemble in Sichomovi's small **Ponsi Hall Community Center**, setting off at regular intervals for a half-hour walk to and around Walpi. By Hopi standards, Walpi is not that old; it was hastily thrown together in the aftermath of the Pueblo Revolt of 1680, as a more secure site in the face of possible Spanish or Navajo attack. The site is absolutely stunning, standing alone at the narrow southernmost tip of the mesa, and connected to the other First Mesa villages by the merest slender neck of stone, with a drop of three hundred feet to either side.

Walpi lacks electricity or running water, and has since 2011 no longer held any permanent inhabitants. Villagers do however come up each day to sell crafts, and return to their family homes here for special events. Depending on the season, you may be in a group of twenty or so, or on your own, but either way there's plenty of opportunity to ask questions and to buy pottery, *kachina* dolls, and fresh-baked *piiki*, a flatbread made with blue cornflour.

Second Mesa
Second Mesa, most easily reached by driving sixty miles north of I-40 on Hwy-67, holds three separate villages – Shungopavi, Mishongnovi and Sipaulovi. As on First Mesa, the original Hopi settlements here stood alongside springs that seeped from the foot of the mesa, and were relocated to the mesa-top after the Pueblo Revolt. Unlike on First Mesa, however, Hwy-264 climbs onto and crosses the mesa itself here, so the villages no longer seem nearly so isolated.

Hopi Cultural Center
Hwy-264, 4 miles northwest of intersection with Hwy-67 • **Museum** summer Mon–Fri 8am–5pm, Sat & Sun 9am–3pm; winter Mon–Fri 8am–5pm • $3 • ☎ 928 734 6650, ⓦ hopiculturalcenter.com

The roadside **Hopi Cultural Center** on Second Mesa makes an obvious first stop for visitors to the Hopi reservation. As well as holding a motel and restaurant (see p.70), it serves as a gift store and information centre. If any forthcoming events are open to tourists, the friendly staff should be able to tell you about them. The small adjoining museum holds some fascinating historical exhibits, old photos, and choice displays of Hopi arts and crafts, while the shop next door is particularly good for silver.

Sipaulovi
Second Mesa, 3 miles south on paved road that starts 0.1 mile east of Hopi Cultural Center • Tours Mon–Fri 9am–4pm • $15 • ☎ 928 737 5426, ⓦ sipaulovihopiinformationcenter.org

The mesa-top village of **SIPAULOVI** was founded in the late seventeenth century by Hopis who migrated north from what's now Homolovi Ruins State Park, outside Winslow. Hour-long walking tours, preceded by a video introduction in the Sipaulovi Visitor Center, include three surviving homes from that era, and offer a chance to buy tribal crafts.

Third Mesa
Fifty miles southeast of Tuba City (see p.51), **Third Mesa** is remarkable as the home of the village of **ORAIBI**, which is regarded as the oldest Hopi settlement of all. No scheduled tours can guide you around, but there's usually a cluster of carvers and craftspeople waiting at the edge of the village who can give permission for you to explore on foot. You're not allowed to walk to the very edge of the mesa, where conspicuous ruins date back as much as a thousand years.

ARRIVAL AND DEPARTURE HOPI INDIAN RESERVATION
Both roads from the interstate up to the Hopi mesas, **Hwy-87** from Winslow and **Hwy-77** from Holbrook, run through a superbly desolate butte-studded segment of the Navajo reservation, on the western fringes of the Painted Desert. If you're coming from the Grand Canyon, take **Hwy-264** east from US-160. Once beyond the Hopi outpost of **Moenkopi**, just outside Tuba City (see p.51), this traverses rugged canyonlands before climbing onto Third Mesa after fifty miles.

TOURS
Joining a Hopi guide for your own private **tour** will show you far more of the reservation than you can see alone. Guides like Gary Tso of the Left-Handed Tour Co (☎ 928 734 2567, ✉ lhhunter68@hopitelecom.net) and Bertram Tsavadawa of Ancient Pathways Tours (☎ 928 797 8145) take visitors around Oraibi and to little-known **petroglyph sites**, as well as to **craftspeople** and **galleries**. Rates depend on how many of you there are; with just two, expect to pay from $75 per person for a three-hour tour, up to $175 per person for a full day.

1

ACCOMMODATION AND EATING

Although the *Hopi Cultural Center Motel* is the only accommodation option on the reservation itself, note that the Hopi opened the larger, more luxurious and more accessible *Moenkopi Legacy* hotel in **Tuba City** in 2010 (see p.51). **Winslow**, on I-40 sixty miles south of Second Mesa, also makes a good base, and is home to the wonderful *La Posada* hotel (see p.261).

Hopi Cultural Center Motel Second Mesa ☎ 928 734 2401, ⓦ hopiculturalcenter.com. Built in a faux-Pueblo architectural style, this motel offers 34 plain but acceptable rooms that are usually booked solid well in advance in summer. The cafeteria serves good, substantial meals, including local delicacy *noqkwivi*, lamb stewed with hominy ($9.25), but be warned that there's precious little to do between the time it closes, at 9pm (or 8pm in winter), and 7am the next morning, when you can indulge your curiosity by having blue cornflakes for breakfast. $105

Southwest Colorado

In ancient times, of course, the straight-line boundaries that divide the states of Arizona, New Mexico, Utah and Colorado – and mark the northeastern limits of the Navajo Nation – did not exist. As a result, although Colorado might not spring to mind as a "Southwestern" state, its far southwest corner holds some fascinating archeological sites. **Mesa Verde National Park** is absolutely unmissable, while the ancient ruins in **Ute Mountain Tribal Park**, which lies well off the beaten track and can only be accessed with a Ute guide, offer adventurous travellers an even more exhilarating sense of discovery.

Once you've crossed the border into Colorado, it's hard to resist the lure of the Rockies, looming along the skyline to the north. There's no scope in this book to do more than sketch out a brief tour, looping up the **San Juan Skyway** from lively **Durango** to historic mining towns such as **Silverton** and **Ouray**.

Four Corners Monument Navajo Tribal Park

Daily: May–Sept 8am–7pm; Oct–April 8am–5pm · $3 · ⓦ navajonationparks.org

The **Four Corners Monument Navajo Tribal Park**, reached by a short spur road half a mile northeast of US-160, is the only place in the United States where four states meet at a single point. However exciting you may find the concept, the reality is bleak and dull. A steady stream of visitors mooch around the pivotal brass plaque, ponderously contorting a limb into each state for demeaning photographs. Navajo stalls on all sides sell crafts, T-shirts, and fry bread.

Ute Mountain Ute Reservation

For a couple of centuries after **Ute Indians** acquired horses from the Spanish, their hunting territory extended east from Utah as far as Nebraska. As miners pushed the Victorian-era frontier westwards, however, the Ute were confined to poorer land. The creation of reservations split them into three separate groups: the **Northern Utes**, who now live in the mountains near Utah's border with Wyoming; the **Southern Utes**, who occupy a strip of southern Colorado south of Durango; and the **Ute Mountain Utes**.

The two-thousand-strong band of Ute Mountain Utes take their name from a long, low mountain ridge in Colorado's far southwestern corner, known to outsiders as **Sleeping Ute Mountain** because of its uncanny resemblance, when seen from the east, to a slumbering warrior. Also known as the Weeminuche, they long ranked among the Southwest's poorest peoples, and draw their income these days from mineral leases and a large **casino** near the main settlement of **Towaoc**.

Although the road through Mesa Verde National Park passes through a tiny corner of the Ute Mountain Ute reservation, only visitors who take a guided tour of the remote, dramatic Ancestral Puebloan ruins in the entirely separate **Ute Mountain Tribal Park** are likely to have any contact with the Utes themselves.

Ute Mountain Tribal Park

Guided tours leave from visitor centre • Usually 9am daily, but schedules vary with demand; in season you can usually join a tour if you turn up at 8.30am, but it's much safer to reserve in advance • Full-day tours, using your own vehicle, cost $48 and get you back to the highway around 5pm, half-day tours cost $28 and finish by 1pm; riding in the guide's van costs an extra $10 • ☎ 970 565 9653 or ☎ 800 847 5485, ⓦ utemountainute.com

The inaccessible but utterly enthralling **Ute Mountain Tribal Park**, which abuts against Mesa Verde National Park, preserves an equally extraordinary but far less visited assortment of ancient **Ancestral Puebloan** – not Ute – remains, which can only be seen on Ute-guided tours.

If you don't have the time to take a full-day tour, the half-day tour makes a very poor alternative. On the half-day trip, you simply leave the group at the end of the morning, having seen a couple of potsherd-scattered mounds, concealing ancient surface-level pueblos, at the foot of the cliffs. On the full-day tour, you continue along a remote and circuitous dirt road to the top of the mesa, and then inch down ladders onto a three-mile ledge skirting **Lion Canyon**. This leads to three beautifully preserved **cliff dwellings**, built at the same time as those on Mesa Verde: Tree House Ruin, the eighty-room Lion House, and the precarious Eagle's Nest, perched in a colossal natural alcove. The whole expedition demands a fair amount of walking and something of a head for heights, but only the final ascent to Eagle's Nest is difficult for vertigo sufferers – you can admire it from below if you prefer.

Visitors are expected to drive their own sturdy vehicles on the tour and to bring food and drink. However, the tour leader's van accommodates half a dozen passengers; if there's room, you can pay extra to ride along, and thus get much more informed commentary on what you're seeing. It's also possible to arrange trips to more remote areas of the park, which involve significantly more **hiking**; groups must consist of four or more members, each of whom pays $60.

INFORMATION   UTE MOUNTAIN UTE RESERVATION

Visitor centre The tribe's visitor centre-cum-museum is housed in a former gas station where US-160 meets US-491, twenty miles up from the Four Corners Monument (April–Oct daily 8am–3pm, but hours subject to fluctuation; ☎ 970 749 1452).

ACCOMMODATION AND EATING

Ute Mountain Casino Towaoc, on US-491 12 miles south of Cortez, 8 miles north of visitor centre ☎ 970 565 8800 or ☎ 800 258 8007, ⓦ utemountaincasino.com. While there's nothing appealing about the smoke-filled casino itself, the hotel rooms are large, clean and good value compared to Cortez; they also have camping space and a cheap restaurant. Tents $19, RVs $25, hotel rooms $55

Ute Mountain Tribal Park Campground Near intersection of US-160 and US-491 ☎ 970 565 9653 or ☎ 800 847 5485, ⓦ utemountainute.com. This primitive campground, just off the main highway, is entirely devoid of facilities, apart from basic cabins and tent sites, but is handy for the park tours and feels deliciously remote at night. Cabin $10, vehicle camping $12

Hovenweep National Monument

Hidden in the fifty-mile-wide swathe of no man's land that straddles the Utah–Colorado border, the Ancestral Puebloan ruins at **HOVENWEEP NATIONAL MONUMENT** lack the scale and setting of the Mesa Verde cliff dwellings or similar Four Corners sites. Instead, sprouting from the rims of shallow desert canyons and dwarfed by the distant mountains, they offer a haunting sense of timeless isolation. They also have one unique feature: the tall **towers** that many archeologists regard as astronomical observatories.

The monument includes five abandoned villages – its name comes from a Ute word meaning "deserted valley" – a few miles apart, in four distinct parcels. Whether you can visit them all will depend on current road conditions, and whether you have a 4WD vehicle. Easy year-round access, however, is restricted to the **Square Tower Unit**.

1

Square Tower Unit

Trail open daily sunrise–sunset • Entrance fee, payable at visitor centre, $6 per vehicle, or $3 per person

A shallow, barely noticeable cleft in the desert expanse, **Little Ruin Canyon** lies immediately behind Hovenweep's smart **visitor centre**. It's no longer possible to walk among or into the structures ranged above and below its rim, which are known collectively as the **Square Tower Unit**; instead, a single trail loops around the edge, keeping visitors at a safe distance.

A complete circuit of the trail takes just under an hour. After meeting the canyon near the fortress-like **Stronghold House**, the trail heads right, past the prosaically named **Unit-type House**, where niches in the walls appear to line up with the angle of the sun at the summer and winter solstices. **Hovenweep Castle**, a four-square building five minutes' walk farther on at the head of the canyon, was constructed around 1200 AD. It may have stood guard over a much larger pueblo complex that nestled on the sandy canyon floor a mere thirty feet below, clustered around the perennial spring that was the site's only source of water. Of that whole complex, only **Square Tower Ruin** can still be discerned, while up above Hovenweep Castle has endured, a perfect illustration of the Biblical admonition that only a house built on rock shall stand. It takes another ten minutes to reach the final significant ruin, the **Twin Towers**. Doubling back on yourself at that point, rather than completing the loop, will spare you the final steep dip and climb through the middle of the canyon, but saves no time overall.

ARRIVAL AND INFORMATION
HOVENWEEP NATIONAL MONUMENT

By car Whatever most tourist maps may suggest, almost all the roads to Hovenweep have now been paved, thanks largely to companies drilling for oil and gas around Aneth. The monument is best reached by driving 35 miles due west from Cortez along County Road G, which leaves US-160 near the air-strip at the south end of town, or 25 miles east from US-191 via Hwy-262, which branches off halfway between Bluff and Blanding in Utah. When conditions are dry, it's also possible to follow a dirt road southwest from Pleasant View in Colorado through Canyons of the Ancients National Monument.

Visitor centre Located at Little Ruin Canyon (daily: April & Oct 8am–5pm; May–Sept 8am–6pm; Nov–March 9am–5pm; ☎ 970 562 4282, ⓦ nps.gov/hove).

ACCOMMODATION

Hovenweep Campground Little Ruin Canyon ☎ 970 562 4282, ⓦ nps.gov/hove. While no accommodation, gasoline, or food is available at or anywhere near Hovenweep, this first-come, first-served 31-site campground, close to the visitor centre, remains open all year. It has a few RV spaces, but no hook-ups. Running water is available in summer only. No reservations. $10

Cortez

The town of **CORTEZ**, twenty miles north of the point where US-160 meets US-491, consists of little more than a long curve of over-developed highway. Were it not so close to Mesa Verde National Park, there would be no reason to visit; as it is, Cortez offers a large, if not exactly broad, selection of roadside motels and diners.

INFORMATION
CORTEZ

Visitor centre The Colorado Welcome Center, 928 E Main St, on the edge of City Park (daily: June–Aug 8am–6pm; Sept & Oct 8am–5pm; Nov–May 9am–5pm; ☎ 970 565 3414, ⓦ swcolo.org), has information on the entire state as well as on Cortez itself.

ACCOMMODATION

A couple of dozen **motels** line Cortez's main strip, with a few of the big-name chains scattered among the local operators. There's no great advantage in staying somewhere central, as the whole place is so spread out you'll almost certainly have to drive to wherever you eat.

Aneth Lodge 645 E Main St ☎970 565 3453 or ☎877 515 8454, ⊛anethlodge.com. The good-sized rooms at this *Budget 6* motel are more kitsch than fancy, but they're clean, cheap, and close to Cortez's pulsating heart. Winter $51, summer $62

Best Western Turquoise Inn & Suites 535 E Main St ☎970 565 3778 or ☎800 547 3376, ⊛bestwestern mesaverde.com. Smart, central two-storey motel, with a small outdoor pool open in summer only and an indoor one for the winter. Winter $80, summer $120

Budget Host Inn 2040 E Main St ☎970 565 3738 or ☎888 677 3738. The "budget" tag doesn't quite do justice to this comfortable and nicely presented motel, as the main road out of Cortez curves east toward Mesa Verde, which has a pool and hot tub. Winter $40, summer $80

Holiday Inn Express Mesa Verde-Cortez 2121 E Main St ☎970 565 6000, ⊛hiexpress.com. Large modern motel at the east end of town, with huge comfortable rooms, attractive landscaped gardens, and a tasteful Navajo theme. Winter $118, summer $155

★ **Kelly Place** 14663 County Rd G ☎970 565 3125 or ☎800 745 4885, ⊛kellyplace.com. Truly exceptional B&B ranch, tucked amid the peach orchards of McElmo Canyon, ten miles west of Cortez towards Hovenweep. Accommodation, all en-suite, is in seven comfortable lodge rooms, three cabins, or a 2-bedroom suite; they also offer tent sites. Breakfast is served in the central dining room. Archeologist-led hikes to Ancestral Puebloan ruins – several are on site – cost $150 for a group of up to four for half a day, or $235 for a full day; it's also possible to ride horses. Rooms $120, suite $215, cabins $145, camping $45

EATING

Dry Dock 200 W Main St ☎970 564 9404, ⊛thedrydock .com. The most upscale traditional restaurant in town, serving delicious seafood specialities – they even have fresh oysters – in a garden decorated with underwater-themed murals. They also offer steaks, fajitas, and burritos, and it's a place you might well choose to linger at the bar. Typical entrees cost $13–22. Daily 5–10pm.

Main Street Brewery 21 E Main St ☎970 564 9112, ⊛mainstreetbrewerycortez.com. Colourful central brewpub with a pressed tin ceiling, a wide range of microbrews, a lengthy wine list, and a full menu of $9 burgers, $12 pizzas, $14 ribs, and $20 steaks. Daily 11am–10.30pm.

Silver Bean 410 W Main St ☎970 946 4404. This eye-catching, old-fashioned silver trailer just west of downtown serves espresso coffees, chais, and smoothies as well as $5 burritos and pastries; drive-through customers welcome. Mon–Fri 6.30am–3pm, Sat 7.30am–1pm.

Stonefish Sushi & More 16 W Main St ☎970 565 9244. Wonders will never cease – this smart, crisply modern Japanese restaurant in the centre of Cortez serves full salmon or steak entrees for $14–19, and noodles, sushi rolls or a "sushi pizza" for $8–13. It may not all be exactly authentic, but it tastes as good as it looks. Mon & Thurs 4.30–9pm, Tues & Wed 11am–2pm & 4.30–9pm, Fri & Sat 4.30–10pm.

Canyons of the Ancients National Monument

While Cortez is very much the largest town in **Montezuma Valley** these days, a thousand years ago the entire valley was densely populated. In fact, it's said to contain the highest density of archeological sites in the United States, which explains why much of it was designated in 2000 as the **Canyons of the Ancients National Monument**. That said, the monument largely consists of several pre-existing small museums and lesser-known sites dotted around the valley. Its creation attracted considerable local opposition, because the local economy depends on extracting gas, oil, and minerals from the canyons all around; all leases, however, which cover 85 percent of the monument, are still being exploited.

Romantic notions that Montezuma Valley was a peaceful agricultural community have been dashed by archeological research that as well as uncovering evidence of warfare and wholesale slaughter has even provided conclusive proof of ancient **cannibalism**. Human excrement discovered alongside the butchered remains of 23 Ancestral Puebloans in Cowboy Wash contained proteins that could only have come from eating their flesh.

Anasazi Heritage Center

27501 Hwy-184, Dolores • Daily: March–Oct 9am–5pm; Nov–Feb 9am–4pm • March–Oct $3, Nov–Feb free • ☎970 882 5600, ⊛co.blm.gov/canm

The **Anasazi Heritage Center**, three miles west of **DOLORES** and six miles north of Cortez, serves as the headquarters of Canyons of the Ancients National Monument. It centres

1

on a couple of twelfth-century pueblos, excavated during the construction of nearby McPhee Dam, responsible for turning the Dolores River into a broad lake at this point. The pueblos were named after the eighteenth-century Spanish friars Domínguez and Escalante, who first noted the traces of prehistoric Indians in the area. A trail leads around the ruins themselves, and there's a well-equipped **museum** of Pueblo life.

Lowry Pueblo

23 miles northwest of Dolores • No fixed hours • Free • Drive 9 miles west along County Road CC from Pleasant View, fourteen miles northwest of Dolores on US-491

There's not a tremendous amount to see at this free-standing **Lowry Pueblo Ruins**, but in summer, it's noteworthy as one of the few sites where at least part of an **Ancestral Puebloan mural** remains in place on the walls of a "Great Kiva" (see p.90). In winter, the mural is taken away for preservation, and the gravel surface of the approach road's last four miles is often impassable to vehicles.

Crow Canyon Archeological Center

23390 County Rd K, 5 miles northwest of Cortez • May–Sept Wed & Thurs 8.45am • $50, week-long course $1525 • ☎ 970 565 8975 or ☎ 800 422 8975, ⓦ crowcanyon.org

Each summer, the **Crow Canyon Archeological Center** runs day programmes for amateur archeologists and week-long residential courses for more serious students of Southwestern prehistory. Both provide the chance to assist on digs at Ancestral Puebloan sites in the valley, such as the 1800-room **Yellow Jacket**, and **Sand Canyon Pueblo**, described below.

Sand Canyon Pueblo

12 miles northwest of Cortez • Either drive straight there on county roads P and N, which leave US-491 5 miles northwest of Cortez, or follow County Road G, which leaves US-491 2 miles south of Cortez, for 10 miles, then hike to the pueblo along the rough, 6-mile Sand Canyon Trail

Sand Canyon Pueblo, a walled city that once covered the cliff-tops at Crow Canyon, is among the sites being excavated under the auspices of the **Crow Canyon Archeological Center**, is a frequent destination on their day programmes. It's also possible to make your own free, unguided visit at any time. Signs on the spot explain how the 420-room pueblo may once have looked, but there are no facilities.

Mancos

Just off US-160 fourteen miles east of Cortez, and seven miles east of the foot of the approach road that climbs into Mesa Verde, **MANCOS** is a spruce, compact attractive little residential community that caters almost exclusively to visitors to the national park.

ACCOMMODATION AND EATING   **MANCOS**

Absolute Bakery & Cafe 110 S Main St ☎ 970 533 1200, ⓦ absolutebakery.com. This welcoming little bakery serves coffees and fresh breads plus breakfast and lunch daily; it also doubles as a bookstore. Mon–Sat 7am–2pm, Sun 7am–noon; closed Tues in winter.

Fahrenheit Coffee Roasters 201 Grand Ave ☎ 970 533 7624. Set back behind a large patio forecourt at Mancos's principal intersection, this local hub offers coffee,

smoothies and $5 burritos, plus wi-fi. Mon–Fri 6.30am–5pm, Sat 7am–5pm, Sun 7am–2pm.

Mesa Verde Motel 191 W Railroad Ave ☎ 970 533 7741 or ☎ 800 825 6372, ⓦ mesaverdemotel.com. The pick of Mancos's small crop of motels, this low-slung single-storey place beside the through highway holds decent clean rooms with a friendly family welcome. Winter $60, summer $75

Mesa Verde National Park

15 miles up from US-160, 10 miles east of Cortez and 35 miles west of Durango • Late May to early Sept $15 per vehicle, $8 for motorcyclists, cyclists, and pedestrians; early Sept and late May $10 and $5 respectively; valid for 7 days • ☎ 970 529 5036, ⓦ nps.gov/meve

MESA VERDE NATIONAL PARK, the only US national park exclusively devoted to archeological remains, is set high in the plateaus of southwest Colorado, off US-160

halfway between Cortez and Mancos. It's an astonishing place, so far off the beaten track that its extensive **Ancestral Puebloan ruins** remained unseen by outsiders until late in the nineteenth century.

Mesa Verde itself – the "green table" – is a densely wooded sandstone plateau, cut at its southern edge by sheer canyons that divide the land into narrow fingers. Hundreds of natural alcoves, eaten high into the canyon walls by seeping water, served as homes for over seven hundred years; by the time they were abandoned,

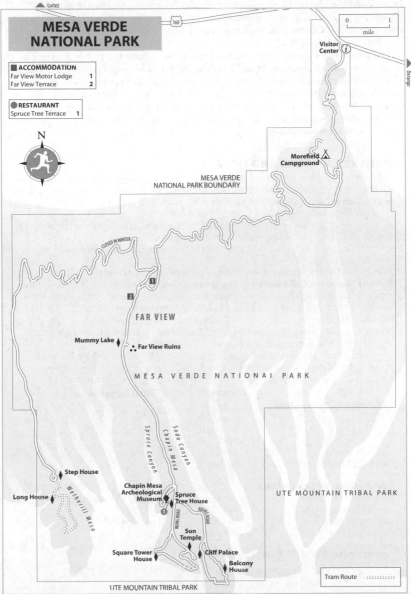

1

around 1300, several held multi-storey **cliff dwellings** that have remained virtually intact to this day.

By Southwestern standards, the mesa is not especially pretty, and it doesn't offer the same **hiking** opportunities as the region's other national parks. Its compelling relics, however, make Mesa Verde an essential stop on any Four Corners itinerary; readers of *Condé Nast Traveler* even voted it the world's top tourist attraction. As things can get very crowded in summer, the **best months** to visit are May, September, and October. The 8000ft elevation means that most of the sights become inaccessible in **winter**, though the park itself, its main museum, and one ruin – Spruce Tree House – remain open year round. **Concessions** such as gas, food, and lodging only operate between late March and early November.

Mesa Verde is not a park to visit on sudden impulse. Quite apart from the time it takes to reach this remote corner of Colorado, even a cursory visit will require a detour off US-160 of at least half a day. The access road climbs south from US-160 ten miles east of Cortez and 35 miles west of Durango. Beyond the visitor centre at the foot of the mesa, it twists and turns for fifteen laborious miles to the point known as Far View, then divides to reach two separate constellations of remains: **Chapin Mesa** to the south, and **Wetherill Mesa** to the west, which is open in summer only.

MESA VERDE TOURS AND TICKETS

The three major ruins in Mesa Verde National Park can only be visited on guided tours, though it is possible to see Cliff Palace and Long House from nearby overlooks. To take a tour, you must first buy **tickets**, which are available up to two days in advance, at either the visitor centre; the Colorado Welcome Center in Cortez (see p.72); or the Morefield Ranger Station (late May to Aug only). While the exact seasons and times of the tours vary according to both funding and climate – the specific times below are for general guidance only – each costs $3, with tickets valid for one specific time only. If you take tours on both Chapin and Wetherill mesas, allow several hours between the two.

On Chapin Mesa, during the busiest months, you will probably not be allowed to tour **Balcony House** and **Cliff Palace** on the same day (though many couples circumvent the regulations by queuing separately for tickets). If you're forced to choose, Cliff Palace can at least be seen from a distance without joining a tour, though on the other hand, touring Balcony House is much more strenuous than Cliff Palace. On days when they let you tour both, photographers should visit Balcony House first, for the best light. For most other ruins, the best time for photography is late afternoon.

In several recent summers, there has been one additional 90-minute Twilight Tour of Cliff Palace each evening between late May and mid-Sept, starting at times varying between 6.45pm & 7.15pm and costing $10, with tickets sold only at the park visitor centre.

	Hours	Tour frequency
Cliff Palace, Chapin Mesa		
early April to mid-May	9am–5pm	hourly
2nd two weeks of May	9am–5pm	half-hourly
late May to early Sept	9am–6pm	half-hourly
early Sept to mid-Oct	9am–5pm	half-hourly
mid-Oct to early Nov	9am–4pm	hourly
Balcony House, Chapin Mesa		
late April to early May	9am–5pm	9.30am, noon, 2pm, 3.30pm
early May to late May	9am–5pm	hourly
late May to early Sept	9am–5pm	half-hourly
early Sept to mid-Oct	9am–5pm	hourly
Long House, Wetherill Mesa		
early Sept to late Sept	10am–4pm	hours vary

1

Visitor centre
Daily: spring and fall 8am–5pm, summer 7.30am–7pm, winter 8.30am–4.30pm

Mesa Verde National Park unveiled a new state-of-the art **visitor centre**, beside US-160 at the entrance to the park, in 2013. As well as holding informative displays on the park and its history, it sells tickets for the timed tours of the various ruins. While you can pay the park entry here, you don't have to; rangers also accept payments at the entrance station at the foot of the park access road just beyond.

Far View
The area known as **Far View**, fifteen miles up from US-160, holds the park's only hotel and principal restaurant. An impressive structure nearby, designed to resemble an Ancestral Puebloan tower and reached via a tunnel and then a spiral walkway, served until the construction of the new facility down by the highway as the main park visitor centre. It's currently expected to reopen as some form of cultural centre.

A couple of miles further on towards Chapin Mesa you'll come to the archeological site from which Far View takes its name – a mesa-top pueblo abandoned in the thirteenth century. Thanks to the coal-burning power plants that stand in the middle distance, it seldom lives up to its name. Archeologists speculate that a large open area nearby, which has been dubbed **Mummy Lake**, doubled as both an open-air plaza and a reservoir which could hold half a million gallons. Some suggest that the rhythmic shuffling feet of ceremonial dancers were deliberately choreographed to wear grooves in the rock along which rainwater would flow to be collected.

Chapin Mesa Archeological Museum
20 miles from park entrance, 2 miles beyond Far View • Daily: mid-May to mid-Oct 8am–6.30pm; early April to mid-May and mid-Oct to mid-Nov 9am–5pm • ☎ 970 529 4631

Although the displays in the venerable **Chapin Mesa Archeological Museum** have to some extent been superseded by the opening of the park's new visitor centre, it's still worth calling in to enjoy historical exhibits that include several 1930s' dioramas depicting how archeologists then saw Ancestral Puebloan life.

Spruce Tree House
Accessible on foot from Chapin Mesa Museum • Mid-March to mid-Nov, free self-guided visits; mid-Nov to mid-Feb, free guided tours 10.30am, 1pm, & 3pm, mid-Feb to mid-March, free guided tours 10.30am, 1pm and 3pm

The short, steep hike down to **Spruce Tree House**, the only ruin that can be seen in winter, drops from alongside Chapin Mesa Museum. Consisting of several well-preserved three-storey structures, snugly moulded into the recesses of a rocky alcove and fronted by open plazas, the neat little village was occupied from 1200 AD until 1276 AD. One *kiva* has been re-roofed, and visitors can enter the dusty, unadorned interior by way of a ladder. Allow around 40min for the complete half-mile loop.

Ruins Road
April to late Oct, daily 8am–sunset

Ruins Road, beyond the Chapin Museum area, has two one-way, six-mile loops. The park's two best-known attractions, Cliff Palace and Balcony House, are on the **eastern** loop, and can be explored on guided tours only. To see them properly, be sure to buy tour tickets before you come this far; once here though, it's well worth exploring the many lesser known, and much less crowded, relics in the vicinity. In particular, try to allow enough time to tour the self-guided sites along the **western** loop as well.

Technically, Ruins Road passes out of the national park just beyond Cliff Palace and briefly enters **Ute Mountain Tribal Park**, where you can pick up information on tours (see p.76).

1

MESA VERDE: A HUMAN HISTORY

Although Archaic sites in Montezuma Valley, below Mesa Verde, date back to 5500 BC, the earliest trace of humans found on the mesa itself is a 550 AD Ancestral Puebloan pithouse. People first moved to the mesa, therefore, at around the time they acquired the skill of pottery. Not so much farmers as gardeners, they continued to gather wild plants and hunt deer and rabbits as well as grow small fields of corn and own dogs and turkeys. For five hundred years, they lived in pithouses dug into the floors of sheltered caves; then, around 1100, they congregated in walled villages on the mesa tops. A century later, they returned to the canyon-side alcoves to build the "palaces" for which Mesa Verde is now famous.

Archeologists believe each settlement held significantly fewer people than it did rooms; the largest, **Cliff Palace**, housed a population of around 120. Two or three people may have slept in a typical living room, measuring six feet by eight feet, while each family had its own *kiva* (see p.461), which when not in ceremonial use was used for weaving and domestic activities. No rigid social hierarchy is indicated either in the architecture, or the relatively few burials to have been found – some in sealed chambers, and some simply, if reverentially, in the trash heaps.

Mesa Verde may well have been a **peripheral community**. While its population is thought to have peaked at around 2500, in the middle of the thirteenth century, there were at least eight larger surface pueblos down in Montezuma Valley, whose inhabitants are thought to have been generally hostile to the Mesa Verdeans.

Ironically, archeologists regard the cliff dwellings that seem so elegant to modern visitors as signs of a declining culture. They say the mesa-top pueblos were more sophisticated in both design and construction, while the alcove complexes are haphazard accretions, contorted by the constraints of the rock and characterized by inferior craftsmanship. These were not ideal homes; older villagers must have found it impossible to get in or out, while children lived in peril of fatal falls. In theory, each complex got its water from the seep or spring that originally created its alcove, but many of those springs had run dry, leaving the occupants forever fetching and carrying.

All of which begs the question of **why** the cliff dwellings were built. Some experts argue that sites like Balcony House were primarily defensive, but there's little evidence they were ever attacked, and dwellings such as Spruce Tree House lie exposed to assault, while the towers are of little use as lookouts. Agricultural space may have been at a premium, with the entire mesa top crisscrossed by dams, terraces and irrigation channels.

In any case, Mesa Verde was **abandoned** by the end of the thirteenth century; no one has lived here since then. The traditional explanation, that a **drought** between 1276 and 1299 drove the Ancestral Puebloans away, only tells part of the story; six previous droughts had been just as bad. It's likely that both firewood and game animals had become seriously depleted, the climate had turned too cold to grow crops, and survival became too much of a struggle. Most Mesa Verdeans migrated into what's now New Mexico, to establish the pueblos where their descendants still live.

THE REDISCOVERY OF MESA VERDE

Although Mesa Verde was named by the Spanish in the seventeenth century, its ruins went unrecorded for two hundred more years. Photographer William Henry Jackson snapped some lesser sites in 1874, and a passing prospector spotted Balcony House in 1884, but the outside world first took notice when **Richard Wetherill** stumbled upon Cliff Palace in a snowstorm in 1888. The Wetherills, a local ranching family, took to selling Ancestral Puebloan artefacts as a way of life, and helped the Swedish Count Gustaf Nordenskïold to ship caseloads of ancient pottery to Europe in 1891. The National Museum of Finland, to which they were donated, now holds the world's finest collection of Mesa Verde artefacts. The activities of the Wetherills prompted both the Antiquities Act of 1906, which prohibited dealing in archeological treasures, and the creation of Mesa Verde National Park in the same year.

Cliff Palace

The first stop on the **eastern** portion of Ruins Road, **Cliff Palace**, is the largest Ancestral Puebloan cliff dwelling that survives anywhere. Tucked a hundred feet below an overhanging ledge of pale rock, it holds 217 rooms and 23 *kivas*, each thought to have belonged to a separate family or clan. It's thought this was a ceremonial or storage centre rather than simply a communal habitation, and may have been home to around 120 people.

Cliff Palace can only be seen close up on guided tours (see p.76), but if you don't have a ticket you can still get a great view from the promontory where the tour groups gather, just below the parking lot. For participants on the tours, the chance to walk through the empty plazas and peer down into the mysterious *kivas*, especially on a quieter day, provides a haunting evocation of a lost and little-known world. Fading murals can still be discerned inside some structures. As you leave, climbing an unalarming metal stairway through a narrow crevice, you may spot the original toe- and footholds used by the Ancestral Puebloans.

Balcony House

Balcony House is one of the few Mesa Verde complexes that was clearly geared toward defence. Built around 1240, it was remodelled during the 1270s to make it even more impregnable; access is very difficult, and it's not visible from above. Guided tours involve scrambling up three hair-raising ladders and crawling through a narrow tunnel, above a steep drop into Soda Canyon. It's a spectacular site, with two circular *kivas* standing side by side in a commanding central position, but those who don't share the fearless Ancestral Puebloan attitude to heights should give it a miss.

Distant views of Balcony House can be had from 1200 yards along the forested **Soda Canyon Overlook Trail**, which starts a short way further around Ruins Road.

The western loop

A 500-foot stroll at the first stop along the western loop of Ruins Road, **Square Tower House**, is rewarded by views of an eighty-room alcove complex, focused around the four-storey Square Tower – at 26 feet, the park's tallest tower. **Sun Point Overlook** looks across Spruce Canyon to as many as twelve distinct cliff dwellings, including Cliff Palace, making it clear just how crowded the canyon was in its heyday. Unlike the alcove sites, the mesa-top **Sun Temple**, next, was built to a premeditated design, and may have been a ceremonial centre for the whole community. It was never finished, however, and its shape and function can only really be appreciated from aerial photos.

Wetherill Mesa
Late May to early Sept, daily 9am–4.15pm

The tortuous twelve-mile drive onto **Wetherill Mesa** from Far View is open in summer only, and even then for ordinary-sized vehicles only. Cycles and RVs are always banned.

From the parking lot at the far end of the road, where there's a ranger station and snack kiosk, a free **miniature train** loops around the tip of the mesa. Priority is given to visitors with tickets for the timed Long House tours (see p.76). Any time spent waiting can be occupied by walking down to nearby **Step House**, where a single alcove contains a restored pithouse, dating to 626, as well as a pueblo from 1226.

The mini-train stops at various trailheads from which hikers can walk to early mesa-top sites or alcove overlooks, but its principal destination is the **Long House**. The park's second largest ruin is set in its largest cave; hour-long tours descend sixty or so steps to reach its central plaza, then scramble around its 150 rooms and 21 *kivas*. These ruins are said to be especially authentic, having been "restabilized" in recent years, rather than subjected to the same extensive rebuilding as the better-known sites were earlier last century. Excavations here uncovered a number of unburied bodies, some of whom had clearly met violent deaths.

TOURS	**MESA VERDE**
Bus tours Half-day bus tours of the park start from the *Far View Lodge* daily between late April and late October. The 8am "700 Years Tour" costs $42 for adults and $34 for ages	5–11, while the slightly shorter 1pm "Classic Pueblo Tour" costs $38 and $20 respectively; both visit Chapin Mesa only and include a tour of Cliff Palace (☎ 800 449 2288,

1

(w)visitmesaverde.com). Taking a tour can ease the laborious business of driving around Mesa Verde, and of queuing for tickets, but the sheer cost makes it hard to recommend them for family groups.

ACCOMMODATION AND EATING

Far View Motor Lodge 15 miles up from US-160 ☏ 970 564 4300 or ☏ 888 896 3831, (w)visitmesaverde .com. This summer-only lodge offers the only rooms at Mesa Verde. It's a peaceful place, away from the bustle of the park itself; guestrooms, which lack phones or TVs but have wi-fi, are in two-storey units dotted around the mesa-top. The standard rooms have private balconies, while the "Kiva" rooms are more luxurious. Though the sweeping views reach into the Rockies to the north, no archeological sites are visible. The *Metate Room*, in the mock-adobe main lodge, is a pretty good restaurant that's open daily for dinner only; entrees such as elk tenderloin are priced at up to $30. Closed late Oct to late April. Standard $145, Kiva $183

Morefield Campground 4 miles up from US-160 ☏ 970 564 4300 or ☏ 888 896 3831, (w)visitmesaverde .com. The park's official campground – so large that it's almost never full – is located a long way from the ruins. No reservations are necessary. Closed early Oct to early May. 1 or 2 vehicles $24, hook-ups $34

Spruce Tree Terrace near the Chapin Mesa museum ☏ 970 564 4300, (w)visitmesaverde.com. The one place in the park to offer food year-round, this straightforward cafeteria serves sandwiches, salads and Navajo tacos at very affordable prices (typically well under $10), and has a pleasant shaded terrace. Daily: mid-March to May & late Aug to Oct 10am–5pm; June to late Aug 9am–6.30pm; Nov to mid-March 11am–3.30pm.

Durango

Named after Durango, Mexico, with which it's also twinned, **DURANGO** was founded in 1880 as a rail junction for the Gold Rush community of Silverton, 45 miles further north. **Steam trains** still run the same high-mountain route, through the Animas Valley, and thanks to their superb close-up views of the mountains are its main tourist attraction. In addition, Durango has become a new-style Wild West boomtown, attracting a large influx of computerized teleworkers. Combine them with outdoors enthusiasts, who come to ride their **mountain bikes** on the gruelling local back roads, and in the morning at least the place has a youthful, energetic buzz. By the evening, most people seem too wiped out to do anything much.

Downtown Durango, located along Main Avenue between 7th and 11th streets, remains the liveliest urban area in the Four Corners, and is worth an hour or two of anyone's time. As well as the outdoors outfitters you might expect, it's packed with funky and upscale fashion and home furnishing stores. That said, in terms of any kind of formal tourist attraction, there's precious little to see. Like, say, Moab, Durango is very much a place where visitors come to do stuff, not see stuff.

THE DURANGO & SILVERTON RAILROAD

Between May and October, the steam trains of the **Durango & Silverton Narrow Gauge Railroad** make up to three daily return trips along a spectacular route through the mountains that parallels the gorgeous San Juan Skyway. Opened in 1882, the track took just nine months to construct. The most memorable of the train's many movie appearances came when it was blown up in *Butch Cassidy and the Sundance Kid* in 1969.

Precise schedules vary, but all trains leave **Durango** in the morning, with the first at 8am, departing from the depot at 479 Main Ave at the south end of town, and allowing time for lunch in **Silverton** at the far end. The journey takes 3 hours 30 minutes in each direction, at a maximum speed of 18mph.

No trains run for most of November, but between late November and April, when the higher mountain reaches are closed by snow, shorter excursions operate on the most scenic section only, as far as Cascade Canyon, departing at 10am, and running daily during the last two weeks of December; Fri–Sun until mid-December; and Thurs–Sat in January and February.

Reservations should be made at least two weeks in advance, via ☏ 970 247 2733, ☏ 888 872 4607, or (w)durangotrain.com. Summer fares are $85 for adults, $51 for ages 5–11; in winter they drop to $59 and $34 respectively. First and Premium Class service is also available.

INFORMATION

DURANGO

Durango's **visitor centre** is in Santa Rita Park south of downtown, near the train station at 111 S. Camino del Rio on the main highway (June–Sept Mon–Fri 8am–6pm, Sat 9am–5pm, Sun 11am–4pm; Oct–May Mon–Fri 8am–5pm; ☏970 247 3500 or ☏800 463 8726, ⓦdurango.org).

ACTIVITIES

Climbing and backpacking Southwest Adventure Guides, 12th St and Camino del Rio (☏970 259 0370 or ☏800 642 5389, ⓦswaguides.com), runs a wide array of guided climbing and backpacking tours.
Mountain bikes Rentals for around $50 per day from Hassle Free Sports, 2615 Main Ave (☏970 259 3874, ⓦhasslefreesports.com).

River-rafting Several operators run river-rafting excursions on the Animas River. Full-day expeditions with Mild to Wild Rafting (☏970 247 4789 or ☏800 567 6745, ⓦmild2wildrafting.com), for example, cost from $80 upwards. If you just want a taster, brief float trips with Flexible Flyers (☏970 247 4628, ⓦflexibleflyersrafting.com) cost from as little as $18.

ACCOMMODATION

Downtown Durango only holds a handful of **accommodation** options, including a couple of fancy but expensive historic hotels. Most of the **motels**, including all the budget ones, are well to the north, on the farther reaches of the forty-block Main Avenue.

Durango Lodge 150 East Fifth St ☏970 247 0955 or ☏888 440 4489, ⓦdurangolodge.com. Small, not particularly attractive but very convenient central motel, close to the railroad station. Spacious rooms plus a pool. Winter $56, summer $125
General Palmer Hotel 567 Main Ave ☏970 247 4747 or ☏800 523 3358, ⓦgeneralpalmerhotel.com. Very smart, old historic hotel, close to the railroad depot, that's slightly chintzier than the similar *Strater* nearby, but still provides an enjoyable taste of old-Western style. Lower-priced rooms face inward, not out on the street. Winter $115, summer $175
Hometown Hostel 736 Goeglein Gulch Rd ☏970 388 415, ⓦdurangohometownhostel.com. This appealing and very well equipped hillside home, 2 miles northeast of downtown and served by local buses #2 (daytime) and #6 (evenings and weekends), holds four bunk-bedded dorm rooms; one male, one female, and two mixed. There's also a cosy communal living room and an outdoor deck. All linens provided. Rates drop for stays of more than two nights. Dorm bed $28
★ **Rochester Hotel** 721 E Second Ave ☏970 385 1920, ⓦrochesterhotel.com. Charming, intimate, romantic – and allegedly haunted – nineteenth-century B&B inn, a block up from Main Ave, where the differing

Wild-West themes of the fifteen very comfortable rooms, some of which have kitchenettes, are inspired in part by classic, locally filmed Westerns. The breakfasts are great, the pleasant patio bar is open Wed–Sat 4–7pm, and free bikes are available. The same owners run the similar, slightly cheaper *Leland House* across the street. Winter $169, summer $219
Siesta 3475 Main Ave ☏970 247 0741 or ☏877 314 0741, ⓦdurangosiestamotel.com. Very inexpensive old-style motor court, at the curve in the highway well north of the centre; all rooms have phone, TV and wi-fi, but little more. Winter $48, summer $72
★ **Strater Hotel** 699 Main Ave ☏970 247 4431 or ☏800 247 4431, ⓦstrater.com. Major downtown landmark that's bursting with frontier elegance and offers almost a hundred mostly small but appealing antique-furnished rooms. Great buffet breakfasts, a reasonable restaurant, and frequent performances of theatrical melodramas. Winter $102, summer $177
United Campground 1322 Animas View Drive ☏970 247 3853, ⓦunitedcampgrounddurango.com. The well-shaded tent sites at this riverside commercial campground, at the northern edge of Durango and equipped with a summer-only heated pool, are the nicest place to **camp** near town. Tents $29, RVs $36

EATING AND DRINKING

Main Avenue downtown, and the streets to either side, are filled with places to **eat** and **drink**; some set their sights on affluent train passengers, others aim at young mountain bikers. There's at least one **espresso bar** on every block; they even hold a coffee festival on the first weekend of September.

Carver Brewing Co 1022 Main Ave ☏970 259 2545, ⓦcarverbrewing.com. Bustling brewpub, with a good menu of big eggy breakfasts, grilled specials like bison bratwurst and dinner entrees from Navajo tacos to seared

ahi stir-fry, for $12–19; and, of course, home-brewed beer, at $4.50 per pint. Daily 6.30am–10pm.
Cyprus Cafe 725 E Second Ave ☏970 385 6884, ⓦcypruscafe.com. Friendly local bistro, a block east of

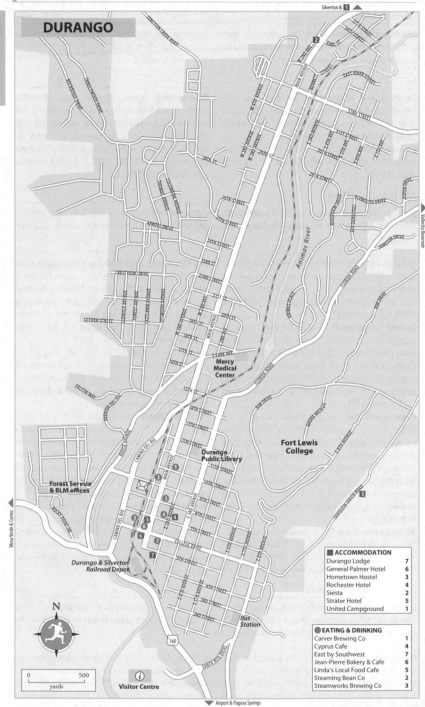

1

DURANGO

Silverton & **1**

Valecito Reservoir

Mesa Verde & Cortez

Animas River

Mercy Medical Center

Fort Lewis College

Durango Public Library

Forest Service & BLM offices

Durango & Silverton Railroad Depot

Bus Station

N

0   500
yards

Visitor Centre

Airport & Pagosa Springs

■ ACCOMMODATION	
Durango Lodge	7
General Palmer Hotel	6
Hometown Hostel	3
Rochester Hotel	4
Siesta	2
Strater Hotel	5
United Campground	1

● EATING & DRINKING	
Carver Brewing Co	1
Cyprus Cafe	4
East by Southwest	7
Jean-Pierre Bakery & Cafe	6
Linda's Local Food Cafe	5
Steaming Bean Co	2
Steamworks Brewing Co	3

Main Ave, with a spacious outdoor patio that features live jazz on summer evenings. The largely Mediterranean menu emphasizes local, sustainable produce, and includes vegetarian options like Greek spanakopita (spinach-and-cheese parcels) as well as steaks, chops and seafood, with entrees ranging $15–29. Mon–Sat 11.30am–2.30pm & 5–9pm.

East by Southwest 160 E College Drive ☎970 247 5533, ⓦeastbysouthwest.com. Ravishing "pan-Asian bistro" a block up from Main Avenue downtown, serving a wide array of delicious Thai, Vietnamese, Indonesian, and, above all, Japanese dishes. Typical entrees cost around $20, while sushi or sashimi platters for two are around $30. Mon–Sat 11.30am–2.30pm & 5–10pm, Sun 5–10pm.

★ **Jean-Pierre Bakery & Cafe** 601 Main Ave ☎970 247 7700, ⓦjeanpierrebakery.com. It may seem a little incongruous in this historic Wild-West building, but this classic French bakery/restaurant offers exquisite breads and pastries, plus sandwiches, salads, and quiches for $10–16, and full meals like mussels or beef with crab for up to $30. Live music on Fri & Sat. Daily 7am–10pm.

★ **Linda's Local Food Cafe** 309 W College Drive ☎970 259 6729, ⓦlindaslocalfoodcafe. It would be easy to overlook this bright, exceptionally friendly little cafe, squeezed into the parking lot alongside Albertson's supermarket. Big mistake; Linda's cooking is quite phenomenal. While the menu is largely Mexican, with burritos from $9, pork or chicken tamales for $11, or a filling tortilla soup for $5, the crucial factor is that Linda works closely with local, largely organic farmers to use ultra-fresh seasonal produce, with delicious daily specials drawn from world cuisines. Mon–Sat 8am–9pm, Sun 8.30am–2pm.

Steaming Bean Co 915 Main Ave ☎970 385 7901, ⓦthebean.com. Early-morning espressos and pastries, as well as speciality drinks; sandwiches, soup and wraps; wi-fi; and live music later on. Mon–Sat 6.30am–9pm, Sun 7am–8pm.

Steamworks Brewing Co 801 E Second Ave ☎970 259 9200, ⓦsteamworksbrewing.com. Large brewpub, perched in a huge corrugated-iron shed a block above Main Avenue. In summer you can enjoy wood-fired pizzas (from $10) on a sunny open-air patio, while in winter you can drink vast quantities of home-brewed beer in its bustling, cavernous interior. Mon–Thurs & Sun 11am–midnight, Fri & Sat 11am–2am.

The San Juan Skyway

North of Durango, the **San Juan Skyway** loops over two hundred miles through the Rockies, up US-550 and then back via Hwy-145 and US-160. En route, it passes through a series of compelling Wild-West towns, including mining communities like **Silverton**, **Ouray** and **Telluride** that have reinvented themselves as year-round mountain resorts.

The Skyway's initial stretch, across invigorating high passes, is known as the **Million Dollar Highway**, for the amount of gold in the ore-bearing gravel used in its construction. As you skirt around the bald, red-striped **Engineer Mountain**, just beyond the Purgatory Ski Area, the views are spectacular.

Silverton

The first town along the San Juan Skyway, **SILVERTON**, spreads across a small flat valley 9318ft up in the mountains fifty miles along, and marks journey's end for the narrow-gauge railroad from Durango. It's one of Colorado's most atmospheric mountain towns, with wide dirt-packed streets leading off toward the hills to either side of the one main road, where the snow lingers year-round. Silverton's zinc- and copper-mining days only came to an end in 1991, leaving it dependent on tourism. The false-front stores along "Notorious Blair Street," paralleling the main drag, recall the days when legendary gunslinger Bat Masterson was the city marshal, and are the scene of frequent staged shoot-outs. Silverton is geared much more toward day-trippers than overnight guests, so even in summer it gets very sleepy at night, with just a handful of Western saloons and steakhouses providing the only sign of life.

Without a 4WD vehicle, it's hard to explore the mountains, but if instead of returning to the main highway you simply keep going beyond the end of Silverton's main street, you can continue for several miles in an ordinary car. The dirt road usually starts to get difficult around the ruins of **EUREKA**, seven miles along the Animas River, which make a good starting point for hikes to nearby waterfalls. The crest of the

1

mountain ridge to the east marks the Continental Divide, with the source of the Rio Grande on the far side.

Ouray

The equally attractive mining community of **OURAY** lies 23 miles north of Silverton, on the far side of 11,018-foot **Red Mountain Pass**, where the bare rock beneath the snow really is red, thanks to mineral deposits. The Million Dollar Highway twists and turns, passing abandoned mine workings and rusting machinery in the most unlikely and inaccessible spots. The best spot for an overview is the Red Mountain Overlook, where the relics of the Idarado Mine lie scattered below a magnificent red peak; tunnels once connected it with Telluride, little more than five miles west but sixty miles by road. Back roads into the mountains hereabouts offer rich pickings for hikers or 4WD drivers.

Ouray itself squeezes into an impossibly slender verdant valley at the head of the Uncompahgre River, with the **Ouray Hot Springs** ranged alongside the river at the north end of town. A mile or so south, a one-way loop dirt road leads to **Box Cañon Falls Park** (daily 8am–dusk; $4), where a straightforward 500-foot trail, partly along a swaying wooden parapet, leads into the dark, narrow Box Cañon. At the far end, the falls thunder through a tiny cleft in the mountain.

Ridgway

North of Ouray, the scenery changes abruptly, with the canyon of the Uncompahgre characterized by red rocks and sparse sagebrush. To complete the San Juan Skyway loop, turn west on Hwy-62 after eight miles at **RIDGWAY**, where the northern limits of the San Juan Mountains stand as a serrated ridge along the southern skyline.

Ridgway was a pivotal location for the 1968 movie *True Grit*. The 62-year-old **John Wayne**, who won his first Oscar as one-eyed Marshal "Rooster Cogburn", met his young sidekick outside the town courthouse, while their subsequent adventures were played out against the magnificent backdrop of the **Wilson Peaks**, which you'll see if you continue west on the San Juan Skyway.

Telluride

As Hwy-62, the San Juan Skyway meets Hwy-145 23 miles southwest of Ridgway, and then turns sharply back eastward on Hwy-145 along the pretty, well-wooded valley of the San Miguel River. The former mining village of **TELLURIDE** is a 74-mile drive from Silverton, even though as the crow flies, across the mountains, the towns are barely ten miles apart.

Telluride was briefly home to the young Butch Cassidy, who robbed his first bank here in 1889. It's now best known as a **ski resort**, rivalling Aspen and Vail as a winter destination for the stars. Telluride has, however, achieved this status without losing its character – the wide main street, a National Historic District with low-slung buildings on either side, still heads directly up toward one of the most stupendous mountain views in the Rockies. Healthy young bohemians with few visible means of support but top-notch ski equipment form the bulk of the 2200 citizens, while most of the glitzy visitors hang out two miles above the town in **Mountain Village**, reached by a free year-round gondola service (daily 7am–midnight).

Although Telluride is generally cheaper to visit in summer than winter, prices do rise during the **Bluegrass Festival** in mid-June (ⓦbluegrass.com), the **Jazz Festival** in early August (ⓦtelluridejazz.org), and the **Film Festival** at the start of September (ⓦtelluridefilmfestival.org).

Bridal Veil Falls

In summer, Telluride offers excellent **hiking** opportunities. One three-mile round-trip walk, which also makes a great if gruelling bike ride, switchbacks up a bumpy 4WD road from the head of the valley to reach Colorado's highest waterfalls, the 365-foot

SKIING AND SNOWBOARDING IN TELLURIDE

Telluride's winter season, which starts as the fall colours fade, usually in late November, continues until early April. The town also hosts US and world **snowboarding** championships, with many former ski trails now reserved for snowboarders.

Prospective visitors should visit ⓦ **telluride.com** for a wide range of lodging and package deals. Guests in certain lodges get discounted lift tickets; otherwise a full-price lift ticket costs around $100 per day. The same website also has full details of the **Telluride Ski and Snowboard School**, which offers expert instruction for visitors of all levels, and of local operators who rent out ski and snowboarding equipment.

Bridal Veil Falls. To join it, follow the main highway all the way through town, park where it ends at Pioneer Mill, and set off uphill. Don't expect to be able to cool off with a swim in the falls, however; it's far too perilous for that.

INFORMATION

SILVERTON

Visitor centre 414 Greene St, at the southern edge of town (daily: May, June & Sept 9am–4pm; July & Aug 9am–5pm; Oct–April 10am–3pm; ☎ 970 387 5654 or ☎ 800 752 4494, ⓦ silvertoncolorado.com).

OURAY

Visitor centre 1230 Main St, outside the hot springs (mid-June to Aug Mon–Wed 9am–7pm, Thurs–Sat 9am–6pm, Sun 10am–4pm; Sept to mid-June Mon–Sat

SAN JUAN SKYWAY

10am–5pm, Sun 10am–3pm; ☎ 970 325 4746 or ☎ 800 228 1876, ⓦ ouraycolorado.com).

Tours Switzerland of America, 226 Seventh Ave (☎ 970 325 4484 or ☎ 866 990 5337, ⓦ soajeep.com) rents out 4WD vehicles and offers guided jeep tours.

TELLURIDE

Visitor centre 700 W Colorado Ave, on the edge of downtown (daily 9am–5pm; ☎ 888 605 2578, ⓦ visittelluride.com).

ACCOMMODATION

SILVERTON

Grand Imperial Hotel 1219 Greene St ☎ 970 387 5527 or ☎ 800 341 3340, ⓦ grandimperialhotel.com. Very central, bright red main street hotel, with plenty of historic ambience and old-style rooms of varying degrees of comfort. The cheapest fall well short of luxury. $79

Silverton Hostel 1025 Blair St ☎ 970 387 0015, ⓦ silvertoninnandhostel.com. This tiny, tin-walled hostel, a block off the main street, offers the cheapest accommodation in town, with dorm beds (bring your own sleeping bag) as well as a few plain, private doubles. Check-in daily 8–10am & 4–10pm. Dorms $20, doubles $50

Teller House Hotel 1250 Greene St ☎ 970 387 5423 or ☎ 800 342 4338, ⓦ tellerhouse.com. Open since 1896, this Victorian guesthouse offers classy antique-furnished rooms, some – not necessarily the cheapest – of which share bathrooms. $89

Triangle Motel 848 Greene St ☎ 970 387 5780, ⓦ trianglemotel.com. Behind its rather ugly facade, this motel at the south end of town is very well maintained, offering good facilities for the price, with two-room suites available. $80

OURAY

Box Canyon Lodge 45 Third Ave ☎ 970 325 4981 or ☎ 800 327 5080, ⓦ boxcanyonouray.com. An old-style

timber motel below the park, where guests can bathe in natural hot tubs. The guest rooms are cosy and snug, with good furnishings and fittings. $105

★ **Hot Springs Inn** 1400 Main St ☎ 970 325 7277 or ☎ 800 706 7790, ⓦ hotspringsinn.com. All of the very pleasant rooms at this comfortable upscale modern inn, at the north end of town, have deck balconies facing the river, and the staff are hugely helpful with area recommendations. $159

TELLURIDE

Manitou Lodge 333 S Fir St ☎ 970 728 3388 or ☎ 888 728 1950, ⓦ telluridehotels.com/manitou-lodge -telluride. While it calls itself a B&B, the *Manitou Lodge* looks more like an outlying segment of an old-fashioned national-park lodge. The cozy comforts of its 11 renovated rooms can't be faulted, though, and neither can its riverside setting – close to the ski lifts and just a short walk from the town centre, via a pedestrian bridge. There's a very pleasant outdoor deck, with a hot tub that's open to the elements when weather permits. $139

New Sheridan Hotel 231 W Colorado Ave ☎ 970 728 4351 or ☎ 800 200 1891, ⓦ newsheridan.com. Restored 1895 hotel in the heart of town, where the large, very luxurious rooms have stylish antique furnishings but modern bathrooms and fittings. The cheapest face inwards,

1

but it costs little more to enjoy great mountain views. They even provide white noise machines to dampen things down when Telluride is in party mode. Winter $204, summer $163

Victorian Inn 401 W Pacific Ave ☎970 728 6601 or 800 611 9893, ⦿victorianinntelluride.com. Despite the name, this is a smart motel rather than a historic inn, lacking a pool or a/c. The rooms are conventional and unexciting, but the location is unbeatable for the price, and it has its own sauna. Winter $99, summer $124

EATING AND DRINKING

SILVERTON

Avalanche Coffee House 1067 Blair St ☎970 387 5282. A welcome contrast to Silverton's crop of rather ordinary Western steakhouses, this friendly hangout offering fresh coffee, pastries, and snacks, plus more substantial pizzas for around $12. Mon, Tues & Thurs–Sun 9am–6pm.

OURAY

Backstreet Bistro 636 Main St ☎970 325 0550. Very central cafe/bakery – despite the name, it's on the main through highway – that makes a good rendezvous for substantial breakfasts, then keeps busy all day doling out coffees, sandwiches and smoothies. Daily 7am–10pm.

Bon Ton 426 Main St ☎970 325 4951, ⦿stelmobonton.com. Snug basement restaurant, below the *St Elmo* B&B, which offers Ouray's most satisfying special-occasion ambience and cuisine. As well as Italian classics for around $18–20, the menu features signature Colorado dishes such as lamb chops with jalapeño mint sauce ($29). Mon & Thurs–Sat 5.30–9pm, Sun 9.30am–1pm & 5.30–9pm.

RIDGWAY

Kate's Place 615 W Clinton ☎970 626 9800. Bright, busy cafe, a block north of the main road west, that's a local legend for its emphasis on regional organic produce in general, and its big breakfast waffles in particular. The lunch menu includes inexpensive daily specials like a

$12.50 lasagne, as well as sandwiches and salads. Tues–Fri 8am–2pm, Sat & Sun 7am–2pm.

TELLURIDE

Baked in Telluride 127 S Fir St ☎970 728 4775. Take-out deli-bakery, just off the main drag, that's great for morning espressos and pastries, and has a nice little terrace where you can enjoy soup, sandwiches, or pizza. Daily 5.30am–10pm.

Chop House New Sheridan Hotel, 231 W Colorado Ave ☎970 728 9100, ⦿newsheridan.com. Cozy, upbeat Western saloon-style dining room, a nice setting for anything from a massive mountain breakfast to a meaty dinner. Prices are more reasonable at lunchtime; an evening steak or chop – especially if you opt for elk! – can cost over $50. Daily 7am–2am.

Cosmopolitan Hotel Columbia, 300 W San Juan Ave ☎970 728 0660, ⦿columbiatelluride.com. At Telluride's fanciest restaurant, set in a high-end, luxury hotel near the ski lifts and open for dinner only, entrees – mostly contemporary Southwestern, but including Thai- and Japanese-influenced options – start at well over $20. Daily 6–10.30pm.

Smuggler Joe's Brewpub and Grille 225 S Pine ☎970 728 0919. Very lively, convivial evening (ideally après-piste) hangout, with a wide-ranging menu of ordinary pub grub but some exceptional house brews, including the likes of raspberry wheat beers. Daily 11am–2am.

Northwest New Mexico

Although **northwest New Mexico** formed the heart of the Dinétah, the Navajo's original homeland in the Southwest, the Navajo territories here are less visited than their more scenic equivalents in Arizona. Archeology buffs are drawn to **Chaco Canyon** and **Aztec Ruins**, which although they rank among the most significant Ancestral Puebloan sites anywhere, are less photogenic than their better-known rivals. None of the towns nearby, whether on or off the reservation, holds any lasting interest.

Instead the region is notorious as the home of the **Four Corners Power Plant**, near Farmington. After this coal-fired generating station opened in the 1960s, it was said to be the single greatest source of pollution in the United States, emitting more noxious gases than either New York City or Los Angeles. Regulations have been tightened since then, but with the **Navajo Mine**, the largest open-pit coal mine in the West, just a mile away, and several other generating plants in the immediate neighbourhood, there's no incentive for outsiders to linger. For the Navajo, of course, who provide much of the industry's workforce, it's a different story.

1

Shiprock

By far the most striking landmark in the dusty red plains of New Mexico's far northwestern corner is the craggy monolith known as **Shiprock**. In Navajo legend, as *Tsé bitTaai* or "Rock Wing," this awesome 1500-foot peak was home to one or two monstrous birds, which were either killed by the hero Monster Slayer or turned into an eagle and an owl. To Anglo eyes, it resembled instead a mighty ocean-going ship. Navajo medicine men continued to use it in sacred ceremonies until 1939, when Sierra Club members including David Brower – the "Arch-Druid" who later founded Friends of the Earth (see p.392) – defiled Shiprock by climbing it.

Roadside signs on **US-491**, which runs within a few miles of Shiprock's vast, eerie bulk, explain that the mountain is a volcanic plug, the hard central core of a volcano that has itself eroded away. There's no point trying to approach it any closer; you can't even walk up to the base, let alone climb it. Neither is it worth stopping at the sprawling mining town six miles north, also known as **SHIPROCK**, other than in early October, when it hosts the **Northern Navajo Fair** (ⓦnorthernnavajonationfair.org).

Farmington

FARMINGTON, the largest town in northwestern New Mexico, lies fifty miles east of the Four Corners Monument; fifty miles southwest of Durango, Colorado; and, more to the point, a mere ten miles west of both the Navajo Mine and the Four Corners Power Plant. Formerly renowned as a definitive "edge-of-the-res" community, rife

---

THE BEAST IS DEAD

Here is wisdom. Let him who has understanding calculate the Number of the Beast, for it is the number of a man: His number is 666.   *Revelation 13:18*

Until 2003, 666 was not merely the Number of the Beast, and the number of a man; it was also the number of the main highway north through the Navajo Nation from Gallup to Shiprock. **US-666** was assigned the dreaded "666" in 1942, as the sixth major road to branch off Route 66, and swiftly acquired such nicknames as the "Devil's Highway" and the "Highway to Hell." Despite being largely straight, and doubtless paved with good intentions, it became renowned for an appalling accident record. *USA Today* rated it as the most dangerous highway in the country, while in 1995 the *Wall Street Journal* ran an article headlined "Beast of a Highway: Does Asphalt Stretch Have Biblical Curse?".

Prompted by state governor Bill Richardson, New Mexico's House and Senate passed a Joint Resolution in 2003 that declared:

WHEREAS, people living near the road already live under the cloud of opprobrium created by having a road that many believe is cursed running near their homes and through their homeland; and
WHEREAS, the number 666 carries the stigma of being the mark of the beast, the mark of the devil, which was described in the book of Revelation in the Bible; and
WHEREAS, there are people who refuse to travel the road, not because of the issue of safety, but because of the fear that the devil controls events along United States route 666; and
WHEREAS, the economy in the area is greatly depressed when compared with many parts of the United States, and the infamy brought by the inopportune naming of the road will only make development in the area more difficult.

…the number of the road should be changed as soon as possible. A state highway official was reported as having no preference concerning the new designation: "As long as it's not 666 and it's nothing satanic, that's OK." The former US-666 therefore duly became US-491 on May 31, 2003.

with racism and violence, Farmington has cleaned itself up and prospered accordingly. Developments like the **Animas Valley Mall**, 4601 E Main St, make it the principal business centre of a wide area.

Farmington's principal concession to tourism is its **museum**, in the Gateway Park on the northeast edge of town at 3041 E Main St (Mon–Sat 8am–5pm; free), which traces town history from the geological "New Mexico Seacoast" up to trading-post times; it also has extensive displays on mining and refining.

ARRIVAL AND INFORMATION   FARMINGTON

By plane Great Lakes Airlines (ⓦflygreatlakes.com) connects the Four Corners Airport, west of town, with Denver, Las Vegas, Page and Phoenix.

Visitor centre 3041 E Main St, in the museum (Mon–Sat 8am–5pm; ☎505 326 7602 or ☎800 448 1240, ⓦfarmingtonnm.org).

ACCOMMODATION AND EATING

Kokopelli's Cave 5001 Antelope Junction ☎505 560 3812, ⓦbbonline.com/nm/kokopelli. This quite extra-ordinary cave dwelling, three miles north of town, was hollowed out in 1980, 75 feet below ground level but opening onto a cliff-face balcony hundreds of feet above the La Plata River. It's rented out on a B&B basis to groups of up to four people. To make the most of its glorious isolation, luxurious ambience, and features like the waterfall shower, stay two nights at least. $260

La Quinta Inn 675 Scott Ave ☎505 327 4706 or ☎800 531 5900, ⓦlq.com. Presentable chain motel, near the

Animas River on the east side of town, with a hundred decent rooms on two storeys, plus a heated pool and free breakfasts. $89

Three Rivers Eatery and Brewhouse 101 E Main St ☎505 324 2187, ⓦthreeriversbrewery.com. Sprawling and very central block-long complex that incorporates a brewery, tap room serving a huge range of speciality beers, and a lively, family-friendly resturant serving the best (and most substantial) food you'll find for miles, including full meals, with entrees at $12–18, as well as lunchtime sandwiches for under $10. Daily 11am–11pm.

Aztec

AZTEC, the county seat of San Juan County, straddles the Animas River fourteen miles northeast of Farmington. While lower-key and more enjoyable than its larger neighbour, its only real interest for visitors is as the site of a major Ancestral Puebloan site, preserved in **Aztec Ruins National Monument**.

Aztec Museum

125 N Main Ave • April–Sept Tues–Sat 11am–5pm • $3 • ☎505 334 9829, ⓦaztecmuseum.org

The quaint Aztec Museum, at the northern end of Aztec's leafy central thoroughfare, celebrates local history with displays on the oil industry and a mock-up barbershop. In its outdoor pioneer village, life-size mannequins hang out in frontier-style buildings like a schoolhouse, a jail, and a bank.

Aztec Ruins National Monument

One mile north of Aztec, across the Animas River • Daily: summer 8am–6pm; winter 8am–5pm • $5 per person • ☎505 334 6174, ⓦnps.gov/azru

The ancient pueblo now protected within **Aztec Ruins National Monument** was erroneously regarded by early Anglo settlers as the work of the dominant civilization of pre-contact Mexico. In fact, it's a large "outlier" Ancestral Puebloan settlement, built from 1111 onwards by people from the Chaco culture (see p.92), and connected with Chaco Canyon, 64 miles south, by a die-straight road now only visible from the air. Aztec stands halfway between Chaco and Mesa Verde, and is thought to have been remodelled by a new wave of settlers from Mesa Verde around 1225.

From the visitor centre, which holds some interesting ancient artefacts, a short trail leads around and through the **West Ruin**, the only part of the site to have been excavated. This 500-room E-shaped structure held only one entrance and was entirely

1

walled. The trail leads through room after room (you'll have to stoop to get through the low doorways) before culminating in the awesome **Great Kiva** – the term for a *kiva* used by an entire community rather than an individual clan or family.

Reconstructed in 1934, this is the only Great Kiva in the Southwest that can be seen in anything approaching its original state. Aspects of the restoration remain conjectural, but there's no disputing the circular chamber's sheer size, which measured fifty feet across. Its 95-ton roof was supported by four pillars that rested on four 375-pound limestone disks, carried here from forty miles away. Archeologists say that the *kiva* may have been in use when the *kachina* religion was first being developed, and that its fifteen side rooms may have been changing rooms from which masked figures would emerge during ceremonies. An informative trail guide, written by an Indian from Santa Clara Pueblo quite possibly descended from the site's original inhabitants, explains much of what you see. A corresponding **East Ruin** lurks mysteriously beneath shapeless hillocks.

INFORMATION   AZTEC

Visitor centre 110 N Ash Ave, east of the river (Mon–Fri 9am–noon & 1–5pm; ☎505 334 9551 or ☎888 543 4629, ⊚aztecnm.com).

THE PUEBLITOS OF DINÉTAH

Although they now lie beyond the boundaries of the Navajo Nation, remote Largo and Gobernador canyons, southeast of Farmington and Aztec, were the original cradles of the **Dinétah**, the traditional Navajo homeland. The earliest known trace of a Navajo presence is a *hogan* in Gobernador Canyon, tree-ring dated to 1541, but the most significant era in its history followed the Pueblo Revolt of 1680. Refugees from the Rio Grande pueblos fled west during the aftermath of the revolt, to be joined by further waves of migrants when the Spaniards reconquered New Mexico from 1692 onwards.

Between 1680 and 1750, Navajo and Pueblo Indians combined to build around 130 stone fortresses in the region, known as the **Pueblitos of Dinétah**. Perched on high eminences close to the canyon rims, or tucked into alcoves just below, these "little pueblos" are reminiscent of Ancestral Puebloan sites like those at Hovenweep (see p.71). Most were too small to house an entire community for any length of time; instead they were intended as lookouts, retreats for elders and religious leaders, and, above all, as shelters during raids. The Spaniards sent punitive expeditions into the area every summer between 1705 and 1716, while from the 1720s onwards Ute war parties threatened Navajo and Spaniard alike.

The *pueblitos* played a crucial role in forging a new synthesis of Navajo and Pueblo cultures. Many of the modern hallmarks of Navajo identity, both in terms of skills such as rug weaving and sheep-herding, and of religious beliefs, were acquired during this period. The driving force seems to have been the inter-marriage of Navajo men with women from the pueblo of Jemez. Their union created the **Coyote Pass People**, still a prominent Navajo clan. Influences are also absorbed from further afield. Not only were Spanish metal-working techniques introduced, but in Three Corn Pueblito, which was abandoned in the 1750s, archeologists have even unearthed a Qing dynasty plate from China.

While you can drive into both Largo and Gobernador canyons, along good-quality dirt roads used by gas-drilling companies, unless you have expert assistance you won't be able to reach or even spot the pueblitos themselves. The Bureau of Land Management office at 1235 La Plata Hwy in Farmington (☎505 599 8900) can provide detailed directions to sites located on BLM lands, but you'd do better to join an **organized tour**.

Aztec Archaeological Consultants ☎505 334 6675, ⊚aztecarchaeology.com. Half-day explorations of the Pueblitos of Dinétah for one or two people for $110, full-day trips for $230.

Chaco Tours ☎505 632 2013, ⊚chacotours.org. The archeologists at Salmon Ruins charge around $300 for an all-day 4WD trip for one or two people, to either Chaco Canyon, the Pueblitos of Dinétah, or other sites of your choosing.

ACCOMMODATION AND EATING

Aztec Restaurant 107 W Aztec Blvd ☎ 505 334 9586. Venerable steak-and-pancake diner, opposite the *Step Back Inn* and frying up a steady stream of inexpensive breakfast eggs, burgers, and breaded fish. Daily 7am–9.30pm.

Main Street Bistro 122 N Main St ☎ 505 334 0109, ⓦ aztecmainstreetbistro.com. A welcome little lunch or breakfast stop, facing the museum, with good coffee and pastries, hearty soups and grilled sandwiches, all for under $10, and an outdoor patio. Mon–Fri 7am–2pm, Sat 8am–noon.

Step Back Inn 123 W Aztec Blvd ☎ 505 334 1200 or ☎ 800 334 1255, ⓦ stepbackinn.com. Despite its modern exterior, this 39-room, twenty-year-old motel-cum-inn, where US-550 meets Main Avenue, holds pleasant rooms furnished with Victorian antiques. $72

Bloomfield

BLOOMFIELD, eight miles south of Aztec or twelve miles east of Farmington, is an unattractive little desert crossroads at the axis of Hwy-64 and Hwy-550. It's notable for its **Salmon Ruins**, two miles west and not much else. Several nondescript restaurants line Broadway Ave (Hwy-64), the main east-west road through town.

Salmon Ruins

6131 US-64, 2 miles west of Bloomfield • May–Oct Mon–Fri 8am–5pm, Sat & Sun 9am–5pm; Nov–April Mon–Sat 8am–5pm, Sun noon–5pm • $3 • ☎ 505 632 2013, ⓦ salmonruins.com

The outlying Chacoan pueblo now known as **Salmon Ruins** was constructed between 1088 and 1094, twenty years before its neighbour at Aztec. It may mark the first attempt to build a "new Chaco," which failed when the San Juan River proved too unruly to tame at this point, whereupon Aztec was built as a replacement. While much of the site consists of the exposed foundation walls of various structures, the central Great Kiva is undeniably impressive, much less fancifully restored than the equivalent at Aztec (see p.90). Replicas of ancient pithouses and modern *hogans* offer insight into the region's successive inhabitants.

Chaco Canyon

Daily 7am–sunset • $8 per vehicle or $4 per individual • ☎ 505 786 7014, ⓦ nps.gov/chcu

Although the **Ancestral Puebloan ruins** of **CHACO CANYON** form the **largest pre-Columbian city** in North America, for sheer beauty and drama they can't compete with lesser settlements such as Canyon de Chelly. The low-walled canyon itself, now protected as **Chaco Culture National Historical Park**, is a mere scratch in the scrubby high-desert plains, and the Chaco Wash that runs through it is often completely dry. Add the fact that the site is a long, bumpy, twenty-mile ride off the nearest paved road, and more than double that from any significant town or facilities, and it's no wonder that visitors on tight itineraries often decide it's more bother than it's worth.

Once you accept that you won't have such amazing photos to show the folks back home, however, there's still plenty about Chaco to take your breath away. Over 3600 separate sites have been logged in the canyon, of which the thirteen principal ones are open to visitors. Six of these, arrayed along the canyon's north wall, are what's known as **Great Houses** – self-contained pueblos, three or four storeys high, whose fortress-like walls concealed up to eight hundred rooms. The largest, **Pueblo Bonito**, is claimed to have been the largest single building in America until structural steel was developed in 1898.

Visitor centre

On the eastern side of the park, where the two approach routes meet • Daily 8am–5pm

An essential first stop, Chaco Canyon's **visitor centre** is the place to pick up maps and brochures, plus schedules of summer-only ranger-led tours. You can also watch videos such

1

THE CHACO PHENOMENON

To archeologists, Chaco Canyon represents the apogee of Ancestral Puebloan achievement. However, what they call the **Chaco phenomenon** remains one of the Southwest's greatest puzzles. How can the canyon's apparent unsuitability for large-scale occupation – if anything, it was slightly drier in Ancestral Puebloan times than it is today – be reconciled with its massive structures and demonstrable influence over an "empire" that covered at least 25,000 square miles?

Although pithouses built by early Ancestral Puebloan Basketmakers are scattered around the canyon, Chaco's first surface pueblo appeared during the ninth century. Around 1000, sophisticated masonry techniques, developed or introduced by migrants from the Mesa Verde region, enabled the construction of larger multistorey apartments. The canyon's heyday came between 1050 and 1125; its last definite tree-ring date is 1132, and by 1200 it was abandoned. Prodigious work went into its construction. Upwards of 200,000 tree trunks, mostly ponderosa pines and corkbark fir, were carried here from hillsides fifty or more miles away, without the use of animals or the wheel.

Since Chaco became a national monument in 1907, estimates of its ancient population have repeatedly diminished. As few burials have been found, there's little sign that the upper floors were ever inhabited, and the canyon's soil is so poor, it's now believed that Chaco never held more than two thousand inhabitants.

Chaco was more of a **ceremonial centre** than a residential community; the Great Houses were not homes, but some combination of warehouses, temples and palaces. Huge quantities of **turquoise** have been discovered – harvester ants, who collect blue and green turquoise to adorn their nests, scavenged fifty thousand pieces in Pueblo Bonito alone. Still precious to contemporary Indian cultures, turquoise was the most valuable trading commodity in the ancient Southwest. The Chacoans acquired it raw from distant mines – mostly to the east, in the Cerrillos region (see p.128) – and crafted it into sacred and ornamental objects, which passed from hand to hand down trading networks into the heart of Mexico. It's said ninety percent of the turquoise found in the Aztec capital of Tenochtitlan was of Southwestern origin. Similarly, the parrots and scarlet macaws whose skeletons have been found here must have come from southern Mexico or beyond.

Chaco's primary significance, however, was much more local. Having started as a small trading settlement, it probably became a place of pilgrimage, where individuals came, with appropriate rituals, to obtain sacred turquoise. Later still, during regular regional **festivals**,

as *Sundagger*, which explains how rocks and petroglyphs atop nearby Fajada Butte were carefully sited to plot not only the annual solstices, but also the moon's 18.5-year cycle.

The loop road

A nine-mile, one-way **loop road** provides the only access to the actual ruins in Chaco Canyon. Its gates are immediately north of the visitor centre, and open the same hours. The major stop is at the far end, where **Pueblo Bonito** can be explored on an easy half-mile trail.

Pueblo Bonito

Work on the four-storey D-shaped structure that's now known as **Pueblo Bonito** – which means "beautiful town" in Spanish, and is almost perfectly aligned east–west – started in 850 AD and continued for around three hundred years. Speculation that hordes of slaves were forced to build it have been deflated by precise dating of its parts; even during its busiest era, a workforce of just thirty men, cutting and hauling trees for a full month each year, and quarrying and shaping stone for four months every two years, could have done the job.

The half-mile trail around Pueblo Bonito heads first to the back of the structure, passing the spot where Threatening Rock, a colossal boulder whose collapse the ancient inhabitants staved off with prayer sticks and supporting walls, finally destroyed thirty rooms in 1941. Entering the ruin via its lowest levels, the path reaches its central plaza, large crowds would assemble for public ceremonies. For most of the year, Chaco held a small, high-caste population, and the upper floors of its pueblos were empty or used for storage; at festival times, they accommodated a large influx of guests.

Evidence for this ceremonial role includes the extraordinary 450-mile network of **roads** that link Chaco with 75 "**outlier**" communities. Averaging thirty feet in width, they were far wider than ordinary human foot-traffic could require; in fact they were more like causeways, built of hard-packed stone and running arrow-straight across cliffs, mesas, and canyons. Most are now only visible from the air. The longest stretched all the way to Aztec Ruins, 64 miles north (see p.89), but if that same line is extended *south*, it makes a virtually perfect alignment with the site known as either **Casas Grandes** or **Paquimé**, over 300 miles away in Mexico. Roadside beacons may have been lit to summon pilgrims to major festivals.

Navajo legends relate that Chaco was ruled by the despotic **Great Gambler**, who was born to a poor Chacoan woman, taught to gamble by his father, the Sun, and won control over the canyon and all it held. When he was eventually defeated, he was shot into the sky, where he once more accumulated great wealth and returned to the region in the shape of the Spanish invaders. Meanwhile, freed of their oppressor, the people of Chaco had dispersed.

Recently, ferocious archeological debate has focused on the signs of large-scale **violence** at Chaco. Human remains found in two-thirds of the Great Houses appear to have been mutilated in a manner that suggests **cannibalism**. In the absence of evidence of warfare, they're seen as possible victims of ritual slaughter. The leading exponent of this theory, Christy Turner III, has even argued that a wandering group of Toltec refugees entered the region from the south around 900, and established a reign of terror at Chaco by introducing the bloodthirsty Mexican practice of **human sacrifice**.

Trying to guess why the Chacoans left the canyon when they did – from 1230 onwards – is probably futile, although even a tiny reduction in rainfall might have been enough to drive them out. Where they went, however, is no great mystery. Both Aztec, at its peak between 1110 and 1275, and Casas Grandes, an even richer commercial centre occupied from 1250 to 1500, can be seen as successive "capital cities" of the same cultural tradition.

Ácoma Pueblo (see p.99) is among the many modern pueblos that show a clear continuity with Chacoan culture. At least nine Hopi clans trace their origins back to what they remember as "the place beyond the horizon," while the Zuni say a medicine society known as the Sword Swallowers joined them from Chaco.

which held at least three **Great Kivas** of the kind restored at Aztec (see p.90). From there, you can walk through the passageways and chambers of the pueblo proper, where the rows of neatly finished doorways, each framed by the next, are Chaco's most photographed feature.

Chetro Ketl

A separate trail from the Pueblo Bonito parking lot heads to the smaller complex of **Chetro Ketl**, a quarter-mile east. Constructed over the course of a century, from 1010 onwards, this shows Chacoan masonry at its most sophisticated – or as some archeologists put it, at its most obviously influenced by Meso-American models. Its horizontal rows of large, squared-off stones are chinked with smaller, flatter stones and set into a bed of adobe mortar with a mosaic-like precision. Many original beams (*vigas*) remain in place, and a vivid fragment of an ancient mural is protected behind a glass panel.

Pueblo del Arroyo

The first stop along the loop road beyond Pueblo Bonito, **Pueblo del Arroyo**, is the only Great House to stand right beside Chaco Wash. Although it rarely holds much water, the stream channel is much deeper and broader than it was in Ancestral Puebloan days. Only half of the pueblo, raised on a small hillock and occupied between 1070 and 1105, has been excavated.

Casa Rinconada

Perched on a mound as the road heads back down the canyon from Pueblo del Arroyo, **Casa Rinconada** is the canyon's largest **Great Kiva**, at 62 feet across. It now lies open to the sun, the subtleties of its astronomical alignments lost but its central features still clearly identifiable. Archeologists are unsure whether the two large vaults in the *kiva* floor served as foot drums, or to propagate seedlings.

ARRIVAL AND INFORMATION   CHACO CANYON

Both the main approaches to Chaco Canyon entail driving at least thirteen miles over rough but **passable dirt roads**. They remain open all year, but should not be attempted during, or within a day of, a **rainstorm**.

From the south Leave I-40 at Thoreau, 28 miles northwest of Grants. Follow Hwy-57 north for another 28 miles, beyond Crownpoint, then turn right onto Arrowhead Hwy-9 for 13 miles to Seven Lakes, where the twenty-mile dirt road to Chaco itself branches off to the left.

From the north or east Turn off US-550 three miles southeast of Nageezi, 36 miles south of Bloomfield; thirteen of the twenty miles from there are on dirt roads.

ACCOMMODATION

Gallo campground Just east of the visitor centre ☎ 505 786 7014, ⓦ nps.gov/chcu. Backcountry camping being forbidden in Chaco Canyon, this basic first-come, first-served campground is the only visitor facility the park has to offer; between April and October it's usually full by 3pm. Bring any firewood you require. Per person $10

Crownpoint

CROWNPOINT, almost forty miles southwest of Chaco Canyon and 24 miles north of the I-40 town of **Thoreau**, is the principal town along the eastern flank of the Navajo Nation. Its only conceivable appeal for tourists is as the site of the **Navajo Rug Auction**, held usually but not always on the second Friday of each month, at Crownpoint Elementary School (☎ 505 786 7386, ⓦ crownpointrugauction.com). Viewing is from 4pm until 6.30pm, with the auction at 7pm, and prices range from $100 up to perhaps $3000 (no credit cards).

Western New Mexico

Even if the reality of today's **I-40** may not match the romance of its predecessor, **Route 66**, crossing **western New Mexico** still has its rewards. The interstate passes through memorable desert scenery, while successive detours to the south lead to crucial sites in Southwestern history. At **Zuni Pueblo**, Spanish conquistadors first encountered the region's indigenous inhabitants, while **El Morro National Monument** records centuries of further incursions. Above all, **Ácoma Pueblo**, the superbly sited "Sky City," makes it worth spending a night in the dreary interstate towns of **Gallup** or **Grants**.

Gallup

As the largest town in I-40's 300-mile run between Albuquerque and Flagstaff, the famous Route 66 stop of **GALLUP**, 25 miles east of the Arizona state line, might be expected to offer a diverting break in a long day's drive. Don't get your hopes up; cheap motels make it a handy overnight pit stop, but there's nothing to hold your interest.

Gallup sprang into being when the railroad arrived in 1881, and its role as the major railhead for the Navajo Nation was augmented by the arrival of first Route 66, and later I-40. The interstate and the railroad tracks still run east–west through the heart of town, paralleled by a ten-mile stretch of the former Route 66 that's lined with endless budget motels and fast-food outlets.

Gallup remains a major commercial centre for the Navajo. An estimated eighty percent of all **silver jewellery** sold in the Southwest passes through the hands of traders like Shush Yaz, 1304 W Lincoln Ave (☎505 722 0130, ⊛shushyaz.com), and Richardson's Trading Company, 222 W 66 Ave (☎505 722 4762, ⊛richardsontrading.com).

Inter-Tribal Indian Ceremonial

Red Rock State Park, 8 miles east of Gallup • some free events, some ticketed, prices vary • ☎505 863 3896, ⊛theceremonial.org

In the week leading up to the second weekend in August, the Navajo and other local Native Americans come together in Gallup for the **Inter-Tribal Indian Ceremonial**, a six-day extravaganza. A two-day pow wow is followed by four days of rodeo, craft shows and dancing, culminating in a Saturday morning parade through town. Be sure to make motel reservations well in advance.

ARRIVAL AND INFORMATION   GALLUP

By train Gallup's Amtrak station at 201 E 66 Ave sees one daily train towards Flagstaff and LA, at 7.08pm, and one east towards Albuquerque and Chicago, at 8.21am.
By bus Buses along I-40 call in at the Amtrak station at 201 E 66 Ave, as do Navajo Transit services to Window Rock,

Arizona System (☎505 729 4002, ⊛navajotransit.com).
Information The Gallup Cultural Center adjoins the Amtrak station at 201 E 66 Ave (summer Mon–Sat 8am–5pm; winter Mon–Fri 8am–5pm; ☎505 863 4131, ⊛southwestindian.com).

ACCOMMODATION AND EATING

Coffee House 203 W Coal Ave ☎505 726 0291. If you're passing through Gallup and simply want a snack or a cappuccino, head for this lively, arty coffee bar, a block off the main drag in the heart of town. Mon–Fri 9am–5pm, Sat 9am–3pm.
Comfort Inn Gallup 1440 West Maloney Ave ☎505 726 2700, ⊛comfortinn.com. Well kept, good-value chain motel, immediately north of the main I-40 exit, across the tracks half a mile west of the centre; look out for discount coupons. Decent rooms, indoor pool, and rates include breakfast. **$89**
Earl's Family Restaurant 1400 E 66 Ave ☎505 863 4201. This inexpensive diner, on the east side of town, serves chile-rich New Mexican specialities at prices that start below $10, and is usually bustling with Navajo crafts sellers. Mon–Sat 6am–9pm, Sun 7am–9pm.
★ **El Rancho Hotel and Motel** 1000 E 66 Ave ☎505 722 2885 or ☎800 543 6351, ⊛elranchohotel.com. Absolutely *the* place to stay, this sumptuous Route 66 roadhouse was built in 1937 by the brother of movie mogul

D.W. Griffith. As its original slogan, still proudly displayed above the door, put it, it combined "The Charm of Yesterday and the Convenience of Tomorrow." From the murals in its opulent Spanish Revival lobby to the gallery of signed photos of celebrity Hollywood guests – Doris Day, W.C. Fields and Ronald Reagan among them – it's bursting with atmosphere, though the guest rooms are small, and the bathrooms even smaller. Some rooms are in the original ranchhouse, the rest in a less characterful two-storey motel building alongside. The decorative dining room (daily 6.30am–10pm) serves burgers named after John Wayne and Humphrey Bogart, plus (separate) Lucille Ball and Errol Flynn sandwiches, and the usual range of barbecue, steaks, and shrimp priced at around $13, while the bar stays open until 1am. **$102**
Red Rock State Park Hwy-566, just north of I-40, 8 miles east of Gallup ☎505 722 3839. This fully equipped campground, complete with showers and toilets plus a small supermarket, is the best place to camp near Gallup. Tents **$17**, RVs **$20**

Zuni Pueblo

Few tourists make the effort to visit the remote and, superficially, unenthralling **ZUNI PUEBLO**, 35 miles south of Gallup and a short way west of Hwy-602. However, it occupies a pivotal role in Southwestern history, as the first point of contact, almost five centuries ago, between the native peoples of the Southwest and the encroaching Spaniards. The invaders never found the gold they were seeking, but Zuni was a major Pueblo trading centre, where the peoples of the Rio Grande exchanged turquoise for birds, feathers, and shells brought up from the south.

Much like the Hopi, the Zuni have since then found themselves restricted to an ever smaller area by Navajo, Apache, Spanish, and Anglo newcomers. Today's **Zuni**

1

FIRST CONTACT WITH THE ZUNI

It was at Zuni, in 1539, that the black African **Esteban** became the first outsider to enter the Pueblo world, and was promptly killed and cut into strips by the Zuni. Fray Marcos de Niza, following close behind him, fled for his life back to Mexico, to report "this land … is the greatest and best of all that have been discovered."

The Zuni call themselves *A:shiwi*, "the flesh," and their country **Shi:wona**, "the land that produces flesh." Fray Marcos, who garbled that name into Cíbola, announced that the six Zuni towns were the **Seven Cities of Cíbola**. Spanish conquistadors had long sought the legendary Seven Cities of Antilla, founded by bishops who sailed west to escape the Moorish invasion of Portugal in 714 AD and said to be rich in **gold**. In 1540, therefore, a Spanish expedition led by Francisco Vásquez de **Coronado** returned to Zuni. Turned back from the now-abandoned town of **Hawikku**, the Spaniards defeated its inhabitants in the first battle ever fought between Europeans and Native Americans (see p.465).

Indian reservation encompasses around three percent of ancestral Zuni lands and, with agriculture rendered marginal by erosion and over-grazing, the Zuni now depend for most of their livelihood on the recently acquired skill of making **silver overlay jewellery**.

The dominant feature on the reservation, the red-and-white-striped mesa of **Dowa Yallane** or **Corn Mountain**, has long served as a refuge for the Zuni people in times of trouble. Immediately below, straddling Hwy-53 three miles west of Hwy-602, stands the main **village**. Now invariably known as **ZUNI**, it was founded as *Halona Idiwan'a*, or "Middle Place of the World," around 1700, when the Zuni came down from Corn Mountain after the Pueblo Revolt.

Simply driving along Hwy-53 through Zuni, it looks like just another rundown desert community. Almost none of the architecture is at all distinctive; an ancient five-storey "apartment block," like the two at Taos Pueblo (see p.151), still stands close to the centre, but its bottom floors are now underground, while the upper levels are concealed beneath modern accretions. As even those buildings used for ceremonial purposes are built to resemble new houses, the only traditional pueblo structures you'll see are the beehive-shaped bread ovens scattered around the plaza, and you get little sense that the traditional life of the pueblo is continuing. There are however several jewellery outlets, crafts shops, and simple diners.

A:shiwi A:wan Museum and Heritage Center

02E Ojo Caliente Rd • Mon–Fri 9am–6pm • Donations welcome • ☎ 505 782 4403, ⓦ ashiwi-museum.org • 3 blocks south of the highway from the only stoplight, along Pia Mesa Road

A former trading post refitted as an excellent modern museum, the **A:shiwi A:wan Museum and Heritage Center** reflects recent attempts by the Zuni to make their culture more accessible to visitors. Documenting Zuni history for tribal members as well as tourists, it centres on a remarkable collection of artefacts that were excavated from the long-abandoned site of **Hawikku** during the 1920s, and only returned by the Smithsonian Institute in 2001. Enthusiastic staff are happy to talk you through the displays, and also provide local information of all kinds.

ZUNI TRIBAL FAIR AND THE SHALAKO DANCE

On a typical day, few visitors make it to Zuni, and even fewer stay very long. Special events can draw crowds, however, most notably the **Zuni Tribal Fair** in late August and the all-night **Shalako** dance, held in late November or early December. Anthropologists believe that this winter-solstice celebration, in which the *kachina* cult appears to blend with Aztec elements, was introduced by Mexican Indians left behind by Coronado.

1

Our Lady of Guadalupe Mission Church

South of the main road, not far east of A:shiwi A:wan Museum • Mon–Fri 8am–4.30pm; for a guide, call Zuni Tourism, below • Donation

The adobe **Our Lady of Guadalupe Mission Church**, erected by the Spanish in 1629, has been restored to more or less its original appearance. In line with historical accounts, the interior once more holds "life-size" murals of Zuni *kachinas*.

Hawikku

Ojo Caliente Rd, 12 miles southeast of Zuni • Contact Zuni Visitor Center to arrange a 2hr 30min tour • $75 for 1–4 people

The mound that conceals the ruins of the ancient settlement of **Hawikku** stands just west of the dirt road leading to the agricultural community of **Ojo Caliente**. Only visit with a guide supplied by the Zuni Visitor Center. There's precious little to see, apart from multicoloured potsherds poking from the rubble, but once you know the history it's an extraordinarily evocative site. Standing at the edge of the Pueblo world, you get a real sense of what a shock it must have been when first Esteban, and later Coronado, appeared across the infinite grasslands.

INFORMATION AND TOURS   ZUNI PUEBLO

Visitor centre The Zuni Visitor Center, 1239 Hwy-53 (☎ 505 782 7238, ⊚ zunitourism.com), offers a varied programme of guided walks through the pueblo, typically priced at $10 for 45min, plus longer visits to Zuni craftsmen and expeditions to archeological sites.

ACCOMMODATION AND EATING

Chu-Chu's Pizzeria 1344 Hwy-53 ☎ 505 782 2100. The pick of the simple restaurants along Zuni's main highway, with burgers, sandwiches and even blue corn enchiladas to complement its decent pizzas. Daily noon–2pm & 5–9pm.

★ **Inn at Halona** ☎ 505 782 4547 or ☎ 800 752 3278, ⊚ halona.com. Spending a night at the *Inn at Halona*, tucked behind the Halona Plaza supermarket and the only accommodation option on the reservation, is a memorable, indeed unmissable, experience for anyone with an interest in Zuni life. Eight charming and individually styled guest rooms, almost all en suite and sharing use of sitting rooms as well as a patio and an extensive library, are located in two separate buildings. The very hospitable owners, who are not themselves Zuni but whose roots here go back over a century, provide excellent breakfasts, and are a mine of information. **$79**

El Morro National Monument

On Hwy-53, 25 miles east of Zuni Pueblo and 42 miles west of Grants • Daily: summer 8am–7pm; spring & fall 9am–6pm; winter 9am–5pm • $3 per person • ☎ 505 783 4226, ⊚ nps.gov/elmo

Hidden away south of the Zuni mountains, **EL MORRO NATIONAL MONUMENT** feels as far off the beaten track as it's possible to be in the modern United States. It seems incredible, therefore, that this sheer sandstone cliff was a regular rest stop for international travellers before the Pilgrims landed at Plymouth Rock. The evidence is plain to see, however. It was first recorded by Spanish explorers in 1583 – *el morro* means "the headland" – and in 1605, **Don Juan de Oñate**, the founder of New Mexico, carved the first of the many messages that earned it the American name of **Inscription Rock**.

Translations and explanations of El Morro's graffiti are displayed in the **visitor centre**. You can see the real thing on a half-mile **trail**, which stays open until an hour before the visitor centre closes.

El Morro is technically a cuesta, a long sloping mesa terminating in an abrupt bluff. The trail's first stop explains why so many people passed this way: a cool, perennial pool of water, collected beneath a waterfall that tumbles through a cleft in the pale pink cliffs. In such a self-evidently sacred spot, it's no surprise to see ancient **petroglyphs** scraped into the desert varnish nearby.

An optional and much more demanding two-mile hike along the **Headland Trail** climbs the cliff beyond the last of the inscriptions to see the recently excavated **A'ts'ina Ruins**, up on top. Its builders, who abandoned it in 1350 AD, were among the ancestors of the modern Zuni.

1

EATING

Inscription Rock Trading Post mile marker 46, Hwy-53 ☎ 505 783 4706, ⓦ inscriptionrocktrading .com. At this log-built cabin, at the foot of a mesa a mile east of El Morro, you can stop off for a snack and browse the display cases of Zuni crafts, or simply sit out on the patio to enjoy coffee, or on occasional summer evenings, live music. Tues–Sat 9am–5pm, Sun 10am–5pm.

El Malpais National Monument

Free • **Northwest New Mexico Visitor Center** 1900 E Santa Fe Ave, Grants • Daily 8am–5pm • ☎ 505 783 4774, ⓦ nps.gov/elma • **BLM ranger station** Hwy-117, nine miles south of I-40 exit 89 • Daily 8am–4.30pm • ☎ 505 240 0300, ⓦ blm.gov

If you had to pick one federal park in the Southwest *not* to visit, **EL MALPAIS NATIONAL MONUMENT** would be the obvious choice. Its creation in the 1980s was bitterly opposed by neighbouring Ácoma Indians, who lost, in part, because they preferred not to reveal the whereabouts of sacred shrines. For tourists, however, the problem with El Malpais is more basic: it's **dull**.

El Malpais is Spanish for "the Badlands," and it preserves a tract of territory covered by **lava flows** from a volcanic eruption two or three thousand years ago – recent enough for the landscape to remain blackened and barren. Hiking any distance across the rough rock is a pretty miserable business.

The map of El Malpais is a peculiar patchwork of desolate lava interspersed with pockets of grassland that the eruption missed. Highways 53 and 117 skirt the periphery of the badlands, to the west and east respectively; in an ordinary vehicle you can only get from one to the other via Grants.

On Hwy-117, the more interesting drive of the two, **Sandstone Bluffs Overlook** near the ranger station, commands views westwards across the flatlands to the jagged peaks of the **Cerritos de Jaspe** and north to Mount Taylor. Not far beyond, **La Ventana Arch** is a chunky natural window three-quarters of the way up a cliff face east of the highway.

Grants

In general, **GRANTS**, sixty miles east of Gallup on I-40, looks better by night than it does by day. Daylight exposes an air of ever-growing dereliction along its old Route 66 frontage that's concealed when the neon signs come on after dark. Even so, Grants has more character than Gallup and is a handy base for detours off the interstate.

Like Gallup, Grants started out as a railroad town. In the 1950s, just as a half-hearted **carrot** boom fizzled out, it struck rich in a rather less wholesome way. A Navajo shepherd, Paddy Martinez, picked up some yellow rocks on nearby Haystack Mountain, and Grants found itself sitting on half the US's reserves of **uranium**. Both the Anaconda mining company, which opened an enormous mine, and the Santa Fe Railroad, which owned the land, made a fortune; Martinez got a monthly pension and the title "official uranium scout".

New Mexico Museum of Mining

100 N Iron Ave • Mon–Sat 9am–4pm • $3 • ☎ 505 287 4802, ⓦ grants.org

Grants' uranium years have receded into history, but they're enjoyably recalled in the **New Mexico Museum of Mining**. Visits consist of a faked descent into a mock-up mine, where you can poke around with no fear of radiation.

INFORMATION	GRANTS

Northwest New Mexico At the east end of town, just south of I-40 exit 85 at 1900 E Santa Fe Ave, this excellent facility, run by the National Park Service, offers information on the region's public lands (daily 8am–5pm; ☎ 505 876 2783).

Visitor centre 100 N Iron Ave, adjoining the mining museum (Mon–Fri 9am–5pm; ☎ 505 287 4802 or ☎ 800 748 2142, ⓦ grants.org).

ACCOMMODATION AND EATING

Holiday Inn Express 1496 E Santa Fe Ave ☎ 505 287 9252, ⊛ hiexpress.com. Grants' smartest motel offers the best rooms in town, though that's not saying all that much; if you're just passing through and aren't too bothered about the size of your pool or TV, you could easily pay half this. **$126**

Super 8 1604 E Santa Fe Ave ☎ 505 287 8811, ⊛ super8 .com. Decent chain motel, near exit 85 off the interstate, across the railroad east of downtown. There's nowhere to

eat nearby, but the rooms are OK, and there's a small pool and complimentary breakfast. **$52**

La Ventana Hillcrest Center, 110 Geis St ☎ 505 287 9393. The most popular place to eat in town, offering pretty much everything from $20 steaks to $12 fajitas, plus lighter sandwich lunches; the dining room is generally dark, so the patio seating can be welcome. Mon–Sat 11am–11pm.

Ácoma Pueblo

The amazing **ÁCOMA PUEBLO**, south of I-40 fifteen miles east of Grants and fifty miles west of Albuquerque, encapsulates a thousand years of Native American history. Focused around the ancient village known as "**Sky City**," atop a magnificent mesa, it has

A HISTORY OF ÁCOMA PUEBLO

Only certain Hopi villages can rival the claim of **Sky City** to be the **oldest inhabited settlement** in the United States. This isolated mesa, 367ft high and 7000ft above sea level, was probably first occupied by Chacoan migrants at some point between 1100 and 1200, when the great pueblos of Chaco Canyon were still in use. The name Ácoma means "people of the white rock"; by the sixteenth century, it's thought to have held around six thousand inhabitants, living in five hundred or so three- to four-storey houses.

The **Coronado** expedition of 1540 described the Acomans as "robbers, feared by the whole country round about." Noting the mesa's strong defences – it could only be reached by climbing ladders through a narrow crevice – the Spaniards commented "no army could possibly be strong enough to capture the village."

In October 1598, **Don Juan de Oñate** visited Ácoma in peace, while exploring his recently proclaimed colony of New Mexico. A month later, however, his nephew **Juan de Zaldivar**, following with reinforcements, arrived at the foot of the mesa, demanded food, and was rejected. Depending on which version you believe, the Spaniards either tricked their way onto the mesa, or the Acomans invited them up and then ambushed them. In the ensuing fight, all the Spaniards were killed, save four who survived being hurled off.

When a punitive Spanish force of seventy men, equipped with cannons, stormed into the village in January 1599, over eight hundred Acomans died in a three-day house-to-house battle. Five hundred women and children and eighty men were taken prisoner. All were sentenced to twenty years of penal servitude, and each man had a foot publicly chopped off, in the plazas of the Rio Grande pueblos. Bitterness persists among the Pueblo peoples to this day; a statue of Oñate erected in Alcalde, New Mexico, in 1999 had its right foot removed within days.

Oñate was eventually called back to Mexico City and removed from office for his savagery. By 1629, Ácoma had a resident Spanish friar – Fray Juan Ramírez is said to have been accepted after he caught a child who fell off the mesa – and the Acomans were hard at work building a huge **mission church**. Ramírez's successors were driven out during the Pueblo Revolt, and a tyrannical eighteenth-century priest was thrown to his death, but in theory the pueblo was permanently converted to Catholicism.

The people of Ácoma clearly never felt inclined to follow the architectural example of the mission, whose mighty beams were carried 25 miles from Mount Taylor without once being permitted to touch the ground. Instead, they went on constructing the same multistorey stone and adobe houses that can still be seen today.

Only thirteen families, forty people in all, now live on the mesa itself. Others make daily trips to sell pottery or fry bread, however, while many more return to their ancestral homes for feast days and other ceremonies. Eighty percent of Acomans call themselves Catholic, but the old religion endures; there are fourteen separate clans, and the Antelope Clan remains in charge of everything. Even now, the priest who serves the community is not himself an Indian, and is only permitted to visit the mesa once a week, on Wednesdays.

1

adapted to repeated waves of invaders while retaining its own strong identity. Although the Acomans have long been happy to take the tourist dollar – so visitors seldom feel the awkwardness possible at other Pueblo communities – Ácoma is the real thing, and its sense of unbroken tradition can reduce even the least culturally sensitive traveller to awestruck silence.

Five hundred years since the Spanish arrived, the **Ácoma Indian Reservation** still has a population of six thousand. Most live in three communities that were originally sited for their proximity to fresh water but now stand conveniently close to I-40 – **ACOMITA, McCARTYS**, and **ANZAC**.

For the most dramatic approach to Sky City itself, which stands twelve miles south of I-40 via any of three connecting roads, leave the interstate I-40 at exit 102 and drive in from the **west**. When the mesa comes into view, glowing in the sunlight as you drop down a hillside roughly three miles distant, you'll understand why the first Spanish explorers spoke of cities of gold.

Sky City

Cultural Center Mid-Feb to mid-Nov daily 8am–7pm; mid-Nov to mid-Feb Sat & Sun 9.30am–4pm; last Sky City tour leaves one hour before closing; Entire pueblo closed to all visitors June 24, June 29, July 9–14, July 25, first and/or second weekend in Oct, first Sat of Dec • Tours $23, plus $13 for photo permit, no camcorders or video • ☎ 505 470 0181 or ☎ 800 747 0181, ⓦ sccc.acomaskycity.org

All visits to Ácoma begin at the **Sky City Cultural Center**, at road's end below the mesa. You can only see Sky City itself on an hour-long **tour**; buses carry groups up from the Cultural Center at regular intervals. While you're waiting, it's well worth paying to see the displays on Ácoma history and pottery in the center's small but very informative **Haak'u Museum** ($4).

Once they reach the mesa-top, tour groups stroll more or less at will, with plenty of opportunities to buy handmade pottery or ears of multi-coloured corn. Don't expect to enter any individual dwellings, however.

While the original walls of Sky City's oldest houses lie concealed beneath several centuries of replastering, the overall appearance of the village changed little in the last millennium. The high windowless wall of the main pueblo, at the northern edge of the mesa, protected its inhabitants against both the chill north wind and potential invaders. Three or four storeys of terraced "apartments" face south to maximize the winter sun. Just one room still has its original tiny "windowpane" of translucent mica. Digging *kivas* down into the sandstone requires too much labour, so seven of the above-ground rooms are *kivas*, each shared by two clans and entered by a tall ladder pointing to the north. Ácoma's sparse rainfall collects in natural depressions in the rock; beside the largest of these cisterns is the mesa's only tree, a slender cottonwood.

Legend has it that the forbidding **Enchanted Mesa**, visible to the east, once held its own Pueblo community. The only access to the top was via a spider's-web of ropes strung between the mesa itself and an adjoining rock pillar. When that pillar collapsed one day while the men were away from the village, two women and a child on top were left stranded, their cries for help fading as they starved.

If you prefer, at the end of your tour you can walk rather than ride back down from Sky City, following the ancient footpath through clefts in the rock.

Church of San Esteban del Rey

The main stop on Sky City tours is the still-active mission church of **San Esteban del Rey**, which measures 120ft long by 40ft wide, with seventy-foot-high walls that taper from 10ft thick at the base to 6ft at the top. The floor is made of hard-packed earth, while the whitewashed interior walls are decorated with a mixture of Christian images and Pueblo motifs. Ácoma's greatest treasure hangs above the altar – a painting of **St Joseph**, said to answer prayers for rain, which was borrowed by

1

Laguna Pueblo in 1800 and only returned after the Acomans took Laguna all the way to the US Supreme Court. As no photography is permitted in the vicinity of the church, you'll never have seen an image of the sublime view as you turn around from the altar, and won't be prepared for the glorious New Mexican light that streams in through the doorway to fill the cavernous space.

There's no soil on the mesa-top, so all the adobe bricks of the church were made with mud carried up from below, and its **cemetery** was filled with endless basket-loads of sand. Only honoured elders can now be buried here – not in coffins, but "replanted," facing east. At first, the churchyard wall looks crenellated, but in fact the bumps are "warriors," placed to guard the dead.

ACCOMMODATION AND EATING

ÁCOMA PUEBLO

Sky City Hotel Beside I-40 exit 102 ☎ 505 552 6123 or ☎ 888 759 2489, ⓦ skycity.com. The only accommodation available at Ácoma is up by the interstate, in this large, comfortable, and reasonably stylish hotel. The adjoining tribal casino is best avoided, other than to eat the good-value food in its *Huwaka* restaurant, which offers cheap buffets as well as a full menu (Mon–Thurs & Sun 7am–1pm, Fri & Sat 7am–midnight). **$79**

YaakYa Café Sky City Cultural Center, below Ácoma mesa, 12 miles south of I-40 ☎ 505 470 0181, ⓦ sccc .acomaskycity.org. Good, inexpensive breakfasts and lunches; a bison or elk burger costs $13, and a Pueblo taco – much the same as a Navajo taco – $7. Mid-Feb to mid-Nov daily 9am–4pm; mid-Nov to mid-Feb Sat & Sun 9.30am–4pm.

Laguna Pueblo

LAGUNA PUEBLO, just north of the interstate six miles east of Ácoma and 44 miles west of Albuquerque, is the **youngest** of the New Mexican pueblos. It was established in 1698 by refugees from several different pueblos, driven here by the disruption of the Pueblo Revolt and the threat of Navajo and Apache raids. It's also the **richest** pueblo, thanks partly to standing above the world's largest **uranium mine**, Anaconda's Jackpile mine, which closed in 1982, after operating for thirty years. **Contamination** from mining has left a sorry legacy of long-term health problems, but thanks to the pueblo-owned Laguna Construction Company, a major contractor with the US military, the tribe remains prosperous.

All of Laguna Pueblo, including its **San José Mission Church**, is visible from a rest stop on the westbound side of I-40, halfway between the tribe's two **casinos** at exits 108 and 140, where traders sell crafts. There's no reason to explore any further.

Santa Fe and northern New Mexico

104 Santa Fe

124 South to Albuquerque

130 West of Santa Fe

135 From Santa Fe to Taos: the northern pueblos

142 The High Road

146 Taos

156 West of Taos

158 The Enchanted Circle

160 Northeast New Mexico

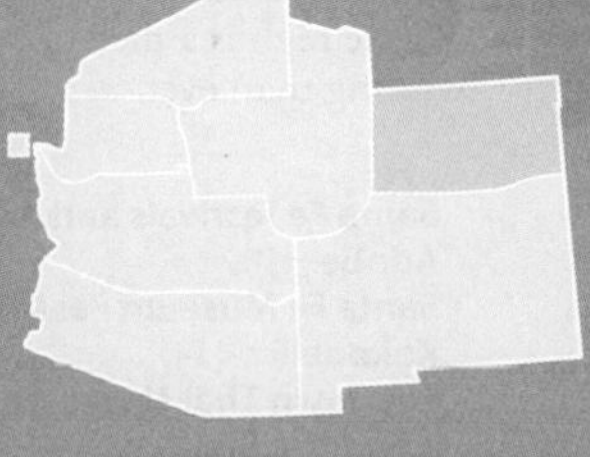

TAOS PUEBLO

Santa Fe and northern New Mexico

2

Basking in the magical "light" that artists – and tourist boards – rave about, stretching beneath the flame-red peaks of the Sangre de Cristo mountains, northern New Mexico is the New Mexico of popular imagination, with its pastel colours, vivid desert landscape, and adobe architecture. Quite apart from its ravishing beauty, nowhere else in North America can boast such a sense of unbroken history. Native American pueblos and Hispanic colonial settlements have stood side by side along the Rio Grande for four hundred years, and the Yankees who arrived on the Santa Fe Trail still seem like relative newcomers.

State capital **Santa Fe**, the only city, more than lives up to its high-profile image as the epitome of Southwestern style, bursting with top-class museums, galleries and restaurants. Nonetheless, it remains less than a tenth the size of Albuquerque, and its central plaza is still recognizable as the frontier marketplace that welcomed trade caravans from Mexico and the Mississippi. **Taos**, 75 miles northeast and even smaller, is almost equally celebrated thanks to a remarkable twentieth-century influx of artists and writers such as **Georgia O'Keeffe** and **D.H. Lawrence**. It too has its share of museums and amenities and is a near neighbour to the Rio Grande's most striking pueblo, multistorey **Taos Pueblo**.

Both Taos and Santa Fe are surrounded by spectacular scenery, and detours away from the river are rewarded with glimpses of countless fascinating communities. These range from the ancient **cliff dwellings** of **Bandelier National Monument** on the Pajarito Plateau west of the river, to Hispanic villages such as **Chimayó** on the **High Road** to the east, Wild West towns like **Las Vegas**, and even the high-tech home of the H-Bomb, **Los Alamos**.

Santa Fe

SANTA FE has long ranked among the most chic cities in the US, a favourite destination for upmarket travellers in particular. That appeal rests on a very solid basis; it's one of America's **oldest** and most **beautiful** cities, founded by Spanish adventurers and missionaries a decade before the Pilgrims reached Plymouth Rock. Spread across a high plateau at the foot of the stunning **Sangre de Cristo** mountains, New Mexico's capital still glories in the adobe houses and baroque churches of its original architects, now complemented by superb art museums and galleries. The busiest season is **summer**, when temperatures usually reach into the eighties Fahrenheit; in winter, the average daytime high is a mere 42°F, though with snow on the mountains the city looks more ravishing than ever.

Santa Fe festivals and markets p.107
Adobe p.109
Santa Fe Museum Passes p.112
Kokopelli p.114
The Town That Never Was: Los Alamos and the Bomb p.131

Visiting the Rio Grande Pueblos p.138
Religious Retreats p.141
The Penitentes p.143
Discount museum tickets in Taos p.149
Cumbres & Toltec Scenic Railroad p.157

SANTUARIO DE CHIMAYÓ

Highlights

❶ The Palace of the Governors, Santa Fe
The oldest public building in the country flew the flags of three other nations before the Americans moved in. **See p.110**

❷ Museum of International Folk Art, Santa Fe The most enjoyable of Santa Fe's many fine museums; a wonderland of folk art objects from around the globe. **See p.116**

❸ La Fonda de Santa Fe Splendidly atmospheric old hotel that once marked the end of the Santa Fe Trail. **See p.120**

❹ Coronado State Monument When the fall colours are at their peak, the sunsets at this historic Pueblo settlement, beside the Rio Grande, are out of this world. **See p.125**

❺ Bandelier National Monument New Mexico's most appealing ancient site, where the ancestors of today's Pueblo peoples carved their homes into soft volcanic rock. **See p.132**

❻ Puyé Cliff Dwellings Seize this rare opportunity to tour extraordinary ancient cliff homes with a pueblo guide descended from the peoples who constructed then. **See p.140**

❼ Santuario de Chimayó Exquisite little adobe pilgrimage church beside the mountainous High Road from Santa Fe to Taos. **See p.144**

❽ Taos Pueblo The multistorey adobe dwellings of Taos are a living legacy of New Mexico's extraordinary history. **See p.151**

HIGHLIGHTS ARE MARKED ON THE MAP ON P.106

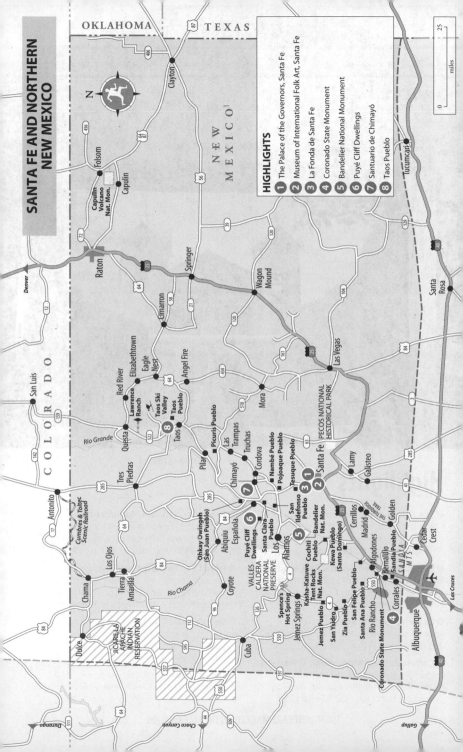

SANTA FE AND NORTHERN NEW MEXICO

HIGHLIGHTS

1. The Palace of the Governors, Santa Fe
2. Museum of International Folk Art, Santa Fe
3. La Fonda de Santa Fe
4. Coronado State Monument
5. Bandelier National Monument
6. Puyé Cliff Dwellings
7. Santuario de Chimayó
8. Taos Pueblo

0 — miles — 25

N

OKLAHOMA   TEXAS

NEW MEXICO

COLORADO

Denver

Santa Rosa

Las Vegas

PECOS NATIONAL HISTORICAL PARK

Santa Fe

Albuquerque

SANDIA MTS

Las Cruces

Tucumcari

Raton

Clayton

Capulin Volcano Nat. Mon.

Capulin

Folsom

Springer

Wagon Mound

Mora

Cimarron

Elizabethtown

Eagle Nest

Angel Fire

Red River

Taos Ski Valley

Lawrence Ranch

Taos Pueblo

Taos

Questa

Rio Grande

San Luis

Antonito

Tres Piedras

Pilar

Picuris Pueblo

Las Trampas

Truchas

Cordova

Chimayó

Nambé Pueblo

Pojoaque Pueblo

Tesuque Pueblo

San Ildefonso Pueblo

Bandelier Nat. Mon.

Los Alamos

Santa Clara Pueblo

Ohkay Owingeh (San Juan Pueblo)

Puyé Cliff Dwellings

Española

Abiquiu

Cumbres & Toltec Scenic Railroad

Los Ojos

Tierra Amarilla

Chama

Dulce

JICARILLA APACHE INDIAN RESERVATION

Rio Chama

Coyote

Cuba

Jemez Springs

Spence's Hot Spring

VALLES CALDERA NATIONAL PRESERVE

Kasha-Katuwe Tent Rocks Nat. Mon.

Cochiti Pueblo

Kewa Pueblo (Santo Domingo)

San Yisdro

Jemez Pueblo

Zia Pueblo

Santa Ana Pueblo

San Felipe Pueblo

Rio Rancho

Corrales

Coronado State Monument

Bernalillo

Algodones

Sandia Pueblo

Cerrillos

Madrid

Golden

Cedar Crest

THE TURQUOISE TRAIL

Lamy

Galisteo

Durango

Chaco Canyon

Gallup

With upwards of a million and a half tourists every year – not to mention twenty thousand daily commuters from Albuquerque – descending on a town of just seventy thousand inhabitants, Santa Fe has inevitably grown somewhat overblown. Long-term residents deplore the increased commercialization, and bemoan what's been lost, while first-time visitors, their initial impressions shaped by the depressing urban sprawl around the interstate, are inclined to wonder what all the fuss is about. Certainly, the rigorous insistence that every downtown building should look like a seventeenth-century Spanish colonial palace takes a bit of getting used to. This must be the only city in the world where it would be illegal to build a gas station that didn't resemble an Indian prayer chamber, and what on first glance appears to be a perfectly preserved ancient adobe turns out to be a multi-storey parking lot.

There's still a lot to like about Santa Fe, however, including a definite, romantic continuity with the Spanish settlement of four hundred years ago. Despite the summer crowds, the downtown area – clustered around its venerable **plaza** – still has the peaceful ambience of a small country town, while holding an extraordinary array of cultural and historic treasures. Above all else, it's rare indeed for it to be such fun simply to stroll around a Southwestern city.

Once you've got your bearings in the plaza, the best places to get a sense of local history and culture are the **Palace of the Governors** and the **Museum of Fine Arts** downtown, and the museums of **Indian Arts and Culture** and **Folk Art** a couple of miles southeast. Two private museums, the **Museum of Spanish Colonial Art** and the **Georgia O'Keeffe Museum**, are also well worth seeing. Alternatively, set about exploring Santa Fe's distinct neighbourhoods, such as the old **Barrio Analco** just southeast of downtown, home to the **San Miguel Mission**; the **Canyon Road** arts district, just beyond; and funkier **Guadalupe Street** to the west, with its lively **Railyard** development.

Brief history

The first homes of **La Villa de Santa Fe** ("Holy Faith") were erected above an abandoned Native American pueblo around 1604. In 1610, after previous Spanish settlements to the northwest had been deemed unsuitable, Santa Fe became the third capital of the infant colony of **New Mexico**. It was laid out as an imposing administrative city; the *casas reales* or "royal houses" that commanded its parade-ground plaza went on, as the **Palace of the Governors**, to house Spanish, Pueblo, Mexican, and American rulers.

Santa Fe was the base from which **horses**, introduced to North America by the Spanish, spread across the continent and were acquired by Native American peoples. During its first two centuries the city presented an inviting target for mounted Apache,

---

SANTA FE FESTIVALS AND MARKETS

The first of the three major events in Santa Fe's annual calendar is **Spanish Market** (ⓦ spanishcolonialblog.org), during the last week in July, when examples of the traditional folk arts of Hispanic New Mexico are sold on the plaza, while contemporary works are on sale in the Palace of the Governors. A smaller-scale **Winter Spanish Market** takes place during the first weekend in December.

Indian Market (ⓦ swaia.org) fills the plaza on the weekend after the third Thursday in August, attracting over 100,000 buyers and craftspeople from all over the world for the premier showcase of Southwestern Native American arts and crafts.

September's **Fiesta de Santa Fe** (ⓦ santafefiesta.org), which takes place over the weekend after Labor Day, has been held annually since 1712 to celebrate the Spaniards' return after the Pueblo Revolt. The ceremonial burning of *Zozobra* ("Old Man Gloom") in Fort Marcy Park on the Thursday prior, which kicks off the parades and processions, is not a Catholic tradition; it was invented in the 1920s by atheist American intellectuals.

Ute, and Comanche raiders. Relations with the **Pueblo** peoples were initially stable, but growing antagonism led to the **Pueblo Revolt** of 1680, when Santa Fe was besieged and conquered by an alliance of many different Indian groups. One thousand Spaniards fled south and lived in exile for twelve years at El Paso before returning under a new governor, **Don Diego de Vargas**. Their fight to regain control of the city is still celebrated in the annual **Fiesta de Santa Fe**.

Santa Fe was always a neglected outpost of the Spanish empire; at the time of Mexican independence in 1821, its garrison was armed merely with bows and arrows. Attempts to improve the economy thereafter focused on the ever-expanding United States. Although American goods were soon pouring across the plains on the **Santa Fe Trail**, US citizens were forbidden to settle in the city. In 1843, the Mexican

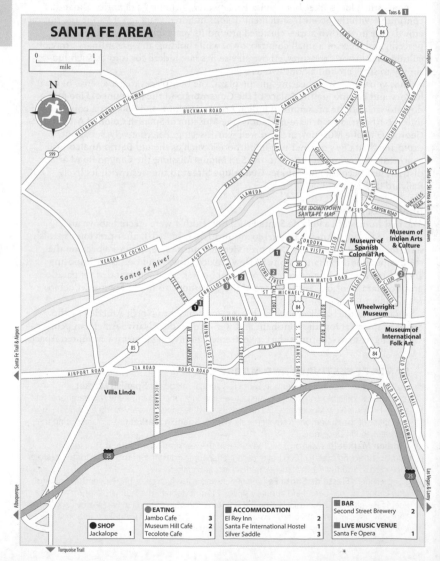

● SHOP	
Jackalope	1

● EATING	
Jambo Cafe	3
Museum Hill Café	2
Tecolote Cafe	1

■ ACCOMMODATION	
El Rey Inn	2
Santa Fe International Hostel	1
Silver Saddle	3

■ BAR	
Second Street Brewery	2

■ LIVE MUSIC VENUE	
Santa Fe Opera	1

ADOBE

For many visitors, the defining feature of New Mexico is its **adobe architecture**, as seen in homes, churches, and even shopping malls and motels. While ancient pueblo villages were constructed using blocks of mud, cut from the riverbeds and mixed with grass, it was early Franciscan missionaries who introduced moulded adobe **bricks**. The Spaniards had themselves learned the technique – in which a mixture of earth, sand, charcoal, and chopped grass or straw is left to bake in the sun in a wooden frame known as an *adobero* – from the Arabs. Built into walls, the bricks are set with a mortar of much the same composition, and then plastered over with mud and straw. The colour of the soil used dictates that of the final building, and thus subtle variations can be seen all across the state. However, adobe is far from being a convenient material: it needs replastering every few years and turns to mud when water seeps up from the ground, so many buildings must be sporadically raised and bolstered by the insertion of rocks at their base.

These days, most of what looks like adobe is actually painted cement or concrete, but even that looks attractive in its own semi-kitsch way. Superb old adobes include the remote **Santuario de Chimayó** on the High Road between Santa Fe and Taos, the formidable church of **San Francisco de Asis** in Ranchos de Taos, and the multi-tiered dwellings of **Taos Pueblo**.

president ordered that the Santa Fe Trail be closed altogether, but a mere three years later New Mexico passed into American hands. A discreet payment of $50,000 to Governor Armijo ensured that there was no opposition to the entry of the US Army on **August 18, 1846**.

The Yankees set about transforming the squat, dusty Mexican town into something more conspicuously American, building in wood rather than adobe, but Santa Fe remained largely unchanged for the rest of the nineteenth century. Even when the old buildings started to disappear, the city was promptly seized by the conviction that it could only retain its identity by turning the clock back again – a campaign ironically inspired by the romantic notions of Anglo newcomers as to how Santa Fe *ought* to look. Since the 1930s, almost every structure within sight of the plaza has been designed or redecorated to suit the **Pueblo Revival** mode. As a result, Santa Fe today – at least at its core – looks much more like its original Spanish self than it did a century ago.

The plaza

Santa Fe's central **plaza** has been the heart of the city since 1610, though the original rectangular parade ground of the Spanish garrison was twice as large as the neat, leafy square of today. As well as witnessing many turning points in New Mexican history – from the public hanging of three Indian "witch-doctors" in 1675 (which helped to trigger the Pueblo Revolt five years later, when Pueblo Indians filled the plaza to lay siege to the Palace of the Governors), to the nineteenth-century celebrations of Mexican independence and annexation by the United States – it served as journey's end for countless weary travellers on the Santa Fe Trail. Just how contentious the city's history remains is illustrated by the **obelisk** at the centre of the plaza, where unknown hands have chiselled the word "savage" out of an inscription that formerly honoured "the heroes who have fallen in the various battles with savage Indians in the territories of New Mexico."

The plaza now serves as a pleasant public park, where visitors and office workers picnic on the grass as they watch the latest bemused arrivals spill out of their tour buses. Under the arcade of the Palace of the Governors, along its northern flank, **Native American traders** shelter from the summer sun or winter wind. They're strictly licensed, so the price, authenticity, and quality of their craftworks and jewellery compare favourably with the stores and galleries that line the other three sides of the square.

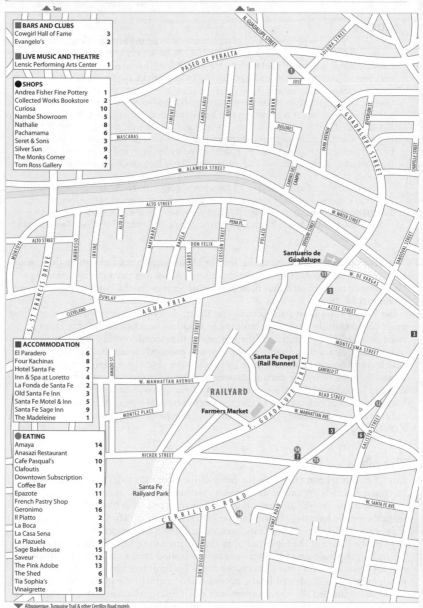

■ **BARS AND CLUBS**
Cowgirl Hall of Fame — 3
Evangelo's — 2

■ **LIVE MUSIC AND THEATRE**
Lensic Performing Arts Center — 1

● **SHOPS**
Andrea Fisher Fine Pottery — 1
Collected Works Bookstore — 2
Curiosa — 10
Nambe Showroom — 5
Nathalie — 8
Pachamama — 6
Seret & Sons — 3
Silver Sun — 9
The Monks Corner — 4
Tom Ross Gallery — 7

■ **ACCOMMODATION**
El Paradero — 6
Four Kachinas — 8
Hotel Santa Fe — 7
Inn & Spa at Loretto — 4
La Fonda de Santa Fe — 2
Old Santa Fe Inn — 3
Santa Fe Motel & Inn — 5
Santa Fe Sage Inn — 9
The Madeleine — 1

● **EATING**
Amaya — 14
Anasazi Restaurant — 4
Cafe Pasqual's — 10
Clafoutis — 1
Downtown Subscription
  Coffee Bar — 17
Epazote — 11
French Pastry Shop — 8
Geronimo — 16
Il Piatto — 2
La Boca — 3
La Casa Sena — 7
La Plazuela — 9
Sage Bakehouse — 15
Saveur — 12
The Pink Adobe — 13
The Shed — 6
Tia Sophia's — 5
Vinaigrette — 18

Palace of the Governors

105 W Palace Ave • Mon–Thurs, Sat, & Sun 10am–5pm, Fri 10am–8pm; closed Mon in winter • $9, free Fri 5–8pm; under-17s free • ☎ 505 476 5100, ⊛ palaceofthegovernors.org

Although it fills the north side of Santa Fe's central plaza, the **Palace of the Governors** often fails to make an immediate impression on visitors. That this long single-storey structure looks so much like every other building in central Santa Fe is

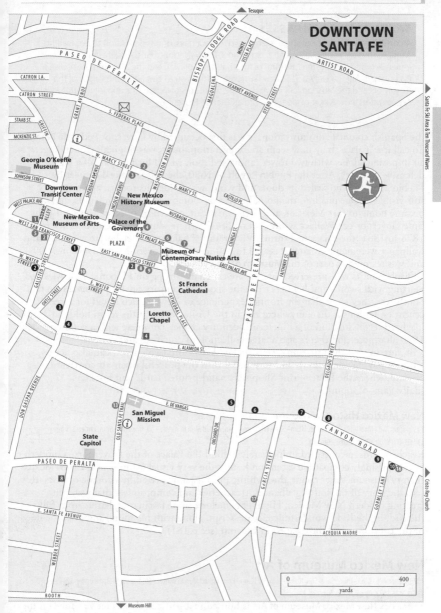

▲ Tesuque

DOWNTOWN SANTA FE

2

Santa Fe Ski Area & Ten Thousand Waves ▶

Cristo Rey Church ▶

N

Georgia O'Keeffe Museum

Downtown Transit Center

New Mexico Museum of Arts

New Mexico History Museum

Palace of the Governors

PLAZA

Museum of Contemporary Native Arts

St Francis Cathedral

Loretto Chapel

San Miguel Mission

State Capitol

0   400
yards

▼ Museum Hill

hardly surprising – it served as a blueprint for the remodelling of the city. It's also as much of a fake, in that until 1913, it was a typical, formal, territorial building with a square tower at each corner; its subsequent adobe "reconstruction" was based on pure conjecture.

Nonetheless, the palace is the oldest public building in the United States, and now serves as a fascinating **historical museum**. Constructed in 1610 as the headquarters of

2

SANTA FE MUSEUM PASSES

A **combination ticket**, costing $20 and valid for four days, grants admission to five leading Santa Fe museums: the Palace of the Governors, the Museum of Fine Arts, the Museum of Indian Arts and Culture, the Museum of International Folk Art, and the Museum of Spanish Colonial Art. Alternatively, a $15 one-day ticket entitles you to visit *either* the Palace of the Governors and the Museum of Fine Arts, *or* the museums of Indian Arts and International Folk Art. No offers, however, include the Georgia O'Keeffe Museum.

the Spanish colonial administration, it was first occupied by Governor **Pedro de Peralta**. To call it a "palace" may now seem an exaggeration, but it was originally much larger, an imposing adobe, with two towers and a sod roof, which formed part of a bigger defensive complex. After the **Pueblo Revolt** of 1680, the palace was taken over by Pueblo peoples, who sealed its doors and windows, divided its rooms, and dug still-visible storage pits into the floor, but it was soon back in Spanish hands, and later became home to first Mexican, and then American, governors of New Mexico. By the time Governor **Lew Wallace** wrote part of *Ben Hur* here, during his term of office from 1878 to 1881, the palace had turned Victorian. Its balustrades, elaborate windows, and wallpaper were removed after it ceased to be the official Governor's residence in 1909, and was restored as part of the **Museum of New Mexico**.

Displays in its well-preserved interior are especially strong on Hispanic New Mexico. Starting with swords and helmets from the sixteenth-century Spanish *entrada* into the Southwest, they stress that the frontier experience of New Mexico lasted for three centuries, far longer than anywhere else in the United States. One room holds an idealized reconstruction of a nineteenth-century chapel, complete with a genuine 1830 altarpiece, and there's also a large collection of crucifixes and *santos*.

Be sure to visit the museum's well-stocked bookstore (which you can also access without paying admission), and to wander into the peaceful open-air courtyard beyond, where the Palace Print Shop sells hand-printed cards and booklets (daily 9am–4.30pm).

New Mexico History Museum

113 Lincoln Ave • Mon–Thurs, Sat & Sun 10am–5pm, Fri 10am–8pm, closed Mon in winter • $9, free Fri 5–8pm, under-17s free • ☎ 505 476 5100, ⓦ nmartmuseum.org

Reached across a courtyard immediately behind the Palace of the Governors, a modern but surprisingly compatible extension houses the very visual exhibits of the **New Mexico History Museum**. After racing through the pre-Hispanic period in a couple of cases, this tells the story of the shifting alliances, treacheries and compromises that went into creating modern New Mexico. Highlights include some fascinating letters from Billy the Kid, in the Kid's wonderfully elegant script, along with his spurs, and even the door of the jail from which he escaped in Lincoln (see p.181).

New Mexico Museum of Art

107 E Palace Ave • Mon–Thurs, Sat & Sun 10am–5pm, Fri 10am–8pm, closed Mon in winter • $9, free Fri 5–8pm, under-17s free • ☎ 505 476 5072, ⓦ nmartmuseum.org

Santa Fe's **New Mexico Museum of Art** is housed in a particularly attractive adobe on the northwest corner of the plaza. Erected in 1917, this was Santa Fe's first example of the "Pueblo Revival" school of architecture, and remains unsurpassed to this day. It focuses around a beautiful garden courtyard with a fountain at its centre, and ornamental beams to all sides. One of the few major art museums to be established by artists rather than educators or collectors, it continues to concentrate on changing exhibits of painting and sculpture by contemporary local artists. Selections from the permanent collection, displayed upstairs, usually include an O'Keeffe or two, while the room devoted to painter and printmaker Gustave Baumann is especially fascinating. A good shop sells Southwestern prints.

Georgia O'Keeffe Museum

217 Johnson St • Mon–Thurs, Sat & Sun 10am–5pm, Fri 10am–7pm • $12, under-19s free • ☎ 505 946 1000, ⓦ okeeffemuseum.org

The ten galleries of the showpiece **Georgia O'Keeffe Museum** house the world's largest collection of O'Keeffe's work. Highlights include many of the desert landscapes she painted near **Abiquiu**, forty miles northwest of Santa Fe (see p.140), where she lived from 1946 until her death in 1986. Most of the museum is given over to touring exhibitions devoted to differing aspects of O'Keeffe's work, so there's little guarantee as to which pieces may be displayed at any one time. The first two rooms however feature selections from the permanent collection, which may include early New York cityscapes that make a surprising contrast among the more familiar sun-bleached skulls and iconic flowers. There's so much material that entire rooms concentrate on paintings of particular motifs, be it flowers or pink seashells, all characterized by O'Keeffe's trademark close focus and voluptuousness. O'Keeffe is also celebrated as an icon herself, via photos by her husband Alfred Stieglitz and others.

St Francis Cathedral

Eastern end of San Francisco St

Santa Fe only acquired its first Catholic bishop in 1851, after New Mexico joined the United States and ceased to belong to the Mexican diocese of Durango. As described in Willa Cather's novel *Death Comes for the Archbishop*, the arrival of **Jean-Baptiste Lamy** – a Frenchman, previously resident in Kentucky – threw the overwhelmingly Hispanic church in New Mexico into turmoil.

Lamy's most lasting achievement, **St Francis Cathedral**, now makes an unlikely spectacle, looming two blocks east of the plaza at the top of San Francisco Street. Eschewing adobe, the first cathedral west of the Mississippi was built of solid stone, between 1869 and 1886, in the formal – and, frankly, dreary – Romanesque style of France. Its walls rose over and around those of its eighteenth-century predecessor, which was progressively removed as rubble. The interior is much brighter than you might expect, adorned with tiles, frescoes and *santos*.

In the only part of the original structure to survive, the side chapel of **Our Lady of the Rosary**, impressive *viga* beams remain conspicuous in its wooden ceiling. Pride of place within goes to a statue of the Virgin known as **La Conquistadora**. Brought from Mexico in 1625, she was credited by the Hispanic population of Santa Fe with facilitating both their escape from the Pueblo Revolt in 1680 and their subsequent reconquest of the province. A disingenuous caption in the chapel explains that while the reconquest may not have been peaceful, it was "less conflicting than it could have been". The statue itself looks more like a Victorian doll than a venerated religious artefact – an effect enhanced by the practice of dressing it in different clothes at different times of the year. She is still paraded through the city each June, on the Sunday after Corpus Christi.

Museum of Contemporary Native Arts

108 Cathedral Place • Mon & Wed–Sat 10am–5pm, Sun noon–5pm • $10, under-17s free • ☎ 505 983 8900, ⓦ iaia.edu/museum

The stimulating **Museum of Contemporary Native Arts** is housed in a modern building – which naturally looks like adobe – facing the cathedral. As they insist on telling you, "we're contemporary, not historical," and most of the artwork exhibited is less than a year old. Encompassing paintings, installations, collages and mixed-media pieces, it's all a long way from the usual stereotyped notion of Native American art. The sculpture garden is especially recommended.

Loretto Chapel

207 Old Santa Fe Trail • Mon–Sat 9am–5pm, Sun 10.30am–5pm • $2.50, ages 7–12 $2 • ☎ 505 982 0092, ⓦ lorettochapel.com

The **Loretto Chapel**, one block from the plaza, was built for the Sisters of Loretto from 1873 onwards, under the auspices of Archbishop Lamy. When the chapel was completed, it was realised that there was no way to reach the choir loft, twenty feet above the nave. Hence the legend of its **Miraculous Staircase**, an elegant wooden spiral – more of a spring, in a sense – that makes two complete 360-degree turns as it rises, and was built without a single nail or any support at either the centre or the sides. It's said to be the work of a mysterious carpenter who arrived in answer to the nuns' prayers and disappeared without demanding payment.

Sadly, the story is more entertaining than the reality. The chapel is now deconsecrated and belongs to the upmarket *Inn at Loretto*; when it's not in use as a wedding chapel, it tends to be packed with tourists. What's more, the nuns found the staircase too frightening to climb, so they disfigured it by adding banisters. The whole thing is now propped up with a metal brace.

San Miguel Mission

401 Old Santa Fe Trail • Mon–Sat 9am–5pm, Sun 1.30–4pm; Mass on Sun at 5pm • $1, under-7s free • ☎ 505 983 3974

San Miguel Mission is said to be the oldest church in the United States to have remained in continuous use. The site is known to have been occupied in 1300 AD, while the church itself was built by Tlaxcalan Indians from central Mexico, who

---

KOKOPELLI

Time was when you could hardly move in Santa Fe without someone trying to sell you a figurine of a turquoise coyote howling at the moon. These days, however, the coyotes have been superseded by a symbol more closely associated with Native American traditions – the hunchbacked flute player known as **Kokopelli**.

Although Kokopelli derives originally from ancient **rock art**, his image has been so extensively appropriated by non-Indian artists that he's now become an all-purpose icon for the Southwest. He's usually depicted in silhouette, as a solid block of a single colour, whether printed, painted, cast in clay or cut from sheet metal. His flute is a simple extension of his face, each leg curves seamlessly from his trunk, and his head is crested with what might once have been feathers but are now often dreadlocks. You might see him cycling, skiing, or dressed in strange costumes, but his basic shape remains instantly recognizable.

But who was Kokopelli? There's no single answer. While he's often referred to as an "Anasazi flute-player" – "Anasazi" being the term formerly used for the Ancestral Puebloans – he dates back longer than that. You can see him in the pictographs in Canyonlands' Horseshoe Canyon (see p.410), created by so-called Archaic peoples more than 1600 years ago. Other ancient cultures familiar with Kokopelli included the Mogollon, the Sinagua, and the Hohokam.

Kokopelli has been viewed in many, inconsistent ways, but there's general agreement that he was not physically deformed, but a trader whose "hunch" is really a pack on his back. As they carried their goods north from Mexico, such traders, possibly carrying seeds for sale, announced their arrival in each new pueblo by blowing a **flute**. Some see him as a benevolent deity who introduced agriculture to the Southwest, bringing new crops to each village and explaining the rituals necessary to their cultivation. Others see him as more of a trickster, a Pied Piper figure who used his flute to seduce impressionable women (hence the enormous phallus in many ancient images).

Today, Kokopelli is most associated with the Hopi, though even within that tribe different groups tell different stories. The Flute Clan, currently based at Walpi on First Mesa, marked their successive homes (they trace their migrations back to Mesa Verde) by depicting their clan symbol, Flute Player, in rock art. They regard Flute Player as distinct from the mischievous Kokopelli, who is remembered by other Hopi clans as a *kachina*, and also exists in a female version – or perhaps it's his wife – Kokolmana.

accompanied New Mexico's earliest Spanish settlers in 1610. Although its roof was destroyed during the 1680 Pueblo Revolt, parts of its graceful, sloping adobe walls survived. That said, before the church was "restored" to its current appearance in the nineteenth century, its external lines were much sharper than they are today; its rounded adobe look is not necessarily authentic.

Inside, a hole in the floor beneath the altar reveals the foundations of an ancient pueblo, as well as the original steps of the sanctuary, while the pale green reredos, or altarpiece, above was painted in 1798 to frame a statue of San Miguel brought by missionaries from Mexico. The mission also holds a buffalo hide and a deerskin, painted with depictions of Jesus on the cross, which date from around 1630. In addition, its gift shop contains what's said to be the oldest bell in the US, cast in Spain in 1356.

The claims of a nearby adobe, immediately north of the church, to be the **oldest house in the United States** are generally dismissed, though it too probably stands on the ruins of the former pueblo. This whole district, the **Barrio de Analco**, is now an appealing residential neighbourhood, abounding in two-hundred-year-old houses.

The Guadalupe District

A few blocks southwest of the plaza, the stretch of **Guadalupe Street** that runs south from the tiny Santa Fe river is the focus of the characterful little **Guadalupe District**. While this has traditionally catered more to local students and artists than to passing tourists, it has inevitably moved somewhat upscale in recent years.

Santuario de Guadalupe

417 Agua Fria St at Guadalupe • Mon–Sat 9am–noon & 1–4pm • Donation • ☎ 505 983 8868, ⓦ ologsf.com/santuario

The small **Santuario de Guadalupe** was built as a shrine between 1776 and 1795 to mark the end of the Camino Real, the trail from Mexico City that for centuries provided Santa Fe's only connection with the outside world. Remodelling in the 1880s added an incongruous New England-style spire and tall windows, and the church became a small museum of its own history to mark its (and the nation's) bicentennial in 1976. It now hosts regular masses, including one at 12.12pm on the 12th of each month, and also hosts occasional concerts, usually of a religious nature.

The Railyard

During the late nineteenth century, the neighbourhood adjoining Guadalupe Street became the point of arrival into Santa Fe for trains on the Atchison, Topeka & Santa Fe, and Denver & Rio Grande railroads. Since it became Santa Fe's terminal for the Rail Runner system (see p.118), it has been redeveloped under the official name of **The Railyard**, with its former warehouses and small factories converted to house boutiques, art galleries and restaurants, along with a Farmers Market (Saturday mornings year-round, plus Tuesday morning in summer).

Canyon Road and Acequia Madre

Before Santa Fe ever existed, **Canyon Road**, which climbs a steady but shallow incline east from Paseo de Peralta, a few hundred yards east of San Miguel Mission, was an Indian trail that led to the pueblo at Pecos. Since the 1920s, however, it has been famous as the centre of Santa Fe's **art colony**. It's now dominated by galleries and high-class stores (see p.123), but even if you don't plan to buy anything it makes for an intriguing half-day stroll out from downtown.

At Canyon Road's far eastern end, the 1940 **Cristo Rey church** is the largest adobe building in the US. It's over three miles out, however, and most walkers prefer either to double back along Canyon Road at some earlier point, or return to town via **Acequia Madre**, one block south. The name of this ancient street literally means the "mother ditch;" following the course of the city's first irrigation canal, it's lined with beautiful adobe homes.

Museum Hill

750 Camino Lejo

The raised plateau known as **Museum Hill** stands two miles southeast of downtown Santa Fe, enjoying magnificent extensive views of the hills and mountains that all but surround the city. At its centre, Milner Plaza is a landscaped area that's home to two superb museums – one dedicated to **Indian Arts and Culture**, the other to **International Folk Art** – as well as a good café (see p.121), and a giant bronze statue of an Apache Mountain Spirit Dancer. Two further museums are located to the immediate north and south – the **Museum of Spanish Colonial Art** and the **Wheelwright Museum of the American Indian**.

Museum of Indian Arts and Culture

Museum Hill · Daily 10am–5pm; closed Mon in winter · $9, under-17s free · ☎ 505 827 6344, Ⓦ miaclab.org

The excellent **Museum of Indian Arts and Culture** provides comprehensive coverage of all the major Southwest tribes, including the O'odham, Navajo, Apache, Pai, Ute, and Pueblo peoples. Its centrepiece, a permanent exhibition entitled **Here, Now, and Always**, is intended as much for Native Americans themselves as for tourists – hence the taped messages that warn Navajo and Tewa visitors to skip certain sections in order to avoid contact with the world of their dead forebears. Myth and history are explained in copious detail. Ancient artefacts ranging from pots and pipes to bells, whistles and spearthrowers are drawn from sites that extend as far south as the Casas Grandes ruins in Mexico (see p.93), while contemporary realities are acknowledged in such forms as the inclusion of computer games, alongside music, architecture, and language, in the exhibit on the modern Apache way of life. Different parts of the exhibit focus on the topography of the Southwest, explaining how native peoples have thrived in such differing terrains as canyons, river basins, mesas and deserts.

The museum also boasts an especially comprehensive array of Native American pottery, from pristine thousand-year-old Ancestral Puebloan and Mimbres pieces up to the works of twentieth-century revivalists.

Museum of International Folk Art

Museum Hill · Daily 10am–5pm; closed Mon in winter · $8, under-17s free · ☎ 505 827 6344, Ⓦ moifa.org

The delightful **Museum of International Folk Art** centres on the huge **Girard Collection** of paintings, textiles and, especially, **clay figurines**, gathered from all over the world. These are arranged in colourful dioramas that include a Pueblo Feast Day, complete with dancing *kachinas* and camera-clicking tourists, and street scenes from countries such as Poland, Peru, Portugal and Ethiopia featuring fabulously ornate churches and cathedrals. The sheer scale of the place has to be seen to be believed – and it makes a pleasant change, for once, for there to be large signs that read "Please Do Take Photos".

An equally eclectic array of folk art objects is displayed in the Neutrogena Collection, where the specific artefacts on show change each year. The traditional New Mexican crafts in the **Hispanic Heritage Wing** are also fascinating. Alongside the expected *santos* (religious depictions of saints, whether carved figures or painted panels of wood), you'll encounter eerie skeletal wooden figures of "Death Personified," associated with the Penitente brotherhoods (see p.143). Excellent temporary exhibitions focus on more recent works such as *paños* – handkerchiefs decorated with religious and secular images in magic marker or pencil by often-anonymous prison inmates.

Museum of Spanish Colonial Art

Museum Hill • Daily 10am–5pm; closed Mon in winter • $5, under-16s free • ☎ 505 982 2226, ⓦ spanishcolonial.org

Focusing on such traditional Hispanic religious artworks as *retablos* (often-naïve painted images of religious scenes and figures) and *bultos* (carved wooden statues of saints), the **Museum of Spanish Colonial Art** makes a valiant attempt to place colonial art in a global context. Statuettes in its World of Art room are drawn from as far afield as Goa and Guatemala. Showcasing work by contemporary New Mexican schoolchildren, another gallery, El Futuro, proves local traditions are in no danger of dying out. The whole collection is appealingly laid out in a former private home, one room of which replicates the living room of an eighteenth-century Spanish captain in New Mexico, and reveals so-called "Santa Fe style" to be more than a mere home decorating invention.

Sadly, however, given the abundance of Hispanic colonial art on display throughout Santa Fe, and in particular the superior exhibits in the neighbouring folk art museum, there may be little here that isn't already familiar to you. In addition, being by definition largely vernacular, the pieces tend not to be of such exceptional quality as to merit a special trip.

Wheelwright Museum of the American Indian

Museum Hill • Mon–Sat 10am–5pm, Sun 1–5pm • Free • ☎ 505 982 4636, ⓦ wheelwright.org

The original purpose of the large, private **Wheelwright Museum of the American Indian**, which resembles a Navajo *hogan*, was to record Navajo sand paintings and ceremonials. These days, however, its permanent collection is seldom on show, and it concentrates instead on changing exhibitions, largely of contemporary art that's similar to what you'll see in the galleries in town. The Case Trading Post downstairs sells jewellery, rugs and *kachinas* of very high quality, at very high prices.

Rancho de las Golondrinas

334 Los Pinos Rd, 15 miles south of Santa Fe, 3 miles from I-25 exit 276 • June–Sept Wed–Sun 10am–4pm; guided tours available by reservation, also on Mon–Fri in April, May & Oct • $6, ages 13–18 $4, under-13s free • ☎ 505 473 4169, ⓦ golondrinas.org

Once a fortified *paraje* (stopping place) on the Camino Real, the **Rancho de las Golondrinas**, or "Ranch of the Swallows", is now a living history museum. The adobe farmstead at its heart is thought to have welcomed the governor of New Mexico in 1698, and strongly resembles Pueblo architecture of the period. As La Cienaga Ranch, it belonged in the eighteenth century to Captain Manuel Delgado, whose living room is reproduced in Santa Fe's Spanish colonial art museum. He was wealthy enough to own a wardrobe of thirteen velvet, cashmere and silk suits.

Topped by a tall *torreon* (watchtower), the 200-acre farmstead incorporates a covered well and plenty of stables and livestock pens within its strongly defensive walls, while planted fields reach down to the river beyond. Other early Hispanic structures – many brought from elsewhere in New Mexico – include a watermill, a replica Penitente *morada* (see p.143), a smithy, and smaller farmhouses. The whole place is staffed by well-informed but unobtrusive "villagers" in period costume, with different sections maintained in the style of the seventeenth, eighteenth and nineteenth centuries. It's an absolutely lovely spot, ranged across the meadows and woodland to either side of the river and bursting with wild flowers and sweet-smelling herbs.

The best time to visit Las Golondrinas is during one of the **theme** or **festival weekends** (from $8), held on the first weekend of each month in summer, as well as several other weekends. Festival season starts with the Spring Festival in June and ends with October's Harvest Festival.

Santa Fe ski area

Hwy-475, 16 miles northeast of the city · Daily lift tickets $66 full-day, $50 half-day · ☎ 505 982 4429, ⓦ skisantafe.com

Santa Fe's **ski area** lies within the Santa Fe National Forest, off the winding and very scenic Hwy-475. Boasting a 12,075ft summit and 1725ft of vertical skiing, its 77 runs are usually open from late November until early April. Skiing is suitable for all levels, and it offers a ski/snowboard school as well as multi-day programmes and workshops for both children and adults. Equipment can be rented on site, but there are **no resort facilities** apart from a café and a grill that provide soups, burgers, sandwiches, and the like.

Pecos National Historical Park

4 miles north of I-25 exit 397, 25 miles east of Santa Fe · **Visitor centre** Daily: summer 8am–6pm; winter 8am–4.30pm · $3 per person · ☎ 505 757 7241, ⓦ nps.gov/peco

A long, low ridge in the heart of the Sangre de Cristo mountains, east of Santa Fe, served for over a thousand years as one of the most significant cultural rendezvous in the Southwest. Excavations during the 1920s so precisely chronicled changes in pottery and architecture as to become the model for all other such digs, and **PECOS NATIONAL HISTORICAL PARK** is thus famed as the "birthplace of Southwestern archeology."

Ninth-century Basketmakers (see p.460) were the first to inhabit this spot, but between 1450 and 1550, as the pueblo of **Cicuyé**, it was home to over two thousand people, including five hundred warriors. Protected behind four-storey walls, it was a major **trading centre**, where Pueblo peoples exchanged turquoise, axes, and shells from as far west as the Pacific for bison meat, hides, and wood for bows brought by Plains nomads who camped outside the walls. **Coronado** stayed here in 1541 and met a captive from the plains who lured his expedition east in search of the nonexistent gold of Quivira (see p.466).

After Franciscan missionaries built a church alongside what they called **Pecos Pueblo**, sixty years later, Spaniards too came to trade, but Apache and Comanche raids eventually forced Pecos into decline. Its last twenty survivors migrated 65 miles west to join Jemez Pueblo in 1838. Their descendants continue to elect a governor of Pecos Pueblo, and return for ceremonies.

Seeing the park

The whole Pecos story is well told in the **visitor centre**, from where a mile-long trail loops onto the ridge itself. Much of the former pueblo area remains unexcavated, though some walls are exposed, and large buried structures are obvious everywhere. Beyond it, the trail leads around and through the high roofless walls of the **mission church**, stark in the bright sunlight and surrounded by the ruined *convento* buildings where its priests once lived. The *kiva* in the heart of the church was dug as a deliberate act of sacrilege during the Pueblo Revolt. Note that if you're pressed for time, you can park close to the church, and spare yourself the hike from the visitor centre, by following the signs off the approach road to the "picnic area."

Two additional parcels of the park, not currently open to visitors, incorporate the site of the **Battle of Glorieta Pass**. Fought on March 28, 1862, it was the turning point of the **Civil War** in the Southwest, when four thousand Union soldiers repelled three thousand Confederate invaders who had already briefly occupied Santa Fe.

ARRIVAL AND DEPARTURE	SANTA FE

By plane Santa Fe's small municipal airport, 10 miles southwest of downtown, is only served by flights from LA, Denver and Dallas/Fort Worth; the nearest major airport is in Albuquerque, 66 miles southeast.

By Rail Runner From the Santa Fe Depot, in the Railyard half a mile southwest of downtown, the Rail Runner train line connects Santa Fe with downtown Albuquerque (journey time 1hr 40min; $9 one-way, $10 all-day pass;

☎ 866 795 7245, ⓦnmrailrunner.com); free shuttle-buses link to Albuquerque airport.

By Amtrak Amtrak does not serve Santa Fe itself, but daily Southwest Chief trains between Chicago and LA stop at

Lamy, 17 miles southeast, where they're met by Lamy Shuttle vans ($28 one-way; ☎505 982 8829).

By bus Greyhound no longer serves Santa Fe.

INFORMATION

New Mexico Department of Tourism 491 Old Santa Fe Trail (daily: June–Aug 8am–7pm; Sept–May 8am–5pm; ☎505 827 7336, ⓦnewmexico.org). The best place to pick up maps, brochures and information on Santa Fe and the whole state.

Santa Fe CVB While the city's own visitor centre at 201 W Marcy St is not worth visiting, the official website, ⓦsantafe.org, is an excellent resource, with full details on attractions and activities, and suggested itineraries.

GETTING AROUND

By bus While downtown Santa Fe is small enough to walk, to get there from your hotel, or to see the farther-flung attractions, you may need to use the Santa Fe Trails bus service (Mon–Fri 6am–10pm, Sat 8am–8pm, Sun 8.30am–6.30pm; ⓦsantafenm.gov). All nine routes start from the Downtown Transit Center, a block northwest of the plaza on Sheridan Ave, with a standard adult fare of $1,

one-day passes for $2, and monthly passes for $20. The most useful for visitors are route #2, which runs up Cerrillos Road at 15-minute intervals, and route #M, which runs hourly to Museum Hill.

By taxi Capital City Cabs (☎505 438 0000).

Bike rental Mellow Velo, 132 East Marcy St (Mon–Sat 9am–5.30pm; ☎505 995 8356, ⓦmellowvelo.com).

ACTIVITIES

Bus tours The Loretto Line, based at the Loretto Chapel, 207 Old Santa Fe Trail, runs bus tours of the city, taking in Museum Hill and Canyon Rd as well as the plaza area (mid-March to Oct daily 10am, noon & 2pm; $15; ☎505 983 3701, ⓦtoursofsantafe.com).

Hiking The Santa Fe area holds excellent opportunities for hiking, with countless trails winding through the surrounding mountains. The greatest concentration can be found along Hyde Park Rd, which leads to the Santa Fe ski area; several trailheads dot either side of the road. On the left-hand side, 5.5 miles from the start of Artist Rd (which becomes Hyde Park Rd), is the trailhead for the Chamisa Trail (5 miles round-trip), a good introduction to the area's hiking possibilities, with plenty of expansive views as it passes alongside several of the region's native tree species, such as white pine, aspens and Douglas fir.

Horseback riding Located a few miles from the plaza on its namesake road, historic *Bishop's Lodge*, 1297 Bishop's Lodge Rd (☎505 412 4067, ⓦwww.bishopslodge.com; check website for current pricing), offers expertly led horseback rides on the numerous trails that lace its thickly-wooded 450 acres as well as into the adjoining Santa Fe National Forest.

Mountain biking The more than twenty miles of trails of the Dale Ball network in the Sangre de Cristos offer numerous challenging rides, all within close proximity to the city centre. Mellow Velo (see above) can provide rentals as well as maps of this network and additional biking trails.

Santa Fe Culinary Academy Located just off the plaza, the highly regarded SFCA, 112 W San Francisco St (call for current prices; ☎505 983 7445,

ⓦwww.santafeculinaryacademy.com), celebrates the city's outsized appeal as an eating destination by offering inventive and accessible cooking classes for locals and travelers alike.

Santa Fe Scenic Railway Excursion trains down to Lamy, drawn by diesel, not steam, leave from the Santa Fe Depot in the Railyard, typically on weekends only (March–Oct; see website for current schedules and fares; ☎505 989 8600, ⓦsfsr.com).

Ten Thousand Waves Many seeking to relax and recharge on their stay in Santa Fe understandably make the 10min drive east into the Sangre de Cristo mountains to the Zen-inspired Ten Thousand Waves, 3451 Hyde Park Rd (check website for current prices; ☎505 982 9304, ⓦwww.tenthousandwaves.com). The distinctive Japanese stylings of its main building and outlying lodges, all fine examples of organic architecture, provide obvious clues to the treatments available within. Ranging from Japanese Anma massages to herbal wraps, all of the services are top-notch and many can be enjoyed outdoors and even under the stars. An onsite teahouse and restaurant was due to open when this book went to press.

Walking tours Historic Walks of Santa Fe runs regular 1hr 45min walking tours of downtown, starting from hotels including *La Fonda*, at 100 E San Francisco St (March–Dec; schedules vary; $14; ☎505 986 8388).

Whitewater rafting Kokopelli Rafting, 802 Early St (ⓦwww.kokopelliraft.com, ☎505 983 3734), leads half-day and full-day rafting tours on the Rio Chama and Rio Grande, ranging from gentle Class I floats to more adrenaline-fuelled Class IV trips in the Taos Box Canyon.

ACCOMMODATION

Even in winter, you won't find a room within walking distance of downtown Santa Fe for under $80, and in summer – when every bed in town is frequently taken – there's little under $125. **Cerrillos Road** (US 85), the main road in from I-25, holds most of Santa Fe's **motels** and its one **hostel**. Everything gets more expensive as you approach the centre, though **B&Bs** make an attractive alternative to paying the sky-high prices demanded by the plush plaza-area hotels.

B&BS

El Paradero 220 W Manhattan Ave ☎ 505 988 1177 or ☎ 866 558 0918, ⓦ elparadero.com. Converted Spanish-era farmhouse near Guadalupe St. The rooms, especially those that open onto the central courtyard, are relatively plain and simple and furnished with folk art; thirteen are en-suite, the remaining two share a bathroom and can combine to make a family suite. Good breakfast and helpful hosts. **$130**

Four Kachinas 512 Webber St ☎ 505 982 2550 or ☎ 800 397 2564, ⓦ fourkachinas.com. Very pleasant, welcoming B&B inn, in a quiet spot near the State Capitol, a short walk from the town centre has the six charming en-suite rooms, with varying themes such as Chimayó style or the prints of Gustav Baumann. Some have their own outdoor patios. If there's no availability, try the same owners' very similar, slightly more expensive nearby property, *El Farolito*. **$160**

The Madeleine 106 Faithway St ☎ 505 982 3465 or ☎ 888 877 7622, ⓦ madeleineinn.com. Large Queen Anne inn with a peaceful garden setting behind the cathedral. The mixture of rooms (not all en suite) and cottages are all furnished with Pueblo and Mexican artworks, and there's an on-site Indonesian spa. **$150**

HOTELS

Hotel Santa Fe 1501 Paseo de Peralta at Cerrillos Rd ☎ 505 982 1200 or ☎ 855 825 9876, ⓦ hotelsantafe .com. Run by Picuris Pueblo, this attractive, elegant and very comfortable adobe hotel on the edge of downtown is within walking distance of the plaza, has its own good restaurant, *Amaya*, and stages free lectures by local experts. **$199**

Inn & Spa at Loretto 211 Old Santa Fe Trail ☎ 800 727 5531, ⓦ innatloretto.com. Rising between the plaza and the river, this upmarket hotel is an extraordinary spectacle, designed with its seven tiers to resemble Taos Pueblo. Besides its opulent rooms and public spaces, a high-class restaurant, and the adjoining Loretto Chapel, it hosts a top-quality spa. **$232**

★ **La Fonda de Santa Fe** 100 E San Francisco St ☎ 505 982 5511 or ☎ 800 523 5002, ⓦ lafondasantafe .com. Gorgeous old inn on the southeast corner of the plaza, marking the end of the Santa Fe Trail; guests have ranged from Kit Carson to John F. Kennedy. Built in 1920 to replace the century-old original, it features hand-painted murals and stained glass throughout, and plenty of nooks and crannies where you can sit and soak up the atmosphere. Each lavishly furnished room is different, with some lovely suites in the newer *La Terrazza* section, and there's a delightful restaurant plus the *Bell Tower* rooftop bar. **$189**

Old Santa Fe Inn 320 Galisteo St ☎ 505 995 0800 or ☎ 800 734 9910, ⓦ oldsantafeinn.com. Former Route 66 motor court, now an appealing inn; many of its tasteful, Mexican-themed rooms have their own gas fireplaces. Avoid the few rooms in the inadequately sound-proofed two-storey buildings. Rates include breakfast. **$224**

HOSTEL AND MOTELS

★ **El Rey Inn** 1862 Cerrillos Rd at St Michael's Drive ☎ 505 982 1931 or ☎ 800 521 1349, ⓦ elreyinnsantafe .com. This white-painted adobe compound, here since the 1930s, offers the most character and best value of the Cerrillos Road motels, with stylish, distinctive and large Southwestern rooms adorned with Art Deco tiles, semi-private patios, some nice suites, complimentary breakfasts, a pool, and a large garden. Ask for a room away from the road. **$105**

Santa Fe International Hostel 1412 Cerrillos Rd at Alta Vista ☎ 505 988 1153, ⓦ hostelsantafe.com. This old-fashioned hostel, housed in a ramshackle former motel a couple of miles southwest of the plaza, is one of those love-it-or-hate-it places. Some travellers find the staff unfriendly, the owner a control freak, and the rooms poorly furnished and dirty; others seem totally satisfied, say there's a good atmosphere, and don't mind the compulsory chores. In winter the whole place can be damp and cold. Dorm bed **$18**, shared-bath double **$35**, en-suite double **$45**

★ **Santa Fe Motel & Inn** 510 Cerrillos Rd ☎ 505 982 1039 or ☎ 800 930 5002, ⓦ santafemotel.com. To call this delightfully stylish yet inexpensive little adobe complex a "motel" barely does it justice; even its most conventional rooms are appealingly furnished, and some have their own kitchens, while there are also several gorgeous little casitas. The staff are very friendly, and the rates, which are great for such a quiet, central location, include a full cooked breakfast. **$139**

Santa Fe Sage Inn 725 Cerrillos Rd at Don Diego ☎ 505 982 5952 or ☎ 866 433 0355, ⓦ santafesageinn.com. Large, clean motel on the edge of the Railyard District with good rates and very helpful staff. Rates include free breakfast and local shuttle. **$95**

Silver Saddle 2810 Cerrillos Rd at Siler Rd ☎ 505 471 7663, ⓦ santafesilversaddlemotel.com. Busy, down-to-earth Western-themed motel, well out from downtown, in the finest Route 66 tradition. Each of the 28 rooms has a little patio, some have cooking facilities, and they feature all kinds of fun cowboy trappings. **$62**

CAMPING

Rancheros de Santa Fe 736 Old Las Vegas Hwy ☎ 505 466 3482, ⓦ rancheros.com. The most appealing commercial campground near Santa Fe, set in the woods 7 miles southeast of town, near I-25 exit 290 on what was once Route 66. There's space for RVs and more secluded areas for tenters, plus a pool, free wi-fi and nightly movie shows in summer. Closed Nov to mid-March. Tents $24, RVs $40

Black Canyon Campground Hwy 475 ☎ 505 753 7331, ⓦ fs.usda.gov/santafe, reservations on ⓦ recreation .gov. Attractive campground in the woods of the Santa Fe National Forest, seven miles northeast of central Santa Fe. Most of its 42 sites, unusual in offering advance reservations, are available to car campers or RVs; it has water and vaulted toilets but no electricity. Two much smaller and more basic campgrounds, free and open year-round, lie further along the same road: *Big Tesuque* and *Aspen Basin*. Closed Oct to late April. $10

EATING

Santa Fe has been renowned as one of America's most exciting places to **eat** since the early 1980s, when a stupendous feat of marketing managed to make dishes such as banana crusted sea bass seem quintessentially Southwestern. It's said to have more high-end restaurants per capita than anywhere else in the US, though that doesn't make it any easier to get a reservation at the latest hotspot in summer. In addition, the fact that so many diners are simply tourists, passing through, makes it hard for restaurants to develop much character. Nonetheless, there's some **memorable dining** to be had, and it doesn't have to be wallet-busting. The sheer **inventiveness** of the city's menus makes up for its shortage of ethnic alternatives (though you will find the odd adobe sushi bar here and there).

CAFÉS AND COFFEEHOUSES

Downtown Subscription Coffee Bar & Newsstand 376 Garcia St ☎ 505 983 3085. Despite the name, this sprawling café, where the large outdoor terrace is usually commandeered by local intellectuals, is a 10min walk from downtown, being just south of Canyon Rd. Inside, take your pick from an enormous range of esoteric papers and magazines. Daily 6.30am–7pm.

French Pastry Shop La Fonda de Santa Fe, 100 E San Francisco St ☎ 505 983 6697. Though it looks and feels more like a diner than a coffeehouse, this hotel café serves fabulous pastries and coffees, along with breakfasts, sandwiches, and crêpes sweet and savoury. Daily 6.30am–5pm.

Sage Bakehouse 535 Cerrillos Rd ☎ 505 820 7243. No-frills bakery on the southern fringe of downtown, open early for delicious fresh-baked sourdough bread and coffees, best enjoyed on the small patio. Daily Mon–Fri 7am–5pm, Sat 7am–2pm.

INEXPENSIVE

Clafoutis 402 N Guadalupe St ☎ 505 988 1809. Hugely popular French cafe/bistro on the northwest edge of downtown (*not* in the Guadalupe Street district), open for breakfast and lunch only. Pastries, coffees, and classic French snacks like *croque-monsieur* and *croque-madame* – both variations on a grilled cheese sandwich, costing around $7 – or meaty onion soup. Mon–Sat 7am–4pm.

Jambo Cafe 2010 Cerrillos Rd ☎ 505 473 1269, ⓦ jambocafe.net. Despite the run-of-the-mill strip-mall setting, Chef Ahmed Obo, who comes from an Indian-Ocean island off the coast of Kenya, has quickly accumulated devoted followers for his skilful adaptation of African and Caribbean traditions to suit Santa Fe tastes. The menu ranges from $13 goat, lamb or coconut lentil stews to a $9 jerk chicken sandwich, with take-out available. Mon–Sat 11am–9pm.

Museum Hill Café 705 Camino Lejo ☎ 505 984 8900, ⓦ museumhillcafe.net. Spacious café, enjoying fabulous mountain views from a terrace on the plaza between the folk art and Indian Arts museums southeast of town, and offering free wi-fi. Inexpensive but good sandwiches – turkey tuna and steak all cost around $11 – plus tacos, flautas, burgers, pasta specials and salads, and a large brunch on Sundays. Tues–Sun 11am–3pm.

Saveur 204 Montezuma St ☎ 505 989 4200. High quality café-cum-salad bar not far west of the State Capitol, serving delicious cooked and raw specialities by the pound, and offering major discounts after 3pm. There's also a choice of three daily soups. Expect to pay around $15 for a good lunch. Mon–Sat 8am–3.45pm.

The Shed 113 E Palace Ave ☎ 505 982 9030, ⓦ sfshed .com. Typical Mexican-flavoured local restaurant in a pleasant garden courtyard not far northeast of the plaza, which serves a steady diet of chile enchiladas, blue-corn tortillas, and even low-fat specialities. There's little over $10 on the lunch menu, but dinner works out a bit more expensive. Reservations accepted for dinner only. Mon–Sat 11am–2.30pm & 5.30–9pm.

Tecolote Café 1203 Cerrillos Rd at Cordova ☎ 505 988 1362, ⓦ tecolotecafe.com. This inconspicuous joint, a couple of miles south of downtown, is renowned for magnificent breakfasts – burritos, *huevos rancheros*, creamy eggs benedict, or shirred eggs (poached on a bed of chicken livers). All dishes cost under $10. Tues–Sun 7am–2pm.

Tia Sophia's 210 W San Francisco St ☎ 505 983 9880. Spicy, very inexpensive Mexican diner, a block or two west of the plaza, that's hugely popular with lunching locals. Daily breakfast and lunch specials for under $10. Mon–Sat 7am–2pm, Sun 8am–1pm.

2

2

Vinaigrette 709 Don Cubero Alley ☎505 820 9205, ⓦvinaigretteonline.com. The principal drawing card for this charming, bright "salad bistro" is its menu of organic salads, drawing on ingredients grown at the owner's farm, and given self-explanatory punning names like "nutty pair-fessor" and "all kale Caesar". Costing around $10, each is also served with fish, scallops, chicken or duck for $5–8 extra, and they have soups and sandwiches as well. Mon–Sat 11am–9pm.

MODERATE

La Boca 72 W Marcy St ☎505 982 3433, ⓦlabocasf .com. Enthusiastic locals squeeze into this little downtown bar/restaurant to enjoy excellent Spanish food, largely served in small tapas portions, and ranging from *gazpacho* to pork *pinchos* (kebabs). Most cost $6–12, but they're half-price in the afternoon, between 3pm and 5pm. The most substantial offering is a satisfying paella, containing chicken, chorizo and seafood, for $24 per person. There's also regular live music, including flamenco. There's a similar, more intimate and informal, spin-off branch, *Taberna La Boca*, at 125 Lincoln Ave. Mon–Sat 11am–9pm.

★ **Epazote** 416 Agua Fria ☎505 988 5991, ⓦepazotesantafe.com. Absolutely wonderful, very stylish Mexican restaurant, housed in a former convent. Chef Fernando Olea takes an infectious delight in good food; forget the menu, and let him cook whatever he fancies – whether it's spiced corn truffles with cheese, slow-cooked lamb in banana leaves, or even *chapulines* (grilled grasshoppers) – it all tastes wonderful. Be sure to sample his three distinct *mole* sauces. A full dinner should cost around $30 per head. Mon–Wed 5.30–9pm, Thurs–Sat 5.30pm–1am.

Il Piatto 95 W Marcy St ☎505 984 1091, ⓦilpiattosantafe.com. Reasonably priced and very good Italian restaurant, festooned with cooking utensils and serving pasta galore, such as a calamari spaghetti for $11 (appetizer) or $19 (entrée), plus a three-course set lunch for $17, and specials like roast duckling for $24. Mon–Sat 11.30am–10.30pm, Sun 4.30–10.30pm.

The Pink Adobe 406 Old Santa Fe Trail ☎505 983 7712, ⓦthepinkadobe.com. This 300-year-old adobe provides a deeply romantic setting for dinner, even if its hybrid New Mexican/Cajun menu is not wildly inspiring. Mexican entrees, like enchiladas or a copious mixed plate, cost around $20, while Louisiana-tinged specialities like avocado shrimp range up to $30. Tues–Sun 5.30–9pm.

★ **La Plazuela** La Fonda de Santa Fe, 100 E San Francisco St ☎505 982 5511, ⓦlafondasantafe.com. Delightful, beautifully furnished Mexican restaurant, which feels like an open-air courtyard even though it's covered by a glass ceiling. All the usual Mexican dishes

are nicely prepared and sold for reasonable prices, with entrees at $11–19 at lunchtime, and ranging, for pricier items such as lamb shank, up to $35 in the evening. Mon–Fri 7am–2pm & 5.30–10pm, Sat & Sun 7am–3pm & 5.30–10pm.

EXPENSIVE

Amaya Hotel Santa Fe, 1501 Paseo de Peralta at Cerrillos Rd ☎505 955 7805, ⓦhotelsantafe.com. Warm, inviting, restaurant in the lovely *Hotel Santa Fe*, serving a rich, hearty version of contemporary Southwestern cuisine. There's a lot of meat on the menu, with $30 entrees including prosciutto-wrapped loin of venison; the prix-fixe $23 dinner is particularly good value. Daily 7–10.30am, 11.30am–2.30pm, & 5.30–10pm.

Anasazi Restaurant Inn of the Anasazi, 113 Washington Ave ☎505 955 7805, ⓦinnoftheanasazi .com. This large, romantic dining room, just off the plaza in one of Santa Fe's finest hotels, is the perfect spot to linger over a long, rich feast of upscale Southwestern cuisine. Typical dinner appetizers include a warm octopus and chorizo salad for $14; entrees like the melting elk tenderloin cost more like $40. Things are simpler earlier in the day, when lunchtime burgers and sandwiches, or breakfast Benedicts and burritos, cost $12–15. Daily 7–10.30am, 11.30am–2.30pm, & 5.30–10pm.

Cafe Pasqual's 121 Don Gaspar Ave ☎505 983 9340, ⓦpasquals.com. Lovely, lively, and ever-innovative Old/ New Mexican restaurant that serves top-quality organic food in an attractive tiled dining room, a block from the plaza. Dinner entrees range from vegetarian *enchiladas* ($24), via a Mexican mixed plate ($28), to chile-rubbed *filet mignon* ($39). Appetizers include spicy Vietnamese scallops ($14). They also serve large, tasty breakfasts, with most menu items costing around $12. Mon–Thurs & Sun 8am–3pm & 5.30–9.30pm, Fri & Sat 8am–3pm & 5.30–10pm.

La Casa Sena 125 E Palace Ave ☎505 988 9232, ⓦlacasasena.com. Lovely courtyard restaurant, a block from the plaza; zestful Southwestern lunches, with most entrees priced at $12–16, are the best deal; the $14 seafood sampler plate is great value. Dinner entrees cost $17–28. At the adjoining, cheaper *La Cantina*, staff perform Broadway show tunes during dinner (Wed–Sun only). Daily 11am–3pm & 5.30–10pm.

Geronimo 724 Canyon Rd ☎505 982 1500, ⓦgeronimorestaurant.com. With its separate small dining rooms, this converted ancient adobe is Santa Fe's most intimate upmarket restaurant, with a streetfront patio and a cool inner courtyard. The menu is mostly contemporary fusion with the odd Mexican touch, with dinner entrees like sweet chile prawns or green miso sea bass priced at $29–45, and a vegetarian set menu at $45. Daily 5.45–9.30pm.

NIGHTLIFE AND ENTERTAINMENT

Santa Fe has the somewhat limited range of **nightlife** you'd expect of a small city, though its **cultural scene** livens up during the summer tourist season. For full **listings** of what's going on, check the free weekly *Reporter* (Ⓦsfreporter.com) or the *Pasatiempo* section of Friday's *New Mexican*. The city runs its own ticket agency for local events (Ⓦticketssantafe.org).

BARS AND CLUBS

Some of the most atmospheric places to drink in town are in the old hotels – the downstairs *La Fiesta* lounge and rooftop bar in *La Fonda* on the plaza are good bets – but otherwise conventional bars are surprisingly few and far between.

Cowgirl Hall of Fame 319 S Guadalupe St ❼505 982 2565, Ⓦcowgirlsantafe.com. Very busy country-themed restaurant and bar, with karaoke on Mondays and live music every other night. Mon–Thurs & Sun 11am–11pm, Fri & Sat 11am–midnight.

Evangelo's 200 W San Francisco St ❼505 982 9014. The only good bare-bones bar in easy walking range of the plaza, with a pool table and a jukebox, plus occasional live music. Be sure to check out the *Underground* dive bar downstairs. Daily noon–midnight.

Second Street Brewery 1814 Second St ❼505 982 3030, Ⓦsecondstreetbrewery.com. This lively brewpub is too far from the centre to attract many tourists, which is half the reason it's so popular with young locals; there's also live music several nights a week. They also run another branch at the Railyard. Mon–Thurs 11am–10pm, Fri & Sat 11am–11pm, Sun noon–9pm.

LIVE MUSIC AND THEATRE

Lensic Performing Arts Center 211 W San Francisco St ❼505 988 1234, Ⓦlensic.org. All year round, this strikingly converted "Pueblo Deco" theatre downtown – originally a movie theatre – hosts musical and theatrical performances, by touring artists as well as local groups.

Santa Fe Opera 7 miles north of Santa Fe, 1.4 miles northeast of US-84 exit 168 ❼505 986 5900 or ❼800 280 4654, Ⓦsantafeopera.org. In its much-anticipated summer season, which runs from late June through August, the Santa Fe Opera stages five separate productions in a magnificent purpose-built amphitheatre. Ticket prices start at $30.

SHOPPING

Secure in the knowledge that many visitors come specifically to **shop**, central Santa Fe is bursting with (generally high-priced) stores and galleries. The galleries alone turn over more than $200 million each year. The city remains largely the preserve of independents, however; few of the international names that move in seem to last long. Don't expect to make an early start; most stores and galleries don't open until 10am. Almost everyone agrees that the best place to buy **Indian crafts**, such as silver and turquoise **jewellery**, is from the Native American sellers outside the Palace of the Governors, ideally during August's Indian Market (see p.107).

CANYON ROAD

Curiosa 718 Canyon Rd ❼505 988 2420. Quirky little store with all sorts of original, unusual and attractively presented gifts, jewellery and general oddities, at reasonable prices. Mon–Sat 10am–6pm, Sun noon–5pm.

Nambe Showroom 924 Paseo de Peralta ❼505 527 4623. Factory outlet at the foot of Canyon Rd with a large stock of Nambe ware – shiny, futuristic table- and ovenware made from a local alloy that looks like silver but has unique heat-retaining properties. Mon–Sat 9am–5pm, Sun 11am–4pm.

Nathalie 503 Canyon Rd ❼505 982 1021, Ⓦnathaliesantafe.com. Little of the Western wear here would be at home on the range – it's all a little too chic and decorative for life on horseback – but it'll still look great when you wear it back home. Mon–Fri 10am–5pm, Sat 10.30am–5pm.

Pachamama 223 Canyon Rd ❼505 983 4020, Ⓦpachamamasantafe.com. Unusually inexpensive Hispanic crafts, mainly from Mexico, including silver and yellow bronze *milagros*, *retablos*, statues, and lots of tin. Mon–Sat 10am–5pm, Sun 11am–4pm.

Silver Sun 656 Canyon Rd ❼505 983 8743, Ⓦsilversun-sf.com. Native American arts and crafts, with a stand-out collection of beautiful turquoise jewellery, and some very affordable prices. Mon–Sat 10am–5pm.

Tom Ross Gallery 409 Canyon Rd ❼505 984 8434, Ⓦhahnross.com. Enjoyable fine art gallery, run by a children's book illustrator and specializing in very bright paintings and sculpture that blend the fantastic with the naïve. Daily 10am–5pm.

THE REST OF SANTA FE

Andrea Fisher Fine Pottery 100 W San Francisco St ❼505 986 1234, Ⓦandreafisherpottery.com. Museum-like gallery, a block west of the plaza, which specializes in Native American pottery and boasts one of the nation's largest selections of Maria Martinez pieces. Mon–Sat 10am–6pm, Sun noon–6pm.

Collected Works Bookstore 202 Galisteo St ❼505 988 4226, Ⓦcollectedworksbookstore.com. This large and very central bookstore is a great source for books on New Mexican history and culture, and has its own in-store coffeehouse. Check the website for upcoming

2

author talks and other events. Mon–Sat 8am–8pm, Sun 8am–6pm.

Jackalope 2820 Cerrillos Rd ☎505 471 8539, ⓦjackalope.com. A Southwestern legend for its pile-'em-high philosophy, this sprawling complex, centred on a disused church well out from downtown, completely takes the mystique out of purchasing folk art. However, the rock-bottom prices for its mostly Mexican and Peruvian arts, crafts, and downright junk make it the ideal spot to pick up inexpensive souvenirs. Mon–Sat 9am–5pm, Sun 10am–5pm.

The Monks Corner 235 Don Gaspar ☎505 982 1915, ⓦthemonkscorner.com. Owned by the Christ In The Desert monastery (see p.140), this unlikely little shop stocks decorative tiles and *santos* as well as devotional books, and honey and even beer produced by the monks themselves. Mon–Sat 10am–5pm.

★ Museum of International Folk Art Museum Hill ☎505 827 6344, ⓦmoifa.org. This wonderful museum gift store stocks some of the best souvenirs in town, ranging from jars from Uzbekistan to tin toys from Zimbabwe. If you're interested in Hispanic folk art, take a look here before you shop downtown. Daily 10am–5pm; closed Mon in winter.

Seret & Sons 224 Galisteo St ☎505 988 9151, ⓦstore.serets.com. Rather lovely, very upscale furnishings emporium, spreading through several adjacent storefronts, and selling sumptuous rugs, cushions and wooden furniture, from Asia in particular. Mon–Fri 9am–5.30pm, Sat 9am–6pm, Sun 9.30am–5pm.

South to Albuquerque

Travellers embarking on the sixty-mile drive southwest from Santa Fe to Albuquerque can choose between two routes. The **interstate**, I-25, is fast and reasonably scenic, but for atmosphere and Old West charm it doesn't begin to match the **Turquoise Trail**, which squeezes between the Sandia and Ortiz Mountains to the east.

Along I-25

While commuters may not give it a second thought, the hour-long journey from Santa Fe to Albuquerque on **I-25** represents a major transition. When it drops down the escarpment known as **La Bajada**, twenty miles from downtown Santa Fe, the interstate leaves the Rocky Mountains and enters the desert. To the north of La Bajada, the Rio Grande was traditionally known as the **Rio Arriba**, or Upper River, and cuts through a deep rocky gorge; to the south, the **Rio Abajo** or Lower River meanders across a broad floodplain.

La Bajada also marks the dividing line between the northern and southern **pueblos**. Below it, the interstate runs through three separate Indian reservations. In 1996, when state legislators considered banning the casinos that have finally brought the pueblos a degree of prosperity, pueblo authorities countered by threatening to place **toll-gates** on the interstate at every boundary.

Cochiti Pueblo

Hwy-22, 10 miles northwest of I-25 exit 259, a total of 24 miles southwest of Santa Fe **Cochiti Lake visitor center** Mon–Fri 8.30am–3.30pm, Sat 10am–2pm, Sun noon–4pm • ☎505 465 0307, ⓦpueblodecochiti.org

COCHITI PUEBLO, at the foot of La Bajada, is home to a thousand Keresan-speaking Indians who trace their ancestry back to the cliff dwellers of Bandelier (see p.132). In the Keresan language, its name is *Kotyete*, meaning "stone *kiva*." Visitors have free access to the pueblo in daylight hours; some residents sell crafts outside their houses, but there are no formal stores. The mission church of **San Buenaventura** still incorporates vestiges of its original adobe form, as built in 1628, but it has been greatly modified over the years, and the contemporary frescoes within are not all that enthralling.

A Cochiti potter, Helen Cordero, fashioned the first ceramic "**storyteller**" here in 1946. Each depicting a mother with up to thirty children, these rank among New Mexico's best-selling souvenirs and are made by over two hundred Indians, including around fifty Cochiti.

In the 1970s, the tribe was forced to lease part of its land to the federal government to create **Cochiti Lake**, by constructing what was then the world's largest earthen dam across the Rio Grande. Though the dam itself is something of an eyesore, the lake now attracts a million recreational users each year – almost exclusively New Mexico residents, with many windsurfers among them – and has a campground as well as a small **visitor centre**.

Kasha-Katuwe Tent Rocks National Monument

Tribal Route 92, Cochiti Pueblo • Daily: mid-March to Oct 7am–7pm, last admission 6pm; Nov to mid-March 8am–5pm, last admission 4pm • $5 per vehicle, national park passes accepted • ☎ 505 761 8700, ⓦ blm.gov/nm • Follow signs for Cochiti Pueblo from I-25 exit 259, turn right onto Tribal Route 92 at a painted water tower, and continue 4.5 miles on what becomes Forest Service Road 266

In 2001, a previously little-known corner of Cochiti Pueblo became **KASHA-KATUWE TENT ROCKS NATIONAL MONUMENT**, jointly administered by the BLM and the pueblo. Kasha-Katuwe means "white cliffs" in Keresan and erosion has sculpted a canyon wall of pale, soft volcanic rock into cone-like shapes that range up to almost one hundred feet tall. Only a few are free-standing pinnacles; most are "hoodoos" that poke from the hillside. While nothing like as dramatic as, say, Utah's Bryce Canyon (see p.367), it makes an interesting half-day venture off the interstate.

From the parking lot at the end of the unpaved access road, the easy two-mile **Cave Loop Trail** circles Peralta Canyon to pass the main formations. While it's not quite long or hard enough to count as a hike, wear decent shoes and carry water. If you want more exercise, and an overview of the whole ensemble, follow the **Canyon Trail** at the furthest point of the loop, which climbs steeply through a narrow slot canyon for another mile to reach Vista Point.

Kewa Pueblo

6.5 miles northwest of I-25 exit 259 • ☎ 505 465 2214

KEWA PUEBLO, which officially changed its name in 2009 from **SANTO DOMINGO PUEBLO**, is the largest Keresan pueblo, with a population of just over 2500. For many centuries, its people have been renowned for making **jewellery**, and especially necklaces of delicate shell and turquoise *heishi* beads. By some accounts, they taught silversmithing to the Navajo in the nineteenth century, and they're now prominent among the Native American vendors in Santa Fe.

Kewa doesn't have a visitor centre or formal opening hours, but as well as an adobe church with a lovely painted facade, its central plaza holds several stores selling jewellery, pottery, and other crafts, and also a simple café.

San Felipe Pueblo

2.4 miles northwest of I-25 exit 252 • ☎ 505 867 3381

Until 1250 AD, the people of **SAN FELIPE PUEBLO**, six miles downriver from Kewa, were a single tribe with their fellow Keresan speakers now known as the Cochiti. Their subsequent migrations only ended in 1693, when they settled here for good after the Pueblo Revolt.

Daytime visits are always permitted here, but photography is not. On the pueblo's **feast day**, May 1, its plaza, worn down over the generations into a bowl-shaped depression, is thronged with dancers performing a day-long corn dance. The tribe runs a large **casino** and **travel centre**, both of which house restaurants, beside interstate exit 252.

Coronado State Monument

US-550, 1 mile west of I-25 exit 242 • Daily except Tues 8.30am–5pm • $3 • ☎ 505 867 5351, ⓦ nmmonuments.org

Enjoying fabulous views of the Sandia Mountains from a spectacular setting on the west bank of the Rio Grande, **CORONADO STATE MONUMENT** is located just outside **BERNALILLO**, an unexciting satellite community of Albuquerque, and five miles south of the languidly riverside village of **ALGODONES**. The monument preserves what

2

remains of the ancient pueblo of **Kuaua**. The Spaniards knew this region as **Tigüex**, and described it as a "broad valley planted with fields of maize and dotted with cottonwood groves;" Francisco de Coronado spent the winter of 1540 in the vicinity, though there's no evidence it was at this precise spot. Kuaua was then a thriving community of well over a thousand rooms; now it's a ruin, of which archeologists have exposed a few eroded adobe walls. The central feature is a restored *kiva*, decorated with vivid reproductions of its multicoloured **murals**. The faded originals, preserved in the visitor centre, include scenes of a rabbit hunt. Rabbits often represent the **moon** in Pueblo art, as Pueblo peoples see a "rabbit in the moon" rather than a "man in the moon". The monument is especially ravishing from late October onwards, when the fall colours along the riverbank are unbelievable.

Rio Rancho

If you're unpleasantly surprised by the volume of traffic climbing US-550 past Coronado State Monument, that's probably because you've never heard of **RIO RANCHO**, reached via a turn-off a short way further up the hill. This ever-expanding community was founded in the early 1960s, after the AMREP Corporation purchased the Koontz cattle ranch for residential development. Though some of its earliest inhabitants, lured here from the East Coast by enticing advertising, were disappointed enough to sue AMREP (successfully) for fraud, Rio Rancho's population has mushroomed to over ninety thousand. With retirees joining Albuquerque commuters, and Intel opening one of the world's largest semi-conductor plants, Rio Rancho is well on the way to become New Mexico's second largest city; it's currently third, just behind Las Cruces. Although it holds half a dozen chain motels, however, there's no reason for tourists to visit.

Sandia Pueblo

I-25 exits 234 and 240 • ☎ 505 867 3317, ⓦ sandiapueblo.nsn.us

SANDIA PUEBLO, between Bernalillo and Albuquerque, dates back to around 1300 AD and was visited by Coronado in 1540. *Sandía* is the Spanish for watermelon; differing stories have it either that the Spaniards mistook the squashes they saw here for watermelons, or they thought that at sunset the mountains to the east resembled segments of pink watermelon. The village's Tiwa name – **Nafiat**, meaning "dry or sandy place" – seems more appropriate to its dusty central plaza. After it was destroyed in 1692 by Spaniards returning after the Pueblo Revolt, many of its inhabitants took refuge with the Hopi, far to the west, and the settlement was not rebuilt for fifty years.

Today the main preoccupation of the three hundred Sandians is protecting their sacred sites in the nearby mountains from blundering hikers. Being so close to Albuquerque, they're also among the chief beneficiaries of the legalization of Indian gaming.

ACCOMMODATION AND EATING   **ALONG I-25**

ALGODONES

Hacienda Vargas 1431 El Camino Real ☎ 505 867 9115 or ☎ 800 261 0006, ⓦ haciendavargas.com. A relaxing rural B&B, set in a lovely adobe trading post not far from I-25 exit 248. All seven rooms have en-suite facilities, *kiva* fireplaces, and private entrances, and several have hot tubs. **$89**

BERNALILLO

While Bernalillo itself holds no accommodation, the nearby Santa Ana Pueblo is home to both the state's

largest and most luxurious resort, the *Hyatt Regency Tamaya* (see p.135), and a top-quality restaurant, the *Prairie Star* (see p.135).

Range Cafe 928 Camino del Pueblo ☎ 505 867 1700, ⓦ rangecafe.com. One of New Mexico's finest restaurants, in a brightly decorated hall east of the river at the south end of Bernalillo, the *Range Cafe* is close to exit 240 off I-25, and makes an easy evening excursion from Albuquerque. Huge Mexican-style appetizers like *chimichangas* cost $10 or less; strongly chile-flavoured main dishes, like the fabulous *quesadillas* garnished with blue-corn chips, a

---

CLOCKWISE FROM TOP KASHA-KATUWE TENT ROCKS NATIONAL MONUMENT (P.125); NEW MEXICO MUSEUM OF ART, SANTA FE (P.112); ALCOVE HOUSE AT BANDELIER NATIONAL MONUMENT (P.132)>

little more. It's a very popular spot, so expect to wait. Mon–Thurs & Sun 7am–9pm, Fri & Sat 7am–9.30pm.

SANDIA PUEBLO

Sandia Resort 30 Rainbow Rd NE ☎ 505 796 7500 or ☎ 800 526 9366, ⓦ sandiacasino.com. The success of the adjoining 24-hour Sandia Casino, alongside I-25, has enabled the tribe to open this striking luxury hotel and conference centre, where full spa facilities complement its plush, opulently furnished rooms, and there's ready access to several restaurants, cafés and lounges to suit all budgets. **$209**

SHOPPING

SANDIA PUEBLO

Bien Mur Indian Market Center 100 Bien Mur Drive NE ☎ 505 821 5400 or ☎ 800 365 5400, ⓦ sandiapueblo .nsn.us/bienmur.html. As well as selling a broad range of Native American ceramics, jewellery and other artefacts, this Pueblo-owned crafts center, just off Tramway Road north of Albuquerque, commands views of a preserve that holds the tribe's herd of buffalo. Mon–Sat 9.30am–5.30pm, Sun 11am–5.30pm.

The Turquoise Trail

The **Turquoise Trail** – less glamorously known as **Hwy-14** – is a modern name for what may be one of the oldest thoroughfares in North America, connecting **mines** along the eastern flanks of the Sandia Mountains with the settlements of the Rio Grande Valley. In the last two hundred years, these mines have yielded copper, coal, and even gold, but **turquoise** production dates back perhaps ten times as far. Long before the coming of the Spaniards, traders carried local stone all over the Southwest and down into Mexico, and wealthy pueblos lined the nearby streams.

Until the recent influx of artists, craftworkers, and small-scale entrepreneurs, communities along the trail had dwindled to become little more than **ghost towns**, but now funky **Madrid**, in particular, makes an appealing day-trip destination for visitors to Santa Fe.

Cerrillos

The northernmost Turquoise Trail town, **CERRILLOS**, just over twenty miles south of Santa Fe, is reached simply by continuing south on Cerrillos Road, which becomes Hwy-14, for fifteen miles beyond its intersection with I-25. The dusty rolling hillocks that surround it – the "little hills" of its name – hold one of the world's greatest concentrations of **turquoise**.

Archeologists estimate that ninety percent of the turquoise treasures seized by the Spaniards from the Aztec capital of Tenochtitlán were crafted using stone from this unprepossessing spot. Prehistoric miners scooped a hundred thousand tons of rock from **Mount Chalchihuitl**, two miles northeast, leaving a cavern 300 feet wide and 200 feet deep. Early Spanish settlers may have forced the Indians to work for them; a mine collapse around 1680, which killed up to eighty Indians, helped to precipitate the Pueblo Revolt. By the time the Spaniards returned, the Indians had deliberately hidden many of the shafts, and tales of fabulously wealthy "**lost mines**" still abound.

Today's Cerrillos, nestled amid the giant cottonwoods along the bank of the broad but usually dry Galisteo River, has changed little since its last boom in the 1890s. Mining not only turquoise but gold, silver, copper and lead, it was briefly rich enough to support eight daily newspapers and numerous hotels and saloons.

There's still a bit of life in the old town; as recently as 1983, robbers made off with $500,000 worth of gold from the nearby Ortiz Mines. In 1988, its unpaved streets and false-front wooden buildings made it an ideal location for the bratpack Western *Young Guns*.

Casa Grande Trading Post, Turquoise Mining Museum, and Petting Zoo

17 Waldo St, Cerrillos • Daily 9am–5pm • $2 • ☎ 505 438 3008, ⓦ casagrandetradingpost.com

Cerrillos' one formal tourist attraction is the **Casa Grande Trading Post, Turquoise Mining Museum, and Petting Zoo**. This endearing shop-cum-museum offers a random assortment of old bills and letters, porcupine quills, rattlesnake skins, and petrified wood, plus the chance to pet a llama or pull on a string to make a plaster Indian hammer on a rock.

Broken Saddle

26 Vicksville Rd • Rides typically last 1–3hr; call for current rates • ☎ 505 424 7774, ⓦ www.brokensaddle.com

For a firsthand look at the area's rich mining legacy, take a **horseback ride** into the nearby **Cerrillos Hills State Park** with **Broken Saddle**, down a dirt road at the northeastern edge of the village. The park holds over 35 miles of trails, some of which pass by long-shuttered mines. As well as providing a fascinating history lesson, the rides traverse a series of gently rolling hills and offer exapnsive views of Mount Taylor (11,301ft) and the Ortiz Mountains.

Madrid

Between 1869 and 1959, the village of **MADRID**, three miles south of Cerrillos, made a good living from mining **coal**, with tunnels running directly beneath the main street. In the early days, coal was hauled by wagon as far as St Louis; later it was consumed in vast quantities by the Santa Fe Railroad.

   After the mine closed down, the whole town was auctioned off piecemeal, and the straggle of wooden cottages to either side of the narrow highway have progressively been taken over by New-Agey newcomers. Several hold genuinely interesting crafts and antiques stores; if you're close enough to home to carry **furniture**, there are some real bargains to be had.

Old Coal Mine Museum

Daily May–Oct only 9am–5.30pm • $5 • ☎ 505 435 3780, ⓦ themineshafttavern.com

At the **Old Coal Mine Museum**, at the southern end of Madrid, an abandoned mine shaft burrows straight into the hillside. The museum itself consists of several barns stuffed with ancient junk like obsolete X-ray machines and decrepit Model "T" Ford trucks. Its main entrance building doubles as the **Engine House Theater**, which stages moustache twirling **melodramas** on summer weekends, and assorted other performances in winter.

Golden

In 1825, **GOLDEN**, fifteen miles south of Madrid, was the site of the Wild West's first-ever gold rush. It has yet to revitalize to any great extent, and you might hardly notice that it's there as the highway races down its former main street. Look out, however, for the tumbledown **adobe church** on the hill at the north edge of town, which served the mining camp of **Tuerto** and has preserved its pioneer graveyard.

Sandia Crest and Cedar Crest

Ten miles south of Golden, the **Sandia Crest Scenic Byway** branches west from Hwy-14, to climb for eight tortuous miles up to the razorback ridge atop the Sandia Mountains. From the mile-high **observation deck** at road's end, you can survey the sprawling city of **Albuquerque**, with the Rio Grande flowing in from the north, and also look east across the endless plains, beyond the Ortiz Mountains. The adjacent *Sandia House* sells tasteless snacks and useless gifts. A fee of $3 is charged for day-use of the nearby trails, but most visitors stay for barely ten minutes before heading back down the hill; there's no through route to Albuquerque.

   In winter, **skiers** exploring the eastern Sandia slopes base themselves down below, in **CEDAR CREST** at the foot of the Scenic Byway. The Turquoise Trail ends six miles south at the intersection with I-40, which sweeps the final dozen miles west to Albuquerque through **Tijeras** – "Scissors" – **Canyon**.

2

INFORMATION   THE TURQUOISE TRAIL

Website For general information on the trail and to download a map, visit ⊛ turquoisetrail.org.

ACCOMMODATION AND EATING

MADRID

Java Junction 2855 Hwy-14 ☎ 505 438 2772 or ☎ 877 308 8884, ⊛ java-junction.com. Attractive old mining home that houses a coffee shop downstairs, serving a limited array of bagels and pastries, and a B&B apartment upstairs, with kitchen and bathroom. **$109**

Mama Lisa's Ghost Town Kitchen/No Pity Cafe 2589 Hwy-14 ☎ 505 471 5769. Good home cooking, in all shapes and sizes with $10 burgers ranging from green chile to salmon pesto as well as healthy salads and daily specials costing up to $15. Summer daily 11.30am–2.30pm & 5.30–9pm; winter hours vary.

Mine Shaft Tavern 2846 Hwy-14 ☎ 505 473 0743, ⊛ themineshafttavern.com. This lively tavern, attached to the Old Coal Mine Museum, claims to have the longest bar in New Mexico. As well as serving a full menu of burgers, fajitas, and the like – typically priced at $10–12 – it stays open late every night, with live music on weekends. Food served Mon–Thurs 11.30am–7.30pm, Fri & Sat 11.30am–9pm; bar open until late.

CEDAR CREST

Elaine's 72 Snowline Rd ☎ 505 281 2467 or ☎ 800 821 3092, ⊛ elainesbnb.com. Very comfortable log-cabin style B&B set in spacious rural grounds. The five guest rooms are decorated according to varying schemes, and include a particularly eccentric "Unicorn" room. **$105**

Sandia Mountain Hostel 12234 Hwy-14 ☎ 505 281 4117. This pleasant, welcoming and exceptionally peaceful purpose-built hostel, up in the mountains far from the crowds, offers eight-bed single-sex dorms, plus a cozy communal lounge with roaring fire, and full kitchen facilities. **$20**

West of Santa Fe

The **Jemez Mountain Trail**, which loops through the mountains west of Santa Fe, can be enjoyed as a long day's excursion or a roundabout route down to Albuquerque. Potential stops range from modern **Los Alamos** – the top-secret "town that never was" – to the ancient dwellings of **Bandelier National Monument**; the scenery encompasses mountain meadows and desert canyons.

The **Pajarito Plateau**, the dominant feature of the landscape, was created just over a million years ago, when colossal **volcanic eruptions** buried four hundred square miles beneath a thousand feet of ash. This solidified into **tuff**, which has eroded away ever since to form an intricate tangle of deep gorges and forested mesas. "Pajarito" means "little bird" in Spanish; it's a translation of the Tewa *tsirege*, the name of an abandoned local pueblo. Only one road climbs onto the plateau, **Hwy-502**, which branches west from US-84 near Pojoaque Pueblo, fifteen miles north of Santa Fe.

Visitors to both Los Alamos and Bandelier should take care to avoid the westbound Hwy-502 **rush-hour** traffic until around 9am and the eastbound from 3pm onwards.

Los Alamos

The wealthy enclave of **LOS ALAMOS**, eighteen miles up Hwy-502, is not so much a town as the overgrown campus of the **Los Alamos National Laboratory**. Home during World War II to the **Manhattan Project**, which first developed the atomic bomb, it remains the leading US centre for the research and development of nuclear weapons.

Los Alamos is a confusing place to visit. Sprawling along several "fingers" at the edge of the Pajarito Plateau, separated by deep canyons, its layout is bizarre in the extreme, and the fact that most of the complex is off-limits to the public doesn't help. Most visitors call in at one of the two local **museums**, then head on to Bandelier.

Bradbury Science Museum

Central Ave & 15th St • Mon & Sun 1–5pm, Tues–Sat 9am–5pm • Free • ☎ 505 667 4444, ⊛ lanl.gov/museum

The **Bradbury Science Museum** presents the authorized version of the history of the Los Alamos National Laboratory. While opponents of nuclear proliferation are given space to state their case – forcefully argued rival displays debate the decision to drop atomic bombs on Japan – the overall line is extremely gung-ho. The central exhibits are full-sized 1940s replicas of "Little Boy," which devastated Hiroshima, and "Fat Man," dropped on Nagasaki. The **visitors' book** is fascinating enough to have been published, while the excellent Otowi Station **bookstore** stands alongside.

Los Alamos Historical Museum

Mon–Fri 10am–4pm, Sat 11am–4pm, Sun 1–4pm • Free • ☎ 505 662 6272, ⓦ losalamoshistory.org

As this book went to press, the **Los Alamos Historical Museum** was about to move to new premises. Assuming its general tenor remains the same, it combines coverage of local history with an inevitable focus on the bomb. Exhibits range from a 360-degree aerial photo of Hiroshima to examples of atomic kitsch, such as a picture of the commander of the 1946 tests at Bikini cutting a mushroom-cloud-shaped cake, some earrings made with "atomsite" fused glass from the Trinity site, and an A-bomb-shaped lamp.

INFORMATION

LOS ALAMOS

Visitor centre 109 Central Park Square (Mon–Sat 9am–5pm, Sun 10am–3pm; ☎ 505 662 8105 or ☎ 800 444 0707, ⓦ visit.losalamos.com).

ACCOMMODATION AND EATING

Adobe Pines B&B 2101 Loma Linda Drive ☎ 505 661 8828, ⓦ losalamoslodging.com. Modern adobe B&B, attached to a private home in a quiet residential area; attractive and much more personal rooms than the chain motels, plus good home-cooked breakfasts. $95

Blue Window Bistro 813 Central Ave ☎ 505 662 6305, ⓦ labluewindowbistro.com. The best-value place to eat in town, with lunchtime sandwiches like the shrimp po-boy

---

THE TOWN THAT NEVER WAS: LOS ALAMOS AND THE BOMB

In 1942, the US and Britain decided to amalgamate the nine research efforts then racing to build the **atomic bomb**. Albert Einstein had suggested the idea to President Roosevelt three years earlier, and a team led by Enrico Fermi was achieving promising results beneath a disused football stadium in Chicago. The search was on for a suitable location in a sparsely populated area, away from the sea. **J. Robert Oppenheimer**, the scientific chief of the **Manhattan Project**, who had backpacked in New Mexico, recommended the exclusive Los Alamos Ranch School on the Pajarito Plateau, and the site was duly bought out. When its final class graduated in February 1943, the scientists moved in.

Working in the utmost secrecy – the words "Los Alamos" were forbidden, and newcomers were told merely to report to 109 Palace Avenue in Santa Fe – scientists took just over two years to make the bomb a reality. The first successful test took place at the **Trinity Site**, 200 miles south (see p.184), on July 16, 1945. Three weeks later, bombs were dropped on **Hiroshima**, on August 6, and **Nagasaki**, August 9; a complete Japanese surrender followed immediately.

For Oppenheimer, who described the development of the bomb with a quotation from the *Bhagavad Gita*, "I am become Death, the shatterer of Worlds," Los Alamos had served its purpose, and the laboratory could now close. Instead, as the Cold War set in, its energies were devoted toward the construction of the **H-Bomb**. Though security was more paramount than ever, ideologically motivated spies such as **Klaus Fuchs** and **David Greenglass** (whose sister and her husband, **Ethel** and **Julius Rosenberg**, were later executed) soon betrayed Los Alamos' secrets to the Russians. Paranoia grew to the point that employees were instructed to "Watch Your Liberal Friends," and Oppenheimer himself was barred by his successor Edward Teller from access to privileged information.

The gate house on the road up from Santa Fe that denied outsiders access to Los Alamos was finally removed in 1957. The laboratory business is still booming, spending well over half its two-billion-dollar annual budget on the research and development of nuclear weapons. While the lab has also drilled a 12,000-foot hole to "mine" heat from hot rocks deep in the earth and worked on the Human Genome Project, its public image remains firmly linked with nuclear experimentation.

from $10, and tasty pasta or steak dinner entrees starting at around $15. Mon–Thurs 11am–2.30pm & 5–8.30pm, Fri 11am–2.30pm & 5–9pm, Sat 5–9pm.
Hilltop House 400 Trinity Drive ☎ 505 662 2441 or ☎ 800 462 0936, ⍟ hilltophousela.com. Formerly a Best

Western, this recently upgraded central hotel is now independently run. Oddly reminiscent of a converted church, it caters largely to visiting scientists, so its moderately-priced dinner-only grill restaurant is open on weekdays only. $95

Bandelier National Monument

10 miles south of Los Alamos, a total of 50 miles northwest of Santa Fe • $12 per vehicle • ☎ 505 672 3861, ⍟ nps.gov/band

Long before the scientists descended on Los Alamos, the "finger canyons" of the Pajarito Plateau were home to Native Americans. The Ancestral Puebloan inhabitants of what's now **BANDELIER NATIONAL MONUMENT** enlarged natural cavities in the soft volcanic rock to create **cliff dwellings**, and also built free-standing pueblos beside the streams on the valley floors. Set amid delightful woodlands and framed against the rose-pink canyon walls, Bandelier's intriguing remains provide an ideal introduction to New Mexico's past.

Although the Ancestral Puebloans are often said to have "disappeared" around 1300 AD, there's little mystery as to where they went. Bandelier is a "missing link," occupied between roughly 1150, as the Four Corners region was being abandoned, and 1550, when many of today's pueblos were established. As successive itinerant groups streamed in, perhaps fleeing drought or invasion, they may have merged here to create the modern Pueblo culture. The peoples of **Cochiti** and **San Ildefonso** in particular trace their ancestry back via Bandelier to Mesa Verde, and it was a Cochiti guide who led amateur archeologist **Adolph Bandelier** to this site in 1880.

Frijoles Canyon

The monument's major sights are concentrated along a 1.5-mile loop trail through **Frijoles Canyon**, open daily from dawn to dusk. From the visitor centre, the trail leads swiftly to the remains of **Tyuonyi** on the canyon floor. Only the ground floor and foundations survive of this circular, multi-storey, 400-room village, whose name means "place of agreement". It's seen as a centre for trade and storage, common to the **Keresan**-speaking peoples, whose pueblos lay to the south, and the **Tewa** speakers to the north. Local obsidian was traded as far as the Dakotas and the Mississippi. Despite the apparently large number of dwellings, the canyon's maximum total population is estimated at between five and seven hundred. Tyuonyi may have still been in use when Coronado's soldiers reached the Southwest (see p.465), though they didn't come this far.

A side path from Tyuonyi leads up to dozens of **cave dwellings**, their rounded chambers scooped into the warmer, south-facing wall of the canyon. (As artificial creations, technically these are "cavates" rather than caves.) Ladders and walkways mean visitors can scramble up to, and even enter, some of them, to peer out across the valley.

The main trail continues to the **Long House**, an 800ft-long series of two- and three-storey houses built against the cliffs. Though most of the upper storeys have collapsed to expose the plastered walls, you can still see the mortised holes that held their pine roof beams or *vigas*. Above these, rows of petroglyphs and pictographs depict figures and abstract symbols.

Though the main trail doubles back to the visitor centre, keen hikers can follow the stream for another half-mile, to the point where **Alcove House** nestles in a rocky overhang 150 feet above the canyon floor. Reaching it entails climbing three hair-raising ladders, as well as steep stairways hacked into the crumbling rock. At the top, *viga*-holes show that the cave once held several structures, but it's now bare except for a reconstructed *kiva*, set down in its sloping sandy floor, and entered by ladder.

Another trail drops south from the visitor centre, coming out after a mile and a half at the **Lower Falls** – at their best in late spring – and then reaches the Rio Grande in another ten minutes. It's also possible to hike up into the backcountry above Frijoles Canyon; a very demanding trek of 6.5 miles each way leads to two very weathered but still remarkable **stone lions**, carved by ancient sculptors.

Tsankawi

Turn south off Hwy-502 onto Hwy-4, 5 miles east of Los Alamos; the Tsankawi parking lot is on the left, a little under a mile along

2

The small, separate **Tsankawi** section of Bandelier lies a dozen miles northeast of the visitor centre, just off Hwy-502 as it climbs from the Rio Grande valley up to Los Alamos. Visits consist of an hour-long loop hike onto an isolated mesa-top that holds the almost indiscernible ruins of an ancient pueblo. If the site itself is disappointing, however, the trail is not; following the same route once used by the Ancestral Puebloans, it's worn waist-deep into the soft tuff in places, and includes a number of prehistoric "stairways." Assuming you're happy to negotiate a couple of short ladders, you're also rewarded with lovely views down into the valley, as well as glimpses of the mysterious Los Alamos laboratories closer at hand.

ARRIVAL AND INFORMATION

BANDELIER NATIONAL MONUMENT

By car Private vehicles are only allowed to drive down into Frijoles Canyon between December and February. Between March and November, drivers have to park at the White Rock Visitor Center, on Hwy-4 in White Rock a couple of miles south of the monument's Tsankawi section, and catch one of the frequent free shuttle buses down to the canyon itself.

Visitor centre The monument's visitor centre is in Frijoles

Canyon, at the bottom of a narrow switchback road down from Hwy-4 (daily: summer 9am–5.30pm, winter 9am–4.30pm). Displays of pottery and jewellery, models and reconstructions, century-old photographs, and an excellent film narrated by Meryl Streep and N. Scott Momaday illuminate the Bandelier story and the region's fascinating geological history, and snacks and sodas are on sale.

ACCOMMODATION

Juniper Campground Hwy-4 ☎ 505 672 3861, ⓦ nps .gov/band. While there's no roofed accommodation at Bandelier, the monument does operate this very pleasant campground, with restrooms but no showers or hookups,

up on Frijoles Mesa at the start of the road down into the canyon. All except a couple of group sites are first-come, first-served, and there's almost always plenty of availability. **$12**

Valles Caldera National Preserve

Hwy-4 • **Information centre** Fri–Sun 9am–5pm • ☎ 866 382 5537, ⓦ vallescaldera.gov

West of Bandelier and Los Alamos, Hwy-4 climbs out of the forests then bursts unexpectedly into the open to skirt the long rim of **Valle Grande**. This 500-foot-deep, 176-square-mile caldera was created by a still-active volcano 1.2 million years ago. Its wide meadows form a lush counterpoint to the dry-as-dust terrain of most of New Mexico, and the basin was much prized by ancient peoples both as prime hunting territory and as a source of obsidian, a volcanic glass that can be chipped to form ultra-sharp blades.

The national government purchased the huge Baca Ranch here for $101 million in 2000, to create the 89,000-acre **VALLES CALDERA NATIONAL PRESERVE**. The basic aim is to run it as a self-sustaining wildlife reserve – it's home to a large elk herd in summer, as well as several rare bird species – funded through commercial activities. You don't need a permit to walk the short trails that lead from a couple of roadside pullouts on Hwy-4, but to take a longer hike, you have to reserve and pay a $10 fee at least 24 hours in advance. The altitude of 8750 feet makes all physical activity demanding, and lightning strikes are such a constant threat, thanks to the almost daily afternoon thunderstorms, that all hikers are advised to leave the area by 2pm. In practice, the preserve remains primarily a drive-through experience.

Spence Hot Springs

Between mileposts 24 and 25 on Hwy-4

Among the most irresistible of the many **hot springs** that bubble from beneath the ground close to Valles Caldera – the most obvious vestiges of the region's volcanic past – are the **SPENCE HOT SPRINGS**. Set on a promontory above the Jemez River, half an hour out of Los Alamos, it consists of half a dozen waterfall-connected pools that provide a range of temperatures to suit anybody, from the high 90°s F in the lower pools to a blissful 104°F at the top. Local custom calls for bathing suits on weekend nights, otherwise it's clothing optional. To get there, cross the river over a fallen tree and then climb up the canyon, keeping to the left for about a ten-minute walk uphill.

2

Jemez Springs

Five miles downhill from Spence Hot Springs, Hwy-4 runs past the bizarre (and very smelly) **Soda Dam**, where calcified deposits all but block the Jemez River, to enter **JEMEZ SPRINGS**. This appealing hamlet, where the river is lined by glowing cottonwoods and flows between high canyon walls that flame gold and red, was once the site of the Towa-speaking pueblo of **Giusewa**, the "Place of the Boiling Waters." The most active of its hot mineral springs was enclosed in the 1870s by a **bath house**, where you can enjoy an hour-long soak for $18, or a massage for $42 (daily 10am–7pm; ☎575 829 3303, ⊛jemezspringsbathhouse.com).

Jemez State Monument

Daily except Tues 8.30am–5pm • $3

The substantial shell of the mission church of **San Jose de los Jemez**, built by Franciscans in 1621 only to be destroyed almost immediately by Navajo raiders, is now preserved in **Jemez State Monument**. Walls that once held bright frescoes are now just stumps, but the principal doorway has been reconstructed. Most of the ruins that surround it were convent outbuildings rather than pueblo dwellings, although you can still spot several subterranean *kivas*. Jemez Springs' religious tradition continues to this day, as it's home to large Christian monasteries as well as a Zen centre.

ACCOMMODATION AND EATING   JEMEZ SPRINGS

Cañon del Rio–Riverside Inn 16445 Hwy-4 ☎575 829 4377, ⊛canondelrio.com. Lovely B&B inn, in a splendid rural setting with its own pool and outdoor spa, where each of the six very comfortable en-suite rooms is themed according to a different Indian tribe. $109

Laughing Lizard Inn ☎575 829 3410, ⊛thelaughing lizard.com. Four simple but appealing and inexpensive en-suite motel-style rooms, opening onto a nice terrace

perched above both highway and river. $70

Los Ojos Restaurant and Saloon ☎575 829 3547, ⊛losojossaloon.com. Very much the social centre for Jemez Springs, this late-opening roadside restaurant offers a full menu of pub food – burgers, wings and the like – for under $10 – as well as pool tables and cheap beer. Mon–Fri 11am–midnight, Sat & Sun 8am–midnight.

Jemez Pueblo

Visitor centre Daily: summer 8am–5pm, winter 8am–4pm • ☎575 834 7235, ⊛jemezpueblo.com

After Giusewa Pueblo, the site of modern Jemez Springs, was abandoned in 1630, its inhabitants built **JEMEZ PUEBLO** fifteen miles downstream. There they participated in the Pueblo Revolt of 1680, sacking their church and killing its priest; when the Spaniards returned, they briefly retreated northwest, establishing cultural and family links with the Navajo that endure to this day. They also assimilated the last twenty survivors of Pecos Pueblo in 1838 (see p.118). Jemez now has a population of around 3400 and is the only surviving Towa-speaking pueblo.

Home for the Jemez Indians is a gorgeous, lush canyon floor, surrounded by low cliffs of rich red rock. In honour of that scenery, they call themselves **Walatowa**, "people of the canyon," and that's also the name of their village. The pueblo itself is only open to visitors on feast days such as August 2, November 12, and December 12. An impressive visitor centre, three miles north on Hwy-4 at Red Rock holds displays on their history, can arrange group tours, and sells a wide range of crafts.

On weekends between April and mid-October, the **Jemez Pueblo Open Air Market**, also at Red Rock, sells food and artwork.

Zia Pueblo

Visitor centre Mon–Fri 8am–noon & 1–5pm • Free • ☎ 505 867 3304

Six miles south of San Ysidro, reached by a short spur road off US-550, little **ZIA PUEBLO** overlooks the Jemez River. Now 750 strong, the Zia Indians have occupied this spot since the sixteenth century. They're best known for the **sun symbol** that features on New Mexico's flag and licence plates. Though they've failed to persuade the courts to grant them royalties for its use, they do at least earn some money as a movie location; both *All The Pretty Horses* and *Ghosts of Mars* were filmed here.

There's little reason for outsiders to visit Zia, but the tribe does maintain a small **visitor centre** not far off the highway.

Santa Ana Pueblo

SANTA ANA PUEBLO, eight miles southeast of Zia Pueblo along US-550, and every bit as small, are like their neighbours also Keresan speakers, who moved in after the Pueblo Revolt. Only since the advent of Indian gaming in the 1990s have they made any effort to welcome visitors. Profits from the roadside **Santa Ana Star Casino** (⊛santaanastar .com), which holds four restaurants and a large bowling centre, have enabled the tribe to branch out in several new directions. These include two top-quality golf courses, 22 soccer fields, and several crafts outlets.

From the end of the Jemez Mountain Trail, when Hwy-44 meets I-25 at **Bernalillo** (see p.125), downtown Albuquerque is a sixteen-mile drive south, while Santa Fe is forty miles northeast, a drive described on p.124 onwards.

ACCOMMODATION	SANTA ANA PUEBLO
Hyatt Regency Tamaya Resort & Spa 1300 Tuyuna Trail ☎ 505 867 1234, ⊛tamaya.hyatt.com. New Mexico's most prestigious luxury resort, a joint venture between Santa Ana Pueblo and Hyatt, is the most conspicuous consequence of the tribe's new gambling-based prosperity. As well as 350 opulent rooms and suites, it features three swimming pools, a fitness centre and spa, four restaurants, a championship golf course, and its own stables and hot-air balloon. **$178**	**Prairie Star** 288 Prairie Star Rd, Santa Ana Golf Club ☎ 505 867 3327, ⊛mynewmexicogolf.com. A popular evening excursion for the affluent of Albuquerque, this excellent restaurant, set in an adobe mansion northwest of the casino, offers contemporary Southwestern cuisine. Typical entrees include grilled organic quail ($27) and bison striploin ($36). Tues–Sun 5.30–9pm.

From Santa Fe to Taos: the northern pueblos

The quickest route between Santa Fe and Taos follows **US-84** as far as the Rio Grande, then continues northeast beside the river on **Hwy-68** – not that the switch from one road to the other, at **Española**, is discernible to the naked eye. US-84 passes through the heartland of the **northern pueblos**. The most interesting of these tiny Tewa-speaking villages for casual visitors are **Nambé**, near the impressive **Nambé Falls**, and **Pojoaque** beside the highway, where a museum and visitor centre provide a quick taste of Pueblo culture. Serious collectors can head instead for **San Ildefonso** and its famous pottery.

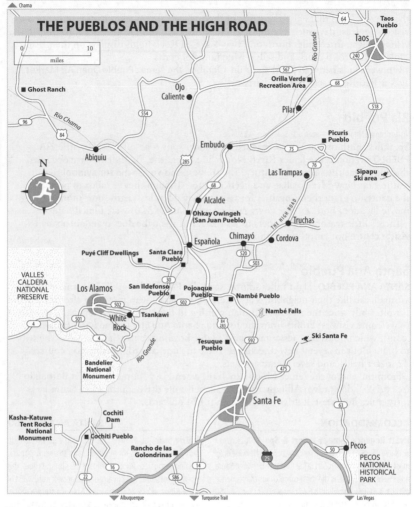

Tesuque Pueblo

Nine miles north of Santa Fe, west of US-84, and overlooked by the remarkable **Camel Rock**, the traditional community of **TESUQUE PUEBLO** studiously turns its back on the city. Its name means "place of the cottonwood trees," and its people were the first to strike against the Spaniards during the Pueblo Revolt. There's no visitor centre, but the tribe operates the **Camel Rock Casino** (ⓦcamelrockcasino.com), which has a good buffet restaurant, and also holds a colourful open-air weekend **flea market**, selling everything from clothing to furniture to hot sauce (March to late Nov Fri–Sun 9am–4pm).

Pojoaque Pueblo

POJOAQUE PUEBLO, twelve miles out of Santa Fe on US-84, was once one of the largest pueblos, but its original settlement was abandoned after a smallpox epidemic in 1895, and in terms of land it's now the smallest in the state. Though some ceremonial activities have resumed, most of the tribe's attention is devoted to running various commercial and cultural enterprises beside the highway. The **Cities of Gold** casino (Ⓦciticsofgold.com) has proved so lucrative that the tribe was able to buy the Santa Fe Downs racetrack, adjoining the pueblo, in order to close it down.

Poeh Museum

Alongside Ó restaurant, Pojoaque Pueblo • Mon–Fri 8am–5pm, Sat 4–9pm • $1 • Ⓣ 505 455 5041, Ⓦpoehmuseum.com

Strangely inconspicuous despite standing very close to US-84, the **Poeh Museum** covers the history and culture of all the Tewa peoples. A walkway leads through a mocked-up cave to reach (uncaptioned) displays that trace Pueblo history from its nomadic origins to the construction of permanent villages and the development of weaving and agriculture. The coming of the Spaniards is represented by a crazy-eyed friar flogging an Indian, followed by a mission church ablaze, while the story ends rather poignantly with a vacant-faced Pueblo child staring at a big-screen TV.

ACCOMMODATION AND EATING   POJOAQUE PUEBLO

★ **Ó Eating House** 86 Cities of Gold Rd Ⓣ 505 455 2000, Ⓦoeatinghouse.com. Although this high-class little restaurant is on Pueblo property, it's independently run, and serves a fundamentally Italian menu, featuring delicious home-made breads and pasta. The $12 steak sandwiches at lunchtime are a real bargain, while typical dinner entrees include bacon linguine for $16, or lamb loin for $26. As well as the conventional dining room, they also have an enclosed patio. Mon 5–9pm, Tues–Sat 11am–9pm.

Nambé Pueblo

Daily: April & May 7am–8pm; June–Aug 6am–8pm; Sept & Oct 7am–7pm • admission $10 per vehicle, still photography $5 extra; Ⓣ 505 455 2304, Ⓦnambefalls.com

The most beautifully sited of the northern pueblos, **NAMBÉ PUEBLO** is reached by turning right on Hwy-503 just beyond Pojoaque. Keep going up the hillside beyond the Sacred Heart church, and turn right after three verdant miles. The pueblo itself, 1.5 miles along, is not visible from the road; apart from a large *kiva*, not much remains in its old plaza area. After another 3.5 miles, you come to a ranger station, where the admission fee of $10 per vehicle is payable.

The steep five-minute hike up to the triple-decker **Nambé Falls** starts from the picnic area and campground ($25 per night) just beyond. At the top of the climb, you can admire the waters as they tumble through a jagged cleft in the surrounding red rocks, but the view is somewhat marred by the colossal concrete dam that towers above. There's no way to reach the foot of the falls, let alone swim there.

San Ildefonso Pueblo

$5 per vehicle, $10 photo permit, $20 video • Ⓣ 505 455 2273 • Tewa Visitor Center Feb–Oct daily 8am–5pm; Nov–Jan Mon–Fri 8am–5pm • Tribal Museum Mon–Fri 8am–4pm • No additional charge

SAN ILDEFONSO PUEBLO, located five miles west of Pojoaque, before Hwy-502 crosses the Rio Grande and climbs up to Los Alamos, is best known as the former home of potter **Maria Martinez**. From 1919 onwards, together with her husband Julian, she was responsible for revitalizing the Pueblo ceramic tradition; the finest collection of the pair's work is in Taos' Millicent Rogers Museum (see p.150).

The people of San Ildefonso trace their ancestry back to Mesa Verde, by way of the Pajarito Plateau. In 1694, when the Spaniards returned after the Pueblo Revolt, refugees from San Ildefonso and its neighbours held out on a nearby mesa, **Black Rock**, until they were starved down.

San Ildefonso now consists of two plazas, one of which holds a replica of its original mission church. Individual artisans sell pottery from their own homes – look out for signs – or you can buy from the selection in the **Tewa Visitor Center** when you pay your pueblo admission fee. The nearby **Tribal Museum** holds some of Martinez's original works.

2

VISITING THE RIO GRANDE PUEBLOS

In 1540, the first Spaniards to explore what's now New Mexico encountered a settled population of around a hundred thousand people, living in a hundred or so villages and towns. These inhabitants did not see themselves as a single people, but the Spaniards collectively named them **Pueblo Indians**, from the Spanish for "village." Smallpox, war and general disruption took their toll, but New Mexico is still home to around forty thousand Pueblo Indians, who live in nineteen autonomous pueblos, each with its own laws and system of government.

Fifteen pueblos are concentrated along the Rio Grande north of Albuquerque. There's a long-standing division between the seven southern pueblos, south of Santa Fe, most of which speak Keresan, and the eight to the north, which mostly speak Tewa (pronounced *tay-wah*). Together with the four pueblos that lie further afield, they jointly promote themselves through Albuquerque's **Indian Pueblo Cultural Center** (see p.171; Ⓦ indianpueblo.org).

Despite their fascinating history, most pueblos aren't the tourist attractions they're often touted to be. While the best-known, **Taos** and **Ácoma**, retain their ancient defensive architecture, the rest tend to be dusty adobe hamlets scattered around a windblown plaza. All the pueblos have to some extent incorporated **Catholicism**, as introduced by the Spanish, into their religious beliefs, and thus tend to centre on an old adobe mission church. Rarely, however, does Christianity amount to more than a syncretic imposition upon more fundamental traditional beliefs, and you'll also see *kivas*, or prayer chambers, nearby.

If you can time your visit to coincide with a feast day, a trip to a pueblo is an extraordinary experience. The spectacle of hundreds of costumed, body-painted tribal members of all ages, drawn from other pueblos as well as the host village, performing elaborate dances in such timeless surroundings, seems like a genuine glimpse of the ancient life of the continent. You won't be allowed to photograph or even sketch the ceremonies, but stalls selling food, jewellery, ceramics and other Pueblo crafts make it possible to take something away with you.

Otherwise, unless you are a knowledgeable shopper in search of Pueblo arts and crafts, visits can be disappointing. You'll certainly be made to feel unwelcome if you fail to behave respectfully – don't "explore" places that are off-limits, such as shrines, *kivas*, or private homes.

Visitors to each pueblo are required to register at a visitor centre; some charge an admission fee of $3 to $10, and those that permit such activities at all charge additional fees of about $5 for still photography, $10–15 for video cameras, and up to $100 for sketching. Many forbid the use of cell phones.

SOUTHERN PUEBLOS

Cochiti (see p.124)	Ⓦ pueblodecochiti.org
Jemez (see p.134)	Ⓦ jemezpueblo.org
Kewa (see p.125)	Ⓦ indianpueblo.org
San Felipe (see p.125)	Ⓦ sanfelipecasino.com
Sandia (see p.126)	Ⓦ sandiapueblo.nsn.us
Santa Ana (see p.135)	Ⓦ santaana.org
Zia (see p.135)	Ⓦ indianpueblo.org

NORTHERN PUEBLOS

Nambé (see p.137)	Ⓦ nambefalls.com
Ohkay Owingeh (see p.141)	Ⓦ indianpueblo.org
Picuris (see p.145)	Ⓦ indianpueblo.org
Pojoaque (see p.136)	Ⓦ citiesofgold.com
San Ildefonso (see p.137)	Ⓦ indianpueblo.org
Santa Clara (see p.140)	Ⓦ indianpueblo.org
Taos (see p.151)	Ⓦ taospueblo.com
Tesuque (see p.136)	Ⓦ indianpueblo.org

PUEBLOS FURTHER AFIELD

Ácoma (see p.99)   🌐 skycity.com
Isleta (see p.173)   🌐 isletapueblo.com
Laguna (see p.101)   🌐 lagunapueblo.org
Zuni (see p.95)   🌐 zunitourism.com

A PUEBLO CALENDAR

Jan 1	Turtle Dance	Taos
Jan 1	Corn Dance	Kewa
Jan 1	Cloud or Basket Dance	Ohkay Owingeh
Jan 6	Three Kings Day	Most pueblos
Jan 22–23	San Ildefonso Feast Day	San Ildefonso
Jan 25	St Paul's Feast Day	Picuris, Ohkay Owingeh
Feb 2	Candelaria Day	Picuris, San Felipe
Feb (1st weekend)	Governor's Feast	Ácoma
Feb (2nd weekend)	Deer Dance	Ohkay Owingeh
March 19	St Joseph's Feast Day	Laguna
Easter	Dances	Nambé, San Ildefonso, Kewa, Zia
May 1	San Felipe Feast Day	San Felipe
May 3	Santa Cruz Feast Day	Taos
May 7	Santa Maria Feast Day	Ácoma
June (1st Sat)	Blessing of the Fields	Tesuque
June 13	San Antonio Feast Day	Most pueblos
June 24	San Juan Feast Day	Ohkay Owingeh, Taos
June 29	San Pedro Feast Day	Santa Ana, Kewa
July 4	Nambé Falls Celebration	Nambé
July (2nd week)	Taos Pueblo Pow wow	Taos
July 14	San Buenaventura	Cochiti
July (3rd week)	Northern Pueblo Arts & Crafts Show	Varying northern pueblos
July 25	Corn Dances	San Ildefonso, Taos
July 26	Santa Ana Feast Day	Laguna, Santa Ana, Taos
Aug 2	Santa Persingula Feast Day	Jemez
Aug 4	Santo Domingo Feast Day	Kewa
Aug 10	Pueblo Revolt Anniversary	Most pueblos
Aug 10	San Lorenzo Feast Day	Ácoma, Picuris
Aug 12	Santa Clara Feast Day	Santa Clara
Aug 15	Assumption	Laguna, Zia
Aug (3rd week)	Indian Market	Santa Fe
Aug (3rd week)	Zuni Tribal Fair	Zuni
Aug 28	San Augustine Feast Day	Isleta
Sept 2	San Estéban Feast Day	Ácoma
Sept 4	Isleta Pueblo Feast Day	Isleta
Sept 8	Corn Dances	Laguna, San Ildefonso
Sept 19	Laguna Pueblo Feast Day	Laguna
Sept 25	Santa Isabela Feast Day	Laguna
Sept 29–30	Feast of San Gerónimo	Taos
Oct (1st week)	Harvest Festival	Zuni
Oct 3–4	San Francisco Feast Day	Nambé
Nov 12	San Diego Feast Day	Jemez, Tesuque
early Dec	Shalako Ceremony	Zuni
Dec 12	Guadalupe Feast Day	Pojoaque
Dec 24–25	Matachina Dance	Most pueblos
Dec 26	Turtle Dance	Ohkay Owingeh
Dec 28	Children's Dances	Picuris, Santa Clara

Santa Clara Pueblo

SANTA CLARA PUEBLO, five miles north of San Ildefonso, or five miles west of Española, is known to its 1500 inhabitants as Kapo, "where the roses grow near the water". Like their neighbours, they too now sell pottery from houses around the central plaza, but the main reason to visit is to see where they used to live: the dramatic **Puyé Cliff Dwellings** in Santa Clara Canyon. The pueblo also runs the successful *Santa Claran* casino/hotel complex in Española (ⓦsantaclaran.com).

2

Puyé Cliff Dwellings

Check in and pay at Valero gas station on Hwy-30, 3 miles south of Santa Clara Pueblo, then drive 7 miles north on Santa Clara Canyon Rd to the ruins • Daily: April–Sept 8.30am–6pm, hourly tours 9am–5pm; Oct–March 9.30am–3pm, hourly tours 10am–2pm; closed week before Easter plus June 13 and Aug 12 • Cliff Tour $20, Mesa Top Tour $20, combined Puyé Adventure Tour $35 • ☎ 888 520 5008, ⓦ puyecliffs.com • If driving from Santa Fe, allow 1hr in total to rendezvous with a particular tour

Like the similar but better-known ruins at Bandelier (see p.132), the ancient community that's now preserved as **Puyé Cliff Dwellings** – "Puyé" means "where the rabbits meet" – was set against the south-facing cliffs at the edge of the Pajarito Plateau, and occupied, presumably by descendants of the Mesa Verdeans, between 1250 and 1550. Two tiers of "apartments" were hollowed into the upper canyon wall – so soft that it could be shaped with wooden tools – while a large free-standing pueblo occupied the mesa-top just above.

Santa Clara Indians now lead hugely informative **guided tours** up to and around the complex, which provide the opportunity, rare indeed in the Southwest, to hear such a site interpreted by members of the same group that used to occupy it. The trail starts from a former Fred Harvey B&B at the base of the cliff that now serves as a visitor centre-cum-museum. Although in principle it's an easy walk, it can feel very exposed in the full heat of midsummer.

To see the whole thing you need to sign up for the full two-hour **Adventure Tour**, but most visitors will be content with the one-hour **Cliff Tour**, which involves climbing at least one steep ladder, as well as some deeply worn "staircases" in the rock. What seem like cozy little cave dwellings were originally interior rooms in larger complexes; each was fronted by several adobe-walled rooms, as the countless holes that once supported roof-beams now testify. Intriguingly, petroglyphs above the entranceways appear to mark specific homes. The second hour of the Adventure Tour continues up onto the mesa, where the ruined foundations of the former pueblo are much less readily understandable. You can also go up there on the stand-alone **Mesa Top Tour**, but that's very much a second choice to the Cliff Tour.

Española

The only sizeable Hispanic settlement between Santa Fe and Taos is **ESPAÑOLA**, roughly halfway between the two and immediately south of the confluence of the Rio Chama and the Rio Grande. While most highway traffic continues northeast at this point toward Taos on Hwy-68, US-84 veers west across the river toward Chama (see p.157) and Colorado.

Other than watching the local youth cruising the streets in their customized "low-riders" or joining them in one of the dozens of neighbourhood fast-food joints, Española has little to offer tourists. However, it can make an alternative base to Santa Fe or Taos.

Abiquiu

O'Keeffe Home Tours June–Oct Tues–Fri 9.30am, 11am, noon, 2pm & 3.30pm, Sat 9.30am, 11am, 1pm & 2pm; late March to May & Nov Tues, Thurs & Fri 9.30am, 11am, noon, 2pm & 3.30pm • Tues–Fri $35, Sat $45 • ☎ 505 685 4539, ⓦ okeeffemuseum.org

Twenty miles up US-84 from Española, the landscape erupts into a riot of red-rock splendour. Cliffs and mesas of Chinle, Entrada, and Windgate sandstone soar above corrugated hillocks of grey, brown and red clays, all strongly reminiscent of southern Utah and the Navajo badlands of northeast Arizona. Surprisingly few visitors pass this way, but it's hardly little known. If it now appears definitively Southwestern, that's largely because the paintings of **Georgia O'Keeffe** have done so much to shape contemporary notions of the Southwest – and it was this very terrain that inspired those paintings. Of one peak, the **Pedernal**, O'Keeffe said, "God told me if I painted that mountain enough, I could have it."

From 1946 until she died, at age 98, in 1986, O'Keeffe's life centred on the pretty adobe village of **ABIQUIU** (pronounced *a-beh-cue*). Originally a settlement of *genízaros* (the Christianized descendants of Plains peoples captured by eighteenth-century Spaniards), Abiquiu village was a trading centre on par with Taos in the late eighteenth and early nineteenth centuries, and was briefly New Mexico's third largest town. These days, it consists of little more than a small plaza, surrounded by tumbledown adobes and centred by the beautiful, restored church of **Santo Tomás**; photography is not permitted.

O'Keeffe maintained homes both at **Ghost Ranch** fourteen miles north of Abiquiu, and in the village itself. The former is not open to the public, but the latter, perched on a hilltop south of the highway and now known as the **Georgia O'Keeffe Home and Studio**, can be visited on guided tours. You must both reserve and pay in advance, and provide full names and addresses of all participants.

ACCOMMODATION ABIQUIU

Abiquiu Inn 21120 Hwy-84 ✆ 505 685 4378 or ✆ 888 735 2902, ⓦ abiquiuinn.com. Exceptionally peaceful B&B inn with wonderful views. A haven for O'Keeffe enthusiasts, it also makes a good base for explorations further afield. As well as 25 comfortable guestrooms and casitas, all en-suite with kiva fireplaces and Southwestern art, it holds a good little bistro and gallery. **$150**

Ohkay Owingeh

Set amid the cottonwoods on the east bank of the Rio Grande off Hwy-68, five miles north of Española, the largest Tewa pueblo, long known as **San Juan Pueblo**, has recently reverted to its Tewa name of **OHKAY OWINGEH**. This is the third village to have stood in this area since 1250, all of which have been called Ohkay, meaning "we are the brothers." The first two capitals of the colony of New Mexico were also built here in 1598. Before they relocated to Santa Fe in 1610, the Spanish took over Ohkay and called it San Juan, and then occupied nearby Yunge and renamed it **San Gabriel**. Later that century, San Juan was the birthplace of **Po'pay**, the medicine man who led the Pueblo Revolt.

The centrepiece of the plaza is the much-restored **mission church**, the first building in the Southwest to be made with adobe bricks as opposed to simple chunks of mud. It's flanked by two rectangular *kivas*, as well as a smaller Catholic chapel. Admission is free in daylight hours, but photography is by permission only.

Alcalde

The previously low-profile community of **ALCALDE**, a couple of miles further up the Rio Grande from Ohkay Owingeh, hit the local headlines in 1999. Shortly after the

---

RELIGIOUS RETREATS

Several religious groups have established retreats in the Abiquiu region, including the international Muslim community that erected the **Dar al-Islam mosque** on the mesa above the village; the Benedictine **Monastery of Christ in the Desert** (ⓦ christdesert.org), thirteen miles west of Ghost Ranch; and the Presbyterian ministry at **Ghost Ranch**, which also holds **museums** of local anthropology and paleontology (summer Tues–Sat 9am–5pm, Sun 1am–5pm; winter closed Sun and all Dec; ⓦ ghostranch.org; $3; ⓦ ghostranch.org).

unveiling of a statue of New Mexico's first governor, Don Juan de Oñate, unknown assailants amputated its right foot – an obvious reference to the barbaric punishment Oñate meted out to the defeated menfolk of Ácoma Pueblo in 1599 (see p.99).

Embudo

The funky little village of **EMBUDO**, five miles northeast of Alcalde, has in recent years become something of an alternative artists' colony. Its handful of crafts and oddities stores include Gasoline Alley, whose forecourt display of 1950s gas pumps is a great little slice of Americana. Inside, you'll find what its owner calls the "shiny stuff," largely consisting of assorted neon and glass advertising signs from the Route 66 era. Open to no fixed hours, it's more of a museum than a shop, though some of the stock is for sale.

Pilar and the Río Grande del Norte National Monument

Visitor centre Daily: May–Oct 8.30am–4.30pm; Nov–April 10am–2pm • ☎ 505 751 4899, ⓦ blm.gov/nm

Perched above the Rio Grande fifteen miles southwest of Taos, **PILAR** started out as a Jicarilla Apache farming village. On May 30, 1854, the Jicarilla defeated sixty US dragoons nearby in the Battle of Cieneguilla; several years of fighting ensued before they were finally confined to a reservation to the west (see p.158).

Pilar today is a base for **rafting** trips (see p.153), and holds a simple roadside diner. It's also the southernmost point of the **Río Grande del Norte National Monument**, created by President Obama in March 2013, which extends north up the **Rio Grande Gorge** all the way to Colorado, and broadens to reach a considerable distance west. Intended primarily to protect the region from exploitation, it's run by the Bureau of Land Management, which operates a visitor centre on the east side of Hwy-68 in Pilar. A minor road drops from across the highway to reach the riverside **Orilla Verde Recreation Area**, which stretches along both banks of the southern end of the gorge. Six miles along, a developed campground charges $7 per vehicle.

Although you can't continue toward Taos along either riverbank, it's possible to meet up with US-285 by following the dirt road that crosses the river beyond the campground. More to the point, the **Vista Verde Trail** shortly after the bridge is an enjoyable 1.25-mile hiking trail that leads across the sagebrush-topped west-bank mesa to an overlook above the Rio Grande Gorge. A longer trail, slightly further up the hillside, runs all the way to the Rio Grande Gorge Bridge (see p.156); at seven miles one way, it's better tackled by bike or horse than on foot.

The High Road

While the most direct route from Santa Fe to Taos heads straight up the Rio Grande Valley, the "**High Road**" over the forested Sangre de Cristo Mountains to the east makes a rewarding alternative if you have a couple of hours to spare. Winding through timeless **Hispanic villages**, it passes some splendid old **adobe churches** and offers good opportunities to sample traditional New Mexican food or buy local folk art. Shopping for crafts is a big deal year-round, reaching its peak in the **High Road Art Tour**, which takes place during the last two weekends of September (ⓦhighroadnewmexico.com).

Chimayó

The first and most famous of the High Road towns, **CHIMAYÓ** is 25 miles north of Santa Fe, eight miles northeast of **Pojoaque Pueblo** via the dessicated Hwy-592 and

THE PENITENTES

During the nineteenth century, the remote hills above Chimayó were renowned as the heartland of the mysterious Hispanic Catholic sect known as the **Penitentes**. Anglo newcomers claimed to have glimpsed hooded figures filing along the ridges at dawn, **whipping** themselves as they went.

A large grain of truth lay beneath the lurid speculation. Self-mortification – the infliction of pain in order to share the suffering of Christ – was widespread in medieval Europe. The Spanish expedition that founded New Mexico performed public self-flagellation on Good Friday 1598, as it marched up through Mexico, and similar acts by early Franciscan missionaries attracted Pueblo Indian scorn. The Penitentes as such, however, emerged after Mexico achieved independence in 1821. Cut off from Spanish funding, the Franciscans vanished from New Mexico within twenty years, leaving the region almost devoid of priests. Hispanic Catholics formed **lay brotherhoods** to keep their faith alive.

The Penitentes – **Los Hermanos de Nuestro Padre Jesús Nazareno**, or the Brothers of Our Father Jesus of Nazareth – may well have modelled themselves on a Guatemalan example, introduced at the same time as the Guatemalan-influenced pilgrimages to Chimayó. From an initial emphasis on individual prayer and penance, they developed a complex system of rituals. While never administering the sacraments, they brought solace to Catholics forced to live – and die – without priests. The Penitente brotherhood in each village became a mutual-aid society, a cultural and political force as well as a spiritual one.

After the American takeover of New Mexico in 1846, the Penitentes were suddenly outsiders not only in their own country but even in their own church. The first Catholic bishop of Santa Fe, Jean-Baptiste **Lamy**, had little sympathy for the unorthodoxies of his Hispanic flock, and denied the sacraments to their most prominent spokesman, Father **Martínez** of Taos. Forced into secrecy, the Penitentes began to gather at night in remote spots. Lacking access to church property, they met in plain adobe structures known as **moradas** – not necessarily distinguished with crosses or towers, but adorned with the handmade sacred images known as **santos**.

The focus of ritual activity was **Lent**, when all Catholics practise some form of self-denial, and the Penitentes attempted to experience the passion and death of Christ. For processions, they divided into *Los Hermanos de Luz* – the **Brothers of Light** – responsible for the candles and music – and *Los Hermanos de Sangre*, the **Brothers of Blood**, who scourged themselves with yucca whips or carried giant wooden crosses. Participants were hooded to ensure humility. Some re-enacted the **crucifixion**, albeit tied rather than nailed to the cross, while others dragged a **Death Cart** – a wooden wagon holding an effigy of Death, armed with a bow and arrow – laden with stones. The Death Cart also figured in the Penitentes' elaborate **funeral** processions. The wayside stone cairns, topped with crosses, seen throughout the High Country are not graves, as outsiders supposed, but *descansos* – places where the coffin-bearers would pause to rest.

A century of conflict ended in 1947, when the Penitentes were officially recognized by the Bishop of Santa Fe. Those that remain now regard themselves as members of the **Third Order of St Francis**, a lay branch of the Franciscan monastic order, and the most lasting Penitente legacy in New Mexico is the *santero* tradition of religious folk art

Hwy-503, or eight miles east of **Española** on Hwy-76. Stretching luxuriantly through the fertile upland meadows that line the Santa Cruz River, and backed by scrubby red-tinged hills, it feels more of a piece with the Rio Grande Valley below than with the mountains to the east.

Chimayó was founded in 1740 as a sort of penal colony for Hispanic troublemakers. In Tewa, the word *tsimayo* means "good flaking stone"; Indians from San Juan Pueblo quarried obsidian here, which they chipped to form sharp blades.

Chimayó has specialized in **weaving** since 1805, when two weavers sent as teachers from Spain chose to live here in preference to Santa Fe. Outlets scattered through the village sell hand-woven goods; other galleries concentrate on wood carving and religious art.

Santuario de Chimayó

Daily: May–Sept 9am–6pm; Oct–April 9am–5pm; Mass Mon–Sat 11am, Sun 10.30am & noon • ☎ 505 351 9961, ⓦ elsantuariodechimayo.us

Before the Spaniards came to Chimayó, Tewa Indians held a dried-up hot spring here sacred, on the basis that the mud from around it, when eaten, had healing properties. That spring, now located in the *barrio* (neighbourhood) of **El Potrero**, at the village's southern end, has become the site of a spell-binding colonial chapel, the **Santuario de Chimayó**.

The church was built between 1813 and 1816, after a visiting priest told the landowner, **Bernardo Abeyta**, about the shrine at Esquipulas in Guatemala, which had arisen at a similar spring venerated by Guatemalan Indians. As a result, Abeyta's church also centred on a crucifix known as **Nuestro Señor de Esquipulas**, supposedly found locally in 1810 (conceivably it had been buried during the Pueblo Revolt).

The church, the crucifix, and the still-exposed *posito*, or dust pit, swiftly became the focus of **pilgrimage** not only for Hispanic peasants but also for Pueblo Indians, for whom the sacred hole in the earth clearly echoed the ancient concept of the *sipapu* (see p.461). To this day, it remains the "**Lourdes of America**."

While devout New Mexican Catholics see Chimayó as much more than a picturesque tourist attraction, the Santuario is an undeniable delight to visit: a ravishing little round-shouldered, twin-towered, tin-roofed adobe beauty set in a walled churchyard beneath the rolling Sangre de Cristo foothills. At the heart of the altar within, the crucifix is framed by a gorgeous *reredos*, with a small equestrian statue of Santiago to the right. Two smaller **side chapels** are filled with mind-boggling votive offerings – paintings, photographs, statues, press cuttings, even rows of discarded crutches. The hole containing the "Holy Dirt" is in the floor at the rear; pilgrims are allowed to take a scoop, as it's replenished regularly with earth from the hills.

The smaller **Santo Niño Chapel**, across the plaza and accessed via an extraordinarily kitsch angel gate, contains a diminutive statue of Santo Niño, the Lost Child – more of a doll, if truth be told – to whom expectant mothers bring offerings such as tiny pairs of shoes.

ACCOMMODATION AND EATING   CHIMAYÓ

Casa Escondida 64 County Rd 100 ☎ 505 351 4805 or ☎ 800 643 7201, ⓦ casaescondida.com. Set back in six acres of gardens on the edge of Chimayó, the "hidden house" is a very tasteful B&B with eight comfortable rooms. All feature *viga* ceilings, tiled floors, and *kiva* fireplaces, and have their own private bathrooms. $109

Hacienda Rancho de Chimayó Hwy-98 ☎ 505 351 2222 or ☎ 888 270 2320, ⓦ ranchodechimayo.com. Immediately across from the *Rancho* restaurant, and run by the same management, this peaceful B&B inn offers seven

appealing en-suite rooms, arranged around a shared courtyard; several have their own patio space. $79

★ **Rancho de Chimayó** Hwy-98 ☎ 505 351 4444, ⓦ ranchodechimayo.com. The best traditional New Mexican restaurant in the state, serving superb *flautas* and a mouthwatering *sopaipilla*, stuffed with meat and chiles and costing $8 for lunch, $12 in the evening, on a lovely sun-drenched outdoor patio. May–Oct Mon–Fri 11.30am–9pm, Sat & Sun 8.30am–10.30am & 11.30am–9pm; Nov–April Tues–Sun 11.30am–9pm.

Truchas

By the time you reach **TRUCHAS**, eight miles northeast of Chimayó on Hwy-76, you're well into the mountains; the views down and across the Rio Grande Valley are tremendous. Villagers from Las Trampas, further up, were granted permission to establish Truchas in 1754, on condition that it was enclosed within a walled square, to defend against Comanche attacks. The settlement took on its present form almost immediately, however, consisting of separate individual farms arrayed along a high ridge above the Río de las Truchas, or "river of trout." As one of New Mexico's least changed Hispanic communities, it was the movie location in 1987 for Robert Redford's *Milagro Beanfield War*.

Hwy-76 makes a right-angle bend to avoid Truchas, but a detour east onto the minor road up the valley takes you along a narrow street of adobe homes and barns – interspersed with the odd incongruous art gallery – and past the fields toward the 13,103-foot **Truchas Peak**.

Las Trampas

Truchas' parent community, the quiet hamlet of **LAS TRAMPAS**, is another eight miles along Hwy-76. It started life as an outpost used by fur-trappers pursuing beaver – hence its name, "the traps" – which by attracting Comanche raids doubled as an early-warning system for Santa Fe. Las Trampas now holds a couple of gift stores, plus a hideous auto scrapyard, but nowhere to eat or sleep.

Five miles on from Las Trampas, Hwy-76 meets Hwy-75 ten miles west of Hwy-68 and the Rio Grande. The quickest route to Taos, twenty miles north, is via Hwy-73 to the east, and then Hwy-518 to the north; more Hispanic villages line the way, but none is of interest to tourists.

San José de Gracia
Daily 10am–4pm

Though no longer walled, the dusty central plaza of Las Trampas, alongside the highway, still holds the evocative adobe church of **San José de Gracia**. Built in 1760, it features a choir loft that extends both inside and out, so that singers could accompany ceremonies on the square as well as in the church. Note the unattached *morada* – Penitente meeting place – beside the cemetery to the east.

Picuris Pueblo

Tiny **PICURIS PUEBLO** is tucked away in a side valley, half a mile toward the Rio Grande from the junction of Hwy-76 and Hwy-75. The last pueblo to be "discovered" by the Spanish, it proudly insists that it has never signed a treaty with any government, the US included. Its population has never risen much above two hundred, and Picuris remains just a cluster of adobe houses spreading across the hillside around a whitewashed church. The best-known tribal enterprise is the excellent *Hotel Santa Fe* in Santa Fe, reviewed on p.120.

There's a model of the pueblo and a reconstructed *kiva* in the village **museum** (daily 9am–5pm; $3 suggested donation). The same building also holds a gift store and a snack bar with views over a small blue lake.

Sipapu

Five miles east of Picuris Pueblo, Hwy-75 meets Hwy-518. Turning left, north, takes you onto the final leg of the High Road to Taos; continue east on Hwy-518, however and in a couple of miles you'll enter the tiny **ski resort** of **SIPAPU**, cradled in the pretty mountain valley known as **Tres Ritos Canyon**. Lift tickets in season, which generally runs mid-December through March, cost $44.

ACCOMMODATION	SIPAPU
Sipapu Lodge Hwy-518, beside the Rio Pueblo ☎ 800 587 2240, ⓦ sipapunm.com. In assorted units to either side of the highway, this ski resort offers every conceivable	grade of accommodation, from dorm beds through private camping cabins, motel rooms, and luxury duplexes. Dorm beds $12, private doubles $59

Taos

Part Spanish colonial outpost, part hangout for bohemian artists and New Age dropouts, and home to one of the oldest Native American communities in the United States, tiny **TAOS** is famous out of all proportion to its size. Not quite six thousand people live in its three component parts: **Taos** itself, around the old plaza; sprawling **Ranchos de Taos** three miles south; and the Indian village of **Taos Pueblo** two miles north. There's one restaurant for every 45 inhabitants, and a massage therapist for every thirty.

Like Santa Fe, Taos – pronounced to rhyme with "house" – stretches languidly across a glorious high-desert plateau. The approach from the south is especially spectacular, as you cross a final bluff on Hwy-68 to be confronted by the pine-forested Sangre de Cristo mountains soaring above the sun-bleached foothills. This far up, the **Rio Grande** is not yet meandering through a well-watered valley, but lies deep in a craggy canyon west of town, occasionally glimpsed as a crack in the plateau.

Beyond the usual unsightly highway sprawl, Taos is a delight to visit. As well as museums, galleries and stores to match Santa Fe, it still offers the unhurried pace and charm, and the sense of a meeting place between Pueblo, Hispanic, and American cultures, that attracted the likes of Georgia O'Keeffe and D.H. Lawrence.

Downtown Taos still centres on the old Spanish **plaza**, which has been remodelled several times over the years, and migrated slightly eastwards in the process. The tiny square is now ringed by galleries and souvenir stores, and its tree-shaded benches make a pleasant spot from which to watch the world go by. The Stars and Stripes have flown day and night from the flagpole at its heart ever since it was erected by Kit Carson during the Civil War; the nearby bandstand was a gift from Mabel Dodge Luhan.

While there's little to see on the plaza itself, a short walk along the narrow, winding streets that stretch away in all directions is rewarded with glimpses of Taos as it used to be. The best central museum is the **Kit Carson Home**, while the **Millicent Rogers Museum**, a few miles north, holds superb Native American and Hispanic artworks.

Brief history

Although the first Franciscan mission at the thousand-year-old **Taos Pueblo** (see p.151) was established in 1598, the modern town of Taos dates from the 1630s, when an uprising at the pueblo induced Spanish colonists to found the separate community of **Fernando de Taos** a few judicious miles south. Its early history was dogged by Pueblo rebellions, but the Spaniards and Pueblos eventually united to resist raids by "horse Indians" like the Apache and Comanche. In the early nineteenth century, despite attempts by the Mexican authorities to restrict contact with the outside world, Taos became the venue for annual **rendezvous**, at which "mountain men" and trappers from the Rockies traded with Indians from the pueblos and plains, and New Mexican merchants.

After the US takeover of New Mexico, Taos' Hispanic and Pueblo citizens once more found common cause. In **1847**, the territory's first American governor, Charles Bent, was killed in his Taos home, but the revolt failed to spread to Santa Fe, and the US Army launched an assault on the Pueblo that succeeded in suppressing further resistance.

Taos' role as an **arts colony** began at the end of the nineteenth century, with the arrival of the painter Joseph Henry Sharp. He was soon joined by two young New York artists, Bert Phillips and Ernest L. Blumenschein; legend has it their wagon lost a wheel outside Taos as they headed for Mexico in 1898, and they liked the place so much they never got around to leaving. The three men established the **Taos Society of Artists** in 1915. Society heiress and arts patron Mabel Dodge turned up soon afterwards, and

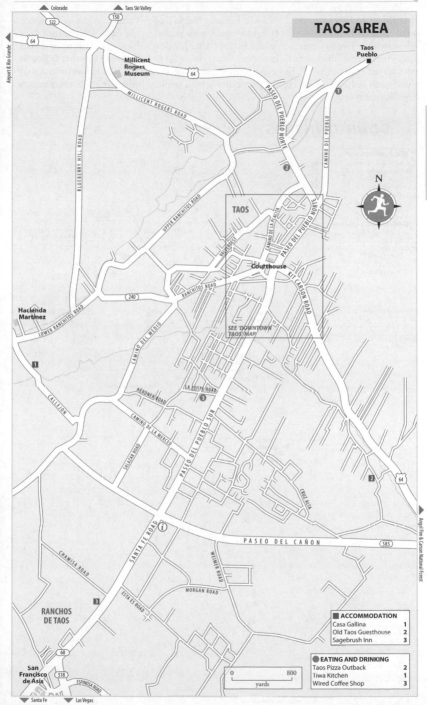

TAOS AREA

Colorado | Taos Ski Valley

522 | 150

64

Airport & Rio Grande

Taos Pueblo

Millicent Rogers Museum

64

MILLICENT ROGERS ROAD

PASEO DEL PUEBLO NORTE

CAMINO DEL PUEBLO

BLUEBERRY HILL ROAD

UPPER RANCHITOS ROAD

TAOS

N

2

CAMINO DE LA PLACITA

VALVERDE ST

PASEO DEL PUEBLO NORTE

Courthouse

RANCHITOS ROAD

KIT CARSON ROAD

240

LOWER RANCHITOS ROAD

Hacienda Martínez

CAMINO DEL MEDIO

SEE 'DOWNTOWN TAOS' MAP

1

CALLEJON

BERDNER ROAD

LA POSTA ROAD

3

CAMINO DE LA MERCED

PASEO DEL PUEBLO SUR

SALAZAR ROAD

CRUZ ALTA

3

64

Angel Fire & Carson National Forest

i

PASEO DEL CAÑON

585

CHAMISA ROAD

SANTA FE ROAD

WEIMER ROAD

MORGAN ROAD

ESTA ES ROAD

RANCHOS DE TAOS

3

68

San Francisco de Asís

518

ESPINOSA ROAD

0 — 800
yards

Santa Fe | Las Vegas

■ **ACCOMMODATION**
Casa Gallina 1
Old Taos Guesthouse 2
Sagebrush Inn 3

● **EATING AND DRINKING** 2
Taos Pizza Outback 2
Tiwa Kitchen 1
Wired Coffee Shop 3

married an Indian from the Pueblo to become **Mabel Dodge Luhan**. In turn, she wrote a fan letter to English novelist **D.H. Lawrence**, who visited in the early 1920s, and whose widow **Frieda** made her home in Taos after his death. New generations of artists and writers have "discovered" Taos ever since, the most famous being **Georgia O'Keeffe**, who stayed here in the 1920s before moving to Abiquiu (see p.140). Her renditions of the church at Ranchos de Taos in particular were a seminal influence on contemporary Southwestern art.

2

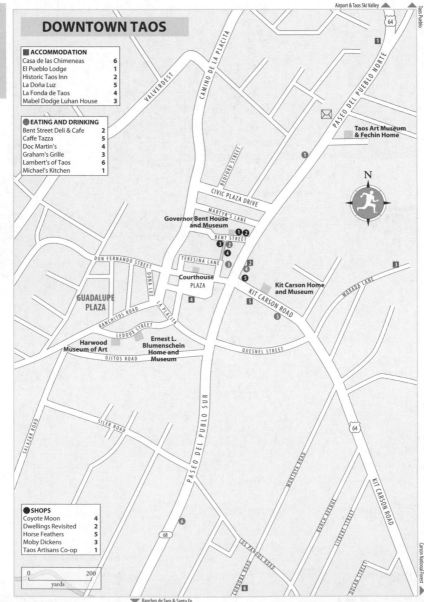

The influx of hippies who converged upon Taos in the late 1960s was followed in subsequent decades by art-loving tourists, gallery-owning entrepreneurs, wealthy divorcées and Hollywood exiles. Even as the urban area has grown larger and more commercialized, however, the population has remained minimal.

Governor Bent House and Museum

117 Bent St • Daily: April–Oct 9.30am–5pm, Nov–March 10am–4pm • $2 • ☎ 505 758 2376

Bent Street, a block north of the plaza, takes its name not from any irregularities but from the first American governor of New Mexico, Charles Bent. His former home is now the **Governor Bent House and Museum**. The imposition of American rule was resented by Taos' Hispanic and Indian population alike, and Bent was killed here by an angry mob on January 19, 1847. Most of his family attempted to escape through a still-visible hole hacked into the adobe walls; they were captured, but their lives were spared. The rest of the small house is a ramshackle museum of frontier Taoseño life, holding Indian artefacts, antiquated rifles, and even an eight-legged lamb.

Kit Carson Home and Museum

113 Kit Carson Rd • Daily 11am–4pm • $5 • ☎ 575 758 4945, ⓦ kitcarsonhomeandmuseum.com

The dusty but evocative adobe home of "mountain man," mason, and part-time US cavalry officer **Kit Carson** stand just east of the plaza, across the highway at the end of Taos' sole surviving stretch of wooden boardwalk. Born in Kentucky in 1809, Carson left home to join a wagon train to Missouri in 1826 – a one-cent reward was offered for the return of the teenage runaway – and spent the ensuing winter in Taos. He was to return repeatedly throughout his life, in between escapades like scouting for the 1840s Frémont expeditions and campaigning against the Navajo in the 1860s (see p.471).

Carson bought the house at the heart of today's museum in 1843, on his marriage to a local woman, Josefa Jaramillo. Sold after their deaths in 1868 to support their seven orphaned children, it now holds a disappointingly small collection of press cuttings and photos relating to Carson himself, plus a mock-up of the family's living quarters, complete with *fogón de campaña*, a bell-shaped adobe fireplace.

Taos Art Museum and Fechin Home

227 Paseo del Pueblo Norte • Wed–Sun 10am–5pm • $8, $25 combination ticket • ☎ 575 758 2690, ⓦ taosartmuseum.org

Russian artist and woodcarver Nicolai Fechin (1881–1955) made his home in Taos between 1927 and 1933 – almost literally so, in that he sculpted and shaped virtually every inch of the interior. As the **Taos Art Museum and Fechin Home**, it's now open to the public. Its ornate decorations are in themselves well worth a quick look, while its walls are adorned with choice pieces by Taos Society of Artists members, including a few lovely Gustave Baumann prints. The house makes a spectacular setting for chamber-music concerts on summer evenings.

> **DISCOUNT MUSEUM TICKETS IN TAOS**
>
> Under a scheme run by the Museum Association of Taos (ⓦ taosmuseums.org), a **$25 combination ticket**, sold at each museum and valid for a year, buys admission to five Taos museums – the Millicent Rogers Museum, the Blumenschein Home, the Harwood Museum, the Taos Art Museum, and the Hacienda Martínez.

Harwood Museum of Art

238 Ledoux St • Tues–Sat 10am–5pm, Sun noon–5pm • $10, or on $25 combination ticket • ☎ 575 758 9826, ⓦ harwoodmuseum.org

The **Harwood Museum of Art**, a complex of interlaced adobes two blocks southwest of the plaza that was originally known as El Pueblito, started life as a combined library and exhibition space almost a century ago. Its educational mission now extends to displaying contemporary local art along with works by twentieth-century Taos artists such as Bert Phillips and woodcarver Patrociño Barelo, and *santos* and *retablos* by their nineteenth-century Hispanic counterparts.

2

Ernest L. Blumenschein Home and Museum

222 Ledoux St • April–Oct Mon–Sat 10am–5pm, Sun noon–5pm; Nov–March Mon, Tues & Thurs–Sat 10am–4pm, Sun noon–4pm • $8, $25 combination ticket • ☎ 575 758 0505, ⓦ taoshistoricmuseums.org

The **Ernest L. Blumenschein Home and Museum** preserves the much-restored 1790 house of the co-founder of the Taos Society of Artists. Paintings by Blumenschein, his daughter Helen, and Zuni and Hopi artists such as Fred Kabotie (see p.308) are on display, but the real star is the house itself. Though Taos has grown to obscure its original uninterrupted views, Blumenschein's studio, made gloriously light by its raised ceiling and enlarged windows, still commands a fine prospect of the mountains.

D. H. Lawrence Forbidden Art

108 South Plaza • Irregular hours • $3 • ☎ 505 758 2211, ⓦ lafondataos.com

Known as **D. H. Lawrence Forbidden Art**, a gallery in the lobby of *La Fonda* hotel on Taos Plaza holds a unique collection of nine paintings by the Nottinghamshire novelist. Although the hotel itself was built in 1937, well after Lawrence's death – his ashes lie in a memorial chapel north of Taos (see p.158) – the paintings were bought from his widow Frieda's second husband. Most were painted in Italy rather than Taos. One, *The Holy Family*, was his first-ever canvas; it shows. Apart from one landscape (a "collaboration" with Frieda and their friend Dorothy Brett), they depict sweaty, fleshy wrestlings such as *The Rape of the Sabine Women*. When first exhibited, in London in 1929, they were regarded as obscene and banned in Britain. They now seem tame, though the *Sunday Times*' original verdict remains accurate: "he can do rather less with a paintbrush than a child of seven without any natural flair."

Millicent Rogers Museum

1504 Millicent Rogers Rd, 4 miles north of the plaza • April–Oct daily 10am–5pm; Nov–March Tues–Sun 10am–5pm • $10, under 17s $2, $25 combination ticket • ☎ 505 758 2462, ⓦ millicentrogers.org

Focussing on both Native American and Hispanic art, and tracing how those cultures have been perceived, the **Millicent Rogers Museum** is one of New Mexico's best galleries. Millicent Rogers herself – a former fashion model, granddaughter of a founder of Standard Oil and "close" to Cary Grant – lived here until her death in 1953.

The museum's highlight is the family collection of San Ildefonso Pueblo potter **Maria Martinez**, whose black-on-black ceramics are the most famous (and valuable) Native American artworks of the twentieth century. Fascinating photos show her creating a pot step by step. Displays also outline the unbroken thousand-year tradition of Pueblo pottery, from the prehistoric Mimbres and Ancestral Puebloan peoples onwards. Other crafts include turquoise jewellery and Navajo blankets.

The development of Spanish colonial religious art in the New World is shown through an array of rugs, looms, carved wooden furniture, *bultos*, and *retablos*, plus a "**Death Cart**" (see p.143), in which a skeleton, known as Doña Sebastiana, rides in a rickety wooden carriage and brandishes a bow and arrow.

Taos Pueblo

Just over 2 miles north of Taos plaza, along either of two separate approach roads off Hwy-68 • Mon–Sat 8am–4pm, Sun 8.30am–4pm, but closed mid-Feb to March, and also frequently closed for tribal events • $10 per person, plus $6 per still or video camera, including cellphones • ⊕ 505 758 1028, ⓦ taospueblo.com

Tiwa-speaking peoples have lived at **TAOS PUEBLO** for almost a thousand years. While they may have originally arrived from the east, across the plains, they have long been at the forefront of the **Pueblo Indian** cultural tradition. Together with Ácoma (see p.99) and the Hopi mesas (see p.66), the pueblo can claim to be the oldest continuously occupied settlement in the United States. It's also stunningly beautiful, centring on two multi-storey adobe "apartment blocks" framed beneath the shining forested peak of Taos Mountain.

The northernmost New Mexican pueblo, Taos is among the few not to have been displaced by the coming of the Spaniards. Its survival has required a long hard struggle; the pueblo was abandoned for two years in the 1630s, to escape retaliation after the killing of a priest, and it later played a central role in the **Pueblo Revolt** of 1680 (see p.467). When the Spanish subsequently reconquered New Mexico, Taos Pueblo was almost completely destroyed. It revolted again under both Mexican and American rule. In 1837, Taos Indians cut off the head of the Mexican governor of New Mexico and used it as a football. Ten years later, they were heavily implicated in the rebellion against Charles Bent (see p.146); when the retaliating US Army besieged and burned the pueblo's church, over 150 women, children and elderly non-combatants were killed.

In the twentieth century, the pueblo was forced to campaign for the return of the sacred **Blue Lake**, high in the mountains. The source of the Río Pueblo de Taos that flows through the heart of the village, and the focus of an annual three-day pilgrimage, Blue Lake was unexpectedly incorporated into a federal forest reserve in 1906. When Richard Nixon finally handed it back in 1970, it marked the first time that land had ever been returned to Native Americans for religious reasons; access is now forbidden to outsiders.

For most of the year, Pueblo life continues with scant regard for visitors, though (camera-less) outsiders are welcome at certain spectacular **feast days** and dances. Most of these take place in summer; the biggest are the Corn Dances (June 13 & 24, July 25 & 26), the Taos Pueblo Pow Wow (second weekend in July), and the Feast of San Gerónimo (Sept 29 & 30).

Hlaauma and Hlaukwima

The admission fee to Taos Pueblo entitles visitors to join one of the regular walking tours, led by Pueblo residents. While taking a tour may help overcome any awkwardness you might feel, however, it won't take you beyond the limited public areas through which you're also free to wander alone.

Visits focus on the two large adobe complexes – **Hlaauma**, the north house, and **Hlaukwima**, the south house – that stand to either side of the Río Pueblo de Taos, also known as Red Willow Creek. In their current form, they almost certainly date from the uncertain years that followed the Pueblo Revolt, at the start of the eighteenth century. This architectural design, consisting of individual dwellings stacked like dice and entered via rooftop ladders, was originally adopted for defence. While the homes have been adapted to include ground-level doorways and windows, their occupants still choose to live without toilets, running water, or electricity. Both complexes remained fully inhabited until the mid-1970s, but due to the lack of conveniences and the constant tourist intrusion, they now hold a mere ten families between them. The remainder of the reservation's population of three thousand live in newer homes nearby. Several rooms facing the plaza function as **craft shops**, but you can't penetrate any further, and you'll only glimpse the *kivas* (ceremonial chambers), distinguished by their long ladders, from a distance.

In the plaza itself, what look like makeshift awnings to shelter parked cars are in fact *ramadas*, wooden racks used for drying corn and chile peppers.

Church of San Gerónimo

Visitors are encouraged to enter, but not photograph, the pretty little **Church of San Gerónimo** on the edge of the plaza. Murals inside feature traditional corn and sun motifs; mass, open to all, is celebrated every Sunday morning at 7am. Tours also lead to the ruins of the pueblo's previous church, all but destroyed by the US army in 1847. Its solitary bell tower dominates a small dusty cemetery beside the adobe wall that surrounds the entire pueblo. Now just a few feet in height, the wall originally stood twelve feet tall.

2

Ranchos de Taos

The distinct community of **RANCHOS DE TAOS**, which spreads to either side of Hwy-68 three miles southwest of central Taos, was founded when Indian farmlands were taken over by the Spanish to grow the crops that fed the townspeople of Taos. Each *rancho* or farm had its own main house, or *hacienda*, and even today Ranchos de Taos retains the feel of a rural village; you can still buy fresh hay for your animals from lots along the highway.

San Francisco de Asis

In the small unpaved plaza of Ranchos de Taos, the mission church of **San Francisco de Asis** turns its broad shoulders, or more accurately its massive adobe buttresses, to the passing traffic on Hwy-68. Built around 1776, it's one of colonial New Mexico's most splendid architectural achievements, with subtly rounded walls and corners that disguise its underlying structural strength. Encountering genuine adobe, which crumbles away after heavy rain or snow, can come as a shock after so much fakery elsewhere in the state; the local congregation is obliged to replaster the whole thing yearly.

The ever-changing interplay of light and shade across the church's golden exterior has fascinated painters from Georgia O'Keeffe onwards. She observed in 1971 that "Everyone paints the Taos church. If you're in Taos for two days you have to paint the Taos church. I asked myself do I have to paint all that church? I'll just paint a little piece of it. That'll do just as well. And I did."

The church's **interior** is equally intriguing. Amid a clutter of devotional objects and artworks, a magnificently ornate green-and-red *reredos* (altarpiece) frames several individual paintings. It was painted by the nineteenth-century *santero* Molleno, who was also responsible for the altarpiece of the Santuario de Chimayó (see p.144). The **plaza** outside – remarkably peaceful considering that the highway is thirty yards away – holds a handful of restaurants and gift stores.

Hacienda Martínez

708 Hacienda Way, off Lower Ranchitos Rd, Ranchos de Taos, 2 miles west of Hwy-68 • April–Oct Mon–Sat 10am–5pm, Sun noon–5pm; Nov–March Mon, Tues & Thurs–Sat 10am–4pm, Sun noon–4pm • $8, $25 combination ticket • ☎ 575 758 0505, ⓦ taoshistoricmuseums.org

One of the few Spanish haciendas anywhere to be preserved in something like its original state, the **Hacienda Martínez** was built in 1804 by Don Antonio Martínez, an early mayor of Taos who was also the father of Padre Antonio Jose Martínez (see p.143). Within its thick, windowless, adobe walls – the place could be sealed like a fortress against then still-prevalent Indian raids – two dozen rooms are wrapped around two separate patios, holding animal pens and a well. Trade goods of the kind Don Antonio once carried south along the Rio Grande are displayed alongside tools, looms, and simple furnishings of the era, while the rooms furthest from the entrance contain a fine collection of Hispanic religious art.

Taos Ski Valley

15 miles north of Taos • Daily lift tickets late Nov to mid-Dec and late March to early April $50, mid-Dec to late March $75 • information
📞 505 776 2291 or 📞 866 968 7386, reservations 📞 800 776 1111, 🌐 skitaos.org

Located on the north flank of **Wheeler Peak** – at 13,161 feet, New Mexico's highest
point – the precipitous slopes of **TAOS SKI VALLEY** are reached via an attractive road that
winds up through a narrow gap in the mountains from the village of **Arroyo Seco**. Its
113 separate runs, served by fourteen lifts, are usually open to skiers and snowboarders
from late November until early April. Experts rate Taos one of the most challenging ski
resorts in the Rockies – just over half the runs are for experts only – but the highly rated
Ernie Blake Ski School teaches novices aged three and upwards on the nursery slopes.

The road up into the Ski Valley dead-ends at a massive parking lot that serves several
lodges, **hotels** and **condo** blocks, as well as a number of cafés, restaurants and bars.
Most accommodation and dining options remain open year-round, but there's little
point staying in summer.

ARRIVAL AND INFORMATION

By car Hwy-68, the main route up to Taos from Santa Fe and Albuquerque, passes first through Ranchos de Taos, then becomes an uninspiring commercial strip as it approaches downtown and is renamed Paseo del Pueblo Sur.

By bus Taos Express buses connect with Rail Runner trains to and from Santa Fe, at weekends only (departs Taos Fri 4.30pm, Sat & Sun 8am & 4.30pm; journey time 2hr;

roundtrip $10, reservations required; 📞 505 751 4459, 🌐 taosexpress.com). Greyhound no longer serves Taos.

Visitor centre 1139 Paseo del Pueblo Sur, 2 miles south of the plaza at the intersection of highways 68 and 585 (summer daily 9am–5pm, winter Mon–Sat 9am–5pm; 📞 505 758 3873 or 📞 800 348 0696, 🌐 taos.org). Brochures and maps, plus accommodation discount coupons and free wi-fi.

GETTING AROUND

By bus On weekdays only, the Chile Line bus runs along a twelve-mile stretch of Hwy-68, between Ranchos de Taos and Taos Pueblo, with a loop around the plaza in the middle (Mon–Fri 7.30am–5.30pm, every 40min; 50¢ one-way;

📞 505 751 4459, 🌐 taosgov.com); some services continue up to the Ski Valley in winter only.

Bike rental Gearing Up, 129 Paseo del Pueblo Sur (📞 505 751 0365, 🌐 gearingupbikes.com).

TOURS AND EXCURSIONS

Cottam's Rio Grande Rafting Full-day whitewater rafting trips through the Taos Box Canyon of the Rio Grande, which offers rapids up to Class V (April–midsummer only, Mon–Fri $104, Sat & Sun $114; 📞 505 758 2822 or 📞 800 322 8267, 🌐 cottamsoutdoor.com). The same operators can also arrange biking, kayaking, and, in winter, snowmobiling expeditions.

Far Flung Adventures Half- and full-day rafting trips on the Rio Grande from Pilar, south of Taos, as well as through the Taos Box Canyon and on the Rio Chama (half-day $55; one-day trips Mon–Fri $105, Sat & Sun $125; 📞 505 758 2628 or 📞 800 359 2627, 🌐 farflung.com).

Pueblo Balloon Company Hot-air balloon flights over the Rio Grande gorge, with advance reservation only ($250 adults, $150 ages 13–18, $100 ages 6–12; 📞 505 751 9877, 🌐 puebloballoon.com).

Taos Trolley Tours In summer, open-air trolley tours visit the main attractions (May–Oct daily 10.30am & 2pm from visitor centre, 10.45am & 2.15pm at plaza; 📞 505 550 5612, 🌐 taostrolleytours.com; $33, including entry fees). All the tours go to Taos Pueblo, except for those on Sundays and Monday afternoons, which visit the Millicent Rogers Museum and Martínez Hacienda instead.

ACCOMMODATION

Taos has accommodation to meet all needs, at prices well below those of Santa Fe. However, midwinter rates are no lower than midsummer, and can even be considerably higher close to the ski area. **High season** runs from Christmas to mid-April and mid-June to mid-October.

HOTELS AND HOSTEL

Abominable Snowmansion Hostel Taos Ski Valley Rd, Arroyo Seco 📞 505 776 8298, 🌐 abominable snowmansion.com. Pleasant, friendly hostel-cum-ski

lodge, on a very tight curve in the road as you enter Arroyo Seco village on Hwy 150 up to the Ski Valley, five miles north of downtown. Office hours are daily 8–11am & 4–10pm, so don't arrive at midday. Two six-bed dorms, one

2

for men and one for women, for which winter rates include breakfast; tipis that sleep up to six; and camping space out back; bargain private rooms and cabins come with and without en-suite facilities. Camping $\overline{\$20}$; dorms summer $\overline{\$22}$, winter $\overline{\$27}$; tipis, June–Sept only $\overline{\$45}$; private rooms summer $\overline{\$42}$, winter $\overline{\$52}$; cabins summer $\overline{\$38}$, winter $\overline{\$48}$

El Pueblo Lodge 412 Paseo del Pueblo Norte ☎505 758 8700 or ☎800 433 9612, ⓦelpueblolodge.com. Southwestern-themed 1940s fake-adobe motel, half a mile north of downtown near the Taos Pueblo, where the nicely furnished rooms have extra-large bathrooms, and there's a decent outdoor pool and hot tub. $\overline{\$110}$

★ **Historic Taos Inn** 125 Paseo del Pueblo Norte ☎505 758 2233 or ☎888 518 8267, ⓦtaosinn.com. Gorgeous, romantic central Taos landmark, consisting of several ancient adobes welded together to create an atmospheric and very Southwestern hotel. Each of the 44 rooms plays some variation on the Pueblo theme, with varying degrees of luxury; the *kiva* fireplaces are just for show, but a real fire burns downstairs, in the cozy, convivial lobby area that was once an open courtyard. Both the excellent *Doc Martin's* restaurant and the *Adobe Bar* are packed nightly. $\overline{\$105}$

La Fonda de Taos 108 South Plaza ☎505 758 2211 or ☎800 833 2211, ⓦlafondataos.com. Vintage 1930s hotel on the plaza that has been totally modernized to hold 24 luxurious suites, with Southwestern furnishings and tiled bathrooms. The lobby even holds a gallery of D.H. Lawrence paintings (see p.150). $\overline{\$149}$

Sagebrush Inn 1508 Paseo del Pueblo Sur ☎505 758 2254 or ☎800 428 3626, ⓦsagebrushinn.com. Attractive three-storey adobe inn, well south of the centre near Ranchos de Taos, which was briefly home to Georgia O'Keeffe and is filled with Southwestern arts and crafts. The hundred guestrooms themselves are nothing very special, but there's a pool and two hot tubs, and live music in the lobby bar most nights. $\overline{\$89}$

B&BS

Casa de las Chimeneas 405 Cordoba Lane ☎505 758 4777 or ☎877 758 4777, ⓦvisit-taos.com. Luxurious

eight-room B&B, set in adobe-walled gardens a couple of blocks southeast of the plaza, with a fitness room and spa. $\overline{\$195}$

Casa Gallina 609 Callejon ☎505 758 2306, ⓦcasagallina.net. This hugely welcoming and very comfortable B&B, in a peaceful rural setting a couple of miles southwest of the plaza, consists of four separate, colourfully furnished adobe guesthouses, with from one to three bedrooms, in spacious gardens. $\overline{\$175}$

La Doña Luz 114 Kit Carson Rd ☎505 758 9000 or ☎888 758 9060, ⓦstayintaos.com. Hispanic-flavoured rooms of differing sizes, prices and standards – all have en-suite facilities, some have fully equipped kitchens and/or hot tubs – in a peaceful adobe B&B a very short walk east of the plaza. $\overline{\$84}$

★ **Mabel Dodge Luhan House** 240 Morada Lane ☎505 751 9686 or ☎800 846 2235, ⓦmabeldodgeluhan.com. This appealing 200-year-old adobe B&B complex, not far northeast of the plaza off Kit Carson Lane, isn't the most luxurious option in Taos, but its historic associations are certainly impressive, with its lovely guestrooms named in honour of former guests like Willa Cather and Ansel Adams. Two rooms, including the light-filled solarium, share a bathroom painted by D.H. Lawrence; the cheaper lodge annexe has more modern fittings. The inn regularly plays host to creative workshops run by writer Natalie Goldberg among others. $\overline{\$105}$

Old Taos Guesthouse 1028 Witt Rd ☎505 758 5448 or ☎800 758 5448, ⓦoldtaos.com. Vintage adobe *hacienda*, a couple of miles east of the plaza, now restored as a spacious B&B complex. Each of the nine rooms offers different facilities – all have private bath and handcarved furniture, some have *kiva* fireplaces – and there's an outdoor hot tub. $\overline{\$120}$

TAOS SKI VALLEY

Amizette Inn 1295 NM-150 ☎505 776 2451 or ☎800 446 8267, ⓦamizetteinn.com. Small but comfortable ski lodge, centred on a former post office building, just over a mile down the valley from the lifts, with an indoor hot tub and sweeping views from its verandas. Rates include breakfast. $\overline{\$79}$

EATING AND DRINKING

Bent Street Deli & Cafe 120 Bent St ☎505 758 5787, ⓦbentstreetdeli.com. Open in daytime only, this airy, partly outdoor place, just north of the plaza is always buzzing with locals and day-trippers. Good-value breakfasts, with eggs Benedict at $8, are followed by sandwich or pasta lunches, with plenty of options for under $10. Mon–Sat 8am–4pm, Sun 10am–3pm.

Caffe Tazza 122 Kit Carson Rd ☎505 758 8706. Central café with nice sunlit terrace, serving coffees and light veggie meals to counter-cultural locals and assorted crazies. Live entertainment most evenings, with anarchic open-mike nights. Free local newspapers. Daily 6.30am–8pm.

Doc Martin's Historic Taos Inn, 125 Paseo del Pueblo Norte ☎505 758 1977, ⓦtaosinn.com. Delicious,

2

inventive New Mexican food in romantic old adobe inn, on the main road just east of the plaza. Typical lunchtime burgers and burritos cost $10–15, while dinner entrees, such as piñon-crusted salmon or roast chicken, range up to $30. Unusual options on the weekend brunch menu include the Kit Carson – poached eggs on yam biscuits. Mon–Fri 11am–10pm, Sat & Sun 7.30am–2.30pm.

Graham's Grille 106 Paseo del Pueblo Norte ☎ 505 751 1350, ⓦ grahamstaos.com. This very popular central bistro stretches a long way back from the main highway; a large, well-shaded patio to the rear complements the copious indoor seating. Tasty lunchtime sandwiches, or "small plates" such as home-made tamales, or mussels with chorizo, cost $6–8, while almost all the dinner steaks, pasta or Mexican entrees are under $20. Mon–Fri 7am–10.30am, 11.30am–2.30pm & 5–9pm, Sat & Sun 8am–2.30pm & 5–9pm.

Lambert's of Taos 309 Paseo del Pueblo Sur ☎ 505 758 1009, ⓦ lambertsoftaos.com. Cozy, low-key restaurant half a mile south of the plaza, with a classy but friendly atmosphere and art on the walls. The cuisine is New American rather than New Mexican, with grilled meat or fish entrees like braised pork ossobucco for $17–35; a half rack of lamb for $49; and opulent desserts. Daily 5.30–9pm.

Michael's Kitchen 304C Paseo del Pueblo Norte ☎ 505 758 4178, ⓦ michaelskitchen.com. Inexpensive Mexican and Southwestern dishes in an old adobe kitchen a few blocks north of the plaza, plus fresh-baked pastries, cinnamon rolls and coffee in the morning. Mon–Thurs 7am–2.30pm, Fri–Sun 7am–8pm.

Taos Pizza Outback 712 Paseo del Pueblo Norte ☎ 505 758 3112, ⓦ taospizzaoutback.com. Hard-to-find pizzeria tucked behind another building to the left of the highway a mile north of town. It has a welcoming youthful ambience and huge portions of great food – the $10 veggie *calzones* are amazing. Daily 11am–10pm.

Tiwa Kitchen 328 Veterans Hwy, Taos Pueblo ☎ 505 751 1020. Indian-run, largely organic restaurant on the road into Taos Pueblo, serving strong chile-flavoured stews, traditional *horno*-baked bread, Indian fry bread, all costing under $10, plus lots of blue corn meal. Daily except Tues, summer 11am–7pm, winter 11am–5pm.

Wired Coffee Shop 705 Felicidad Lane ☎ 505 751 9473, ⓦ wiredcoffeeshop.com. Friendly cyber café near the visitor centre, with breakfast pastries and cereals, sandwiches and chilli later on, as well as coffee, smoothies, wi-fi access and computers for public use – plus a very pleasant garden. Daily 8am–5pm.

SHOPPING

Coyote Moon 120C Bent St ☎ 505 758 4437, ⓦ johndunnshops.com. A riot of colour, this is Taos' best selection of Mexican folk art, with plenty of Oaxacan carved animals and Day of the Dead souvenirs. Mon–Sat 11am–6pm, Sun noon–6pm.

Dwellings Revisited 10 Bent St ☎ 505 758 3377. Quirky store where the owners have imported trinkets, oddities, furniture and folk art from all over the world. Unusual Greek and Indian items sit alongside the more familiar Mexican stuff. Daily 11am–6pm.

Horse Feathers 109B Kit Carson Rd ☎ 505 758 7457. A great source for all things Western, from Stetson hats and

colourful cowboy boots at bargain prices to off-the-wall antiques. Daily 10am–6pm.

Moby Dickens 124A Bent St ☎ 505 758 3050, ⓦ mobydickens.com. Central bookstore with an extensive array of local fiction and history, and lots more on the Southwest in general, plus New Age material. Daily 10am–6pm.

Taos Artisans Co-op 107A Bent St ☎ 505 758 1558, ⓦ taosartisansgallery.com. Individually styled jewellery, clothing and sculpture, created by an assortment of Taoseño artists. Daily 11am–6pm.

West of Taos

Assuming your plans already cover Santa Fe and points south, the obvious day-trip drive from Taos follows the **Enchanted Circle** to the northeast; see p.158. However, a longer and wilder route heads **west** on US-64, across the Rio Grande and over the dramatic **San Juan Mountains**. Branching west off Hwy-68 four miles out of downtown Taos, this reaches the awesome 650-foot-high **Rio Grande Gorge Bridge** seven miles on. Be sure to take the time to park at the end and walk out to the middle, otherwise you'll barely get a glimpse of the narrow chasm as you drive across.

After a magnificent seventy-mile mountain run, punctuated by scenic overlooks, US-64 finally drops into **Chama Valley**. From there, either head south into Georgia O'Keeffe country around **Abiquiu**, or north to **Chama** itself, the base for excursions on New Mexico's best-known **steam railroad**.

Tierra Amarilla

US 64 meets the north–south US-84 in **TIERRA AMARILLA** ("yellow earth"), at the foot of the sheer, furrowed **Brazos Cliffs**. This pastoral village, founded in 1832 when the valley was prone to constant Ute, Apache and Navajo raids, provides a classic example of the consequences to New Mexico's Hispanic population of the American takeover of the territory. In 1860, the US Congress refused to recognize that shared grazing lands belonged to the community as a whole, and instead sold them off to a Yankee landowner from Santa Fe.

Bitter disputes have raged ever since, culminating in an incident commemorated by a defaced roadside marker in the heart of the village. In 1967, a group led by Chicano activist **Reies López Tijerina** seized a nearby campground in the Kit Carson National Forest. Declaring independence from the United States, they burned down Tierra Amarilla's Rio Arriba Courthouse, destroying land-grant records and injuring a policeman and a jailer. The government responded by sending in two hundred military vehicles, including tanks. After a series of trials, Tijerina eventually served two years in federal prisons. He remains an active campaigner on lands-rights issues to this day. Passions hereabouts still run high – hence the sign reading *TIERRA O MUERTE* ("Land or Death") on the outskirts of town.

While Tierra Amarilla remains the county seat, it has declined to the point where parts are all but derelict.

2

Tierra Wools

91 Main St, Los Ojos • April to mid-May Mon–Sat 10am–5pm; mid-May to mid-Oct Mon–Sat 10am–6.30pm, Sun 11am–4pm; mid-Oct to Nov Tues–Sat 10am–5pm; Dec–March Mon–Sat 10am–4.30pm • ☎ 505 588 7231, ⓦ handweavers.com

In the village of **LOS OJOS**, one mile west of Tierra Amarilla, a cooperative effort to revitalize the local economy has proved a resounding success. Based at the clearly signposted Los Ojos Trading Post, **Tierra Wools** maintains local **weaving** traditions by breeding Spanish Churro sheep in the valley, and selling hand-dyed rugs and clothing.

Chama

Tiny **CHAMA**, set in the meadows at the head of the Chama Valley, a dozen miles north of Tierra Amarilla and a total of 85 miles northwest of Taos, is a former mining camp that has reinvented itself as a base for summer hunters and winter skiers.

INFORMATION   CHAMA

Visitor centre Where US-64 meets Hwy-17, half a mile south of town (daily: summer 8am–6pm; winter 8am–5pm; ☎ 505 756 2306 or ☎ 800 477 0149, ⓦ chamavalley.com).

CUMBRES & TOLTEC SCENIC RAILROAD

The pretty yellow station just below the centre of Chama is the western terminus of the highest narrow-gauge railroad in the nation, the **Cumbres & Toltec Scenic Railroad** (late May to mid-Oct; ☎ 505 756 2151 or ☎ 888 286 2737, ⓦ cumbrestoltec.com). This exhilarating, if not entirely comfortable, 64-mile steam-train ride crosses the High Brazos mountains into Colorado by way of **Cumbres Pass**, then runs through the deep **Toltec Gorge** and out onto the plains before ending in **Antonito**, Colorado. Its many movie credits include the opening sequence of 1989's *Indiana Jones and the Last Crusade*.

It's not possible to do the entire round-trip by train in one day; passengers either go by van to Antonito and return by train (depart Chama 8.30am), or catch the train from Chama at 10am, and either go through the most scenic segment as far as Osier, and pick up a return train there, or ride the train all the way to Antonito, and catch a bus back from there. Each of those options costs $89 in coach class (child fare $49); $129 in Deluxe Tourist Class (child fare $69); or $169 in Parlor Class (no children allowed). Dress warmly; it gets pretty cold up in the mountains.

ACCOMMODATION AND EATING

Carlatte's 425 Terrace Ave ☎ 505 756 2555. In the heart of town, *Carlatte's* serves coffee and simple meals, and has an outdoor patio. Mon–Sat: summer 7am–9pm, winter 7am–2pm.

Vista del Rio 2595 US-64/84 ☎ 505 756 2138 or

☎ 800 939 9943, ⓦ vistadelriolodge.com. Among the best of several very similar log-cabin riverfront lodges along the main highway into town, with 19 comfortable motel-style rooms. $100

The Cumbres Pass and Antonito, Colorado

North of Chama, **Hwy-17** follows much the same route as the railroad, first climbing far above the single track and then crisscrossing it repeatedly as it makes its way up to the 10,022-foot **Cumbres Pass**. In July 1848, legendary "mountain man" Bill Williams was injured here in a confrontation between the US Army and a combined force of Ute and Apache.

Beyond the pass, highway and railroad part company, not to meet again until they reach **ANTONITO**, Colorado, fifty miles out of Chama – a dreary, depressing little town that's home to the **Cumbres & Toltec Scenic Railroad** terminus.

Jicarilla Apache Indian Reservation

US-64 and US-84 join forces for twelve miles **west of Chama**, then once across the Continental Divide – not at all dramatic at this point – US-64 continues alone for another fifteen miles to **DULCE**, the headquarters of the **Jicarilla Apache Indian Reservation**. Today's three-thousand-plus Jicarilla are descended from separate Apache groups who lived further east, some as Plains nomads in the Cimarron area, and some in adobe villages near the pueblos of the Rio Grande. Their name is often said to come from the little baskets (*jicarillas*) they now sell to tourists, but the Jicarilla say they only started making baskets after they were confined to this remote reservation in the nineteenth century, and that the name comes from a Mexican word connected with chocolate.

There's little for tourists to see or do on the Jicarilla reservation, whose economy is based on oil and gas revenues and raising sheep. Dulce itself is just a very sharp dog-leg in the highway, where US-64 turns south rather than climb onto sheer Archuleta Mesa; after a few miles the road turns west again to head through Vaqueros Canyon and Gobernador Canyon (see p.90).

The Enchanted Circle

While the driving circuit through the Sangre de Cristo range northeast of Taos doesn't quite live up to its tourist-brochure billing as the **Enchanted Circle**, it does pass a handful of long-abandoned ghost towns amid the mountain scenery. Oklahomans and Texans flock to the closest **ski slopes** to home, but visitors from further afield are more likely to spin off east to the hard-bitten frontier town of **Cimarron**.

The Lawrence Ranch

Lawrence Ranch Rd, 1.5 miles east of Hwy-522

Starting seventeen miles north of Taos on Hwy-522, a rutted, muddy road climbs for five miles east to the **Lawrence Ranch**. The English novelist **D.H. Lawrence** made three six-month visits to Taos in the early 1920s, having been enticed across the Atlantic by Mabel Dodge Luhan (see p.148). Staying at her mountain cabin, then known as Kiowa Ranch, he wrote "there are all kinds of beauty in the world, but for greatness of beauty I have never experienced anything like New Mexico." **Georgia O'Keeffe** was also a guest here, in 1929, when she painted the tree right in front of the main cabin as

The Lawrence Tree. As seen from below, the painting makes the tree look more like a giant squid; it's usually on display in the Georgia O'Keeffe Museum in Santa Fe.

Lawrence died in France in 1930, but five years later his widow Frieda shipped his ashes back to New Mexico. They now rest in a small **shrine** that enjoys panoramic views of the upper Rio Grande valley, at the top of a zigzag cement footpath cleared through the forest; according to some stories, the ashes were actually poured into a wheelbarrow of cement, to ensure they could never be taken away. Frieda is said to have acquired the ranch from Mabel Dodge Luhan in exchange for the manuscript of *Sons and Lovers* – which Mabel in turn used to pay her psychiatrist – and lived in it until her death in 1956. It now belongs to the University of New Mexico, which holds weekend retreats in the main cabin; only the shrine is accessible to visitors, with no fixed hours or admission fee.

Red River

Half a dozen miles north of the turn-off to the Lawrence Ranch, as Hwy-522 gathers itself for the final climb into Colorado, **Hwy-38** follows the Red River east from **QUESTA**, an ugly little village ravaged by opencast mining. After twelve more attractive riverside miles, it reaches **RED RIVER**, a former gold-mining town whose rough-shod timber architecture is more authentic than it looks. Summer visitors hike in the surrounding forests, but Red River is at its busiest during the winter **ski** season, when there's cross-country skiing in the valley and a downhill resort in the mountains. The season typically lasts from late November until late March (lift tickets $65 per day; ☏575 754 2223, ⓦredriverskiarea.com).

Cimarron

East of Red River, Hwy-38 negotiates the 9820-foot **Bobcat Pass** – often closed in winter – then drops southwards, by way of the ruins of long-abandoned **Elizabethtown**, down to **Eagle Nest**. Just a cluster of cabins and RV parks, Eagle Nest sprang up around a lake formed when the **Cimarron River** was dammed in 1920, and is popular with fishing enthusiasts. US-64 parallels the river to enter impressive **Cimarron Canyon** four miles east, beneath the towering 800-foot **Palisade Cliffs**. This route provided access to Taos for nineteenth-century travellers who split from the Santa Fe Trail's "mountain branch" at **CIMARRON** itself, 24 miles east of Eagle Nest.

Cimarron means "wild" or "untamed," and in its heyday the town was as wild as the West could be. It stood at the heart of the 1.7-million-acre **Maxwell Land Grant**, the largest private landholding in the US, accumulated by Lucien Bonaparte Maxwell after the American takeover of New Mexico. Maxwell's main business was cattle ranching, but with gold and silver mines booming and busting all over the mountains, Cimarron lured a vast profusion of gamblers, gunfighters, outlaws and cowboys. Its old downtown now stands relatively intact half a mile south of the main highway. Local history is lovingly chronicled in the **Aztec Mill Museum** (June–Aug Mon–Wed, Fri & Sat 9am–5pm, Sun 1–5pm; May & Sept Sat 9am–5pm, Sun 1–5pm; $3).

Angel Fire

The Enchanted Circle loops back to Taos from Eagle Nest along US-64, passing, after ten miles, through the part-**golf**, part-**ski** resort of **ANGEL FIRE** in Moreno Valley, developed in the late 1960s. Despite upgrading, Angel Fire shows few signs of maturing beyond its current brash, unappealing sprawl. As at Red River, the ski slopes are usually active between late November and late March, but here they're considerably more suitable for novices, and there's also a snowboard park (lift tickets $66 per day; ☏575 377 6401, ⓦangelfireresort.com).

RED RIVER

Alpine Lodge 417 W Main St ☎ 575 754 2952 or ☎ 800 252 2333, ⊛ alpinelodgeredriver.com. This very central Red River option, handy for the ski lifts and downtown alike, offers spacious river-view cabins as well as hotel rooms and kitchenette apartment. Rooms $103, cabins $119

CIMARRON

St James Hotel 617 S Collinson St ☎ 505 376 2664 or ☎ 888 376 2664, ⊛ exstjames.com. Cimarron's most famous relic, built by President Lincoln's former White House chef in 1873, has witnessed 26 murders; names in the guest register include Jesse James and Buffalo Bill. It now has its own grand, tin-ceilinged restaurant, open for all meals daily and serving everything from $7 burgers and $13 *sopapillas* to $32 steaks; twelve authentically furnished nineteenth-century rooms, not all en-suite; and ten more conventional motel-type rooms in a less romantic annexe. Shared-bath hotel room $85, motel room $95, en-suite hotel room $120

Northeast New Mexico

Successively traversed by Pueblo Indian traders, pioneers on the **Santa Fe Trail**, and passengers on the transcontinental railroad, the traditional route between New Mexico and the plains is now followed by the **I-25** interstate. The Wild West town of **Las Vegas** provides a good send-off into New Mexico's **northeast corner**, as the Sangre de Cristo mountains gradually recede below the western horizon and the Great Plains begin to unfurl in all their relentless monotony. There's no great reason to stray off the interstate until the Rockies start to loom above **Raton**, a hundred miles on, though with time to spare the detour to **Capulin Volcano** at that point is worth making.

Las Vegas

The sleepy backwater of **LAS VEGAS**, New Mexico, 73 miles east of Santa Fe, has more in common with its upstart Nevada namesake than may be immediately obvious. Once a wild, lawless frontier outpost, where almost anything went, it consists of two distinct sections. The **old Plaza** area, above the fertile meadows (*vegas*, in Spanish) that line the Gallinas River, was established in 1835, when Hispanic settlers drove away the Comanche and set about capturing trade on the burgeoning **Santa Fe Trail**. When the **railroad** arrived in 1879, focus shifted across the river to the grid of streets around the new station. Incomers included the legendary **"Doc" Holliday**, who briefly owned a saloon on Center Street before scurrying back to Dodge City to escape a murder charge. In a single month, Las Vegas witnessed 29 gunshot deaths.

At the end of the nineteenth century, Las Vegas was the principal city in New Mexico, and almost all its buildings still date from the Victorian era. The conspicuous lack of adobe makes it easy to forget you're in the Southwest, but it ranks among the state's most authentic Wild West towns, and while it offers no particular stand-out tourist attractions, it's a delight to stroll around.

Grand Avenue – the main business drag – and I-25 alike now closely parallel the railroad, leaving the **Plaza** high and dry a mile to the west. Its four-square layout resembles something from the Deep South, though a Victorian bandstand rather than a courthouse stands at its centre. The only significant building on the perimeter is the *Plaza Hotel* (see opposite), but **Bridge Street**, which leads up from the highway, is lined with antiques stores and cafés.

Theodore Roosevelt recruited around forty percent of his volunteer **Rough Riders**, who invaded Cuba in 1898, in Las Vegas. Their exploits, plus the minutiae of local history, are recorded in the **City Museum**, 727 Grand Ave (Tues–Sat 10am–4pm; $2 suggested donation).

Hwy-518 leads due north from Las Vegas into some of New Mexico's most appealing mountain scenery, and serves as an eighty-mile shortcut to **Taos**. The Hispanic farming village of **MORA**, thirty miles out, is the seat of Mora County, ranked by the *Wall Street Journal* as one of the three poorest counties in the US.

ARRIVAL AND INFORMATION

LAS VEGAS

By train Two Amtrak trains pull into Las Vegas each afternoon, one heading west to Albuquerque, the other east to Chicago.

Visitor centre 513 Sixth St (Mon–Fri 9am–5pm; ☎505 425 8631 or ☎800 832 5947, ⓦlasvegas newmexico.com).

ACCOMMODATION AND EATING

Plaza Hotel 230 Old Town Plaza ☎505 425 3591 or ☎800 328 1882, ⓦplazahotel-nm.com. Much the nicest place to stay in Las Vegas, this restored, antiques-furnished hotel on the main plaza holds 71 very pleasantly updated rooms, plus the excellent *Landmark Grill*, open daily for all meals (most dinner mains $15–22), and a saloon. Rates include breakfast. If it all looks somehow familiar, it may be that you recognize it from the Coen Brothers' movie, *No Country for Old Men*. **$89**

Raton

Appealing little **RATON** is tucked into the foothills of the Rockies a hundred miles north of Las Vegas on I-25, a mere eight miles south of the Colorado border. Once a way-station on the Santa Fe Trail, it reached its present size after becoming the site of a railroad repair shop in 1880, and can have changed little since then.

Few passengers now bother to dismount from the two sleek Amtrak Starliners that pull into the Santa Fe Depot each day, but an hour or two's stroll in **downtown Raton** can be fun. Photos and oddments in the **Raton Museum**, facing the station at 216 S First St (May–Sept Tues–Sat 9am–5pm, Oct–April Wed–Sat 10am–4pm; free; ☎575 445 8979), recall highlights from Raton's first century. Until 1938, the town was dominated by the seven-storey *Hotel Swastika*, which then "found it necessary to change its name" to the *Yucca*, and is now a bank. Sadly, the landmark *El Portal* hotel, which was by far the most appealing modern-day lodging option, was destroyed by a fire in November 2012.

EATING

RATON

Enchanted Grounds 111 Park Ave ☎575 445 2219. The best place for a quick snack as you pass through Raton, this welcoming espresso café serves excellent coffee and fresh pastries, plus lunchtime sandwiches and, in summer, a daily hot soup special, all for under $10. They also have free wifi and a selection of books, and operate an espresso cart at the station nearby. Daily 7.30am–4.30pm.

Capulin Volcano National Monument

30 miles east of Raton on US-64/87, then 3 miles north on Hwy-325 • Gates open daily: summer 7.30am–6.30pm; winter 8am–4.30pm • $5 per vehicle • ☎505 278 2201, ⓦnps.gov/cavo

The remote **CAPULIN VOLCANO NATIONAL MONUMENT** preserves the neatest and most symmetrical of a chain of cinder cones that last exploded around ten thousand years ago. Most people drive straight past the **visitor centre** on up the two-mile spiral of road that leads to the summit. Once there, a thousand feet above the plains, you can **hike** for a mile around the rim, enjoying views to the Sangre de Cristo mountains in the west and Oklahoma to the east, or make the slightly more demanding descent down to the vent where it all began.

Albuquerque and southern New Mexico

164 Albuquerque and around

176 East of Albuquerque

178 Southeast of Albuquerque

185 Southeast New Mexico

190 The Rio Grande valley

195 Southwest New Mexico

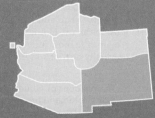

ALBUQUERQUE INTERNATIONAL BALLOON
FIESTA

Albuquerque and southern New Mexico

While New Mexico's tourist destinations lie largely to the north, its often-neglected central and southern portions hold many sites of interest. Prime among them is the state's largest city, Albuquerque, where the relics of its Route 66 heyday remain visible everywhere, and several stimulating museums celebrate a fascinating and varied history.

Much of the region remained dominated by the nomadic Apache until well into the nineteenth century. Even Albuquerque was founded long after Santa Fe, while towns such as **Silver City**, **Mesilla** and **Lincoln** only really got going after New Mexico joined the United States in 1846. All three went on to play significant roles in the career of **Billy the Kid**, and all still look today much like the frontier outposts Billy must have known. Together with the pre-Columbian remains of the **Gila Cliff Dwellings** in the remote southwest corner, they're the most appealing historic attractions in southern New Mexico. The region also holds a couple of **geological** wonders, however. The subterranean labyrinths of **Carlsbad Caverns National Park** lure a million tourists across the plains each year, while the dazzling dunes of **White Sands National Monument** make an extraordinary spectacle against the San Andres Mountains. Top-secret missile tests and bomb blasts give this desolate landscape an added sense of mystery, making its role in popular myth as the site of the notorious **Roswell Incident** a tiny bit more plausible.

Albuquerque and around

Sprawling at the heart of New Mexico, where the main cross-country road and rail routes cross both the Rio Grande and the old road south to Mexico, **ALBUQUERQUE**, with half a million people, is the state's only major metropolis, even if it isn't the capital. Though many tourists race north from the airport to Santa Fe without a thought for Albuquerque, the "**Duke City**" has a good deal going for it. Although, like Phoenix, it's grown a bit too fast for comfort, and the architecture is often uninspired, Albuquerque's original Hispanic core remains discernible, and its diverse, cosmopolitan population gives a rare cultural vibrancy. Above all, the city enjoys a magnificent setting, sandwiched between the Rio Grande to the west, lined by stately cottonwoods, and the dramatic, glowing **Sandia Mountains** to the east. Specific highlights for visitors include the intact **Spanish plaza**, the neon-lit **Route 66** frontage of Central Avenue, the fascinating **Indian Pueblo Cultural Center**, and October's **hot-air balloon** extravaganza.

Albuquerque consists of several distinct districts, interspersed between anonymous residential areas and threaded through by the twenty-mile artery of **Central Avenue**, the most authentic remnant of the classic Route 66, alive with flashing neon. **Old Town** remains the most interesting area for visitors, with **downtown** two miles east and the **university district** and the fashionable **Nob Hill** area beyond that. Further east, the

---

The balloons of Albuquerque p.167
Billy the Kid and the Lincoln County War p.180
All-American Futurity p.182
Trinity Site p.184

Lechuguilla Cave p.188
The bats of Carlsbad p.189
The Final Frontier p.192
The Mogollon and the Mimbres p.198

WHITE SANDS NATIONAL MONUMENT

Highlights

❶ Albuquerque International Balloon Fiesta It's hard to imagine a more photogenic spectacle than hundreds of colourful hot-air balloons soaring above the Rio Grande on a crisp fall morning. **See p.167**

❷ Indian Pueblo Cultural Center Albuquerque's premier museum provides a great opportunity to learn about New Mexico's nineteen surviving pueblos. **See p.171**

❸ Lincoln This quintessential Wild West town has barely changed since Billy the Kid blasted free from the county courthouse. **See p.179**

❹ White Sands National Monument An utterly amazing landscape of pure white sand dunes, lined against the azure sky. **See p.184**

❺ The Underground Lunchroom A perfect slice of 1950s Americana, this space-age subterranean cafeteria makes a surreal climax to a tour of Carlsbad Caverns. **See p.189**

❻ Silver City A wonderful Wild West relic, this mountain retreat from the heat of the desert is by far the most appealing town in southwest New Mexico. **See p.196**

❼ Gila Cliff Dwellings Remote ancient ruins, set in a lovely valley high in the mountains of southern New Mexico. **See p.198**

HIGHLIGHTS ARE MARKED ON THE MAP ON P.166

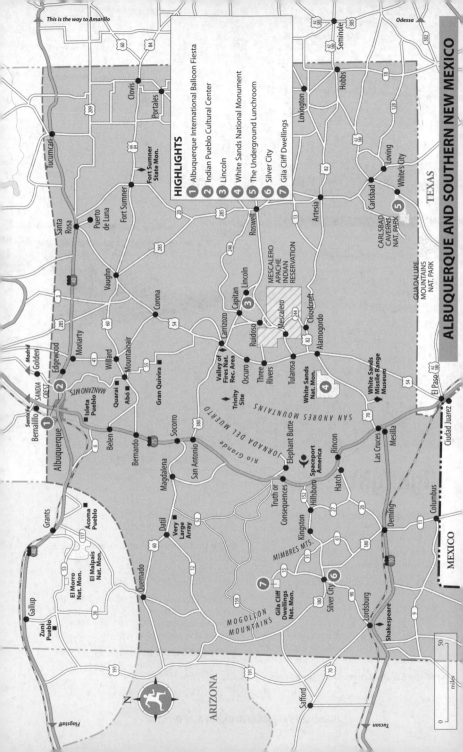

ALBUQUERQUE AND SOUTHERN NEW MEXICO

HIGHLIGHTS

1 Albuquerque International Balloon Fiesta
2 Indian Pueblo Cultural Center
3 Lincoln
4 White Sands National Monument
5 The Underground Lunchroom
6 Silver City
7 Gila Cliff Dwellings

This is the way to Amarillo

Odessa

TEXAS

MEXICO

ARIZONA

N

miles
0   50

Sandia Mountains finally call a halt to the Sunbelt sprawl. The city has instead pushed west of the Rio Grande, where only **Petroglyph National Monument** holds any appeal for tourists.

Brief history

Three centuries ago, in 1706, Hispanic colonists named a new town beside a sweeping curve of the Rio Grande in honour of the Spanish **Duke of Alburquerque**. Albuquerque's earliest surviving adobe buildings, however, still the nucleus of **Old Town**, date from the 1790s, when it occupied a pivotal position on the **Camino Real** – the "Royal Road" from Mexico to Santa Fe, which later linked up with the **Santa Fe Trail** from Missouri. Modern Albuquerque began to grow with the arrival of the railroad in 1880, when its epicentre shuffled a couple of miles east toward the new station. Around that time, Albuquerque managed to lose its first "r," possibly thanks to a misspelling by a railroad signpainter.

What really transformed Albuquerque was the decentralization of **defence** industries during World War II. Weapons research at **Sandia National Laboratories**, on the giant **Kirtland Air Force Base**, southeast of the city, brought a massive influx of money and jobs. In the 1950s, "Atomic City" was the best-educated city in the nation, in terms of PhDs per capita, and acquired enough federal offices to earn the nickname "Little Washington." It even achieved the dubious distinction of surviving an **H-bomb**: in 1957, a B-36 bomber accidentally dropped a 42,000-pound nuclear device near the air base. Its conventional explosives went off, creating a sizeable crater, but failed to trigger the intended one-megaton thermonuclear blast. Kirtland base these days is effectively a self-contained city, now more sealed-off than ever from the rest of Albuquerque.

Old Town

Albuquerque's tree-filled **Old Town Plaza** may lack the cachet of its counterpart in Santa Fe, but makes an appealing focus for the old Spanish settlement. Adobe buildings on all four sides have been restored as souvenir stores and tourist restaurants, with crafts sellers congregating under the porticos on the eastern side. The whole ensemble is still presided over by the twin-towered facade of **San Felipe de Neri church** to the north.

THE BALLOONS OF ALBUQUERQUE

First held in 1972 as a 50th anniversary stunt for a local radio station, when it featured just thirteen balloons, Albuquerque's annual **International Balloon Fiesta** (@balloonfiesta.com) has grown to become the most important event in world ballooning. By a freak of geography, the **"Albuquerque Box"** offers ideal conditions for balloonists. After takeoff, the prevailing winds consistently blow balloons toward the east, until they clear the top of the Sandia Mountains. Then stronger winds propel them back westwards, making it possible to land more or less where they were launched. As a result, Albuquerque regularly hosts major gas and hot-air ballooning championships, such as the unlikely sounding Coupe de Gordon Bennett.

A photographer's dream, the Balloon Fiesta lasts from the first Saturday until the second Sunday of October. It attracts roughly a thousand balloons and well over a million visitors, so book several months in advance if you need a room, or even a rental car, in early October. The fun focuses on **Balloon Fiesta Park**, half a mile west of I-25 and seven miles north of downtown. Admission costs $8 (under-12s free), with a further $10 for parking. The busiest times are the "mass ascensions" at 7am on the four weekend mornings, as well as the "Special Shapes" events, when balloons in shapes ranging from beer bottles to dumptrucks, and dragons to doughnuts, take to the air. Volunteers are always welcomed to help set the things up, and may be rewarded with a quick flight.

Various companies run hot-air balloon flights year round, from around $160 per person, including World Balloon (@worldballoon.com) and Rainbow Ryders (@rainbowryders.com).

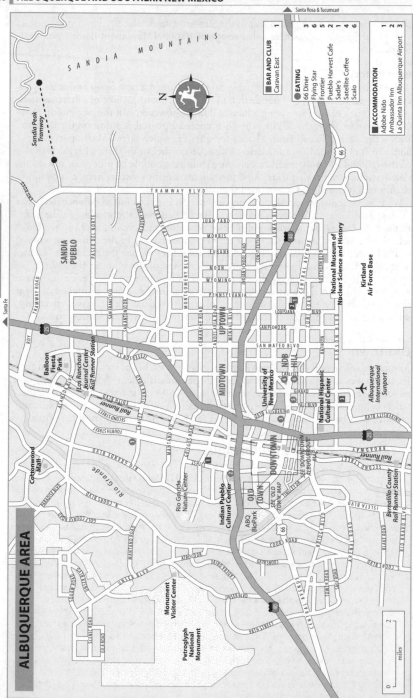

Santa Rosa & Tucumcari

ALBUQUERQUE AREA

3

SANDIA MOUNTAINS

SANDIA PUEBLO

Sandia Peak Tramway

Santa Fe

BAR AND CLUB
Caravan East   1

EATING
66 Diner   3
Flying Star   6
Frontier   5
Pueblo Harvest Cafe   2
Sadie's   1
Satellite Coffee   4
Scalo   6

ACCOMMODATION
Adobe Nido   1
Ambassador Inn   2
La Quinta Inn Albuquerque Airport 3

National Museum of
Nuclear Science and History

Kirtland
Air Force Base

TRAMWAY BLVD

JUAN TABO
MORRIS
EUBANK
MOON
WYOMING
PENNSYLVANIA

LOMAS BLVD

CONSTITUTION

CENTRAL AVENUE

INDIAN SCHOOL ROAD

PASEO DEL NORTE

TRAMWAY ROAD

ROY

COMANCHE ROAD

MONTGOMERY BLVD

CANDELARIA RD

MENAUL BLVD

SAN FRANCISCO

SAN ANTONIO DR

SAN MATEO BLVD

SAN PEDRO DR.

LOUISIANA

CARLISLE

EUBANK BLVD

JUAN TABO

WASHINGTON BLVD

UPTOWN

NOB HILL

MIDTOWN

University of
New Mexico

National Hispanic
Cultural Center

Albuquerque
International
Sunport

Balloon
Fiesta
Park

Los Ranchos
Journal Center
Rail Runner Station

JEFFERSON ST

OSUNA RD

2ND STREET

Rail Runner

FOURTH STREET

SECOND STREET

CHAVEZ

MENAUL RD

Rio Grande
Nature Center

Indian Pueblo
Cultural Center

ABQ
BioPark

Rio Grande

RIO GRANDE BLVD

N COORS BLVD

PARADISE BLVD

GOLF COURSE ROAD

ALAMEDA

EDITH

CARLISLE

GIRARD

YALE BLVD

UNIVERSITY BLVD

DOWNTOWN

SEE OLD TOWN MAP

SEE DOWNTOWN
ALBUQUERQUE MAP

OLD
TOWN

Cottonwood
Mall

COORS ROAD

ATRISCO DR.

BRIDGE BLVD

UNSER BLVD

98TH STREET

CENTRAL AVENUE

Bernalillo County
Rail Runner Station

Rail Runner

SECOND STREET

ISLETA BLVD

BROADWAY

RIO BRAVO BLVD

COORS BLVD

TOWER ROAD

SAGE ROAD

BLAKE ROAD

ARENAL ROAD

KREHL ROAD

Monument
Visitor Center

Petroglyph
National
Monument

MONTANO ROAD

UNIVERSE BLVD

SCENIC ROAD

GILAR ROAD

N

Acoma & Gallup

0   miles   2

Albuquerque Museum of Art and History

2000 Mountain Rd • Daily except Mon 9am–5pm • $4, free Sun 9am–1pm • ☎ 505 743 7255, ⓦ cabq.gov/museum

The **Albuquerque Museum of Art and History**, a couple of blocks northeast of the plaza, makes a great introduction to the city's story. As well as an impressive array of the armour and weaponry carried by the Spanish conquistadors – though the paucity of local finds means that the exhibits are drawn from sixteenth-century Europe rather than New Mexico – it holds delicate religious artefacts, plus paintings and photos showing Albuquerque through the centuries. There's a lot on the history of weaving along the Rio Grande; Coronado brought five thousand sheep on his expedition here in 1542, so the region has the longest tradition of sheep-rearing of anywhere in the US.

New Mexico Museum of Natural History and Science

1801 Mountain Rd NW • Daily 9am–5pm; closed Mon in Jan & Sept • $8 • ☎ 505 841 2800, ⓦ nmnaturalhistory.org

With its full-scale models of dinosaurs, and a replica of a Carlsbad-like snow cave, the **New Mexico Museum of Natural History and Science** is aimed primarily at kids. Its fascinating "Start Up" exhibition uses Microsoft's origins in Albuquerque in 1977 as the springboard for a history of the computer revolution. Albuquerque was where the first Altair personal computer was developed, prompting an incredibly young-looking Bill Gates and Paul Allen to move here in 1977 and establish "Micro-Soft" to write software for the first generation of home-based programmers. Fascinating displays also cover the stories of the internet and Apple. A Dynamax theatre shows the usual limited array of giant-screen movies for an additional charge.

American International Rattlesnake Museum

202 San Felipe St NW • June–Aug Mon–Sat 10am–6pm, Sun 1–5pm; Sept–May Mon–Fri 11.30am–5.30pm, Sat 10am–6pm, Sun 1–5pm • $5 • ☎ 505 242 6569, ⓦ rattlesnakes.com

The bizarre **American International Rattlesnake Museum**, southeast of the Old Town plaza, has live rattlers on display and rattlesnake curios for sale. Visits consist of walking through a small room at the back of the gift store, where spiders and scorpions as well as snakes are kept in tiny glass cases.

Turquoise Museum

2107 Central Ave NW • Guided tours only, by reservation, Mon–Sat 11am & 1pm • $10 • ☎ 505 247 8650, ⓦ turquoisemuseumcom

The intriguing little **Turquoise Museum**, half a block west of the plaza, looks like just another mall store. Step inside, however, on one of the two daily 90-minute tours, and you'll find you've entered a fortified vault, filled with rare and beautiful turquoise nuggets. The story of worldwide turquoise production is told in copious detail, and there's lots of useful advice on the tricks of the trade; unfortunately, the only definitive way to tell if a piece of turquoise is genuine involves destroying it. Of course, visits end with the chance to buy a few trinkets.

The riverfront

The Rio Grande has shifted its course in the past three hundred years, so there's an unexpectedly low-key gap **west** of Old Town, much of it left undeveloped in deference to the unruly river. That allows space on the wooded eastern riverbank for a couple of welcome natural attractions – the **ABQ BioPark**, which is home to an aquarium and botanical gardens, and, further north, the **Rio Grande Nature Center**.

ABQ BioPark

June–Aug Mon–Fri 9am–5pm, Sat & Sun 9am–6pm; Sept–May daily 9am–5pm • $12.50 • ☎ 505 768 2000, ⓦ cabq.gov /culturalservices/biopark

In the **ABQ BioPark**, immediately north of the bridge where Central Avenue crosses the river, the **Albuquerque Aquarium** offers such diverse experiences as eating in a

3

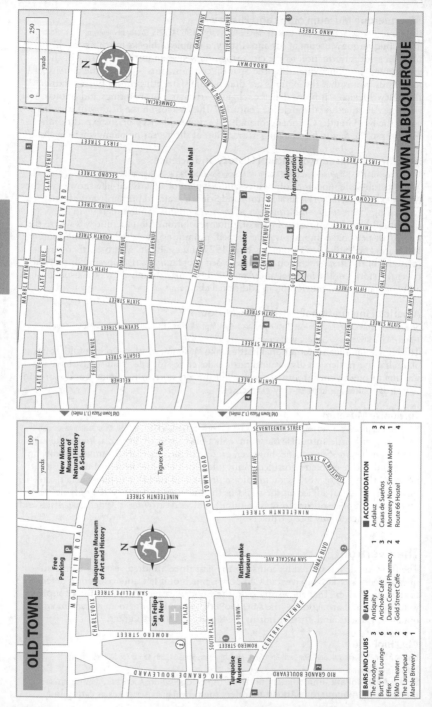

DOWNTOWN ALBUQUERQUE

Galeria Mall

Alvarado Transportation Center

KiMo Theater

CENTRAL AVENUE (ROUTE 66)

OLD TOWN

New Mexico Museum of Natural History & Science

Tiguex Park

Free Parking

Albuquerque Museum of Art and History

San Felipe de Neri

Rattlesnake Museum

Turquoise Museum

■ BARS AND CLUBS

The Anodyne	3
Burt's Tiki Lounge	6
Effex	5
KiMo Theater	4
The Launchpad	4
Marble Brewery	1

● EATING

Antiquity	1
Artichoke Café	6
Duran Central Pharmacy	2
Gold Street Caffe	4

■ ACCOMMODATION

Andaluz	3
Casas de Sueños	3
Monterey Non-Smokers Motel	2
Route 66 Hostel	4

restaurant beside a glass-walled tank filled with live sharks, and walking through a tunnel surrounded on all sides by fierce-eyed moray eels. The whole place has been designed with a great eye for aesthetics, with lots of sculpture outside and beautifully lit tanks filled with ethereal, wispy jellyfish within.

Across the park's central plaza, the **Botanic Garden** consists of two large conservatories – one holding rare plants from the Sonoran and Chihuahua deserts, the other more temperate Mediterranean species – plus a series of formal walled gardens. The river itself is not visible from either section.

Rio Grande Nature Center
2901 Candelaria Ave NW • Daily 8am–5pm • $3 per vehicle • ☎ 505 344 7240, ⓦ rgnc.org

Two miles north of Old Town, by way of Rio Grande Boulevard, the 270-acre **Rio Grande Nature Center** has informative displays describing local wildlife. Two short but pleasant nature trails, each around a mile long, follow the riverside, feeling far removed from the city.

The rest of the city

Downtown Albuquerque may be where New Mexico's largest city conducts its daily business, but it holds little that's likely to detain tourists for long; unless you're staying in a hotel nearby, you may bypass it altogether.

A couple of miles east of downtown, the campus of the **University of New Mexico** stretches along the northern side of Central Avenue. The 25,000-strong student body keeps the southern side of the highway lively around the clock with funky hangouts of all kinds, from bookstores and laundromats to cafés and diners.

Indian Pueblo Cultural Center
2401 12th St NW • **Museum** Daily 9am–5pm • $6 **Gift store** Daily 9am–5.30pm • Free • ☎ 505 843 7270, ⓦ indianpueblo.org

The **Indian Pueblo Cultural Center**, north of I-40 a few blocks north of Old Town, is a highly informative **museum** and **giftstore** that's collectively run by the nineteen New Mexican pueblos. Its horseshoe-shaped design deliberately echoes the architecture of the Ancestral Puebloan city of Pueblo Bonito, in Chaco Canyon.

This is New Mexico's one major museum about Native Americans to be curated by Native Americans, and the displays in the two basement-level galleries have a clear and distinct point of view. The shared heritage at the root of Pueblo culture is explained in detail, as is the impact of the Spanish conquistadors. Describing the Pueblo Revolt of 1680 as the "first civil war," it states that by allowing the defeated Spaniards to leave unharmed, the Pueblo peoples "showed them more mercy than they showed us." There's also as good an explanation as you're ever likely to get of a topic Pueblo Indians rarely discuss with outsiders: how indigenous Pueblo religion has managed to coexist with imported Catholicism. Films illustrate modern Pueblo life, while a separate display case is devoted to each individual Pueblo.

An outstanding selection of pottery and jewellery is sold in the larger shopping area upstairs, which you can visit without paying the museum admission fee. A separate **art gallery** hosts changing exhibitions of Native American art. The good-quality *Pueblo Harvest Café* on site is reviewed on p.174. On weekends throughout the year, **Pueblo dances** take place in the central courtyard, with additional performances at 2pm on Thursdays and Fridays between June and August.

The National Hispanic Cultural Center
1701 Fourth St • Daily except Mon 10am–5pm • $3 • ☎ 505 246 2261, ⓦ nhccnm.org

Whether you choose to visit the impressive **National Hispanic Cultural Center**, a mile south of Old Town, is likely to depend on what's on in its spacious **art gallery**. Stimulating temporary exhibitions complement permanent displays that focus on

"Hispanidad," with lots of New Mexican religious iconography. A good **café**, *La Fonda del Basque*, serves breakfast and lunch daily. The local Barelas neighbourhood traditionally marked the point where the Camino Real trail from Mexico entered Albuquerque.

Maxwell Museum of Anthropology

Tues–Sat 10am–4pm • Free • ☎ 505 277 4405, ⓦ unm.edu/~maxwell

Of the six museums on the campus of the University of New Mexico, non-academic visitors are most likely to enjoy the **Maxwell Museum of Anthropology**, which documents the peoples of the Southwest, past and present. There's some fine Mimbres pottery (see p.198), as well as material from Chaco Canyon, while the Ancestors segment traces human evolution from the three-million-year-old Lucy, just 3ft 7in tall, unearthed in Ethiopia in 1974.

National Museum of Nuclear Science and History

601 Eubank Blvd SE • Daily 9am–5pm • $8 • ☎ 505 245 2137, ⓦ nuclearmuseum.org

The **National Museum of Nuclear Science and History** has since 2009 occupied a new home immediately outside Kirtland Air Force Base; as the National Atomic Museum, it used to stand within the base, until the threat of terrorism rendered that location inappropriate. Displays range from the early discoveries of Madame Curie, via newspaper advertisements promoting the health-giving properties of drinking the Radithor brand of radioactive water, to a 1953 *Life* magazine cover reading "we are in a life and death bomb race." You'll be soothed to learn how much more precise and sophisticated today's weapons are compared with the "primitive city-busting concepts" of the Cold War era, just how safe nuclear waste disposal can be, and a host of other little-known facts. A gift store sells space-age novelties.

The Sandia Mountains

Sandia Peak Tramway Summer daily 9am–9pm; winter Mon & Wed–Sun 9am–8pm, Tues 5–8pm • $20 **Ski season** Mid-Dec to mid-March; lift tickets $50 • ☎ 505 242 9052, ⓦ sandiapeak.com

The forested **Sandia Mountains** tower 10,500ft over Albuquerque to the east; views from the summit are especially beautiful at and after sunset, when the city lights sparkle below. In summer it's a good 25°F cooler up here than in the valley, while in winter you can go downhill or cross-country **skiing**.

The most exciting way to reach the top is by riding the world's longest tramway, the 2.7-mile **Sandia Peak Tramway**, which departs from the end of Tramway Road a dozen miles northeast of town. During the uppermost 1.5 miles of its exhilarating 15-minute climb, not a single support tower interrupts the progress of the cable car.

If you'd rather **drive** to the top of the mountains, you have to circle around the back on I-40, then approach from the east, by way of the Turquoise Trail (see p.128).

Petroglyph National Monument

Unser Blvd NW • Daily 8am–5pm • Mon–Fri $1 per vehicle, Sat & Sun $2 • ☎ 505 899 0205, ⓦ nps.gov/petr

Set beneath a chain of burned-out cinder cones thrown up by a 150,000-year-old volcanic eruption, a low seventeen-mile escarpment west of the Rio Grande, protected as the **PETROGLYPH NATIONAL MONUMENT**, holds some unusually accessible ancient Native American **rock art**. Other than to enjoy the spectacular views of the valley and mountains, there's no need to go to its **Las Imágenes visitor centre**, reached by crossing the river on I-40 then driving four miles north on Unser Boulevard. Instead, continue to the petroglyphs themselves, another mile north in **Boca Negra Canyon**.

Three short trails off the canyon's one-way loop road lead up to the escarpment, which on close inspection turns out to consist of tumbled black lava boulders; only the half-hour **Mesa Trail** demands any energetic climbing. Most of the crudely scratched images you'll pass, ranging from simple spirals to masked figures and eagles with Bart Simpson hairdos, date from 1300 to 1680 AD. During the eighteenth century, shepherds from the nearby Hispanic settlement of Atrisco added a number of Christian crosses and symbols.

Petroglyph National Monument has for many years been the focus of intense controversy, because city boosters see it as a major obstacle to any future westward expansion of Albuquerque. Despite opposition from the nineteen New Mexican pueblos as well as local activists, the east–west Paseo del Norte road has indeed been pushed through monument land.

Isleta Pueblo

☎ 505 869 3111, ⓦ isletapueblo.com

The only New Mexican pueblo south of Albuquerque, **ISLETA PUEBLO**, lies just off the interstate a dozen miles from downtown, to which it's also connected by the RailRunner light rail system (ⓦ nmrailrunner.com). The sole survivor of the many pueblos encountered by Spanish explorers along the lower Rio Grande, it served in the seventeenth century as a refuge where Tiwa peoples gathered to resist the threat of Apache raids. During the Pueblo Revolt, some Isletans accompanied the Spanish retreat southwards to found the pueblo of **Tigua**, outside El Paso, while others fled west to join the Hopi. Isleta itself was repopulated in 1718, and remains home to around three thousand people.

Although the tribal lands mark a verdant interruption amid the dormitory communities that line the interstate's first fifty miles, the reservation is plagued by river-borne pollution from the industries of Albuquerque. Economically, it's dependent on its huge neighbour; a high proportion of Isletans work in the city.

Every day during daylight hours, visitors have free access to the principal pueblo village – also known as **SHIAW-IBA** – where the main attraction is the white-walled **mission church** of San Agustín de Isleta. In addition, Isleta stages major festivals on August 28 and September 4, and runs a 24-hour **casino**.

ARRIVAL   ALBUQUERQUE AND AROUND

By plane Albuquerque's International Sunport, four miles southeast of downtown, is served by all major US airlines. All the national rental car chains have outlets, while a taxi into town with Albuquerque Cab (☎ 505 883 4888, ⓦ albuquerquecab.com) costs $15 and up. Sunport Shuttle (☎ 505 883 4966, ⓦ sunportshuttle.com) runs door-to-door shuttles at similar rates. Many hotels and motels also run free shuttles. Buses also connect the airport with the Rail Runner network, Mon–Sat only (see below).

By train One daily train in each direction on Amtrak's Los Angeles–Chicago Southwest Chief service calls at the Alvarado Transportation Center, at First and Central.

By bus Long-distance Greyhound buses use the Alvarado Transportation Center.

INFORMATION, GETTING AROUND AND TOURS

Tourist information 303 Romero St NW, in the Plaza Don Luis in the Old Town (daily: April–Oct 10am–6pm, Nov–March 9.30am–4.30pm; ☎ 505 842 9118, ⓦ itsatrip .org), and at the airport (Mon–Fri 9.30am–8pm, Sat 9.30am–4pm).

By train Albuquerque has its own light-rail system, Rail Runner (fares from $2; ☎ 866 795 7245, ⓦ nmrailrunner .com). Commuter trains from its Downtown Albuquerque station, in the Alvarado Transportation Center at First and Central on the eastern edge of downtown, run south to Belen and north to Bernalillo, but the main appeal for tourists is that services also continue all the way north to Santa Fe (see p.118). Connecting buses from the airport run to both the Downtown station and the first Rail Runner stop south of downtown, the Bernalillo County station at 113 Rio Bravo SE, Mon–Sat only.

By bus The Alvarado Transportation Center is also the hub of the ABQ Ride city bus network (☎ 505 843 9200, ⓦ cabq.gov/transit). Its free D-Ride route circles downtown, while commuter buses further afield cost $1 a ride.

Walking tours The Museum of Art and History, 2000 Mountain Rd, organizes walking tours of Albuquerque's historic Old Town (mid-March to mid-Dec, Tues–Sun 11am; ☎ 505 743 7255, ⓦ cabq.gov/museum).

ACCOMMODATION

The twenty-mile length of **Central Avenue**, the old Route 66, is lined with the flashing neon signs of $50-per-night **motels**. Try to have a good look in daylight, to spot those that may turn scary at night. You'll have to pay a little extra to stay in the heart of **Old Town** – which holds few accommodation options – or downtown. Larger convention **hotels** are congregated along the interstates and near the airport – look out for discount coupons in New Mexico's welcome centres – while **B&Bs** are scattered across the city.

Adobe Nido 1124 Major Ave NW ☎ 505 344 1310, ⓦ adobenido.com. Garden-set adobe B&B, a mile north of I-40 beyond the Indian Pueblo Cultural Center, with three attractively furnished double rooms. All have private bathrooms with jetted tubs, and as well as the patio there's an outdoor sauna. The welcoming owners serve a great breakfast. $129

Ambassador Inn 7407 Central Ave NE ☎ 505 265 1161, ⓦ reservation.magnusonhotels.com. There's nothing fancy or exciting about the *Ambassador*, and it's well to the east of the liveliest part of Central Ave, but for a clean, presentable, ordinary motel room, the price is great. $43

Andaluz 125 Second St NW ☎ 505 242 9090 or ☎ 877 987 9090, ⓦ hotelandaluz.com. As *La Posada de Albuquerque*, this historic, elegant hotel, built in Mexican style by Conrad Hilton in 1939, has long been downtown's most appealing upscale option. It has now been exquisitely revamped to the latest eco-conscious standards, while retaining its beautiful wood-panelled lobby, top-class restaurant and cosy bar. $159

Casas de Sueños 310 Rio Grande Blvd SW ☎ 505 247 4560 or ☎ 800 665 7002, ⓦ casasdesuenos.com. Beautifully furnished, exotic and friendly B&B, very close to

Old Town, with themed adobe *casitas* (cottages) and smaller rooms of varying degrees of luxury – some have kitchenettes and whirlpool baths. Rooms $129, hot-tub suites $159

La Quinta Inn Albuquerque Airport 2116 Yale Blvd SE ☎ 505 243 5500 or ☎ 800 531 5900, ⓦ lq.com. Large, relatively upscale motel, served by frequent shuttles from the nearby airport, and offering accommodation that's far from memorable but safe, good-value and quiet; rates include breakfast. $75

★ **Monterey Non-Smokers Motel** 2402 Central Ave SW ☎ 505 243 3554 or ☎ 877 666 8379, ⓦ nonsmokersmotel.com. Clean, fifteen-room motel, two blocks west of Old Town, run by a friendly Polish couple, and offering a pool and laundry, as well of course as a strict nonsmoking policy. $72

Route 66 Hostel 1012 Central Ave SW ☎ 505 247 1813, ⓦ www.rt66hostel.com. Albuquerque's only hostel, a friendly place in what was once a private house, between Old Town and downtown, offers dorm beds and very plain but bargain-priced private doubles, plus kitchen facilities and abundant books and board games. Office hours daily 7.30–10.30am & 4–11pm. Dorm $20, shared-bath double $30, en-suite double $35

EATING

The chefs of Santa Fe may be trying to redefine Southwestern cuisine, but Albuquerque still knows what it likes – mountainous **Mexican** meals. This is the place to come to grips with what real New Mexican food is all about, with family diners all over the city competing to create the spiciest *chile rellenos*, enchiladas, and *sopaipillas*. If you don't mind driving a few miles out of town, fine dining options within easy reach of Albuquerque include the *Range Cafe* in Bernalillo (see p.126) and *Prairie Star* at nearby Santa Ana Pueblo (see p.135).

CAFES AND DINERS

Duran Central Pharmacy 1815 Central Ave NW ☎ 505 247 4141, ⓦ durancentralpharmacy.com. Mexican dining counter attached to a working drugstore, not far from Old Town, with delicious, inexpensive tortillas, enchiladas, and plenty of chile, both green and red. Mon–Fri 9am–6.20pm, Sat 9am–2pm.

Flying Star 3416 Central Ave SE ☎ 505 255 6633, ⓦ flyingstarcafe.com. Lively, crowded University District café serving eclectic international cuisine to a largely student clientele, who linger with coffee and smoothies over the free wifi and huge stock of magazines. The vast menu ranges through breakfast specialities, salads, and blue-plate specials such as Vietnamese noodles, mac cheese or pasta pomodoro for $10. Other branches throughout northern New Mexico. Sun–Thurs 6am–11pm, Fri & Sat 6am–midnight.

Frontier 2400 Central Ave SE ☎ 505 266 0550, ⓦ frontierrestaurant.com. Legendary diner across from the university – no longer (quite) open around the clock – where an unceasing parade of characters chow down on burgers, burritos, and great vegetarian enchiladas. As you enjoy your $7 *huevos rancheros*, see how many John Wayne portraits you can count on the walls. Daily 5am–8am.

Gold Street Caffe 218 Gold Ave SW ☎ 505 765 1633, ⓦ goldstreetcaffe.com. Having started out as an espresso café catering to busy office workers, this smart downtown space has expanded to serve lunch and dinner as well. The day still kicks off with great coffee, wonderful pastries, and full breakfasts, but now you can get a steak or Mexican meal later on. Mon & Sun 7am–4pm, Tues–Sat 7am–9pm.

The Grove Cafe & Market 600 Central Ave SE ☎ 505 248 9800, ⓦ thegrovecafemarket.com. With its emphasis on fresh organic ingredients, this lively Route 66 café makes a great spot for breakfast, lunch or a bit of both – locals flock here for Sunday brunch. Poached eggs with ham and fresh fruit costs $9, a lunchtime salad or sandwich, such as roasted turkey with havarti cheese, around $10. Tues–Sat 7am–4pm, Sun 8am–3pm.

Pueblo Harvest Cafe Indian Pueblo Cultural Center, 2401 12th St NW ☎ 505 843 7270, ⓦ indianpueblo.org. While still serving Pueblo specialities like Indian fry bread at lunchtime, this unusual Native American restaurant is also open both for breakfast (try the $10 cornmeal pancakes) and for fine dining in the evening, when braised bison ribs are among its good $20–30 entrees. Mon–Thurs 8am–8.30pm, Fri & Sat 8am–9pm, Sun 8am–4pm.

Sadie's 6230 Fourth St NW ☎ 505 345 5339, ⓦ sadiesofnewmexico.com. Huge, great-value Mexican restaurant – the stuffed *sopaipillas* are irresistible, as indeed are the margaritas. Giant TV screens ensure it's too bright and loud to be romantic, but it's a good place to bring kids. Mon–Thurs 11am–10pm, Fri & Sat 10am–10.30pm, Sun 10am–10pm.

Satellite Coffee 3513 Central Ave NE ☎ 505 256 0345, ⓦ satellitecoffee.com. This University District coffee bar, marked by the sign of the flying saucer, also serves daily specials like split pea soup. It's proved so popular with locals, and students in particular, that it now has branches all over the city. Daily 6am–8pm.

66 Diner 1405 Central Ave NE ☎ 505 247 1421, ⓦ 66diner.com. Classic Fifties diner near the university, with white-capped waiting staff, a soda fountain, and a lively late-night clientele. Mon–Fri 11am–11pm, Sat 8am–11pm, Sun 8am–10pm.

FINE DINING

Antiquity 112 Romero St NW ☎ 505 247 3545, ⓦ antiquityrestaurant.com. Old Town cottage turned dinner-only romantic restaurant. The menu consists largely of French cuisine, some of which is given a New Mexican twist by a leavening of chile. Typical meat and seafood entrees cost $21–33. Mon–Thurs 5–9pm, Fri & Sat 5–10pm.

Artichoke Café 424 Central Ave SE ☎ 505 243 0200, ⓦ artichokecafe.com. Simple but classy restaurant in the heart of downtown, serving a good, varied menu of California-influenced modern American cuisine; typical entrees cost $12–15 at lunch, $20–30 for dinner. Mon–Fri 11am–2.30pm & 5.30–10pm, Sat 5.30–10pm, Sun 5–9pm.

Scalo 3500 Central Ave SE ☎ 505 255 8781, ⓦ scalonobhill.com. Large but romantic and stylish Northern Italian restaurant near the university. Appetizers like steamed mussels or beef carpaccio cost $12–15, entrees such as roasted salmon are more like $27, and there are plenty of pasta and vegetarian options. Mon–Thurs 11am–2.30pm & 5–10pm, Fri & Sat 11am–2.30pm & 5–11pm, Sun 11am–2.30pm & 5–9pm.

DRINKING AND NIGHTLIFE

Many of downtown Albuquerque's **bars** and **nightclubs** have long doubled as small theatres or music venues. The free weekly *Alibi* magazine (ⓦ alibi.com) carries full listings of what's coming up or going down.

The Anodyne 409 Central Ave NW ☎ 505 244 1820, ⓦ theanodyne.com. Downtown's most popular bar, tucked away upstairs, offers pool tables, pinball, a good jukebox, and an eclectic mix of customers, from beer guzzlers to martini sippers. Mon–Fri 4pm–1.30am, Sat 7pm–1.30am, Sun 7–11.30pm.

Burt's Tiki Lounge 313 Gold Ave SW ☎ 505 247 2878, ⓦ burtstikilounge.com. Thursday night, the Freaky Tiki Bass dance party, is the big night at this tiki-bar cocktail-lounge, though the Polynesian-cum-pirate decor makes a good backdrop for live bands every weekend. Wed–Sat 8.30pm–2am.

Caravan East 7605 Central Ave NE ☎ 505 265 7877, ⓦ caravaneast.com. Enormous honky-tonk, where tenderfeet can do the two-step with throngs of urban cowboys, and the live music includes plenty of mariachi and conjunto as well as country. Tues, Fri & Sat 5pm–2am, Sun 6pm–midnight.

Effex 420 Central Ave SW ☎ 505 842 8870, ⓦ effexabq .com. Huge, multi-storey and very central gay club, across the street from the landmark KiMo Theater, with masses of room for shirtless posing as well as dancing. Tues–Sat 7pm–2am.

KiMo Theater 423 Central Ave NW ☎ 505 768 3544, ⓦ cabq.gov/kimo. Gorgeous, city-owned "Pueblo Deco" theatre, dating from the late 1920s, which puts on an eclectic programme of opera, dance and theatre performances, kids' movies, and everything from burlesque to Beethoven, as well as regular live bands.

The Launchpad 618 Central Ave SW ☎ 505 764 8887, ⓦ launchpadrocks.com. Dance and live music space that showcases touring indie and world music bands; besides the fabulous space-age decor, there's also a cluster of pool tables.

Marble Brewery 111 Marble NW ☎ 505 243 2739, ⓦ marblebrewery.com. Bustling brewpub, just north of downtown, where you can see the giant vats in the brewery itself behind the bar. There's no kitchen, but takeout food trucks park outside, and the (summer-only) outdoor patio makes a good place to eat. Mon–Sat 1pm–midnight, Sun 1–10.30pm.

East of Albuquerque

The first twenty miles of I-40's eastward run from Albuquerque are scenic, as the interstate threads between the Sandia Mountains. Once through the hills, however, if you don't turn north onto the **Turquoise Trail** toward Santa Fe (see p.128), you're in for a long hard slog out into the plains. The only place before Texas that might pique your curiosity is **Fort Sumner**, which played a heart-rending role in Navajo history and also holds the grave of **Billy the Kid**.

Santa Rosa

A hundred unutterably boring miles east of the Sandia Mountains, weary drivers reach their first potential overnight stop. South and west of the interstate, a four-mile stretch of the former Route 66 runs through **SANTA ROSA**. Named **Parker Avenue** in the small downtown, and **Will Rogers Drive** further east, it's dotted with diners and motels, but there's little to see, apart perhaps from the restored classic cars at the **Route 66 Auto Museum**, 2866 Route 66 (daily: April–Oct Mon–Sat 7.30am–6pm, Sun 10am–5pm; Sept–April Mon–Sat 8am–5pm, Sun 10am–5pm; $5; ⓦroute66 automuseum.com). Thanks to the bright yellow car atop a pole outside, you won't have any difficulty finding it.

The Blue Hole

Scuba-divers desperate for a dip cross the plains to plunge into Santa Rosa's **Blue Hole**, a crystal-clear natural pool that's sixty feet across and eighty feet deep, though to anyone who's seen the ocean it may come as an anti-climax. You'll find it by turning left off Fifth Street, south of the main drag, and driving half a mile on Blue Hole Road. An onsite dive centre provides tank rentals.

Tucumcari

Sixty miles east of Santa Rosa, **TUCUMCARI** is the definitive Route 66 pit-stop. Known at this point as Tucumcari Boulevard, Route 66 cuts a broad five-mile swath through town. If you expect its abundant truck stops, diners and motels to yield a kitsch fascination, you'll be sorely disappointed, but their glittering neon signs make a welcome sight as dusk descends on the plains.

No one in their right mind stays two nights in Tucumcari; an hour spent admiring the barbed-wire collection of the **Tucumcari Historical Museum**, in a former schoolhouse at 416 S Adams St (Tues–Sat 9am–3pm; $5; ☎505 461 4201), should convince you it's time to hit the road again.

INFORMATION   **TUCUMCARI**

Visitor centre 404 W Route 66 (Mon–Fri 9am–5pm; ☎575 461 1694, ⓦtucumcarinm.com).

ACCOMMODATION AND EATING

★ **Blue Swallow** 815 E Route 66 ☎575 461 9849, ⓦblueswallowmotel.com. Everyone loves the *Blue Swallow*, a classic, beautifully restored Route 66 motel where the appealing retro-furnished rooms are bursting with memorabilia. **$65**

Del's Family Restaurant 1202 E Route 66 ☎575 461 1740, ⓦdelsrestaurant.com. While dining choices in Tucumcari may be plentiful, they're also limited – this is as good a diner as you're going to find, serving New Mexican

specialities like sopaipillas as well as inexpensive chicken and steak dinners. Mon–Sat 11am–9pm.

Historic Route 66 Motel 1620 E Route 66 ☎575 461 1212, ⓦrte66motel.com. As well as simple clean rooms at great prices, this impeccably maintained old-fashioned motor court also offers the very friendly little early-morning *Circa Espresso Bar*, which serves excellent coffee and smoothies and also has wi-fi. **$37**

Fort Sumner

A 45-mile detour south of I-40 near Santa Rosa brings you to modern **FORT SUMNER**, a small town named after a nineteenth-century Army outpost that stood seven miles southeast, on what's now **Fort Sumner State Monument**.

Fort Sumner State Monument

3647 Billy the Kid Rd • Daily 8.30am–5pm • $5 • ⓦ nmmonuments.org

The fort was infamous as the headquarters of the **Bosque Redondo Indian reservation**, where nine thousand Navajo and Mescalero Apache captives were incarcerated during the 1860s after being rounded up by General James Carleton and Kit Carson and forced here on the Long Walk (see p.481). The idea was for the reservation to be self-sufficient and for the Indians to become accustomed to an agricultural lifestyle. In fact, the Pecos River proved too salty to drink, let alone use for irrigation. In the words of Navajo headman Barboncito:

Whatever we do here causes death. Some work at the acequias, take sick, and die; others die with the hoe in their hands; they go to the river to their waists and suddenly disappear; others have been struck and torn to pieces by lightning. A rattlesnake bite here kills us; in our country a rattlesnake before he bites gives warning which enables us to keep out of its way and if bitten, we readily find a cure – here we can find no cure.

The Mescalero escaped in November 1865, only to be chased by Carson and suffer further slaughter. The Navajo remained until General William T. Sherman arrived to replace Carleton on May 28, 1868; the treaty that allowed them to return home was signed on June 1. Over three thousand prisoners had died.

Only a low ridge of adobe bricks on the eastern riverbank remains of the fort the Navajo built for their captors, but the dead are honoured by a large visitor centre-cum-museum. The **Bosque Redondo Memorial** details the whole sorry story, including photos of soldiers guarding large groups of Native American captives.

Old Fort Sumner Museum

3501 Billy The Kid Rd • Daily 9am–5pm • $5 • ☎ 575 355 2942

After the Bosque Redondo reservation closed, rancher Lucien Maxwell bought Fort Sumner and the surrounding land. **Billy the Kid** was hiding in his son Peter's bedroom here in 1881 when **Pat Garrett** tracked him down and shot him dead (see p.180). His **grave** is located in the backyard of the **Old Fort Sumner Museum**, a few hundred yards east of the fort. Billy was buried alongside two fellow outlaws, Tom O'Folliard and Charlie Bowdre; all remain imprisoned to this day, as their joint tombstone, poignantly inscribed "*PALS*," is protected from would-be thieves behind steel bars. Originally erected by film director King Vidor, the tombstone was stolen so often that participants in an annual festival, held on the second weekend of June, now compete to "steal" an eighty-pound replica, and then throw it as far as possible.

The museum itself holds jumbled items that may or may not have belonged to Billy, plus displays relating to local history.

Billy the Kid Museum

1601 E Sumner Ave • Mid-May to Sept daily 8.30am–5pm; Oct to mid-May Mon–Sat 8.30am–5pm • $5 • ☎ 575 355 2380, ⓦ billythekidmuseumfortsumner.com

While the **Billy the Kid Museum**, in the town of Fort Sumner, has no immediate connection with the life of the Kid himself, it's a vast and entertaining treasurehouse of Wild West relics that purportedly include his rifle, his spurs and even some of his hair. Endless warehouses stretch back from the highway, filled with old cars, wagons, typewriters and other rusty hardware.

Southeast of Albuquerque

Although the Rio Grande Valley, south of Albuquerque – and covered on p.190 onwards – has always held a larger human population, the terrain **southeast** of the city offers greater scenic and historic appeal. Here you'll find the ancient pueblos of **Salinas National Monument**, the eerie gypsum wastelands of **White Sands**, and the mountain resorts of **Ruidoso** and **Cloudcroft**. Most compelling of all, however, is the rough-hewn frontier town of **Lincoln**. Scene of the bloodiest exploits in the career of **Billy the Kid**, it has remained all but untouched since his death.

Salinas National Monument

Each section Daily: summer 9am–6pm; winter 9am–5pm • Free • **Visitor centre** On US-60 in Mountainair, 36 miles east of I-25 • Daily 8am–5pm • Free • ☎ 575 847 2585, ⓦ nps.gov/sapu

Early Spanish colonists ranked the precious salt deposits of **Salinas Valley**, east of the Manzano Mountains seventy miles southeast of Albuquerque, among New Mexico's greatest treasures. Franciscan missionaries targeted the Pueblo peoples of the valley, erecting massive churches atop their existing settlements, but due to epidemics and Apache raids, the entire region had been abandoned before the Pueblo Revolt of 1680. Three separate ruined pueblos now form **SALINAS NATIONAL MONUMENT**. Each has its own "contact station", and they share a **visitor centre** in little **MOUNTAINAIR**.

Only at the largest and most interesting Salinas pueblo, **Gran Quivira**, on a low hill 26 miles south from Mountainair along Hwy-55, has the pueblo itself been more than minimally excavated. That process has revealed an impressive 300-room structure complete with hidden *kivas*, built in secret to avoid the wrath of the Spanish priests. The adjoining Mission of San Buenaventura church probably remained incomplete when the pueblo was abandoned. Juan de Oñate, who visited Gran Quivira in 1598, reported that its inhabitants painted stripes on their noses.

The main feature of **Quarai**, a mile west of Hwy-55 eight miles north of Mountainair, is the fortress-like stone church of La Purísima Concepción, whose golden walls tower above the rubble-strewn mounds that conceal the pueblo village. At **Abó**, just north of US-60 nine miles west of Mountainair, the church of San Gregorio dominates an even more tantalizing expanse of ruins.

Carrizozo

Fifty miles southeast of Gran Quivira, where US-54 meets US-380, the parched desert outpost of **CARRIZOZO** replaced better-known Lincoln as the seat of Lincoln County in 1909. Other than a potential halt on a long drive, and the **Valley of Fires Recreation Area** nearby, there's nothing much to it.

Valley of Fires Recreation Area

US-380, 4 miles northwest of Carrizozo • Daily dawn–dusk • $5 per vehicle • ☎ 575 648 2241, ⓦ blm.gov

The **Valley of Fires Recreation Area** preserves a jet-black river of lava that poured for over forty miles down the Tularosa Valley five thousand years ago. Though it ranges from four to six miles wide and up to 150 feet deep, the one trail across the lava is less than a mile long. It's so rough underfoot, and so exposed to the sun, that you're unlikely to want to hike any further, but there's a good **campground** alongside ($12). At its southern end, the lava flow abuts the utterly contrasting White Sands National Monument; see p.184.

Capitan

A twenty-mile drive up into the mountains east of Carrizozo brings you to the crossroads known as **CAPITAN**, notable only as the birthplace of a little bear named

Smokey. Rescued from a forest fire in 1950, the five-month-old Smokey was taken to the National Zoo in Washington DC, where he survived another 26 years and became a national fire prevention symbol. His words of wisdom, seen on anti-fire billboards across the country – "Only YOU Can Prevent Forest Fires" – live on. Smokey's grave is the centrepiece of **Smokey Bear Historical State Park**, which also features exhibits on his life and a short nature trail (daily 9am–5pm; $2; ⓦsmokeybearpark.com).

Capitan is plagued, incidentally, by a running feud between people who say "Smokey Bear" (good) and wilful misfits who insist on "Smokey *the* Bear" (bad).

ACCOMMODATION	**CAPITAN**
Smokey Bear Motel 316 Smokey Bear Blvd ☎ 575 354 2253 or ☎ 800 766 5392, ⓦ smokeybearmotel .com. Transformed and upgraded by new management,	this simple but appealing motel offers cabin-style rooms near the park. **$60**

Lincoln

3

Lincoln State Monument Each site $3.50, joint admission to all sites $5; not all sites remain open throughout the winter • ☎ 575 653 4372, ⓦ nmmonuments.org

Though not strictly speaking a ghost town, tiny **LINCOLN**, twelve miles east of Capitan on Hwy-380, is a perfectly preserved Wild West settlement. During the late nineteenth century, around 750 people made their home in this cattle-ranching centre and Army outpost of **Fort Stanton**, including the legendary outlaw Billy the Kid. Bypassed by the railroads, however, it soon dwindled, and time seems to have stood still ever since. No new buildings have joined the venerable false-front structures that line Main Street, and the entire town is now **Lincoln State Monument**. Visitors can stroll its length at any time, while the cheapest way to visit its various historical sites is via a joint admission ticket, sold at each.

During the first weekend of August, the streets of Lincoln echo with gunfire once again during the three-day **Old Lincoln Days** festival, which features living history demonstrations, fiddle competitions and the like.

Historic Lincoln Visitors Center

Daily 8.30am–5pm

The **Historic Lincoln Visitors Center**, at the east end of town, offers the fullest displays on local history, and its short opening movie makes a good introduction to Lincoln's complicated story. After exhibits covering Hispanics, cowboys, "Buffalo Soldiers" – the black cavalrymen stationed at Fort Stanton – and Apache, the museum moves on to the Lincoln County War. Its account of Billy's life is extremely thorough, extending to the coroner's handwritten report on the men shot during his April 1881 escape; however, none of the artefacts definitely belonged to Billy himself.

Lincoln's oldest building, the **Torréon**, stands alongside. While resembling the masonry of Ancestral Puebloans, this circular tower was erected by Hispanic settlers during the 1850s, as a refuge against Apache raids. It's too small to admit visitors; a glance from the street makes it easy to imagine quite how cramped it must have been and speaks volumes about the miserable, unglamorous reality of frontier life.

Tunstall Store

March–Nov daily 9am–5pm

The **Tunstall Store**, a few yards west of the Historic Lincoln Visitors Center, is an extraordinary time capsule. The "mercantile" over which the Lincoln County War was fought must have failed to sell a single item in the ensuing century. It remains stocked with dusty date-expired groceries, plus Victorian paraphernalia like weighing scales and cash registers, cases of photos and artefacts, and even Lincoln County's first-ever light bulb, installed in 1914 and allegedly still capable of burning. The wounded Billy the

BILLY THE KID AND THE LINCOLN COUNTY WAR

The Hispanic farming community of Las Placitas del Río Bonito, founded during the 1850s, was renamed **Lincoln** in 1869. It became the seat of **Lincoln County**, which at 27,000 square miles was the largest county in the United States, occupying a quarter of New Mexico. Rival Anglo ranchers and their political allies were then competing for economic control throughout the Wild West. The **Western Civil War of Incorporation** pitted large cattle-raising conglomerates, federal lawmen and Republican capitalists against small-scale Democrat ranchers and cowboys. Such tensions were everywhere exacerbated by individual antagonisms; Tombstone's **Gunfight at the OK Corral** is a classic example (see p.238).

The "ring" of men who dominated Lincoln in the 1870s centred on the mercantile, or store, of **Lawrence G. Murphy**, an Irish former theology student, Freemason and alcoholic whose business affairs were run by **James J. Dolan**. Their racketeering included rustling cattle from rancher **John Chisum** to supply beef at knock-down prices to the US Army at nearby Fort Stanton. The arrival of a wealthy 23-year-old Englishman, **John Tunstall**, who opened a rival mercantile in Lincoln with lawyer **Alexander McSween**, triggered the **Lincoln County War**.

On February 18, 1878, Tunstall was murdered on the road to Ruidoso by a posse of Dolan's men. Among Tunstall's hired hands who witnessed the slaying was the gunslinger **Billy the Kid**. Born Henry McCarty in Brooklyn in 1859, Billy had been brought west by his mother, who married William Antrim in Santa Fe in 1873. Within a year she had died in Silver City, and young Billy Antrim was cast adrift. A life of petty teenage crime culminated with the shooting in 1877 of a bullying Irish blacksmith in Fort Grant, Arizona. As **Billy Bonney**, the fledgling outlaw fled to Lincoln.

After Tunstall's death, his men formed the **Regulators** and were deputized by the local justice of the peace to seek out his killers. Ten of them, including Billy, killed the two chief culprits in March, then gunned down **Sheriff William Brady**, a Dolan man, on Lincoln's main street on April 1. That July, forty of Dolan's supporters laid siege to the Regulators in the adobe home of Alexander McSween; after five days, they summoned soldiers from Fort Stanton, who trained a Gatling gun on the house and set it ablaze. McSween and three Regulators were killed trying to escape, but Billy and ten others sprinted to safety.

Billy spent two years on the run, mostly rustling cattle near Fort Sumner, where he also dealt cards in the saloon of Texan buffalo hunter **Pat Garrett**. In 1880, New Mexico's governor **Lew Wallace** offered an amnesty to all participants in the Lincoln County War who would testify against Dolan. Billy accepted the deal and surrendered, only to escape when he realized that Wallace – then busy writing *Ben Hur* – was not going to keep his word. Later that year, Garrett was elected as sheriff of Lincoln County, on a pledge to recapture Billy (who naturally lobbied for his opponent). Garrett knew exactly where to look. Just before Christmas, after ambushing and killing two of Billy's friends at Fort Sumner, he duly captured Billy himself at nearby Stinking Springs. Reporting his arrest, the *Las Vegas Gazette* made the first-ever reference to "Billy the Kid."

Billy was taken by train to Santa Fe and on to **Mesilla**, where he was convicted of Sheriff Brady's murder. As he awaited the hangman's noose in Lincoln's courthouse – the former Murphy store, its owner James Dolan having by now taken over the Tunstall mercantile down the street – Billy pulled off his most daring **escape**. Taking advantage of a trip to the outhouse, on April 28, 1881, he shot Deputy J.W. Bell with his own gun. Meanwhile, Marshal Bob Olinger, a long-time Dolan ally, was having lunch with prisoners in the *Wortley Hotel*. Hearing the shots, he raced across the street, to be felled by a blast from an upper window. Billy then struggled unsuccessfully for an hour to break his shackles, repeatedly falling off the horse he was attempting to commandeer, watched all the while by a crowd who dared not intervene.

With a **$500 reward** on his head, Billy fled back to Fort Sumner. Late on the night of July 14, Garrett crept into the bedroom of rancher **Pete Maxwell**, whose family owned Fort Sumner, to ask if he had seen his friend Billy. Moments earlier, Billy had climbed through the window to find out if Maxwell knew Garrett's whereabouts. Garrett recognized the voice that called "*quien es?*" (who's there?), and shot Billy dead.

The next year, Garrett wrote a bestseller, *The Authentic Life of Billy The Kid, the Noted Desperado of the Southwest*. He was not re-elected as sheriff, however, and embarked on a life of wandering that saw him ranching in Texas, a guest of Theodore Roosevelt at the White House, and a customs collector in El Paso, before he was eventually murdered for no apparent reason near Las Cruces in 1908.

Kid hid beneath the floorboards after shooting Sheriff William Brady on the street outside, on April 1, 1878.

Lincoln County Courthouse

Daily 8.30am–5pm

L.G. Murphy's original store, across the road and a hundred yards west from the Tunstall Store, became the **Lincoln County Courthouse** after James J. Dolan took over Tunstall's operation. It served as Billy's prison when he was brought back from Mesilla to be hanged. Billy felt he was being railroaded; his increasingly bitter letters to Governor Lew Wallace are displayed upstairs in the courtroom where his cell formerly stood. A bullethole at the foot of the stairs shows where he shot Deputy Bell during his famous escape. You can stand at the window through which he then shot Marshal Olinger. Stones in the garden mark where the two men died. That the courthouse is now so old and musty only adds to the atmosphere of it all.

ACCOMMODATION AND EATING   LINCOLN

Wortley Hotel US-380 ☎ 575 653 4300, ⓦ wortley hotel.com. Once owned by Pat Garrett, this old-style roadside hotel, across from the courthouse, offers seven plain but appealing rooms, furnished with functional Victorian antiques. Its dining room serves breakfast and lunch daily, Wed–Sun only; the simple stews and sandwiches include the pot roast and mashed potatoes that constituted Marshal Bob Olinger's final meal. April to mid-Oct only. $95

Ruidoso

For visitors from the flatlands of west Texas and Oklahoma – not to mention valley towns like Alamogordo – the hilltop community of **RUIDOSO**, nestling almost 7000 feet up in the forested Sacramento Mountains thirty miles southwest of Lincoln, offers an enticing retreat from the heat of summer. As a result, motels and mountain lodges line several miles of the Ruidoso ("Noisy") River. Tourists from further afield, however, may well feel it lacks interest, though it makes a reasonable overnight stop en route to Carlsbad.

In winter, attention turns to the 12,000ft slopes of **Ski Apache**, a downhill ski area northwest of town (lift tickets $52; ☎ 575 464 3600, ⓦ skiapache.com). Though operated by the Mescalero Apache, it's not on tribal land.

Hubbard Museum of the American West

26301 US-70 • Daily 10am–4.30pm • $6 • ☎ 575 378 4142, ⓦ hubbardmuseum.org

Outside the **Hubbard Museum of the American West**, alongside the Ruidoso Downs racetrack, stands a sculpture ensemble of eight lifesize galloping horses, *Free Spirits of Noisy Water*. Inside, you'll find displays on all aspects of Western history. The principal emphasis is on horses, but each year sees temporary exhibitions on various subjects.

INFORMATION   RUIDOSO

Visitor centre 720 Sudderth Ave (Mon–Sat 9am–5pm, Sun 1–4pm; ⓦ ruidoso.net).

ACCOMMODATION AND EATING

Cornerstone Bakery & Cafe 359 Sudderth Drive ☎ 575 257 1842, ⓦ cornerstonebakerycafe.com. In addition to its coffee, bread and pastries, this friendly little café, open for breakfast and lunch only, serves good cooked breakfasts, including huevos rancheros, and a great green-chile stew. Daily 7am–2pm.

Grill Caliente 2800 Sudderth Drive ☎ 575 630 0224, ⓦ grillcaliente.com. As the name suggests, this Ruidoso newcomer specializes in spicy New Mexican cuisine, with burgers smothered in chipotle or green-chile sauce, as well as tacos and salads for under $10, fiery pork chops for $18, and steaks for over $20. Tues–Sat 11am–2.30pm & 5–9pm.

Inn of the Mountain Gods Carrizo Canyon Rd ☎ 575 257 5141 or ☎ 800 545 9011, ⓦ innofthe mountaingods.com. This glitzy resort, 3 miles southwest of central Ruidoso, is, like the ski resort, owned by the Mescalero Apache, and holds a lucrative

> ## ALL-AMERICAN FUTURITY
>
> Ruidoso's major claim to fame is the **All-American Futurity**, which was, until the 1980s, the world's richest **horse race** of any kind – and with prize money totalling over $2 million, it remains the highest-paying event for quarter horses. (Quarter horses, the world's most popular breed, are so-called because they excel at quarter-mile races.) The race takes place each Labor Day at the **Ruidoso Downs** racetrack, just east of town, as the climax of a 77-day season that runs from late May to early Sept (ⓦraceruidoso.com). Also at the track, the **Billy the Kid Casino** offers year-round slot-machine gambling.

casino as well as several restaurants to suit all budgets and luxury accommodation. $100
Shadow Mountain Lodge 107 Main St ☏575 257 0132, ⓦsmlruidoso.com. Central but exceptionally peaceful property, where the main wooden lodge holds 19 very comfortable rooms encircled by a wraparound veranda, and there are also four individual cabins with whirlpool baths and private decks. Room $125, cabin $145

Mescalero Apache Indian reservation

Immediately south of Ruidoso, US-70 runs for around fifteen miles through the highlands of the **Mescalero Apache Indian reservation**. The Mescalero trace their history as a distinct Apache group back to the early eighteenth century, when they were driven from the plains by the Comanche and turned to a lifestyle split between farming and raiding Pueblo and Hispanic settlements. In 1862 Kit Carson rounded up five hundred Apache to be confined with the Navajo at Bosque Redondo (see p.176). The Apache were eventually granted this small reservation in 1873, which was too high to grow or gather many traditional foods. The Mescalero were later joined by other Apache refugees, such as those remnants of Geronimo's Chiricahua who chose to return to the Southwest in 1913 from their enforced exile in Oklahoma.

Thanks to their successful investments in Ski Apache and the *Inn of the Mountain Gods*, the Mescalero's tribal economy has greatly strengthened in recent years. Tourists don't see much from the highway, and most roads leading off it are barred to outsiders. It's well worth driving through the open-range country between Ruidoso and Cloudcroft, however, where wildflowers dot the quasi-alpine meadows and Apache cowboys gallop in pursuit of their errant cattle.

Cloudcroft

Much smaller and cozier than Ruidoso, the picturesque mountain village of **CLOUDCROFT** – forty miles south, and almost two thousand feet higher – has been a vacation resort from the word go. It was built in 1898, after a railroad spur was pushed up into the Sacramento Mountains to carry timber down to El Paso, and immediately attracted day-trippers escaping the sweltering valley below. The railroad is long gone, but drivers still twist their way up US-82 from Alamogordo, leaving behind the bare sandstone hills, scattered with creosote bushes, as they penetrate the forested uplands.

Cloudcroft itself is a pretty little Western community in which to while away an afternoon. The souvenir stores and cafés that line the boardwalk of **Burro Avenue**, one block north of the highway, get a bit more kitschy each year, so **hiking** makes an enjoyable alternative to shopping. Cloudcroft stands at the heart of the southern segment of the Lincoln National Forest, which features maintained and waymarked trails of varying lengths. Starting near the west end of town, the **Cloud Climbing Rail Trail** follows the old railroad route for a mile down to a vast ruined trestle that drivers on US-82 may have already noticed. Spectacular views extend right across the valley; it's usually possible to glimpse the White Sands (see p.184), as a thin white line at the foot of the San Andres Mountains on the far side.

Cloud Cafe 505 Burro Ave ☎ 575 682 5843. Pies, crepes, coffee and free wi-fi make this bright, friendly little place, set just back from the main drag, a welcome addition to the Cloudcroft scene. One Friday a month, they serve tasty dinners, with live music. Tues–Fri 11am–4pm, Sat & Sun 10am–5pm.

Cloudcroft Hotel 306 Burro Ave ☎ 575 682 3414, ⓦ cloudcrofthotel.com. Freshly renovated old hotel in the heart of town, with comfortable, antique-furnished rooms of widely varying sizes – some have kitchenettes – and balconies overlooking the main strip. $94

Cloudcroft Mountain Park Hostel 1049 US-82 ☎ 575 682 0555, ⓦ cloudcrofthostel.com. Perched in the woods

six miles west of town, on the way down towards Alamogordo, this lurid blue-painted double-decker hostel is a smart motel-style affair that offers two dorms, two private doubles, and one large family room that sleeps four. Cash only. Dorm $17, private double $30, family room $50

The Lodge at Cloudcroft 601 Corona Place ☎ 575 682 2566 or ☎ 800 395 6343, ⓦ thelodgeresort.com. South of the highway, a mile up Hwy-130, the *Lodge* is a prestigious historic hotel. As well as well-priced B&B rooms, it features some absurdly plush suites and private cottages, and also *Rebecca's*, an attractive continental restaurant with panoramic views. It even has its own golf course, at an elevation of 9000ft. $125

Alamogordo

3

Sprawled at the foot of the Sacramento Mountains seventy miles northeast of Las Cruces, **ALAMOGORDO** is, like Los Alamos, a child of the Bomb. Once a quiet ranching centre, it has grown since World War II to a town of well over thirty thousand inhabitants, most of whom owe their living to the military bases and research facilities tucked away in the surrounding deserts. It's conservative enough to have held public burnings of the Harry Potter books in 2002.

Alamogordo's original central streets remain surprisingly unchanged, but they're a neglected backwater compared to the frenzy of commercial activity along the five-mile strip of US-54, here known as **White Sands Boulevard**. Given pride of place at the **Tularosa Basin Historical Society Museum**, 1301 N White Sands Blvd (Mon–Sat 10am–4pm; free), an old electric toaster from *Howards Café* bears witness to quite how little ever happens around these parts.

New Mexico Museum of Space History

3198 Hwy-2001 • Daily 9am–5pm • Museum $6, movie theatre/planetarium $6; combined admission $10 • ☎ 575 437 2840, ⓦ nmspacemuseum.org

Any five-storey building in Alamogordo would probably be a tourist attraction; that the gleaming glass cube on the hillside east of town holds the **New Mexico Museum of Space History** is gilding the lily. Displays inside trace the history of rocketry from eleventh-century China onwards, covering New-Mexico-based pioneers Robert Goddard and Wernher von Braun – one snap of von Braun's cheery crew sitting astride a V2 rocket is straight out of *Dr Strangelove* – up to the craft that will offer the first commercial space flights. A diorama depicts the unfortunate Ham, the first chimp in space, who was trained at Alamogordo in 1961 by receiving electric shocks or banana-flavoured pellets according to which lever he moved. The adjoining **Clyde W. Tombaugh Imax Theater** shows giant-screen movies and doubles as a **planetarium**; there's also a "garden" of abandoned rockets outside.

Visitor centre Alongside Tularosa Basin museum, at 1301 N White Sands Blvd (Mon–Fri 8am–5pm, Sat 9am–4pm,

Sun 10am–3pm; ☎ 575 437 6120, ⓦ alamogordo.com).

Best Western Desert Aire 1021 S White Sands Blvd ☎ 575 437 2110, ⓦ bestwestern.com. Welcoming motel, renovated to a high standard, and offering kitchenette suites as well as standard rooms, plus a sauna, hot tub and

outdoor pool. Rates include breakfast. $83

Memories 1223 N New York Ave ☎ 575 437 0077, ⓦ memories-restaurant.com. "Continental" restaurant set in a very floral old house in Alamogordo's sleepy downtown – quite a contrast to the highway – where entrees such as steaks, salmon, or swordfish, cost around $20 including soup or salad. Mon–Sat 11am–9pm.

Tia Lupe 1200 N White Sands Blvd ☎575 437 0820, ⓦtialupes.com. Lively, large and very popular Mexican restaurant, across from the visitor centre, with a friendly local atmosphere and a good menu of dishes like the $8 stuffed sopaipillas, oozing green chile and cheese.

Mon–Sat 10am–8pm.

White Sands Motel 1101 S White Sands Blvd ☎575 437 2922 or ☎877 437 2922, ⓦwhitesandsmotel.biz. This old-fashioned roadside motel looks unremarkable from the outside, but it's well managed and cared for, while the accommodation itself is clean and spruce, and there are some great-value extra-large family rooms. Standard rooms ~~$60~~, family rooms ~~$80~~

White Sands National Monument

US-70, 14 miles west of Alamogordo • **Visitor centre** Daily: summer 8am–7pm; spring & fall 9am–6pm; winter 9am–5pm • ☎575 479 6124, ⓦnps.gov/whsa

The glistening, towering dunes of **White Sands** fill 275 square miles of the broad Tularosa Basin, between the Sacramento and San Andres mountains. Though their whiteness is beyond dispute, they're not sand but fine **gypsum**, deposited on an ancient sea bed 250 million years ago. Anywhere else, the gypsum would have dissolved and been carried off by rivers; here, however, it's trapped in a riverless ring of mountains. The southern portion of this surreal landscape, immediately north of US-70 fourteen miles west of Alamogordo, has been set aside as **WHITE SANDS NATIONAL MONUMENT**. Be warned that roughly twice each week, US-70 **closes** for up to two hours while missile tests are under way.

Beside the highway, the **visitor centre** illustrates the unique life-forms that populate this pallid environment.

While there's no developed **campground** at White Sands, backcountry camping is allowed, by permit only ($3 per person per night). Once or twice a year, rangers lead vehicle convoys up to Lake Lucero, the actual source of the sands.

Dunes Drive

Hwy-7/Carlsbad Cavern Hwy • Daily: summer 7am–9pm; winter 7am–sunset • $3 per person

From the visitor centre, you have to drive five more miles along the paved portion of **Dunes Drive** to reach the heart of the dunes. In this initial stretch, as you get your first glimpses of white sand beneath the scrubby vegetation, you may wonder what the fuss

---

TRINITY SITE

Twice each year, sightseers make a peculiar pilgrimage to the **Trinity Site**, out on the **White Sands Missile Range** in the desert thirty miles west of Carrizozo (see p.178), where the first **atomic bomb** was detonated at 5.30am on July 16, 1945. Brought by road from Los Alamos in the back of a '42 Plymouth, the bomb, code-named **Fat Man**, was not dropped but placed atop a steel tower. As well as destroying a nearby "doom town" built to study its effects, the blast was strong enough to shatter windows in Silver City, 120 miles west, and to fuse the sands below "Ground Zero" into a thick slab of radioactive green glass known as **trinitite**. The eight-feet-deep crater it created was subsequently filled in to minimize radiation.

The Missile Range has witnessed thousands more weapons tests since then, and remains off-limits to non-military personnel except for the first Saturdays of April and October. Visitors on those days can either join a "caravan" that sets off from **Alamogordo** at 8am, or enter the range unaccompanied via the **Stallion Gate** (8am–2pm), on US-380 fifty miles west of Carrizozo. You're forbidden to stop or take photos other than at the site itself, or to make political speeches, and urged not to pick up any trinitite you may spot. Not only is it part of a National Historic Landmark, it's radioactive.

For more information on tours, and on the range itself, access ⓦwww.wsmr.army.mil – where the authorities helpfully explain "In the end, if it's a missile, we fire it" – or drop in at the White Sands Missile Range Museum (see p.185).

is about. Unless you have either an abundance of time or walking difficulties, skip the unenthralling nature trail along the **Interdune Boardwalk**.

A little further along, the plants thin out, and you come to a bizarre world of dazzling white knife-edge ridges and graceful slopes. The drive now loops around a six-mile one-way labyrinth, where the roadway is at times hundreds of yards wide, and then narrows again to a slender channel, as the west winds that constantly replenish the dunes pile sand in your path in luxuriant drifts. Plentiful pull-outs, some equipped with fabulous 1950s-style curving picnic shelters, enable you to leave your vehicle and plough through pristine sand to the top of the ridges, which offer long-range mountain views. Slipping and sliding back down again is even better.

White Sands Missile Range Museum

Hwy-213, 4 miles south of US 70 and 26 miles east of Las Cruces • Mon–Fri 8am–4pm, Sat 10am–3pm • Free • ☎ 575 647 1116, Ⓦ wsmr-history.org

A couple of miles north of the boundary of White Sands National Monument, on the top-security White Sands Missile Range – the largest military installation in the US – the **White Sands Space Harbor** held one of the three seven-mile runways where the **Space Shuttle** was able to land. While it was used extensively for training, it only welcomed one actual landing, the Space Shuttle *Columbia*, in 1982.

For the full story, head for the **White Sands Missile Range Museum**, thirty miles southwest of the monument en route to Las Cruces. The open-air **Missile Park** alongside displays all the missiles ever tested at White Sands. These date back to "Vengeance Weapon 2," the **V2** rocket, almost four thousand of which were fired across the English Channel by the Nazis during World War II. After the war, the weapon's designer, Dr Wernher von Braun, directed the firing of sixty more V2s at White Sands – one went astray and crashed across the border near Ciudad Juarez, Mexico. He moved on to Huntsville, Alabama, in 1950.

Southeast New Mexico

East of the mountains, at the edge of the Great Plains, **southeast New Mexico** has little in common with the rest of the Southwest. It's not quite as dull as it looks, however; all its treasures are tucked away underground, from its oil and mineral wealth to the fairytale labyrinth of **Carlsbad Caverns National Park**. Traditionally, Carlsbad was the only reason tourists ever strayed this way, but these days a steady influx of pilgrims come to contemplate the extra-terrestrial wonders of **Roswell**.

Roswell

The small ranching town of **ROSWELL,** 57 miles east of Lincoln and 75 miles north of the national park at Carlsbad, is renowned as the spot near which an **alien spacecraft** supposedly crashlanded on the night of July 4, 1947. The commander of the local air force base authorized a press statement announcing that the wreckage of a flying saucer had been retrieved and taken away for examination. Despite a follow-up denial within a day, claiming that it was in fact a weather balloon – and President Clinton's categorical assertion that "No, an alien spacecraft did not crash in Roswell, New Mexico, in 1947" – the story of the so-called "**Roswell Incident**" has kept running. As 100,000 *X-Files* fanatics descended upon Roswell in 1997 for a six-day festival to mark the "Incident's" fiftieth anniversary, the US Air Force revealed that the errant balloon had been monitoring the atmosphere for evidence of Soviet nuclear tests. Witnesses were also said to have confused the balloon crash with parachute experiments in 1953, which involved dropping dummies from high-altitude planes. UFO theorists, however, remain unconvinced.

Incidentally, considerable vagueness surrounds exactly where the crash took place. Since a local entrepreneur bought up one purported site, the original witnesses have started to "remember" that it all happened somewhere else entirely. With TV series such as *Roswell* and *Taken* having perpetuated the myth, Roswell's curious tourist boom shows no signs of abating.

International UFO Museum

114 N Main St • Daily 9am–5pm • $5 • ☎ 575 625 9495, ⓦ roswellufomuseum.com

Despite its best intentions, and the wishful thinking of the truly weird clientele who drift in from the plains, the central **International UFO Museum** inadvertently exposes the whole tawdry tale of the Roswell Incident as transparent nonsense. Set up by the military press officer responsible for the 1947 announcement, it reveals such gems as that John F. Kennedy was shot because he was about to reveal the secret, and that Neil Armstrong, astonished at encountering flying saucers on the moon, blurted out "Boy, were they beige!" (You'd have to assume that "big" was the word he was fumbling for.) Murals depict "what might have happened," while the showpiece exhibit is a model of a so-called "**alien autopsy**." Note the "fiction" and "non-fiction" sections in the museum bookstore.

Roswell Museum

100 W 11th St • Mon–Sat 9am–5pm, Sun 1–5pm • Free • ☎ 575 624 6744, ⓦ roswellmuseum.org

The long-standing **Roswell Museum** boasts an excellent, multifaceted collection with nary an alien corpse to be seen. Its most sensational section celebrates pioneer rocket scientist **Robert Goddard** (1882–1945), one of whose early experiments prompted the newspaper headline *"Moon Rocket" Man's Test Alarms Whole Countryside*. His entire laboratory has been reconstructed, and entertaining footage shows him wheeling a rudimentary rocket in a wagon to the launch pad, then racing to escape the blast in a Model T Ford.

There's also a huge, top-quality **art gallery**, displaying Southwestern landscapes by Henriette Wyeth and Peter Hurd as well as a solitary Georgia O'Keeffe, *Ram's Skull With Brown Leaves*.

Carlsbad

Considering that a million tourists per year pass through **CARLSBAD** en route to Carlsbad Caverns National Park – covered below – the town itself is astonishing in its blandness. A century of ranching and potash-mining has given it a sizeable if characterless downtown area, which holds nothing whatsoever to see.

Quite the reverse, in fact – Carlsbad possesses the dubious distinction of being home to the **Waste Isolation Pilot Plant** (ⓦ wipp.energy.gov). Hollowed from a thick layer of salt two thousand feet below ground level, this subterranean facility is the world's first repository for radioactive waste created during the production of nuclear weapons.

Living Desert Zoo and Gardens State Park

1504 Miehls Drive N • Daily: summer 8am–5pm; winter 9am–5pm; last admission 1hr 30min before closing • $5 • ☎ 575 887 5516, ⓦ emnrd.state.nm.us

Carlsbad's one significant attraction is the **Living Desert Zoo and Gardens State Park**, a couple of miles northwest of town. This botanical garden of desert plants doubles as a zoo that houses elk, rattlesnakes, a prairie dog village, and even "Maggie the Painting Bear", an adept, if strictly non-representational, watercolourist.

CLOCKWISE FROM TOP ART GALLERY, SILVER CITY (P.196); THE INDIAN PUEBLO CULTURAL CENTER, ALBUQUERQUE (P.171); INTERNATIONAL UFO MUSEUM AND RESEARCH CENTER, ROSWELL (OPPOSITE)>

Carlsbad Caverns National Park

20 miles southwest of Carlsbad on US 62/180, then 7 miles west from White's City on Hwy-7 • $6 for 3 days, under-16s free; national park passes cover up to four adults; optional tours extra • ☏ 575 785 2232, tour reservations ☏ 877 444 6777, ☜ nps.gov/cave, tour reservations ☜ recreation.gov

CARLSBAD CAVERNS NATIONAL PARK consists of a tract of the Guadalupe Mountains that's so riddled with underground caves and tunnels as to be virtually hollow. Tamed in classic park-service style with concrete trails and electric lighting, this subterranean wonderland is now a walk-in gallery, where tourists come in droves to marvel at its intricate limestone tracery. Before you decide to join them, however, be sure to grasp that the park is a *long* way from anywhere else – three hundred miles southeast of Albuquerque and 150 miles northeast of El Paso, Texas.

The Guadalupe Mountains are the remnants of the **Capitan Reef**, a 400-mile-long horseshoe-shaped reef that formed beneath a primeval ocean. Made up of algae and sponges rather than coral, it was thrust above the plains a mere three million years ago. Surface moisture has trickled through the resultant cracks ever since, gnawing at the rock within.

Almost all park visitors confine their attention to the main cave, **Carlsbad Cavern** itself, where the summer crowds can be intense. Strangely, though, that's part of the fun – coming to Carlsbad feels like a real throwback to the 1950s boom in mass tourism. If you're not convinced, wait until you see the gloriously kitsch **Underground Lunchroom**.

Note that there's no **camping** at the national park; the nearest campgrounds and motels are at White's City and Carlsbad.

Visitor centre

Hwy-7/Carlsbad Cavern Hwy • Daily: late May to early Sept 8am–7pm; early Sept to late May 8am–5pm

Atop the mountains, and commanding sweeping views east across the plains, the **visitor centre** for Carlsbad Caverns National Park stands at the end of the narrow, twisting seven-mile road up from White's City. Part of a complex that also includes a restaurant, a gift store, a crèche, and even a kennel, it's a compulsory port of call, to pay entrance fees and pick up details of the day's programme of tours.

Carlsbad Cavern

Natural Entrance Route Daily: last entry late May to early Sept 3.30pm, early Sept to late May 2pm • **Elevator** Daily: summer first down 8.30am, last up 6.30pm; winter first down 8.30am, last up 4.55pm

The centrepiece of Carlsbad Cavern, the **Big Room**, lies 750 vertical feet below the visitor centre – as it's inside the mountain, it's also 400ft horizontally from the open air in some places. Measuring up to 1800ft long and 250ft high, it's festooned with stalactites, stalagmites, and countless unnameable shapes of swirling liquid rock. All are a uniform stone grey; the rare touches of colour are provided by slight red or brown mineral-rich tinges, improved here and there with gentle pastel lighting. Most visitors take an hour or so to complete the reasonably level trail around its perimeter. Whatever

---

LECHUGUILLA CAVE

Revealed in 1986, after cavers cleared a thirty-foot plug of bat dung and rubble in a little-known area of Carlsbad Caverns National Park, the astonishing **Lechuguilla Cave** system is not only deeper than Carlsbad Cavern but, at 1600ft, has turned out to be the deepest in the US. Over 130 miles of tunnels have been mapped so far, but they're so dangerous that Lechuguilla is off-limits to all but the experts. It's expected to remain a "wilderness cave" – even its location is kept secret – so the rest of us will have to content ourselves with the marvellous pictures of its delicate crystalline formations in the visitor centre.

THE BATS OF CARLSBAD

The recesses of Carlsbad Caverns are the summer home of approaching a million Mexican (or Brazilian) free-tailed **bats**. Each evening from April to mid-October, having slept all day suspended from the ceiling of the imaginatively titled **Bat Cave** – to which there's no public access – they emerge in cloud-like spirals at dusk or a little later, and disperse across the desert in search of delectable insects. Visitors watch the spectacle from the amphitheatre seating that faces the cave mouth; rangers can tell you what time sunset is due.

It was the bats that first brought the caves to human attention, in the 1890s. Miners employed to dig bat dung or **guano**, which was greatly prized as fertilizer, started to explore what lay beyond the cave mouth. As word of their discoveries spread, sightseers began to arrive. Early visitors were dropped down in buckets and guided through on ropes. The present trail system was constructed after the caverns became a national park in 1930.

the weather up top – summer highs exceed 100°F – the temperature down here is always a cool 56°F, so dress warmly.

Direct **elevators** drop to the Big Room from the visitor centre. They arrive alongside the **Underground Lunchroom**, a vast formation-free side cave paved over in the 1950s to create a diner-cum-souvenir-store that sells indigestible lunches in polystyrene containers, plus Eisenhower-era souvenirs such as giant pencils and Viewmaster reels. To modern eyes, this strange installation seems absurd, but moves by the park service to close it down have repeatedly been stymied by its place in popular affections. Indeed, thanks to Republican New Mexican congressman Joe Skeen, it has since 2004 been illegal to spend any money that "permits or requires" the closure of the lunchroom.

To get a better sense of the depth of the cavern, eschew the elevator and **walk** down via the **Natural Entrance Route**. This steep paved footpath switchbacks into the guano-encrusted maw of the cave, a short way from the visitor centre. It takes fifteen minutes to reach the first formations and another fifteen to reach the Big Room itself. All visitors are obliged to ride the elevator back out.

The walk-down trail used to meander through beautiful side caves such as the **King's Palace**, filled with translucent "draperies" of limestone. However, formations are broken at the rate of two thousand per year, so these have long been closed to casual visitors. They're now open on guided tours only, which start from the Big Room (2–4 tours daily; $8). Additional tours can take you along the **Left Hand Tunnel** route down from the visitor centre ($7), or on a much more demanding descent into either **Spider Cave** or the **Hall of the White Giant** (both $20; under-12s not permitted).

Slaughter Canyon Cave

25 miles southwest of park visitor centre • Guided tours only, late May to mid-Aug Fri–Sun 8.30am; mid-Aug to late May Sat & Sun 8.30am • $15

Much less frequented, and much less developed, than the main Carlsbad Cavern complex, **Slaughter Canyon Cave** can only be explored on strenuous guided tours. If you're physically fit, and up for a demanding (and claustrophobic) wilderness adventure on which you'll see spectacular formations in a relatively pristine state, these are well worth the effort.

Lasting almost six hours, the tours start with an orientation session in the park visitor centre; participants then pool cars and drive together to a point half a mile below the cave entrance, to start the steep hike up. There's a minimum age of eight; you're provided with a flashlight, but expected to bring batteries; and you're not allowed to walk with a stick within the cave itself.

Slaughter Canyon Cave still appears as "New Cave" on some maps, but it's been renamed to avoid confusion since the discovery of **Lechuguilla Cave**.

3

White's City

Twenty miles southwest of Carlsbad at the turn-off for Carlsbad Caverns, **WHITE'S CITY** is not a town but a privately owned tourist complex. A notorious eyesore, it was built in 1926 by entrepreneur Charlie White, who cannily anticipated the imminent advent of automobile tourism and bought up the land at this crucial road junction without ever having seen it. The park service has deplored its very existence ever since, and has attempted to avoid the same situation arising at parks elsewhere.

Although White's City provides the closest accommodation and camping to the national park, none is currently worth recommending.

INFORMATION   SOUTHEAST NEW MEXICO

ROSWELL
Visitor centre 912 N Main St (Mon–Fri 8am–5pm; ☎ 575 624 6860, ⓦ roswellnm.org).

CARLSBAD
Visitor centre 302 S Canal St (Mon–Fri 8am–5pm; ☎ 575 887 6516, ⓦ carlsbadchamber.com).

ACCOMMODATION AND EATING

ROSWELL
Cattle Baron 1113 N Main St ☎ 575 622 2465, ⓦ cattlebaron.com. Large, good-value steakhouse, with traditional Wild West decor, big slabs of meat, including steaks at $20–26, and an extensive salad bar. Mon–Thurs 11am–9.30pm, Fri & Sat 11am–10pm, Sun 11am–9pm.
Farley's 1315 N Main St ☎ 575 627 1100, ⓦ farleyspub .com. Lively sci-fi-themed pub and diner, not far up the hill from the Roswell Museum, with lots of gleaming chrome and neon; things can get noisy, but the food and drink keeps flowing, and it's reasonably priced. Mon–Thurs noon–11pm, Fri & Sat 11am–midnight, Sun 11am–9pm.
La Quinta Inn 200 E 19th St ☎ 575 622 8000 or ☎ 800 753 3757, ⓦ lq.com. Very dependable motel, just off the main through highway north of the centre; new, clean and well managed, with an indoor pool and free breakfasts. $109

CARLSBAD
Best Western Stevens Inn 1829 S Canal St ☎ 575 887 2851, ⓦ bestwesternnewmexico.com. This large, old-fashioned roadside motel complex, a mile south of the centre towards the national park, has been given a thorough makeover thanks to the recent influx of oil-company workers. The rooms are generally big but otherwise unremarkable, and there's an outdoor pool. Rates include a breakfast buffet at the *Flume Room* restaurant, which is as good a place to eat as you're likely to find (Mon–Sat 6am–10pm, Sun 6am–9pm). $132
Blue House Bakery 609 N Canyon St ☎ 575 628 0555. Set on a broad and very sleepy residential road slightly northeast of downtown Carlsbad, this popular cottage cafe/bakery serves early-morning coffee and pastries, then salads and sandwiches later on. Mon–Fri 6am–2pm, Sat 6am–noon.
★ **Trinity Hotel** 201 S Canal St ☎ 575 234 9891, ⓦ thetrinityhotel.com. An unexpected find for this part of New Mexico, this former bank in downtown Carlsbad – not that that's an area you'd explore on foot – has been beautifully converted into a nine-suite boutique hotel. Most rooms have walk-in showers, and there's also an excellent restaurant, open for all meals but, unlike the hotel itself, closed on Sundays. $149

The Rio Grande valley

The 260-mile route between Albuquerque and the Mexican border at El Paso, Texas, follows one of America's oldest and most romantic trails. For 250 years, the **Camino Real** or "Royal Road" beside the Rio Grande gave the Hispanic colonists of New Mexico their one tenuous link with the outside world. However, travellers on the Camino Real were so prone to Apache attack if they followed the curve of the Rio Grande between **Socorro** and **Las Cruces** that they preferred to take a hundred-mile shortcut behind the mountains that lie east of the river. This route too had its perils – not least a complete lack of water – and became known as the **Jornada del Muerto**, or Dead Man's Route, after Juan de Oñate's chaplain Fray Cristóbal de Salazar died here in the early 1600s. To this day there's no north–south road through the desert.

The Camino Real is now paralleled by I-25, a monotonous four-hour drive relieved only by distant views of the mountains. You don't even see much of the river itself, except where it's been dammed to form incongruous turquoise lakes around the town of **Truth or Consequences**. Of the old way-stations en route, only **Socorro** in the north and **Mesilla** in the south are particularly worth visiting.

Socorro

Historic **SOCORRO**, eighty miles south of Albuquerque, received its unusual name – "help," in Spanish – from Don Juan de Oñate in 1598, after local Pueblo peoples fed his expeditionary party from their reserves of corn. The first Hispanic settlement was destroyed during the Pueblo Revolt of 1680, whereafter the site was abandoned for over a century. The picturesque **plaza** at its core, a block west of the main road, California Street, and the spruced-up adobe church of **San Miguel**, a couple of blocks north (daily 6am–6pm; free), were rebuilt during the 1820s. Sixty years later, triggered by the arrival of the railroads and the discovery of extensive **silver** deposits nearby, Socorro briefly became New Mexico's largest town. When the silver ran out, so too did most of the population, leaving behind some fine Victorian architecture.

The Very Large Array (VLA)

US-60, 50 miles west of Socorro • **Visitor centre** Daily 8.30am–sunset; guided tours first Sat of month, 11am–3pm • Free • ☎ 505 835 7243, ⓦ vla.nrao.edu

A must-see for astronomy enthusiasts and fans of the unusual, the aptly named **Very Large Array**, or VLA, spreads across the Plains of San Agustin fifty lonely miles west of Socorro. One of the world's most powerful observatories, it comprises 27 separate moveable radio dishes, each 25 metres across, which can be arranged in permutations that vary from a dense cluster to a twenty-mile line. The array's visitor centre, clearly signed on Hwy-52 just south of US-60, holds assorted displays, but is usually not staffed. Instead, visitors can simply check out the attached gift shop and follow a well-marked walking route that takes them closer to, but not right up to, however many dishes are currently nearby.

While the VLA makes a striking, photogenic spectacle, reaching it requires a long detour from the interstate. Neither **Magdalena**, twenty miles east of the array, nor **Datil**, fifteen miles west, hold much for visitors apart from a basic diner or two, so the trek is probably only worth it if you're en route to or from Arizona.

Bosque del Apache Wildlife Refuge

About 8 miles south of San Antonio on NM-1 • **Refuge** Daily from 1hr before sunrise to 1hr after sunset • **Visitor centre** Mon–Fri 7.30am–4pm, Sat & Sun 8am–4.30pm • $3 per vehicle • ☎ 575 835 1828, ⓦ fws.gov or friendsofthebosque.org

Hispanic colonists heading south from Socorro along the Camino Real, beside the Rio Grande, would avoid the encampments at Bosque del Apache (forest of the Apache) by crossing the river twenty miles south of Socorro, and heading towards the Jornada del Muerto trail. This point off Hwy-1 is now the **Bosque del Apache Wildlife Refuge**, the Southwest's most spectacular **birdwatching** site. As many as twenty thousand sandhill cranes and almost fifty thousand snow geese migrate here in early December for the winter; and even in summer its riverine marshes and forests are bursting with birds and mammals. A twelve-mile, one-way road loops around the entire refuge, but to make the most of a visit you need to hike at least one of the hiking trails en route, which range in length from under one mile to over four miles. Allow at least two hours in total.

El Camino Real International Heritage Center

Exit 115 off I-25, 30 miles south of Socorro • Wed–Sun 8.30am–5pm • $5 • ☎ 575 854 3600, ⓦ caminorealheritage.org

The story of the Camino Real, which is very much the history of New Mexico as a Spanish colony, is recounted in lavish and fascinating detail at the impressive **El Camino Real International Heritage Center**, overlooking the Rio Grande thirty miles south of

Socorro. The trail was the lifeblood of New Mexico, linking Santa Fe with Mexico City, 1500 miles south, and the exhibits stress ongoing cultural connections. Smaller-scale trails have been laid out nearby as short nature hikes.

Truth or Consequences

Until 1950, the minor spa town seventy miles south of Socorro was appropriately known as **Hot Springs**. Then the radio show *Truth or Consequences* promised that any community prepared to change its name would receive the meagre reward of hosting its tenth anniversary edition. Hot Springs prostituted itself for fifteen minutes of fame, and **TRUTH OR CONSEQUENCES** was saddled with the world's worst name – though locals habitually abbreviate it these days to "**T or C**." Its small downtown now consists of just a couple of blocks, sandwiched between two busy one-way streets, Broadway and Main Street.

Scattered throughout downtown, several **thermal springs** – where Apache warriors such as Geronimo used to soak away the worries of the warpath – are now run as private bathhouses, with prices starting at around $3 for a twenty-minute session.

3

Geronimo Springs Museum
211 Main St • Mon–Sat 9am–5pm, Sun noon–4pm • $6 • ⓦ geronimospringsmuseum.com

Native American memorabilia, including Mimbres pottery (see p.198), form a prominent part of the historical collection at the **Geronimo Springs Museum**. You can also learn fascinating snippets about **Ralph Edwards**, the late presenter of the long-defunct *Truth or Consequences* show, who managed to return each year for the first fifty times the **Truth or Consequences Fiesta** was celebrated, on the first weekend in May. He died aged 92 in 2005.

Hillsboro

Hwy-152 branches west from I-25 fifteen miles south of T or C, crossing the Mimbres Mountain en route to **Silver City** (see p.196). **HILLSBORO**, less than twenty miles off the interstate in the fertile foothills, is a former gold-mining settlement that has since turned its hand to apple-growing instead, as celebrated in an annual **Apple Festival** held on Labor Day weekend. Now it is no more than a village, with a small crop of arts-and-crafts galleries.

THE FINAL FRONTIER

Appropriately enough, given its long-standing association with cutting-edge technology, frontier adventurism and strange alien spacecraft, New Mexico is due to become home to the world's first **commercial space flights**. The state government and Virgin Galactic are building **Spaceport America** (ⓦ spaceportamerica.com) in the empty desert of the Jornada del Muerto, roughly 45 miles northeast of Las Cruces and 25 miles southeast of Truth or Consequences.

While no specific dates have been announced, most of the details are already known. The craft to be used, SpaceShipTwo, is an updated version of the prototype that in 2004 became the first space vehicle to fly to an altitude of over 100km twice within two weeks, thereby claiming the $10 million Ansari X-Prize. Carried aloft by the WhiteKnightTwo launch plane, the ship is released and then fires its own rocket engines to reach suborbital space. Amazingly, it uses a combination of nitrous oxide – laughing gas – and solid rubber as fuel. Virgin Galactic is ultimately hoping to operate a fleet of five spacecraft from New Mexico, each capable of carrying eight astronauts, and to offer its space voyagers a "five-star destination experience" on the ground as well. The actual flight will last around three hours, culminating in perhaps three minutes of weightlessness; it won't go into Earth orbit. Reservations for US$200,000 tickets are already being accepted; contact ⓦ virgingalactic.com for details.

Hatch

Forty miles south of T or C, along I-25 en route to Las Cruces, tiny **HATCH** is noteworthy only as the home of New Mexico's leading **chile farms**. All year, roadside stalls sell fresh peppers and the dried garlands known as *ristras*, while Labor Day weekend sees a **Chile Festival** (☎575 267 5050, ⊚hatchchilefest.com) with fiercely competitive chile cook-offs.

Fort Selden State Monument

15 miles north of Las Cruces • Mon & Wed–Sun 8.30am–5pm • $3 • ☎ 575 526 8911, ⊚ nmstatemonuments.org

Just south of **RADIUM SPRINGS**, not far north of downtown Las Cruces, **Fort Selden State Monument** stands on the east bank of the Rio Grande. It preserves the ruined adobe walls of a US Army fort built to protect Las Cruces in 1865. Its small museum focuses largely on the black troops stationed here just after the Civil War, who became known as Buffalo Soldiers, and are also commemorated by a bronze statue outside. The fort was decommissioned in 1891, so it basically consists of rounded stumps surrounding its former parade ground, but it still comes alive on summer weekends during regular re-enactments.

Las Cruces

Named after the crosses that marked the graves of early travellers killed by the Apache, **LAS CRUCES** is now a major crossroads, where the east–west I-10 meets the north–south I-25. Once a riverside farming community, it has grown beyond recognition, though the boom in industrial and military employment has been at the expense of any scenic beauty Las Cruces may once have possessed. It has very little to offer visitors. As New Mexico's second largest city, it boasts a wide array of shops and services, but these days they're all housed in the malls that line I-25 to the east, leaving downtown a rather desolate sprawl. Any time you can spare for sightseeing is better spent in neighbouring Mesilla.

Mesilla

The little-changed Hispanic village of **MESILLA** stands just south of I-10 two miles south of Las Cruces, an easy drive down Avenida de Mesilla from downtown. When New Mexico passed into American hands in 1846, the Mesilla Valley still belonged to Mexico; Mesilla itself was founded in 1850 by New Mexicans who preferred to remain Mexican. Under the **Gadsden Purchase**, however, signed here in 1853, it passed to the US and soon became one of the Southwest's largest towns, with over eight thousand inhabitants. During the Civil War, Mesilla even served briefly as the Confederate capital of the territory of Arizona, but it went into swift decline when the railroad bypassed it in favour of Las Cruces in 1881.

Mesilla's Old West **plaza** has a real frontier feel, though most of the old adobes that surround it – including the former courthouse where **Billy the Kid** was tried and sentenced to death in 1881 – now house art galleries and souvenir shops. Gift stores stock interesting Southwest souvenirs and jewellery leavened with some much cheaper Mexican crafts, while the Mesilla Book Center has an excellent selection of local literature. Two blocks east at 1875 Boutz Rd, the small **Gadsden Museum** (Mon–Sat 9–11am & 1–5pm, Sun 1–5pm; $2) recounts the town's history and details the events that led to the Gadsden Purchase.

INFORMATION   **RIO GRANDE VALLEY**

SOCORRO
Visitor centre 217 Fisher Ave, a block west of the plaza (Tues–Fri 9am–5pm, Sat 10am–2pm;

☎575 835 8927, ⊚socorronm.gov). Self-guided walking tour maps available.

LAS CRUCES
Visitor centre 211 N Water St (Mon–Fri 8am–5pm, Sat 9am–1pm; ☎ 575 541 2444, ⊛ lascrucescvb.org).

MESILLA
Visitor centre 2231 Avda de Mesilla (daily 9am–5pm; ☎ 575 524 3262, ⊛ oldmesilla.org).

ACCOMMODATION

SOCORRO
Motel 6 807 S US-85 ☎ 575 835 4300, ⊛ motel6.com. Socorro holds pretty much all the national chains, but with none being exceptional you might as well opt for this well-run *Motel 6*, just off I-25 exit 147. The rooms are very ordinary but perfectly adequate, and there's an outdoor pool; wi-fi costs $3 extra per night. **$37**

TRUTH OR CONSEQUENCES
Blackstone Hot Springs 410 Austin St ☎ 575 894 0894, ⊛ blackstonehotsprings.com. The seven spacious modern rooms in this fancy downtown option are enjoyably themed in honour of 1950s TV shows, from *I Love Lucy* to *The Twilight Zone*. Each has its own spring-fed hot tub or shower, as well as a kitchenette, and some have patios. **$75**
Riverbend Hot Springs 100 Austin St ☎ 575 894 7625, ⊛ nmhotsprings.com. As well as spring-fed hot tubs, this lovely lodge, beside the Rio Grande in the heart of town, offers comfortable suites as well as "budget doubles" that share baths and can sleep up to four and small, individually decorated "artist rooms". All guests must be aged 12 or over. Artist rooms **$70**, budget doubles **$120**, suites **$150**
Sierra Grande Lodge & Spa 501 McAdoo St ☎ 575 894 6976, ⊛ sierragrandelodge.com. Gorgeously restored 1920s lodge where each of the opulently furnished rooms

and suites has its own private hot tub, and massages and spa treatments are available. **$99**

LAS CRUCES
★ **Best Western Mission Inn** 1765 S Main St ☎ 575 524 8591 or ☎ 800 390 1440, ⊛ bwmissioninn.com. The cream of Las Cruces' motels; it may not look all that special from the outside, but the large rooms are surprisingly attractive, featuring lovely Mexican tilework and murals. Rates include a full cooked breakfast, and there's a heated outdoor pool. The one drawback is its proximity to the railroad tracks. **$82**
Lundeen's Inn of the Arts 618 S Alameda Blvd ☎ 575 526 3326 or ☎ 888 526 3326, ⊛ innofthearts.com. Century-old B&B inn downtown, in which each of the twenty rooms is named for a regional artist, such as Maria Martínez or Georgia O'Keeffe, and furnished appropriately. The public spaces include two huge and impressive common rooms. **$100**

MESILLA
Mesón de Mesilla 1803 Avda de Mesilla ☎ 575 652 4953, ⊛ mesondemesilla.com. B&B inn, 5 minutes' walk east of the plaza, which offers fifteen rooms of varying degrees of luxury, gorgeous mountain views, and an outdoor pool. **$119**

EATING AND DRINKING

SOCORRO
Old Town Bistro 115 Abeyta Ave ☎ 575 838 3976, ⊛ oldtownbistronm.com. More pub than bistro, this very laidback adobe nightspot consists of two large dining rooms, one of which also holds a bar and a stage on which local musicians perform, plus several tables on the patio outside. As for the food, it's part Asian, part Mexican, with appetizers like shrimp rumaki and green chile wontons; Mexican dishes such as chile rellenos for $10; and steaks, eggplant chicken and so on for $14 and up. Mon–Sat 11am–10pm.
Socorro Springs Brewing Company 1012 California St ☎ 575 838 0650, ⊛ socorrosprings.com. As well as a good range of beers that are in fact brewed in Colorado, this conspicuous pub serves calzones and pizzas ($10–12) from its wood-fired oven, along with sandwiches ($8–10). Daily 11am–10pm.

TRUTH OR CONSEQUENCES
Cafe Bella Luca 303 Jones St ☎ 575 894 9866, ⊛ cafebellaluca.com. Friendly Italian restaurant with indoor and outdoor seating and an emphasis on local organic produce. The lunch menu includes $8 calzones, and

sandwiches and pasta specials for $10; dinner entrees range from classics like eggplant parmigiana for $13 up to fish or steak for around $25. Mon, Wed & Thurs 11am–9pm, Fri & Sat 11am–10pm, Sun 11am–8pm.

HILLSBORO
Barbershop Café 200 Main St ☎ 575 895 5283, ⊛ barbershopcafe.com. This friendly local restaurant is only open for lunch, a few times a week, but if you're passing through it makes a good pitstop, with tasty green-chile burgers for $7 and soups. Thurs–Sun 11am–3pm.

HATCH
B&E Burritos 303 N Franklin St ☎ 575 267 5191. Absolute hole-in-the-wall place in New Mexico's chile capital that's not surprisingly renowned for its fiery Mexican cuisine ($6–10). Mon–Sat 8am–9pm.

LAS CRUCES
The most promising area for restaurants in Las Cruces is along University Avenue, which marks the northern limits of the New Mexico State University campus at the south

end of town. The entire neighbourhood is also buzzing with student-oriented coffeehouses.

Mix Pacific Rim 1001 E University Ave ☎575 532 2042, ⓦmixpacificrim.com. University-district fusion restaurant, specializing in Japanese and Asian cuisine, with a sushi bar, and entrees like Thai green curry or Vietnamese stir-fries priced at up to $20. The adjoining *Mix Express* serves cheaper takeout. Mon–Sat 11am–2pm & 5–9pm.

Nellie's Café 1226 W Hadley Ave ☎575 524 9982. The slogan – "*Chiles with Attitude*" – tells you what to expect: sublimely spicy Mexican food. All the classics are here, from huevos rancheros for breakfast to the burritos and green chile at lunchtime ($6–10). Tues–Sat 8am–2pm.

MESILLA

Double Eagle 308 Calle de Guadalupe ☎575 523 6700, ⓦdouble-eagle-mesilla.com. The smartest restaurant on the plaza, with indoor seating in a grand Victorian edifice, plus a courtyard. You can pay up to $45 for steaks, but most of the Continental meat and seafood entrees cost $20–25. Strictly speaking at lunchtime, when it serves burgers, salads, and Mexican dishes for $10–12, it goes by the name of *Peppers* – and just to confuse things further, you can also order from the *Peppers* menu in the evening as well. Mon–Sat 11am–10pm, Sun noon–9pm.

La Posta 2410 Calle de San Albino ☎575 524 3524, ⓦlaposta-de-mesilla.com. Mexican *cantina*, just off the plaza in the former offices of the Butterfield Stage Coach, a nineteenth-century adobe that was here before Mesilla itself. Expect your south-of-the-border specialities to cost $12–15, and arrive smothered in cheese and green chile. Daily 11am–9.30pm.

Southwest New Mexico

Most of New Mexico's sparsely populated **southwest corner** – also known as the "**Boot heel**" – consists of open rangeland. Interstate towns like **Deming** and **Lordsburg** are entirely forgettable, though a detour north into the mountains takes you to the mining historic town of **Silver City** and the ancient **Gila Cliff Dwellings**.

Deming

A bonanza of billboards sixty miles due west of Las Cruces announces your arrival at **DEMING**, a typical desert outpost scattered with motels and diners. Half-hearted attempts at agriculture have left their traces on the landscape, but the main sign of activity comes from the ever-present swirling dust devils (as the noncommittal highway signs would have it, "Dust Storms May Exist").

In Deming's biggest event of the year, late August's **Great American Duck Race** (ⓦdemingduckrace.com), live ducks waddle down a dry track and paddle down a wet one. If your duck wins – they're assigned by a lucky draw – you can win big money.

Museum and Custom House

301 S Silver Ave • Mon–Sat 9am–4pm, Sun 1.30–4pm • Free • ☎575 546 2382, ⓦcityofdeming.org

The highlight of Deming's downtown **Museum and Custom House** is an extensive collection of Mimbres pottery (see p.198), donated by local residents. The complex also includes the Harvey House restaurant that formed part of the town's old railroad station, and its original one-room "custom house".

INFORMATION   DEMING

Visitor centre 800 E Pine St, at the east end of downtown (Mon–Fri 9am–5pm, Sat 9–11am; ☎575 546 2674, ⓦdemingchamber.com).

ACCOMMODATION AND EATING

Holiday Inn Deming 4600 E Pine St ☎575 546 2661, ⓦholidayinn.com. This large chain motel, at the eastern interstate exit, is as good as it gets in Deming, with clean rooms, an outdoor pool, and a decent **restaurant**, too. $69

Joe Perk Coffee Shop 122 E Spruce St ☎575 544 014. Friendly little coffee shack, a block south of the main drag, that also sells smoothies and pastries. Tues–Sun 11am–7pm.

Pancho Villa State Park

Daily: park 24hr; museum 8am–5pm • $5; camping $10 • ☎ 575 531 2711, ⊛ emnrd.state.nm.us

Sleepy Columbus, thirty miles south of Deming, just north of the Mexican border, is where Mexican revolutionary Pancho Villa led five hundred guerrillas in an attack on the US cavalry on March 9, 1916. "Raid Day" commemorates the anniversary each year in **PANCHO VILLA STATE PARK**. A small museum chronicles the last invasion of the US, and the adjoining sixty-acre desert botanical garden makes a nice place to **camp** (except in midsummer, when it's baking hot).

If you fancy a *cerveza* or two, the frontier with neighbouring **LAS PALOMAS**, three miles south in Mexico, remains open day or night. Border formalities are minimal, though foreign travellers must be sure to carry their passports.

Silver City

Six thousand feet up in the Mogollon Mountains, **SILVER CITY** stands roughly fifty miles from either Deming or Lordsburg on I-10. As you drive up from the interstate, however, it's easy not to notice that you're climbing – the region has been so extensively **mined** that many of the hills that once lay south of Silver City have now been completely carved away.

Ancient peoples knew this region as a source of top-quality **turquoise**, but the Hispanic settlement of La Cienaga de San Vicente was only founded in 1804, after friendly Apache showed the Spanish soldier Jose Manuel Carrasco where to find **copper**. The Santa Rita copper mine was repeatedly attacked by the Apache, however, and abandoned altogether in 1838. Only when **silver** was discovered after the Civil War was the town re-established, with a new name and a rip-roaring reputation. **Billy the Kid** spent most of his childhood here; he's said to have committed his first robbery – of a Chinese laundry – in Silver City, and also his first murder.

Things having calmed down when the silver ran out, Silver City today is a rundown, but nonetheless appealing, Victorian relic, scattered with ornate old buildings, antique shops and a couple of good museums. The two thousand students of Western New Mexico University, whose campus is on the western edge of downtown, keep things reasonably lively for most of the year, and they're replaced in summer by a large influx of tourists. Copper mining, meanwhile, continues unabated; neighbouring Santa Rita, a fully fledged community in its own right that was the birthplace of Apollo 17 astronaut Harrison Schmitt, disappeared into the bowels of an open-pit copper mine in 1966.

A massive flood ripped the heart out of downtown Silver City in 1895, washing away its original Main Street. No buildings survive from the days of **Billy the Kid**; Wild West devotees have to settle instead for inspecting the places where they *used* to be. The former site of Main Street is now occupied by **Big Ditch Park**; stand on its eastern edge, at 11th and Hudson, and you're on the spot where Billy grew up, in a simple one-room cabin. His mother is buried in the town cemetery, on Memory Lane a couple of miles east. After her death, Billy found work as a busboy in the *Star Hotel*, which survives in much-altered form at Broadway and Hudson, but soon turned to crime. The jail where he was imprisoned, and from which he made the first of his many escapes, stood at 304 N Hudson Street

Silver City Museum

312 W Broadway • Tues–Fri 9am–4.30pm, Sat & Sun 10am–4pm • $3 • ☎ 575 538 5821, ⊛ silvercitymuseum.org

A classic little small-town gem, the **Silver City Museum** concentrates on the boom-and-bust mining years, with photos of the frontier era and personal accounts of the vanished community of Santa Rita. It also holds Indian pottery, rugs, and basketry.

Western New Mexico University Museum

12th and Alabama • Mon–Fri 9am–4.30pm, Sat & Sun 10am–4pm; closed during university hols • Free • ☎ 575 538 6386, ⓦ wnmuseum.org

The emphasis at Silver City's **Western New Mexico University Museum** is on an absolutely beautiful collection of the **Mimbres pottery** for which the region is famous (see p.198), tracing its development over a thousand-year period. Further displays cover more recent Native American ceramics and other artefacts, as well as Silver City's mining era.

INFORMATION   SILVER CITY

Visitor centre 201 N Hudson St, on Hwy-90 as it enters downtown (April–Oct Mon–Fri 9am–5pm, Sat 10am–2pm, Sun noon–1pm; Nov–March Mon–Fri 9am–5pm; ☎ 575 538 3785 or ☎ 800 548 9378, ⓦ silvercity.org).

ACCOMMODATION

Room rates are surprisingly inexpensive in Silver City, but with most of the **motels** strung along US-180 east of town there's a dearth of options within walking distance of downtown.

Bear Mountain Lodge Bear Mountain Rd ☎ 575 538 2538, ⓦ bearmountainlodge.com. A 1920s adobe ranch house four miles northwest of downtown, where the eleven B&B guest rooms include four luxurious suites; the bathrooms are excellent, and there are cosy fireplaces aplenty (but no TVs). Breakfast is served in the on-site *Cafe Oso Azul*, which also serves lunch and, for $30 and with 24hr notice, dinner. $145

Holiday Inn Express 1103 Superior St ☎ 575 538 2525, ⓦ hiexpress.com/silvercitynm. The pick of Silver City's chain motels, with a heated spa and free continental breakfasts. Three miles east of downtown, it's hard to find, hidden behind a *Wendy's*. $110

Murray Hotel 200 W Broadway ☎ 575 956 9400, ⓦ murray-hotel.com. The biggest building in downtown Silver City, this Art Deco beauty originally opened as a hotel in 1938, but lay defunct for twenty years before remodelled and reopened by sympathetic new owners in 2012. The eighty guest rooms have been refurbished with a knowing retro touch – the en-suite bathrooms are particularly tasteful – and the public spaces remain impressive. $149

Palace Hotel 106 W Broadway ☎ 575 388 1811, ⓦ silvercitypalacehotel.com. Small nineteenth-century hotel downtown, nicely restored to suit budget travellers. Some rooms have showers instead of baths, and they all have historic rather than contemporary fittings, but the ambience – and the rates, which include a continental breakfast – are great. The lack of air conditioning can be a problem in high summer, as can weekend noise from the neighbouring bars. Doubles $51, suites $82

EATING AND DRINKING

What few interesting **restaurants** and **diners** Silver City has are concentrated downtown, along with a few hair-raising **bars**, so don't expect to find anything more exciting along the highways further out. The annual **Blues Festival** attracts big names at the end of each May (ⓦ mimbresarts.org).

Buckhorn Saloon and Opera House 32 Main St, Pinos Altos ☎ 575 538 9911, ⓦ buckhornsaloonandoperahouse.com. Enjoyable Wild West-themed steakhouse in the ghost town of Pinos Altos, seven miles north of Silver City (see below). Dinner entrees range from pasta or chicken for around $20 up to $30 for a big steak or surf'n'turf, and there's usually live music – generally folky singer-song writers or acoustic indie bands – on Wed, Fri & Sat. Mon–Sat 4–10pm.

Diane's Restaurant and Bakery 510 N Bullard St ☎ 575 538 8722, ⓦ dianesrestaurant.com. Welcoming downtown restaurant where the menu ranges from steak and meatloaf via Italian seafood stews to Thai green curries, pretty much all at $14–20; lots of wine by the glass, and they have their own bakery across the street. Closed Sun after 4pm, & all Mon. Tues–Fri 11am–2pm &

5.30–9pm, Sat 5.30–9pm, Sun noon–4pm.

Javelina Coffee House 210 N Bullard St ☎ 575 388 1350. Bright, friendly community rendezvous in the heart of downtown, open daily from very early indeed, and attracting arty types to drink coffee, eat pastries and use the free wi-fi. Mon–Thurs 6am–9pm, Fri & Sat 6am–10pm, Sun 6am–7pm.

Shevek and Co 602 N Bullard St ☎ 575 534 9168, ⓦ silver-eats.com. A full menu of beautifully prepared Mediterranean and, especially, Italian dishes, including seafood, with patio seating in summer. It's undeniably pricey, but all dishes are available in three sizes, from tapas tasters, typically costing $6–8, via mezze, to full entrees for around $30. Mon, Tues & Sun 5–9pm, Fri & Sat 5–9.30pm.

3

The Mogollon and Mimbres mountains

North of Silver City, the volcanic **Mogollon** and **Mimbres mountains** are among the remotest wilderness areas in the US, mostly belonging to the **Gila National Forest**. Until the late nineteenth century, this was an Apache stronghold; **Geronimo** was born at the headwaters of the Gila River and returned throughout his free adult life. Before that, they were home to the **Mogollon** peoples, and the main reason to make the fifty-mile dead-end trip into the mountains on **Hwy-15** is to see the dramatic Mogollon ruins of the **Gila Cliff Dwellings National Monument**.

Hwy-15 is, however, a beautiful drive in its own right, albeit a slow one. It's never especially steep, let alone dangerous, but the twists and turns seem endless. Potential stops along the way include **Pinos Altos** – a fun little semi-ghost town in the woods a few miles out of Silver City that's home to the *Buckhorn Saloon* (see p.197) – and the **Vista Viewpoint** above the Gila River near the far end.

Gila Cliff Dwellings National Monument

45 miles north of Silver City on Hwy-15 • **Visitor centre** Daily: summer 8am–5pm; winter 8am–4.30pm • **Dwellings access** Summer 8am–6pm; winter 9am–4pm • $3 per person or $10 per family • ☎ 575 536 9461, ⓦ nps.gov/gicl

Occupied for just a brief moment in history, between 1270 AD and 1300 AD, the Mogollon pueblo, now preserved as the **GILA CLIFF DWELLINGS NATIONAL MONUMENT**, is southern New Mexico's most spectacular archeological site. While not on the scale of the Ancestral Puebloan "cities" of the Four Corners region, it's much less visited, and you may well have the place to yourself. To modern eyes, ancient Southwestern peoples often seem to have chosen to live in inhospitable places, but here there's no such problem. The dwellings are tucked into sheltered south-facing recesses along the wall of

---

THE MOGOLLON AND THE MIMBRES

Archeologists identify the three major cultures of the prehistoric Southwest as the **Ancestral Puebloans** of the Colorado Plateau, the **Hohokam** of the Salt River Valley around modern Phoenix, and the **Mogollon**, based in the **Mogollon mountains** of what's now southwest New Mexico. Thanks to their proximity to Mexico, Mogollon peoples were among the first to acquire both **agriculture** – in the shape of corn and squash, around 1200 BC – and **pottery** around 200 AD.

At its peak, between 100 AD and 1300 AD, the Mogollon culture extended well into modern Arizona and Mexican Chihuahua. Its heartland, however, remained the **Gila** and **Mimbres** rivers, north and east of modern Silver City. The Mogollon sub-group known as the **Classic Mimbres** culture is considered to represent the ancient Southwest's finest artistic flowering. Above all, the Mimbres people – their name comes from the Spanish for "willows" – were superb **potters**. While the intricate stylized borders of their plates and bowls are typical of many pueblo peoples, their vivid naturalistic images of birds, insects and animals are quite extraordinary. Usually executed in black on white, they also hint at a complex mythology; some show bees or rabbits juxtaposed with strange humanoid creatures, others are what may be prototype *kachina* figures (see p.67), and there are even scenes of decapitation, suggesting human sacrifice.

The Mimbres culture reached its apogee around 1100 AD, when around five thousand people were farming beside the Mimbres River. While depictions of Pacific fish suggest that they travelled extensively, there's little evidence of trade. No Mimbres ceramics have been discovered elsewhere, and it's believed that the finest bowls were created for specific individuals at birth, used in ceremonies throughout their lifetime, and finally **buried** with them. The bowl would be inverted over the head of the corpse, always with a "**kill hole**" punched through it, which according to modern Pueblo Indians released its "spirit" to accompany that of the deceased. As a result, undamaged Mimbres bowls are extremely rare, and Mimbres pottery in general is so valuable that the few known Mimbres sites have been extensively looted, rendering the detective work of archeology almost impossible. As far as anyone can tell, the Mimbres stopped producing pottery around 1150 AD, and left the valley soon afterwards, possibly because overuse had depleted its soil.

a shallow canyon, a couple of hundred feet above a perennial creek and thus in earshot of running water and the constant rustle of small game. "Gila," incidentally, is pronounced "heela," and comes from an Apache word meaning "mountain".

Even when there's no traffic, Hwy-15 requires such care that driving the full 45 miles from Silver City is likely to take two hours. You won't have time to see the monument if you set off from Silver City later than 4pm in summer, or 2pm in winter. If you're coming from the east, Hwy-35, which branches off Hwy-152 fifty miles west of I-25, is not so slow or mountainous, but it's still a hell of a long drive. Either way, the final eight miles follow the broad valley of the Gila River to reach the **visitor centre**, poised near the confluence of the Gila's Middle and West forks.

The **trail** to the dwellings starts a mile further on, crossing the Gila on a long footbridge. Only half a mile along the creek do you get your first glimpse of the pueblo. What from below looks like three separate caves turns out after you climb the hillside to be a single, deep, long alcove with three entrances. Each entrance was sealed with stones and mortar, but behind them lay around forty interconnected rooms, sharing a communal – and presumably very dark – plaza at the rear. As the trail leads into and through the complex, keep an eye out for the pictographs that mark certain dwellings, as well as a granary that still holds a desiccated cache of tiny corn.

| ACCOMMODATION | THE MOGOLLON AND MIMBRES MOUNTAINS |

Forks Campground Hwy-15, 5 miles south of Gila Cliff Dwelling National Monument ☎ 575 536 2250, ⓦ fs.usda.gov. The northernmost of the two small, free Forest-Service campgrounds located either side of the Gila River, at the point where Hwy-15 crosses the river. As at the *Grapevine Campground* immediately across the bridge, campers are dependent on water from the river itself. Another two undeveloped campgrounds are located half a mile south of the monument. First come, first served. **Free**

Gila Hot Springs Ranch Hwy-15, 8 miles south of Gila Cliff Dwelling National Monument ☎ 575 536 9551, ⓦ gilahotspringsranch.com. Spreading comfortably amid verdant green meadows, this high-mountain ranch offers tent camping, RV hookups and a couple of large well-equipped rental units at bargain rates – they can sleep up to ten, with an extra per-person charge payable – and also has its own hot-springs pool. The owners offer single- and multi-day hunting and horseback trips into the mountains. Tents **$15**, RVs **$20**, rental units **$92**

Lordsburg

Sixty miles down the interstate from Deming, 44 miles southwest of Silver City, and just twenty miles short of Arizona, **LORDSBURG** is southwest New Mexico's last gasp. John Wayne went to a lot of trouble to get here in *Stagecoach*, but the desultory strip of gas stations and motels today make you wonder why he bothered.

Far more redolent of the Old West is **SHAKESPEARE**, two miles south, a privately owned **ghost town** that's only open for infrequent guided tours (March–Dec only, on the second Sat & Sun of each month, plus occasional other weekends, 10am & 2pm; $4; ☎ 575 542 9034, ⓦ shakespeareghostown.com). If you go at any other time, there's no access to the site and nothing to see.

| INFORMATION | LORDSBURG |

New Mexico Welcome Center 191 Stagecoach Road, just south of I-10 exit 20 at the west end of town (Mon–Fri 8am–4pm; ☎ 575 542 8149).

ACCOMMODATION AND EATING

Econolodge 1408 S Main St ☎ 575 542 3666, ⓦ econolodge.com. It would be hard to claim there's much to distinguish this large *Econolodge* from its similar neighbours along the few blocks of Main Street that lie south of I-10, but the mom-and-pop motels along Lordsburg's Motel Drive are so consistently dismal that you're better off

settling for one of the sizeable, bland rooms here. **$69**
Kranberry's 1405 S Main St ☎ 575 542 9400. The pick of a humdrum crop of diners, and serves a tasty $9 green chile stew that comes with two flour tortillas. Pretty much every entree, from burrito to burger, costs just under $10. Daily 6am–10pm.

O.K. CORR
"WALK WHERE THE
THE MOST FAMOUS
IN ARIZONA
TOMBSTONE
HISTORAMA
OUTFITTER

Phoenix and southern Arizona

202 Phoenix and around

214 East of Phoenix

218 From Phoenix to Tucson

220 Tucson

230 The Mission Trail

235 Southeast Arizona

244 Southwest Arizona

OK CORRAL, TOMBSTONE

Phoenix and southern Arizona

Despite every conceivable geographic and climatic disadvantage, ninety percent of Arizonans live in Southern Arizona, mainly concentrated in two of the most unlikely cities on earth – Phoenix and Tucson. Not only does Southern Arizona for the most part lack the compelling scenery of the state's northern half, it also lacks the water to support either Phoenix or Tucson. However, although the very existence of either city defies normal logic, they have accrued sufficient political leverage to persuade the federal government to spend ever more money on vast canal projects to meet their needs.

Phoenix in particular can be seen as the bloated spider at the centre of the web, sucking the juices from the rest of the state. By far the largest city in Arizona, it has minimal appeal for tourists wanting to do anything more than lounge by the pool in ultra-expensive resorts. **Tucson** at least has a spark of life, thanks to its long and fascinating history; it started out as a Mexican frontier outpost, and is still surrounded by such missionary relics as the churches of **San Xavier del Bac** and **Tumacácori**. It's also at ease with its desert surroundings, accessible to **Saguaro National Park** and the **Arizona-Sonora Desert Museum**. Beyond Tucson, **southeast Arizona** is the one area of southern Arizona where the landscapes rival those of the Colorado Plateau. As well as intriguing flora and fauna, its "sky islands" hold evocative Wild West sites like **Tombstone**, now an entertaining if slightly tacky theme park of a town, and the mining settlement of **Bisbee**.

Phoenix's fragile grip on reality is highlighted by the fact that it was built on the ruins of a long-lost desert civilization. Until 1350 AD, the valleys of southern Arizona were home to the **Hohokam** people, and crisscrossed by sophisticated irrigation canals. The Hohokam eventually depleted the land too much for their way of life to endure. Their name means "people who have vanished" in the language of the **O'odham** (once known as the Pima and the Papago) who later took their place. The O'odham now occupy vast reservations in southwest Arizona, while their old enemies, the **Apache**, dominate the mountains to the east.

Phoenix and around

When it began life in the 1860s, as a sweltering little farming town, **PHOENIX** must have seemed like a good idea. Set in the heart of the **Salt River Valley**, which measures forty miles east to west and twenty miles north to south, with a ready-made irrigation system left by ancient Indians, it had lots of room to expand. Within a century, however, Phoenix had turned into what writer Edward Abbey called "the blob that is eating Arizona," acquiring as it did so the money and political clout to grow way beyond its natural limitations. Today, Arizona's capital has filled the entire valley and is the sixth largest city in the US. Over 1.5 million people live within the city boundaries, and around four million

Excursions from Phoenix p.209
The legend of the Lost Dutchman p.216
The unbelievable story of Biosphere 2
  p.219
The saguaro cactus; a desert saga p.226

Opening the House of the Wind p.232
The gunfight at the OK Corral p.240
A fortified frontier p.242
Hi Jolly's final camp p.249

THE HEARD MUSEUM, PHOENIX

Highlights

❶ The Heard Museum Arizona's finest collection of Native American artefacts, including hundreds of superb Hopi *kachinas*. See p.208

❷ Desert Botanical Garden A tremendous assortment of fascinating desert plants thrives in the heat of the Valley of the Sun. See p.210

❸ Hotel Congress Downtown Tucson's hippest hangout; not just a hotel and a hostel, but also a great café and nightclub. See p.225

❹ Saguaro National Park There's nowhere quite like it; hordes of towering multi-armed saguaro cactuses march across the desert hills of Tucson. See p.227

❺ San Xavier del Bac The spectacular "White Dove of the Desert" has to be the Southwest's most beautiful mission church. See p.230

❻ Tombstone From the OK Corral to *Big Nose Kate's*, Tombstone is an irresistible throwback to the wildest days of the West. See p.237

❼ Bisbee Atmospheric old mining town that has reinvented itself as a cozy, arty, mountain hideaway for overheated Arizonans. See p.240

❽ Chiricahua National Monument Apache such as Geronimo and Cochise once hid among the weird rock formations of this remote mountain fastness. See p.242

HIGHLIGHTS ARE MARKED ON THE MAP ON P.204

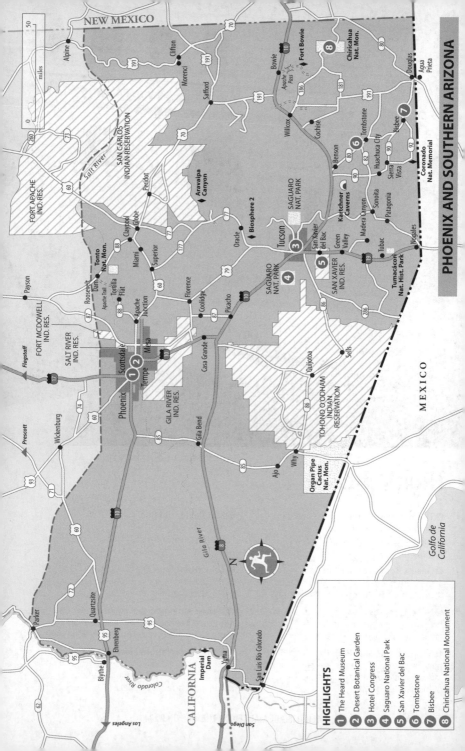

PHOENIX AND SOUTHERN ARIZONA

NEW MEXICO

CALIFORNIA

MEXICO

Golfo de California

HIGHLIGHTS

1. The Heard Museum
2. Desert Botanical Garden
3. Hotel Congress
4. Saguaro National Park
5. San Xavier del Bac
6. Tombstone
7. Bisbee
8. Chiricahua National Monument

miles · 0 · 50

people inhabit the twenty separate incorporated cities, such as **Scottsdale, Tempe** and **Mesa**, which together make up the metropolitan area. The entire Phoenix area is also known colloquially as the **Valley of the Sun**, but the term has no official meaning.

Perhaps the single most defining characteristic of Phoenix, even more than its sheer size, is that it's **hot**; between June and August daytime highs average over 100°F, making it one of the world's hottest cities outside the Middle East. While that may put off visitors in summer, when local room rates are at their lowest, tourists flock here from colder climes in winter, to enjoy temperatures that rarely drop below 65°F. They pay vast sums to warm their bones in the luxury resorts and spas, concentrated especially in Scottsdale, that are the modern equivalent of the 1930s dude ranches. Unlike golf, tennis, and shopping in the city's plentiful upscale malls, **sightseeing** rarely ranks high on the agenda. In fact, apart from the **Heard Museum**'s excellent Native American displays, the cactuses at the **Desert Botanical Garden**, and Frank Lloyd Wright's architecture studio at **Taliesin West**, Phoenix is short of must-see attractions. If you're on a touring vacation, there's no reason to spend more than a night or two, and you could easily choose to bypass it altogether.

Brief history

Phoenix epitomizes the Western maxim that "water flows uphill to money"; its history revolves around its manoeuvrings to obtain ever more water, from ever further afield. The first Anglo-American settler in the Salt River Valley was John Smith in 1865, who supplied hay to Camp McDowell, thirty miles northeast. However, the obvious traces of over three hundred miles of canals dug by the ancient Hohokam people (see p.463) made it clear that the valley had once supported a large population. By clearing one such canal in 1867, Confederate deserter Jack Swilling established Phoenix. It was named by British adventurer "Lord" Darrel Duppa, who saw it as rising like the mythical bird from the ashes of the Hohokam civilization.

4

Phoenix was laid out in 1870 on a 98-block grid measuring one mile long by half a mile wide. Avenues and streets (now numbered) were named for Indian tribes, and cross streets for presidents. By 1889 it was **capital** of Arizona, and home to over ten thousand people. Catastrophic floods and droughts during the 1890s convinced the city-dwellers that their future depended on ensuring a safe, dependable source of water. The building of the **Roosevelt Dam** in the mountains to the east, in 1911 (see p.216), marked the first step in a process that culminated with the completion of the **Central Arizona Project**, a 336-mile canal from the Colorado River to Phoenix and Tucson, in the 1990s.

By the 1920s Phoenix was promoting itself as the "winter playground of the Southwest," a healthy refuge from the smog-laden cities of the East. Its citizens were exhorted to landscape their properties with gardens, under the slogan "**Let's Do Away With the Desert**," and lavish resort hotels began to open. Exponential growth truly began during World War II, when the city acquired three major air bases, and **industrialization** continued apace during the 1950s. The development of **air-conditioning** finally made the desert heat bearable, and the population swelled from 107,000 to 439,000 between 1950 and 1960 alone. As it swallowed a host of neighbouring communities, the city's endless sprawl swiftly covered the "golden fields of ripened grain" described in one 1940s guidebook. By the time it topped one million, around 1990, it had grown by over four hundred square miles in forty years.

Central Phoenix

Although **Downtown Phoenix** – defined as the few blocks east and west of Central Avenue and north and south of **Washington Street** – remains too hot and too spread out to walk around in any comfort, determined efforts have been made to regenerate and revitalize the area. A ninety-block district, focusing on two massive side-by-side sports stadiums, the **US Airways Center** and **Chase Field** (home respectively to the

Phoenix Suns and Arizona Diamondbacks) has even been rebranded under the name of **Copper Square**.

What little remains of Phoenix's nineteenth-century architecture now constitutes **Heritage Square**, a couple of blocks southeast of the Arizona Center at 115 N Sixth St. Rather than original adobe ranch houses, however, it preserves a quaint assortment of Victorian homes converted into tea rooms and toy museums.

ACCOMMODATION	
Aloft Tempe	7
Arizona Biltmore Resort & Spa	4
Four Seasons Resort Scottsdale	1
Hermosa Inn	3
Holiday Inn Express Phoenix Airport	9
Maricopa Manor	5
Sleep Inn Airport	8
Sleep Inn at North Scottsdale Rd	2
Tempe Mission Palms Hotel	6

NIGHTLIFE	
Four Peaks Brewing Company	2
Marquee Theatre	1

Arizona Science Center

600 E Washington St • Daily 10am–5pm • $15, ages 3–17 $11 • ☎ 602 716 2000, ⓦ azscience.org

The **Arizona Science Center** ranks as Arizona's second-favourite tourist attraction, welcoming barely fewer visitors each year than the Grand Canyon. Aimed primarily at children, it's a hands-on museum of learning games and interactive gimmicks that centres on a giant-screen movie theatre.

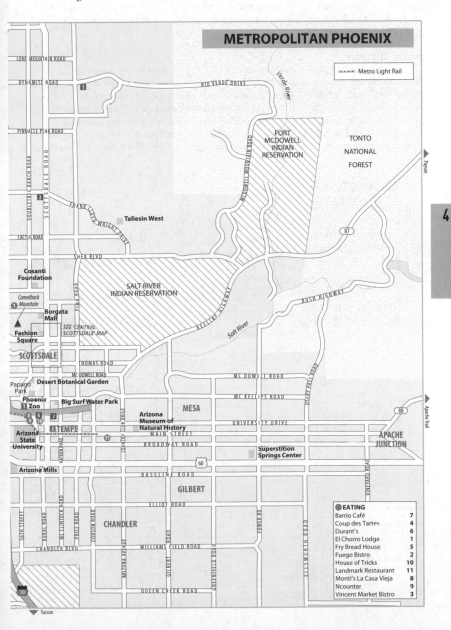

4

4

Phoenix Art Museum

1625 N Central Ave • Wed 10am–9pm, Thurs–Sat 10am–5pm, Sun noon–5pm • $15, ages 6–17 $6 • ☎ 602 257 1222, ⓦ phxart.org

The permanent collection at the vast and hugely rewarding **Phoenix Art Museum**, a mile north of dowtown, is sensibly rooted in an extensive array of Western art, with all the names you'd expect – Frederic Remington, Georgia O'Keeffe – and including an enjoyable room devoted to Arizona artist Philip Curtis. Anish Kapoor's black sculpture *Upside Down Inside Out* is another highlight, and temporary exhibitions range through all eras and styles. A top-quality gift store stocks Mexican crafts items and jazzy modern ceramics.

Heard Museum

2301 N Central Ave • Mon–Sat 9.30am–5pm, Sun 11am–5pm • $18; ages 6–12 $7.50 • ☎ 602 252 8848, ⓦ heard.org

Much the finest museum in Phoenix, the **Heard Museum** has been greatly enlarged in the last few years, while still showcasing its lovely old original buildings. It provides a good introduction to the culture of the **Native Americans** of the Southwest, and their arts and crafts in particular. A sumptuous pottery collection includes stunning Mimbres bowls (see p.198), clay dolls made by the Quechan and Mohave peoples as souvenirs for nineteenth-century railroad passengers, and modern Hopi ceramics. You'll

EXCURSIONS FROM PHOENIX

If a family visit or business trip to Phoenix brings you to Arizona for the first time and you'd like to see a little more of the state, you'll have to rent a car to get anywhere interesting.

Great **day-trips** include driving a hundred miles north on I-17 and visiting some combination of **Montezuma Castle** (see p.280), **Sedona** (see p.271), and **Jerome** (p.277), or following the **Apache Trail** northeast from Mesa, as described on p.216. With a **weekend** to spare, the **Grand Canyon** is an obvious possibility, though it is a 450-mile round-trip excursion. Alternatively, **Flagstaff** is a good base for several lesser known attractions (see p.262), while Wild West fans will enjoy **Tombstone**, 180 miles southeast (see p.237). Best of all, if you're up to driving three hundred miles each way, is northeast Arizona's stupendous **Canyon de Chelly** (see p.58).

---

also find a complete Navajo *hogan* (see p.62), some fine old Havasupai baskets, Apache beadwork, and painted buffalo-skin shields from New Mexican pueblos. Best of all are the Hopi **kachina dolls** – see p.67 – four hundred of which were donated by arch-conservative Arizona senator Barry Goldwater. Additional galleries upstairs tell the heartbreaking story of how the federal government shattered traditional family life by shipping Native American children to boarding schools. The museum also holds a superb store, and a good café.

Scottsdale

Now home to almost 250,000 people and stretching more than twenty miles from north to south, the town of **SCOTTSDALE**, founded ten miles northeast of Phoenix in the 1880s, is a remarkable success story in its own right. Despite being almost wholly subsumed into the metropolitan maw, it has carved itself an eccentric double niche as both the city's chic-est destination, home to opulent resorts and designer-led malls, and its most determinedly "Western" quarter.

Southeast of **Camelback Mountain** and the **Scottsdale Fashion Square** mall, downtown Scottsdale centres on a few pleasant blocks of sidewalk cafés and souvenir stores. West of Scottsdale Road counts as the **Main Street Arts and Antiques District**; to the east, **Old Town** plays the Wild West theme for all it's worth.

Taliesin West

114th St and Frank Lloyd Wright Blvd • Oct–May daily 10am–4pm; June & Sept daily 9am–4pm; July & Aug Mon & Thurs–Sun 9am–4pm; see website for tour schedules • Panorama Tour $24, Insight Tour $32, Behind The Scenes Tour $60 • ☎ 480 860 2700, ⓦ franklloydwright.org

Whatever its general appearance may suggest, Phoenix has managed to attract some visionary designers. Notable among them was **Frank Lloyd Wright**, who came to the city to work on the *Biltmore Hotel* and returned to spend the winter for most of the 25 years before his death in 1959. His studio, **Taliesin West** – at Scottsdale's far northeastern edge, a dozen miles from the Old Town – is now an architecture school and a working design studio, with multimedia exhibits of the man's life and work.

Seventy years after Wright first came here, Taliesin West is still a splendidly isolated spot, where his trademark "organic architecture" makes perfect sense. Wright and his students camped out and assessed the terrain long before building any permanent structures, and the complex blends seamlessly into the desert. It can only be seen on guided visits, the main options being the hour-long "Panorama Tour"; the ninety-minute "Insight Tour", which grants access to Wright's private living area; and the three-hour "Behind The Scenes Tour". The expertise and enthusiasm of the guides makes the experience well worth the relatively high price.

Scottsdale Fashion Square

Main St Arts & Antiques District

EATING
Arcadia Farms	2
Bandera	5
Cowboy Ciao	1
Malee's Thai on Main	3
The Mission	4

■ ACCOMMODATION
Motel 6 Scottsdale	1
The Phoenician	2

CAMELBACK ROAD

Arizona Canal

INDIAN SCHOOL ROAD

OLD TOWN

MAIN ST

Scottsdale Museum of Contemporary Arts

OSBORN ROAD

0   400
yards

N

CENTRAL SCOTTSDALE

Cosanti Foundation

6433 Doubletree Ranch Rd • Mon–Sat 9am–5pm, Sun 11am–5pm • $1 donation • ☎ 480 948 6145, ⓦ arcosanti.org

Designed by **Paolo Soleri**, an Italian-born former student of Frank Lloyd Wright, and constructed out of rammed earth and concrete, the buildings at the **Cosanti Foundation** have a similar organic feel to those at Taliesin West, four miles northeast. Crafts workshops cast bells and bronzes, and a small museum shows drawings and models of Soleri's life work, the planned community of **Arcosanti** (see p.281).

Desert Botanical Garden

1201 North Galvin Parkway • Daily: May–Sept 7am–8pm; Oct–April 8am–8pm • $18, ages 3–12 $8 • ☎ 480 941 1225, ⓦ dbg.org

In **Papago Park**, at the south end of Scottsdale, the fascinating **Desert Botanical Garden** is filled with an amazing array of cactuses and desert flora from around the world. Prime specimens include spineless "totem pole" cactuses from the Galápagos Islands and "living stone" plants from South Africa that at a glance you'd never suspect were alive. Separate enclaves are devoted to **butterflies** – seen at their best in August and September – and to **hummingbirds**, of which Arizona boasts fifteen indigenous species.

Tempe

Contemporary Phoenix's major success story has been the transformation of the community of **TEMPE** into the liveliest and most dynamic portion of the Valley of the Sun. It lies south of Scottsdale, across I-60, and six miles east of downtown Phoenix. The seventy thousand students of **Arizona State University** keep the cafés, clubs, stores and restaurants of the red-brick **Mill Avenue** constantly buzzing. Several minor museums and galleries are dotted across the college campus, immediately east, while a couple of blocks north the Salt River has been dammed and its surroundings landscaped to create an appealing park, the **Tempe Town Lake**.

Mesa

Built on the site of the Mormon settlement of Fort Utah, which lasted for three years from 1877, **MESA**, east of Tempe, is now Arizona's third-largest city. Covering more than a hundred square miles, it has a population of around 450,000. Spread among its endless broad boulevards are twenty golf courses, several large malls, some of Phoenix's most affordable residential districts, and dozens of cheap motels. With the Superstition Mountains rising to the east, it's not a bad base for passing visitors.

Arizona Museum of Natural History

53 N MacDonald St • Tues–Fri 10am–5pm, Sat 11am–5pm, Sun 1–5pm • $10, ages 6–12 $6 • ☏ 480 644 2230, ⓦ arizonamuseumofnaturalhistory.org

As well as displays on dinosaurs, including skeletons and animatronic models, the enjoyable **Arizona Museum of Natural History** features a fascinating reconstruction of a block of Mesa's Main Street as it looked a century ago. Other sections cover the Hohokam, and the story of the Lost Dutchman Mine (see p.216).

ARRIVAL

PHOENIX AND AROUND

By plane Sky Harbor International Airport is 3 miles east of downtown (ⓦphxskyharbor.com). Free shuttles connect it with the nearest Metro Light Rail station at 44th and Washington (ⓦvalleymetro.org), while SuperShuttle (☏602 244 9000 or ☏800 258 3826, ⓦsupershuttle.com) operates door-to-door shuttle buses costing around $13 for downtown destinations and more like $25 for Scottsdale. Arizona Shuttle Services runs shuttles to other towns in

Arizona, including Tucson, Sedona and Prescott (☏520 795 6771 or ☏800 888 2749, ⓦarizonashuttle.com).
By train Amtrak trains don't serve Phoenix, though bus connections coincide with Amtrak services to Tucson and Flagstaff.
By bus Greyhound buses arrive at 2115 E Buckeye Rd (☏602 389 4200, ⓦgreyhound.com), close to the airport.

GETTING AROUND

By car Phoenix is so vast, and so utterly dependent on car travel, that it's much easier to drive than to use public transport – even driving, it can take hours to get across town.
By Metro Light Rail The Metro Light Rail System (one-way ride $2, one-day pass $4; ☏602 253 5000, ⓦvalleymetro.org) follows a twenty-mile route, from

Camelback Road north of downtown Phoenix to Apache Boulevard in Mesa. There are stations in downtown Phoenix and Tempe, and also close to the airport, but it's much more useful for commuters than visitors.
By taxi Yellow Cab (☏480 888 8888, ⓦaaayellowaz.com).

INFORMATION

Phoenix 125 N Second St, downtown (Mon–Fri 8am–5pm; ☏602 254 6500 or ☏877 225 5749, ⓦvisitphoenix.com).
Scottsdale 4343 N Scottsdale Rd (Mon–Fri 8am–5pm; ☏480 421 1004 or ☏800 782 1117, ⓦscottsdalecvb.com).

Tempe 51 W Third St (Mon–Fri 8am–5pm; ☏480 894 8158 or ☏866 914 1052, ⓦtempetourism.com).
Mesa 120 N Center St (Mon–Fri 8am–5pm; ☏480 827 4700 or ☏800 283 6732, ⓦvisitmesa.com).

ACCOMMODATION

Metropolitan Phoenix is so huge that it's essential to stay near the places you want to visit. **Downtown Phoenix** is relatively inexpensive, with cheap motels lining the somewhat rundown **Van Buren Street** a few blocks north of the centre. Room rates are considerably more expensive in **winter**, when snowbirds from all over the US fill the upscale resorts of **Scottsdale** in particular; arrive between June and August, and you could well get a swanky room for half-price or less.

CENTRAL PHOENIX

Arizona Biltmore Resort & Spa 2400 E Missouri Ave ☏602 955 6600 or ☏800 950 0086, ⓦarizonabiltmore .com. Extraordinarily lavish 750-room resort, built under the influence of Frank Lloyd Wright in the 1930s and still retaining its Art Deco trimmings and extravagant gardens despite subsequent renovations. Low-season rates can be a real bargain. Two golf courses, four restaurants, eight pools, plus afternoon teas, tennis and spa. Winter $327, summer $167
Budget Lodge Motel 402 W Van Buren St ☏602 254 7247, ⓦblphx.com. For a no-nonsense room at a very attractive rate, this unexciting motel offers the best deal within walking distance of the downtown core; you won't want to walk here after dark, though. $69
CamelBackpackers Hostel 1601 N 13th Ave ☏602 258 4143, ⓦcamelbackpackers.com. Clean, friendly hostel in

a former private home on the northern fringes of downtown, opened by a keen traveller in 2012 and aimed at young international backpackers. As well as two mixed 6–8-bed dorms, and one private room capable of sleeping up to 4, there's a shared lounge and kitchen. Check in 3–8pm, free (basic) breakfasts and wi-fi. Dorm $26, double $60
HI Phoenix – Metcalf House 1026 N Ninth St above Roosevelt St ☏602 254 9803, ⓦhiusa.org/phoenix. Dorm beds in a slightly rundown location in a residential district, 15min walk north of the Arizona Center. No phone reservations, but space is usually available in the ten-bed men's dorm and four-bed "ladies" dorm. No curfew, plus use of kitchen and laundry; rates include breakfast. Check in 8–10am & 5–10pm, $3 surcharge if you're not a member of Hostelling International. Closed July. Dorms $23.50

4

4

Holiday Inn Express Phoenix Airport 3401 E University Drive ☎ 602 453 9900, ⊛ hiexpress.com. This very presentable, good-value motel, between Phoenix and Tempe, may not be a place to spend very much time, but its large modern rooms make a handy overnight stop before or after a flight from nearby Sky Harbor – connected by free shuttles – and there's a pool and complimentary breakfast. Winter $136, summer $106

Maricopa Manor 15 W Pasadena Ave ☎ 602 264 9204 or ☎ 800 292 6403, ⊛ maricopamanor.com. The pick of the valley's B&Bs is handily poised between Phoenix and Scottsdale, near a light-rail station. Housed in a 1928 hacienda-style home, it holds six all-suite rooms, equipped with kitchenettes, sleeping up to four, and decorated to widely varying themes, from Arts and Crafts to Mexican. Winter $229, summer $119

Hotel San Carlos 202 N Central Ave ☎ 602 253 4121 or ☎ 866 253 4121, ⊛ hotelsancarlos.com. To appreciate this historic, very central 1920s hotel, you have to be the kind of traveller who positively prefers an old-fashioned, frazzled and often noisy downtown hotel to a crisp, new, deathly quiet motel. That said, the rooms are very tastefully furnished, if small, and there's a nice Vietnamese restaurant, and a rooftop swimming pool. Winter $189, summer $119

SCOTTSDALE

Four Seasons Resort Scottsdale at Troon North 10600 East Crescent Moon Drive ☎ 480 515 5700, ⊛ fourseasons.com/scottsdale. Magnificent desert resort, with very luxurious rooms and suites arrayed in separate casitas around spacious swimming pools in the cactus-studded mountains to the north of Scottsdale, plus a good spa and fine restaurants. Winter $474, summer $164

Hermosa Inn 5532 N Palo Cristi Rd ☎ 602 955 8614 or ☎ 800 241 1210, ⊛ hermosainn.com. 1930s guest ranch, set in desert gardens halfway between Phoenix and Scottsdale in Paradise Valley, that's been converted into a tranquil 35-room boutique hotel, with a genuine Southwestern ambience to its large, luxurious rooms and a good restaurant. Winter $319, summer $209

Motel 6 Scottsdale 6848 E Camelback Rd ☎ 480 946 2280, ⊛ motel6.com. Cut-price lodgings are few and far between in Scottsdale, so this totally unremarkable budget motel, just off I-17 close to the Fashion Mall and downtown Scottsdale, is well worth considering. Winter $86, summer $52

The Phoenician 6000 E Camelback Rd ☎ 480 941 8200 or ☎ 800 888 8234, ⊛ thephoenician.com. Gorgeous 250-acre resort, spread out at the base of Camelback Mountain at the northern end of Scottsdale and offering every conceivable luxury, with golf course, waterfalls and lush gardens as well as lavish rooms and restaurants. Winter $479, summer $249

Sleep Inn at North Scottsdale Rd 16630 North Scottsdale Rd ☎ 480 998 9211 or ☎ 888 767 8809, ⊛ sleepinnscottsdale.com. Dependable, upscale chain motel, convenient for visiting Frank Lloyd Wright's Taliesin West with a pool, hot tub and free breakfasts. A free shuttle bus will take you anywhere within 5 miles, but downtown Scottsdale is actually 10 miles south. Winter $129, summer $89

TEMPE

Aloft Tempe 951 E Playa Del Norte Drive ☎ 480 621 3300 or ☎ 877 462 5638, ⊛ alofthotels.com/tempe. Aimed at younger, hipper travellers, the Aloft chain is a much more affordable and frankly more likeable offshoot of the rather snooty designer W hotel group, and with its bright palette and pool table in the lobby bar it's a good fit for Tempe. The rooms themselves are spacious with high (loft-like) ceilings and rainfall showers. Winter $119, summer $79

Sleep Inn Airport 2621 S 47th Place ☎ 480 967 7100 or ☎ 800 631 3054, ⊛ sleepinn.com. Above-average chain motel, three miles south of the airport but served by 24hr free shuttles; breakfast is free. Winter $95, summer $70

Tempe Mission Palms Hotel 60 E Fifth St ☎ 480 894 1400 or ☎ 800 547 8705, ⊛ missionpalms.com. Very comfortable Southwestern-themed, largely business-oriented hotel in Tempe's revitalized Mill Ave district, with an opulent rooftop swimming pool. Come in summer, and it's a pretty good deal. Winter $239, summer $150

EATING

Unless you're prepared to pay resort prices, it's hard to find a good **restaurant** in Phoenix with very much atmosphere. Apart from a block or two in **central Scottsdale**, and Tempe's lively **Mill Avenue**, no areas are small enough to walk around while you look for a place to eat, but if you're happy to drive, **neighbourhood diners** – especially Mexican – can still be found, and the major thoroughfares are the usual fast-food heaven.

CENTRAL PHOENIX

Alice Cooper'stown 101 E Jackson St ☎ 602 253 7337, ⊛ alicecooperstown.com. Barbecue restaurant-cum-sports bar, owned by the rock star and local resident, filled with huge TV screens, and located alongside downtown's US Airways Center. While far from fine dining, the food's better

than you might expect, with barbecue sandwiches at $9 and mixed plates for $14, and the atmosphere is fun, with waiters in full Alice make-up. Mon–Thurs 11am–9.30pm, Fri & Sat 11am–11pm, Sun noon–8pm.

Barrio Café 2814 N 16th St ☎ 602 636 0240, ⊛ barriocafe.com. Reservations are not taken at this

wildly popular little local Mexican place, but it's worth the wait – you can always bide your time sampling the huge array of tequilas, and there's live music Thurs–Sun – to enjoy authentic southern Mexican food, including succulent *cochinita pibil* (pork) for $12, and guacamole freshly made at your table. Tues–Thurs 11am–10pm, Fri 11am–10.30pm, Sat 5–10.30pm, Sun 11am–9pm.

Coup des Tartes 4626 N 16th St ☎602 212 1082, ⊛nicetartes.com. Unassuming 1930s farmhouse that conceals a romantic little restaurant, serving classic French appetizers like brie with caramelized apples ($12), a broader range of entrees from Moroccan lamb shank ($24) to rosemary pork tenderloin ($29), and succulent French tarts ($9). The lunch menu is more limited, with sandwiches and sliders at $12–15. Bring your own wine, with a corkage charge of $10 per bottle. Mon 11am–2pm, Tues–Thurs 11am–2pm & 5.30–10pm, Fri 11am–2pm & 5–11pm, Sat 5–11pm, Sun 10am–2pm.

Durant's 2611 N Central Ave ☎602 264 5967, ⊛durantsaz.com. This old-style downtown restaurant is a venerable institution for Arizona's elite, complete with red-leather banquettes and velvet wallpaper, and specializing in rich all-American food such as oysters Rockefeller ($17.50) and steaks, at $33 and up; if you can down the 48-oz Porterhouse, your name gets added to a plaque on the wall. They stop serving food at 10pm weekdays, 11pm weekends, but locals also drop in for late-night drinks at the atmospheric central bar. Mon–Thurs 11am–midnight, Fri 11am–1am, Sat 5pm–1am, Sun 4.30pm–midnight.

Fry Bread House 4140 N Seventh Ave ☎602 351 2345. You'll find fry bread on native American reservations throughout the Southwest; here, though, thanks to Tohono O'odham chef Cecelia Miller, it's raised to fluffy perfection and sold with both savoury (say, chile or chorizo) and sweet (chocolate!) toppings, for $5–8. Mon–Thurs 10am–8pm, Fri & Sat 10am–9pm.

Fuego Bistro 713 E Palo Verde Rd ☎602 277 1151, ⊛fuegobistro.com. Delicious contemporary Latin American food, in a hard-to-find spot five miles north of downtown. Dinner entrees like panko-crusted tilapia or the seafood-stuffed chile relleno cost $21–25, but lunch, of chicken tortilla soup for example, is less than half that. Tues–Sat 11am–2pm & 3–9pm.

Pizzeria Bianco Heritage Square, 623 E Adams St ☎602 258 8300, ⊛pizzeriabianco.com. High-quality brick-oven pizzas at $12–16, in a very convenient downtown location, with ultra-fresh ingredients including home-made mozzarella; no wonder it's so popular. No reservations. Mon 11am–9pm, Tues–Sat 11am–10pm.

Vincent Market Bistro 3930 E Camelback Rd ☎602 224 3727, ⊛vincentsoncamelback.com. Very inexpensive but high-quality French-style bistro/deli, with a tiny outdoor seating area, squeezed around the back of *Vincent's* much more upscale fine-dining restaurant (also recommended).

When the thriving farmers' market to which it's attached is in full swing, on Saturdays between Oct and May, there's no table service. Lunchtime salads and omelettes cost around $8, thin-crust pizzas are $10, and dinner entrees like coq au vin or beef bourguignon cost just $12–14; specials include seafood kebab or paella. They'll also deliver, as Vincent Van Go. Mon–Sat 7am–8pm, Sun 7am–2pm.

SCOTTSDALE

Arcadia Farms 7014 E First Ave ☎480 941 5665, ⊛arcadiafarmscafe.com. The most popular lunch rendezvous in Scottsdale's Old Town – salads, sandwiches and entrees, including daily specials like crepes, crab cakes and quesadillas, cost $13–16 – also serves healthy Southwestern breakfasts, and there's open-air courtyard seating. Daily 8am–3pm.

Bandera 3821 N Scottsdale Rd ☎480 994 3524, ⊛hillstone.com. Chicken cooked in the wood-burning oven ($17) is the speciality in this busy, inexpensive rotisserie on the southeast edge of downtown, though other meats and fish are almost as good. Mon–Thurs & Sun 4.30–10pm, Fri & Sat 4.30–11pm.

Cowboy Ciao 7133 E Stetson Drive at Sixth ☎480 946 3111, ⊛cowboyciao.com. Appropriately enough, considering a decor that blends an Old West roadhouse with an Italian feel, this hip downtown option serves "modern American food with global influences." At lunchtime, a burger or seared tuna sandwich costs $13–19; the $13 "Stetson" chopped salad is also available in the evening, when a "mucho mushrooms" stir-fry is $25 and the cumin-rubbed pork shank is $33. Mon–Thurs & Sun 11.30am–2.30pm & 5–10pm, Fri & Sat 11.30am–2.30pm & 5–11pm.

El Chorro Lodge 5550 E Lincoln Drive ☎480 948 5170, ⊛elchorrolodge.com. Spacious, classy Paradise Valley lodge that's been catering to Phoenix sophisticates since 1937; dine alfresco in summer, or by the cozy fireside in winter. Dinner entrees range from $16 buffalo burgers and $19 vegetarian pasta up to rack of lamb at $49, while Sunday brunch is a local tradition, with the signature Eggs Benedict costing $18. Mon–Sat 5–10pm, Sun 9am–3pm (Oct–May only) & 5–10pm.

Malee's Thai on Main 7131 E Main St ☎480 947 6042, ⊛maleesthaibistro.com. Somewhat inconspicuous but very popular and dependably good Thai place downtown, serving all the usual items – pad thai noodles, chicken green curry – at reasonable prices (typically $15), in a smart date-night setting. Mon–Wed 11am–9pm, Thurs–Sat 11am–9.30pm, Sun 4.30–9pm.

The Mission 3815 N Brown Ave ☎480 636 5005, ⊛themissionaz.com. Named for the whitewashed adobe church alongside, and with stunning decor – including one wall made of salt blocks – that's designed to echo its architecture, this "modern Latin" restaurant draws equally on

4

Old- and New-World cuisines. Classics like made-to-order guacamole ($12) are complemented by $24–28 meat and seafood entrees, prepared on either a wood-fired or flat-top "a la plancha" grill. The tequila bar stays open until 2am. Mon–Thurs & Sun 11am–10pm, Fri & Sat 11am–11pm.

TEMPE

House of Tricks 114 E Seventh St ☏ 480 968 1114, ⓦ houseoftricks.com. Tiny modern-American place in the University district, named for chefs Robin and Robert Trick, with lots of vegetarian options and some lovely, well shaded courtyard seating. Dinner entrees range from $23 for mushroom gnocchi up to $39 for poached lobster tail with cornbread pudding. Mon–Sat 11am–10pm.

Monti's La Casa Vieja 100 S Mill Ave ☏ 480 967 7594, ⓦ montis.com. Tempe's oldest adobe house, built beside the Salt River ferry landing in 1873, is now an atmospheric Western-themed diner, serving a conventional steak-and-chicken menu at surprisingly low prices, with burgers at $13 and steaks $18–30. Mon–Thurs & Sun 11am–10pm, Sat & Sun 11am–11pm.

Ncounter 310 S Mill Ave ☏ 480 968 9288, ⓦ ncounter .com. Large, very popular canteen in the thick of Tempe's buzzing downtown, with some outdoor seating. Open for breakfast and lunch only, it's an ideal stop-off for anything from a $5.50 stack of pancakes to an $8.50 Waldorf salad, a $9 cheesy croque-monsieur, or simply a $5 fresh-fruit smoothie. Daily 7am–3.05pm.

MESA

The Landmark Restaurant 809 W Main St ☏ 480 962 4652, ⓦ landmarkrestaurant.com. Classic mid-American diner housed in a former Mormon church, serving hearty baked and roasted meats for $22–32, including a trip to the excellent salad bar. Mon–Thurs 11am–8pm, Fri & Sat 11am–9pm, Sun 11am–7pm.

NIGHTLIFE AND ENTERTAINMENT

Phoenix's **nightlife** has less of a Western identity than you might expect, with Tempe and Scottsdale respectively cultivating an alt-rock, college crowd, and a glitzier clubbing scene. For a rundown of what's happening musically, pick up the free weekly *New Times* (ⓦ phoenixnewtimes.com), or check out the bars and clubs listed below.

BARS AND CLUBS

Bar Smith 130 E Washington St, Phoenix ☏ 602 229 1265, ⓦ barsmithphoenix.com. The best thing about this stylish downtown bar and lounge is its fabulous outdoor dance floor, upstairs. Mon–Thurs 11am–2pm, Fri 11am–2am, Sat 10pm–2am.

Bikini Lounge 1502 Grand Ave, Phoenix ☏ 602 252 0472, ⓦ thebikinilounge.com. A real gem of a dive bar, this veteran tiki bar attracts a fascinating, eclectic mix of local characters. Daily 3pm until late.

Four Peaks Brewing Company 1340 E Eighth St, Tempe ☏ 480 303 9967, ⓦ fourpeaks.com. The best brewpub in the metropolitan area, near the university a mile or so east of Mill Ave, with good beer and a full menu of pub grub, plus some outdoor seating. Mon–Sat 11am–2am, Sun 10am–2am.

Last Exit Live 717 S Central Ave, Phoenix ☏ 602 271 7000, ⓦ lastexitlive.com. Formerly a staple of the Tempe scene, this rock-oriented live music venue has moved to a new downtown location, where it continues to programme acts ranging from country-rock to local punks. Hours vary.

Marquee Theatre 730 N Mill Ave, Tempe ☏ 480 829 0607, ⓦ luckymanonline.com. The best venue to see big-name touring acts, with an open floor rather than seating, and good beer. Hours vary.

Monarch Theatre 122 E Washington St, Phoenix ☏ 602 692 9633, ⓦ facebook.com/monarchtheatre. Downtown Phoenix's hottest new club opened in 2012, in a former nightclub space overhauled with a huge dancefloor and stage to pus the biggest names in electronica. Hours vary.

East of Phoenix

Almost two hundred miles of mountainous terrain stands between Phoenix and New Mexico to the east, much of it belonging to two huge Apache reservations. Although sweltering Phoenicians spend summer weekends in hill towns to the northeast, like Payson and Pinetop, there's little to detain ordinary tourists on the long drive east.

US-60 and US-70 are the quickest routes to New Mexico, but if you want a quick escape from the desert heat, head instead up the **Apache Trail** into the **Superstition Mountains**, the site in legend of the **Lost Dutchman Mine**.

THE LEGEND OF THE LOST DUTCHMAN

The **Superstition Mountains** east of Phoenix are famous in Wild West lore as the site of the legendary **Lost Dutchman Mine**. The story goes that around 1870, two German prospectors, Jacob Waltz and Jacob Weiser, discovered rich deposits of gold, and turned up repeatedly in the town of Florence bearing priceless nuggets. Before his death in Phoenix in 1890, Waltz is said to have murdered not only Weiser but another seven men who tried to shadow him back to the motherlode. Ever since, expeditions have attempted to follow his deathbed directions to the mine – guarded, according to different accounts, by pygmies or a never-discovered group of Apache – and thirty gold-seekers are rumoured to have lost their lives.

The Apache Trail

The closest accessible wilderness to central Phoenix lies along **Hwy-88**, which climbs northeast into the Superstition Mountains from Apache Junction, almost twenty miles east of Mesa and a good thirty miles from downtown Phoenix. Constructed in 1904 to reach the Roosevelt Dam, then being built at the confluence of Tonto Creek and Salt River, this fifty-mile highway was later renamed **The Apache Trail** to attract tourists. Still a popular scenic drive, it's a long, slow haul, taking around two hours end to end.

Goldfield Ghost Town

4650 N Mammoth Mine Rd; 4 miles northeast of Apache Junction • Daily 10am–5pm • Attractions individually priced • ☎ 480 983 0333, Ⓦ goldfieldghosttown.com

As the cactus-studded foothills of the Superstition Mountains start to rise, ramshackle **Goldfield Ghost Town** provides an appealing photo opportunity, complete with discarded mine machinery and a street of tumbledown timber-frame stores. Much of what you see is either fake or brought from somewhere else, but it's all quite atmospheric. **Activities** including descents into mine shafts and open-air train rides cost from around $8 per person, and various on-site businesses offer pricier jeep tours, horserides and even helicopter flights in the vicinity. Alternatively, you can pick up coffee or a full steakhouse meal.

Canyon Lake

Many day-trippers go no further up the Apache Trail than **Canyon Lake**, fifteen miles along. Created by a more recent dam, it's a bit too narrow to satisfy pleasure-boaters, who find themselves having to turn around every time they get up a bit of speed. However, if you're happy to take it easy, a cruise on the *Dolly Steamboat* (☎ 480 827 9144, Ⓦ dollysteamboat.com) is an enjoyable way to pass a couple of hours. Cruises run five days weekly at noon, costing $20; Saturday-night twilight dinner cruises cost $60.

TORTILLA FLAT, at the east end of Canyon Lake, is not so much a town as a hundred-yard stretch of boardwalk with an Old West flavour, equipped with a saloon, diner and souvenir store. Named for the nearby flat-topped boulders, Tortilla Flat has no connection with the Steinbeck novella.

Roosevelt Dam

Northeast of Tortilla Flat, as the Superstition Mountains finally start to get serious, Hwy-88 responds by turning to gravel. After a few hair-raising hairpin bends, with stomach-lurching views across the saguaro-studded canyons, it returns to undulating gently along beside the river. An optional detour drops down to **Apache Lake**, another busy boating and picnicking spot. Keep going to reach **Roosevelt Dam** itself, which was recently raised and strengthened to cope with Phoenix's bottomless thirst for water.

Tonto National Monument

Hwy-88; 3 miles east of Roosevelt Dam • Daily 8am–5pm • $3 per person • ☎ 928 467 2241, ⓦ nps.gov/tont

Set half a mile above Hwy-88, overlooking Theodore Roosevelt Lake, the **cliff dwellings** of **TONTO NATIONAL MONUMENT** are reached from the **visitor centre** along a very steep trail, which shuts an hour before closing time. Not a walk to schedule for the middle of a summer's day, it leads to the remarkably complete **Lower Ruin**, set in a deep alcove near the top of the rocky ridge, with great saguaro cactuses standing sentinel.

This large pueblo, dating from the mid-fourteenth century, was built by the **Salado** Indians, now regarded as less sophisticated than the Ancestral Puebloans to the north. Their masonry is much cruder, using lumps of rock that had fallen from the cliff face and were then thickly plastered with mud that still bears thousands of ancient fingerprints. Visitors can walk through several rooms of the ruin, some of which retain original beams and saguaro-rib ceilings. "Shelves" and storage niches are tucked into the cave walls, as well as notches that once supported additional rooms.

Between November and April only, rangers lead guided hikes to the similar, forty-room **Upper Ruin**, reached by a separate trail up the next ridge along.

Globe

The mining town of **GLOBE** stands where Hwy-88 meets US-60, the direct route east from Phoenix. Dating from the 1880s, when a twelve-mile strip of land on which a globe of pure silver had just been discovered was grabbed from the Apache reservation, it has made its living from copper since the silver and gold ran out.

Downtown Globe's few central blocks still hold several Victorian-era brick structures, though the claim that these include "the West's oldest Woolworth's" betrays quite how little there is of interest. On the third Saturday in October, Native Americans from all over the Southwest pour in for the **Apache Jii** fair.

If you prefer your Wild West utterly unvarnished and unromantic, head a mile or two west of Globe to the twin communities of **CLAYPOOL** and **MIAMI**. All but engulfed by monstrous mountains of copper-mine tailings, these flyblown towns are packed with gun stores, all-day saloons and pick-up trucks, and are certainly not a vacation destination to be chosen in preference to Miami, Florida.

Besh-Ba-Gowah

1324 S Jesse Hayes Rd; 1 mile southeast of Globe • Daily 9am–5pm • $5 • ☎ 928 467 2241, ⓦ nps.gov/tont

The ruins of **Besh-Ba-Gowah** demonstrate that Native Americans lived in the mountains around Globe long before the Apache arrived. Home first to the Hohokam and later to the Salado, they take their modern name from the Apache for "metal-its-house." Visitors can enter reconstructed living quarters and a *kiva*.

INFORMATION	GLOBE

Visitor centre 1360 N Broad St (Oct–April Mon–Fri 8am–5pm, Sat & Sun 10am–4pm; May–Sept Mon–Fri 8am–5pm; ☎ 928 425 4495 or ☎ 800 804 5623, ⓦ globemiamichamber.com).

ACCOMMODATION AND EATING

Days Inn 1630 E Ash St ☎ 928 425 5500, ⓦ daysinn .com. Set just back from the highway, as it curves away east of the centre, this is the most salubrious of Globe's dozen or so **motels**, with an outdoor pool and hot tub. **$85**

Libby's El Rey Cafe 999 N Broad St ☎ 928 425 2054. You'd never guess it from the plain exterior, but this tiny shed-like adobe, north of the centre, offers the best Mexican food in town, with $6 green chile burritos to die for. Daily noon–8pm.

4

Boyce Thompson Arboretum

US-60, Superior; 40 miles east of Apache Junction or 15 miles southwest of Miami • Daily: May–Aug 6am–3pm; Sept–April 8am–5pm;
last entry 1hr before closing • $9, ages 5–12 $4.50 • ☎ 520 689 2723, ⓦ ag.arizona.edu/bta

The **Boyce Thompson Arboretum**, in the former silver-mining town of **SUPERIOR**, is a
landscaped public garden that spreads through two parallel canyons, and contains
desert plants from around the world. Cactuses are of course abundant, but there are
also spectacular oddities like the towering boojum tree from Baja California. A brisk
walk along the main hiking trail takes around an hour, though you could spend much
longer exploring additional side trails like the themed "Plants of the Bible" walk. The
fall colours are usually at their best from late November to early December.

San Carlos Indian Reservation

The two-million-acre **SAN CARLOS INDIAN RESERVATION**, which extends a hundred
miles east and north of Globe, was created in 1872 to protect the **Apache** from such
outrages as the Camp Grant massacre of 1871 (see below). In the words of one tribal
member, the reservation was "the worst place in all the great territory stolen from the
Apache. If anybody ever lived there permanently, no Apache knew of it. The heat was
terrible. The insects were terrible. The water was terrible."

Around eight thousand Apache now live on the reservation, which offers few activities
for tourists apart from sailing or fishing on **San Carlos Lake**, twenty miles east of Globe.
After the original reservation town of **San Carlos** was drowned when the lake arose
behind the new Coolidge Dam in 1930, the community previously known as **Rice**,
ten miles north, was simply renamed San Carlos.

Aravaipa Canyon

Permits $5 per day, max 2-night stay • ☎ 928 348 4400, ⓦ blm.gov/az/aravaipa

The beauty of **ARAVAIPA CANYON**, which lies just below the southern boundary of the
San Carlos Reservation, belies its sad history as the site of one of the most notorious
tragedies in the whole sorry tale of Anglo–Apache relations. In 1871, when it was
home to a semipermanent Apache encampment under the nominal protection of the
US Army, 144 women and children were slaughtered in the **Camp Grant massacre**.
Their killers were an unholy party of Tucson vigilantes who called themselves the
Committee of Public Safety (see p.220).

Reached along a well-maintained eleven-mile dirt road that heads east from
Hwy-77 fifty miles south of Globe, Aravaipa Canyon is now a **wilderness area**. The
terrain ranges from sun-drenched hillsides covered with saguaros to the deep-red
gorge carved by Aravaipa Creek – a rare perennial desert stream – and lined by giant
cottonwoods. Visitors keen to experience the desert in its wild state need to come
prepared; the canyon has no trails, no established campgrounds, and no signs, and
is home to rattlesnakes and scorpions. Entry to the thirty-square-mile wilderness is
by permit only, with only fifty permits sold for any one time.

From Phoenix to Tucson

The hundred-mile sprint from Phoenix to Tucson along I-10 is one of Arizona's less
inspiring drives. The chief distraction en route is the molar-shaped promontory of **Picacho
Peak**, at the base of which the roadside **Rooster Cogburn Ostrich Farm** is as good a place
to stretch your legs, and possibly buy a feather duster, as any (9am–5.30pm, closed
Tues–Thurs May–Sept; ⓦ roostercogburn.com). By taking a slightly more circuitous route,
however, it's possible to break the journey at a couple of equally unlikely and enigmatic
structures – ancient **Casa Grande** and ultra-modern **Biosphere 2**.

Casa Grande Ruins National Monument

Just outside Coolidge; 15 miles east of I-10 exit 185, or 20 miles north of I-10 exit 210 • Daily 9am–5pm • $5 per person • ☏ 520 723 3172, Ⓦ nps.gov/cagr

CASA GRANDE RUINS NATIONAL MONUMENT preserves the most substantial surviving example of **Hohokam** architecture. It shares its name – Spanish for "Great House" – but little else, with the I-10 pit stop of Casa Grande, thirty miles southwest, and the much larger ancient site of Casas Grandes, far south in northern Mexico.

The Casa Grande itself, a four-storey building completed early in the fourteenth century, is made of the concrete-like natural stone known as caliche. Spanish priest Father Eusebio Kino, who passed this way in 1694 – by which time the site had been abandoned for three centuries – said the main structure was "as large as a castle", and surrounded by thirteen smaller houses and many ruins. It was clear to him that "in ancient times there had been a city here." The house stood in a walled compound in the flood-plain of the **Gila River**, where villagers used a network of canals to grow crops, harvested fruit from saguaro cactuses, and traded for shells and macaws with peoples from the south.

It's now protected beneath a spider-like canopy; visitors can enter the compound but not the structure itself. Its exact purpose is unknown, though as its windows and wall niches are aligned with key moments in the cycles of both the sun and moon, archeologists think it was an astronomical observatory that doubled as a fortress.

Biosphere 2

Mile-marker 96.5 on Hwy-77; 30 miles north of Tucson or 8 miles southwest of Oracle • Daily 9am–4pm • $20, ages 6–12 $13 • ☏ 520 838 6200, Ⓦ b2science.org

At one point, twenty years ago, the vast complex of Plexiglas pyramids known as **BIOSPHERE 2** ranked among Arizona's most popular tourist destinations. Now that no would-be space adventurers are locked inside, however, the crowds have dwindled. Run by the University of Arizona, it's primarily a historical attraction. Even so, the standard

4

THE UNBELIEVABLE STORY OF BIOSPHERE 2

When **Biosphere 2** was completed, in 1991, it was extensively publicized as a major laboratory for environmental science. Containing five separate "**biomes**," or self-contained ecosystems – rainforest, marsh, savanna, desert, and a 25-foot-deep ocean – it was designed as a miniature working model of Biosphere 1, planet Earth itself, and stocked like a real-life Noah's ark with almost four thousand species of plants and animals. Investigative journalists soon revealed, however, that it was staffed largely by ex-actors from an experimental theatre group, assembled by a certain "Johnny Dolphin" in the hope of colonizing Mars and thus escaping nuclear holocaust on Earth. A hundred million dollars' worth of support from Texas oil tycoon Ed Bass got this farfetched scheme off the ground, and top academics were recruited to add a veneer of respectability.

Eight "Biospherians" were sealed into Biosphere 2 in 1991, their "mission" being to survive in isolation for two full years. This they more or less did, growing 88 percent of their own food, and losing 13.65 percent of their body weight. Much of what transpired was replete with irony; hungry Biospherians found themselves planting bananas and papayas in what they had resolved would be the inviolate wilderness of the rainforest, and destroying parts of the desert to boost oxygen, while the ocean proved impossible to keep clean. As for their fellow inhabitants, the bush babies caught the hummingbirds, and the only birds to survive were unwanted sparrows that snuck in during construction. After "crazy ants" killed all the pollinating insects, all the plants had to be pollinated by hand.

By the time the next crew moved in, conditions had degenerated into farce. Two of the original crew, who had been acrimoniously fired, broke the Biosphere's seals from the outside, thus aborting the second mission after just six months; they later sued and won compensation for their dismissal.

two-and-a-half-hour guided tours are still worth taking. Most of that time is spent peering into the greenhouses hoping to spot any sign of life larger than an ant, and marvelling at the fact that, whatever you may have assumed, Biosphere 2 is not solar powered but depends on an external natural-gas power plant. Tunnels take you down beneath the "Coral Biome;" the guides insist it isn't an aquarium, but it doesn't half look like one. Visitors are also allowed into the Biospherians' futuristic living quarters, tacked like a space capsule onto the back of the main block, where they appear to have suffered no privations whatsoever. An all-day café serves meals and snacks on an appealing terrace.

Tucson

For over two hundred years, under five separate flags, **TUCSON** has been southern Arizona's leading city. Spreading across a mountain-ringed basin at the northern limits of the **Sonoran Desert**, it's now home to almost a million inhabitants, who pride themselves on being more cosmopolitan, cultured and liberal than those of its upstart rival Phoenix. Like Phoenix, the "Old Pueblo" has grown way past the point where the region's rivers, such as the Santa Cruz, could ever quench its thirst. All are now dry sandy washes for most of the year, though flash floods rage through the cross-town culverts after summer thunderstorms. However, Tucson embraces rather than denies the desert, eschewing lawns and fountains in favour of directing visitors toward the landscapes of **Sabino Canyon** and the **Arizona-Sonora Desert Museum** and the cactus-strewn hillsides of **Saguaro National Park**.

By Southwestern standards, Tucson (pronounced *too-sonn*) is a diverse, attractive, and lively city, home to the forty thousand energetic students of the **University of Arizona** as well as a large influx of retirees, and strongly influenced by its long association with Mexico, a mere sixty miles south. While prone to the same Sunbelt sprawl as Albuquerque and Phoenix, it still has a compact and recognizably historic centre, some good parks and museums, affordable accommodation and enjoyable restaurants, and a pretty good nightlife.

Brief history

The valley of the Santa Cruz had already been inhabited for many centuries by the time Spanish priest Eusebio Kino visited the **Pima Indian** settlement of Stjukshon, or "dark spring," in 1700. Archeological excavations west of downtown have even suggested that this may be the oldest inhabited site in North America. In 1776, under the direction of **Hugo O'Conor**, one of the Catholic "Wild Geese" who had fled English-controlled Ireland to fight for Spain, the Spanish relocated their main Arizona fortress here from Tubac (see p.232). That forty-mile move northwards brought them closer to **Apache** territory, and the energies of the Hispanic and Pima citizens of **San Agustín de Tucson** were largely devoted to resisting Apache raids and sieges. The severed heads of Apache warriors were displayed as trophies on the city walls.

When Tucson was sold to the US in the **Gadsden Purchase** of 1854 (see p.470), the incoming Anglos were generally welcomed. Most of the valley's Mexican farmers remained in Arizona, and were even joined by more of their former compatriots. Soon, however, travellers were describing Tucson as "a place of resort for traders, speculators, gamblers, horse-thieves and vagrant politicians ... a paradise of devils."

Although the **Confederates** who occupied southern Arizona in 1862 were swiftly driven away by Union forces from California, suspicions of lingering Confederate sympathies led to Tucson being passed over as capital of the new Territory. Conflict with the Apache continued, and a vigilante force of Mexicans, Anglos and O'odham Indians from Tucson was responsible for the notorious **Camp Grant massacre** of 144

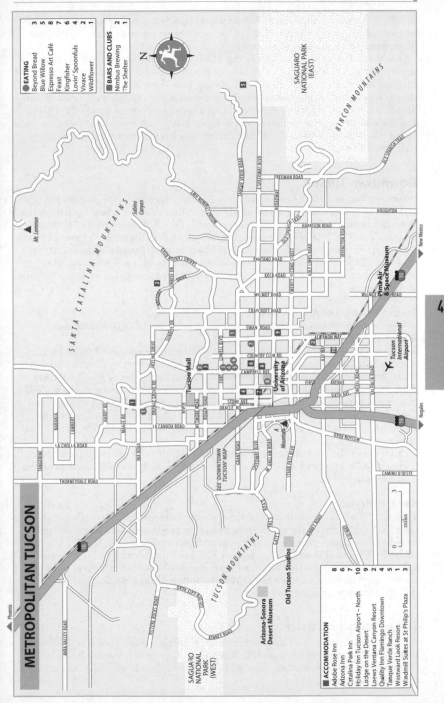

METROPOLITAN TUCSON

EATING
Beyond Bread	3
Blue Willow	5
Espresso Art Café	8
Feast	7
Kingfisher	6
Lovin' Spoonfuls	4
Vivace	2
Wildflower	1

BARS AND CLUBS
Nimbus Brewing	2
The Shelter	1

ACCOMMODATION
Adobe Rose Inn	8
Arizona Inn	6
Catalina Park Inn	7
Holiday Inn Tucson Airport – North	10
Lodge on the Desert	9
Loews Ventana Canyon Resort	2
Quality Inn Flamingo Downtown	4
Tanque Verde Ranch	5
Westward Look Resort	1
Windmill Suites at St Philip's Plaza	3

Apache in Aravaipa Canyon in 1871 (see p.218). US Army commanders came to believe that a shadowy "**Tucson Ring**" of businessmen was provoking the Apache to profit from the resultant military spending.

After the end of the Apache Wars in the 1880s coincided with the coming of the transcontinental **railroad**, trade with Mexico rapidly declined, and Tucson's wealthy Mexican merchants were driven out of business. Ever since, Mexican labourers have streamed back and forth across the border as the economy expands and contracts, but Tucson has become ever more American. Outstripped by Phoenix during the 1920s, and home to under forty thousand people (in an area of just nine square miles) as recently as 1940, by conventional standards the city has nonetheless grown at a phenomenal rate.

Downtown Tucson

Downtown Tucson, which centres on the area where the east–west Congress Street and Broadway Boulevard cross the north–south Stone Avenue, is largely characterized by undistinguished modern architecture, though the 1928 **Pima County Courthouse** is an eclectic mix of Southwestern and Moorish influences. The adobe fortress of San Agustín de Tucson occupied what's now the four-block **El Presidio Historic District**, a couple of blocks northwest. None of its original structures is still standing, but several of their nineteenth-century successors have been restored as cafés, art galleries, and B&Bs.

Tucson Museum of Art

140 N Main Ave • Wed, Fri &Sat 10am–5pm, Thurs 10am–8pm, Sun noon–5pm • $10, under-19s free; free first Sun of month • 🕿 502 624 2333, 🔊 tucsonmuseumofart.org

The **Tucson Museum of Art** devotes its main building to changing exhibitions of modern painting and sculpture, and the gift shop stocks interesting contemporary crafts. An adjoining adobe, the **Palice Pavilion**, displays magnificent pre-Columbian artefacts, including Mochica ceramics from northern Peru, with extraordinarily life-like faces; textiles from the later Peruvian Chancay culture; and gold from Colombia and Costa Rica. Mexican artefacts range from masks and effigies created by the ancient Olmec and Mixtec peoples to eighteenth-century religious pieces and nineteenth-century oil-on-tin family portraits.

The museum also controls access to much of El Presidio. The oldest house in the complex, **La Casa Cordova** at 175 N Meyer Ave (same hours), contains displays on the city's Mexican heritage.

Barrio Historico

Tucson's 1880s business district, now known as the **Barrio Historico**, stretches south from Cushing Street, on the southern fringes of the modern downtown. While the neighbourhood holds plenty of century-old adobes, its most notable landmark is the sidewalk shrine of **El Tiradito**, "the castaway." Said to mark where a young man was killed by his father-in-law for committing adultery with his mother-in-law, and was buried where he fell, it's famous as the **Wishing Shrine**. Light a candle that burns through the night, and your prayers will be answered.

The university district

Apart from downtown, the other main area of interest in central Tucson is the **University of Arizona**, which spreads between Sixth Street and Speedway Boulevard a mile east of downtown. Park Avenue, on its western flank, is lined with funky cafés and stores that cater to students.

Arizona State Museum

1013 E University Blvd • Mon–Sat 10am–5pm • $5, under-18s free • ☎ 520 621 6302, ⓦ statemuseum.arizona.edu

In the **Arizona State Museum**, the highlight of the university campus, the Pottery Project traces the history of Southwestern ceramics. There's a stunning case devoted to fabulous "burden carrier" pots made by the Hohokam between 850 and 1000 AD, as well as some very modern pieces that challenge all preconceptions about Native American pottery. The large **Paths of Life** exhibition illuminates the cultures of the

DOWNTOWN TUCSON

FIFTH STREET

FIFTH STREET
SEVENTH AVENUE
SIXTH AVENUE
ARIZONA AVENUE
FIFTH AVENUE
HERBERT AVENUE
FOURTH AVENUE

NINTH AVENUE
STONE AVENUE
SIXTH STREET

TOOLE AVENUE

SEVENTH STREET

FRANKLIN STREET
MEYER AVENUE
COURT AVENUE
CHURCH AVENUE
COUNCIL STREET
EIGHTH STREET

MAIN AVENUE
WASHINGTON ST
TOOLE AVENUE
NINTH STREET

La Casa Cordova
Tucson Museum of Art
ALAMEDA STREET
Pima County Courthouse
Amtrak Station

El Presidio Park
E PENNINGTON STREET
ARIZONA AVENUE

CONGRESS STREET
Greyhound Depot

GRANADA AVENUE
BROADWAY BOULEVARD
FIFTH AVENUE
HERBERT AVENUE
RAILROAD AVENUE

JACKSON STREET

Sosa-Carrillo-Frémont House
OLHOA STREET
12TH STREET
FOURTH AVENUE

Tucson Convention Center
St Augustine Cathedral
SCOTT AVENUE
Armory Park

CHURCH AVENUE
MC CORMICK ST
13TH STREET

N

SIXTH AVENUE

CUSHING STREET
14TH STREET
FIFTH AVENUE

EL PASO AVENUE
MAIN AVENUE
CONVENT AVENUE
MEYER AVENUE
STONE AVENUE
SIMPSON STREET
15TH STREET
ARIZONA AVENUE

El Tiradito

0   200
yards

KENNEDY STREET

ACCOMMODATION
| Hotel Congress | 1 |
| Roadrunner Hostel | 2 |

EATING
Café à la C'Art	1
Café Poca Cosa	2
Cup Café	3

BARS, CLUBS AND MUSIC VENUES
Club Congress	3
IBT's	1
Rialto Theatre	4
Sky Bar	2

4

major native peoples of the Southwest and northern Mexico, with a heavy emphasis on Arizona. They also have a wonderful collection of baskets.

Center for Creative Photography

1030 North Olive Rd • Mon–Fri 9am–5pm, Sat & Sun 1–4pm • Free • ☎ 520 621 7968, ⓦ creativephotography.org

The **Center for Creative Photography** holds one of the world's finest photography archives. Ansel Adams left his negatives, prints and journals to the university, and his collection has been complemented by images from all eras. Temporary exhibitions only show a tiny selection, however, and the archive is primarily intended for serious scholars.

UA Museum of Art

1031 North Olive Rd • Tues–Fri 9am–5pm, Sat & Sun noon–4pm • Free • ☎ 520 621 7567, ⓦ artmuseum.arizona.edu

An eclectic affair, the **UA Museum of Art** has acquired its permanent collection via a number of unconnected bequests. Its treasures therefore includes a somewhat morbid altarpiece from the cathedral of Spanish city Ciudad Rodrigo, along with prints and drawings and canvases by Rembrandt, Picasso and Warhol; a solitary O'Keeffe; and some fine cubist sculpture by Jacques Lipchitz.

Arizona Historical Society Museum

949 E Second St • Mon–Sat 10am–4pm • $5 • ☎ 520 628 5774, ⓦ arizonahistoricalsociety.org

The **Arizona Historical Society Museum**, across Park Avenue from the campus, surveys the history of southern Arizona with a replica mine tunnel; exhibits on the Apache Wars that include a rifle that belonged to Geronimo; and a good "Oxcart to Auto" section, on travel in the frontier era. If it's specifically the history of Tucson itself that interests you, call in also at the museum's downtown offshoot, at 140 N Stone Ave (Tues–Fri 10am–4pm; $3).

Sabino Canyon

5900 N Sabino Canyon Rd • Daily dawn–dusk • Free, but parking $5 • ☎ 520 749 8700, ⓦ sabinocanyon.com

For an enjoyable taste of the **Santa Catalina Mountains**, which form Metropolitan Tucson's northern boundary, head to **Sabino Canyon**, in the Coronado National Forest ten miles northeast of downtown. The canyon was cut into the lower reaches of Mount Lemmon by Sabino Creek, which manages to flow for up to eleven months of the year, and is lined by green vegetation. Assorted trails lace into the hills from a four-mile riverbank road – barred to private vehicles, but served by jump-on, jump-off **tram rides** ($8.50) – that's popular with early-morning joggers.

Mount Lemmon

Mount Lemmon Ski Valley Full-day lift ticket $40; half-day $35 • Rentals available • ☎ 520 576 1321, ⓦ www.skithelemmon.com

The 9157ft summit of **Mount Lemmon**, which towers above Sabino Canyon, is a two-day hike beyond the canyon or a one-hour drive on the undeniably scenic Mount Lemmon Highway. After branching off Tanque Verde Road, an eastward continuation of Grant Road, a few miles east of the Sabino Canyon turn-off, this winds for 25 slow miles up the mountain, with countless panoramic viewpoints to either side. The summit is largely given over to the **Mount Lemmon Ski Valley**, which holds more than twenty runs, including several black diamonds, and a few restaurants that collectively offer a surprisingly well-rounded selection of meals.

Pima Air & Space Museum

6000 E Valencia Rd; 2 miles east of I-10 • Daily 9am–5pm • Nov–May $15.50, ages 7–12 $9; June–Oct $13.75, ages 7–12 $8;
☎ 520 574 0462, ⓦ pimaair.org

The **Pima Air & Space Museum** boasts an amazing collection of vintage and modern aircraft. Some exhibits, like the Wright Brothers' 1903 Flyer and the Apollo capsule, are replicas, but the great majority are the real deal, including plenty of World War II bombers, prototype helicopters, and the superfast X-15 fighter. The whole place is so huge, with vast tracts of sun-scorched concrete between the various hangars, that you may well prefer to pay $6 extra to tour it by tram.

As you approach the museum, you pass rows of defunct aircraft lined up in the Boneyard of the adjoining Davis-Monthan Air Force Base; on weekdays, the museum offers bus tours that go in there as well, costing an extra $7.

Old Tucson Studios

201 S Kinney Rd; 12 miles west of downtown • May Fri–Sun 10am–5pm, Oct Thurs–Sun 6pm–midnight, Nov–April daily 10am–5pm,
closed June–Sept • $17, under-12s $11 • ☎ 520 883 0100, ⓦ oldtucson.com

The focus of **Old Tucson Studios**, an entertaining Wild West theme park, is a movie-set mock-up of nineteenth-century Tucson itself, constructed for the 1939 western *Arizona*, which has been used for TV shows and movies up to *Tombstone* and *Geronimo*. Visitors can ride a stagecoach or a coal-fired steam train, and watch gunfights on Main Street or a bawdy show in the saloon. Since Old Tucson had to be almost entirely rebuilt after a fire in 1995, it's now even more spurious than ever. Kids love it all the same.

Arizona-Sonora Desert Museum

2021 N Kinney Rd • March–May & Sept daily 7.30am–5pm; June–Aug Mon–Fri & Sun 7.30am–5pm, Sat 7.30am–10pm; Oct–Feb
8.30am–5pm • June–Aug $12, ages 4–12 $4; Sept–May $14.50, ages 6–12 $5 • ☎ 520 883 2702, ⓦ desertmuseum.org

Part zoo, part garden, the **Arizona-Sonora Desert Museum** makes a hugely satisfying adjunct to visiting nearby Saguaro National Park. Displays in the museum proper explain regional geology and history, while dioramas are filled with tarantulas, rattlesnakes and other creepy crawlers. In enclosures along the loop path beyond – a hot walk in summer – bighorn sheep, mountain lions, jaguars and other seldom-seen desert denizens prowl in credible simulations of their natural habitats. An artificial cave is home to a colony of real bats, and impish prairie dogs go about their impenetrable business. Hawks and bald eagles fly about a large aviary, thankfully separated from the greenhouse full of hummingbirds. Spectacular displays by free-flying Harris hawks are scheduled most winter afternoons. The outdoor terrace of the museum's restaurant is a great stop-off for a light lunch; it also has a good coffee bar.

Saguaro National Park

In two sections, east and west of Tucson • Admission to either or both, valid for a week, costs $10 per vehicle • ⓦ nps.gov/sagu

Flanking Tucson to either side, the two sections of **SAGUARO NATIONAL PARK** offer visitors a rare and enthralling opportunity to stroll through desert "forests" of monumental, multilimbed **saguaro** (pronounced *sa-wah-row*) **cactuses**. Both tend to be seen on short forays from the city; there's no lodging, or even permanent campground, in either segment, and in summer, it's far too hot to do more than pose for photographs, dwarfed beneath some especially eccentric specimen.

As saguaros prefer sloping foothills, which offer a little run-off after rain, to level desert, both sections include rugged mountain tracts. Most of the **Rincon Mountain**

District in the east, which became a national monument in 1933, is much higher, and the one road only penetrates its low-lying fringes. It was joined in 1961 by the **Tucson Mountain District** in the west, which incorporates the world's densest stand of saguaro.

Backcountry camping is by permit only; contact park rangers for details.

The western park: Tucson Mountain District
15 miles west of downtown Tucson • **Visitor centre** Daily 8am–5pm • ☎ 520 733 5158

The **Tucson Mountain District** of Saguaro National Park is located on the western flanks, logically enough, of the Tucson Mountains. The Red Hills **visitor centre** stands two miles along Kinney Road from the Desert Museum. Turn right off the highway 1.5 miles further on to start the six-mile **Bajada Loop Drive**, which although not fully paved is always passable to ordinary vehicles, and leads through a wonderland of weird saguaro, offering plentiful short hiking trails and photo opportunities. Although you can join the road at either of two intersections, which are less than half a mile apart, its central mile or so is one-way, so the only way to complete a full loop is by starting at the south.

The easiest walk, the **Desert Discovery Nature Trail**, sets off just before the one-way section. It follows a small gully before climbing onto a low brow for sweeping westward views, with abundant saguaro all around; in principle it's half a mile long, though you can choose how far you want to walk before you turn back. If you've only time for one hike in the park, however, head further along the road and walk at **Signal Hill** instead, ideally timing your arrival to enjoy its magnificent sunset panoramas. You're not the first to pass this way; boulders at the top are marked with Hohokam petroglyphs. Gluttons for punishment can follow the longer **Hugh Norris Trail** up a ridge to the 4687ft summit of Wasson Peak.

Branching onto Golden Gate Road from the northeastern limit of the loop drive brings you in around five miles to Picture Rocks Road, which joins **Ina Road** a few more miles along and thus makes an alternative route back to northern Tucson.

THE SAGUARO CACTUS: A DESERT SAGA

As the mighty, multi-armed **saguaro cactus** is unique to the Sonoran Desert, and Tucson stands near the desert's northeastern extremity, the Tucson region is one of very few places in the Wild West where real-life saguaro grow. Whatever you may have seen in the movies, you can drive a long way in Arizona without seeing a saguaro; finally encountering a thousand at once is a genuine thrill.

Each saguaro can grow up to fifty feet tall and weigh up to eight tons, but it takes a very long time to reach that size. A teenage cactus is a foot high, a 50-year-old more like seven feet. At 75, it sprouts the first of what may amount to forty "arms," and it only reaches its full height at around 150, with perhaps another fifty years to go before it dies. Its roots radiate as much as a hundred feet in all directions, barely three inches below the surface, and can draw enough water from one rainstorm to last for two years.

Each year from the age of 30 onwards, between late April and June, a saguaro grows up to a hundred white flowers, each of which blossoms for a single night and dies by the next afternoon. In its lifetime, each saguaro produces as many as forty million seeds, but few, if any, germinate and thrive. It's also home to an intricate community of birds, insects, mammals and reptiles. Woodpeckers and owls burrow holes into the trunk for their nests, which the cactus heals over with hardened "scar tissue" to create permanent hollows. The **Tohono O'odham** Indians traditionally cut away these depressions for use as bowls; they also mashed the saguaro's succulent crimson fruit to make jam, syrup, and even wine, and used its long, wood-like ribs to construct dwellings and fences.

Thanks to the thriving black market in stolen saguaros, many cactuses in Saguaro National Park are now micro-chipped against theft.

The eastern park: Rincon Mountain District

Old Spanish Trail; 17 miles east of downtown Tucson • Visitor centre Daily 8am–5pm; Cactus Forest Drive: Daily: April–Oct 7am–7pm;
Nov–March 7am–5pm • ☎ 520 733 5153

To reach the eastern section of Saguaro National Park, the **Rincon Mountain District**,
head east from downtown Tucson along first Broadway Boulevard and then Old
Spanish Trail. The **visitor centre** is at the end of the road. Although short trails such as
the quarter-mile **Desert Ecology Trail** lead off the eight-mile **Cactus Forest Drive**, this
area of the park is less immediately rewarding for casual visitors than its western
counterpart. Instead, most of those who make their way here come specifically to hike
far from the road, up into the mountains. The saguaro cactuses thin out almost as soon
as you start climbing the **Tanque Verde Ridge Trail**, which leads in due course to a
hundred-mile network of remote footpaths through thickly forested canyons. Permits
to use the district's six wilderness campgrounds, only accessible on foot or by horse,
cost $6 per night. Water is seasonally available – check with rangers – but should be
treated before you drink it.

ARRIVAL AND DEPARTURE   TUCSON

By plane Tucson International Airport, 10 miles south of
downtown (ⓦflytucsonairport.com), receives flights from
all over the Southwest, but for long-distance services it's
very much second fiddle to Phoenix. It's connected to
central Tucson by the slow Sun Tran bus #6 or #11 ($1.50;
ⓦsuntran.com) and the $25 shuttle vans of Arizona
Stagecoach (☎520 889 1000, ⓦazstagecoach.com). For
taxi service, contact Discount Cab (☎520 200 2000,
ⓦdiscountcab.com).

By train The Amtrak station, downtown at 400 E Toole
Ave, is served by three trains weekly in each direction
between Los Angeles and points east; connecting Amtrak
buses run north to Phoenix.

By bus Greyhound buses stop very centrally, at 471 W
Congress St (☎520 792 3475, ⓦgreyhound.com). Arizona
Shuttle Services runs a shuttle-van service between Tucson
and Phoenix's Sky Harbor airport (one way $39; ☎520 795
6771 or ☎800 888 2749, ⓦarizonashuttle.com).

GETTING AROUND AND INFORMATION

By streetcar As this book went to press, Tucson was
constructing, and hoping shortly to open, a new light-rail
system connecting downtown and the university area. For
the latest details, visit ⓦtucsonstreetcar.com.

Visitor centre 100 S Church Ave, in downtown's lurid
little La Placita development (Mon–Fri 9am–5pm, Sat &

Sun 9am–4pm; ☎520 624 1817 or ☎800 638 8350,
ⓦvisittucson.org).

Maps and guides Tucson Map & Flag Center, 3239 N First
Ave (Mon–Fri 9am–5.30pm, Sat 9am–5pm; ☎520 887
4234, ⓦmapsmithus.com), stocks Arizona's best selection
of maps and local guides.

ACCOMMODATION

Tucson offers a broader range of accommodation than Phoenix, with plenty of reasonably priced **hotels** and **motels**
downtown as well as some atmospheric **B&Bs** both in the historic centre and out in the surrounding desert. It also has its
fair share of **resorts** and **dude ranches**. Once again, rates drop when the mercury rises.

HOSTELS AND B&BS

★ **Adobe Rose Inn** 940 N Olsen Ave ☎520 318 4644
or ☎800 328 4122, ⓦaroseinn.com. Charming, great-
value B&B in a peaceful residential area near the university,
with plenty of good restaurants nearby. The six en-suite
rooms feature attractive fireplaces, tilework and ceramics,
and the courtyard pool and outdoor seating areas are very
welcome. The copious communal breakfasts are superb –
the friendly hosts have their own scone business.
June–Aug $90, Sept–May $135

Catalina Park Inn 309 East First St ☎520 792 4541 or
☎800 792 4885, ⓦcatalinaparkinn.com. Beautiful yet not
overly fussy historic B&B across from a quiet park; all but one
of the six en-suite rooms are large, some have hot tubs or

private balconies. Within walking distance of the university
and happening Fourth Ave. Closed June–Sept. $139

Roadrunner Hostel 346 E Twelfth St ☎520 940 7280,
ⓦroadrunnerhostelinn.com. Small and very central
independent hostel in a downtown home, popular with
international travellers and in easy walking distance of
eating and nightlife. Accommodation is in six-bed dorms or
private doubles, with discounted weekly rates, and there's a
communal kitchen and patio. Closed noon–3pm daily.
Dorms $22, doubles $45

HOTELS AND MOTELS

★ **Hotel Congress** 311 E Congress St ☎520 622 8848
or ☎800 722 8848, ⓦhotelcongress.com. Central,

4

bohemian hotel, a short walk from Amtrak and Greyhound, with vintage Art Deco furnishings. In the 1930s, bank-robber Dillinger was arrested here after pleading for his strangely heavy luggage to be rescued from a blaze on the third floor; now it offers forty plain en-suite guest rooms, with vintage radios rather than TVs. With the *Cup Café* (see p.229) and *Club Congress* (see p.229) downstairs, this is one of the hottest spots in town, with loud music and dancing at night; if you're simply looking for a quiet place to sleep, don't even dream of staying here. June–Aug $69, Sept–May $89

Holiday Inn Tucson Airport – North 4550 S Palo Verde Blvd ☏ 520 746 1161, ⓦ holidayinn.com. Six-storey, Southwestern-styled hotel with reasonable rooms, a nice pool, and a waterfall in the lobby, located roughly halfway between the airport – served by free shuttles – and downtown. $90

Quality Inn Flamingo Downtown 1300 N Stone Ave ☏ 520 770 1910, ⓦ flamingohoteltucson.com. Now officially a *Quality Inn*, with nicely revamped rooms, the Western-themed *Flamingo* motel is a much-loved Tucson fixture, even from the outside it still looks straight out of the 1950s – Elvis himself slept here. Standing barely a mile north of downtown Tucson, it has a reasonable pool and spa. $60

Windmill Suites at St Philip's Plaza 4250 N Campbell Ave ☏ 520 577 0007 or ☏ 800 547 4747, ⓦ windmillinns .com. These large two-room suites, near the foothills north of downtown and alongside a shopping mall that holds a number of good restaurants, are ideal for families. There's also a pool, plus free breakfasts and bikes for local explorations. $90 June–Aug $109, Sept–May $149

RANCHES AND RESORTS

Arizona Inn 2200 E Elm St ☏ 520 325 1541 or ☏ 800 933 1093, ⓦ arizonainn.com. Elegant, family-owned desert oasis that's been a winter favourite for numerous presidents, Rockefellers, and the Duke and Duchess of Windsor, and still offers croquet on the lawn. With just 95 rooms, it remains surprisingly unstuffy and far from expensive in low season. Rates include gourmet breakfast. June–Aug $139, Sept–May $299

Lodge on the Desert 306 N Alvernon Way ☏ 520 320 2000 or ☏ 877 498 6776, ⓦ lodgeonthedesert.com. 1930s adobe resort a couple of miles east of downtown, tastefully restored to resemble a Mexican hacienda, with large, comfortable rooms and a good restaurant, though the pool is somewhat small. June–Aug $109, Sept–May $199

Loews Ventana Canyon Resort 7000 N Resort Drive ☏ 520 299 2020 or ☏ 800 234 5117, ⓦ loewshotels .com. Grand red-brick resort, reaching majestically across a hundred acres at the foot of the Santa Catalina mountains northeast of the city, with its own on-site waterfall. Four restaurants, two golf courses, plus tennis and spa, and the desert on your doorstep. June–Aug $169, Sept–May $299

Tanque Verde Ranch 14301 E Speedway Blvd ☏ 520 296 6275 or ☏ 800 234 3833, ⓦ tanqueverderanch.com. Arizona's most authentic dude ranch, an irresistibly romantic 400-acre spread adjoining Saguaro National Park twenty miles east of downtown. The accommodation in individual *casitas* is luxurious and the stable is home to more than a hundred horses. The quoted rates include all meals and a full programme of rides, from early-morning cowboy cookouts to all-day pack trips; there's also tennis, swimming and hiking. At times, during quiet periods, it's possible to stay on a room-only basis, for much cheaper rates. Three-day minimum. May–Oct $425, Nov–April $525

Westward Look Resort 245 E Ina Rd ☏ 520 297 1151 or ☏ 800 722 2500, ⓦ westwardlook.com. Fancy but very affordable resort, in attractive landscaped grounds north of the city, which retains its atmospheric 1912 core while modernized to eco-friendly standards, and now holds almost 250 extra-large rooms and suites in very private low-slung *casitas*. The emphasis on physical fitness, and tennis in particular, doesn't preclude having a top-quality restaurant. June–Sept $104, Oct–May $169

EATING

Though downtown Tucson shuts down pretty early each evening – it's hard to find anywhere to eat after 9pm – the city has a fine selection of **restaurants**. Mexican joints and cowboy-style Wild West steakhouses abound in the central districts, while fancier restaurants congregate further north in the Foothills, and especially in the resort hotels.

CAFÉS AND COFFEEHOUSES

Beyond Bread 3026 N Campbell Ave ☏ 520 322 9965, ⓦ beyondbread.com. The most central of this hugely popular cafe-bakery's four Tucson outlets has little atmosphere, but it's great for a take-out sandwich – most, from "classics" named for staff members like Bob's BLT to specials like a New Orleans-style shrimp po'boy – cost $5 for a half-portion or $7 for the whole thing – a breakfast omelette, or a daily hot special. Mon–Fri 6.30am–8pm, Sat 7am–8pm, Sun 7am–6pm.

Blue Willow 2616 N Campbell Ave ☏ 520 327 7577, ⓦ bluewillowtucson.com. Tasty, fruity breakfasts – with nothing priced over $9, that's when it's most likely to be crowded – and light lunches and dinners (entrees like their signature meatloaf cost $15), served on a pleasant garden patio. Mon–Fri 7am–9pm, Sat & Sun 8am–9pm.

Café à la C'Art Tucson Museum of Art, 150 N Main Ave ☏ 520 628 8533, ⓦ tucsonmuseumofart.org. With such a good café in the art museum courtyard serving sandwiches, salads and daily specials for $9–12, museum visitors have

4

no need to look further afield. Note, though, that it's also open at times – breakfast, for example – and even on days when the museum itself isn't. Mon–Wed 7am–2pm, Thurs–Sat 7am–2pm & 5–9pm, Sun 7–11.30am.

★ **Café Poca Cosa** 110 E Pennington St 520 622 6400, cafepocacosatucson.com. Popular and stylish downtown café that serves tasty but inexpensive Mexican – or to be more precise, Sonoran – cuisine with a great deal of contemporary Southwestern flair. Typical highlights on the short blackboard menu include shredded beef, or cod with clams. Lunch entrees cost around $10; at dinner they're more like $20. Tues–Thurs 11am–9pm, Fri & Sat 11am–10pm.

Cup Café Hotel Congress, 311 E Congress St 520 798 1618, hotelcongress.com. Jazzy downtown café, straight out of the 1930s but updated to include an espresso bar. As well as making a good morning rendezvous, with eggy breakfasts for around $12, it offers lunchtime sandwiches and salads for $11–14, and a full dinner menu that includes fish'n'chips for $16. Mon–Thurs & Sun 7am–10pm, Fri & Sat 7am–midnight.

Espresso Art Café 942 E University Blvd 520 624 4126. Grungy, alternative coffee bar, in the heart of the University District, with a sideline in selling artworks and hosting regular live music. Daily 7am–midnight.

Lovin' Spoonfuls 2690 N Campbell Ave 520 325 7766, lovinspoonfuls.com. Far and away Tucson's best vegetarian restaurant, *Spoonfuls* serves a totally vegan menu – even the $11.25 "country fried chicken" and the breakfast chorizo-and-bacon "deluxe scramble" contain soya and tofu rather than meat and eggs. More importantly, it all tastes delicious. Mon–Sat 9.30am–9pm, Sun 10am–3pm.

RESTAURANTS

Feast 3719 E Speedway Blvd 520 329 9363, eatatfeast.com. Thanks to its combination of top-notch modern cooking at affordable prices, plus takeout if you'd prefer a picnic, *Feast* has gone from strength to strength, and moved into larger, more comfortable premises. The precise menu changes monthly, but typical dishes include crispy duck salad ($12) and braised lamb shank with honey-hop sauce ($24). Tues–Sat 11am–9pm, Sun 10am–9pm.

Kingfisher 2564 E Grant Rd 520 323 7739, kingfishertucson.com. Upmarket restaurant that serves seafood – from Maine lobsters and Maryland soft-shell crabs to Oregon oysters – with an eclectic mix of American cooking styles from Cajun to New Pacific. Fish entrees start with the $18 ruby trout, and strict meat-eaters can opt instead for roast chicken ($17) or ribs ($26). The reduced late-night menu (also, confusingly, served 3–5pm on weekdays) can be a life-saver. Mon–Fri 11am–midnight, Sat & Sun 5pm–midnight; closed first 2 weeks of July.

Vivace 4310 N Campbell Ave 520 795 7221, vivacetucson.com. Good, honest Italian food in an attractively faked Italian setting. It's particularly good value at lunchtime, when sandwiches and specials cost $8–12; in the evening, pasta or risotto costs $16–20, and more substantial mains like *osso bucco* or veal piccata $28–32. Mon–Thurs 11.30am–9pm, Fri & Sat 11.30am–10pm.

Wildflower 7037 N Oracle Rd 520 219 4230, foxrc .com. While you can't help being a bit wary of a place that calls itself a "progressive, on-trend restaurant concept", the fusion "New American" cuisine in this stylish mall restaurant, well north of the centre, just plain tastes nice and that's all that matters. Choose between casual dining on the spacious patio, or nestle into the plush indoor seating, in sight of the open kitchen, and enjoy appetizers like edamame dumplings with shiitake mushrooms ($9); entrees including lemongrass scallops with forbidden rice ($23); and the fabulous $5 butterscotch dessert. Mon–Thurs & Sun 11am–9pm, Fri & Sat 11am–10pm.

ENTERTAINMENT AND NIGHTLIFE

Downtown, Tucson **nightlife** focuses on Congress Street with its gaggle of arty cafés and nightclubs; most venues double as bars or restaurants. A handful of student places can be found near the university, while country saloons are scattered on the outskirts of town. Check listings in the free *Tucson Weekly* (tucsonweekly.com).

Club Congress Hotel Congress, 311 E Congress St 520 622 8848, hotelcongress.com. Hectic, trendy, late-opening bar with live music, including some surprisingly big names, three or four nights each week, and club nights on the rest. Nightly until late.

IBT's 616 N Fourth Ave 520 882 3053, ibtstucson .com. Tucson's premier gay downtown dance club features contemporary DJs most nights and also puts on drag acts and revue, with a huge dancefloor indoors and another on the patio outside. Daily noon–2am.

Nimbus Brewing 3850 E 44th St 520 745 9175, nimbusbeer.com. Tucson's best local beer, served right in front of the brewery responsible, in the shape of pale,

brown and red Nimbus ales (but no lagers); spend long enough here and you'll see the little monkey mascot dancing before your very eyes. *Nimbus* also runs a bistro/pub at 6464 E Tanque Verde Rd. Mon–Thurs 11am–11pm, Fri & Sat 11am–1am, Sun 11am–9pm.

Rialto Theatre 318 E Congress St 520 740 1000, rialtotheatre.com. 1920s vaudeville theatre that's reincarnated as Tucson's hottest venue for touring bands. Hours vary, showtime usually 8pm.

The Shelter 4155 E Grant Rd 520 326 1345, thesheltercocktaillounge.com. Take a trip back to groovier times in this round, windowless "go-go boot-wearing lounge"; all lava lamps, pinball machines and velvet paintings. It's barely changed since 1961, but still shakes up a mean martini, and has occasional live music and DJs. Daily 3pm–2am.

Sky Bar 536 N Fourth Ave ☎520 622 4300, ⓦ skybartucson.com. While the USP here is astronomy, with telescopes set up on the (smoking allowed) patio so patrons can learn about the night sky, it's a great bar in its own right, with live jazz on Tues, open mic on Wed, and Happy Hour all day on Sunday. They also serve smoothies and $1 coffees, and offer takeout from *Brooklyn Pizzas* next door. Daily 9am–2am.

The Mission Trail

The first part of Arizona settled by the Spanish – they called it **Pimería Alta** – the southern tract between Tucson and the Mexican border remained its most populous region until well into the nineteenth century. Scattered **mission churches** and abandoned forts still testify to Spanish efforts to Christianize the **Pima** peoples from 1692 onwards. Epidemics and Apache raids meant that of the early towns, only Tucson grew to any size, but as recently as 1870, the Pima were still Arizona's largest ethnic group.

Now known as the **Akimel O'odham**, twelve thousand Pima survive on the **San Xavier Reservation** a few miles south of Tucson. The magnificent church of San Xavier, and the Titan Missile Museum and artistic community at **Tubac** not far beyond, are the prime attractions for modern travellers who drive south on the I-19 interstate. Sadly, though, the notion of taking a day-trip to Mexico, via the border town of **Nogales**, is less appealing than it used to be.

San Xavier del Bac

1950 W San Xavier Rd; 9 miles south of downtown Tucson, just west of I-19 • Daily: church 7am–5pm, museum 8am–4.30pm • Donation • ⓦ sanxaviermission.org

Even today, the white-plastered walls and towers of **San Xavier del Bac**, the best-preserved mission church in the US, seem like a dazzling desert mirage. How much more dramatic they must have been two centuries ago, when to Christian missionaries and Apache warriors alike they symbolized the Spanish quest to subdue and convert the native peoples of the Southwest.

Nicknamed the "White Dove of the Desert" – the church stands on the eastern fringes of the arid San Xavier Reservation. The Jesuit **Father Eusebio Kino** founded it in 1700, beside the Santa Cruz River and next to the Pima village of W:ak ("where the water emerges"), which soon became Bac. Kino's church was destroyed by Apache in 1767; what survives is its replacement, built for the Franciscans between 1783 and 1797. No one knows the name of the architect responsible for its Spanish Baroque, even Moorish lines – it consists almost entirely of domes and arches, making only minimal use of timber – let alone the O'odham craftsmen who embellished its every feature.

Although the church attracts a constant stream of tourists, the ideal time to come is on Sunday morning, when masses at 8am, 11am and 12.30pm pack in the parishioners from the reservation. As you approach the main entrance across the dusty plaza, with saguaro cactuses to the right and ocotillo to the left, take a moment to appreciate its ornate facade. On the top level, a cat squats on the spiral flourish to the right, eyeing a mouse in the corresponding position on the left. The tower on the right was never completed, possibly to avoid the need to pay a levy to the authorities back in Mexico.

Inside, the church is almost entirely adorned with frescoes. A huge gilded altarpiece dominates the main altar, the approach to which is guarded by two naive gilt-headed lions, representing the royal lions of León and Castille in Spain. The left alcove holds a recumbent, articulated statue of **St Francis Xavier**, covered with metal *milagros* (images of healed body parts). Devout Catholics can lean in and lift his head.

CLOCKWISE FROM TOP BIGHORN SHEEP, ARIZONA-SONORA DESERT MUSEUM (SEE P.225); TUMACÁCORI NATIONAL HISTORICAL PARK (SEE P.233); BIOSPHERE 2 (SEE P.219)>

OPENING THE HOUSE OF THE WIND

The little hillock immediately east of the church of San Xavier del Bac is now topped by a replica of the shrine of Saint Bernadette at Lourdes, France. Back in November 1699, however, Juan Mateo Manje, who accompanied Father Kino to W:ak, described finding a **white stone** on top of this hill:

We guessed it might be some idol that the heathen Indians worshipped, so with great effort we pulled out the stone, thereby exposing a large hole. At the time, we did not know what it could be. While we were coming down the hill, a great and furious hurricane developed. We could scarcely walk because of the terrific windstorm. None of the Indians had gone with us to the top of the hill; but when the furious wind arose they started to yell, saying in sort of rebellion, "Vbiriqui cupioca", which meant that the House of the Wind (god) had been opened.

Still within the mission walls, to the right of the church, a small **museum** displays a gigantic illuminated sheepskin psalter and photos of other remote churches on the Tohono O'odham reservation.

Ramada-shaded stalls in the square-cum-parking lot in front of the church sell snacks and sodas. This square also hosts the mission's major **feast days**, of St Francis of Assisi on October 4, and St Francis Xavier on December 3.

Titan Missile Museum

1580 W Duval Mine Rd; I-19 exit 69 • Daily 8.45am–5pm • $9.50 • ☎ 520 625 7736, ⓦ titanmissilemuseum.org

Sixteen miles south of San Xavier, the main attraction at the **Titan Missile Museum** is an underground silo that, until 1982, held two Titan II nuclear missiles. Each was primed and ready to fire at a choice of three specific targets, as much as five thousand miles away; what those targets were remains classified even today, but they never changed during the 22 years that the site was operational. A total of 54 such missiles were deployed at 27 separate locations, in Arizona, California and Arkansas, but only this site survived the end of the Cold War. One of its missiles is actually still down there – no longer primed, of course – and can be examined close-up on hour-long subterranean **guided tours**.

The whole installation was designed to remain functional in a nuclear war. Its vast sliding door could open through eight feet of post-holocaust debris; the crew could live beneath the surface for up to thirty days; and the whole place could even operate on two 28-volt batteries in case of electrical outage. Tours culminate in the control room, still scattered with top-secret manuals, where two keys had to be turned simultaneously to fire the missile.

As you might imagine, inspecting colossal rocket launchers and other military hardware is very much a "guy thing." Casual visitors who take the tours may well run out of steam before the excitable gun nuts in the crowd find time to draw breath. Check the website for schedules of the five-hour "Top-to-Bottom" tours (four times monthly, starting 8am; $70).

Tubac

These days, the village of **TUBAC**, fifty miles south of San Xavier, is a thriving **arts colony**. Originally, however, this was the first permanent Spanish settlement in Arizona, founded in 1752 as a **presidio** or fortress to guard against repetitions of the previous year's Pima Revolt against the Jesuits. In 1775, its commander, Juan Bautista de Anza, launched the expedition that established **San Francisco**, but Tubac soon declined, after its garrison was shifted to the new city of Tucson in 1776. For the next century, it was alternately abandoned and resettled as Apache raids permitted.

Tubac's successful new incarnation has enabled it to grow almost beyond recognition, with all new real-estate developments echoing Taos and Santa Fe in their use of the faux-adobe architectural style. The broad streets in its central core are now paved and lined with studios, galleries, folk-art stores and boutiques, while each year yet another identical little plaza seems to sprout from the surrounding fields. Most of what's on sale lies firmly within the established genres of contemporary Southwestern arts and crafts – lurid O'Keeffe-esque sunsets and blanket-swathed native Americans, turquoise ironwork, and the like – but there are also plenty of inexpensive imports, especially ceramics, from south of the nearby Mexican border.

Tubac Presidio State Historic Park

1 Burruel St • Daily 9am–5pm • $5 • ☎ 520 398 2252, ⓦ tubacpresidiopark.com

Although the foundations of Tubac's original adobe fortress now lie beneath an earthen mound, they can be admired from a cool underground viewing gallery in the **Tubac Presidio State Historic Park**. A large museum alongside contains pieces from all periods of Tubac's long history, including beautiful naïve *retablos*, the press that was used to print Arizona's first newspaper, *The Weekly Arizonan*, in 1859, and a crucifix depicting the black "Christo Negro" – a Native American Christ.

On alternate Sundays between October and March, from 1pm until 4pm, costumed locals re-enact the daily life of the eighteenth-century presidio.

Tumacácori National Historical Park

3 miles south of Tubac; I-19 exit 29 • Daily 9am–5pm • $3 per person • ☎ 520 398 2341, ⓦ nps.gov/tuma

A **Spanish mission** founded by Father Kino in 1691, before its more celebrated neighbour at San Xavier (see p.230), is now the focus of the **TUMACÁCORI NATIONAL HISTORICAL PARK**. Like San Xavier, the church here was built at the end of the eighteenth century, but having failed to withstand Apache raids, Tumacácori was abandoned in 1848, five years before the region passed into US control.

It's now an evocative ruin, topped by a whitewashed dome but home only to the birds that fly down from the Patagonia Mountains. Behind its weatherbeaten red-tinged facade, the plaster has crumbled from the interior walls to reveal bare adobe bricks. A few traces of a mural can be discerned in the raised sanctuary, but little remains of the priests' living quarters alongside.

A fascinating **museum** holds a replica of a banner carried by missionaries; one side depicts the Madonna and Child, the other shows an Indian burning in hell. Opposite the gate, the *Tumacácori Restaurant* serves Mexican and Greek specialities as well as deli sandwiches.

Nogales

NOGALES, an hour's drive south from Tucson and the largest of the Arizonan–Mexican border towns, consists in effect of two separate towns, one in the US and one across the border in Mexico, both of which were founded in 1880. The contrast between the sedate, ordered streets of the American town – the unlikely birthplace of iconoclastic jazz great **Charles Mingus** – and the jumbled whitewashed houses clinging to the slopes in Mexico hits you as soon as you come in sight.

There's never been anything much to see on either side of the border, and these days the tourist novelty of dipping into Mexico has become overshadowed, literally and metaphorically, by the construction of a huge new security wall to deter illegal immigrants. While considerable numbers of people still cross the frontier every day, on foot as well as driving, American Nogales is now home to the largest Border Patrol facility in the country, while Nogales in Mexico has filled up with deportees who have nowhere else to go. The day-trippers who venture there now tend to be looking for cut-price medicines or dental work rather than rugs or hammocks.

Patagonia and Sonoita

A longer but even more attractive route back from Nogales to Tucson avoids the interstate by following highways 82 and 83 northeast from Nogales through the lush **Sonoita Valley**, in the craggy mountains of the Coronado National Forest.

The appealing little Wild West mining and cattle-ranching town of **PATAGONIA**, twenty miles up from Nogales, attracts weekend crowds of **birdwatchers**. Twelve miles further along, **SONOITA** itself is a wide-open desert crossroads, lined with a few false-front stores, at the point where Hwy-83 veers northwest to rejoin I-10 two miles east of Saguaro National Park, while Hwy-82 cuts east toward Tombstone, 35 miles away (see p.237).

Patagonia-Sonoita Creek Sanctuary

150 Blue Haven Rd, Patagonia • April–Sept Wed–Sun 6.30am–4pm; Oct–March Wed–Sun 7.30am–4pm • $5 • ☎ 520 394 2000

At the far southwestern end of a mile-long dirt road that leads off Patagonia's Fourth Street, the **Patagonia-Sonoita Creek Sanctuary** is a dense riverbank stand of oaks and cottonwoods that's home to an amazing range of songbirds and raptors, including finches and flycatchers, kingbirds and kestrels, and woodpeckers and cardinals. With all this colourful collection to choose from, the sighting most prized by twitchers is a drab little specimen called the northern beardless tyrannulet.

ARRIVAL, DEPARTURE AND INFORMATION

THE MISSION TRAIL

NOGALES

Visitor centre 123 W Kino Park (Mon–Fri 9am–5pm; ☎ 520 287 3685, ⓦ thenogaleschamber.com).

TO MEXICO

Crossing the border into Mexico from Nogales is straightforward, as only travellers heading more than 21km south of the border require Mexican visas. US citizens must, however, carry their passports, while foreign visitors should check their visa status entitles them to re-enter the

US; if you're on or eligible for the visa waiver scheme (see p.41), you're fine. There's no need to change money; US dollars are freely accepted by stores and businesses in Mexico.

If you plan to set off further south, pick up a tourist visa just beyond the border crossing. Then take a taxi (around $10) a couple of miles to the long-distance bus station, from which regular buses head to Hermosillo, Guaymas on the Gulf of California (a good overnight stop), and Los Mochis, the start of the Copper Canyon Railroad.

ACCOMMODATION AND EATING

TUBAC

Tubac Country Inn 13 Burruel St ☎ 520 398 3178, ⓦ tubaccountryinn.com. The nicest of the B&Bs in the centre of old Tubac, this timber-framed inn has five very substantial en-suite rooms that share a common veranda and use of an attractive garden. Breakfast is delivered outside your door. **$125**

Tubac Deli & Coffee Company 4 Plaza Rd ☎ 520 398 3330, ⓦ tubacdeli.com. Busy coffeehouse, snack place and all-round community rendezvous, just off the main highway; salads and sandwiches to take out or eat in typically cost $8. Daily 6.30am–7pm.

Shelby's Bistro 19 Plaza Rd ☎ 520 398 8075, ⓦ shelbysbistro.com. The best place to get a full meal in Tubac, with a long, consistently good menu that ranges from delicious black bean soup via pizzas up to substantial meat and seafood entrees for $15–18 – but watch for bugs on the cooled outdoor patio. Mon, Tues & Sun 11am–4pm, Wed–Sat 11am–4pm & 5–8.30pm.

NOGALES

Holiday Inn Express 850 W Shell Rd ☎ 520 281 0123 or ☎ 800 465 4329, ⓦ hiexpress.com. This smart hundred-room motel, part of a cluster near the interstate three miles out from the centre, is considerably more appealing than the alternatives closer in. **$114**

PATAGONIA

Duquesne House 357 Duquesne Ave ☎ 520 394 2732, ⓦ theduquesnehouse.com. Century-old adobe boarding house that's been converted into a delightful little B&B. As well as three large suites that sleep up to four, there's a smaller studio apartment; each is en-suite, and effectively has its own area of the tranquil gardens, which offer great birdwatching. Rates are $15 cheaper on Tues & Wed, when the usual tasty breakfast is not available. **$125**

Gathering Grounds 319 W McKeown Ave ☎ 520 394 2097. The ideal stop for a lunchtime snack or an evening meal of steak, fish or a *clayuda*, a kind of Mexican pizza costing around $10. Mon–Wed & Sun 7am–5pm, Thurs–Sat 7am–9pm.

Stage Stop Inn 303 W McKeown Ave ☎520 394 2211, ⓦ stagestophotelpatagonia.com. Despite appearances, this convenient hotel in the heart of old Patagonia was actually built as a Western-movie set in the 1970s. It holds a dozen retro-furnished rooms, some of which have private balconies and/or kitchenettes. $89

SONOITA

The Café 3280 Hwy-82, Sonoita ☎520 455 5278. Originally *Café Sonoita*, this popular restaurant, just west of town, is now run by an enterprising new chef, but is serving a somewhat less imaginative menu, with lunchtime burgers and sandwiches for around $10, complemented by dinner entrees like chicken breast stuffed with green chiles for $14, and slow-roasted prime rib for $16–20. Mon–Thurs 11am–2pm, Fri & Sat 11am–2pm & 5–8pm, Sun 10am–2pm.

Southeast Arizona

Although the I-10 interstate remains consistently dull as it crosses **southeast Arizona**, the rugged territory to the south holds some spectacular scenery and memorable historic sites. While the much-mythologized Wild West outpost of **Tombstone** does its best to entertain the hordes of cowboy fanatics who troop this way, the mining town of **Bisbee** is in many ways a more evocative relic of frontier times.

Further east, the **Chiricahua Mountains** witnessed the final saga of Native American resistance to federal encroachment, in the 1880s guerrilla campaign of Geronimo's **Apache**. The Chiricahua is merely one of around a dozen separate ranges that soar from the deserts, known as "**sky islands**" because each harbours its own unique ecosystem of plants, birds and animals.

Kartchner Caverns

Signposted west off Hwy-90, 7 miles south of Benson and 52 miles southeast of Tucson • Park entrance $6 per vehicle, Rotunda/Throne tour $23, Big Room tour $23 • ☎ 520 586 2283, ⓦ azstateparks.com

When **Kartchner Caverns** became a state park in 1999, it was expected to become one of Arizona's premier tourist attractions. Unlike counterparts such as Carlsbad Caverns in New Mexico, these caves are very unusual in being "live;" they're still being hollowed out of the Whetstone Mountains by each new dose of rainfall, and the formations within are still growing. While the caves may be an exciting novelty for local residents, however, they're not really worth travelling across the country – let alone the world – to see, and with a visit for a family of four costing at least $70, they're also wildly overpriced.

Kartchner Caverns were discovered in 1974 when cavers Gary Tenen and Randy Tufts, investigating a strange-smelling hole in the mountainside, squeezed into what turned out to be a vast open space. Eventually the two explorers mapped out the subterranean complex at over two miles long, with around 13,000 feet of passageways. They told no one until 1987, whereupon it took a further twelve years, and $28 million, for the Arizona state authorities to prepare the caverns for display.

The caves themselves can only be seen on one of the two distinct **guided tours** detailed below. Overall numbers are limited, and during busy periods all tours may be fully booked months ahead, though two hundred unreserved "walk-ins" are allowed each day. Try to reserve as far in advance as possible. You have to pay the full fee by credit card when you book; the fees are not refundable, though you can change the precise time of your tour. If you're hoping to turn up without a reservation, call on your chosen day to assess your chances; if you fail to get in, you can at least content yourself with the displays in the large **Discovery Center** instead (daily 7.30am–6pm).

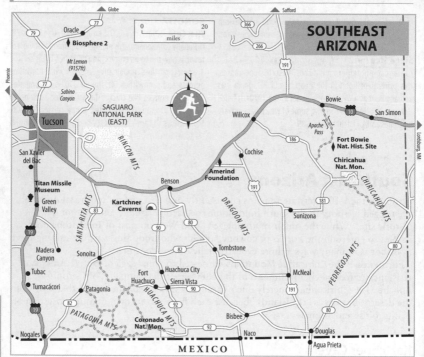

The Rotunda/Throne tour

The shorter of the two tours, the **Rotunda/Throne** tour follows a narrow, switchbacking cement trail of a third of a mile through the caverns' two upper "rooms". It lasts for something over an hour, including a tram ride to the cave entrance and 45 minutes spent underground. Formations en route include precarious stalactites (the ones that dangle from the ceiling) and towering stalagmites (which rise from the floor) – to add to the confusion, there's also a 21ft hollow soda straw, a combination of both that stretches from floor to ceiling. However, the most spectacular feature is the striated **colouring** of the cavern walls, created by eons of unseen flooding and illuminated by the dramatic sound-and-light show with which the tour culminates.

The Big Room tour

The **Big Room** tour, available between mid-October and mid-April only, delves deeper into the cave system than the Rotunda/Throne tour, and requires visitors to pass through no fewer than six separate airlock doors. Taking ninety or more minutes, it goes into a little more technical detail, while showcasing unusual wet formations such as a bizarre "fried egg."

Amerind Foundation Museum

1 mile southeast of I-10 exit 318; 65 miles southeast of Tucson • Daily except Mon 10am–4pm • $8 • ☎ 520 586 3666, ⒲ amerind.org

The privately run **Amerind Foundation Museum**, in remote Texas Canyon, offers the one point of interest on the barren run east from Benson towards New Mexico on I-10. It's a rather highbrow affair, with the declared ambition to "increase the world's knowledge of ancient man by excavation and collection." Displays cover native cultures from North, Central and Southern America, but specialize in the Southwest, featuring fine Apache, Navajo and Hopi crafts, plus older pieces from the Mimbres and Hohokam peoples. While not quite on a par with the museums in Flagstaff, Phoenix or Santa Fe, it's worth an hour or two of your time if you're passing this way.

Sierra Vista

The characterless modern town of **SIERRA VISTA**, 30 miles south of Benson on Hwy-90, has grown in tandem with the Army base at **Fort Huachuca**. One of the few nineteenth-century military outposts to remain active, the fort still employs over eighteen thousand people. As the headquarters of the United States Army Intelligence Center, it's widely reported to have played a major role in developing the interrogation techniques made infamous at Abu Ghraib – not that you'll find much on the subject in the **US Army Intelligence Museum** (Mon–Sat 9am–4pm; $5 donation).

Ramsey Canyon Preserve

Off Hwy-92; 7 miles south of Sierra Vista • Mon & Thurs–Sun 8am–5pm • $5 • ☎ 520 378 2785, ⓦ nature.org

Owned by the Nature Conservancy, the **Ramsey Canyon Preserve** squeezes into a slender gorge in the Huachuca Mountains, south of Sierra Vista. This well-watered spot is dedicated to safeguarding local wildlife in general, but the main reason everyone comes here is for its mind-boggling summer array of colourful **hummingbirds**, which reach their peak population in August. Guided walking tours explore the preserve in summer only (March–Oct Mon, Thurs & Sat 9am). Be warned that there's not much room for cars; the 23 parking spaces are first-come, first-served, so there's a risk you'll be turned away.

4

ACCOMMODATION	SIERRA VISTA

Ramsey Canyon Inn 29 Ramsey Canyon Rd ☎ 520 378 3010, ⓦ ramseycanyoninn.com. Just outside the namesake preserve, seven miles south of Sierra Vista and a mile above sea level, the *Ramsey Canyon Inn* is a plush B&B where all six rooms in the main house are en suite; there are also two separate suites which sleep four and are the only options for families travelling with children. A battery of sugar-water feeders attracts countless hummingbirds in summer. **$135**

Coronado National Memorial

5 miles south of Hwy-92; a total of 20 miles south of Sierra Vista • **Visitor centre** Daily 8am–4pm • Free • ☎ 520 366 5515, ⓦ nps.gov/coro

Tucked into the southernmost notch of the Huachuca Mountains, **CORONADO NATIONAL MEMORIAL** commemorates the approximate spot where in May 1540 the expedition of **Francisco Vásquez de Coronado** first entered what is now the United States (see p.465). Displays in the **visitor centre** explain the history, but the memorial basically exists to offer a selection of scenic **hiking trails**. The best short hike climbs south from **Montezuma Pass**, the highest point along the washboard dirt road west of the visitor centre. The 0.4-mile **Coronado Peak Trail** culminates in huge views in all directions, and especially to the pyramidal Mexican mountains across the border.

Tombstone

Perhaps the most famous town in the Wild West, **TOMBSTONE** lies on US-80, 22 miles south of I-10 and 67 miles southeast of Tucson. Well over a century has passed since its mining days came to an end, but "The Town Too Tough to Die" clings to an afterlife as a tourist theme park. With its dusty streets, wooden sidewalks, and swinging saloon doors, it's surprisingly unchanged, though these days the emphasis is on entertaining kids with tacky dioramas and daily shoot-outs. While much more commercialized than Lincoln, its counterpart in New Mexico (see p.179), to be honest it's also more fun.

Prospecting in the Dragoon Mountains in 1877, **Edward Schieffelin** was told by soldiers stationed nearby that all he'd find would be his own tombstone. Hence the name of the town that rose from the desert when he made Arizona's largest **silver** strike, in March 1878. Schieffelin sold his stake for $500,000, but the mine yielded $30 million in seven years, and by 1880 Tombstone was home to over ten thousand people. Drifters arrived from the played-out gold-fields of Canada and Australia, and gamblers came in from Dodge City, only for the mine to hit water 500 feet down in 1886, and be flooded beyond repair.

Most of the buildings that fill modern Tombstone's simple grid date from the early 1880s. Decaying wagons are parked on the street corners, and signs along the boardwalks mark the sites of famous shoot-outs. It's all quite surreal, as groups of disconsolate, ornery **gunslingers** still pace the streets, snarling at each other and generally creating enough trouble that the town council has repeatedly attempted to outlaw public gunfighting. Assuming you visit when no ban is in place, whenever a posse of cowboys manage to round up enough tourists, usually at around $4 per head, they gun each other down on some appropriate vacant lot. During **Helldorado Days**, held on the third weekend of each October, you can hardly move for corpses.

OK Corral

Allen St, between Third & Fourth • Daily 9am–5pm; gunfights Tues–Thurs 2pm & 4pm, Fri–Mon 2pm & 5pm • $6, or $10 with gunfight • ⓦ ok-corral.com

Although the real gunfight at the OK Corral in fact took place on Fremont Street, the **OK Corral** itself, on Allen Street, remains a big attraction. The first thing you see on entering is the hearse used to take the victims away. Crude dummies in the second of two baking-hot adobe-walled courtyards beyond show the supposed locations of the Earps and the Clantons. In the original studio of photographer C.S. Fly alongside, you can pose for your own souvenir photo or tintype (Thurs–Mon 10am–5pm; $25).

Bird Cage Theater

Allen St and Sixth Ave • Daily 8am–6pm • $10 • ☎ 800 457 3423, ⓦ tombstonebirdcage.com

The **Bird Cage Theater** was Tombstone's leading venue for entertainment of all kinds. Seven "bird cages," much like theatre boxes but curtained off and used by prostitutes, hang from either side of the main hall. Those on the left were frequented by the Earps and their cronies, while the ones on the right were the preserve of Sheriff Behan and the Clantons. The theatre now holds a motley collection of curiosities, including a revolting foot-long "merman" from China and another ornate hearse, while downstairs you can see the old gaming tables and bordello rooms.

Tombstone Courthouse State Historic Park

Third and Toughnut streets • Daily 9am–5pm • $5 • ☎ 520 457 3311, ⓦ azstateparks.com/Parks/TOCO/

Centring on Cochise County's original, red-brick 1882 courthouse, the **Tombstone Courthouse State Historic Park** holds displays on the Apache and early outlaws, and documents several rough episodes of frontier justice.

Boothill Graveyard

Half a mile north of downtown Tombstone on US-80 • Daily 7.30am–6pm • Free • ⓦ boothillgraves.com

Tombstone's fabled **Boothill Graveyard** closed in May 1884, having been filled by 276 burials. In keeping with the souvenir store that now guards the entrance, several of the graves bear dubious jokey epitaphs, and country music is piped from concealed speakers. The losers at the OK Corral, however, still rest in relative peace.

INFORMATION   **TOMBSTONE**

Visitor centre 395 E Allen (Mon–Thurs 9am–4pm, Fri–Sun 9am–5pm; ☎ 520 457 3929, ⓦ tombstonechamber.com).

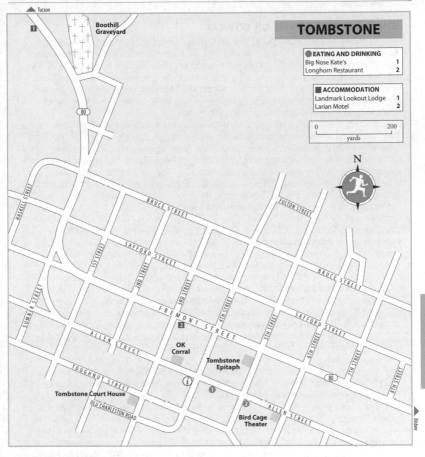

4

ACCOMMODATION

Landmark Lookout Lodge 781 N US-80 ☎ 520 457 2223, ⓦ lookoutlodgeaz.com. Classy, tasteful Western-themed rooms with splendid mountain views; the one snag with this modern chain motel is that it's a mile north of downtown, out on its own with only the neighbouring *Holiday Inn Express* for company. **$99**

★ **Larian Motel** 410 E Fremont St ☎ 520 457 2272, ⓦ tombstonemotels.com. Much the best of the old-style motels in the middle of Old Tombstone, in walking distance of all the attractions. Clean well-maintained rooms and exceptionally friendly and helpful owners. **$79**

EATING AND DRINKING

Big Nose Kate's 417 E Allen St ☎ 520 457 3107, ⓦ bignosekates.info. Very fancy Wild West saloon, with lots of stained glass and period fittings, where the waitresses wear period costume, country musicians entertain most afternoons, and everyone strives to keep the atmosphere authentically raucous. Prices on menu of burgers, pizzas and calzones start around $8. Daily 10am–midnight.

Longhorn Restaurant 501 Allen St ☎ 520 457 3405, ⓦ bignosekates.info/longhorn.html. Tombstone's oldest restaurant – once the *Bucket of Blood* – is now run by *Big Nose Kate's* nearby. More of a family steakhouse than a saloon, it serves all meals daily, with a lunchtime barbecue hoagie for $8, and dinner entrees ranging from $11 pot roasts to a $20 T-Bone. Daily 7.30am–9pm.

THE GUNFIGHT AT THE OK CORRAL

Despite the fame of the **gunfight at the OK Corral** – which ended the feud between the **Earps** and the **Clantons** – how the clannish dispute began remains obscure. To Hollywood, the Earps have always been the heroes, with Wyatt Earp played by firm-jawed stars like Henry Fonda and Kevin Costner. They were, after all, officers of the law, although it was **Virgil** who was Tombstone's marshal, and his brothers **Wyatt** and **Morgan** merely temporary deputies. Ike Clanton, his brother Billy, and their "gang" were freebooting cattle rustlers, who raided Mexican ranches to feed Tombstone's hungry miners.

Such family-based clans were typical of the West, where individuals seldom prospered alone but trustworthy partners were few and far between. Just as typically, both factions had allied themselves with more powerful forces. Though the Earps dreamed of establishing their own cattle empire, they were the hired guns of Tombstone's **Republican** elite. For the owners and managers of the local mines, a federally imposed end to Arizona's frontier anarchy was essential for future investment. Their mouthpiece, Republican mayor John Clum, was also editor of the *Tombstone Epitaph*. The Clantons, like most cowboys and small-scale ranchers, were aligned with the county sheriff, **Democrat** John Behan.

In the spring of 1881, masked gunmen held up a stagecoach near Tombstone and killed two passengers. Some say the robbers were Clanton associates; others, that a familiar cough betrayed one as **John "Doc" Holliday**, a consumptive dentist from Georgia who was close to the Earps, and that the victims were Clanton's men. The hold-up may even have been a joint operation by both groups, who fell out when the plan went awry.

By October, each faction had sworn to shoot the other on sight. The final showdown came at 2pm on **October 26, 1881**. Virgil, Wyatt and Morgan Earp, together with Doc Holliday, confronted the Clanton brothers, Tom and Frank McLaury and Billy Claiborne, not in the OK Corral itself, but on Fremont Street nearby. Two of the Clanton group were unarmed, whereas all the Earps had pistols, and Holliday was carrying a shotgun. The Earps fired first. When the shooting stopped, Billy Clanton and the McLaury brothers were dead; Virgil and Morgan Earp and Doc Holliday were wounded; and Ike Clanton had fled.

Under the headline "Three Men Hurled Into Eternity in the Duration of a Moment," the next day's *Tombstone Epitaph* reported that "the feeling among our best citizens is that the Marshal was entirely justifiable." However, Wyatt and Holliday were charged with murder and were held in jail before being acquitted towards the end of November.

In March 1882, Morgan Earp was killed as he played billiards in Tombstone's *Campbell & Hatch* saloon. Three days later, Wyatt Earp shot the chief suspect, Clanton associate Frank Stilwell, in Tucson. He also killed two more of the Clanton gang that summer before leaving Tombstone with his surviving brothers, and moving to Los Angeles. Lionized by early moviemakers, he died in 1929. Tombstone's Episcopalian minister at the time of the shoot-out – Endicott Peabody – went on to be Franklin Roosevelt's White House chaplain.

Bisbee

Crammed into a narrow gorge 25 miles south of Tombstone, **BISBEE** is among Arizona's most atmospheric Victorian towns, rivalled only by Jerome (see p.277). Its fortunes were similarly built on a century of mining mundane, dependable **copper** from the surrounding mountains, rather than a few ephemeral years of gold and silver. Its solid brick buildings testify to the days when Bisbee was the largest city between New Orleans and San Francisco. In 1910, its population stood at fifteen thousand, outstripping both Phoenix and Tucson, and it even started to develop its own suburbs.

George Warren, who first discovered copper in Mule Pass Gulch, the site of modern Bisbee, in 1877, swiftly lost his claim in a fit of drunken bravado, betting he could outrun a man on horseback. The Copper Queen and Phelps Dodge companies soon moved in, then amalgamated rather than fight over which owned a vast ore body found between their two mines.

Phelps Dodge finally closed down in 1975, having extracted over six billion dollars' worth of metals. As the miners moved away, however, artists and retirees moved in, preserving Bisbee's original architecture while turning it into a thriving, friendly little community that caters to tourists without being overwhelmed by them.

Walking Bisbee's narrow central streets, lined with galleries and antiques stores, is a pleasure in itself, though you may grow weary of climbing the high staircases built by the WPA during the 1930s.

Bisbee Mining and Historical Museum

5 Copper Queen Plaza • Daily 10am–4pm • $7.50 • ☎ 520 432 7071, ⓦ bisbeemuseum.org

Excellent displays at the **Bisbee Mining and Historical Museum** explore local history in fascinating detail. As well as a thorough account of the enforced deportation in 1917 of 1200 "Wobblies" – members of the International Workers of the World, who were seen by the mining corporations as communist troublemakers – it holds evocative photos of the town's early days, and lots of material on the immigrants who arrived here from all over the world.

INFORMATION AND TOURS	BISBEE

Visitor centre 478 Dart Rd (Mon–Fri 9am–5pm, Sat & Sun 10am–4pm; ☎ 520 432 3554 or ☎ 866 224 7233, ⓦ discoverbisbee.com).
Queen Mine Tours Hour-long **underground tours** of

Bisbee's actual mines, starting from 478 Dart Rd, adjoining the visitor centre (daily 9am, 10.30am, noon, 2pm & 3.30pm; adults $13, ages 4–12 $5.50; ☎ 520 432 2071, ⓦ queenminetour.com).

ACCOMMODATION

Copper Queen Hotel 11 Howell Ave ☎ 520 432 2216, ⓦ copperqueen.com. The venerable *Copper Queen* – Arizona's oldest hotel, in the heart of town – is more of a historic experience than an up-to-the-minute lodging option; the plumbing in particular remains antiquated. In terms of both size and comfort, its 48 rooms cover a very broad spectrum; the smallest really are quite pokey, while those named for famous guests such as John Wayne or Teddy Roosevelt are quite sumptuous. There's also a plush bar and a good restaurant with terrace seating. $99
School House Inn 818 Tombstone Canyon ☎ 520 432 2996 or ☎ 800 537 4333, ⓦ schoolhouseinnbb.com. Quirky B&B in a converted school a mile west of the centre,

where the nine attractively furnished en-suite rooms are still named for the original use – the History Room, the Library, even the two-room Principal's Office – with a large common lounge and high-quality breakfasts. $89
★ **The Shady Dell** 1 Douglas Rd ☎ 520 432 3567, ⓦ theshadydell.com. Truly unique accommodation on the southern outskirts of town. The *Shady Dell* is home to nine beautifully restored, irresistibly kitsch 1950s trailers – each neatly fenced into its own desert-garden lot, and furnished with authentic period memorabilia – and even a 1947 yacht. This is not a place to bring your own RV, but a great opportunity to sample how a Southwest road trip used to be, complete with 1950s-style diner. $87

EATING AND DRINKING

Once-notorious **Brewery Gulch**, which runs north from Main Street, still holds a handful of spit-and-sawdust saloons and diners, while the less atmospheric **Copper Queen Plaza** mall to the south has its own brewpub and espresso café.

Café Roka 35 Main St ☎ 520 432 5153, ⓦ caferoka .com. Smart, very modern dinner-only restaurant in downtown Bisbee, where the menu changes twice monthly according to what's in season, and normally includes plenty of seafood. Appetizers like steamed clams or Spanish tortilla cost $5–10, entrees like prosciutto-stuffed roasted quail or risotto cakes $16-23. There's live jazz on Friday nights. Summer Fri–Sat 5–9pm; spring &

fall Wed–Sat 5–9pm; winter Thurs–Sat 5–9pm.
High Desert Market & Cafe 203 Tombstone Canyon ☎ 520 432 6775, ⓦ highdesertmarket.net. Part deli, part cafe, at the west end of town, this friendly hangout has indoor and outdoor seating, good salads and sandwiches for $8 – hummus on pitta, for example – and wholesome all-fruit smoothies for $4. Daily 7am–7pm.

Douglas

As you'll see if you drive south from Bisbee, the endless tailings that spill from the canyons hereabouts left little room to build in or near the town. In 1900, therefore, the new town of **DOUGLAS** was constructed 25 miles east, nestled against the Mexican

A FORTIFIED FRONTIER

Douglas has long been renowned as the number-one port of entry for **illegal immigrants** from Mexico. At its peak, in the late 1990s, 61,000 such entrants were arrested in Douglas in a single month – a rate of almost one hundred per hour, but nonetheless a small proportion of those who attempted the crossing. Those figures have dropped enormously since then, partly as a result of economic recession but also due to a major US crackdown that saw the construction of a permanent border wall. Head south anywhere in Douglas, and you'll soon find yourself confronted by a colossal, forbidding fence.

These days would-be migrants attempt to cross the fearsome Sonora Desert on foot, far from urban areas. Around 250 per year die of dehydration, while Douglas itself is racked by controversy, with unauthorized vigilante patrols vying with church and humanitarian groups to find distressed wanderers.

border, to hold a smelter that processed copper from Bisbee's mines. Although Douglas has diversified into ranching and industry, the relocation of Phelps Dodge following a bitter 1980s strike has left the local economy too depressed for it to make an appealing stop for tourists.

Illegal trade with the much larger city of **AGUA PRIETA** across the border – home to almost 100,000 people – is a major source of income. One notorious drug smuggler hired surveyors and labourers to dig a deep tunnel between his houses in either town, then had them executed to preserve his secret.

With its whitewashed adobe homes and churches, Agua Prieta is a considerably more attractive place to stroll around than Douglas, and offers plenty of opportunities to eat spicy Sonoran food and buy cheap souvenirs.

ARRIVAL AND INFORMATION   DOUGLAS

Visitor centre Douglas has a visitor centre at 345 Sixteenth St (Mon–Fri 9am–4pm, Sat 10am–3pm; ☎ 520 417 7344, ⓦ douglasaz.gov).
Crossing the border Cars and pedestrians alike cross

into Mexico at the foot of Pan American Avenue, a mile or so southwest of downtown Douglas; US citizens should carry passports.

ACCOMMODATION AND EATING

Gadsden Hotel 1046 G Ave ☎ 520 364 4481, ⓦ hotelgadsden.com. The one noteworthy building in downtown Douglas, this 160-room hotel opened in 1907, and still boasts an extraordinarily opulent lobby with a white marble staircase leading to a 42ft Tiffany glass

window. The guest accommodation is not nearly so classy, and the plumbing unreliable, but both its *Saddle and Spur Lounge* and *El Conquistador* restaurant, which serves reasonable meals for around $10, have a real frontier-town air. $60

Chiricahua National Monument

36 miles southeast of I-10 exit 340, Willcox, via Hwy-186 • **Visitor centre** Daily 8am–4.30pm • $5 per person • ☎ 520 824 3560, ⓦ nps.gov/chir

Stretching northeast of Douglas toward New Mexico, the **Chiricahua Mountains** were the homeland and stronghold of the **Chiricahua Apache**. Led by legendary warriors like **Cochise** and **Geronimo**, the Chiricahua – the name means "land of wild turkeys" – were the last Native Americans to hold out against the US Army. The 25-year **Apache Wars** began at Apache Pass in 1861, when Cochise met Lt George Bascom under a flag of truce, and was falsely accused of kidnapping a 12-year-old boy. He escaped into the mountains, but his brother and two nephews were hanged, precipitating a vicious cycle of raids and killings that only ended with Geronimo's fourth and final surrender in 1886.

Had the small Chiricahua band not fought so long and hard, they might still be living on the **Chiricahua reservation**, established during a period of relative peace in

1872. Occupying the entire southeastern corner of Arizona, it was disbanded in 1876, when the Chiricahua were forcibly decamped to join their distant cousins on the San Carlos Reservation to the north. No sign of the Apache presence remains, but the core of the former reservation now constitutes **CHIRICAHUA NATIONAL MONUMENT**. The monument was designated to protect the bizarre **rock formations** created in the 27 million years since volcanic eruptions covered the landscape with a 2000ft coating of dark rhyolite rock. That layer has now cracked and fragmented into strange towers and columns of stacked and balanced stones, a bewildering maze that always defeated Army attempts to pursue the Apache into the mountains.

Although Chiricahua National Monument is not as spectacular as the desert canyons of Utah, this remote fastness preserves a tract of barely touched wilderness that conjures up haunting images of the Wild West, and it's also a sanctuary for rare animals and birds. These include a colony of thick-billed **parrots**, once common here and reintroduced in 1986. No food, gas or lodging is available in the monument, and overnight backpacking is forbidden.

Just one paved road – the eight-mile **Bonita Canyon Drive** – penetrates, but does not cross, the mountains, and stays open 24 hours. From the monument entrance it runs for two miles to the **visitor centre**, then follows Bonita Canyon east before climbing south to reach **Massai Point**, 6870ft up. This high vantage point looks out over the main concentration of rocky pinnacles, in **Echo Canyon** and **Heart of Rocks**; trails drop from the parking lot to circle the promontory below.

Hiking in Chiricahua

Massai Point is only a good spot from which to start **hiking** if you have a few hours to spare. It is possible to walk down into the labyrinth from the point, but then you're faced with either a long climb to get back out again, or a one-way walk of at least four miles to reach the visitor centre. For a shorter and less demanding stroll, set off instead along **Echo Canyon Trail**, which starts half a mile or so back down the road. This level footpath leads in ten minutes to some dramatic formations, and you can turn back whenever you've had your fill. The highest peak in the monument at 7310ft, **Sugarloaf Mountain**, can be climbed on a separate mile-long trail, but it's a much less rewarding hike.

ACCOMMODATION AND EATING	**CHIRICAHUA NATIONAL MONUMENT**
Bonita Canyon Campground Chiricahua National Monument ☎520 824 3560, ⓦnps.gov/chir. Small, first-come, first-served campground that offers the only opportunity to spend the night in Chiricahua National Monument. All 22 sites remain open year-round, and tend to fill up every day during spring. **$12**	☎520 824 3344 or ☎866 786 4569, ⓦsunglowranch .com. This 475-acre guest ranch, just south of the monument, holds luxurious *casitas* of varying sizes, with bathrooms, fireplaces and private patios; six have one bedroom, and five have two. Rates include breakfast and dinner at the on-site *Sunglow Café*, which is also open for all meals to non-guests. **$269**
Sunglow Ranch 14066 S Sunglow Rd, Pearce	

Fort Bowie

3203 S Old Fort Bowie Rd; 13 miles south of I-10 exit 366, at Bowie • **Visitor centre** Daily 8am–4.30pm • Free • ☎520 847 2500, ⓦnps.gov/fobo

The ruins of **FORT BOWIE**, the original focus of the Chiricahua Reservation and now a national historic site, lie just beyond the northern boundary of Chiricahua National Monument. They're reached by a demanding but exhilarating 1.5 mile trail that starts on the north side of **Apache Pass**, a total of 22 miles from the monument visitor centre.

Apache Pass today is an insignificant back route. The central nine miles of the **Apache Pass Road** across it are not even paved, though when it hasn't been raining they're usually passable to ordinary vehicles. This low saddle between the Dos Cabezas and Chiricahua mountains is now overgrown with mesquite bushes, but when the Apache were here it ran through clear, open grassland. Its perennial natural **springs** made it a crucial way station for the **Butterfield Overland Mail**, which started regular runs through Apache Pass in 1857, as part of a 25-day, 2800-mile service between St Louis and San Francisco. The US Army soon established a permanent military presence at the pass.

Allow at least two and a half hours for the round-trip hike up to the fort itself. The first significant relic comes after half a mile, with the stone walls of the **Apache Pass Stage Station**, built in 1858. Shortly after crossing the old stage route, now a mere furrow in the soil, you reach the **cemetery** where Little Robe, Geronimo's two-year-old son, lies alongside several US soldiers. Not far beyond, the trail reaches the glorious lush creek that flows from **Apache Spring** – the source of all the trouble, but now the preserve of a myriad of playful coatis and bobcats.

There are no views to speak of as you climb; instead, the **fort** itself sits in a deep, broad bowl, ringed by mountains and dominated by a granite knob known as **Helen's Dome**. Only the rounded, sun-baked stumps of its adobe walls now survive, though a flag still flutters above the parade ground, and a visitor centre nearby provides much-needed shade and water. An optional, slightly longer route back continues up the adjacent hillside before circling down to the trailhead. En route, you step over the geological fault that created the springs, and the surrounding vegetation instantly transforms from yucca and flowering cactuses (on limestone) to beargrass (on granite).

Willcox

Only one significant community interrupts I-10 in its ninety-mile run east from Benson to the New Mexican border: **WILLCOX**, 36 miles out from Benson. In its small but atmospheric downtown area, the **Chiricahua Regional Museum**, 127 E Maley St (Mon–Sat 10am–4pm; $2 donation), is a storefront that holds informative displays on both Cochise and Geronimo.

INFORMATION   WILLCOX

Visitor centre 1500 N Circle I Rd, close to I-10 exit 340 (Mon–Fri 8am–5pm, Sat 9am–4pm, Sun 9am–1pm; 📞 520 384 2272 or 📞 800 200 2272, 🌐 willcoxchamber.com).

ACCOMMODATION AND EATING

Bucko's 114 S Railroad Ave 📞 520 384 2575. Very welcoming espresso café housed in a charming old store opposite the railroad depot. Tues–Sun 9am–6pm.

Holiday Inn Express 1251 N Virginia Ave 📞 520 384 3333 or 📞 800 315 621, 🌐 willcoxlodging.com. The newest and best equipped of Willcox's chain motels, out in the desert on the other side of the interstate from the old centre, with clean rooms and a decent breakfast buffet. $81

Rodney's 118 N Railroad Ave 📞 520 384 6317. Friendly hole-in-the-wall barbecue joint in town; not the cleanest or smartest of places, to be sure, but the food is good, with ribs, hot wings and tacos too for under $10. Tues–Sun 11am–8pm.

Southwest Arizona

Two interstates, **I-8** and **I-10**, run west across central and southern Arizona toward California, 35 miles apart near Phoenix and more than twice that by the time they reach the state line. There's virtually nothing of interest in these vast desert plains, apart perhaps from the strange prototype military airplanes glimpsed above the Barry M. Goldwater Air Force Range, which stretches south from I-8 to Mexico. A long detour south will take you to the wild terrain of **Organ Pipe Cactus National Monument**, but the only town you might conceivably want to visit is **Yuma**, a venerable river crossing on the far southwest border with California, whose mundane present fails to live up to its wild past.

Tohono O'odham Indian Reservation

Known as **Papaguería** to the Spanish, the high country east of Tucson is now dominated by the **TOHONO O'ODHAM INDIAN RESERVATION** (formerly known as the Papago Indian Reservation). The **Tohono O'odham**, whose name means "desert people," are one of three related groups who together call themselves the **O'odham** – "The People." Unlike the **Akimel O'odham** (or Pima), the "river people" who lived in permanent villages, the Tohono O'odham were traditionally "two-villagers," who divided their time between a summer "field" village in the valleys and a winter "well" village near a spring in the foothills. Apart from the mission at San Xavier del Bac (see p.230), the O'odham are best known these days for the music they call *waila*, derived from Mexican accordion and polka music, which may be more familiar as "**chicken scratch**".

Around twenty thousand Tohono O'odham now live on the reservation, which was established in 1916. They share it with the less numerous **Hia C–ed O'odham**, formerly known as the Sand Papago – desert nomads who in 1976 accepted $26 million as compensation for the loss of the lands now enclosed by Organ Pipe Cactus National Monument and the Barry Goldwater Air Force Base.

For tourists, the only reward in driving the hundred-mile width of the reservation, which starts 25 miles out of Tucson on **Hwy-86**, is its sheer sense of desolation. The only signs of human occupation, since most Tohono **O'odham** live far from the road, are a handful of roadside buildings at **Sells**, the administrative headquarters 56 miles southwest of Tucson, and **Quijotoa**, another 23 miles northwest.

Organ Pipe Cactus National Monument

Visitor centre Daily 8.30am–4.30pm • $8 per vehicle • ☎ 520 387 6849, ⓦ nps.gov/orpi

Located at the heart of the Sonoran Desert, right on the Mexican border, the five-hundred-square-mile **ORGAN PIPE CACTUS NATIONAL MONUMENT** is a treasure-trove of rare desert plants and animals, but focuses especially on the **organ pipe**, found almost nowhere else in the United States. Whereas the saguaro stands alone, the organ pipe grows in clusters of tubular "pipes," thrusting up from a shared central root system.

To reach the monument, detour south on Hwy-85 from the Y-shaped intersection, fifty miles south of Gila Bend, that has over the years acquired the formal name of **WHY**. Head through the straight, flat **Sonoyta Valley**, between the jagged ridge of the dry Ajo Mountains to the east and the lower Puerto Blanco Mountains to the west, and after twenty miles you'll come to the monument.

The monument **entrance fee** is payable only if you leave the main road. From the **visitor centre**, just west of the highway, two separate **scenic drives** loop off into the mountains. Both are unpaved and steep, but generally passable for ordinary vehicles; the 21-mile **Ajo Mountain Drive** takes around two hours to complete, the 53-mile **Puerto Blanco Drive** at least half a day. This remote area is so prone to illegal border crossings that it receives virtually constant attention from security forces; roads are often closed altogether for significant periods, and even when they're not, the activities of the border patrols may make you feel too uncomfortable to linger.

In summer, **hiking** anything more than the hundred-yard nature trail at the visitor centre would be far too gruelling to consider. Between October and April, however, you might feel more inclined to walk several short trails that lead further afield. The cooler months are also the only time when the **campground** (first-come, first-served; $12), a mile south of the visitor centre, is likely to fill up.

Ajo

Ten miles north of Why, almost halfway to Gila Bend and the interstate, **AJO** is a former copper-mining town that's nicer than the hideous open-pit mine to the south might suggest. Hispanic settlers were digging for copper by 1750; they named the town in honour of the garlic (*ajo*) that grows wild in the hills nearby.

Since Phelps Dodge closed the mine in 1984, after a bitter strike, Ajo has defied the sceptics and clung to life by attracting a steady trickle of tourists and retirees. There's a welcoming bustle about its tidy, grassy plaza, surrounded by palm trees and holding two whitewashed Spanish-colonial churches, even if the streets behind hold little of interest.

ACCOMMODATION   AJO

Guest House Inn 700 Guest House Rd ☎ 520 387 6133, ⊛ guesthouseinn.biz. Ajo's most central and comfortable lodging option was originally a mining-company guesthouse; now it's a comfortable B&B with four en-suite rooms that feature evocative antique furniture. **$89**

La Siesta 2561 N Hwy-85 ☎ 520 387 6569, ⊛ ajolasiesta.com. The better of the two simple roadside motels that stand a couple of miles north of Ajo. As well as the conventional motel rooms visible from the highway, it also offer tiny wooden cabins, plus a small pool. **$65**

Gila Bend

At the intersection of Hwy-85 and I-8, **GILA BEND** is a minor farming community whose rather scanty history is celebrated in the tiny **museum** that adjoins its rudimentary **visitor centre** at 644 W Pima St (daily 8am–4pm; ☎ 520 683 2002, ⊛ gilabendaz.org). The distance between here and Yuma (100 miles to the west) makes Gila Bend worth considering as a stopover, if not much else.

ACCOMMODATION   GILA BEND

Best Western Space Age Lodge 401 E Pima St ☎ 928 683 2273 or ☎ 866 683 7722, ⊛ bestwestern spaceagelodge.com. In this dramatic relic of the 1950s' obsession with all things space-related, the Sputnik motif extends to a giant neon flying saucer sign over the

run-of-the-mill on-site diner. The actual motel rooms are less themed, and there are cheaper alternatives; staying a night here is pretty much the one thrill Gila Bend has to offer. **$119**

Yuma

The sheer size of **YUMA** surprises most visitors; its numbered streets start a full fifty miles out from the centre, and while its population remains under 100,000, it's Arizona's third largest conurbation. According to the *Guinness Book of Records*, it's also the sunniest place on earth, with less than three inches of rain per year and 339 sunny days. Average July highs are 107°F (42°C), while the record maximum is 124°F (51°C).

Yuma is not a vacation destination in the usual sense, but its warm, dry winters, when temperatures seldom drop below the mid-70°s F, have made it a goal for hordes of "**snowbirds**" who keep an astonishing 72 local RV and trailer parks busy. During summer, on the other hand, Yuma is too much of an inferno for anyone to linger very long.

Neither is Yuma an attractive town; it's much too large to explore on foot, while its historic downtown is small and insignificant, and only Gateway Park offers appealing access to the riverside.

Brief history

Commanding the confluence of the Gila and Colorado rivers, the site of modern Yuma was recognized as being significant as early as 1540, when **Hernando de Alarcón**, in charge of the naval wing of Coronado's expedition (see p.465), sailed past its high bluffs. It later became the major river crossing for California-bound travellers, though Spanish attempts to establish a permanent mission settlement were destroyed by the **Yuma Revolt** of 1781, when **Quechan** Indians (known to the Spaniards as the Yuma) massacred over 150 settlers during Mass.

At the height of California's **Gold Rush**, sixty thousand passengers in a single year paid $2 each to be ferried across the Colorado at **Yuma Crossing**. This lucrative trade was at first controlled by the Quechan, but freebooting entrepreneurs wrested it out of their hands, with the US Army at Fort Yuma on hand to stifle Indian resistance. (A phenomenally bloodthirsty account of the struggle appears in Cormac McCarthy's *Blood Meridian*; see p.488.) Known initially as Colorado City, and later Arizona City, Yuma took on its current name in 1873, by which time it was experiencing a gold rush of its own.

Now that intricate hydraulic engineering has tamed the Colorado – one California-bound canal actually siphons beneath the river – it would take a major dam-burst to cause a repeat of the river's formerly devastating floods. In theory, Arizona could use its share of the Colorado's water to irrigate the land around Yuma and create a rival to California's nearby **Imperial Valley**, one of the world's richest farming areas; instead, although Yuma's economy is indeed largely founded on agriculture, the vast bulk of the water is channelled across the desert to Phoenix and Tucson at astronomical expense.

Yuma Territorial Prison State Historic Park

1 Prison Hill Rd • June–Sept Mon & Thurs–Sun 9am–5pm, Oct–May daily 9am–5pm • $4 • ☎ 928 783 4471, ⓦ azstateparks.com

The best place to get a feel for Yuma's tempestuous past is the **Yuma Territorial Prison State Historic Park**, set high above the Colorado a few blocks east of downtown. Built in 1876, the "Hell Hole of Arizona" was the state's principal prison for 33 years. Its restored wooden guardtower gives great views of the green-lined river meandering in from the north; this spot originally marked the precise confluence of the two rivers, but that has now shifted five miles further upstream. The "Ocean to Ocean" bridge here was built in 1915, not only superseding the ferry but also completing the southernmost transcontinental railroad route.

Displays inside the prison compound's adobe walls tell the stories of its three thousand prisoners. These ranged from teenage burglars to Harvard lawyers, and included nine Mormon polygamists, several Mexican revolutionaries, and a handful of women, such as the colourful Pearl Hart, who served five years for committing Arizona's last stagecoach robbery in 1899. You can also enter several cells.

Quartermaster Depot

201 N Fourth Ave • June–Sept Tues–Sun 9am–5pm, Oct–May daily 9am–4.30pm • $4 • ☎ 928 783 0071, ⓦ azstateparks.com

All supplies originally reached Yuma via a fifty-mile river journey from the ocean via Port Isabel on the Gulf of California. Now a state park, the former **Quartermaster Depot**, near the river bridge, still holds two warehouses where Colorado paddle-steamers used to moor. Various ancient wagons, carriages and even trains have been stabled indoors or set out to pasture on the lawns, but unless transportation history is your thing, it's not desperately exciting.

Camel Farm

15672 S Ave 1E; 4 miles south of town • Oct–May Tues–Sun 9am–5pm • $4 • ☎ 928 627 7511

Until you get within smelling distance, it's fiendishly difficult to find Yuma's most unusual attraction, the **Camel Farm**. Avenue 1E only starts, as a dirt road, south of the airport. Assuming you do manage to get here, you'll be able to inspect a large herd of slobbery, drooling dromedaries, bred here for circuses and zoos – there's no camel riding here – plus a cross-section of other wildlife such as ostriches, water buffalo and Watusi cattle.

Algodones and San Luis (Mexico)

Many visitors to Yuma take day-trips south into **Mexico**, whether to little **Algodones**, across from California a mere ten miles east, or to the much larger city of **San Luis**, 23 miles south. Both offer the usual array of souvenir stores and restaurants, together with cut-price drugstores.

ARRIVAL, INFORMATION AND TOURS
YUMA

By train Amtrak trains from LA to Tucson stop at 281 Gila St, at hideously unsocial hours.

By bus Greyhound buses run from 1245 Castle Dome Ave (☎928 783 4403) to Phoenix, Tucson, and San Diego.

Visitor centre Quartermaster Depot, 201 N Fourth Ave (June–Sept Tues–Sun 9am–5pm, Oct–May daily 9am–5pm;

☎928 783 0071 or ☎800 293 0071, ⓦvisityuma.com).

Yuma River Tours Colorado cruises from Fisher's Landing, 32 miles upstream from Yuma (☎928 783 4400, ⓦyumarivertours.com), including trips on jet boats (five-hour $75, seven-hour $95, both starting at 10am daily) and a replica sternwheeler (three-hour, $48; 11am daily).

ACCOMMODATION

As well as a plethora of RV parks, the "business loop" that parallels the interstate for six miles through the heart of Yuma holds dozens of **hotels** and **motels**, with plusher chains along its east–west segment on **32nd Street**, and old-fashioned budget options on the north–south **Fourth Avenue** closer to the river.

Best Western Coronado Motor Hotel 233 S Fourth Ave ☎928 783 4453 or ☎877 234 5567, ⓦbwcoronado .com. Veteran, nicely updated, central motel, within easy walking distance of downtown, and built in appealing Mission Revival style, complete with a little museum of pioneer life. **$80**

Yuma Cabaña 2151 S Fourth Ave ☎928 783 8311 or ☎800 874 0811, ⓦyumacabana.com. Traditional roadside motel, with a lovely old neon sign, a couple of miles up from the river. Clean, quiet, and very good value, with some larger kitchenette suites. **$46**

EATING

Garden Cafe 248 S Madison Ave ☎928 783 1491, ⓦgardencafeyuma.com. Tasteful café with indoor and outdoor seating, behind a small free museum of pioneer life, that's open for breakfast and lunch only and serves salads, sandwiches and burgers for $8–12. A separate espresso cafe in the stand stays open until 5pm. Tues–Fri 9am–2.30pm, Sat & Sun 8am–2.30pm; closed June–Sept.

Lutes Casino 221 S Main St ☎928 782 2192, ⓦlutescasino.com. This downtown landmark may look like a dull old barn from the outside, but inside it's bursting with quirky oddities and paraphernalia, and does a brisk

trade in surprisingly tasty $6.50 hamburgers, served with their secret-recipe hot sauce. There's no gambling, but plenty of pool and domino players. Mon–Thurs 10am–8pm, Fri & Sat 10am–9pm, Sun 10am–6pm.

River City Grill 600 W Third St ☎928 782 7988, ⓦrivercitygrillyuma.com. Bright "international" restaurant, serving an eclectic and relatively expensive menu that concentrates on Asian-influenced seafood options like Thai crab cakes or seared *ahi*, with dinner entrees priced at up to $27 (for mustard-crusted halibut). Outdoor dining available. Mon–Fri 11am–2pm & 5–10pm, Sat & Sun 5–10pm.

North from Yuma

North of Yuma, three **wildlife refuges** – the Kofa, Cibola, and Imperial – line the Colorado River. Established to protect mule deer and bighorn sheep as well as migratory Canadian geese, the parks aren't really designed for visitors, and are virtually inaccessible without a four-wheel-drive vehicle. Granted that you'd rather not get caught up in the tank battles staged by the army in its enormous, 1300-square-mile **Yuma Proving Ground**, there's nowhere to stop on the main north–south highway, **US-95**, until you reach **Quartzsite**.

Quartzsite

With the Colorado now twenty miles west, **QUARTZSITE** is even bleaker and drier than Yuma, eighty miles south. While it has a nominal population of two thousand, it, too, experiences a major winter influx of snowbirds. Literally hundreds of thousands of RV-owners descend on this desert outpost between early January and mid-February each year, ostensibly to bargain for precious, semi-precious, and merely pretty stones, but also to ride out the coldest months with like-minded fellow retirees.

Despite, or perhaps because of, its endless expanse of RV parks, Quartzsite has just four tiny and flyblown **motels**, with fewer than ten rooms each.

HI JOLLY'S FINAL CAMP

Topped by a brass camel, a pyramidal monument in Quartzsite's dusty central cemetery commemorates an odd episode in Southwestern history. Inscribed "The last camp of **Hi Jolly**, born somewhere in Syria about 1828, died Quartzsite December 16 1902," it marks the grave of Haiji Ali, who arrived at Indianola, Texas, in 1856, in charge of 33 **camels** that had been requisitioned by the then Secretary of War, Jefferson Davis.

Although the camels adapted well to the desert, army mule handlers and cowboys lacked the patience or inclination to care for them properly, and experiments to test their suitability as beasts of burden petered out during the Civil War. "Hi Jolly" became just another prospector; the abandoned camels bred in the wild into the twentieth century. To this day, it remains against the law to shoot a camel in Arizona.

Parker

Quartzsite's winter crowds spill over to **PARKER**, beside the river 35 miles north. The main activity here is boating on the placid waters downstream of the **Parker Dam**, a Depression-era project designed to divert Colorado water to the thirsty cities of southern California. Since 1985 the dam has also provided water for the **Central Arizona Project**, whose 336 miles of aqueducts stretch as far as Phoenix and Tucson. Almost twenty miles out of Parker, it's the deepest dam in the world, dug 235 feet into the riverbed. Jet-skiers glide up to its base for a closer look, and it can also be seen on free self-guided **tours** (daily 7.30am–4pm).

Colorado River Indian Reservation

Parker started life in 1905 as the principal settlement on the **Colorado River Indian Reservation**. Not far from the dam, clearly signposted from Hwy-95, visitors can examine prehistoric rock art, or **intaglios**, made by "carving" the darker top layer of rock away from the desert floor, to reveal lighter layers of sand beneath (daily 8am–sundown; $3). The figures are so huge (up to 160ft) that it's hard to tell what you're looking at, but gaze long enough and you can discern a four-legged animal, and a human and spiral design.

4

ACCOMMODATION AND EATING   PARKER

Bluewater Resort & Casino 11300 Resort Drive ☎ 928 669 7000 or ☎ 888 243 3360, ⓦ bluewaterfun.com. Overlooking the Colorado just under two miles northwest of Parker, this huge casino resort, owned by the Colorado River Indians, has two hundred very comfortable guest rooms, plus three restaurants, including a steakhouse, a buffet, and one with a riverside patio, four pools, and its own indoor water park. Sun–Thurs $85, Fri & Sat $135

Flagstaff and central Arizona

252 New Mexico to Flagstaff

262 Flagstaff

267 Around Flagstaff

271 South of Flagstaff

285 West of Flagstaff

PETRIFIED FOREST NATIONAL PARK

5

Flagstaff and central Arizona

With the state's northernmost hundred miles, from the rugged Navajo and Hopi reservations across to the Grand Canyon, impassable to east–west traffic, the I-40 corridor is the focus of a huge tract of north and central Arizona. Before the interstate was pushed through, the legendary Route 66 followed much the same path; before either road, there was the Santa Fe Railroad; and before the railroad arrived, not much more than a century ago, there were no significant Anglo settlements in the region at all.

Even today, only charming, characterful **Flagstaff** of the I-40 towns, set in the world's largest stand of sweet-smelling ponderosa **pine forest**, amounts to much more than an overnight pit stop. It also makes a great base for visits not only to the Grand Canyon (detailed in Chapter 6) but to the dramatic ancient sites of **Wupatki** and **Walnut Canyon**, and the superbly positioned New Age mecca of **Sedona**.

The highlight of the long drive between Flagstaff and New Mexico is **Petrified Forest National Park**, where giant fossilized remains lie strewn like matchsticks across the eerie desert badlands. To the west, the road to California is less inspiring; it makes more sense to detour south by way of the historic hilltop mining town of **Jerome** and pristine Victorian **Prescott** or, further west, to take a timewarp spin along Route 66 to the ghost town of **Oatman**.

New Mexico to Flagstaff

During its 150-mile run west from the New Mexico border to Flagstaff, **I-40** passes few towns of any size, let alone interest. The **landscape**, however, while barren in the extreme, is consistently beautiful, with double rainbows reaching across the desert plain and fiery dawns blazing along the horizon. The most accessible section of this **Painted Desert** lies within **Petrified Forest National Park**, which makes an intriguing half-day detour.

For many, this relentless desolation is exactly what they came to see; few join the locals in escaping south to the cool uplands of the **White Mountains**.

Petrified Forest National Park

Straddling I-40, 108 miles east of Flagstaff and 25 miles east of Holbrook • $10 per vehicle, or $5 for motorcyclists, cyclists and pedestrians • ☎ 928 524 6228, ⊕ nps.gov/pefo

PETRIFIED FOREST NATIONAL PARK serves a dual purpose. While its chief role is to protect a prehistoric "forest" of fossilized trees, south of I-40, it also stretches north of the interstate to include picturesque stretches of the **Painted Desert**, an ill-defined area of multicoloured badlands that covers much of northeast Arizona. Its blue-tinged clays and crumbling sands support little vegetation or life, and continue to erode at a fearsome rate.

Stone trees in the sand p.255
Getting to the Grand Canyon from Flagstaff p.264
The end of the New Age? p.272
Parking in Sedona p.274
Verde Canyon Railroad p.277
London Bridge is falling down p.290

WUPATKI NATIONAL MONUMENT

Highlights

❶ Petrified Forest National Park As noteworthy for the bizarre coloured sands of the Painted Desert as for its namesake stony trees, this isolated park makes a great break on the long haul across northeast Arizona. **See p.252**

❷ La Posada Glorious old restored hotel, straight from the heyday of Route 66, that's a great reason to spend a night in Winslow. See p.261

❸ Downtown Flagstaff Flanking both sides of Route 66 and the Santa Fe Railroad, Flagstaff's bustling downtown streets abound with the flavour of the West. **See p.262**

❹ The Museum of Northern Arizona Superb museum, just outside Flagstaff, that explains the history and geography of the Colorado Plateau in fascinating detail. **See p.262**

❺ Wupatki National Monument Extraordinary site northeast of Flagstaff, where the ancient Sinagua people raised multi-storey pueblos out of the desert floor. **See p.269**

❻ Jerome Former mining town, now turned artists' colony, perched high on a hillside with magnificent views. **See p.277**

❼ Prescott Once the state capital, Prescott remains one of its most charming little towns. **See p.281**

HIGHLIGHTS ARE MARKED ON THE MAP ON P.254

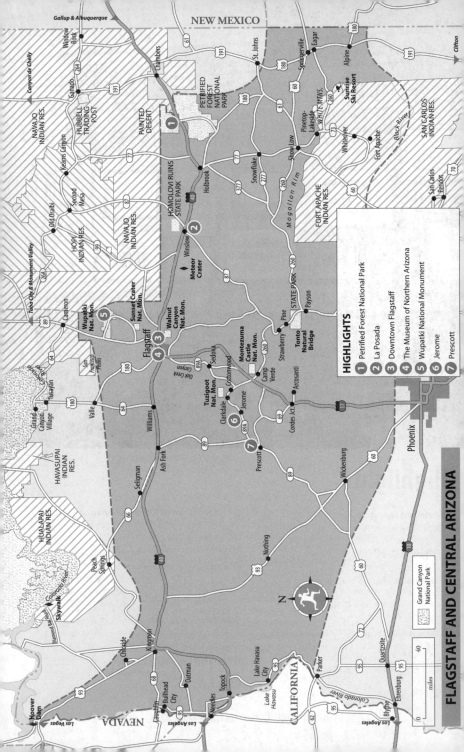

FLAGSTAFF AND CENTRAL ARIZONA

HIGHLIGHTS

1. Petrified Forest National Park
2. La Posada
3. Downtown Flagstaff
4. The Museum of Northern Arizona
5. Wupatki National Monument
6. Jerome
7. Prescott

Grand Canyon National Park

N

miles
0   40

5

STONE TREES IN THE SAND

Fossilized wood is not in fact all that rare; it's the sheer abundance of the stuff in **Petrified Forest National Park** that's extraordinary. Each year, ongoing erosion exposes more and more lithified logs to view, lying in haphazard profusion on the barren slopes. The wood-bearing layer, also rich in dinosaur bones and other fossils, extends three hundred feet beneath the ground.

The **gigantic trees** of Petrified Forest, drawn from long-extinct species such as *Auracarioxylon*, *Woodworthia* and *Schilderia*, **date back 225 million years**. When alive, they resembled ponderosa pines. This is not, however, the site of an actual forest. Its mighty trunks are horizontal, not vertical; they didn't grow here, they accumulated as a vast log jam in an ancient river. Settling onto the riverbed, they were buried by layers of silt and ash, thereby slowing decay. Bit by bit, silica seeped in and replaced the original wood cells, then crystallized into quartz.

Cross-sections of petrified wood, cut with diamond saws and then polished, look stunning; prize specimens are displayed in the park's two visitor centres, while lesser examples, gathered outside the park, are sold in commercial outlets nearby.

Petrified Forest became a national park in 1962, when large-scale **pilfering** threatened to deplete its stocks altogether. A similar park in the Dakotas had to close in the 1930s after visitors carried off all its fossil treasures, and even today twelve tons of rock disappears from the Petrified Forest each year. In theory, rangers can search your vehicle as you leave and impose heavy fines on anyone caught with a pocketful of petrified wood-chips. They rarely bother, however, preferring the subtler approach of displaying letters in the visitor centres from repentant rock thieves who have been punished by the loss of hair, health, pets or progeny.

Petrified Forest effectively divides into three sections, with an area rich in ancient Indian remains separating the desert in the north from the forest in the south. To see its full range, you have to complete the entire 27-mile **Scenic Drive**, but there's no need to stop at every overlook along the way.

Although the eerie desertscape is never less than stunning, the trees themselves, as seen on the ground from trails along the scenic drive, are not always all that exciting. Segmented, crumbling, and very dark, they can just seem like a bunch of logs lying in the sand, even if they are stone logs. The best viewing comes in late afternoon, when the setting sun brings out rich red and orange hues.

Exploring the park

Although the main road through Petrified Forest National Park crosses I-40, there's no access to or from the interstate at that point. Instead, the park has two separate entrances, at the north and south ends of its scenic drive. Which you use will depend on how much time you can spare, and which way you're heading.

If you're coming from New Mexico – or if you're heading east and only have time for a quick look – leave the interstate at exit 311, and within a mile you'll come to the **Painted Desert Visitor Center**. Anyone who's driving east and wants to see the entire park, however, would do better to leave I-40 at Holbrook and take US-180 for twenty miles southeast to the southern entrance, near the **Rainbow Forest Museum**.

Painted Desert Visitor Center

1 mile north of I-40 exit 311 • Daily: early May to late Sept 8am–6pm; late Sept to early May 8am–5pm

As well as displays on the geology of the park and forest, the **Painted Desert Visitor Center** holds most of the park's few facilities, including a *Fred Harvey* **restaurant** that serves overpriced café meals all day, a large gift store, and a gas station.

5

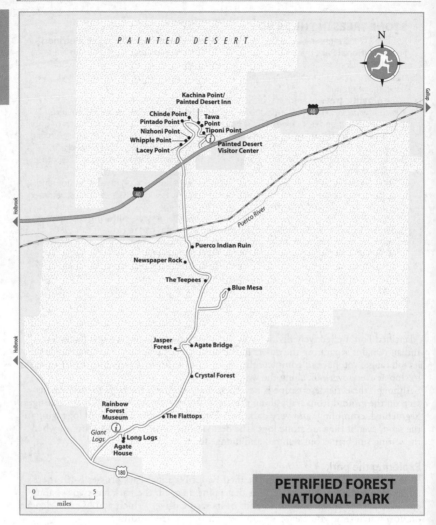

PETRIFIED FOREST
NATIONAL PARK

The Painted Desert

Painted Desert Inn Daily 9am–5pm • Free

Assuming you enter the park in the north, continue past the Painted Desert
Visitor Center and you'll soon find yourself skirting the edge of a giant mesa,
which drops away northwards to reveal long-range views across the **Painted Desert**
itself. At different times of day, the undulating expanse of clay-topped mounds
takes on different colours, with an emphasis on blueish shades of grey and reddish
shades of brown.

This astonishing vista is best admired through the panoramic windows of the **Painted
Desert Inn**, a mile or two along, a long-defunct adobe hotel that has been restored as a
museum. Mexican-style murals inside, painted by Hopi artist Fred Kabotie in 1948,
depict Hopi pilgrimages and dances, while a stone slab bears a thirteenth-century
petroglyph depiction of a fierce-clawed mountain lion.

From the promontory behind the inn, **Kachina Point**, backcountry **trails** drop down into the Painted Desert Wilderness. Only by walking these can you truly appreciate the scale of the place, but even the shortest hike involves a hot climb back up again.

The scenic drive continues past several similar overlooks before crossing first the interstate, and then, in quick succession, the Santa Fe Railroad and the Puerco River.

Puerco Indian Ruin

At the **Puerco Indian Ruin**, immediately south of the broad but usually dry Puerco river, a short trail leads around a small, partially excavated pueblo, abandoned in 1300 AD by its Ancestral Puebloan inhabitants. Patches of black desert varnish on nearby rocks show well-preserved petroglyphs, including one you'd swear depicted a stork bringing a baby. A little further along, a bunch of bigger petroglyph-covered boulders – known collectively, like many such sites, as **Newspaper Rock** – lie at the foot of a rocky incline. Closer access is forbidden, but free binoculars allow you to peer at the indistinct scribbles. In time, some resolve themselves into male and female figures.

The Petrified Forest

The bizarre pyramidal hillocks of the **Teepees**, south of Newspaper Rock, mark the northern limit of the **Petrified Forest**. At roadside halts south from here, rough concrete walkways have been laid over the terrain – and often over the tree trunks too – so visitors can ramble through the larger concentrations of logs. At **Blue Mesa**, certain tree-trunks are raised on muddy "pedestals" above the surrounding desert; at **Agate Bridge**, one even spans a little gully.

The park's busiest trail, the **Long Logs Walk** near the southern entrance, is so popular that its parking lot is closed in the mornings, and hikers have to walk a few hundred extra yards up from the Rainbow Forest Museum. Here at the edge of the desert, a little grass manages to survive, making the half-mile main trail especially surreal. The large, shattered logs are simply strewn across the grasslands, with not another stone or rock in sight. A side trail leads in another half-mile to a knoll holding the remains of a seven-hundred-year-old Indian pueblo constructed entirely from petrified wood. **Agate House** might sound amazing, but, thanks perhaps to its clumsy restoration, it's oddly banal.

When the Long Logs Walk looks busy, the **Crystal Forest** trail, five miles north, makes a good alternative.

Rainbow Forest Museum

Off US-180, 20 miles southeast of Holbrook • Daily: early May to late Sept 8am–6pm; late Sept to early May 8am–5pm

The **Rainbow Forest Museum**, at the park's southern entrance, is the smaller of its two visitor centres. Along with exhibits on local history and the prehistoric past, it sells simple snacks. The short Giant Logs Trail, which starts just behind the museum, leads to some especially fine ancient specimens. During peak periods, when parking is hard to find, it makes sense to leave your car here while you hike the nearby Long Logs Walk as well.

ACCOMMODATION AND EATING · PETRIFIED FOREST NATIONAL PARK

You can pick up something to **eat** at either entrance, but there are no **lodges** or **campgrounds** in the park. The only way to spend a night is to camp in the backcountry, with a free permit from the visitor centre.

Holbrook

From 1886 to 1900, **HOLBROOK**, halfway between Gallup and Flagstaff, was the rowdy headquarters of the "Hashknife" cattle outfit, the third largest in the country. Not much seems to have happened since, but traffic on Route 66 and I-40 has kept Holbrook ticking.

5

Unless you're ready to stop for the night, there's no great reason to stray off the interstate, though a romantic patch of Route 66 frontage survives along **Navajo Boulevard**, the main road through the centre of town.

Old West Museum

100 E Arizona St • Daily 8am–5pm • Free • ☎ 928 524 6558

Housed in Holbrook's former courthouse is the town's only diversion to speak of, the **Old West Museum**. The appealing small-town melange holds Ancestral Puebloan pots, fading photographs, and dioramas of Wild West shootouts.

ACCOMMODATION AND EATING · HOLBROOK

Holiday Inn Express 1308 E Navajo Blvd ☎ 928 524 1466, ⓦ hiexpress.com. Decent, unremarkable but clean and well-equipped chain motel, one of a clutch located up the hill north of the interstate at exit 286. **$114**

Mesa Italiana 2318 N Navajo Blvd ☎ 928 524 6696. The best bet for a good meal in town, this above-average roadside Italian joint offers pizzas and pasta mains like cheese ravioli or fettucini Alfredo for around $12, and veal or shrimp entrees for $17. Mon–Fri 11am–2pm & 4–9pm, Sat & Sun 4–9pm.

★ **Wigwam Motel** 811 W Hopi Drive ☎ 928 524 3048, ⓦ galerie-kokopelli.com/wigwam. By far the most unusual and exciting place to stay in Holbrook. Each room in this Route 66 relic – one of three such *Wigwams* left in the country, the others being in Kentucky and California – is a miniature teepee of white concrete, filled with 1950s' furnishings and memorabilia. It's all enjoyably retro, and fortunately they've brought it up to date by buying new mattresses. **$58**

The Mogollon Rim

Although the spellbinding northern Arizona desert appears to stretch away forever to either side of I-40, the southern limit of the Colorado Plateau is in fact just beneath the horizon to the south – the 2000ft escarpment of the **Mogollon Rim**, curving two hundred miles from west to east and extending well into New Mexico. Heading south from I-40 feels like you're heading into the back of beyond, but you're soon within a hundred miles of the megalopolis of **Phoenix**.

For sweltering city-dwellers, the highland forests – especially in the **White Mountains**, near **Show Low** – make ideal destinations for weekend breaks. Visitors from beyond the Southwest rarely stray this way, and unless you're looking to hunt, fish, or, in winter, ski, the only point in doing so is to reach **southern Arizona** without passing through Phoenix. While no Mogollon Rim town amounts to more than the sum of its dreary parts, all do at least offer abundant motels. Both roads south, **US-60** and **US-191**, are exhilarating drives, passing through untamed mountainous terrain that evokes the early days of the Wild West.

Springerville and Eagar

The easternmost White Mountain towns, **SPRINGERVILLE** and neighbouring **EAGAR**, stand near the edge of the plains in **Round Valley**, a few miles west of New Mexico. They're only significant as base camps for trips into the mountains, which you'll encounter a couple of miles south on US-191, or ten miles west on Hwy-260, across the innocuous Little Colorado River.

Casa Malpais

2 miles north of Springerville; tours from 418 E Main St • March–Nov Tues–Sat 9am, 11am & 2pm • $10, under-19s $5 • ☎ 928 333 5375, ⓦ casamalpais.org

Known as **Casa Malpais**, a pueblo that was built by the Mogollon people to exploit natural caves is located a couple of miles north of Springerville. It can only be visited on guided tours, which take around ninety minutes, include some potentially demanding hiking, and lead you past the outline of a Great Kiva as well as individual homes. Tours leave from the local visitor centre, 418 E Main St (Mon–Sat 8am–4pm), which also holds a small **museum** about the site that stays open year-round.

Coronado Trail Scenic Road

South of Springerville, the tortuous high-mountain US-191, designated the **Coronado Trail Scenic Road**, doesn't so much follow the route taken by Francisco de Coronado in 1540 – see p.96 – as vaguely parallel it. Driving all the way to **Clifton**, 120 miles south, can take up to four hours, and it leads through stretches that were devastated by Arizona's largest-ever wildfire, the **Wallow Fire** of 2011, but much of it remains spectacular.

At the only village to interrupt the pine woods – **Alpine**, 25 miles south of Springerville – US-180 branches off west into New Mexico. Just a tiny T-junction in a meadow, Alpine is said to be the chilliest spot in Arizona. Beyond Alpine, snow frequently closes US-191 between mid-December and mid-March. When it's open, roadside trailheads, used mainly by hunters, make it possible to hike into the **Apache-Sitgreaves National Forest**, which also holds several rudimentary campgrounds.

Show Low

SHOW LOW, fifty miles south of Holbrook on Hwy-77 and 43 miles west of Springerville on US-60, is the largest town on the Mogollon Rim. It stands on the site of a 100,000-acre ranch, whose cofounders played cards in 1876 to decide who should get to keep it. With the game all square, one invited the other to "show low and take the ranch"; his rival drew the deuce of clubs and duly took possession. He went on to sell the ranch to the Mormon church, which built a small settlement before selling it on again.

These days, Show Low amounts to little more than a strip of motels and diners ranged along US-60, or **Deuce of Clubs Avenue**. The nearby slopes of Sunrise Ski Park ensure it remains busy year round.

Fort Apache Indian Reservation

One reason why the mountains of eastern Arizona are not better known is that a large proportion of the central massif still belongs to the **Apache**. The Apache are not a single "tribe", however, so there are two separate but contiguous reservations here. The **FORT APACHE INDIAN RESERVATION**, which starts just a mile or two out of Pinetop and Show Low, stretches south to the Salt and Black rivers; beyond it the **San Carlos Indian Reservation** extends for another hundred miles past Globe.

The Fort Apache Reservation is headquartered in the town of **WHITERIVER**, cupped in a mile-high valley twenty miles south of Pinetop. **US-60**, the only north–south road across the reservation, is also the most direct route between northeast Arizona and Tucson. All of its 87-mile run from Show Low to **Globe** (see p.217) is awe-inspiring, but the most dramatic moment comes fifty miles along, where it takes five miles of switchbacks to get to the bottom of gaping **Salt River Canyon**.

Fort Apache

Hwy-73, 5 miles southeast of Whiteriver • Summer Mon–Sat 8am–5pm, winter Mon–Fri 8am–5pm • $5 • ☎ 928 338 4625, ⓦ mat.nsn.us

FORT APACHE itself, at the confluence of the north and east forks of the White River, is a US Army outpost that was founded in 1870 to support the campaigns of General Crook. Even though he was allied with the White Mountain Apache, Crook wanted to keep an eye on them. Several buildings still survive, and hold displays on the period.

Payson

Until 1959, **PAYSON**, ninety miles west of Show Low on Hwy-260, was a sleepy cowboy town that had started out in a gold-rush frenzy and then relaxed into a yearly round of ranching punctuated by the odd rodeo. Then the paving of Hwy-87 placed Payson within two hours' drive of Phoenix, eighty miles southwest. It's now a mountain retreat whose population doubles or triples at weekends, as urban refugees flock to their second homes or at least rent cabins in the forest.

5

On first glance, Payson, if not exactly appealing, is at least mildly impressive in its quiet, bucolic prosperity. Somehow, however, as you drive down its long, broad streets, passing representatives of every national fast-food and lodging chain, you never seem to find a compelling reason to stop.

Tonto Natural Bridge State Park

Hwy-87, 15 miles north of Payson • Mon & Thurs–Sun: May–Aug 8am–7pm; April, Sept & Oct 8am–6pm; Nov–March 9am–5pm • $5 • ☎ 928 476 4202, ⊕ azstateparks.com

The world's widest and longest (but not quite highest) **travertine bridge**, formed from minerals deposited by constantly flowing springs, is preserved in **TONTO NATURAL BRIDGE STATE PARK**. In 1877, a Scottish gold prospector, David Gowan, supposedly hid in a cave inside the bridge as he fled the Apache who used the surrounding meadows as a summer camp. He stayed and built a cabin nearby. When a description of the natural wonder appeared in an English newspaper in 1896, David Goodfellow spotted the name of his long-lost uncle and wrote to Gowan, who offered him the site. Goodfellow's ten-room lodge no longer accepts guests but still serves as the park's giftshop and visitor centre (same hours).

The bridge itself, reached by a network of short trails, doesn't really live up to the build-up. Spanning a gully that's roughly 150ft wide, it's more of a tunnel, or a dank cave with openings at both ends. With effort, you can scramble down to a boardwalk at the base, but you can't go through it.

INFORMATION

SPRINGERVILLE
Visitor centre 418 E Main St (Mon–Sat 8am–4pm; ☎ 928 333 2123, ⊕ springerville-eagarchamber.com).

FORT APACHE INDIAN RESERVATION
Visitor centre Hwy-260, milepost 357, Fort Apache (summer Mon–Sat 8am–5pm, winter Mon–Fri

THE MOGOLLON RIM

8am–5pm; ☎ 928 369 2036, ⊕ wmat.us).

PAYSON
Visitor centre 100 W Main St (Mon–Fri 9am–5pm, Sat & Sun 10am–2pm; ☎ 928 474 4515 or ☎ 800 672 9766, ⊕ rimcountrychamber.com).

ACCOMMODATION AND EATING

SPRINGERVILLE
Reed's Lodge 514 E Main St ☎ 928 333 4323 or ☎ 800 814 6451, ⊕ k5reeds.com. Plain, no-frills old-fashioned motel, part of a complex that also includes a bookshop and gallery. The cheapest, "Bunkhouse" rooms are rundown, but a more comfortable option costs little more. **$49.50**
Safire 411 E Main St ☎ 928 333 5883. Something of a community centre, this friendly roadside diner serves meats and beers to match any hunter's appetite, with dinner plus salad bar costing under $15. Friday night is fish-fry night. Daily noon–10pm.
X Diamond Ranch CR4036, 8 miles southwest of Springerville ☎ 928 333 2286, ⊕ xdiamondranch.com. Seven individual cabins, each with kitchen and sleeping up to 8, on a working ranch beside the Little Colorado River that also holds horse riding, a Wild West museum and an ancient Indian ruin. **$110**

SHOW LOW
KC Motel 60 W Deuce of Clubs Ave ☎ 928 537 4433 or ☎ 800 531 7152, ⊕ kcmotelinshowlow.com.

Clean, efficient motel offering good-value central accommodation, with free, albeit simple, breakfasts. **$57**

PAYSON
Best Western Payson Inn 801 N Beeline Hwy ☎ 928 474 3241, ⊕ bestwesternarizona.com. Everything a small-town motel should be: clean, comfortable and very dependable, with a nice rural feel. **$90**
Gerardo's Firewood Cafe 512 N Beeline Hwy ☎ 928 464 6500, ⊕ gerardosbistro.com. Far and away the best restaurant in Payson, this friendly pizzeria emphasizes local organic ingredients, and draws weekenders from Phoenix to dine Italian-style on sandwiches and simple pasta specials for $8–10 at lunchtime – there's an $8 all-you-can-eat pizza buffet on Wednesdays – and dinner entrees like the $24 *cioppino* seafood stew plus a full menu of 12-inch pizzas for $11–16 all day. Tues 3–8.30pm, Wed & Thurs 11am–8.30pm, Fri & Sat 11am–9pm, Sun 3–8pm.

Winslow

On I-40, 56 miles east of Flagstaff, **WINSLOW** is yet another Route 66 town kept alive by transcontinental truckers. It's also the closest the interstate comes to the Hopi mesas (see p.66), which jut from the desert across sixty miles of butte-studded wilderness to the north.

Winslow was founded as a railroad stop in 1882, not far from the recently established Mormon community of **Brigham City**, now lying derelict a mile northeast. If you only know of it thanks to the line about "standin' on the corner in Winslow, Arizona," in the Eagles' *Take It Easy*, you'll be glad there's an official **Standin' on the Corner Park** at Kinsley Avenue and Second, where you can have your photo taken with a bronze statue of a guitar-toting hitchhiker. Local history is recalled in the diverting **Old Trails Museum** at 212 Kinsley Ave (Tues–Sat: April–Nov 10am–4pm, Dec–March 11am–3pm; free; ⓦoldtrailsmuseum.org).

Homolovi Ruins State Park

Hwy-87, 3 miles northeast of Winslow • Daily 8am–5pm • $7 per vehicle • ☎ 928 289 4106, ⓦ azstateparks.com

Homolovi Ruins State Park holds four pueblo villages and hundreds of lesser sites that were occupied by the Hisatsinom people – the ancestors of today's **Hopi** – until perhaps the fourteenth century. Most remain unexcavated, though archeologists are usually hard at work in June and July, when visitors are welcome to join them.

ARRIVAL AND INFORMATION   WINSLOW

By train Winslow's Amtrak station welcomes one daily train west to Flagstaff and one east to Albuquerque.

Visitor centre 523 W Second St (Mon–Fri 8am–5pm; ☎ 928 289 2434, ⓦ winslowarizona.org).

ACCOMMODATION AND EATING

★ **La Posada** 303 E Second St ☎ 928 289 4366, ⓦ laposada.org. Winslow's grandest accommodation option is so totally magnificent – a worthy candidate for the best in the world, in fact – that it's worth going a very long way out of your way to spend a night here. It was originally designed during the late 1920s by Mary Jane Colter of Grand Canyon fame (see p.299), though she invented an entire fictional history of its former life as a Spanish hacienda. The last and greatest of the railroad hotels built for the Fred Harvey company, it closed in 1959 when the railroads had been superseded by private cars. In 1999, however, it was restored as a true labour of love by a small group of enthusiasts who proclaim "we are not hoteliers – for us this is about art." Dazzlingly colourful modernist canvases by one of them, Tina Mion, bedeck the public spaces, but the whole place is so enormous that there's also plenty of the earthy Southwestern style you might expect. The surrounding gardens are a delight too, while doors from the lobby lead straight to the old railroad platform (be warned you'll hear the trains at night). Best of all are the guest rooms, where the fixtures and fittings, and especially the tiling, feel like a real throwback to the heyday of transcontinental travel. All are named for illustrious former visitors ranging from Clark Gable to Roddy McDowell, and have en-suite baths or even whirlpool tubs, but they're without phones. The excellent *Turquoise Room* restaurant is reviewed separately, below. $119

★ **Turquoise Room** La Posada, 303 E Second St ☎ 928 289 2888, ⓦ theturquoiseroom.net. Like the hotel itself, *La Posada*'s showcase restaurant is irresistible in terms both of its decor and contemporary Southwestern cuisine. Dinner entrees range from chile-tinged south-of-the-border specialities like grilled chicken breast with tomatillo sauce ($19) to Colorado elk medallions with huckleberries ($34), but it's all in a different league from anywhere else along a hundred-mile stretch of highway. Daily 7am–9pm.

Meteor Crater

6 miles south of I-40 exit 233, 18 miles west of Winslow and 38 miles east of Flagstaff • Daily: late May to early Sept 7am–7pm; early Sept to late May 8am–5pm • $16, under-18s $8 • ☎ 800 289 5898, ⓦ meteorcrater.com

Around 22,000 years ago, a meteorite slammed into northern Arizona, blasting a huge hole, nearly a mile across and over five hundred feet deep, into the scrubby plateau. The site of that impact, **METEOR CRATER** now lies six miles south of the interstate, almost forty miles east of Flagstaff.

5

Though the staff dress up in mock Park Service uniforms, Meteor Crater is privately owned and frankly offers poor value for money. A modern gallery beside the parking lot holds the unimaginative **Astronauts Hall of Fame**, which commemorates the fact that the first men on the moon were trained on the cavity's otherworldly surface (some sceptics claim that they faked their entire mission here). Walkways climb from there to the lip of the abyss, where you'll probably find that there's a limit to how long you can spend staring at a featureless hole in the ground. Hour-long guided walking tours, included in the price, set off hourly from 9.15am to 2.15pm, but you can't hike into the actual crater.

Flagstaff

Northern Arizona's liveliest and most attractive town, **FLAGSTAFF**, occupies a superbly dramatic location beneath the San Francisco Peaks, halfway between New Mexico and California. Straddling the I-40 and I-17 interstates, and a major waystation for tourists en route to the Grand Canyon eighty miles northwest, it's also a worthwhile destination in its own right.

Flagstaff's little-changed **downtown**, where barely a building rises more than three stories, oozes Wild West charm. Its main thoroughfare, Santa Fe Avenue, used to be **Route 66**, and before that the pioneer trail west. During the 1960s, downtown Flagstaff had become seriously rundown, and was about to be demolished to construct car parks for Route 66 visitors; the flaw in the plan was that it would have left no Route 66 to visit. Instead ongoing restoration efforts have brought the place back to life.

While the central few blocks hold no specific tourist attractions, old-style diners and saloons jostle for space with modern restaurants, brewpubs and espresso cafes, and souvenir stores selling Route 66 and Native American crafts stand alongside outfitters aimed at outdoor adventurers. Simply strolling around is gloriously evocative of the past. Cowboys and Indians share the sidewalks with liberal-minded students from Northern Arizona University, and with the tracks of the Santa Fe Railroad still dividing downtown in two, life in Flagstaff remains punctuated by the mournful wail of passing trains.

With a population of a little over fifty thousand, Flagstaff makes an ideal base for travellers. As well as the abundant amenities within easy walking distance of downtown, outlets of the national food and lodging chains line the interstates slightly further afield. There are also a couple of good museums nearby, together with wonderful scenery and ancient sites in the close vicinity. Just one word of warning: at almost seven thousand feet above sea level, the nights may well be colder than you're expecting. It can even snow in July.

Brief history

Flagstaff's first settlers arrived in 1876, lured from Boston by reports of mineral wealth and fertile land. They soon moved on, disappointed, toward Prescott, having stayed long enough to celebrate the centenary of US independence by flying the Stars and Stripes from a towering pine tree. As this flagpole became a familiar landmark on the route west, the town became known as Flagstaff. Right from the start, it was a cosmopolitan place, with a strong black and Hispanic population working in the (originally Mormon-owned) lumber mills and the cattle industry, and Navajo and Hopi heading in from the nearby reservations to trade.

Museum of Northern Arizona

3101 N Fort Valley Rd, 3 miles northwest of downtown Flagstaff on US-180 • Daily 9am–5pm • $10, ages 10–17 $6 • ☏ 928 774 5213, ⓦ musnaz.org

Flagstaff's exceptional **Museum of Northern Arizona** makes an essential first stop for any visitor to the Colorado Plateau. Although it covers local geology, geography, flora and

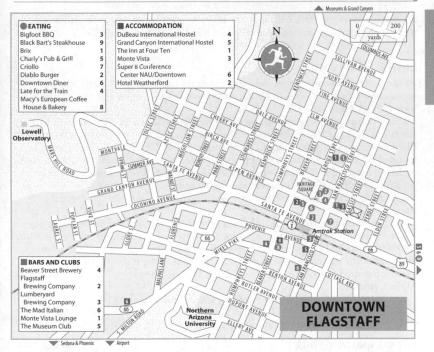

▲ Museums & Grand Canyon

● EATING

Bigfoot BBQ	3
Black Bart's Steakhouse	9
Brix	1
Charly's Pub & Grill	5
Criollo	7
Diablo Burger	2
Downtown Diner	6
Late for the Train	4
Macy's European Coffee House & Bakery	8

■ ACCOMMODATION

DuBeau International Hostel	4
Grand Canyon International Hostel	5
The Inn at Four Ten	1
Monte Vista	3
Super 8 Conference Center NAU/Downtown	6
Hotel Weatherford	2

■ BARS AND CLUBS

Beaver Street Brewery Flagstaff	4
Brewing Company	2
Lumberyard Brewing Company	3
The Mad Italian	6
Monte Vista Lounge	1
The Museum Club	5

DOWNTOWN FLAGSTAFF

fauna – and can help you come to grips with the various theories as to the origins of the Grand Canyon – its main emphasis is on documenting **Native American** life. It starts with an excellent run-through of the Ancestral Puebloan past, featuring stone knife blades still set in their wooden handles, an intact ancient loom and a collection of pottery miniatures whose purpose remains unknown. Attention then turns to contemporary Navajo, Havasupai, Zuni and Hopi cultures, with rooms devoted to pots, rugs, *kachina* dolls, and silver and turquoise jewellery. There are also temporary shows of local (not always Native American) arts and crafts, a well-stocked bookstore and a **nature trail** that runs through the small piñon-fringed canyon outside.

Ever since it was established, in 1928, the museum has actively encouraged traditional and even new skills among Native American craftworkers. The exquisite inlaid silver jewellery now made by the Hopi, for example, resulted from a museum-backed programme to find work for Hopi servicemen returning from World War II. During its annual Native American Marketplaces, every item is for sale; the **Hopi** show takes place on the weekend closest to July 4, the **Zuni** one in late May, and the **Navajo** one at the start of August. Late October sees the **Celebraciones de la Gente**, honouring local Hispanic traditions.

For details of **Museum of Northern Arizona Ventures**, an extensive programme of tours and expeditions, which include multi-day Grand Canyon trips, check on ⊛ mnaventures.org.

Pioneer Museum

2340 N Fort Valley Rd, 2 miles northwest of downtown Flagstaff on US-180 • Mon–Sat 9am–5pm • $5, under-15s free • ☎ 928 774 6272, ⊛ arizonahistoricalsociety.org

Run by the Arizona Historical Society, and housed in what was once the county hospital, the **Pioneer Museum** holds a random but reasonably entertaining assortment

5

of objects and images from old Flagstaff. The downstairs rooms focus on childhood, while an impressive steam train stands guard beside the highway outside.

Lowell Observatory

1400 West Mars Hill Rd, 1 mile west of downtown • March–May & Sept–Oct Mon, Wed, Fri & Sat 9am–9.30pm, Tues, Thurs & Sun 9am–5pm; June–Aug daily 9am–10pm; Nov–Feb Mon, Wed, Fri & Sat noon–9.30pm, Tues, Thurs & Sun noon–5pm • $12, under-18s $5 • ☎ 928 774 3358, ⓦ lowell.edu

Flagstaff's **Lowell Observatory**, in the pine forest atop Mars Hill west of downtown, is famous as the place where the existence of the dwarf planet Pluto was first confirmed. Many of the necessary calculations were performed by Dr Percival Lowell, who founded the observatory in 1894 and also deluded himself that he'd discovered canals on Mars. Lowell died in 1916 – he's buried in a small domed mausoleum of blue glass on the hilltop – and Pluto was eventually spotted in 1930 by Clyde Tombaugh. Regarded for many years thereafter as the ninth planet, it was finally demoted in status in 2006.

From the **visitor centre**, where only very technically minded visitors are likely to get much joy from playing with computers or watching explanatory videos, the **Pluto Walk** footpath climbs up to the tiny original observatory. Signs tick off the relative positions of the planets; if it kept going on the same scale, it would have to extend over six hundred miles, beyond Boise, Idaho, to show the position of the nearest star, Alpha Centauri.

Astronomy remains a passion in Flagstaff, and the town has won awards for minimizing night-time light pollution. The observatory stays open four evenings a week for after-dark **stargazing sessions**.

ARRIVAL AND DEPARTURE   FLAGSTAFF

By train Though the Santa Fe Railroad is still busy with freight, Amtrak's daily Southwest Chief between Chicago and Los Angeles is now the only passenger train that stops at Flagstaff's venerable wooden stationhouse, in the heart of town (ⓦ amtrak.com). In summer, the eastbound service arrives from Los Angeles at 4.36am and the westbound arrives from Albuquerque at 8.51pm; winter times are one hour later.

By bus Greyhound, 880 E Butler Ave (☎ 928 774 4573, ⓦ greyhound.com), runs five daily buses to Phoenix and also heads east toward Albuquerque and west to Las Vegas, LA, San Diego, and San Francisco.

By plane Tiny Pulliam Airport, off I-17 five miles south of downtown Flagstaff, at 6200 S Pulliam Drive, is connected several times daily with Phoenix on US Airways (ⓦ usairways.com).

INFORMATION AND GETTING AROUND

Visitor centre Flagstaff's helpful visitor centre occupies half of the Amtrak stationhouse at 1 E Route 66 (Mon–Sat 8am–5pm, Sun 9am–4pm; ☎ 928 774 9541 or ☎ 800 379 0065, ⓦ flagstaffarizona.org). Even when it's not staffed, the

GETTING TO THE GRAND CANYON FROM FLAGSTAFF

Arizona Shuttle (☎ 928 226 8060 or ☎ 800 888 2749, ⓦ arizonashuttle.com) runs daily buses from Flagstaff's Amtrak station, via Williams, to *Maswik Lodge* in Grand Canyon Village (one-way $29). Year-round, a bus leaves Flagstaff at 7.45am and reaches the *Maswik* at 9.30am, and another leaves Flagstaff at 3.45pm and gets to the *Maswik* at 5.45pm. Between March and October, a third bus leaves Flagstaff at 12.45pm and arrives at the *Maswik* at 2.45pm. Arizona Shuttle also offers twelve daily buses between Flagstaff and Phoenix ($45), and two to Sedona ($25).

Flagstaff companies offering day-trip tours to the Grand Canyon, at typical rates of just over $100 per day, include All-Star (☎ 928 814 8887 or ☎ 800 940 0445, ⓦ allstargrandcanyontours .com), Angel's Gate Tours (☎ 928 814 2277 or ☎ 800 957 4457, ⓦ seegrandcanyon.com), and Seven Wonders (☎ 928 221 6164 or ☎ 888 298 7477, ⓦ sevenwondersscenictours.com).

Two local **hostels**, the *DuBeau* and the *Grand Canyon*, also offer inexpensive Grand Canyon excursions.

building remains open for rail passengers, so visitors can still pick up brochures and discount coupons for local motels. You'll also find a courtesy phone in the Amtrak lobby for making hotel and hostel reservations (daily 8am–5pm).

Car rental The least expensive car rental agency is Budget, 175 W Aspen Ave (☎ 928 213 0156); Avis, Hertz, Enterprise, and National also have outlets.

Bike rental Absolute Bikes, 202 E Route 66 (open daily; ☎ 928 779 5969, ⓦ absolutebikes.net), rents out mountain bikes.

Outfitters Among the best of several local outfitters offering equipment for outdoor activities and backpacking expeditions is Aspen Sports, 15 N San Francisco St (☎ 928 779 1935, ⓦ aspensportsflagstaff.com).

ACCOMMODATION

As Flagstaff is considerably more than just another interstate pit stop, its dozens of **motels** and **B&Bs** charge higher rates than its I-40 neighbours. They're still not bad value, however, while **budget** travellers can choose between two hostels. Most chain motels are clustered well to the east, but staying close to downtown is much more fun. Plan ahead on summer weekends, when the town is likely to be booked solid.

CABINS AND HOSTELS

Coconino National Forest ☎ 928 282 4119, reservations on ☎ 877 444 6777, ⓦ coconinoforest.us. The national forest's "Rooms With A View" programme offers four separate century-old cabins, way out in the woods up to an hour's drive from Flagstaff, at rock-bottom rates. They sleep six to ten guests, who have to bring their own food and bedding, and in low season, water too. Mid-April to mid-Nov only. $75

DuBeau International Hostel 19 W Phoenix Ave ☎ 928 774 6731 or ☎ 800 398 7112, ⓦ dubeauhostel .com. Welcoming independent hostel just south of the tracks, whose spotless, appealingly converted en-suite motel rooms serve as four-person dorms, or private en-suite doubles of two distinct sizes. Breakfast is free, and there's free wi-fi, but the common areas, complete with pool table, can get noisy at times. Contact them in advance if you plan to arrive between 1.30pm & 4.30pm. Free pick-up from Greyhound, car rental discounts and tours to the Grand Canyon ($85; March–Oct Tues, Thurs, & Sat; Nov–Feb Wed & Sat). They also offer minivan connections with Utah's national parks. Dorms $20, economy doubles $56, deluxe doubles $64

Grand Canyon International Hostel 19 S San Francisco St ☎ 928 779 9421 or ☎ 888 442 2696, ⓦ grandcanyonhostel.com. Independent hostel, under the same friendly management as the similar nearby *DuBeau* – and offering the same programme of tours – but with a significantly quieter overall ambience. Four-bed dorms plus eight private rooms, sharing bathrooms. Rates include breakfast. Dorms $24, doubles $52

HOTELS AND B&BS

Holiday Inn Express 2320 E Lucky Lane ☎ 928 714 1000 or ☎ 877 859 5095, ⓦ hiflagstaff.com. Large motel in a rather characterless area just off the interstate, with a handful of diners nearby. While it's not one of this chain's newer properties, it's maintained to a good standard, and offers free hot breakfasts. $117

★ **The Inn at Four Ten** 410 N Leroux St ☎ 928 774 0088 or ☎ 800 774 2008, ⓦ inn410.com. Bright Craftsman-style home, a very short walk up from downtown, that's now a luxurious antique-furnished B&B. All nine rooms are en-suite, most with fireplaces and three with whirlpool tubs. On summer evenings, the porch and patio make welcoming, convivial retreats, while breakfasts are superb. $165

Little America 2515 E Butler Ave ☎ 928 779 7900 or ☎ 800 865 1401, ⓦ flagstaff.littleamerica.com. Large motel-cum-resort near the interstate, where the 1950s-style ambience conceals a higher standard of accommodation than you might expect. Good pool. $139

Monte Vista 100 N San Francisco St ☎ 928 779 6971 or ☎ 800 545 3068, ⓦ hotelmontevista.com. Attractive landmark 1920s hotel in the heart of downtown. The assorted restored rooms, with and without attached bathrooms, are named for celebrity guests, from Bob Hope to Michael Stipe; Paul McCartney stayed here in 2008. Don't expect luxury, let alone tranquillity; in truth, the ambience is more like a hostel than a hotel. Many of the guests are young international travellers, drawn by the local nightlife, including the hotel's own bar (see p.267). Weekend rates typically rise by $20. $65

Super 8 Conference Center NAU/Downtown 602 W Route 66 ☎ 928 774 4581 or ☎ 800 800 8000, ⓦ super8 .com. The best-value chain motel that's at all near the centre, less than a mile southwest of downtown, just past the US-89 turnoff toward Sedona. Focused on an enclosed swimming pool, it offers a decent standard of no-frills accommodation adjacent to a Barnes & Noble bookstore. $70

Hotel Weatherford 23 N Leroux St ☎ 928 779 1919, ⓦ weatherfordhotel.com. This old downtown hotel, with elegant wooden fittings, has been progressively restored as a true labour of love. The finest rooms offer tasteful accommodation, with antique furnishings and clawfoot tubs plus phones and TVs; five more en-suite rooms are smaller and cheaper; and three large but basic ones share a bathroom. The upstairs lounge offers Wild West ambience, but can make for a noisy night. Shared-bath doubles $49, en-suite doubles $89

5

EATING

While surprisingly short of high-end **restaurants**, central Flagstaff holds a lively assortment of both old-style Western **diners** and eclectic **budget** options. Thanks to all those students, the area around San Francisco Street, both north and south of the tracks, is filled with vegetarian cafés and espresso bars.

Bigfoot BBQ Old Town Shops, 120 N Leroux St ⓣ928 226 1677, ⓦbigfootbbq.com. Lively, friendly and very affordable barbecue stand, downstairs in a funky downtown mall. It's no place for a romantic soiree, but the meat can't be faulted, with a pulled-pork sandwich costing $7, and a mixed plate $13. Daily 11am–9pm.

Black Bart's Steakhouse & Musical Revue 2760 E Butler Ave ⓣ928 779 3142, ⓦblackbartssteakhouse.com. Enjoyable Western-themed steakhouse, across from Little America on the east edge of town, with waiting staff who sing and dance onstage between servings of barbecued steak, ribs and chicken ($19–36). Daily 5–10pm.

Brix 413 N San Francisco St ⓣ928 213 1021, ⓦbrixflagstaff.com. Flagstaff's smartest contemporary restaurant, set in a former carriage house a couple of blocks up from the downtown hub, serves a seasonally changing menu of delicately prepared appetizers such as shrimp and grits ($13), and entrees like lamb ragout ($24) or pan-roasted scallops ($29). Note that portion sizes tend to be significantly smaller than the Wild West norm. Daily 5–9pm.

Charly's Pub & Grill Hotel Weatherford, 23 N Leroux St ⓣ928 779 1919, ⓦweatherfordhotel.com. This café-restaurant is more a place to come to for its classy Western ambience than gourmet food, but it's open for all meals, with good $10 lunchtime sandwiches and dinner entrees like "broken-hearted chicken" for around $20. There's also live music (cocktail piano at lunch, bands at night). Daily 8am–10pm.

Criollo 16 N San Francisco St ⓣ928 774 0541, ⓦcriollolatinkitchen.com. Smart, spacious restaurant, serving Latin American food worth lingering over. The full menu includes tapas as well as substantial dishes like pork belly tacos ($10), *ropa vieja* (braised beef; $12), and their own delicious take on paella, with fish, shellfish and chorizo ($18). Mon–Thurs 11am–10pm, Fri 11am–midnight, Sat 9am–midnight, Sun 9am–10pm.

Diablo Burger 120 N Leroux St ⓣ928 774 3274, ⓦdiabloburger.com. Stylish joint in the centre of town, with outdoor seating beneath a great mural on Heritage Square. The $10–13 burgers feature exclusively local ingredients, most obviously free-range hormone-free cattle from the Diablo ranch. Cash only. Mon–Wed 11am–9pm, Thurs–Sat 11am–10pm.

Downtown Diner 7 E Aspen Ave ⓣ928 774 3492, ⓦfacebook.com/downtowndinerflag. Classic Route 66 diner a block north of the main drag, featuring leatherette booths and hefty burgers and sandwiches, mostly priced at or under $10. Mon–Sat 5.30am–9pm, Sun 7am–6pm.

Late for the Train 107 N San Francisco St ⓣ928 779 5975, ⓦlateforthetrain.com. Little coffee bar opposite the *Monte Vista* that serves excellent home-roasted coffee and pastries to a slightly older, literary crowd. Mon–Thurs & Sun 6am–6pm, Fri & Sat 6am–9pm.

Macy's European Coffee House & Bakery 14 S Beaver St ⓣ928 774 2243, ⓦmacyscoffee.net. Not merely superb coffee, but heavenly pastries to go with it, in a chaotic but friendly, student-oriented atmosphere. Substantial entrees (all vegetarian) include black bean pizza ($8), and there's even couscous for breakfast ($5). You'll also find free wi-fi and an adjacent coin laundry. Daily: summer 6am–10pm, winter 6am–10pm.

NIGHTLIFE

Milling with international travellers in summer and students the rest of the year, Flagstaff is the liveliest **nightspot** between Las Vegas and Santa Fe. Wander a block or two to either side of San Francisco Street downtown, and you can't go wrong.

Beaver Street Brewery 11 S Beaver St ⓣ928 779 0079, ⓦbeaverstreetbrewery.com. Popular microbrewery that has won awards for both its ales and its lagers, and also serves inventive and inexpensive food, including fondues, with an outdoor BBQ in the beer garden on Wednesday nights in summer. Mon–Wed & Sun 11am–1am, Thurs–Sat 11am–2am.

Flagstaff Brewing Company 16 E I-40 ⓣ928 773 1442, ⓦflagbrew.com. Bustling downtown pub, with outdoor patio seating right by Route 66, big windows and live music Thurs–Sat, plus a morning espresso bar. Daily 11am–2am.

Lumberyard Brewing Company 5 S San Francisco St ⓣ928 779 2739, ⓦlumberyardbrewingcompany.com. This recent addition to Flagstaff's brewpub scene, immediately south of the tracks and run by the same team as the *Beaver Street Brewery*, serves a full menu of home-brewed beers, sandwiches (around $10) and deli snacks. Mon–Tues & Sun 11am–11pm, Wed–Sat 11am–2am.

The Mad Italian 101 S San Francisco St ⓣ928 779 1820, ⓦmaditalianpublichouse.com. This highly sociable downtown dive bar, a staple student haunt for over three decades, has recently moved into new

5

ownership, but still features several pool tables, a long cocktail list, and regular live music. Mon–Fri 2pm–2am, Sat 11am–2am, Sun 10am–2am.

Monte Vista Lounge Monte Vista, 100 N San Francisco St ☎ 928 779 6971, ⓦ hotelmontevista.com. Hip little bar and dance club in the basement of a venerable old hotel, with frequent live music and DJs. Daily noon–2am.

The Museum Club 3404 E Route 66 ☎ 928 526 9434, ⓦ themuseumclub.com. A real oddity, this log-cabin taxidermy museum, popularly known as "The Zoo", somehow transmogrified into a classic Route 66 roadhouse, saloon and country music venue – live bands typically Thurs–Sat – that's a second home to hordes of dancing cowboys. Daily 11am–2am.

Around Flagstaff

Dominated by the striking **San Francisco Peaks**, the area around Flagstaff is extraordinarily rich in natural and archeological wonders. Three national monuments – **Sunset Crater**, **Wupatki** and **Walnut Canyon** – lie within 25 miles. All are generally seen as day-trips from Flagstaff; the monuments offer almost no practical facilities, with only **Sunset Crater** having so much as a campground.

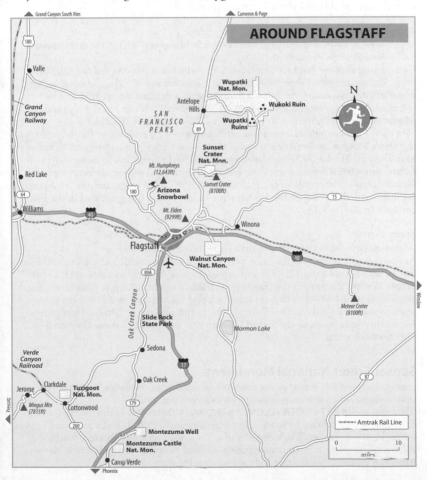

5

The San Francisco Peaks

The **San Francisco Volcanic Field**, north of Flagstaff, consists of around four hundred distinct volcanic cones, which have formed over the past two million years. During that time, the region has also been covered by glacial ice on three separate occasions, shaving around 3000ft off the top of the volcanoes.

The serrated **SAN FRANCISCO PEAKS** are the remnants of a single mountain; their highest point today, at 12,643ft, is the summit of **Mount Humphreys**. They were named by Spanish missionaries in honour of St Francis of Assisi, though the Hopi already knew them as *Nuvatukya'ovi*, the home of the *kachina* spirits, and to the Navajo this was *Dook'o'oosliíd*, one of the four sacred mountains. Seen from afar, topped by a semi-permanent layer of clouds, it's obvious why the Hopi and Navajo regarded them as the source of life-giving rain. Ironically, it's because the mountains were sacred sites for both tribes that they now belong to neither; as federal law stipulates that Native American reservations can only include lands of which a tribe can prove it has "exclusive use," the very fact that both held them holy precluded either from claiming them, and left them open to Yankee exploitation.

The Hopi in particular still make annual pilgrimages on foot from their mesas, 65 miles east, to shrines hidden in the mountains.

Arizona Snowbowl

9300 N Snowbowl Rd · Mid-Dec to mid-April · Lift tickets $55 9am–4pm, $41 for noon–4pm · ☎ 928 779 1951, ⓦ arizonasnowbowl .com · At the end of a seven-mile spur road north of US-180

Considering that the San Francisco Mountain, which has not erupted for 220,000 years, is dormant rather than extinct, the time may come when the gods decide that Flagstaff's own **ski resort**, the **Arizona Snowbowl**, is a desecration no longer to be tolerated. For the moment, it survives, nestling between Mount Humphreys and Mount Agassiz and featuring ski runs such as "Boo-Boo" and "Bambi."

As there's not enough water to make artificial snow – an early name for the peaks was the **Sierra Sinagua**, or "waterless range" – the season typically runs from mid-December to mid-April. The Forest Service has however received permission to make snow in the future, using treated wastewater from Flagstaff's municipal sewage system. Hopi and Navajo tribal leaders consider the plan a violation of sacred lands, and the resultant lawsuits went all the way to the US Supreme Court before being decided in the Forest Service's favour in 2011.

Scenic Skyride

Mid-May to mid-Oct Fri–Sun 10am–4pm · $15, under-13s $10 · ☎ 928 779 1951, ⓦ arizonasnowbowl.com

In summer, the longest of the Snowbowl's four chairlifts, which climbs to within a few hundred feet of the 12,350ft summit of Mount Agassiz, remains open as the **Scenic Skyride**. To protect the fragile vegetation, onward hiking is prohibited, but you'll find plenty of other day-use **trails** in these mountains, most of them also open to mountain-bikers. One switchbacks to the summit of Mount Humphreys for seventy-mile views to the Grand Canyon and beyond. For more information, visit ⓦ azhikers.org.

Sunset Crater National Monument

12 miles north of Flagstaff on US-89, then 2 miles east on FR-545 · Visitor centre Daily: May–Oct 8am–5pm, Nov–April 9am–5pm · $5 per person, includes Wupatki National Monument; under-16s free · ☎ 928 526 0502, ⓦ nps.gov/sucr

The focus of **SUNSET CRATER VOLCANO NATIONAL MONUMENT** is the youngest of the San Francisco volcanoes. Its most recent eruption, in 1065 AD, had a profound impact on the local population. Thick deposits of ash opened previously infertile land to cultivation, accelerating – if not triggering – a land rush that threw different Native American cultures into contact and competition for the first time.

John Wesley Powell named Sunset Crater for its multicoloured cone, which swells from a black base through reds and oranges to a yellow-tinged crest. Unfortunately, however, its shifting cinders are too unstable to allow hikers to climb up to the rim. Instead, after you've seen displays about the crater in the visitor centre, the one-mile **Lava Flow Trail** at its base offers a close-up look at the jagged black lava that streamed out across the desert. The steeper one-mile **Lenox Crater Trail** ascends a lesser cone nearby.

Sunset Crater is just one of dozens of cones in the vicinity; trees have been steadily climbing up some of them for a thousand years, while others remain all but untouched by vegetation. Artist James Turrell has spent over thirty years turning one such pristine cone, **Roden Crater** (⟳rodencrater.com) into a sculptural installation-cum-astronomical observatory, inside which it will one day be possible for paying guests to spend the night.

ACCOMMODATION	SUNSET CRATER NATIONAL MONUMENT

Bonito Campground Opposite Sunset Crater visitor centre ☎928 527 0866, ⟳nps.gov/sucr. Run by the Forest Service, this 44-site, summer-only campground offers simple camping among the woods; running water available. Closed mid-Oct to early May. $18

Wupatki National Monument

20 miles north of Sunset Crater on FR-545, or 26 miles north of Flagstaff on US-89, then 14 miles east on FR-545 • $5 per person, includes Sunset Crater • ☎928 679 2365, ⟳nps.gov/wupa

A cluster of several exceptionally well-preserved ancient ruins, dramatically poised between the volcanoes and the desert north of Sunset Crater, jointly constitute **WUPATKI NATIONAL MONUMENT**. They appear to testify to a period in which different tribal groups lived side by side in harmony. At some time after the Sunset Crater eruption – though not necessarily because of it, as archeologists formerly believed – the Sinagua people already present here, who surely witnessed the explosion, were joined by many others, including the Ancestral Puebloans and the Hohokam. When the rich new soil had been exhausted, around 150 years later, all moved on once more.

Visitor centre

FR-545, 21 miles from east from the US-89 junction • Daily 9am–5pm

Although the first of the five separate pueblo complexes you see as you approach from Sunset Crater is Wukoki, it's best to start your visit at the monument's excellent **visitor centre**, slightly further along the highway. Displays explain the history of the Sinagua and their neighbours, placing them firmly with the context of the traditional migration story of their modern descendants, the Hopi.

Wupatki Pueblo

Accessed via a paved loop trail that leads down from the visitor centre, the main three-storey, hundred-room pueblo block of **Wupatki** ("long cut house") itself is moulded to a sandstone hillock and thus conceals a number of natural caves. The site's most intriguing features, however, lie a little further along.

First comes what seems to be an amphitheatre, a walled circular plaza of unknown purpose. Beyond it is an oval **ball court**, the northernmost such court ever found. Similar arenas throughout central America were used for a game – part ritual, part sport – in which players tried to propel a rubber ball through a stone hoop high on a wall, using their knees and elbows alone, much like modern basketball (except that the losers were sacrificed at the end). Alongside the ball court, cracks in the ground have created a natural **blowhole**, through which air is either sucked or blown depending on pressure and temperature. The audible "breathing" of the earth made this a sacred shrine for Wupatki's ancient inhabitants.

5

Wukoki Pueblo

Wukoki, at the end of its own 2.5-mile spur road near the visitor centre, takes its name from a modern Hopi word meaning "big house." Reminiscent of the castle-like structures at Hovenweep in southern Utah, it's located within sight of a procession of rounded cinder cones, but was probably positioned for its commanding prospect of the Painted Desert to the north and east. Windows in its central tower – again moulded to the contours of a red-rock outcrop, and built with bricks of the same material – look out in all directions. Archeologists believe some are precisely aligned to monitor the sunrise at significant moments. With the Little Colorado River a full five miles distant, the pueblo's inhabitants must have been desperately short of water.

The Citadel

The loop road past Sunset Crater and Wupatki rejoins US-89 twenty miles south of Cameron (see p.328). Outcrops along its final few miles hold more pueblos, such as one known for obvious reasons as **The Citadel**, perched on and fully occupying a hilltop. While its interior, which appears to contain a large circular *kiva*, remains unexcavated, much of its outer wall is still standing, incorporating striped bands of black lava boulders. It too is dotted with tiny "windows" that may have served defensive or astronomical purposes.

Walnut Canyon National Monument

Just south of I-40, 10 miles east of Flagstaff • Visitor centre Daily: May–Oct 8am–5pm; Nov–April 9am–5pm; $5 • ☎ 928 526 3367, ⓦ nps.gov/waca

Between 1125 and 1250 AD, the shallow canyon now preserved as **WALNUT CANYON NATIONAL MONUMENT** was home to a thriving Sinagua community, who lived in small family groups rather than in communal pueblos. Literally hundreds of their **cliff dwellings** still nestle beneath overhangs in the canyon walls. They simply walled off alcoves where softer strata of rock had eroded away, and put up partitions to make separate rooms. No single dwelling is on the same scale as, say, the Sinagua pueblo of Wupatki, and only a handful are accessible to visitors, but cumulatively they make an impressive spectacle.

A large scenic window in the **visitor centre** gives an excellent overall view. **Walnut Creek** itself, long since diverted to provide Flagstaff's drinking water, now runs dry, but you can see how fertile this valley must have been when the Sinagua first arrived. Trees cling to the porous rock to shade the ancient dwellings, and the vegetation thickens down to a valley floor dense with black walnut and oak.

While the main attraction is to hike the Island Loop Trail around the main ruins, each summer rangers lead two- to three-hour **guided hikes** to lesser-known and otherwise inaccessible sites within the monument (see website for current schedule).

No accommodation, and only minimal snack food, is available at the canyon.

Island Loop Trail

Only visitors who arrive an hour or more before closing time are allowed to set off down the mile-long **Island Loop Trail**; as the dwellings are at their most photogenic in late afternoon, that calls for careful timing. Having dropped steeply down from the visitor centre, the trail crosses a narrow causeway to an isthmus of rock high above a gooseneck of the creek. Once there, you can go inside a few Sinagua homes; note the T-shaped doorways, which could only be entered headfirst, and the ceilings blackened by the smoke of generations of fires. Petroglyphs have been found in the other ruins visible on all sides, but none remain on the trail.

South of Flagstaff

US-89A threads its way south from Flagstaff down **Oak Creek Canyon** to emerge after 28 miles at **Sedona**, on the threshold of the extraordinary **Red Rock Country**. Up from the valley rise giant mesas and buttes of stark red sandstone, where Zane Grey set several Wild West adventures. The boom-and-bust mining town of **Jerome** looks down from a mountainside to the south. Hwy-260 links both US-89A and I-17 and the haunting Sinagua ruins of **Tuzigoot** and **Montezuma Castle**.

Oak Creek Canyon

Local claims that **OAK CREEK CANYON**, the largest of several slender chasms that cut into the 2000ft escarpment of the **Mogollon Rim**, is a serious rival to the Grand Canyon are somewhat exaggerated. However, you *can* drive right through it, and with its sheer walls striped in vivid bands of colour, its sparkling streams and densely wooded glens, and its facilities for camping, eating, and general playing around, this would be an unmissable attraction anywhere else in the world. The canyon's narrow floor has been heavily developed, though leisure facilities are hidden where possible by careful landscaping.

Lookout Point, its northern end, appears suddenly a dozen forested miles south of Flagstaff on US-89A. Native American craft stalls surround the parking lot, and several overlooks within easy walking distance command prospects of the narrow gorge below. The road then switchbacks sharply down to run alongside **Oak Creek** itself. The lowest level in the rocks to either side, often obscured by maples, cedars, oaks and pines, is the bright-red Supai sandstone. Above that, layers of white sandstone, buff limestone, and finally black basalt testify to a geological history which has fluctuated from harsh desert to sea bottom. Temperatures are cool enough to make fishing, picnicking and hiking expeditions welcome escapes.

Slide Rock State Park

6871 N US-89A • Daily: March to mid-May 8am–6pm; mid-May to mid-Oct 8am–7pm; mid-Oct to Feb 8am–5pm • $10 per vehicle in winter, $20 in summer • ⓦ 928 282 3034, ⓦ azstateparks.com

Seven miles before US-89A reaches Sedona, **Slide Rock State Park** preserves what was originally a 43-acre apple orchard. The reason it's so full in summer, though, is that Oak Creek at this point forms a natural water chute, where you can swim and slide across smooth boulders set in the riverbed. The absence of still water means that it's almost insect-free.

ACCOMMODATION

OAK CREEK CANYON

★ **The Canyon Wren** 6425 N US-89A ⓣ 928 282 6900 or ⓣ 800 437 9736, ⓦ canyonwrencabins.com. Four large and hugely comfortable, private two-person cabins, each with a kitchen and a whirlpool tub, six miles north of Sedona; they're especially cosy in winter. No wi-fi. $155
Garland's Oak Creek Lodge 8067 N US-89A ⓣ 928 282 3343, ⓦ garlandslodge.com. The loveliest place to stay beside Oak Creek, 7 miles north of downtown Sedona, has to be in one of these individual log cabins, set in gorgeous gardens and reached across a small ford half a mile north of Slide Rock. Rates include breakfast and dinner in the top-quality dining room in the central lodge. 2-night minimum stay. Closed Sun, and mid-Nov to late March. $265

Sedona

There's no disputing that the New Age resort of **SEDONA** enjoys a magnificent setting, amid definitive Southwestern canyon scenery. Sadly, however, the town itself adds nothing to the beauty of its surroundings. In fact, it's a real mess, with several miles of ugly sprawl interrupted by the occasional mock-historical mall monstrosity. Some visitors, particularly Europeans, experience a strong negative reaction, feeling

5

THE END OF THE NEW AGE?

Sedona's big break as a destination for **New Age** travellers came in 1981, when Page Bryant, author and psychic, "channelled" the information that Sedona is in fact "the heart *chakra* of the planet." After she pinpointed her first **vortex** – a point at which, it is claimed, psychic and electromagnetic energies can be channelled for personal and planetary harmony – the town achieved its own personal growth, and blossomed as a focus for New Age practitioners of all kinds.

However, the image of Sedona as a centre of New Age spirituality suffered a devastating setback in October 2009, when three people died of burns and dehydration during a sweat lodge exercise, and a further eighteen were hospitalised. Each had paid almost $10,000 to participate in a "Spiritual Warrior" retreat organized by self-styled guru James Arthur Ray, who was subsequently found guilty of negligent homicide and jailed for two years.

The tragedy served to focus attention on Native American views that such New Age practitioners have grossly misrepresented Native American practices and beliefs. While Sedona still abounds in New Age tour operators and therapists many have since toned down any claims to be associated with Native American spirituality.

there are plenty of beautiful landscapes elsewhere in the Southwest that haven't been sullied by this sort of over-development. Other travellers, by contrast, absolutely love it, for its combination of luxurious accommodation and fancy restaurants, and almost limitless opportunities for active outdoor vacationing. In particular, artists, healers, and wealthy retirees have flocked here in the last few decades. Whether you love or hate Sedona may depend on whether you share their wide-eyed awe for angels, crystals, and all matters mystical – and whether you're prepared to pay over-the-odds prices for the privilege of joining them. Whatever your attitude, it's still an intriguing place to visit, where even the most hard-nosed commercial operation can seem a front for the real business of holding earnest conversations about the state of each other's psyches. **John McCain** certainly likes it; he spends almost every weekend on his ranch nearby.

Established in 1902 by Theodore Schnebly and named after his wife, Sedona remained a small farming settlement for most of the twentieth century, unmarked on most maps. German surrealist painter **Max Ernst** moved here in the 1940s – the bizarre backdrops of his later canvases seem less surreal once you've seen where they were painted – and Hollywood moviemakers filmed in the area from the 1950s onwards. **Elvis Presley** came here to shoot his 27th movie, *Stay Away Joe*, in 1967.

The prevailing pay-no-taxes ethos of Sedona's ardent libertarians has ensured that few of the side roads off the main highways are paved. That dovetails neatly, of course, with the booming business in off-road tours. Nonetheless, much of the best scenery is visible from the highway, and in any case many jeep roads are perfectly passable in ordinary vehicles. So long as you're happy to remain ignorant as to which rocks are really electromagnetic tuning forks vibrating in harmony with Alpha Centauri, there's no great need to take a commercial tour.

The "Y" and around

Sedona centres on the road junction known as the "Y", poised above Oak Creek, where Hwy-89A branches southwest toward Cottonwood, while Hwy-179 heads by way of the village of Oak Creek to meet I-17, fourteen miles south. The town itself holds little to detain sightseers, though strolling the two or so blocks that count as **uptown** – the one area where the stores and businesses are close enough together to make walking a possibility – just north of the "Y," is pleasant enough. Above the roaring traffic, you can usually still hear the synchronized chirruping of crickets in **Oak Creek** below, while your eyes are repeatedly drawn to the superb red rocks that tower above the banal buildings along Hwy-89A. A little way south of the "Y," on Hwy-179, **Tlaquepaque Shopping**

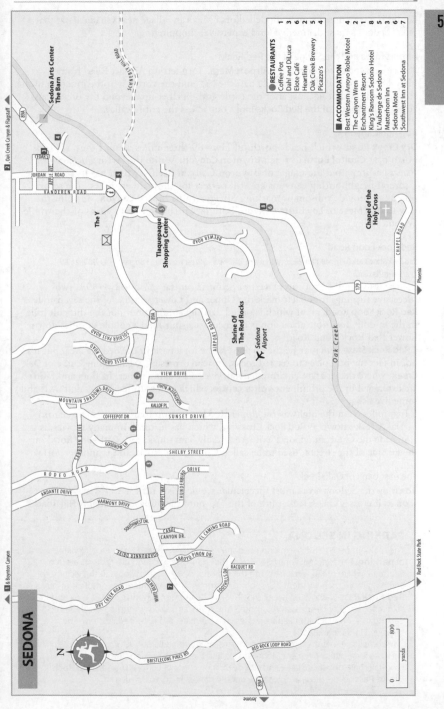

SEDONA

N

0 _____ 800
yards

● RESTAURANTS

Coffee Pot — 1
Dahl and DiLuca — 3
Elote Café — 6
Heartline — 2
Oak Creek Brewery — 5
Picazzo's — 4

■ ACCOMMODATION

Best Western Arroyo Roble Motel — 4
The Canyon Wren — 2
Enchantment Resort — 1
King's Ransom Sedona Hotel — 8
L'Auberge de Sedona — 5
Matterhorn Inn — 3
Sedona Motel — 6
Southwest Inn at Sedona — 7

Sedona Arts Center
The Barn

The Y

Tlaquepaque
Shopping Center

Shrine Of
The Red Rocks

Sedona Airport

Chapel of the
Holy Cross

Oak Creek

▲ Oak Creek Canyon & Flagstaff
▲ & Boynton Canyon
▼ Phoenix
▼ Red Rock State Park
◄ Jerome

5

Center is a very upscale mall, modelled on a Mexican village near Guadalajara, that offers Sedona's most distinctive (and expensive) shopping.

Airport Mesa and the Shrine of the Red Rocks

The closest **vortex** to town is on **Airport Mesa**. Turn left up Airport Road from Hwy-89A as you head west, a mile past the "Y," and the vortex is at the junction of the second and third peaks, just after the cattle grid. Further up, beyond the precarious airport, the **Shrine of the Red Rocks** looks out across the entire valley.

Boynton Canyon

Dry Creek Road, which heads north off Hwy-89 three miles west of the "Y", runs north past **Capitol Butte** to reach **Boynton Canyon**. While the lavish *Enchantment Resort* has impaired the magic of Boynton Canyon itself – which has its own vortex – several neighbouring canyons are still perfect for short desert hikes. The resort office can provide trail maps marking Sinagua ruins in **Red Canyon**, or point the way to **Doe Mesa** or **Loy Butte Canyon**, both of which offer great views of the whole Sedona valley.

Red Rock Loop Road

Red Rock State Park Daily: park 8am–5pm, visitor centre 9am–5pm • $10 per vehicle or $3 per person • ☎ 928 282 6907, ⓦ azstateparks.com

Four and five miles respectively west of Sedona's central "Y" on Hwy-89A, two successive turnings to the left mark the Upper and Lower sections of the seven-mile **Red Rock Loop Road**, all of which is paved barring a bumpy but not too difficult mile in the middle. Its prime attraction is reached via a spur road a couple of miles down Lower Red Rock Loop Road.

Red Rock State Park may be the obvious name for a park in the Sedona area, but it's not in fact the best place to see red rocks. Instead it preserves a sweeping curve of **Oak Creek**, where the riparian environment survives reasonably intact. Its flora and fauna are explained in the prominent **visitor centre**, which holds stuffed hawks and owls and some live fish.

Two miles from the highway on Upper Red Rock Loop Road, a picturesque ford in Oak Creek known as **Red Rock Crossing**, which has featured in many movies, is alongside the Crescent Moon Picnic Area (daily 9am–dusk; $9). **Cathedral Rock**, on the far side of the stream, used to be called Courthouse Rock, and is another vortex.

The east bank of Oak Creek

To enjoy the Sedona area's most spectacular scenic drive, turn left off Hwy-179 as soon as it crosses Oak Creek south of the "Y," onto the unpaved **Schnebly Hill Road**.

PARKING IN SEDONA

The major impediment to exploring Sedona in your own vehicle is the inconvenience of **parking**. The National Forest Service requires anyone parking in the forests around Sedona – which means anyone using the majority of roadside pullouts in the vicinity, for anything more than "incidental stopping", reckoned at fifteen minutes or more – to buy a **Red Rock Pass** (1-day $5, 1-week $15, 1-year $20; ⓦ redrockcountry.org). The passes are sold in local visitor centres, stores, motels and B&Bs, and also by vending machines in parking lots. Annual national park passes (see p.36) are also accepted, but must be displayed in the parked car.

To complicate matters further, four popular scenic spots – Banjo Bill, Grasshopper Point, Red Rock Crossing (site of Crescent Moon Ranch), and Call O'The Canyon (trailhead for the West Fork Trail) – are on private land, and charge their own fees of up to $10; a $40 **Red Rock Grand Pass** covers those areas as well, but the national park passes do not.

In summer, the road remains open all the way to I-17, twelve rough miles east. Alternatively, continue south for three miles and then take Chapel Road to the left, which soon brings you to the **Chapel of the Holy Cross** (daily 9am–5pm). This tall and very narrow concrete chapel, whose facade is shaped like a massive cross, is squeezed into a cleft in the red cliffs. Another two miles down the highway, **Bell Rock**, on the east as you enter the village of Oak Creek, is Sedona's fourth major vortex.

ARRIVAL AND DEPARTURE — SEDONA

By car Sedona is 28 miles south of Flagstaff on Hwy-89A and 120 miles north of Phoenix. Its road system is utterly unable to cope with the level of visitation; expect bumper-to-bumper traffic on weekends.

By bus Arizona Shuttle (☎ 928 226 8060 or ☎ 800 448 7988, ⓦ arizonashuttle.com) runs shuttles to Sedona from Phoenix (9 daily; $47) and Flagstaff (2 daily; $25).

GETTING AROUND AND INFORMATION

Visitor centre 331 Forest Road at Hwy-89A, just north of the "Y" (Mon–Sat 8.30am–5pm, Sun 9am–3pm; ☎ 928 282 7722 or ☎ 800 288 7336, ⓦ visitsedona.com).

Bike rental Companies that rent out bikes include Bike &

Bean, 75 Bell Rock Plaza, Hwy-179 (☎ 928 284 0210, ⓦ bike-bean.com), which has its own espresso bar.

Car rental Barlow Jeep Rentals (☎ 928 282 8700, ⓦ sedonajeeprentals.com) can provide 4WD vehicles.

TOURS

Arizona Helicopter Adventures ☎ 928 282 0904 or ☎ 800 282 5141, ⓦ arizonahelicopteradventures.com. Chopper flights, from the 12min Red Rock RoundUp ($89) to the 30min Sedona Deluxe ($179).

Northern Light Balloon Expeditions ☎ 928 282 2274 or ☎ 800 230 6222, ⓦ northernlightballoon.com. Comparatively unspiritual balloon trips from $195, with champagne picnics.

Pink Jeep Tours (☎ 928 282 5000 or ☎ 800 873 3662, ⓦ pinkjeep.com). You can't miss this lot in uptown Sedona.

Quite exceptionally garish "4-wheelin' vehicles" crunch around in off-road tours, from $59.

Red Rock Biplane Tours ☎ 928 204 5939 or ☎ 888 866 7433, ⓦ sedonaairtours.com. Fly over Sedona in an open-cockpit biplane, from $129 for 20min.

Trail Horse Adventures ☎ 928 634 5276 or ☎ 866 958 7245, ⓦ trailhorseadventures.com. Horseback trips, largely geared around eating (in traditional cowboy style), in Cottonwood's Dead Horse Ranch State Park, from $64 up to $125.

ACCOMMODATION

Sedona is an expensive place to **stay**, and away from the "Y" it's too spread out to walk around. For those who don't mind spending well over $100 per night, Sedona has some extremely fancy options, including around twenty upscale **B&Bs** and several full-service **resorts**; budget travellers can get better deals at Cottonwood and Jerome (see p.276 & p.278). **Oak Creek Canyon** (see p.271), just north of Sedona, provides a couple of worthwhile alternatives to staying in town.

Best Western Arroyo Roble Motel 400 N US-89A ☎ 928 282 4001 or ☎ 800 773 3662, ⓦ bestwesternsedona .com. This comfortable multi-tiered motel, stacked up above Oak Creek not far north of uptown Sedona, has a separate deluxe wing, *Arroyo Roble North*. Even the standard rooms have private patios or balconies, with fabulous view, and rates include good, free hot breakfasts. $244

Enchantment Resort 525 Boynton Canyon Rd ☎ 928 282 2900 or ☎ 800 826 4180, ⓦ enchantmentresort .com. Extremely luxurious resort, equipped with four pools and seven tennis courts, that has taken over ravishing Boynton Canyon eight miles west of town. Accommodation is in fully equipped one- and two-bedroom adobe *casitas*. $295

King's Ransom Sedona Hotel 771 Hwy-179 ☎ 928 282 3132 or ☎ 877 480 0044, ⓦ kingsransomsedona .com. Nicely refurbished upper-range motel, half a mile

south of the Tlaquepaque mall, with rather small rooms – most with balconies – but a nice garden, a pool and spa, and a highly recommended Mexican restaurant, reviewed below. $104

L'Auberge de Sedona 301 L'Auberge Lane ☎ 928 282 1661 or ☎ 855 905 5745, ⓦ lauberge.com. Plush two-part resort in the heart of the town, with fancy if somewhat incongruous French-themed motel rooms at road level looking out onto the red rocks, and a cable-car connection to the individual guest cottages ranged along the tranquil banks of Oak Creek below. $225

Matterhorn Inn 230 Apple Ave ☎ 928 282 7176 or ☎ 800 372 8207, ⓦ matterhorninn.com. Central motel, on the right as you come into town on Hwy-89A from the north, with two tiers of rooms that face across to the red rocks. $129

Sedona Motel 218 Hwy-179 ☎ 928 282 7187 or ☎ 877 828 7187, ⓦ thesedonamotel.com. Small

5

motel, amazingly inexpensive by local standards, in an ideal and attractive location close to the "Y" uptown, with a friendly atmosphere on its shared communal deck. $89

Southwest Inn at Sedona 3250 W US-89A

☎928 282 3344 or ☎800 483 7422, ⓦswinn.com. The classiest of Sedona's many highwayside motels, with very welcoming staff, an outdoor spa, and comfortable sound-proofed rooms; to get a view, though, you have to pay a bit extra. $125

EATING

Sedona is bursting with expensive Southwestern-style **restaurants**, not all of which are particularly good, and still has a smattering of old-fashioned diners. There's a shortage of places where you can just sit and watch the world go by over a coffee and a sandwich; most of its cafés are twee little places intended mainly to entice tourists into pastel-trimmed gift stores.

Coffee Pot Restaurant 2050 W Hwy-89A ☎928 282 6626, ⓦcoffeepotsedona.com. Sedona's largest, oldest diner – named for a nearby rock formation – serves a hundred kinds of omelettes ($7–12), and all the burgers ($7–10), Mexican dishes ($8–10), and fried specials you could hope for. Daily 6am–2pm.

Dahl and DiLuca 2321 W Hwy-89A ☎928 282 5219, ⓦdahlanddiluca.com. Northern Italian dinners served in a romantic mock-up of a Tuscan villa; specials like veal and prawn pasta cost up to $29, but standard, well-prepared pasta entrees are more typically priced around $20. Daily 5–10pm.

Elote Café King's Ransom Sedona Hotel, 771 Hwy-179 ☎928 203 0105, ⓦelotecafe.com. High-quality Mexican restaurant a mile south of town, including delicious *salsa verde* salmon ($20), buffalo ribs with mole sauce ($25), and smoked chicken enchiladas ($18.50). No reservations. Tues–Sat 5–9.30pm.

Heartline 1610 W Hwy-89A ☎928 282 0785, ⓦheartlinecafe.com. Tasteful white-table-linen

restaurant, with an attractive garden courtyard, that serves determinedly healthy – though not exclusively vegetarian – Southwestern cuisine. Dinner entrees like pecan-crusted trout cost $25–30, a "Sedona Sunrise" salmon breakfast $10.50. Daily 8am–9.30pm.

Oak Creek Brewery 336 Hwy-179 ☎928 282 300, ⓦoakcreekpub.com. Sedona's first-ever brewpub, in the Tlaquepaque mall, closes remarkably early for a pub, but it offers a fine selection of lagers and ales, brewed on site, plus a full menu ranging from rotisserie chicken for $14 and large pizzas for $20. No reservations. Daily 11.30am–9pm.

Picazzo's 1855 W Hwy-89A ☎928 282 4140, ⓦpicazzos.com. Part of an arty Arizona chain, this fancy organic-pizza place enjoys pretty red-rock views, with outdoor seating on a shaded patio. Pizza flavours include fig and mozzarella ($15.75) and "meaty meaty" ($18.50), and they have plenty of vegetarian and even gluten-free options. Mon–Thurs & Sun 11am–9pm, Fri & Sat 11am–10pm.

Cottonwood

Describing **COTTONWOOD**, eighteen miles southwest of Sedona, the 1930s WPA guide to Arizona wrote, "Familiar figures in the town are the cowboys from the range and the prospector or 'desert rat' who wanders in from his camp in the mountains to break the monotony of his lonely life." Today's Cottonwood is not nearly so romantic, though thanks to an influx of retirees it's much larger. It's not really even the same place, as the former downtown is stranded a couple of miles north of Hwy-89A, now lined by modern strip development.

Cottonwood does, however, make an inexpensive base for Sedona and Jerome, and its old main street still possesses a certain charm.

ACCOMMODATION AND EATING   COTTONWOOD

Old Town Cafe 1025A N Main St ☎928 634 5980, ⓦoldtownroaster.com. Housed in a small gallery in downtown Cottonwood, this friendly café offers the perfect opportunity for latterday desert rats to break the monotony, with a breakfast coffee or pastry, or lunchtime smoothie ($3.50) or sandwich ($6–9). Tues–Sat 8am–3pm.

Pines Motel 920 S Camino Real ☎928 634 9975 or ☎800 483 9618, ⓦazpinesmotel.com. Great-value family-owned motel, just off Hwy-89A a short way south of the centre, with clean, good-sized rooms, some with kitchenettes, and a pool; you won't find rates like this in Sedona. $59

VERDE CANYON RAILROAD

Although an unremarkable little place itself, the town of Clarkdale, three miles northwest of Cottonwood, is the starting point for Arizona's most scenic **vintage train ride**.

The **Verde Canyon Railroad** operates 25-mile round-trip excursions, along the otherwise inaccessible Verde Canyon as far as Perkinsville, with plenty of dramatic red-rock scenery and archeological ruins en route. The trips run year-round, varying in frequency from twice weekly to daily, and almost always leaving at 1pm. See the website for precise schedules, and note that the actual trains are powered by diesel engines, not steam ($55, ages 2–12 $35; ☎800 582 7245, ⓦverdecanyonrr.com).

Tuzigoot National Monument

2 miles northeast of Cottonwood on Hwy-89A, then 0.6 miles east on Tuzigoot Rd • Daily 8am–5pm • $5 per person • ☎928 634 5564, ⓦ nps.gov/tuzi

During the fourteenth century, there were fifty major pueblo sites in the valley of the Verde River, south of Sedona, occupied by the ancient people now known as the **Sinagua**. One of the largest, perched on a hillock across the river from **Clarkdale**, now constitutes **TUZIGOOT NATIONAL MONUMENT**.

The ground floor alone had 86 rooms; with fifteen more rooms on the upper level, it may have been home to some 225 people. Some archeologists think it was a final enclave, where the Sinagua gathered against encroaching drought before abandoning the area early in the fifteenth century. Artefacts displayed in the recently modernized visitor centre include turquoise mosaics and shell jewellery.

Unfortunately, Tuzigoot is among the least satisfying of such sites. When it was restored in a 1930s make-work programme, a little too much work was done, and a broad cement trail was laid over, across, and through the pueblo. Furthermore, while the river, lined with cottonwoods, still flows past the pueblo, the "fields" below are just a sickly orange mass of tailings from the nearby copper mines.

Jerome

The tiny mining-town-turned-arts-colony of **JEROME**, high above the Verde Valley on Hwy-89A, is conspicuous from quite a distance; not only is an enormous letter "J" etched deep into the hillside above it, but a large chunk of that hillside is missing altogether, having been blown apart for **opencast copper mining**.

As recently as the 1970s, Jerome was a **ghost town**, where it was possible to turn up and move into an empty house. Many who did so are still here, making a living from arts and crafts, and the town itself has made a dramatic recovery. The fact that it's now solely geared towards the needs of visitors makes it something of a tourist trap, but it's nonetheless fascinating to explore. While most of the shops only stock souvenirs, there are some interesting crafts showrooms and art galleries around, as well as fine old saloons.

Thanks to the steep angle of the hillside, Jerome's streets are stacked one atop the other, and its stone houses tend to have two storeys at the front and four or five at the back. Under the concussion of two hundred miles of tunnels being blasted into the mountainside, the whole town used to slip downhill at the rate of five inches per year; the **Sliding Jail** on Hull Avenue came to rest 225 feet from where it was built (it's still there, but it's not open to the public).

Brief history

Although Mingus Mountain abounds in mineral wealth – thick veins of copper are interspersed with gold and silver, and an endless supply of limestone is still extracted for cement – serious exploitation only started in 1876.

5

The **United Verde** mine was partly financed by New Yorker Eugene Jerome (a cousin of Winston Churchill's mother, Jennie Jerome), who insisted the new town bear his name. The United Verde has been called "the richest mine ever owned by an individual"; it made William Clark $100 million, and by 1953 had produced enough copper to give a thirteen-pound lump to every person on earth. Until the tortuous highway was built, the only way up to Jerome was the rail line that corkscrewed down from the mine to the world's largest copper smelter, at Clarkdale.

Jerome was a hard-drinking, hard-living town. The young **Pancho Villa** started out in life by supplying its drinking water, using a relay of two hundred burros, and the International Workers of the World (the "**Wobblies**") were briefly a strong presence; several hundred miners and "outside agitators" were literally railroaded out of town in 1917 and dumped unceremoniously in the remote deserts of southwest Arizona.

Harsh economic realities have always determined local fortunes. Plenty of copper remains in the earth; although the Depression hit hard, the mine was only closed in the 1950s, when cheap imported copper made it uneconomic to continue, and as prices rise, it may reopen. To keep the mineral rights from reverting to the state, the present owners are obliged to keep on researching and prospecting; in fact, they do more than they have to, and reportedly find enough gold to cover their expenses.

Jerome State Historic Park

100 Douglas Rd • Daily 8am–5pm • $5 • ☎ 928 634 5381, ⓦ azstateparks.com

Built for mine owner "Rawhide Jimmy" Douglas in 1917, the **Douglas Mansion**, below town, is now open as **Jerome State Historic Park**. Given the sweeping views, it can be hard to concentrate on the displays detailing the history of the mines and the lifestyles of the bosses.

Mine Museum

200 N Main St • Daily 9am–5pm • $2 • ☎ 928 634 5477, ⓦ jeromehistoricalsociety.org

Located in the former *Fashion Saloon*, in the heart of old Jerome, the **Mine Museum** displays an amateurish but enjoyable collection of Wild West oddities ranging from milk bottles to laundry machines and firearms. Its most memorable feature is the pressed-tin ceiling of the saloon itself.

ARRIVAL AND INFORMATION   JEROME

By car Though on paper, Hwy-89A is a direct through route between Sedona, thirty miles northeast of Jerome, and Prescott, thirty miles southwest, the formidable Mingus Mountain makes reaching Jerome a slow business. Coming from Cottonwood, it's a painstaking switchback climb; if you approach from Prescott, you descend into Jerome, with gorgeous views of the valley spread out below. Hwy-89A branches in two in the heart of town, where a one-way system takes westbound traffic along Hull Avenue and eastbound along Main Street.

Visitor centre A tiny shack provides local information at 310 N Hull Ave (Mon–Fri 10am–4pm, Sat & Sun 11am–3pm; ☎ 928 634 2900, ⓦ jeromechamber.com).

ACCOMMODATION

There's no room to build **motels** on Jerome's uncertain slopes, so accommodation is restricted to a couple of turn-of-the-century hotels and a few former homes converted into **B&Bs**.

Connor Hotel 164 Main St ☎ 928 634 5006 or ☎ 800 523 3554, ⓦ connorhotel.com. Small central hotel, offering twelve attractive antique-furnished rooms, each with a tasteful tiled private bathroom, above the *Spirit Room* bar, which gets busy on weekends. $95

Ghost City Inn 541 N Main St ☎ 928 634 4678 or ☎ 888 634 4678, ⓦ ghostcityinn.com. Century-old house, at the entrance to town as you come up from Cottonwood, with huge views from its wooden veranda. Some of the six guest rooms, which vary in price, are resolutely Western, others more flowery, but all have en-suite bathrooms. $105

5

Jerome Grand Hotel 200 Hill St ☎ 928 634 8200 or ☎ 888 817 6788, ⓦ jeromegrandhotel.com. Restored hotel, housed in a former hospital that spills down five storeys from the highest point in town; the views are fabulous, but the accommodation merely evokes bygone days, rather than being particularly luxurious. There's also a good on-site restaurant; see below. $120

Surgeon's House B&B 101 Hill St ☎ 928 639 1452 or ☎ 800 639 1452, ⓦ surgeonshouse.com. Smart, upmarket B&B, set in lovely gardens at the top of town; three of the four plush en-suite rooms enjoy dramatic views. $145

EATING AND DRINKING

Day-trippers tend to fill Jerome's **tearooms** and **snack bars** at lunchtime – especially on weekends – but come the evening, in bars like the *Spirit Room* in the *Connor Hotel*, you can still get a faint sense of its riproaring past.

★ **The Asylum** Jerome Grand Hotel, 200 Hill St ☎ 928 639 3197, ⓦ asylumrestaurant.com. "Fun" restaurant that makes the most of its dramatic, quirky setting in a former hospital, but nonetheless serves excellent Southwestern cuisine. All that plus a fabulous wine list and astonishing views – what more could you ask for? Dinner entrees like maple leaf duck breast range $21–31; lunch salads and sandwiches cost $10–13. Daily 11am–3.30pm & 5–9pm.

Bobby D's BBQ at the English Kitchen 119 Jerome Ave ☎ 928 634 6235, ⓦ facebook.com /bobbydsbbqjerome. Supposedly Arizona's oldest restaurant, built in 1899, and successively an opium den and a meeting hall for the Wobblies. These days it specializes in barbecue, serving meaty breakfasts and then later on succulent pulled pork and smoked chicken, with sandwiches for around $10, mixed plates more like $15, and take-out available. The terrace offers commanding views over the valley. Mon & Tues 7am–4pm, Wed, Thurs & Sun 7am–8pm, Fri & Sat 7am–10pm.

Flatiron Cafe 416 N Main St ☎ 928 634 2733, ⓦ theflatironjerome.com. Small, friendly joint at the southern apex of the one-way system. Espresso coffees, scrambled-egg breakfasts, and fancy salad-and-sandwich lunches for around $10. Mon & Wed–Sun 8am–4pm.

Montezuma Castle National Monument

2 separate sites, just east of I-17, 40 miles south of Flagstaff and 20 miles southeast of Sedona

Toward the east end of the Verde Valley, two dramatic ancient sites, roughly five miles apart, jointly constitute **MONTEZUMA CASTLE NATIONAL MONUMENT**. If you only have time to see one, Montezuma Castle itself is more rewarding, but each offers a fascinating snapshot of the Sinagua culture.

Montezuma Well

4 miles east of I-17 exit 293 • Daily 8am–5pm • Free • ☎ 928 567 4521, ⓦ nps.gov/moca

Montezuma Well, the northernmost of the two components of Montezuma Castle National Monument, is a natural lake that measures 368 feet across by 55 feet deep. Set like a volcanic crater into a small hill, it formed when the roof of an underground cave collapsed 11,000 years ago. It's still fed by a spring that produces a phenomenal 1.9 million gallons of warm water per day, naturally heated to a constant 75°F.

Not surprisingly, the well was sacred to Native Americans; the **Yavapai** people (see p.322) say they emerged into the world here. The **Hohokam**, who arrived around 600 AD, were the first to divert its water for irrigation, while the **Sinagua** followed in 1125 AD. Traces of their ruined pueblos can be discerned on the hilltop, reached by a five-minute walk from the parking lot, and a more complete **cliff dwelling** is set into the inner crater wall. It's now inaccessible, though you get a good view from the staircase that leads down to the lakeside, where a couple more dwellings stand at ground level. No fee is charged to visitors.

Montezuma Castle

Half a mile east of I-17 exit 289 • Daily 8am–5pm • $5 per person • ☎ 928 567 3322, ⓦ nps.gov/moca

In an idyllic setting above Beaver Creek, **Montezuma Castle** itself is a superbly preserved Sinagua **cliff dwelling** that dates from the twelfth century. Filling a hillside alcove with a wall of pink adobe, and originally reached by three separate ladders from the valley floor, its five storeys taper up to fit the contours of the rock. Apparently, the sycamore beams are still in place, and the fingerprints of the masons are still visible on the bricks, but visitors are not permitted to climb up.

The ruins of a much larger, though now much less photogenic, dwelling "next door" were exposed to view by a fire in about 1400 AD. Once again you can't go inside, but holes in the limestone show that it had 45 rooms, as well as little "cupboards" recessed into the walls. It may have housed a hundred people, as opposed to thirty or so in the castle.

Displays on the Sinagua in the castle **visitor centre**, where you pay your entry fee, are stylish and modern, if not all that detailed. The collection includes a macaw skeleton, which suggests trade with the Mexican civilizations thousands of miles south. There's no connection with the Aztec ruler Montezuma, though the well is said to appear on a deerskin map that belonged to Cortes himself.

Arcosanti

1.5 miles northeast of I-17 exit 263, near Cordes Junction • Guided tours daily 9am–5pm; tours hourly 10am–4pm except noon • $10 • ☎ 928 632 7135, ⓦ arcosanti.org

The space-age project known as **ARCOSANTI** has been gradually rising from the rim of a beautiful high desert canyon since 1970. Designed to be a self-sufficient community of five thousand people – someday, it's currently estimated at around five percent completion – Arcosanti is the clearest embodiment of **Arcology**, a blend of architecture and ecology created and still overseen by Italian architect **Paolo Soleri**, a former student of Frank Lloyd Wright who's also responsible for the bell foundry at Cosanti, near Phoenix (see p.210).

Though far from any sizeable settlement, Arcosanti is intended as a model of future urban environments. Part construction site, part theme park, with buildings shaped to maximize the benefit of the sun's energy, it can be seen on hour-long guided tours. You can also pay extra for longer, more specialized tours, or sign up for five-week, $1550 workshops and help with the construction. In summer, Arcosanti hosts a popular series of outdoor **concerts**.

Prescott

The neat little Victorian town of **PRESCOTT** makes an unlikely sight in the Arizona wilderness, a hundred miles north of Phoenix by way of I-17 and Hwy-69 (which branches off the interstate at Cordes Junction). In 1863, when President Lincoln acceded to pressure from mining interests and granted Arizona territorial status, he chose to establish a new capital well away from Tucson, the obvious choice, which he saw as a hotbed of Confederate sympathizers. His first pick, **Fort Whipple**, was replaced in 1864 when gold was discovered near Prescott, which became the site of both fort and capital. It was named in honour of William H. Prescott, author of the classic *History of the Conquest of Mexico*, who never visited the town.

Although Tucson duly supplanted it as capital within three years, Prescott survived, with cattle ranchers joining the gold miners to make it a rowdy, liquor-loving town. Those days are long gone, however, and while Prescott refused to die, neither has it grown.

Still centring on its venerable courthouse square, it's a charming little town with a real Wild West flavour. While few out-of-state visitors find their way here, as it's not on any obvious itinerary, it makes a rewarding overnight stop, with a thriving infrastructure of hotels and restaurants.

5

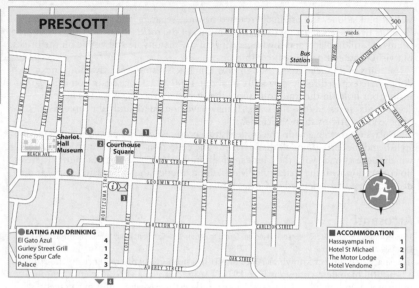

EATING AND DRINKING
El Gato Azul	4
Gurley Street Grill	1
Lone Spur Cafe	2
Palace	3

ACCOMMODATION
Hassayampa Inn	1
Hotel St Michael	2
The Motor Lodge	4
Hotel Vendome	3

Courthouse Square

Downtown Prescott focuses on the kind **of Courthouse Square** you'd expect to find in the Deep South, not the Wild West. Apart from the Courthouse itself, its central feature is the **Rough Rider Memorial Monument**, a bronze equestrian statue that commemorates William Owen "Buckey" O'Neill. While mayor of Prescott, this frontier character recruited many of Theodore Roosevelt's Rough Riders in 1898 and was killed in Cuba at the Battle of San Juan Hill. A colourful timeline set into the concrete footpath nearby traces local history from a visit by the Spanish explorer Espejo in 1581 up to the opening of the "Automated Flight Service Station" in 1985. Especially on summer weekends, the square plays host to community events and arts fairs.

Sharlot Hall Museum

415 W Gurley St • May–Sept Mon–Sat 10am–5pm, Sun noon–4pm; Oct–April Mon–Sat 10am–4pm, Sun noon–4pm • $5 • ☎ 928 445 3122, ⍟ sharlot.org

The best place to get a feel for Prescott's past is the **Sharlot Hall Museum**, a short walk west of the centre. Sharlot Hall herself arrived in Prescott with her pioneer parents in 1882, aged twelve, and went on to become Arizona's official historian. She also started this collection, which now fills a dozen buildings and an entire city block. In its modern headquarters, you can admire the attractive flapper-esque gown of copper she wore when taking Arizona's three electoral college votes to Washington DC to elect Calvin Coolidge in 1925. Structures nearby include the 1864 Governor's Mansion and the contemporaneous Fort Misery, which became Arizona's first law office and courthouse as well as a church, general store and boarding house.

The main **Sharlot Hall Building** covers the town's early history and also explores the travails of the Yavapai, tracing their story from baskets, bows and arrows up to their current ownership of two casinos and the luxurious local Conference Center. The most popular section, the **Transportation Building**, holds a gorgeous Wells Fargo stagecoach, painted red with yellow wheels, which was in use – and held up by bandits – in Tombstone in 1881.

ARRIVAL AND INFORMATION

By bus Coconino/Yavapai Shuttle buses connect Prescott with Flagstaff (2 daily Mon–Fri, 1 on Sat; $25 one-way, $40 round-trip; ☎928 775 8929 or ☎888 440 8929, ⓦcoconinoyavapaishuttle.com), while Shuttle "U" runs here from Phoenix's Sky Harbor Airport ($30 one-way;

PRESCOTT

☎928 442 1000 or ☎800 304 6114, ⓦshuttleu.com).

Visitor centre 117 W Goodwin St, on Courthouse Plaza (Mon–Fri 9am–5pm, Sat & Sun 10am–2pm; ☎928 445 2000 or ☎800 266 7534, ⓦprescott.org).

ACCOMMODATION

For a small town, Prescott has an ideal range of **accommodation** options. Besides assorted historic **hotels** around the main square, several small-scale **B&Bs** lurk in Victorian homes in the surrounding streets. The usual chain motels can be found on the fringes, but it would be a shame to stay too far from the centre.

Hassayampa Inn 122 E Gurley St ☎928 778 9434 or ☎800 322 1927, ⓦhassayampainn.com. Grand 1920s hotel just off the square, offering plenty of Art Deco flourishes amid its overall Southwestern theme, and equipped with comfortable, individually styled guest rooms that vary considerably in size. The *Peacock Room*, open for all meals daily, serves upscale, expensive Continental cuisine. **$102**

Hotel St Michael 205 W Gurley St ☎928 776 1999 or ☎800 678 3757, ⓦstmichaelhotel.com. Atmospheric old downtown hotel – some say it's haunted – with a wide range of inexpensive rooms, all en suite, plus its own coffee bar and mall of antique and speciality stores. Rates include breakfast, and are at their cheapest on weekdays. **$69**

★ **The Motor Lodge** 503 S Montezuma St ☎928 717 0157, ⓦthemotorlodge.com. While the *Motor Lodge* might look like a vintage motel, its twelve individual en-suite cabins actually date from 1910. Playfully refurbished with colourful retro flourishes, equipped as a rule with gas fireplaces and/or private porches, they make an excellent and very memorable budget option. **$89**

Hotel Vendome 230 S Cortez St ☎928 776 0900, ⓦvendomehotel.com. Century-old lodging house, modernized in the ways that matter while retaining its period charm. Twenty en-suite rooms, spread over two storeys and sharing long verandas; rates include top-quality breakfasts. **$89**

EATING AND DRINKING

The streets around Prescott's Courthouse Square hold a plethora of places to **eat** and **drink** at reasonable prices. **Bars** are concentrated on Montezuma Street on its western side, in the block once known as **Whiskey Row**.

El Gato Azul 316 W Godwin St ☎928 445 1070, ⓦelgatoazulprescott.com. Actually bright yellow, this friendly little café with indoor and outdoor seating serves a wide-ranging Southwestern menu that draws on Spanish as well as Mexican traditions. A full Spanish paella costs $18, pork carnitas $17, but many diners come simply for the tasty $4–9 tapas. There's live jazz and acoustic music Thurs, Fri & Sun. Daily 11am–late.

Gurley Street Grill 230 W Gurley St ☎928 445 3388. Large, extremely popular restaurant, downhill from the centre, where several dining rooms cater to almost every taste, style, and budget, from foreign tourists to students on dates to farmers celebrating anniversaries. The menu includes chicken, ribs and steaks, as well as pizzas, pasta specials and stir-fries, all prepared to above-average standards, with most entrée prices well below $20. Daily 11am–late.

Lone Spur Cafe 106 W Gurley St ☎928 445 8202, ⓦthelonespur.com. Good old-fashioned Western diner, right on Courthouse Square and always busy in the daytime for massive pancake-and-eggs breakfasts, and burgers-and-steaks lunches. The daily lunch special costs just $10. Dinner options include a full rack of ribs ($21) or pork chops ($16). Mon–Thurs, Sat & Sun 8am–2pm, Fri 8am–2pm & 4.30–8pm.

Palace 120 S Montezuma St ☎928 442 9208, ⓦhistoricpalace.com. Majestic old saloon, complete with double swinging doors, was originally the centrepiece of Whiskey Row. Still a genuine Western bar, it now also serves $10–13 lunchtime salads and burgers as well as full meaty dinners for $18–27. Mon–Thurs & Sun 11am–9pm, Fri & Sat 11am–10pm.

Wickenburg

WICKENBURG, sixty miles southwest of Prescott and as far northwest of downtown Phoenix, is another former mining and ranching town now kept humming by tourism. It's only a little higher, and a little cooler, than Phoenix, so the main visitor season is in winter, between November and April.

5

Wickenburg stands beside the **Hassayampa River**, whose Apache name, meaning "river that runs upside down," refers to the fact that it often flows underground. This spot marks the "pumpkin patch" where Prussian prospector Henry Wickenburg built a mill in 1864 to process the gold he'd discovered in the Vulture Mountains, fifteen miles south. His **Vulture Mine** was seldom profitable, and finally closed down in 1942. By then, however, Wickenburg had established a successful sideline running **dude ranches**, where well-heeled Easterners could dabble with the Wild West lifestyle for a few carefree days.

In general, Wickenburg is spruce and prosperous, with little sense of a desert outpost, though the wooden sidewalks and false-front stores along **Frontier Street** in the heart of town must look much as they did in Wickenburg's heyday. You can still see the mesquite tree that served as the original town "jail"; miscreants were simply chained to its trunk.

Desert Caballeros Western Museum

21 N Frontier St · Mon–Sat 10am–5pm, Sun noon–4pm; closed Mon May–Aug · $9, under-18s free · ☎ 928 684 2272, ⓦ westernmuseum.org

For the full saga of Wickenburg's history, drop in at the **Desert Caballeros Western Museum**. As well as 1900s street scene, it features paintings by Remington and Russell, lots of sculptures of noble native American warriors, several little dioramas, masses of spurs and bits and hats and chaps, and all the barbed-wire you could want.

Vulture Mine

36610 N 355th Ave, 16 miles southwest of central Wickenburg · Sat 10am · $10, under-6s free · ⓦ vultureminetours.com

The long-abandoned workings of the **Vulture Mine** itself, which can only be visited on once-weekly guided tours, rear from the streets of the well-preserved ghost town of **Vulture City**. Stick to the walking trail as you wander round; the various buildings, which include a blacksmith's shop and the mine's head office, are not as sturdy as they appear.

INFORMATION   WICKENBURG

Visitor centre The friendly visitor centre, 216 N Frontier St (summer Mon–Fri 9am–5pm; winter Mon–Fri 9am–5pm, Sat 9am–2pm, Sun 10am–3pm; ☎ 928 684 5479, ⓦ outwickenburgway.com), hands out a sunny guide on local attractions.

ACCOMMODATION AND EATING

Best Western Rancho Grande 293 E Wickenburg Way ☎ 928 684 5445 or ☎ 800 854 7235, ⓦ bestwestern arizona.com. The most attractive of Wickenburg's conventional **motels**, part genuine adobe and part Spanish colonial mock-up, with good-sized rooms, some with kitchenettes, and a pool. **$75**

Flying E Ranch 2801 W Wickenburg Way ☎ 928 684 2690 or ☎ 888 684 2650, ⓦ flyingeranch.com. The only working cattle ranch in Wickenburg that still accepts paying guests spreads across twenty thousand acres. Rates include all meals in the central lodge (no alcohol served) but not riding; one 2hr ride costs $45. Nov–April only. **$325**

Joshua Forest Parkway

Northwest of Wickenburg, US-93 runs for 108 dramatic miles across some of Arizona's wildest and most scenic mountains, to meet I-40 twenty miles east of Kingman (see p.287). If you're heading up from Phoenix, this slow two-lane highway bears witness to just how much of the state remains wilderness. Apart from the hamlet of **NOTHING** – which might sound enticing on the map, but really is nothing, other than the home base of a towing company that rescues unfortunate stranded motorists – there's almost no sign of human life. Instead, the vegetation is the main source of interest, with saguaro and ocotillo **cactuses** scattered across the impressive rocky outcrops. These eastern fringes of the Mojave Desert are among the few places in Arizona where you'll encounter an abundance of **joshua trees** – hence the road's official designation as the **Joshua Forest Parkway**.

West of Flagstaff

5

Though the two hundred miles of I-40 that run **west from Flagstaff** to California are kept busy by traffic heading to, from, and between the Grand Canyon and Las Vegas, few towns along the way are especially interesting. However, most became reliant on tourism during the heyday of **Route 66**, and driving through any of them can bring on a frisson of that era's romance.

If you have the time to indulge your 1950s fantasies, then take the 120-mile side trip on the longest surviving section of what John Steinbeck called the "**Mother Road**," which starts at **Seligman**, loops back down to **Kingman**, and then crosses wild and mountainous country to the ghost town of **Oatman**. Otherwise, it makes little difference where or even whether you choose to take a break from the interstate.

Williams

Although Flagstaff is generally regarded as the obvious base for visitors to the Grand Canyon's South Rim, **WILLIAMS**, 32 miles west, is in fact the closest interstate town to the national park. While it can't boast half the charm or pizazz of its neighbour, it's a nice enough little place, filled with Route 66-era motels and diners and retaining a certain individuality despite the stream of tourists. Its setting, cupped in a high grassy valley amid pine-covered hills, helps; the largest peak, the 9264-foot **Bill Williams Mountain** to the south, was named for pioneer trapper and "mountain man" Bill Williams (1787–1849), and gave its name in turn to the town, founded thirty years after his death.

Like Flagstaff, Williams originally based both its architecture and its economy on the ponderosas of the surrounding forests. Since 1901, however, when the Santa Fe Railroad first connected it with the canyon rim, sixty miles due north, Williams has lived off tourism. Though the railroad went out of business in 1968, it reopened in 1989 as the **Grand Canyon Railway**, promoted as a fun ride rather than a serious means of transportation. Most people who spend the night in Williams are here to take the morning train up to the canyon.

Highlights of Williams' annual calendar are **Rendezvous Days**, on Memorial Day weekend in late May, when locals dress up as pioneer "buckskinners," and the Labor Day **rodeo**.

Route 66 and Railroad Avenue

Williams holds a definite romantic appeal as the very last town on the old **Route 66** to have been bypassed by the I-40 interstate. Until October 13, 1984, when Bobby Troup of (*Get Your Kicks On*) *Route 66* fame fronted a closing ceremony, the only stoplight on the interstate between Chicago and Los Angeles stood outside the Williams visitor centre. To this day, the centre of town remains a major rendezvous for bikers, and on summer Saturdays especially it's usually thronging with Harley-Davidsons.

Much of the former Route 66 frontage remains barely changed, with quirky antiques stores selling vintage memorabilia alongside Native American crafts and jewellery. However, while it's fun to explore the central blocks along the two main one-way streets – Route 66, running west to east, is paralleled by the east–west **Railroad Avenue** – an hour's evening or morning stroll is enough; Williams is not really a place to spend the day, just the night before or after you visit the Grand Canyon.

ARRIVAL, INFORMATION AND TOURS	WILLIAMS
By train Amtrak's *Southwest Chief* train calls in at Williams Junction, three miles east of town, twice daily, heading east at 3.50am in summer, and west at 9.33pm. The *Grand*	*Canyon Railway Hotel* runs free connecting shuttle buses into town. **Visitor centre** 200 W Railroad Ave, near the railroad depot

5

(daily: summer 8am–6.30pm; winter 8am–5pm; ☎928 635 1418 or ☎800 863 0546, ⓦexperiencewilliams.com). Also holds an entertaining museum of neighbourhood history, and covers the nearby national forests as well.

Grand Canyon Railway Schedules and prices for the Grand Canyon Railway (☎303 843 8724 or ☎800 843 8724, ⓦthetrain.com), which sets off daily, usually at 9.30am, from the Williams Depot in the centre of town, appear on p.315.

Guided tours Marvelous Marv's Tours run daily guided van tours of the Grand Canyon South Rim from Williams, with the $10 adult rate including park admission (☎928 707 0291, ⓦmarvelousmarv.com).

ACCOMMODATION

Although the *Grand Canyon Railway Hotel* is Williams' leading accommodation option, plenty of alternatives exist. The downtown streets are lined with **vintage motels** as well as the odd **B&B**, while national chains congregate near the interstate exits at either end of town.

Best Western Plus Inn of Williams 2600 W Route 66 ☎928 635 4400 or ☎800 635 4445, ⓦbestwestern williams.com. Spacious, well-equipped motel-resort, perched near I-40 exit 161 at the west end of town, and generally a cut above usual chain standards. Large comfortable rooms plus a pool, hot tub and on-site restaurant. $190

Canyon Motel & RV Park 1900 E Rodeo Rd ☎928 635 9371, ⓦthecanyonmotel.com. The word "motel" hardly does this restored Route 66 relic justice. Perched on the edge of the forest east of downtown, it offers accommodation in individual brick cottages and, best of all, converted railroad cars; two 1929 cabooses sleep 5–6 each, while a larger carriage holds three separate en-suite units. Don't expect luxury, but it's a much more memorable experience than just another highway motel, and there are also fifty RV spaces. RV sites $38, motel rooms $79, carriage rooms $105, caboose $159

Grand Canyon Hotel 145 W Route 66 ☎928 635 1419, ⓦthegrandcanyonhotel.com. Not to be confused with the much larger *Railway Hotel*, this attractively restored downtown "boutique hotel" offers individual beds in a clean, crisp dorm, plus themed private doubles with and without en-suite facilities. Dorm $35, shared-bath room $65, en-suite room $73

Grand Canyon Railway Hotel 1 Fray Marcos Blvd ☎928 635 4010 or ☎800 843 8724, ⓦthetrain.com /hotel. The Grand Canyon Railway's flagship hotel opened in 1908 as the *Fray Marcos*. Rebuilt and renamed, it lacks character, though the large open lobby is pleasant enough, and there's also an indoor pool, spa, and saloon. All rooms provide two queen beds. $169

The Lodge on Route 66 200 E Route 66 ☎877 563 4366, ⓦthelodgeonroute66.com. Restored Route 66 motor-court motel in the heart of town, with spotless and very comfortable rooms and friendly management. $90

Red Garter Bed & Bakery 137 W Railroad Ave ☎928 635 1484 or ☎800 328 1484, ⓦredgarter.com. Plush four-room B&B in a former downtown bordello, serving fresh-baked breakfasts from its own downstairs bakery. Look for discounted rates online. Closed mid-Dec to mid-Feb. $135

Red Lake Hostel AZ-64, 9 miles north of Williams ☎928 635 4753 or ☎800 581 4753, ⓦgrand canyontexaco.com. Adjoining a gas station at a lonely curve on AZ-64, this bright red converted motel offers very rudimentary accommodation; some of its tiny bare rooms serve as dorms, with two beds rented individually, others hold a double bed. All other facilities are in a separate building. Also tent and RV camping. Dorms $20, RVs $25, private room $40

EATING

Williams' **restaurant** selection is frankly disappointing. A few spots conjure up the feel of its Route 66 heyday, but nowhere serves interesting food. That said, you will find filling meals and affable places to eat.

Cafe 326 326 W Route 66 ☎928 635 0777, ⓦamericanflyercoffeeco.com. Funky, friendly café that serves espressos, juices and pastries, with a couple of outdoor tables and free wi-fi. Daily 7am–7pm.

Dara Thai Grand Canyon Hotel, 145 W Route 66 ☎928 635 2201, ⓦthegrandcanyonhotel.com. Dependable outpost of Flagstaff's longstanding Thai restaurant, serving good Thai dishes for $8 at lunch, $10 at dinner. Mon–Sat 11am–2pm & 5–9pm.

Pancho McGillicuddy's 141 W Railroad Ave ☎928 635 4150, ⓦvivapanchos.com. Popular but very average Mexican cantina, housed in an attractive tin-ceilinged building downtown, with its own authentic-looking saloon. South-of-the border standards like flautas, tostadas, tamales or carnitas, cost just over $10, while mixed platters go for $16, and you can also get steaks and grills. Daily 11am–10pm.

★ **Pine Country Restaurant** 107 N Grand Canyon Blvd ☎928 635 9718, ⓦpinecountryrestaurant.com. Traditional, very central diner with friendly waitstaff, where the food is actually pretty good, and you can have a full dinner, like pork chops or country-fried steak, for $11. An enticing glass cabinet is stacked with each day's fresh-baked delights; slices of the irresistible homemade pies – the menu lists around forty, in flavours like raspberry cream cheese – go for $4.59. Daily 6.30am–9pm.

Ash Fork

The ranching community of **ASH FORK**, stretched along a brief curving fragment of Route 66 north of the interstate twenty miles west of Williams, is smaller, less picturesque and far less involved in catering to travellers. By this point I-40 has pulled clear of the forests, so downtown Ash Fork is constructed not from timber but using the yellowish sandstone that's the basis of the local economy – it calls itself the "flagstone capital of the US". While the major motel chains haven't bothered to set up shop, Ash Fork holds a few rundown, homespun lodging alternatives.

ACCOMMODATION · ASH FORK

Ash Fork Inn 859 Route 66 ☎928 637 2514. Sprawling, reasonably spruced up and rather pink old motel, at the west end of town near I-40 exit 144. The simple rooms can be cold in winter, but otherwise they're not a bad deal. $65

Seligman

Starting a few miles west of Ash Fork, the old Route 66 parallels its modern replacement at a discreet distance for the twenty or so miles to **SELIGMAN**. This dusty desert halt now feels more than a little stranded, a mile or two north of the interstate, but if you're in the mood to be seduced by its kitsch diners and drive-ins, it makes a mildly diverting stop in a long day's drive. Every business strives to outdo the others with eye-catching displays – mannequins of Elvis and Marilyn waving from oddball parked vehicles and the like – and the passing traffic is worth watching, too, with all kinds of vintage roadsters making pilgrimages along the "Mother Road."

You might even choose to follow Route 66's original course as it curves northwards, through a dozen fading villages and part of the **Hualapai reservation** (see p.326), and back south to Kingman. That's a total drive of 88 miles, as opposed to the dreary 65-mile run west on I-40. It also provides access to **Havasu Canyon**, in the depths of the Grand Canyon, one of the Southwest's least-known marvels (see p.320).

ACCOMMODATION AND EATING · SELIGMAN

★ **Canyon Lodge** 114 E Chino Ave ☎928 422 3255 or ☎800 700 5054, ⓦroute66canyonlodge.com. From the outside, this blue two-storey structure on Route 66 might look like just another highway motel; each room, though, has been lovingly refurbished as a tribute to a different 1950s theme. The Elvis and Marilyn rooms are especially recommended. Rates include breakfast. $55

Delgadillo's Snow Cap 301 E Chino Ave ☎928 422 3291. Seligman's wackiest local diner, with a fine assortment of vintage jalopies and roadsters parked outside. Every malt or $5 burger comes with a side order of outrageous puns and put-ons. Daily 10am–6pm; closed mid-Nov–Feb.

Kingman

With a population of over thirty thousand, **KINGMAN**, 65 miles west of Seligman and thirty miles short of California, ranks second to Flagstaff among Arizona's I-40 towns. As all traffic between Phoenix or the Grand Canyon and **Las Vegas** – a mere hundred miles northwest on US-93 – is obliged to pass this way, Kingman's thirty-plus motels stay busy year-round. The best that can be said for it, however, is that it's not particularly ugly – apart from the long sprawl beside the railroad tracks north of the

5

interstate – and it's not lifeless. Apart from that, it's a humdrum pit stop with a slight tinge of Route 66 quaintness.

Kingman's main street, curving alongside the railroad tracks, is named in honour of native son **Andy Devine**, the actor who drove the eponymous *Stagecoach* in John Ford's 1939 movie. As a local brochure puts it, "there must be somebody who hasn't heard of Andy Devine, but that person sure doesn't live in Kingman." 1939 was clearly a big year for Kingman: Carole Lombard and Clark Gable were married here on March 29.

Route 66 Museum

Powerhouse, 120 W Andy Devine Ave · Daily 9am–4.30pm · $5, same ticket as Mohave Museum · ☎ 928 753 9889, Ⓦ gokingman.com

Upstairs in Kingman's Powerhouse, which also holds the local visitor centre, the **Route 66 Museum** is much larger than it might seem at first glance, and to be honest considerably better too. Displays cover the original surveying and construction of Route 66 in these parts, with several fine old roadsters to admire, and good details on John Steinbeck's description of the Dustbowl era in *The Grapes of Wrath*. Other exhibits illustrate mining in Oatman and Chloride, and there's even an old organ you can play.

Mohave Museum of History & Arts

400 W Beale St · Mon–Fri 9am–5pm, Sat 1–5pm · $5, same ticket as Route 66 Museum · ☎ 928 753 3195, Ⓦ mohavemuseum.org

The **Mohave Museum of History & Arts** explores the various unlikely components of Mohave County's heritage, including the movie career of local boy Andy Devine and the culture and basketwork of the Hualapai. For no obvious reason, there's also a display of pictures of every American First Lady.

ARRIVAL AND INFORMATION

KINGMAN

By train Kingman's central Amtrak station still welcomes trains between Flagstaff and LA, but only at unearthly hours of the night

By bus Greyhound buses, between Phoenix and Las Vegas as well as east–west, use a terminal near the interstate at

3264 E Andy Devine Ave (☎ 928 757 8400).

Visitor centre Kingman's large Powerhouse visitor centre, at the western edge of downtown at 120 W Andy Devine Ave (daily 8am–5pm; ☎ 928 753 6106 or ☎ 866 427 7866, Ⓦ gokingman.com), also sells lots of Route 66 memorabilia.

ACCOMMODATION

Granted that you're unlikely to spend more than one night in Kingman – or linger in the morning, either – its ordinary but inexpensive **motels** should easily meet your needs.

Best Western A Wayfarer's Inn 2815 E Andy Devine Ave ☎ 928 753 6271 or ☎ 800 548 5695, Ⓦ bestwesternarizona.com. Upscale hundred-room chain property, a couple of miles northeast of town near I-40 exit 53, charging reasonable rates for its smart if anonymous rooms, and offering a pool and indoor spa. **$105**

Hualapai Mountain Park 6250 Hualapai Mountain Rd ☎ 928 681 5700 or ☎ 877 757 0915, Ⓦ mcparks.com. This beautiful county-run park, in the hills 15 miles southeast of Kingman, offers around twenty rental cabins,

which have fireplaces and en-suite bathrooms, but you bring your own bedding (and note that rates rise at weekends) plus tent and RV camping. **Tent sites $15**, **RVs $25**, **cabins $55**

Quality Inn Kingman 1400 E Andy Devine Ave ☎ 928 753 4747 or ☎ 800 228 5151, Ⓦ qualityinn.com. Standard motel half a mile from downtown, with small but adequate rooms, which offers a bit of character via a strong Route 66 theme, including a retro breakfast room and outdoor vintage gas pumps. **$46**

EATING

Most Kingman **restaurants** play on the Route 66 angle. It's all too spread out to wander around comparing menus, but hop in your car and you'll find something.

Dambar & Steakhouse 1960 E Andy Devine Ave ☎ 928 753 3523, Ⓦ facebook.com/DambarSteakhouse.

Classic Western steakhouse atop the hill, all sawdust and bare timber, serving grilled and barbecued ribs and chicken, as well as massive steaks. Main dishes around $20 at dinner, more like $7–12 at lunch. Daily 11am–10pm.

Mr D'z Route 66 Diner 105 E Andy Devine Ave ☎928 718 0066, ⓦmrdzrt66diner.com. Loving recreation of a classic Route 66 roadhouse, across from the visitor centre and bursting with memorabilia, neon and lurid moulded trimmings. Good burgers and shakes, malts and floats, and fries with everything, with pretty much all of it costing under $10. Daily 7am–9pm.

Redneck's Southern Pit BBQ 420 E Beale St ☎928 757 8227, ⓦredneckssouthernpitbbq.com. Large portions of tangy Southern BBQ, ordered cafeteria style and enjoyed in a family atmosphere. Beef, pork or chicken plates cost under $10, ribs up to $22 for a full rack. Mon–Sat 11am–9pm.

Chloride

Fifteen miles northwest of Kingman, as US-93 tears through the flat, prosaically named **Detrital Valley** toward Las Vegas, a paved road climbs away into the mountains to the right. Its goal, the former silver mining centre of **CHLORIDE** four miles up, was established in 1864 and boasts Arizona's oldest still-functional post office. As well as silver, vast quantities of gold, copper, lead and turquoise were also extracted from the roadless **Cerbat Mountains** beyond, but Chloride these days lives by its wits, exploiting its ramshackle Wild West appearance to attract tourists.

Some of Chloride's erstwhile neighbours – such as **Cerbat** and **Mineral Park** – have become genuine **ghost towns**.

Bullhead City and Laughlin

While both the old Route 66 and the interstate head southwest from Kingman, Hwy-68 barrels due west for thirty miles to **BULLHEAD CITY** on the Colorado River. Built as a work camp for the construction of nearby Davis Dam, Bullhead City somehow survived the dam's completion in 1953 and is prospering these days due to its proximity to the casinos of **LAUGHLIN**, Nevada, just across the river.

In terms of temperature, **Bullhead** is the hottest town in the US, exceeding 120°F day after day each summer. In most other respects, however, it's not the least bit hot. Thirty thousand people now live along a ten mile riverfront stretch of Hwy-95; why on earth you'd join them, even for a night, is hard to imagine.

Not that **Laughlin** is much better, despite the endless hype of its tourist authorities. If you've never been to Las Vegas, you may well be impressed by the dozen or so huge, glittering **casinos** that jostle for position beside the Colorado. They lack the panache of their Vegas counterparts, however, as well as the will to cater to anyone other than hardened gamblers. The only real reason to come here is that **accommodation** rates are so cheap, though it is also fun to take a **paddle-wheeler cruise** on the Colorado, costing about $10 for a little over an hour, from either the *Riverside Resort* or the *Edgewater Hotel*.

INFORMATION   LAUGHLIN

Visitor centre 1555 S Casino Drive (Mon–Fri 8am–4.30pm; ☎702 298 3321 or ☎800 452 8445, ⓦvisitlaughlin.com).

ACCOMMODATION AND EATING

At least eight casinos in Laughlin offer well over a thousand **rooms** each, with weekday rates that can drop below $30 per room. Each holds several **restaurants** ranging from buffet joints whose all-you-can-eat specials start at under $5, to steakhouses and dimly lit Italian schmoozeries. It's really not worth eating anywhere other than where you're staying, however – it takes a long time to walk from one casino to the next, and you'll only find the same bland choices you had before you set off.

Don Laughlin's Riverside Resort Hotel 1650 S Casino Drive ☎702 298 2535 or ☎800 227 3849, ⓦriversideresort.com. Laughlin's oldest casino traces its ancestry all the way back to an eight-room motel that opened in 1966. It has consistently kept pace with its neighbours, and now holds over 1400 rooms, plus assorted restaurants and lounges. Mon–Thurs & Sun $49, Fri & Sat $79

Golden Nugget 2300 S Casino Drive ☎702 298 7222

5

or ☎ 800 950 7700, ⓦ goldennugget.com/laughlin. The upscale, glittering *Golden Nugget* counts as Laughlin's top-of-the-range lodging option, with smart river-view rooms and a pool by the Colorado, and the classiest selection of restaurants around. Mon–Thurs & Sun $30, Fri & Sat $60

Oatman

If you're heading west towards **Needles**, California, from Kingman, but don't mind how quickly you get there, following Route 66 over the **Black Mountains** to the south makes an enjoyable alternative route. It also has the bonus of passing through one of Arizona's most appealing **ghost towns**, the former gold-mining community of **OATMAN**. In total it's a drive of fifty miles to Needles if you head this way, as opposed to 64 on the interstate, but it's a long, slow drive, with lots of tricky mountain bends.

The eastern approaches to the mountains, at the edge of the Sacramento Valley, are guarded by a splendid solitary rock pinnacle that was a beacon to early travellers. Following a laborious climb up to a gap between the peaks, the road twists down the far side and eventually enters Oatman itself. Established in 1906, Oatman went bust in 1942, but a second career as a movie backdrop and tourist stop-off has ensured that it's never truly been abandoned.

Gift and craft stores now occupy most of the false-front structures along Oatman's raised wooden boardwalk. The streets are still roamed by semi-wild burros descended from animals left by the miners; stores sell carrots, the only food you're allowed to offer them.

Lake Havasu City

Forty miles southwest of Kingman on I-40, ten miles from the California border, a twenty-mile detour south on Hwy-95 brings you to the most incongruous sight of the Southwestern deserts. At **LAKE HAVASU CITY**, the old grey stones of **London Bridge** reach out across the stagnant waters of the dammed Colorado River. However, it's not often you see anything quite as **boring** in Arizona as London Bridge; unless you've never seen a bridge before, it's one to miss.

Lake Havasu City has an undeniable attraction for the parched urbanites of cities such as Phoenix, who flock to fish on the lake or charge up and down in motorboats and on jet skis, but it holds minimal appeal for travellers from further afield. Many of its copious clubs, bars and restaurants used to be heavily London-themed, but these

---

LONDON BRIDGE IS FALLING DOWN

Californian chainsaw manufacturer **Robert P. McCulloch** moved his factory to the remote Arizona desert in 1964, to try out his new sideline in outboard motors on Lake Havasu. Three years later, he heard Johnny Carson mention that London Bridge was up for sale; in the words of the nursery rhyme, it really was falling down, unable to cope with all those newfangled automobiles. McCulloch bought it for $2,460,000, and painstakingly shipped ten thousand numbered blocks of granite across the Atlantic. Lacking anything for the bridge to span, he dug a channel that turned a riverbank promontory into the island of **Pittsburg Point**.

Despite the jibes that McCulloch thought he was buying London's picturesque Tower Bridge – the turreted one that opens in the middle – his investment in London Bridge, merely the latest in a long line of London Bridges and dating only from 1831, paid off handsomely. The bridge now ranks second among Arizona's tourist attractions, after the Grand Canyon, and Lake Havasu City has become a major vacation resort and retirement centre, with a population of over fifty thousand. For its part, London Bridge is listed in the **Guinness Book of Records** as the largest antique ever sold.

5

days it's styled more like a generic tropical resort. What's more, between March and June, it's almost permanently filled with students on **Spring Break**, drinking and partying around the clock.

English Village and London Bridge Beach

Only when you cross the bridge onto the island, and look back, do you appreciate how large Lake Havasu City has grown, sprawling up the gentle slope away from the river. Most of those broad hillside streets are lined with condo blocks and minor malls; the only place tourists bother to visit is the **English Village**, a mock-Tudor shopping mall, which also holds a handful of riverview restaurants, at the base of the bridge. Several operators offer short **river cruises** from the quayside of the English Village, and jet ski rentals are also widely available.

Out on the island, if you head south from the bridge you'll soon come to **London Bridge Beach**. The "beach" is more grit than sand, and few people swim from it. With its bizarre fringe of date palms, however, and its panorama of weird desert buttes and the Chemehuevi Mountains, it does at least linger in the memory.

INFORMATION	LAKE HAVASU

Visitor centre 422 English Village (daily 9am–5pm; ☎ 928 855 5655, ⓦ golakehavasu.com).

ACCOMMODATION AND EATING

Heat Hotel 1420 W McCulloch Blvd ☎ 928 854 2833 or ☎ 888 898 4328, ⓦ heathotel.com. Lake Havasu isn't really the sort of place where you expect to find a boutique hotel, but there's really no faulting the stylish contemporary taste with which the *Heat Hotel*, on the island across from town, has been kitted out. Most rooms have private bridge-view patios. Expect to pay a heavy premium at weekends. **$129**

London Bridge Resort 1477 Queen's Bay ☎ 928 855 0888 or ☎ 866 331 9231, ⓦ londonbridgeresort.com. Once you get past the lobby, which is all but filled by a gilt replica stagecoach, this extravagant all-suite resort feels more like a beach hotel, with a huge pool with waterslides, and lots of lake frontage too. Rates are usually higher on weekends. **$129**

Mudshark Brewing Co 210 Swanson Ave ☎ 928 453 2981, ⓦ mudsharkbeer.com. Buzzing brewpub, not far south of the bridge on the mainland (with no lake views), with a decent selection of its own beers, and a menu of burgers, pasta and pizzas, typically priced at $9–12.50. Mon–Thurs & Sun 11am–9pm, Fri & Sat 11am–10pm.

Shugrue's 1425 W McCulloch Blvd ☎ 928 453 1400, ⓦ shugrues.com. The best place to combine eating with views over the bridge and lake, across from the mainland in the Island Fashion Mall, *Shugrue's* is a traditional, upscale American restaurant. Lunchtime salads, sandwiches and daily specials cost around $12, while in the evening you can get fresh halibut or tuna for around $25, and rack of lamb for $32. Mon–Thurs & Sun 11am–9.30pm, Fri & Sat 11am–10.30pm.

The Grand Canyon

299 The South Rim

320 The Havasupai reservation

326 The Hualapai reservation: Grand Canyon West

328 The road between the rims

331 The North Rim

335 The Arizona Strip

SUNSET AT DESERT VIEW

The Grand Canyon

Although almost five million people come to see the Grand Canyon of the Colorado every year, it remains beyond the grasp of the human imagination. No photograph, or statistics, can prepare you for such vastness. At more than one mile deep, it's an inconceivable abyss; varying from four to eighteen miles wide; an endless expanse of bewildering shapes and colours, glaring desert brightness and impenetrable shadow, stark promontories and soaring, never-to-be-climbed sandstone pinnacles. While no one is disappointed with their first stunning sight of the chasm, visitors often struggle to understand what can appear as a remote and impassive spectacle.

They race frantically from viewpoint to viewpoint, constantly imagining that the next one will be the "best," the place from which the whole thing will finally make sense. The secret to transcending that initial frantic excitement is to slow down, to appreciate whatever small portion of the canyon may be displayed in front of you at any one moment, and to allow enough time for the bigger picture to develop. And visiting the Grand Canyon need not be a passive experience. In addition to touring the **overlooks** along each rim, the views from all of which shift and change unceasingly from dawn to dusk, you can **hike** down into the depths; ride down on a **mule**; hover above the canyon in a **helicopter**; raft through the **whitewater rapids** of the river itself; spend a night at **Phantom Ranch** on the canyon floor; or swim beneath the waterfalls of the idyllic **Havasupai reservation**.

Mapping and defining precisely what constitutes the "Grand Canyon" has always been controversial; **Grand Canyon National Park** covers a relatively small proportion of the greater Grand Canyon area. Only in the past forty years has it included the full 277-mile length of the Colorado River from Lees Ferry in the east to Grand Wash Cliffs near Lake Mead in the west, and even now it's restricted for most of that way to the narrow strip of the inner gorge. Ranchers whose animals graze in the federal forests to either side, mining companies eager to exploit the mineral wealth hidden in the rocks, engineers seeking to divert the river to irrigate the deserts, and the Native Americans who live in the canyon, have combined to minimize the size of the park.

The vast majority of visitors arrive at the **South Rim** – it's much easier to get to, holds far more facilities (mainly at **Grand Canyon Village**, inside the park), and remains open year round. Another lodge and campground are located at the **North Rim**, which by virtue of its isolation can be a lot more atmospheric, but at one thousand feet higher this entire area is usually closed by snow from November until mid-May. Few people visit both rims on a single trip; to get from one to the other demands either a three-day hike down one side of the canyon and up the other, or a 215-mile drive. On both rims, the main activity consists of gazing over the gorge from lookouts spaced along the

Park admission p.207
The formation of the Grand Canyon p.298
Grand Canyon tours p.300
The return of the condor p.304
Sunset and sunrise p.306
Hiking in the Grand Canyon p.310
Backcountry camping p.314
The Havasupai p.322

Havasupai horses, helicopters and hiking tours p.324
The sheer cost of visiting Grand Canyon West p.327
The Skywalk falls to earth p.327
Flying to Grand Canyon West p.328
The extraordinary saga of Colorado City p.336

A VIEW OF WOTAN'S THRONE FROM CAPE ROYAL

Highlights

❶ Shoshone Point Little-known viewpoint, accessible only on foot, that feels a world away from all the other South Rim overlooks. **See p.306**

❷ Desert View Watchtower Circular mock-Puebloan tower, blending into the rocks at the east end of the South Rim, that provides stunning canyon views. **See p.308**

❸ The Bright Angel Trail Deservedly the most popular hiking trail within the park; a superb introduction to life below the rim. **See p.310**

❹ The South Kaibab Trail This hair-raising descent to the canyon floor offers the finest day-hikes in the park. **See p.313**

❺ El Tovar Hotel The jewel of Grand Canyon Village, this historic hotel provides the South Rim's best food and lodging. **See p.317**

❻ Havasu Falls Astonishing, lush turquoise waterfalls buried deep within the canyon on the Havasupai reservation. **See p.324**

❼ Cape Royal The perfect vantage point from which to appreciate the overall shape of the canyon. **See p.332**

❽ Toroweap Overlook The remotest canyon viewpoint within the national park offers unique views into the Granite Gorge. **See p.337**

HIGHLIGHTS ARE MARKED ON THE MAP ON P.296

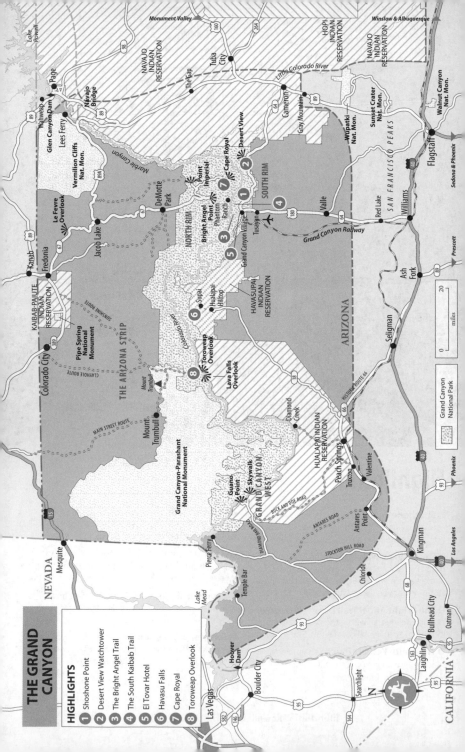

THE GRAND CANYON

HIGHLIGHTS

1. Shoshone Point
2. Desert View Watchtower
3. The Bright Angel Trail
4. The South Kaibab Trail
5. El Tovar Hotel
6. Havasu Falls
7. Cape Royal
8. Toroweap Overlook

PARK ADMISSION

Admission to Grand Canyon National Park, valid for seven days on either rim, costs $25 for one private, noncommercial vehicle and all its passengers, or $12 per pedestrian or cyclist. All the park-service **passes** detailed on p.36 are sold and valid.

For an even more detailed account of the entire Grand Canyon region, see the **Rough Guide to the Grand Canyon**, also by Greg Ward.

6

canyon-edge roads. In the 1920s the average visitor stayed for two or three weeks, whereas these days it's more like two or three hours – of which forty minutes are spent actually looking at the canyon.

If you're visiting the Grand Canyon as part of a longer Southwest itinerary, you may be wondering whether you "should" visit both rims, or which rim is "better." It really depends on how much time you have and what time of year it is. Though wilderness enthusiasts tend to find the summer crowds at the South Rim unbearable, even there it's possible to escape the throng, and there's great scope for day-hiking. The North Rim is convenient to Zion and Bryce parks and northeast Arizona and has nicer accommodation options. It's probably best to choose whichever rim fits in with your planned route, and not to feel you ought to see the other one as well.

Brief history

It may look forbidding, but the Grand Canyon is teeming with life – sheep and rabbits, eagles and vultures, mountain lions, and, of course, spiders, scorpions and snakes all thrive here. The earliest signs of any **human** presence are twig figurines of animals from around 2000 BC, found hidden in caves in the canyon walls and probably created to ensure successful hunting. Remains of later dwellings built by the **Ancestral Puebloans** are scattered throughout the canyon – the most accessible now is **Tusayan Ruin** (see p.307). A separate tribal group, the **Havasupai** (see p.322), arrived around 1300 AD.

The Spaniards arrive

In 1540 – less than twenty years after Cortés conquered the Aztec of Mexico – the first **Spaniards** reached the Southwest. At the Hopi mesas, a detachment of Coronado's company were told of a great river not far west, inhabited by people with very large bodies (presumably the Havasupai, who tend to be significantly bigger than the Hopi). A small party, led by **García López de Cárdenas**, was despatched to investigate. Their Hopi guides led them to a spot somewhere near Grandview Point, but chose not to reveal the trails down to the river. The Spaniards spent three days on the South Rim, only appreciating the scale of the canyon after an abortive attempt to reach the river. They identified the Colorado as being the Tíson or "Firebrand" River, up which a simultaneous naval expedition was attempting to sail (it managed 225 miles, reaching what's now the site of the Hoover Dam).

Mapping the canyon

When jurisdiction over the Grand Canyon passed from Mexico to the United States in 1850, it had never been surveyed and did not even have a fixed **name**. To the Havasupai, it was *Wikatata* ("Rough Rim"); Spanish maps showed it as *Río Muy Grande* ("Very Big River"); and trappers and prospectors knew it as the Big Cañon. The name Grand Canyon, first used on a map in 1868, was popularized by the one-armed Civil War veteran **John Wesley Powell**, whose expeditions along the fearsome and uncharted Colorado in 1869 and 1871–72 – see p.401 – captured public imagination.

Mining, logging and the growth of tourism

As the Grand Canyon was being recognized as the most extraordinary natural wonder in the US, American settlers arrived nearby in ever greater numbers. Tensions have

6

THE FORMATION OF THE GRAND CANYON

Although the Grand Canyon could be called the world's clearest geological textbook, scientists continue to argue over how to read the story written in the stone. Layer upon layer of different rocks, readily distinguished by colour, and each with its own fossil record, recede down into the canyon and back through time, until the riverbed lays bare some of the oldest exposed rocks on earth. Almost all the successive strata of sandstone and limestone were deposited during periods when the entire region was submerged beneath shallow primeval seas. The bottom layer, the two-billion-year-old **Vishnu Schist**, is so ancient that it contains no fossils; it dates back to the Precambrian era, when life had barely begun.

That same tale of sedimentation, of course, holds true for much of the planet. Two major factors transformed what, until five million years ago, was an unremarkable landscape into the Grand Canyon. First of all, the chronic shortage of rain in this desert area prevented the growth of vegetation to bind the brittle surface together. Secondly, there was the fast-flowing **Colorado River**, cascading down from the Rocky Mountains with a gradient over 25 times steeper than the Mississippi. In full flood, charged with mighty boulders, it can blast deep crevices into the earth.

However, a crucial mystery remains. The Colorado Plateau is not flat at this point; it's an enormous hill, known to the Paiute Indians as the **Kaibab**, or mountain with no peak, which slopes southwards from a ridge that runs roughly a dozen miles north of the North Rim. Thus the Colorado has eaten away a chunk of the hillside, around a third of the way up the southern slope – which explains why the North Rim is a thousand feet higher than the South. Why, or how, the Colorado River cuts straight through that hill, rather than flowing around it, has long perplexed geologists. The hypothesis currently in favour, "**stream piracy**," suggests that until five million years ago, the river did indeed skirt the Kaibab – along some unknown course – but was then "captured" by another river and began to flow through it instead. That may have occurred when a powerful stream, at the head of its own canyon, cut so far back that it breached the barrier that separated it from the Colorado. The Colorado then rushed through, abandoning its own course and usurping this alternative channel.

Crudely speaking, while the Colorado is responsible for the **depth** of the canyon – and continues to scour its way deeper – it did little to create its **width**, which owes more to flash-flooding along its tributary streams and extreme cycles of heat and cold. Vast slabs of stone are chiselled away when water that trickles into cracks in exposed rock later freezes and expands, thereby sculpting the fantastic pyramids and mesas that tower above the central gorge. Some layers of rock are much harder than others; thus the solid Tapeats Sandstone of the **Tonto Platform**, a mile-wide shelf above the river that runs through most of the national park, was left behind when the weaker Bright Angel Shale above it eroded away. Because the general slope of the Kaibab runs from north to south, rain that falls north of the canyon flows down toward the gorge, while rainfall to the south flows away. As a result, the North Rim is deeply cut by tributaries and pushed back further from the Colorado, while the lower South Rim is much more regular.

The most striking features were named for their supposed resemblance to the great temples of India and China – **Brahma Temple**, **Shiva Temple**, **Vishnu Temple** and so on – by Clarence Dutton, a student of comparative religion who wrote the first Geological Survey report on the canyon in 1881. The tradition was followed by later cartographers such as François Matthes, who named **Krishna Shrine** and **Walhalla Plateau**.

arisen ever since between this new permanent population, determined to survive in such an unforgiving environment, and visitors hoping to find unspoiled wilderness. Broadly speaking, **logging** and **grazing** interests retain control of the plateau forests, while in the canyon itself most attempts at **mining** were defeated by the difficulty of the terrain, and **tourism** soon proved a far more lucrative proposition.

When the **railroad** first crossed northern Arizona in 1882, visitors were taken by stagecoach from the nearest station to the Grand Canyon, at **Peach Springs**, to stay at the *Diamond Creek Hotel* by the river. With the growth of the timber towns to the east, that site soon declined; by the 1890s, **Flagstaff** was the main terminus, connected with the canyon by three weekly stages. The railroad reached the canyon itself, via a branch line from **Williams**, in 1901. That triggered the growth of **Grand Canyon**

Village, built by a subsidiary of the Santa Fe Railroad. The Fred Harvey Company's grand *El Tovar Hotel* – still the showpiece canyon-edge lodging – opened in January 1905, and its early marketing strategies influence the experience of Canyon visitors to this day. Following an internal memo to "get some Indians to the Canyon at once," the Hopi House souvenir store was built, modelled on the Pueblo village of Old Oraibi (see p.69) and staffed with Hopi craftspeople. Similarly, Navajo weavers were exhorted to produce rugs to suit tourist tastes, using previously unfavoured "earth" colours such as brown. Pseudo-Pueblo architecture became the dominant theme, with a single architect, **Mary Jane Colter**, designing such structures as Hermit's Rest (1914), the Desert Watchtower (1932), and *Bright Angel Lodge* (1935).

6

A national park

Late nineteenth-century proposals to create a **Grand Canyon National Park** aroused vigorous local opposition. In due course, however, naturalist **John Muir** – who declared the Grand Canyon to be "unearthly … as if you had found it after death, on some other star" – found a powerful ally in President **Theodore Roosevelt**. Only entitled to protect sites of historical, rather than geological, interest, Roosevelt used the pretext of preserving Ancestral Puebloan ruins to proclaim Grand Canyon National Monument in 1908. Arizona politicians finally came round to the idea after Arizona achieved statehood in 1912. Even then, by the time the boundaries of the Grand Canyon National Park were fixed in 1919, they had trimmed away large tracts of grazing land. The new park covered around 1000 square miles and included just 56 miles of the actual canyon.

Meanwhile, tourism to the South Rim had not stood still. Thanks to his bogus mining claims, **Ralph Cameron** was charging a toll of $1 to riders on the Bright Angel Trail. In 1905, he built his own hotel alongside the railroad terminal, thereby forcing the Fred Harvey Company to relocate the station out of sight of the upstart rival. Cameron continued to be a thorn in the side of the new national park. Elected to the US Senate in 1920, he spent a few years hacking at its budget before his mining claims were eventually invalidated. His presence had by then spurred the development of the **Kaibab Trail**, stretching from rim to rim of the canyon by way of the Kaibab suspension footbridge (see p.313). Plans to pave that route never materialized, but a small enlargement of the park in 1927 permitted the construction of a road east to Desert View, which with the completion in 1928 of the Navajo Bridge across Marble Canyon reduced the previous 600-mile drive between the rims to a more feasible 215 miles.

The first **automobile** arrived at the Canyon in 1902, despite running out of gas twenty miles short. By 1926, more visitors were coming by car than by train, and Flagstaff was once again the major point of access. Advance reservations for both mule rides and lodging have been necessary since 1938; annual visitor numbers first exceeded a million in 1956, and ran at over five million through most of the 1990s. Anticipating that visitation would continue to increase, the park service drew up plans to construct a huge new tourism complex close to the South Rim, to be known as "**Canyon Forest Village**", and also a **light rail** network. However, for reasons no one can explain, numbers then dropped back down below five million, and the political will to make major changes has disappeared.

The South Rim

When someone casually mentions visiting the "Grand Canyon," it's almost certainly the **South Rim** to which they're referring. To be more precise, it's the thirty-mile stretch of the South Rim that's served by a paved road; and most specifically of all, it's **Grand Canyon Village**, the small canyon-edge community, sandwiched between the pine forest and the rim, that holds the park's **lodges**, **restaurants**, and **visitor centre**.

6

GRAND CANYON TOURS

PARK BUS TOURS

To reserve a guided South Rim **bus tour**, contact the "transportation desk" in any lodge, book on ⓦgrandcanyonlodges.com, or call ☎888 297 2757. Adults can take any two tours, not necessarily on the same day, for $60, while accompanied under-17s travel free.

Desert View Tour 52-mile, 4-hr round-trip skirting the East Rim along Desert View Drive – a route open to private vehicles but not served by park shuttle buses. Stops include Yavapai Geology Museum, Lipan Point, and Desert View at road's end. $47.

Hermit's Rest Tour 2-hour jaunt west of the village

along the same route as the free Hermit's Rest shuttle bus (see p.316). $28.

Sunrise 90-minute early-morning tour east of the village. $21.50.

Sunset 90-minute late afternoon tour west of the village. $21.50.

HORSE RIDING

Apache Stables ☎928 638 2891, ⓦapachestables .com. Based at *Moqui Lodge* in Tusayan (which is itself permanently closed), charges $48.50 for a one-hour

trail ride through the Kaibab Forest, and $88.50 for two hours, and in the evening offers campfire rides on horseback for $58.50, or by wagon for $25.50.

MULE RIDES

Joining a mule train from Grand Canyon Village is a fine old canyon tradition. Riders must be at least four feet seven inches tall (1.38m), speak fluent English and weigh not more than 200 pounds (91kg) for the overnight rides, or 225 pounds (102kg) for the day-trips. Places are limited, so make a reservation as early as possible, on ☎303 297 2757 or ☎888 297 2757. If you arrive without a reservation, put yourself on the waiting list at the *Bright Angel Lodge* Transportation Desk and turn up there at 6am on the morning you want to ride; there are usually a few last-minute cancellations each day. Precise timings vary.

Overnight Rides Spend the morning descending the Bright Angel Trail to the riverside *Phantom Ranch*, where you'll sleep in two-person cabins. Soon after sunrise the next day, the mules set off back up the South Kaibab Trail. You should be back at *Bright Angel Lodge* in time for lunch. Trip costs, including lodgings and all meals, are $507 for one person, $896 for two. Two-night rides, available between November and

March only, follow the same route but stay another night down at the ranch, and cost $714 for one, or $1192 for two.

Day-trips The three-hour round-trip through the woods to the Abyss Overlook, west of Mohave Point, takes 75 minutes each way; only during the half-hour at the overlook do you get any canyon views. Twice daily March to mid-October, once daily otherwise, it costs $123.

GRAND CANYON FIELD INSTITUTE

The **Grand Canyon Field Institute** offers well-priced, expert-led guided tours and hikes in and around the canyon (☎928 638 2481 or ☎866 471 4435, ⓦwww.grandcanyon.org/learn /grand-canyon-field-institute).). Different tours, some restricted to women only, specialize in geology, history, natural history, photography, wilderness techniques and other topics. Most involve camping and backpacking, others include lodge accommodation or even llama

The reason nine out of every ten canyon visitors come here is not, however, because this is a uniquely wonderful spot from which to see the canyon; Grand Canyon Village just happens to be where the canyon's tourist facilities have been concentrated ever since the arrival of the railroad a century ago.

As the millennium approached – and despite the emergence of the small gateway community of **Tusayan** just outside the park – it looked as though the village could no longer take the strain. An ambitious scheme was drawn up under which visitors would explore the South Rim using a **light rail** network rather than their own vehicles. Visitor numbers, however, unexpectedly dropped, and the plan was abandoned.

Instead, the brand-new **Canyon View Information Plaza**, built as the hub of the rail network a mile or so east of the village, was kitted out with a new visitor centre and plentiful car parking space, and became the centre instead of a network of free seasonal trekking; all are graded according to the difficulty of any hiking involved. Prices range from $560 for a three-night hike down to Indian Garden to $770 for a four-night rim-to-rim backpack.

FLIGHT-SEEING TOURS

For safety reasons and to diminish **noise**, strict **regulations** surround flights above the national park. Airplanes and helicopters have to fly at different altitudes; no one can fly below the level of the rim; and 75 percent of the park, including the airspace above the South Rim lookouts and the central rim-to-rim "Corridor," is off-limits. All flights operate from Grand Canyon Airport at **Tusayan**, just south of the park.

Helicopters

Helicopters typically fly **three standard routes**: a half-hour western tour, straight across the canyon and back a few miles west of the village, for around $160; a forty-minute eastern tour, flying along the rim as far as the confluence of the Colorado and Little Colorado rivers, for roughly $190; and a fifty-minute loop trip that combines the two by flying across the forest of the North Rim, for perhaps $240.

Grand Canyon Helicopters T 928 638 2764 or T 800 541 4537, W www.grandcanyonhelicoptersaz.com. **Maverick** T 928 638 2622 or T 888 261 4414, W www.maverickhelicopter.com. **Papillon** T 928 638 2419 or T 888 635 7272, W www.papillon.com.

Airplanes

Airplane or "fixed-wing" tours can cover much greater distances, but they're obliged to fly at least 1000ft above rim level, and thus don't offer quite such good views. Prices range upwards from $100 for half an hour to as long as you like for as much as you've got.

Grand Canyon Airlines T 928 638 2359 or T 866 235 9422, W grandcanyonairlines.com.

WHITEWATER RAFTING

Places on commercial **whitewater rafting trips** tend to be reserved as much as a year in advance. Such trips vary in length from three days to three weeks, with the main choice being whether to cut the 300-mile voyage from Lees Ferry to Diamond Creek in half by leaving or joining the expedition at Phantom Ranch. An estimated 161 sets of rapids interrupt the full route. You can also choose between a quieter, slower oar-powered trip or a motorized expedition; both tend to cost between $250 and $350 per person, per day. A list of authorized operators, most of whom offer trips of both kinds and of varying lengths, appears online at W nps.gov/grca/planyourvisit/river-concessioners.htm.

No **one-day** rafting trips are available within Grand Canyon National Park. There are two alternatives, however, one at either end of the canyon.

Colorado River Discovery T 928 645 9175 or T 888 522 6644, W raftthecanyon.com. Based in Page, Arizona, and offering one-day trips ($89) that start below Glen Canyon Dam and finish at Lees Ferry. **Hualapai River Runners** T 928 769 2636 or T 888 868 9378, W grandcanyonwest.com/rafting.php. This tribal-run operation offers pricey one-day trips ($381) on the Hualapai Reservation near the west end of the canyon, starting at Diamond Creek. March–Oct only.

shuttle buses. While certain canyon overlooks are no longer accessible by car year-round, it remains perfectly possible to visit the South Rim using your own vehicle. The village still gets clogged with traffic in summer, but it rarely comes to a standstill, and is a nicer and more attractive place to spend time than you might imagine. The major drawback, or rather the price for keeping things bearable, is that all its accommodation tends to be booked up way in advance.

Grand Canyon Village and around

Naturally enough, the first thing that every visitor wants to do is to see the canyon. Where you see it for the first time doesn't actually matter all that much; of the twenty or so major, named viewpoints along the South Rim, plus any number of others in

6

between, no single one can be said to be the "best". In any case, you don't have to move from place to place to obtain radically different views of the canyon; staying in one spot, and watching the colours and shadows change as the day progresses, achieves much the same end.

However, contrary to what you might expect, the views from **Grand Canyon Village** itself are not exceptionally good. To enjoy long-range panoramas, you have to head at least as far from the central village as **Maricopa** or **Yavapai** points. Both of those, as well as the majority of the overlooks along the two rim-edge sightseeing routes – **Hermit Road** to the west, and **Desert View Drive** to the east – make ideal vantage points from which to see an unforgettable canyon sunrise or sunset.

The Grand Canyon Village viewpoints

Grand Canyon Village ranges along the inner curve of a recess that cuts well back into the South Rim. Such features are known to geologists as "arenas"; this one is also a "swale", in that the middle is significantly lower than the two sides. As a result, from the paved, railed terrace that follows the rim for the length of the village you can only see straight across the canyon. The long promontories to either side end at **Maricopa Point** to the west, the ridge beneath which stretches into a sturdy sandstone mesa known picturesquely as the Battleship, and **Grandeur Point** to the east. Straight down below, the Bright Angel Trail threads through the oasis of Indian Gardens before disappearing into a deep crevice, while another long trail leads across the flat, pale-green Tonto Platform to its dead end at **Plateau Point**.

The defining absence in the view is the **Colorado River** itself. Although the mighty walls of the Granite Gorge – the chasm that holds the actual river – are visible on the far side, you can't see their full 1300ft depth, and the river remains out of sight at the bottom. Thanks to the Bright Angel geological fault, however, there is a gap in the gorge, where Bright Angel Canyon slices into the North Rim. Just to the left at the top is *Grand Canyon Lodge* (see p.334), though you're only likely to spot it after dark, when the lights come on.

Mather Point

An easy walk of just a few hundred yards from the information plaza, busy **Mather Point** centres on a pair of rocky outcrops that jut out just below the rim. When the crowds prove too much, there's always space somewhere along the railed rim trail nearby, with subtly changing views at every step.

Mather Point faces northeast, toward Bright Angel Canyon on the far side, which is the route followed by the North Kaibab Trail down from the North Rim (see p.333). Two other rim-to-river trails can be spotted closer at hand. To the east, the South Kaibab Trail zigzags down from Yaki Point, while the further west of the two visible stretches of the Colorado River marks the point where it's reached by the Bright Angel Trail. From there, the trail heads east to Phantom Ranch, which is also visible, nestling close to the other tiny patch of river.

Yavapai Point

Walk west for around ten minutes from Mather Point, and you'll come to **Yavapai Point**. The easternmost point served by shuttle buses on the Village Route, this also offers parking for private vehicles. Long-range views are similar to those from Mather, meaning that the full range of pyramid-shaped buttes known as "temples" line up in front of the North Rim. Two different segments of the river are now on view, one of which includes both the Kaibab Suspension Bridge, or "Black Bridge," across the Colorado, and Phantom Ranch.

Nearby, if you can tear your eyes away from the view through its tinted bay windows, the **Yavapai Geology Museum** (daily: hours vary from 8am–8pm in summer down to 8am–5pm in winter; free) holds illuminating displays on how the canyon may have been formed. It takes another ten minutes' walk west along the rim before rounding

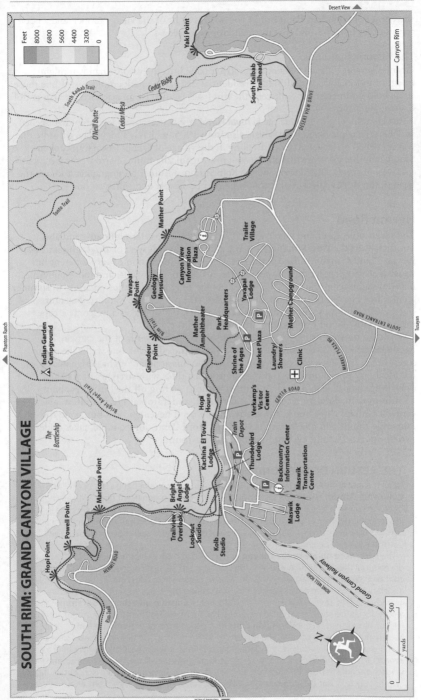

SOUTH RIM: GRAND CANYON VILLAGE

Desert View

— Canyon Rim

Feet
8000
6800
5600
4400
3200
0

Yaki Point

South Kaibab Trailhead

South Kaibab Trail

Cedar Ridge

Cedar Mesa

O'Neill Butte

DESERT VIEW DRIVE

Tonto Trail

Mather Point

Canyon View Information Plaza

Trailer Village

Yavapai Point

Geology Museum

Yavapai Lodge

Mather Campground

Phantom Ranch

Indian Garden Campground

Mather Amphitheater

Park Headquarters

SOUTH ENTRANCE ROAD

Tusayan

Rim Trail

Grandeur Point

Shrine of the Ages

Market Plaza

Laundry/Showers

Clinic

MARKET PLAZA RD

Bright Angel Trail

Hopi House

Kachina El Tovar Lodge

Verkamp's Visitor Center

CENTER ROAD

The Battleship

Maricopa Point

Bright Angel Lodge

Train Depot

Thunderbird Lodge

Backcountry Information Center

Maswik Transportation Center

Powell Point

Hopi Point

Trailview Overlook

Lookout Studio

Kolb Studio

HERMIT ROAD

Maswik Lodge

ROWE WELL ROAD

Grand Canyon Railway

Rim Trail

Hermit's Rest

N

0   500

yards

the corner of Grandeur Point brings you within sight of the village proper, and a good ten minutes more beyond that to reach Hopi House.

The historic buildings

Grand Canyon Village stretches a lot farther back into the woods than you might imagine and includes a well-hidden residential district for park employees. While those parts hold no interest for sightseers, the rim itself is lined by an attractive assortment of historic buildings.

Particular highlights include the **El Tovar Hotel**, a vast overgrown log cabin that opened in 1905; the triple-tiered **Hopi House**, also from 1905, which is a high-class gift store that was modelled on an actual Hopi dwelling in the village of Oraibi (see p.69); **Lookout Studio**, another gift store that appears to grow organically from a narrow protuberance just west of *Bright Angel Lodge*; and the **Kolb Studio**, a former photographic studio at the head of the Bright Angel Trail that now holds a bookstore and gallery.

Hermit Road

The seven-mile, dead-end scenic drive officially known as **Hermit Road** – and also unofficially as the **West Rim Drive** – starts a hundred yards west of *Bright Angel Lodge*, just as Grand Canyon Village peters out. Offering a succession of very different but consistently impressive canyon panoramas, it's the most obvious, and most enjoyable, half-day sightseeing trip from the village. As the only vehicles allowed access in summer are the free Hermit's Rest Route **shuttle buses** (see p.316), the Xanterra bus tours (see p.300), and those displaying disabled permits, it also makes a welcome escape from the crowds and traffic elsewhere along the rim.

While for most of its length the road runs within a few yards of the canyon, it's paralleled, as ever, by the **Rim Trail**, even closer to the edge. No one walks the entire seven miles, but since you can get on and off the bus at any of eight designated stops, the ideal way to explore is to combine shuttle bus rides with stretches of **walking**. Travelling the full length of Hermit Road without getting off the bus takes about 75 minutes. To allow for a couple of short hikes, and a stop at Hermit's Rest, give yourself perhaps three hours. Alternatively, you need never get on a bus at all; the four-mile round-trip hike from the village to Hopi Point, for example, takes under two hours. And finally, **cycling** is permitted year-round.

THE RETURN OF THE CONDOR

Of all the awesome spectacles along the South Rim, few can match the sight of a fully grown **California condor** soaring on the canyon updrafts. These magnificent birds, with a wingspan of more than nine feet and a lifespan of up to sixty years, were reintroduced to Arizona in 1996. Progress has been slow but steady, and around seventy free-flying, but tagged and monitored, condors now live in the Grand Canyon. They can frequently be seen hovering above Grand Canyon Village, or perching just below the rim.

The birds **were native to the canyon**, and indeed to most of North America, for thousands of years, but their population was dwindling long before the first Europeans arrived. The last condor in the Grand Canyon area was recorded as nesting near Lees Ferry in the 1890s, while a solitary bird was seen circling Williams in 1924. During the 1980s, the last remaining 22 individuals of the species were trapped in California. A **captive breeding programme** reintroduced the birds first in California, and subsequently in northern Arizona. At the Arizona release site, located on the **Vermilion Cliffs** fifty miles northeast of the South Rim – scientists keep contact between condors and humans to a minimum, so the birds don't learn to associate humans with food. Condors are very inquisitive creatures, however, and to the delight of tourists almost all the Arizona birds spend much of their time near the village. Project workers and park rangers discourage them from approaching too close, and leave animal carcasses out for them in remote places. Natural scavengers, they also manage to find carrion by themselves.

Maricopa Point

The first two viewpoints along the way, known as **Trailview I** and **II**, show prospective Bright Angel Trail hikers (see p.310) exactly what they're in for, with its red-dirt switchbacks clearly etched against the canyon walls below. After just over a mile, as you round the corner to pass out of sight of Grand Canyon Village, the railed, rocky overlook at **Maricopa Point** commands an almost 360° view, though only the tiniest sliver of the churning Colorado is visible. This is a prime spot for identifying the majestic buttes on the far side of the river, such as the Brahma and Zoroaster "temples," each with its capping layer of hard red sandstone.

6

Powell Point

Beyond Maricopa, road and trail alike have long detoured inland around the site of the **Orphan Mine**, which was America's largest uranium mine in the 1950s. At the headland immediately west, **Powell Point**, a short walk from the next shuttle stop leads to the spot where the park was officially dedicated on April 30, 1920. From the paved but rail-less viewing area on its far side, you can look across the river to the curious semicircular cliff wall of the "temple" known as the Tower of Set; shaped like an opening bracket, it's mirrored by a similar wall on Isis Temple to the east.

Hopi Point

Two miles out from Grand Canyon Village, **Hopi Point** is the busiest of the western viewpoints. Its reputation as the perfect place to watch the sunset rests on the fact that this promontory thrusts further north than any of its neighbours, with the vast panoply that spreads to the west forming just part of what's virtually a 360-degree canyon prospect.

The most dramatic of several distinct stretches of the Colorado on view lies immediately below Plateau Point (see p.312). It's hard to believe that the river is 350ft wide down there, lying at the foot of gnarled and impossibly ancient walls of black schist, streaked through with vertical pink faults. To the west, the river threads its tortuous way toward the ocean between interleaved spurs of red rock, and a maze of lesser canyons twists among the mighty buttes.

Mohave Point and Pima Point

Road and trail curve gracefully west of Hopi Point for three-quarters of a mile to **Mohave Point**, a large railed promontory from which the long-range vista remains substantially unchanged. **Pima Point** is four miles further on, beyond a sheer-walled recess known as **The Abyss**. The river is by now less than two miles from the South Rim – look almost straight down to admire the three-quarter-mile Granite Rapid – but from the far bank it's another twelve labyrinthine miles to the North Rim.

Hermit's Rest

Way station Daily: summer 8am–7.30pm; otherwise 9am–sunset

Hermit Road ends slightly over a mile beyond Pima Point, at the **Hermit's Rest** way station, appealingly laid out in 1914 to evoke the dwelling of some imaginary canyon prospector, which sells gifts and simple snacks. The **Hermit Trail**, abandoned by the Santa Fe Railroad in 1931 but still popular with inner-canyon hikers (see p.314), starts a short way further along.

Desert View Drive

Desert View Drive, which runs for 23 miles east from Mather Point to Desert View itself, just inside the park's eastern boundary (and beyond that to Cameron and, potentially the North Rim), is the one part of the South Rim that's open year-round for self-guided driving tours. Allow two hours at the very least to get to the end and back. In addition

6

SUNSET AND SUNRISE

"What's the best place to watch the sunset?" is probably the single question Grand Canyon park rangers most tire of being asked. There is no best place, neither for sunset, nor for sunrise. How could there be? Each rim of the canyon is almost three hundred miles long. Every yard of the way, the views are different, while the weather, cloud cover and visibility change every day.

That said, the Grand Canyon *does* look especially dramatic at the start and end of each day. When the sun is high in the sky, the colours tend to be bleached out, and heat and dust diminish visibility. By contrast, when the sun is low, the rich reds and oranges of the sandstone formations emerge, etched against sharp black shadows, and the whole spectacle can be simply stunning.

It's definitely worth ensuring that you're at a major canyon viewpoint as sunset approaches, and, to a lesser extent, at dawn. On the South Rim, that means getting away from the village itself, to somewhere that commands long-range canyon views to either east or west, or ideally, both – like **Hopi, Mohave or Pima** points to the west, or **Yavapai, Yaki or Desert View** to the east. The most popular spots tend to be Hopi Point for the sunset and Yavapai for sunrise; the down side of that, however, is that often a thousand or more people cram into those single small areas at the relevant moment. It's always better to play things by ear, and simply hope to find a quiet area where you can wander at will, rather than jostle for position. Shoshone Point is strongly recommended; because it's a twenty-minute walk from the nearest road, it rarely sees more than a handful of visitors.

Finally, bear in mind that it's not the sunset that's the spectacle, it's the canyon; if you aim to arrive five minutes before the precise time the sun goes down, you'll see very little. To illuminate anything within the canyon itself, the sun has to be significantly above the horizon, so **the finest viewing comes in the final hour or so before sunset**, and it comes from looking east, away from the sun and towards those buttes and temples that continue to catch direct sunlight, not west into the shadows. Similarly, it doesn't matter if you miss the moment of dawn; it's the ensuing hour, in which the rising sun picks out the pinnacles one by one, that will live in your memory.

to the formal viewpoints described below, the road occasionally runs very close to the rim; you're not supposed to stop for picnics and sightseeing, but plenty of people do.

Yaki Point
2 miles east of Yavapai Point

The first of the Desert View Drive lookouts, **Yaki Point**, is accessible in your own vehicle only between December and February, though it's served year-round by free shuttle buses. Two miles east of Yavapai Point, it commands much the same trans-canyon views as its neighbour.

The most prominent of several inner-canyon trails on show is the **South Kaibab Trail** (see p.313), which starts its quickfire descent to Phantom Ranch from its own separate parking lot nearby. From the main overlook, you can spot it far below, switchbacking down an exposed scree slope of red rock between two buttes. Scramble out onto the rocks beyond the viewpoint for clearer views down to the trail's principal staging post, O'Neill Butte.

Shoshone Point
2 miles east of Yaki Point

Shoshone Point is the least-known and least-visited of the South Rim viewpoints, for the simple reason that it's only accessible on **foot**, along an easy one-mile trail from Desert View Drive. It's an absolute gem of a place, offering beautiful views along with an unparalleled sense of peace and privacy. An hour's round-trip hike from the road may well offer your only chance to be alone with the canyon on the South Rim, and it's arguably the finest viewpoint on either rim.

The trail to Shoshone Point begins from an unpaved parking lot 1.4 miles east of the turn-off to Yaki Point; look for a grey gate barring a dirt road, and a brown park notice reading "Site Use by Permit Only." The sign is there because the park service does not publicize Shoshone Point to casual visitors, as it's used for weddings in summer, but there's no system for issuing permits to hikers. Instead, you're simply asked to respect the privacy of any group that may be out there, and not to hike out at all if there are a lot of cars at the parking lot. The point itself is truly spectacular. A solitary pale hoodoo marks the tip of its slender neck, while the sublime views range along the full panoply of the North Rim.

Grandview Point
8 miles east of Yaki Point, 12 miles east of Grand Canyon Village

Grandview Point was where Europeans first saw the Grand Canyon, in 1540 (see p.314). It's suggested that their Hopi guides deliberately led them to a spot from which no trails were visible, to make the canyon appear even more impassable. Grandview was also the place where Grand Canyon tourism first took off, after prospector Peter Berry constructed the Grandview Trail down to his Last Chance copper mine in 1892, and visitors began to gravitate to the site.

In terms of views Grandview is unarguably superior to Grand Canyon Village. There's no need to set foot on the precarious **Grandview Trail** (see p.314) to plot the sinuous course of the Colorado, which makes its broad and languorous entrance off to the east before disappearing into the stunning sandstone labyrinth. Down below, the twin prongs of **Horseshoe Mesa** reach out towards the North Rim. The left points to the mesa of Wotan's Throne, detached from the rim but still towering a couple of hundred feet taller than Grandview itself; in the centre is Cape Royal, and to the right Cape Final juts out at the far eastern end of the North Rim.

Tusayan Ruin
10 miles east of Grandview Point, 22 miles east of Grand Canyon Village

Tusayan Ruin, in the forest south of the highway (and not to be confused with modern Tusayan), is what remains of a genuine **Ancestral Puebloan pueblo**. One of two thousand known such sites in the Grand Canyon area, it's not comparable in scale to relics elsewhere in the Southwest, but its existence enabled President Theodore Roosevelt to accord National Monument status to the entire Grand Canyon. Only low stone walls survive of the original complex of buildings, occupied for perhaps 25 years by a group of up to thirty people, around 1185 AD. A small museum (daily 9am–5pm; free) holds displays on the contemporary Navajo and Hopi, as well as 4000-year-old twig figurines and Ancestral Puebloan pottery found nearby.

Desert View

Desert View, 25 miles east of Grand Canyon Village, is the last viewpoint along Desert View Drive. As Hwy-64, however, the road continues another 34 miles to meet US-89 at Cameron (see p.328), so Desert View also provides visitors approaching from the east with their *first* opportunity to see what all the fuss is about.

To the north, four miles distant, the Colorado River can be seen approaching its sudden westward turn. Just north of its last visible curve lies the confluence of the Colorado and Little Colorado rivers. The stark cliffs known as the **Palisades of the Desert** delineate the South Rim, while above them the pallid plains of the **Marble Plateau** stretch to the horizon, beneath an overwhelming sky. Sixty-five million years ago, this entire landscape was buried beneath an additional four or five thousand feet of sandstone. Thanks to erosion, all that remains are a few tiny vestiges, such as reddish **Cedar Mountain**, a mile or two back from the rim.

Over to the west, by contrast, the river disappears deep into the Granite Gorge, engulfed on all sides by buttes and mesas, temples, shrines and tabernacles. During the morning they present an extraordinary panoply of colours and shapes; the rich golds and reds are the first to go, leached out by the midday sun, while as dusk draws on they seem to lose all form as well, turning into mysterious interleaving shadowy screens, devoid of all three-dimensional quality.

6

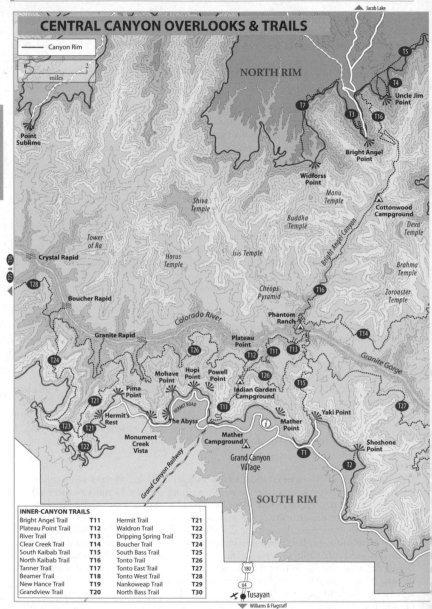

CENTRAL CANYON OVERLOOKS & TRAILS

Canyon Rim

miles

Jacob Lake

NORTH RIM

T5

T4

Uncle Jim
Point

Point
Sublime

T7

T3

T16

Bright Angel
Point

Widforss
Point

Manu
Temple

Cottonwood
Campground

Deva
Temple

Shiva
Temple

Buddha
Temple

Bright Angel Canyon

Tower
of Ra

Isis Temple

Brahma
Temple

Crystal Rapid

Horus
Temple

T28

Cheops
Pyramid

Zoroaster
Temple

Boucher Rapid

T16

Colorado River

Phantom
Ranch

T14

Granite Rapid

Plateau
Point

Granite Gorge

T26

T12

T11

T13

T24

Mohave
Point

Hopi
Point

Powell
Point

T126

T15

Pima
Point

Indian Garden
Campground

Yaki Point

T21

T11

Hermit's
Rest

HERMIT ROAD

The Abyss

Mather
Point

Shoshone
Point

T23

T21

Monument
Creek
Vista

Mather
Campground

T27

T22

Grand Canyon Railway

Grand Canyon
Village

T1

T2

SOUTH RIM

INNER-CANYON TRAILS			
Bright Angel Trail	**T11**	Hermit Trail	**T21**
Plateau Point Trail	**T12**	Waldron Trail	**T22**
River Trail	**T13**	Dripping Spring Trail	**T23**
Clear Creek Trail	**T14**	Boucher Trail	**T24**
South Kaibab Trail	**T15**	South Bass Trail	**T25**
North Kaibab Trail	**T16**	Tonto Trail	**T26**
Tanner Trail	**T17**	Tonto East Trail	**T27**
Beamer Trail	**T18**	Tonto West Trail	**T28**
New Hance Trail	**T19**	Nankoweap Trail	**T29**
Grandview Trail	**T20**	North Bass Trail	**T30**

180

64

Tusayan

Williams & Flagstaff

Desert View Watchtower

Daily 8am–sunset • Free

Rather than the canyon itself, what immediately draws the eye is the remarkable **Desert View Watchtower** perched at its lip, built in Ancestral Puebloan style by Mary Jane Colter in 1932. Stairs from the gift store at its base climb through three chambers, decorated with murals by the Hopi artist Fred Kabotie, as well as reproduction petroglyphs.

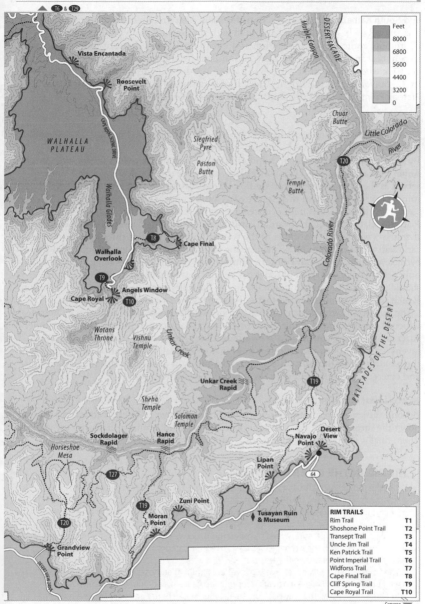

RIM TRAILS	
Rim Trail	**T1**
Shoshone Point Trail	**T2**
Transept Trail	**T3**
Uncle Jim Trail	**T4**
Ken Patrick Trail	**T5**
Point Imperial Trail	**T6**
Widforss Trail	**T7**
Cape Final Trail	**T8**
Cliff Spring Trail	**T9**
Cape Royal Trail	**T10**

South Rim hikes: into the canyon

Hiking any of the trails that descend into the Grand Canyon offers more than just another view of the same thing. Instead you pass through a sequence of utterly different landscapes, each with its own climate, wildlife, and topography.

Eight major trails lead into the canyon from the South Rim, but most either start from inaccessible places or are in poor condition. Traffic is heaviest on the **Bright Angel** and **South Kaibab** trails, the two "**Corridor Trails**" that link up in the gorge to lead to Phantom Ranch. They can be combined with the North Kaibab Trail to form a continuous route between the South and North rims. If you do want to hike from rim to rim, bear in mind that Transcanyon Shuttle runs from one to the other, so you can get back where you started (see p.334). The Corridor trails also offer the best **day-hikes** in the canyon; down the Bright Angel Trail as far **Indian Garden**, or at most out to **Plateau Point**, and down the South Kaibab Trail to **Cedar Ridge**.

6   The Bright Angel Trail

Trailhead: Grand Canyon Village • Day hike to Indian Garden 9.2 miles round-trip, 5–7hr; day hike to Plateau Point 11.2 miles round-trip, 8–10hr; Phantom Ranch 9.6 miles one-way, 5–6hr descent, 7–9hr ascent

By far the busiest inner-canyon hiking route – with mules as well as hikers – the **Bright Angel Trail** starts in Grand Canyon Village, alongside the wooden shack that once served as the Kolb photographic studio. An old Havasupai route, it was improved by miners a century ago, and then operated as a toll trail when the mines failed to prosper.

Although the side canyon immediately below the village makes access to the Tonto Platform relatively straightforward, it's still a long, hard climb. Most **day-hikers** content themselves with walking to either of the two resthouses in the first three miles, but with an early start you should be able to manage the round trip of nine miles to Indian Garden, or even eleven miles to Plateau Point. In summer, you can obtain water along the trail and only need to carry one quart of water per person; in winter, when there is none, you should carry two. Only try to reach the river – 7.8 miles from the trailhead, with Phantom Ranch almost two miles beyond that – if you've reserved a campsite for the night.

The trail begins with a long, exposed set of switchbacks down the dry, rocky hillside, which changes from pale pink to sheer red. Two short tunnels punctuate its first mile. After another mile, you start to see more wildlife – deer, rodents, and the ubiquitous ravens – while various rock surfaces hold pictographs, all but obscured by graffiti. Both the basic 1930s **resthouses**, after 1.6 and 3.1 miles, have water in summer (May–Sept) and emergency phones, but only the 1.6-mile one has restrooms.

Jacob's Ladder and Garden Creek

Beyond the second resthouse, a set of switchbacks known as **Jacob's Ladder** carries you down the sheer Redwall cliff, a major obstacle throughout almost the entire canyon. Then, finally, the trail starts to level out, and the vegetation gets greener, with

---

HIKING IN THE GRAND CANYON

While the canyon can offer a wonderful wilderness experience, it's a hostile and very unforgiving environment, gruelling even for expert hikers. Park rangers have one simple message for all would-be hikers: **Don't try to hike to the river and back in one day**. It might not look far on the map, but it's harder than running a marathon. Several hikers each year die in the attempt, and several hundred more receive emergency medical treatment. If you do want to reach the Colorado, it's best to reserve campgrounds for two nights, so you have a day to recover before the trek out.

The South Rim is 7000 feet above sea level, an altitude that most people find fatiguing in itself. Furthermore, all hikes start with a long, steep descent, and unless you camp overnight you'll have to climb all the way back up again when you're hotter and wearier. As a rule of thumb, keep track of how much time you spend hiking down and allow twice that much to get back up again. Average summer temperatures inside the canyon exceed 100°F; to hike for eight hours in that sort of heat, you have to drink an incredible thirty pints of water. Always **carry at least a quart per person** – and much more if there are no water sources along your chosen trail. You must have food as well, as drinking large quantities without also eating can cause water intoxication. Ideally, the best seasons to hike are spring and fall.

OPPOSITE THE BRIGHT ANGEL TRAIL (P.310)>

yellow- and red-blossomed cactuses scattered to either side. Soon you hear the astonishing sound of trickling water in **Garden Creek**, lined by dazzling green trees.

Indian Garden

The spring at **Indian Garden**, 4.6 miles from the rim, is the reason the Bright Angel Trail exists. Native peoples really did have a garden here, planted in prehistoric times and used by the Havasupai from around 1300 AD until the nineteenth century. Now this unexpected little oasis holds a ranger station, restrooms, separate camping and day-use areas, and a staging post for mules.

Plateau Point

From Indian Garden, the Bright Angel Trail continues to the river, while the **Tonto Trail** runs both east and west for a phenomenal total length of 92 miles along the flat, arid Tonto Platform. A spur trail off the Tonto Trail – reached by heading left at Indian Garden, crossing Garden Creek, and then turning right at an obvious intersection three-quarters of a mile along – threads its way out to **Plateau Point**, a superb overlook above the Granite Gorge from which it is not possible to descend any further. Barren even by inner-canyon standards, the desert landscape is spectacular, with the mighty red buttes and mesas of the canyon now framed against the blue sky.

Shortly after you get your first awesome glimpse of the black tumbling walls of the gorge, the Plateau Point spur trail comes to an end. Precariously perched on the rocky outcrops, you can see a long stretch of the dark-green Colorado, though both the bridges and Phantom Ranch lie out of sight around the next promontory to the east.

Devil's Corkscrew and the Colorado River

As it continues beyond Indian Garden, the Bright Angel Trail first drops through the fertile margins of Garden Creek, then switchbacks down the **Devil's Corkscrew**, hacked into the rock during the 1930s to create a shortcut to the river. Once beside the Colorado, dwarfed beneath thousand-foot walls of dark-grey granite, it undulates through sand dunes scattered with yucca and prickly pear.

Hikers can cross the river around a mile along, using the 1960s **Silver Bridge**; mules, which balk at the prospect of seeing the river between its slats, have to continue a little further. The 400ft **suspension bridge** they prefer was set in place in 1928, hanging from twin cables that were carried down the Kaibab Trail on the shoulders of 42 Havasupai. Not far away on the other side – though you'll have to cross Bright Angel Creek twice to reach it – is **Bright Angel Campground**, with **Phantom Ranch** a short distance up beyond.

The temperature at river level tends to be around 20°F higher than on the South Rim, and there's significantly less rainfall. The **ecology** down here has changed since Glen Canyon Dam was completed in the mid-1960s (see p.395). Previously, up to a million tons of earth and rock hurtled past Phantom Ranch each day. Now it's more like forty thousand; trees that would previously have been swept away are establishing themselves, and fish that were perfectly adapted to such conditions are now becoming extinct.

Phantom Ranch

Bright Angel Creek flows down Bright Angel Canyon from the North Rim to meet the Colorado below Grand Canyon Village. John Wesley Powell named it in 1869, contrasting this "clear beautiful creek" with the muddy Dirty Devil River, upstream in Utah, and identified a small **Ancestral Puebloan ruin** that's still visible today.

This confluence now marks the only place where inner-canyon hikers and mule riders can not only cross the Colorado River but also camp and even sleep in a real bed at the bottom of the canyon. **Phantom Ranch**, beside Bright Angel Creek, consists of assorted cabins, corrals and outbuildings clustered amid huge cottonwoods and fruit orchards around a central lodge. Overnight accommodation is in individual cabins and dorms (see p.318), while the **Bright Angel Campground** is nearby (see p.318).

6

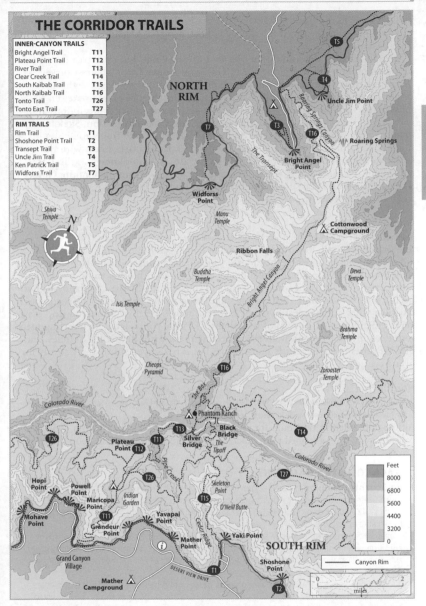

THE CORRIDOR TRAILS

INNER-CANYON TRAILS
Bright Angel Trail	**T11**
Plateau Point Trail	**T12**
River Trail	**T13**
Clear Creek Trail	**T14**
South Kaibab Trail	**T15**
North Kaibab Trail	**T16**
Tonto Trail	**T26**
Tonto East Trail	**T27**

RIM TRAILS
Rim Trail	**T1**
Shoshone Point Trail	**T2**
Transept Trail	**T3**
Uncle Jim Trail	**T4**
Ken Patrick Trail	**T5**
Widforss Trail	**T7**

South Kaibab Trail

Trailhead: First shuttle-bus stop on green route, around 500 yards before Yaki Point • Day-hike to Cedar Mesa 3 miles round-trip, 2–4hr;
day-hike to Skeleton Point 6 miles round-trip, 4–6hr; Phantom Ranch 7.1 miles one-way, 4–6hr descent, ascent not recommended

The **South Kaibab Trail**, the most direct route from the South Rim to Phantom Ranch, is never as busy as the Bright Angel Trail. And no wonder – taking just six miles to drop to the river, it's an even steeper haul, and the trailhead lies three miles east of the information plaza. If you plan to combine the Bright Angel and South Kaibab trails in hiking to and from Phantom Ranch, make the Kaibab the one you go *down*. Even if you can only spare the time for a short day-hike, however, you'll be rewarded by superb views.

The trail starts by descending slightly west of **Yaki Point**, but once past the end of the promontory it runs along the top of **Cedar Ridge**. This high crest surveys a thirty-mile stretch of the canyon in both directions and also faces straight up Bright Angel Canyon toward the North Rim. In the absence of any water en route, most hikers turn back after 1.5 miles. If you keep going, down a precipitous and very exposed slope, you reach another potential day-hike destination, **Skeleton Point**, 1.5 miles further along, and eventually meet the **Tonto Trail** a total of 4.4 miles down. A long, if level, trek east enables backpackers to connect with the Grandview Trail but the obvious way to go is west. At a spot known as the **Tipoff**, a few hundred yards along, you're poised to plunge down into the Granite Gorge. The river, and the 1928 suspension bridge that leads to Phantom Ranch, are little more than a mile away.

Grandview Trail

Trailhead: Grandview Point • Day-hike to Horseshoe Mesa 6.4 miles round-trip, 5–7hr

The **Grandview Trail**, down from **Grandview Point**, was built during the 1890s to aid copper mining on **Horseshoe Mesa**, which remains littered with abandoned mine workings. Although it's possible, by connecting with other trails, to use the Grandview to reach the Tonto Platform and thus eventually the Colorado, it's not itself a rim-to-river route. Instead, the hike down to the mesa and back is a popular **day-hike**. That doesn't mean it's easy, however; now officially "unmaintained," it's a very demanding trail. Several of its switchbacks were constructed by inserting metal rods deep into the canyon wall, then covering them with juniper logs, stones, and dirt. At times it can be a little hair-raising, but it has stayed surprisingly sturdy for over a century.

Hermit Trail

Trailhead: Hermit's Rest • Day-hike to Santa Maria Spring 4.6 miles round-trip, 3–4hr; day-hike to Dripping Spring 6.5 miles round-trip, 3–5hr; Colorado River 9.7 miles one-way, 6–7hr descent, 7–9hr ascent

Although the **Hermit Trail,** built for mule riders in 1912 and abandoned in 1931, is considered an unmaintained trail, much of its engineering remains in good shape.

BACKCOUNTRY CAMPING

Backcountry camping below the canyon rim is by permit only, with permits costing $10, plus $5 per person per night. Applications are accepted in person, by mail (PO Box 129, Grand Canyon, AZ 86023), or by fax (☎928 638 2125), but not by email or phone. Full details can be found at ⓦ nps.gov/grca.

All applications have to specify an exact itinerary, detailing where you'll spend each night – either named campgrounds or the wider-ranging "Use Areas" coded on official park maps, also available online. Between March and mid-November, there's a limit on the most popular trails of two nights per party per campsite.

Mailed or faxed applications are accepted for dates until the end of the fourth complete month after they're submitted; thus if you're planning a trip in the peak month of July, you'd better mail your application on March 1. To apply in person, turn up at either the **Backcountry Information Center**, in the Maswik Transportation Center near *Maswik Lodge* in Grand Canyon Village (daily 8am–noon & 1–5pm; ☎928 638 7875; or at the **North Rim Backcountry Office**, a quarter-mile north of the *North Rim Campground* (daily 8am–noon & 1–5pm; ☎928 638 7868). Even in peak season, your chances of a last-minute cancellation are pretty good. Your name is added to a waiting list, and each morning at 8am that day's cancellations are reassigned – though you have to be there on the spot to get one.

Named in honour of Louis Boucher, a nineteenth-century prospector, it's now used mainly by solitary types, setting off on long backcountry camping expeditions away from the crowds.

From the Hermit's Rest parking lot at the end of Hermit Road (see p.305), the trail drops into a side canyon, then switchbacks into Hermit Gorge and slowly descends a high rock wall far above Hermit Creek. A detour less than two miles along allows for the popular day-hike to **Dripping Spring**, not recommended for anyone with a fear of heights. Alternatively, if you press on, rockfalls tend to make for slow progress, but the resthouse at **Santa Maria Spring**, 2.3 miles down from the trailhead, is a lovely day-hike destination. Beyond that, views of the Granite Gorge eventually open up. The *Hermit Camp* is not far west of the junction with the Tonto Trail, 7miles along. Turning right (north) shortly before the campground brings you to the Colorado itself, almost ten miles from the trailhead, at **Hermit Rapid**, where the wave-like surge of the river can reach over twenty feet high.

ARRIVAL AND DEPARTURE   THE SOUTH RIM

The South Rim is separated from I-40 by the sixty-mile expanse of the **Coconino Plateau**, covered by the largest **ponderosa pine forest** in the world. Crossing this undramatic landscape, you get no sense of the impending abyss until you reach the very edge of the canyon.

BY CAR
Driving to the Grand Canyon The vast majority of visitors reach the park entrance at Tusayan by **driving** north from I-40. AZ-64 from Williams (52 miles south; see p.285), also known as the Bushmaster Memorial Highway, joins US-180 from Flagstaff (75 miles southeast; see p.262), at Valle, thirty miles south of the canyon itself. The route from Flagstaff, by way of the San Francisco Peaks (see p.268), is more scenic, and is followed by most commercial **buses**. It's also possible to drive to Grand Canyon Village from the east, by turning onto AZ-64 from US-89 at Cameron (see p.328).

BY TRAIN
Amtrak Amtrak trains come no closer to the South Rim than the stations at Flagstaff and Williams. In summer, westbound services, originating in Chicago, arrive at Flagstaff at 8.51pm and Williams Junction at 9.33pm daily, while eastbound trains, which start in LA, call at Williams Junction at 3.50am and Flagstaff at 4.36am daily. Times in winter are one hour later. Bus connections are detailed on p.264.
Grand Canyon Railway Trains on the restored Grand Canyon Railway (☎928 773 1976 or ☎800 843 8724, ⓦthetrain.com) run for 64 miles from a separate station in the heart of Williams to the picturesque station at Grand Canyon Village. The railway is a tourist attraction in its own right, with passengers riding in historic cars of varying levels of comfort and entertained throughout the day by Wild West shoot-outs, hold-ups, pistol-packing marshals, singing conductors, and the like. The scenery en route – part desert scrubland, part pine forest – is far from spectacular, and you never actually see the canyon from the train, but it's a fun way to make

a short visit to the park without having to drive. Services operate daily all year, with varying schedules but typically leaving Williams at 9.30am and reaching the canyon at 11.45am, and then leaving the canyon at 3.30pm to arrive back in Williams at 5.45pm. Only in summer is the train pulled by steam engines. Round-trip fares range from $75 in Coach Class (under-13s $45) up to $199 (under-13s not permitted) in the Luxury Parlor Car. No Amtrak passes are accepted, and if you don't have a national park pass, an additional fee of $8 is charged for park admission.

BY BUS
Arizona Shuttle Daily buses from Flagstaff's Amtrak station, via Williams, to *Maswik Lodge* in Grand Canyon Village (☎928 226 8060 or ☎800 888 2749, ⓦarizonashuttle.com; one-way $29). Year-round, a bus leaves Flagstaff at 7.45am and reaches the *Maswik* at 9.30am, and another leaves Flagstaff at 3.45pm and gets to the *Maswik* at 5.45pm. Between March and October, a third bus leaves Flagstaff at 12.45pm and arrives at the *Maswik* at 2.45pm.
Tours Various companies operate **one-day tours** to the Canyon from Flagstaff (see p.262) and Williams (see p.285).

BY AIR
Tusayan airport The small airport (ⓦgrand canyonairport.org) at Tusayan, six miles from the South Rim, just outside the park boundary, is used primarily by "flight-seeing" tour companies (see p.301). The only airlines that currently fly here offer excursions from Las Vegas; almost all passengers come on day-trips, but it is possible to arrange a one-way flight. The major

6

operators are Scenic Airlines (📞702 638 3200 or 📞800 634 6801, 🌐scenic.com), and Grand Canyon Airlines (📞928 638 2359 or 📞866 235 9422, 🌐grandcanyonairlines.com).

INFORMATION

The Guide So long as you have the park's free newspaper, *The Guide*, handed out at the two entrance stations on AZ-64 (one's just north of Tusayan, the other a mile east of Desert View), there's no real need to stop at a visitor centre. As well as listing opening hours and shuttle-bus schedules, *The Guide* carries a full programme of activities such as free ranger talks and guided hikes.

Canyon View Information Plaza The main source of information for the South Rim, and the hub of its free shuttle-bus system, is immediately north of the spur road that heads west into the village from AZ-64. Despite its name, however, the plaza offers no canyon views; for those, you have to walk a few hundred yards north, to Mather Point. Well-illustrated open-air displays explain different aspects of the canyon, and detail its various hiking trails.

Grand Canyon Visitor Center The official visitor centre, on Canyon View Information Plaza, holds very little information you can't find elsewhere, but is staffed by helpful rangers eager to advise on any topic you care to mention (daily: May to mid-Oct 8am–6pm, mid-Oct to April 9am–5pm; 📞928 638 7888, 🌐nps.gov/grca). Across the plaza, there's an excellent separate bookstore.

Information desks Additional information desks are located at Kolb Studio, Yavapai Geology Museum (see p.302), Tusayan Museum (see p.307), and Desert View (see p.307).

Maps None of the free maps on offer at the park is adequate for backcountry hiking, so invest in the waterproof and tearproof maps published by National Geographic–Trails Illustrated, costing $11.95 each (🌐maps.nationalgeographic.com). No. 261 focuses specifically on Bright Angel Canyon and the Corridor Trails, at 1:35000, while nos. 262 and 263 cover the eastern and western portions of the canyon respectively, at 1:90000.

GETTING AROUND

PARK SHUTTLE BUSES

Grand Canyon Village is always accessible to private vehicles and so, too, is the road east from the village to Desert View. Both the road west from the village to Hermit's Rest, however, and the short access road to Yaki Point, east of Mather Point, are only open during the months of December, January and February. You're almost certain, therefore, to use one of the park's free shuttle bus routes, which interconnect but do not overlap, and are listed in *The Guide* newspaper.

Village Route Coded blue on official park maps, the busiest shuttle-bus route loops between Grand Canyon Village and Canyon View Information Plaza, stopping at *Bright Angel*, *Maswik* and *Yavapai* lodges and *Mather Campground*, as well as Yavapai Point. Starting an hour before sunrise, buses run at half-hourly intervals until 6.30am, and then at fifteen-minute intervals till 7.30pm (May & Sept) or 9pm (June–Aug), after which they revert to half-hourly intervals until either 10pm (May & Sept) or 11pm (June–Aug).

Kaibab Trail Route Coded green, this connects Canyon View Information Plaza with Yaki Point, off Desert View Drive a couple of miles east of the village. Buses start running at half-hourly intervals an hour before sunrise, then from either 6.30am (May–Aug) or 7.30am (Sept) they run at fifteen-minute intervals until an hour after sunset. In order to use this route, you have first to catch a village bus to the information plaza.

Hikers' Express For anyone planning to hike along the South Kaibab Trail from the Yaki Point trailhead (see p.313), it's much quicker to catch this direct early-morning service to Yaki Point from *Bright Angel Lodge*, via the Backcountry Information Center and the information plaza (daily June–Aug 4am, 5am & 6am; March & Nov 7am, 8am & 9am; April & Oct 6am, 7am & 8am; May & Sept 5am, 6am & 7am; Dec–Feb 8am & 9am). Note that you can also use a taxi on this route.

Hermit's Rest Route Coded red, this route operates between March and November only, and follows Hermit Road, a scenic seven-mile drive west of the village that holds eight canyon overlooks (see p.304). The whole point of the trip is to take your time and enjoy the views; allow at least two hours. Buses run from an hour before sunrise until an hour after sunset, at fifteen-minute intervals between 7.30am and sunset and at half-hourly intervals otherwise. Demand is always high for buses out from the village to see the sunset, so be sure to get to the stop at least an hour in advance, and for buses back to the village once the sun has gone down.

Tusayan Route Coded purple, and offering regular twenty-minute runs between Tusayan, where there are four separate stops, and Canyon View Information Plaza. The first bus leaves Tusayan at 8am daily, and the information plaza at 8.40am; the last service from both is at 9.30pm. All passengers entering the park must already have permits.

CYCLING

Cycling is permitted on any paved road in the park, including Hermit Road when it's closed to private vehicles. You can also ride on the Greenway network of paths, which includes a stretch of the Rim Trail on either side of Mather Point, a trail that links the information plaza with the village and a newer segment that starts at Monument Creek Vista, four miles west of the village on Hermit Road, and runs another three miles west to Hermit's Rest.

Bright Angel Bicycles Based in its own café at Canyon View Information Plaza (daily: April–Nov 6am–8pm, Dec–March 7am–7pm; ☎928 638 0355,

ⓦbikegrandcanyon.com), Bright Angels rents bikes for $12 per hour, $30 for four hours, $40 for a full day and $35 per day for multi-day rentals, with reduced rates for under-17s. Trailers to pull children behind are also available. An hourly cyclists' shuttle to Hopi Point and two other stops on Hermit Road costs $34 including bike rental, and 3hr cycle tours are $48.

ACCOMMODATION

6

Roughly two thousand **guest rooms** are available close to the South Rim: half of them in and around **Grand Canyon Village**, and a further thousand in **Tusayan**, an unattractive strip-mall of a town that stands seven miles from Grand Canyon Village, a mile south of the park entrance. Given the choice, the best place to stay has to be on the very lip of the canyon, but very few rooms indeed enjoy canyon views, and they tend to be booked as much as two years in advance. In fact, for most of the summer it's very unusual for any same-day bookings to be available in the park. While the more basic in-park lodges, away from the rim, still make more convenient bases than Tusayan, the hotels in Tusayan do tend to be more modern and better equipped. On the other hand, some of the rates available inside the park represent extraordinarily good value. If you are stuck, other possibilities include **Cameron** (see p.328), **Flagstaff** (p.262), and **Williams** (p.285).

GRAND CANYON VILLAGE

★ **Bright Angel Lodge** Grand Canyon Village same-day ☎928 638 2631, advance ☎303 297 2757 or ☎888 297 2757, ⓦgrandcanyonlodges.com. Designed by Mary Jane Colter and built in 1935, the *Bright Angel* complex consists of an imposing central lodge and a westward sprawl of rustic but delightful detached log cabins, of which only the Rim Cabins enjoy canyon views. Though reasonably sized and appealingly furnished, many of the lodge rooms share bathrooms and/or toilets; a few do offer private showers. Best of all is the Buckey O'Neill Suite, which boasts a large living room with working fireplace and two front doors that open on the rim. Lodge rooms $72, Historic Cabins $120, Rim Cabins $154, Buckey O'Neill Suite $362

★ **El Tovar** Grand Canyon Village same-day ☎928 638 2631, advance ☎303 297 2757 or ☎888 297 2757, ⓦgrandcanyonlodges.com. Named for an early Spanish explorer, this log-construction rim-side hotel remains the centrepiece of Grand Canyon Village, and exudes the same combination of rough-hewn charm and elegant sophistication that made it the very peak of fashion when it first opened. Only three suites offer extensive canyon views; the rest of the 78 tastefully furnished guest rooms come in two different sizes, but are otherwise very similar. Almost all provide just one bed. Standard $183, larger $281, suites $348

Kachina Lodge Grand Canyon Village same-day ☎928 638 2631, advance ☎303 297 2757 or ☎888 297 2757, ⓦgrandcanyonlodges.com. Anonymous but perfectly adequate motel-style rooms, each with two queen-size beds and full bath, set in a low and utterly undistinguished two-storey block separated by just twenty yards of grass from the rim. The upper-floor rooms on the canyon side – which cost $11 extra – provide great panoramas. $180

Maswik Lodge Grand Canyon Village same-day ☎928 638 2631, advance ☎303 297 2757 or ☎888 297 2757, ⓦgrandcanyonlodges.com. This large complex, a few hundred yards back from the rim, includes two distinct blocks of motel-style rooms – the Maswik North building is much nicer than the smaller, cramped Maswik South – plus a cluster of basic summer-only cabins, each holding two double beds and thus the closest the village comes to budget lodging. Cabins $94, Maswik South $92, Maswik North $176

Thunderbird Lodge Grand Canyon Village same-day ☎928 638 2631, advance ☎303 297 2757 or ☎888 297 2757, ⓦgrandcanyonlodges.com. Built of grey brick in the 1960s and intended to last only ten years, the *Thunderbird* is still going strong without being in any way distinctive. 37 of its 55 rooms are on the canyon side of the building and cost $11 extra; all have twin beds and full bath. $180

Yavapai Lodge Grand Canyon Village same-day ☎928 638 2631, advance ☎303 297 2757 or ☎888 297 2757, ⓦgrandcanyonlodges.com. With 358 rooms, *Yavapai* is the largest in-park lodge and the last to fill up, so it's most likely to be available at short notice. The main drawback is that it's set back in the woods half a mile from the rim, and twice that from the heart of Grand Canyon Village. In late fall and early spring, either of the two similar sections, the air-conditioned Yavapai East or the smaller Yavapai West, which has ceiling fans only, may be closed, while the whole lodge shuts down in winter. The rooms themselves offer perfectly decent motel-style accommodation, most with twin beds. Yavapai West $125, Yavapai East $166

TUSAYAN

Best Western Grand Canyon Squire Inn 100 Hwy-64 ☎928 638 2681 or ☎800 622 6966,

6

ⓦgrandcanyonsquire.com. While Tusayan's most lavish option bills itself as the canyon's "only resort hotel", with an outdoor pool, indoor spa and even its own four-lane bowling alley, its rates compare favourably with those of its neighbours. Most rooms are spacious and very comfortable, if unremarkable; paying a little extra gets you an enormous deluxe room with oval bath. $230

The Grand Hotel 149 Hwy-64 ⓣ928 638 3333 or ⓣ888 634 7263, ⓦgrandcanyongrandhotel.com. The overall look of this modern hotel is a nod towards traditional park lodges. Once you get past the smart public spaces, however – designed with tour groups in mind – the rooms themselves are no better than those at its cheaper neighbours or lesser in-park options, although there is a nice figure-of-eight indoor pool, and it's also home to the *Canyon Star* restaurant (see p.319). $229

Red Feather Lodge 106 Hwy-64 ⓣ928 638 2414 or ⓣ800 538 2345, ⓦredfeatherlodge.com. This long-established motel was joined a few years back by a large new hotel block. They share a pool, the rates aren't bad and the newer rooms offer a reasonably high standard. $126

Seven Mile Lodge AZ-64 ⓣ928 638 2291. The last remaining little roadside motel in Tusayan, this twenty-room place is very plain beyond its Pueblo-style doorway and hanging flowers, but it's the least expensive option around. Reservations are not accepted; rooms are simply doled out from 9am daily. Despite the slight premium charged for housing three or four guests in the same room, it's still great value for groups of (close) friends. $99

PHANTOM RANCH

★ **Phantom Ranch** Colorado River ⓣ303 297 2757 or ⓣ888 297 2757, ⓦgrandcanyonlodges.com. Located at river level, beside Bright Angel Creek near the bottom of the Bright Angel, South Kaibab and North Kaibab trails, *Phantom Ranch* can only be reached on foot or mule. First call on its fully equipped individual cabins goes to mule riders (see p.300), but they're also let to hikers when available, which is more likely in winter. Otherwise, hikers can get beds in one of the four ten-bunk, single-sex dormitories – two for men and two for women – with bedding, showers, towels and soap provided. Reservations are essential, while cancellations are handed out first-come, first-served, at the *Bright Angel Lodge* early each morning. All supplies reach *Phantom Ranch* the same way you do, so family-style meals in its restaurant are expensive, at $21 for breakfast and $28–44 for dinner. Dorms $46, cabins $149

CAMPING IN THE PARK

★ **Bright Angel Campground** Phantom Ranch area, Colorado River; details on ⓦnps.gov/grca; reserve via Backcountry office PO Box 129, Grand Canyon, AZ 86023 ⓣ928 638 2125. Accessible only on overnight backpacking trips, the beautiful *Bright Angel Campground*, amid the cottonwoods alongside Bright Angel Creek a quarter of a mile up from its confluence with the Colorado, holds 32 separate sites, each with its own picnic table. Camping is by backcountry permit only (see p.314); do not hike down without a reservation. $5

Desert View Campground Desert View ⓦnps.gov /grca. The park opens up this simple campsite, set back from the rim 25 miles east of Grand Canyon Village, in summer only (May to mid-Oct), on a first-come, first-served basis, with no RV hook-ups available. No reservations. $12

Mather Campground Grand Canyon Village, south of the main road not far from Market Plaza ⓣ928 638 7851, advance reservations ⓣ877 444 6777, ⓦrecreation.gov. Tent and RV camping (without hook-ups) is available year-round at *Mather Campground*, south of the main road through Grand Canyon Village, not far from Market Plaza. Sites holding up to two vehicles and six people can and should be reserved up to six months in advance for dates between March and mid-Nov. In winter, they're first-come, first-served, and the fee is lower. They also have walk-in sites for hikers and bikers year round. Walk-in sites $6, vehicle sites March to mid-Nov $18, mid-Nov to Feb $15

Trailer Village Adjacent to Mather Campground, Grand Canyon Village ⓣ303 297 2757 or ⓣ888 297 2757, ⓦgrandcanyonlodges.com. Exclusively RV sites with hook-ups, and open between May and mid-Oct only. Basic rates are for two people, with charges for each additional adult. $35

CAMPING OUTSIDE THE PARK

Camper Village 549 Camper Village Lane, Tusayan ⓣ928 638 2887, ⓦgrandcanyoncampervillage.com. Commercial campsite, just east of AZ-64 in central Tusayan, in easy walking distance of restaurants (though not the canyon itself) and equipped with its own small store. Open year-round. Tents $29, RVs $46

Flintstone's Bedrock City 332 AZ-64, Valle ⓣ928 635 2600. Run-down commercial campsite, 20 miles south of the park, with a simple store, snack bar and its own prehistoric theme park based on the cartoon series. Closed Nov to mid-March. Tents $20, RV hook-ups $25

Ten-X Campground AZ-64, 2 miles south of Tusayan ⓣ928 638 2443, ⓦfs.usda.gov; advance reservations ⓣ877 444 6777, ⓦrecreation.gov. Minimally equipped campground, with no hook-ups or showers, run by the Kaibab National Forest. Enjoying a peaceful forest setting, fifty of its seventy sizeable sites are first-come, first-served – and seldom full – while the remaining twenty can be booked in advance. Closed Oct–April. $10

EATING AND DRINKING

Grand Canyon Village offers a reasonably wide choice of places to **eat**, and prices in the budget cafeterias are not bad. Summer crowds can lead to endless queueing, however, and it's worth bringing at least some food with you. A few stores – notably the Canyon Village Marketplace, which has a pretty good **deli counter** (summer daily 7am–6pm, otherwise daily 8am 5pm) – sell basic supplies. Tusayan holds several fast-food options in addition to the places listed below. Both the *Bright Angel* and the *El Tovar* have atmospheric, traditional **bars** open until 11pm nightly.

Arizona Room *Bright Angel Lodge* ⓦgrandcanyon lodges.com. Informal, plain but good-quality restaurant, just a few yards from the rim; no views to speak of, but you do get a strong sense of the vast space nearby. The open kitchen serves conventional meat and seafood meals, with sandwiches, salads and simple main dishes costing $8–12 at lunchtime, and typical dinner prices including a slab of baby back ribs for $26, a 10oz steak for $24, or a cilantro lime chicken breast for $16.50. No reservations; nip in a little before sunset, or you may have to wait in the bar by the entrance for up to two hours. Daily 11.30am–3pm (March to mid-Sept only) & 4.30–10pm; closed early Jan to mid-Feb.

Bright Angel Dining Room *Bright Angel Lodge* (s e e p.317). Straightforward, windowless diner that serves pretty much anything you might want, from snacks and salads for around $10 to steaks at up to $26. No reservations. Daily 6am–10pm.

Canyon Cafe *Yavapai Lodge* ⓦgrandcanyonlodges .com. Locals prefer the *Yavapai*'s large cafeteria to the *Maswik*'s for its salad bar and fried chicken, and slightly lower prices, but if you're not staying here, it's not worth a special trip. All main dishes cost under $10, with daily specials at $9 and a two-piece chicken dinner for $6.50. The lines are often long, but it's possible to skip straight to the chicken counter. Beyond the central dining area, which has a dull canteen-like feel, there's a nicer glassed-in annexe. Summer daily 6am–10pm, spring and autumn daily 6am–9pm; shorter hours and closures in low season.

Canyon Coffee House *Bright Angel Lodge* (s e e p.317). Early-morning organic coffees and scones, served in the *Bright Angel*'s bar. Daily 5.30–11am.

Canyon Star *Grand Hotel*, 149 Hwy-64, Tusayan

ⓣ638 3333 or ⓣ888 634 7263, ⓦgrandcanyon grandhotel.com. Large, attractive hotel restaurant, where dinner is a choice between "hardy ranch fare", like $32 steaks or $22 barbecue ribs, or lighter salads and fish dishes. Lunchtime salads, sandwiches and Mexican staples mostly cost around $10. The food's nothing special, but the central dance floor hosts "Native American Experience" dances (6.30pm & 8pm nightly), often featuring hoop dancers, and live country music. The adjoining saloon has big-screen live sports. Daily 7–10am, 11am–2pm & 5–9pm.

★ **El Tovar** *El Tovar Hotel* ⓣ928 638 2631 ext 6432 ⓦgrandcanyonlodges.com. Very grand, very classy dark-wood dining room, with subdued lighting and great big windows that focus all attention outwards, especially at sunset – though only the front tier of tables have actual canyon views. Reservations are accepted for dinner only, and tend to be grabbed long in advance. The food itself is rich and expensive, especially at dinner, when main dishes such as roast duck or salmon tostada cost around $26, and steaks more like $35. Appetizers are a bit more imaginative, with devilled crab cakes at $12 and French onion soup at $7. Lunchtime sandwiches, tacos and so on cost more like $10–15. Daily 6.30am–11am, 11.30am–2pm & 5–10pm.

Maswik Cafeteria *Maswik Lodge* ⓦgrandcanyon lodges.com. Self-service fast food, aimed especially at tour groups, with separate Mexican and Italian sections, as well as burgers and standard plate lunches. Breakfast can come in under $5, but main dishes at lunch and dinner are closer to $10. Offers two spacious seating areas plus an adjoining "Pizza Pub", with sports TV and a substantial menu of $20, 16-inch pizzas, also available by the slice. Daily 6am–10pm; pub daily 11am–11pm.

DIRECTORY

Bank In Market Plaza, with 24hr ATM machine. Mon–Thurs 9am–5pm, Fri 9am–6pm.

Camping equipment Can be bought or rented at the Canyon Village Marketplace. Daily: summer 7am–8.30pm, spring & fall 8am–8pm, winter 8am–7pm.

Travellers with disabilities The *Accessibility Guide*, available at all visitor centres and lodges, provides full accessibility details; for further information, visit ⓦnps.gov /grca. At either park entrance station, you can obtain a permit enabling you to drive on Hermit Road. All shuttle buses except along Desert View Drive are wheelchair accessible.

Gas The closest gas stations to the South Rim are in Tusayan and at Desert View.

Internet access Wi-fi access at all lodges; free public computers in Park Headquarters, near Market Plaza.

Laundromat Near *Mather Campground*. Daily: summer 6am–11pm; spring and fall 7am–9pm; winter 8am–6pm.

Medical help Call ⓣ911 for emergencies; ⓣ928 638 2551 for the village clinic (daily 8am–6pm; emergencies only at other times); ⓣ928 638 2460 for the pharmacy; and ⓣ928 638 2395 for dentist.

Post office In the Market Plaza. Mon–Fri 9am–4.30pm, Sat 11am–1pm.

Showers Coin-operated showers, available to all visitors, are located in the laundromat building (hours as above).

6

The Havasupai reservation

92 miles north of I-40 exit 123, via AZ-66 and Arrowhead Hwy-18, then 8 miles on foot, horseback or helicopter • No entry to reservation without advance lodging reservation • Entrance fee $35 • ☎ 928 448 2121, ⓦ havasupaifalls.net

Havasu Canyon, one of the most spellbindingly beautiful places in the entire Southwest, nestles deep in the Grand Canyon, a mere 35 miles west of the park headquarters as the condor flies. The only approach is from the southwest, however, so it's a road trip of almost two hundred miles from the national park; once you leave the interstate, the last ninety miles lie across the endless Coconino Plateau.

Those visitors who brave the eight-mile desert hike down into the canyon are rewarded by a stunning oasis of **turquoise waterfalls** and lush vegetation, a Shangri-La that has been home for centuries beyond record to the same small group of Native Americans. They're here thanks to a geological fluke; although the canyon receives only nine inches of rain each year, all the water that falls for three thousand square miles around funnels down into this one narrow gorge, to create the year-round torrent of Havasu Stream. The down side of that is that the canyon is prone to repeated, devastating **flash floods**. The major flood in 2008, which caused immense damage and carved out a new set of waterfalls, was the fifth such in twenty years.

Havasu Canyon forms the heart of the **Havasupai reservation**, said by a 1930s anthropologist to be "the only spot in the United States where native culture has remained in anything like its pristine condition." Since then, tourism has become the mainstay of the tribal economy, but visitor numbers are kept deliberately low, at about 35,000 per year. Suggestions of building a road – or even a tramway – down into the canyon have always been rejected, to minimize the impact on the traditional way of life. Instead, the five hundred or so Havasupai earn their keep by ferrying non-hikers up and down the trail on horses and pack mules, and by operating a thriving **campground** beside the stream as well as a comfortable lodge in the village of **Supai**. Although visitors should not expect sweeping views of the Grand Canyon itself – or to have much interaction with the tribal members – for spectacular desert scenery and sheer romance, the Havasupai reservation is beyond compare.

The road to the reservation

The only way to get to the Havasupai reservation is via I-40, turning off at Seligman if you're coming from Flagstaff or Grand Canyon Village, or at Kingman from Las Vegas or California. In total, it takes between three and four hours to drive from Flagstaff, more like five from Las Vegas. Stock up with food, water and gas when you leave the interstate, then follow AZ-66 – the only surviving segment of Route 66 not superseded by newer roads – to the poorly marked intersection with Arrowhead Hwy-18, six miles east of Peach Springs.

Hwy-18 runs for its entire sixty-mile length with hardly a building in sight, across bare sagebrush desert interrupted by patches of thick ponderosa forest. Eventually it starts to wind down through burgeoning canyonlands, coming to an end at the large plateau known as **Hualapai Hilltop**.

At an elevation of 5200ft, the plateau commands a long view of the white-walled Hualapai Canyon, cutting into the tablelands as it stretches north toward its meeting with Havasu Canyon. Although the hilltop holds no more than a small cluster of dilapidated shacks, with no accommodation, food or gas available, there are usually far more vehicles parked here than you might anticipate for such a remote spot.

Hikers are free to set off from Hualapai Hilltop whenever they choose. From the end of the car park, the Hualapai Trail to Supai village zigzags steeply down the hillside to the right, and can then be seen threading its way across the valley floor below. As stressed above, do not attempt to go down unless you have already reserved accommodation.

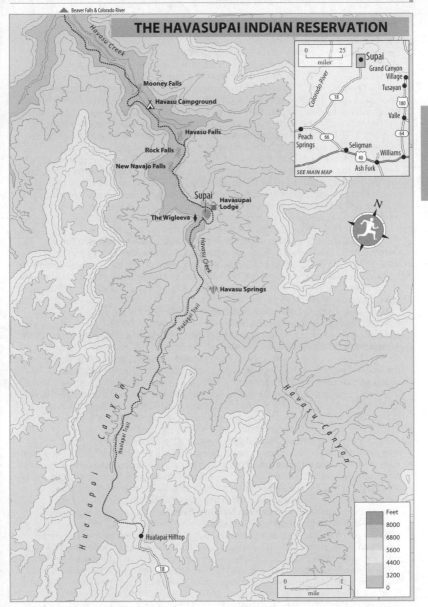

The trail to Supai

Beyond its initial switchbacks, the **Hualapai Trail** is not especially difficult. It is, however, a long eight-mile walk, with no shade for the first three miles and no reliable water source until very near the end. Allow around three hours to reach **Supai village** (and four or more to come back up again), and be sure to carry enough food and water for a day in the desert.

6

THE HAVASUPAI

The **Havasupai** – the "people of the blue-green water" – trace their occupation of Havasu Canyon back at least as far as 1300 AD. The word "**Pai**" means people and refers to a Yuman-speaking group that reached the Southwest via California well over a thousand years ago. They soon quarrelled, splitting to form the **Hualapai** ("People of the Tall Pines") of northwest Arizona, and the **Yavapai** ("Almost-People," who no longer quite deserved to be regarded as people) who settled along the Colorado further south. The Hualapai established close links with Pueblo groups such as the Hopi and Zuñi, from whom they eventually acquired the art of raising sheep and horses, as well as the seeds and skills to grow such crops as peaches. Until the Havasupai were allocated their own reservation toward the end of the nineteenth century, they regarded themselves not as a separate "tribe" but as just another band of Hualapai.

Although the Havasupai took their name from the turquoise river that watered their fields, they only lived on the canyon floor in summer, in houses of hide-covered branches. In winter, the canyon made a cold, miserable home, lacking big game and wood for fuel and receiving as little as five hours of sunlight per day. Instead, the Havasupai moved up onto the plateau to hunt deer, elk and antelope. Their territory extended beyond the San Francisco Peaks (near modern Flagstaff), and took in the region now occupied by Grand Canyon Village.

In the summer of 1776, as the Declaration of Independence was being signed in Philadelphia, the Havasupai welcomed their first white visitor, **Father Francisco Tomás Garcés** from San Xavier del Bac near Tucson (see p.230), with five days of feasting. Describing the Grand Canyon as a "calaboose of cliffs and canyons," he dubbed it the Puerto de Bucareli in honour of the Viceroy who had despatched him; more enduringly, he was the first to name the Río Colorado. Meanwhile, as Garcés explored the canyon, the rest of his expedition blazed a trail to California, where they founded San Francisco.

The Havasupai then remained undisturbed for eighty years, until Anglo prospectors and surveyors began to enter the region. Conflict arose in 1866, when Congress granted the Atlantic and Pacific Railroad company ownership of swathes of land adjoining its tracks across northern Arizona. Native resistance escalated into **war**, and the defeated Hualapai spent several years confined to a reservation near Ehrenberg on the Colorado. Because the Havasupai did not participate in the fighting, they were allowed to remain in their traditional territory. In negotiations over the extent of a permanent Havasupai reservation, the US government was as usual only prepared to acknowledge Native American "ownership" of land that held permanent settlements and cultivated fields. Fearful of being deported themselves, the Havasupai settled in 1882 for a tiny 518-acre plot at the bottom of Havasu Canyon. Restricted to a fraction of their former range, they were obliged to farm as intensively as possible.

During the ensuing century of hardship, the Havasupai repeatedly petitioned to have their reservation enlarged. Suffering great spiritual uncertainty, both the Havasupai and Hualapai took part in the 1890s **Ghost Dance** movement, joining in trance-like rituals designed to ensure that white men would vanish from the land and the old ways would return. The Havasupai also briefly adopted the rain-making *kachina* dances of the Hopi (see p.67), until a catastrophic **flood** on January 1, 1910, destroyed their village, which then stood half a mile from its current site.

At first, the creation of **Grand Canyon National Park** placed yet more restrictions on Havasupai use of traditional lands. The Havasupai survived largely through disobeying whatever unenforceable regulations outsiders sought to impose, continuing to spend their winters up on the plateau. Many Havasupai in due course found jobs in Grand Canyon Village, while tourism to Havasu Canyon itself became an important element in the tribal economy.

After endless legal battles, the Havasupai finally won their struggle in 1975. Almost 200,000 acres were added to the reservation, the largest tract of land ever returned to Native Americans. It came only just in time; almost immediately, the Grand Canyon region experienced a boom in **uranium** mining, with over 3500 claims filed in the Arizona Strip during the ensuing decade.

In 1988, Energy Fuels Nuclear was granted rights to develop **Canyon Mine**, at a site outside the reservation, close to **Red Butte** in the Kaibab National Forest, which is sacred to the Havasupai as *Mat Taav Tijundva*. Despite fears that the mine might contaminate Havasu Creek, Havasu Canyon and ultimately the Colorado itself, federal courts blocked Havasupai attempts to stop it. The mine was built, but did not go into operation at the time, thanks to a drop in world uranium prices. As this book went to press in 2013, it was looking very possible that Canyon Mine would finally resume production in 2015.

The route is very obvious and kept busy throughout the day with small supply trains of mules and horses. Once on the valley floor, it follows the bed of a dry wash between red-rock walls that slowly but inexorably climb to form a deep, narrow canyon. The sand underfoot is so thick that it shifts at every step, but the potential for flash floods is clear from the much-scoured rocks to either side. Mighty boulders occasionally all but block the path, while solitary cottonwoods reach up toward the thin strip of sky overhead.

After almost seven miles, the trail reaches the intersection where Havasu Canyon comes in from the right; until the disastrous flood of 1910, this was the site of Supai village. Do not continue straight ahead into Cataract Canyon at this point – it took three weeks to find a dehydrated camper who did so in 1975. Bear left instead, at a dense cluster of small trees. The sound of rushing water soon signals the emergence of Havasu Stream from hidden crevices in the rock; before long it's flowing through the parched landscape in all its blue-green splendour.

Not far beyond a footbridge across the creek, you cross a low rise to be confronted by the meadow that holds the modern village, and the two red-rock pillars that watch over Supai from the high canyon wall on the far side. Known as the **Wigleeva**, these twin sentinels, of which one is considered to be male and the other female, are regarded as the guardian spirits of the Havasupai.

Supai

Though located in a superb natural setting – a wide flat clearing surrounded on all sides by forbidding walls of red sandstone – the village of **SUPAI** is not in itself attractive. The Havasupai were only obliged to build a year-round settlement down in the canyon after losing their lands on the plateau above (see p.322), and this site was their second choice after the first proved prone to flooding. It too has suffered repeated damage ever since, most recently in the catastrophic flood of 2008. It therefore consists of just a scattering of basic timber-frame houses and prefabricated cabins. Even the name itself is a flimsy fabrication; "Supai" is a meaningless abbreviation of "Havasupai," invented by the US Post Office.

Once the Hualapai Trail, running alongside a line of irrigation ditches, has shepherded you into the village, the first building you come to holds the tribal **registration office**. Only campers are obliged to pay the $35 reservation **entrance fee** here; for lodge guests, it's added to their bill. A back room holds a small **museum** (daily 7am–7pm; donations welcome), with a reasonably interesting assortment of early twentieth-century photos and cuttings. The Havasupai are famous for crafts such as basket-making, so there's a case of assorted baskets, one of which has been coated with pine pitch to make it waterproof. On the whole, though, ancient artefacts have become too expensive for the museum to afford, so the finest old Havasupai baskets in Arizona are in Phoenix's Heard Museum (see p.208).

Fifty yards further on, beyond the only post office in the US still to receive its mail by pack mule, lies Supai's dusty, wind-blown **plaza**. Benches outside the village's one **grocery store** form its main social centre, where the older Havasupai gather each evening. The younger set, together with a vast population of dogs, are more likely to be found on the terrace of the **café**, opposite. Once past that, the trail skirts the edge of the village school, then branches left down toward the campground. Visitors are forbidden to wander off the main trail into the farm lands around the village.

Below Supai: the falls

All the **waterfalls** for which the Havasupai reservation is famous lie further down the canyon beyond Supai. To get there, follow the footpath out of the village from near the lodge; it takes several minutes to get clear of the straggle of farms and homes.

6

HAVASUPAI HORSES, HELICOPTERS AND HIKING TOURS

HORSE AND MULE RIDES

To ride rather than walk down the Hualapai Trail, you need to make a reservation when you book your accommodation. Each day, the mule train leaves the hilltop at some point between 10am and noon; if you arrive any later than noon, you won't be able to ride down, and you'll lose both your reservation and your deposit. To ride as far as the **village** costs $70 per person one-way and $120 round-trip, and should be arranged via the lodge (☎ 928 448 2111); riding to the **campground** costs $93.50 each way, and is arranged by the camping office (☎ 928 448 2121 or 2141); full details on ⓦ havasupaifalls.net. Riders' baggage weighing over ten pounds has to be carried separately – one animal can carry up to four packs, again for $70 one-way, $120 round-trip – and many hikers also arrange to have their bags carried.

HELICOPTER SHUTTLES

A **helicopter shuttle** service connects Hualapai Hilltop with Supai village. Call AirWest Helicopters on ☎ 623 516 2790 to check whether it's currently operational, and see schedules on ⓦ havasupaitribe.com. In recent years, it's been active between 10am and 1pm on Thurs, Fri, Sun, and Mon between mid-March and mid-October, and on Fri & Sun only between mid-October and mid-March. Passengers are carried on a first-come, first-served basis, without any advance reservations, for a one-way fare of $85.

It's also possible to charter a helicopter from the South Rim to the reservation, for around $600 per person, via Papillon (☎ 928 638 2419 or ☎ 888 635 7272, ⓦ papillon.com).

GUIDED TOURS

Arizona Outback Adventures ☎ 480 945 2881 or ☎ 866 455 1601, ⓦ aoa-adventures.com. Luxurious four-day trips with accommodation at their own "Base Camp." Prices start at $1499, with extra charges if you ride or fly rather than hike.

Discovery Treks ☎ 520 404 1151 or ☎ 888 256 8731, ⓦ discoverytreks.com. Three-day trips with a choice of hiking, horseback riding and helicopter rides, and camping or staying in the lodge. Prices range upwards from $895.

Grand Canyon Field Institute ☎ 928 638 2481 or ☎ 866 471 4435, ⓦ grandcanyon.org /fieldinstitute. Three highly recommended four-day hiking and camping tours each summer, one of which is reserved for women only, for a fee of around $750.

New Navajo Falls and Rock Falls

The riverbed immediately below Supai village is forever being reshaped by flash floods and fresh erosion. The flood of August 2008 scoured out a great new chasm, well over 100ft deep. Leaving the former Navajo Falls high and dry, it created two spectacular new cascades. The first you come to, known as **New Navajo Falls**, is a short walk left of the trail roughly a mile down. Tumbling over a wide cliff face in countless separate strands, it shrouds a regrowth of young ferns and saplings in a mist of white spray.

From the foot of the falls, Havasu Creek has carved a new course through a churned-up landscape of bare mud. The riverbed itself is extraordinarily green and verdant, but scores of dead aspens, whose roots no longer reach the water table, look down forlornly from the high cliffs on its far side.

Another quarter-mile along, the second of the new falls, **Rock Falls**, usually consists of a single expansive cascade. The full width of the river roars over a 20ft drop, immediately before making a sharp turn; it's possible to swim in the pool immediately below the falls.

Havasu Falls

When the trail appears to divide, half a mile beyond Rock Falls, take the left fork and follow it down to a footbridge over the creek (the right fork climbs briefly to an unimportant overlook). You're now approaching the stupendous double cascade of **Havasu Falls**. First seen from an overlook more or less level with the top, this is an absolutely breathtaking sight. The creek foams white as it hurtles over a 150ft cliff, to crash into shallow terraces filled with limpid turquoise water. The rock formations all around are formed from water-deposited limestone known as **travertine** – the same stuff that creates the stalactites of Carlsbad Caverns and clogs the inside of domestic kettles. It's the light travertine coating on the riverbed that gives the water its astonishing blue-green glow. Be sure not to walk barefoot on it, however; travertine is horrendously sharp stuff.

In the days when it was known to the park service as **Bridal Veil Falls**, Havasu Falls used to be a long broad expanse of water, which explains the solidified sheets and curtains of travertine that run right across its wide brim. Then a flash flood punched out a notch right in the centre, through which the falls now gush to either side of a small outcrop that's knitted together by a frail cottonwood sapling.

Side trails off the main path lead down to an idyllic shaded "beach" beside the largest, deepest pool, where the ceaseless roar makes conversation difficult, but swimming is all but irresistible. Cross to the far side of the river, traversing the travertine dams that divide the various terraces, to reach a group of picnic tables standing in a cottonwood grove at the mouth of a side canyon.

Havasu Campground

A short distance beyond Havasu Falls, two miles down from Supai village, you finally reach **Havasu Campground**, set in an especially narrow and high-walled segment of the canyon. Once a tribal burial ground, this site was only added to the reservation in 1975, having originally been considered to be too rich in mineral deposits to be left to the Indians.

Today, the campground stretches for around three-quarters of a mile. Sadly, this entire area sustained major damage in the 2008 flood, and was heavily denuded of its formerly luxuriant cottonwood trees. Although villagers are barred from the area in summer by tribal edict, groups of horses stand tethered at the entrance, waiting to carry campers back up the hill.

Mooney Falls and the Colorado River

Havasu campground is brought to an abrupt end by the precipitous, and once again luridly turquoise, 196ft **Mooney Falls**. This natural barrier was long regarded, even by the Havasupai, as impassable. Its modern name comes from an unfortunate prospector who fell to his death here in 1880, after a rope snagged as he was being lowered to the bottom. It took several months before his companions managed to bore through the travertine to retrieve his body, which lay by then beneath a fresh coating of limestone.

Though Mooney Falls was barely affected by the 2008 flood, the trail to the bottom remains little better today. Having scrambled down the travertine ledges to reach the two successive tunnels that drop through the cliff face, you come to a sheer section that was blasted away in a 1993 flood, and now consists of a vertical series of footholds aided by an iron chain fixed into the rock. The prospect of having to climb back up is terrifying enough to make many hikers turn back at this point; if you press on, there are also two steep ladders to contend with. Assuming you do make it to the bottom, the pools and swimming holes at the foot of the falls are once again gorgeous.

A long day-hike from the campground continues on for three miles to **Beaver Falls**, a quick-fire set of rapids that's as far as the Havasupai recommend any visitors should try to go. Negotiating an onwards route involves climbing up to and along a high ledge, after which it takes four more miles to reach the Colorado itself. Quite possibly, you'd be greeted by river-runners who preferred to get here the easy way, shooting 157 miles of whitewater from Lees Ferry (see p.329).

ACCOMMODATION AND EATING   HAVASUPAI RESERVATION

Havasu Campground Havasu Canyon ☎928 448 2121 or ☎448 2141, ⱳhavasupaifalls.net. Facilities in the creekside campground, which holds around three hundred campers, are primitive in the extreme, though at least safe drinking water is provided by fresh springs in the canyon wall. Tents can be pitched to either side of

6

the creek, which is usually shallow and is in any case crossed by makeshift footbridges. There are no showers or phones, and fires are not permitted. Reservations are compulsory. $23.70

Havasupai Lodge Supai Village ☎ 928 448 2111 or ☎ 448 2201, ⓦ havasupaifalls.net. Set slightly apart from things on the edge of the village, close to the canyon wall behind the school, this simple two-storey structure, a functional motel rather than an atmospheric park lodge, holds plain but comfortable air-conditioned rooms, without phones or TVs. All sleep four people. Advance bookings are compulsory, and very hard to get between May and October. $159.50

Tribal Café Main Plaza, Supai Village ☎ 928 448 2981. The food, in the only place to get a **meal** in Supai, is far from exciting, with fried breakfasts, and a lunch or dinner of beef stew, Indian fry bread, or burritos; pretty much everything seems to cost around $9, or more if you want grated cheese on top. Daily: summer 6am–7pm, winter 8am–5pm.

The Hualapai reservation: Grand Canyon West

Immediately west of the Havasupai reservation, and also inhabited by descendants of the Pai people, the **Hualapai Indian reservation** spreads across almost a million acres, bounded to the north by a 108-mile stretch of the Colorado River.

A cluster of overlooks above that river frontage is promoted as **Grand Canyon West**, and also sometimes known as the "**West Rim**" of the Grand Canyon. While it's been tremendously hyped in the last few years, thanks to the construction of the glass-floored **Skywalk** over the canyon, it's very far from being a must-see attraction – and it's also extraordinarily **expensive** and time-consuming to visit. If you're an outdoors type, eager to immerse yourself in the magnificent desert wildernesses of the Southwest, this probably isn't for you. If you're happy to pay premium prices for a once-in-a-lifetime thrill, on the other hand, it may be.

It can't be emphasized enough that Grand Canyon West bears no relation to the canyon at its best. This far west, the canyon is starting to peter out; it lacks the colossal depth and width of its central section, and holds none of the towering mesas, buttes and temples so conspicuous from the South or North Rim viewpoints. The so-called West Rim is really just a canny piece of marketing aimed at Las Vegas' forty million annual tourists. This is the closest spot to Las Vegas where it's possible to see the Grand Canyon, and most of its visitors are day-trippers who don't realize that this isn't the canyon proper. That said, the West Rim is undeniably an impressive spectacle, and offers several unique experiences, including helicopter flights down to the Colorado, and short river trips, as well as the Skywalk.

The only entrance to Grand Canyon West is at the **airport**, a few hundred yards short of the rim. To reach the Skywalk and other viewpoints, further down the road, you have to join a **bus tour** from here. If you've flown in, some package will already be included in the overall price you've paid; otherwise, the prices are outlined in the box on p.327.

The Skywalk

Eagle Point, a short distance from Grand Canyon West airport • $33

The **Skywalk** is a horseshoe-shaped glass-bottomed walkway that juts out a short way from the rim, four thousand feet above the canyon floor. However, whatever impression the publicity may give, it's not on the main canyon rim, and not directly above the Colorado, but on one rim of a narrow, unnamed side canyon, the cliff face on the other side of which bears an uncanny resemblance to a massive eagle with its wings outstretched. Supposedly to protect its glass floor, **cameras are forbidden** on the walkway, so you have to pay an official photographer if you want to capture the big moment.

6

THE SHEER COST OF VISITING GRAND CANYON WEST

Any independent traveller planning to visit Grand Canyon West needs to be aware that it's much, much more **expensive** than any other outdoors destination covered in this book. The following charges apply to all independent visitors to Grand Canyon West; if you buy a flight-seeing or other tour from Las Vegas, check exactly what the quoted price includes.

All visitors have to buy at least the $44 Hualapai Legacy package; the price includes tribal taxes and an $8 "impact fee", and covers use of the shuttle-buses to reach Eagle Point, Guano Point and Hualapai Ranch, but not the Skywalk or any food. Note that, in theory at least, you are not permitted to bring your own food or drink onto the reservation.

The $57 Legacy Silver package includes one meal at any of the viewpoints, which would otherwise cost $17 if bought separately, while the $88 Legacy Gold package additionally includes a ticket for the Skywalk, which costs $33 if bought separately. Having your photo taken on the Skywalk – you can't take your own camera – costs another $30.

Further optional extras include horseback rides ($11 for 10min in the arena; rim rides $38 for 30min, $82 for 90min); a sightseeing helicopter flight ($138 for 15min); and a helicopter flight down to the river, where you take a pontoon boat ride ($171).

Thus two adults who drive to the West Rim, and walk on the Skywalk, will pay a minimum of $176 for the day. With no reductions for children, families can expect to pay double that.

Full details can be found on ⓦ www.grandcanyonwest.com.

Guano Point

At the dead end of the road, two miles from the terminal, the unfortunately named **Guano Point** surveys long stretches of the Colorado in both directions. Though the Grand Canyon looks as if it could go on forever, in fact it comes to an end not far beyond the next bend in the river to the west, where it bisects the Grand Wash Cliffs.

The Colorado River

No hiking trail connects Grand Canyon West with the Colorado River below, but many visitors take the four-minute **helicopter** ride down from the terminal. The flight in itself is a major adventure, and it's also a real thrill to find yourself walking down by the river in the depths of the inner gorge.

A short footpath leads down from the landing site to the river's edge, where wooden jetties act as the base for the pontoons and jet boats that sweep visitors out for a quick swirl on the river. The adjoining beach is the terminus for the Hualapai's one-day rafting trips (see p.301); participants fly out from here.

ARRIVAL AND DEPARTURE   GRAND CANYON WEST

By car The best routes to Grand Canyon West approach not from the east via Peach Springs, but on two separate paved roads from the west and south. The busier **Pearce Ferry Road** heads northeast from US-93, thirty miles north of Kingman and forty miles south of the Hoover Dam. Twenty-eight miles along, you'll turn east on Diamond Bar Road. The other paved route to this same spot, the forty-mile **Stockton Hill Road**, runs due north from central Kingman to meet Pearce Ferry Road around twelve miles short of Diamond Bar Road.

THE SKYWALK FALLS TO EARTH

Although the Hualapai built the **Skywalk** as a joint venture with Las Vegas-based developer David Jin, the partnership had already broken down by the time it was opened to visitors in 2007. As a result, a proposed visitor centre alongside the walkway has never been completed. The tribe seized control of the Skywalk from Jin in 2012, and then **declared bankruptcy** in 2013 after a federal Judge ruled that move illegal. As this book went to press, Grand Canyon West was still open for business, ostensibly run by a separate Hualapai entity; **check before you visit**, though, as the future is not looking bright.

6

FLYING TO GRAND CANYON WEST

Flight-seeing tours to Grand Canyon West from Las Vegas start at around $135 by plane (without landing) or $250 by helicopter. Expect to pay at least $250 by plane or $300 by helicopter for a tour that includes walking on the Skywalk, and up to $500 for a helicopter tour that lands down by the river as well.

Note that many flights depart not from Las Vegas itself, but from Boulder City, thirty miles southeast.

Grand Canyon Airlines ☎928 638 2359, ⓦgrandcanyonairlines.com.
Maverick ☎702 261 0007, ⓦmaverickhelicopter.com.

Papillon ☎702 736 7243, ⓦpapillon.com.
Scenic Airlines ☎702 638 3300, ⓦscenic.com.
Sundance ☎702 736 0606, ⓦsundancehelicopters.com.

Diamond Bar Road itself climbs for fourteen rocky miles to reach the Hualapai reservation, where the airstrip and Grand Canyon West headquarters lie five miles farther up the road.

Peach Springs

The only town on the Hualapai reservation, **PEACH SPRINGS**, is fifty miles southeast of Grand Canyon West as the crow flies, but not connected to it by road. Instead you have to reach it along Route 66 from I-40, by heading either fifty miles northeast of Kingman, or 35 miles northwest of **Seligman**. Home to just under a thousand of the total Hualapai population of around 1500, Peach Springs is no more than a straggle of buildings along the highway.

ACCOMMODATION   PEACH SPRINGS

Hualapai Lodge 900 AZ-66, Peach Springs ☎928 769 2230 or ☎888 255 9550, ⓦwww.grandcanyonwest.com/lodge.php. This shiny, modern lodge, prominent in the heart of Peach Springs, holds sixty good-sized motel bedrooms and a reasonable restaurant, open for all meals. **$140**

The road between the rims

Although the South and North rims of the Grand Canyon stand just eleven miles apart, the shortest driving route between them takes 215 miles, and at least four hours. Very few towns lie along the way, but the scenery is seldom less than spectacular. Starting from Grand Canyon Village, you follow first Desert View Drive and then AZ-64 east, which runs close to the gorge of the **Little Colorado** (look out for Navajo trinket stalls) until it meets US-89 at **Cameron**. Head north to cross **Marble Canyon** on Navajo Bridge, then continue west on US-89A to **Jacob Lake**, where you take AZ-67 44 miles south to the North Rim. As most of this route is on the Navajo reservation, which observes daylight savings time, for six months of each year clocks at any establishment en route are set one hour later than at the Grand Canyon.

Cameron

Tiny **CAMERON**, which amounts to little more than a handful of buildings, lies a mile or so north of the intersection of AZ-64 and US-89, on the south side of the suspension bridge spanning the Little Colorado River.

The **Cameron Trading Post** here, established in 1911, stocks a huge array of Southwest arts and crafts, from mass-produced trinkets and jeans to genuine Hopi *kachinas* and museum-quality Navajo rugs. While busy with tourists in summer, it remains at heart a trading centre for the Navajo Nation, still conducting some of its business by barter.

Marble Canyon and Navajo Bridge

Fifteen miles north of Cameron, US-160 branches northeast toward Monument Valley and Colorado via **Tuba City** (see p.51). Continuing north, after another forty miles of emptiness US-89 climbs up the mesa to the right, heading for Page and Glen Canyon Dam (see p.393). US-89A, however, presses on at the foot of the **Echo Cliffs**, to reach **Navajo Bridge** after a further fifteen miles.

There are in fact two Navajo Bridges. The 1929 original is now reserved for pedestrians only; a wider facsimile opened 150ft downstream in 1995. The Colorado at this point cuts through the chasm of **Marble Canyon** – it's such a narrow interruption in the vast flat plains that you can't tell it's there until you're right on top of it.

On the west bank, the **Navajo Bridge Interpretive Center** (daily: mid-April to mid-Oct 9am–5pm; ☎928 355 2319, ⓦnps.gov/glca) is not so much a visitor centre as a good bookstore, stocking literature about the Glen Canyon region.

Lees Ferry

Before the construction of Navajo Bridge, ferries struggled across the river at **LEES FERRY**, six miles north. Mormon elder Jacob Hamblin was guided to this remote spot – the only place within hundreds of miles to offer easy land access to both banks of the Colorado – by Naraguts, a Paiute, in 1858.

Thirteen years later, **John Doyle Lee** was sent here to set up a ferry service to help Mormon missionaries en route south into Arizona. Lee was on the run after the **Mountain Meadows Massacre** in Utah in 1857, when a wagon train of would-be settlers was slaughtered by an armed white band clumsily disguised as Indians, Lee among them. He was finally arrested in 1874 and executed in 1877, but his (seventeenth) wife Emma remained here. Determined not to honour Lee, Congress passed a special act to remove the apostrophe from what used to be "Lee's Ferry."

The ferry service was always perilous, with the boats in constant danger of being swept downstream, and was finally abandoned after a fatal accident in 1928. A crucial piece of equipment needed to finish the bridge on the left bank was stranded on the right bank; the only way to get it across was to take it eight hundred miles by road, via Las Vegas.

Lees Ferry marks the confluence of the Paria River with the Colorado; **Paria River Beach**, at the foot of the gently sloping road from Marble Canyon, is the official start of the Grand Canyon. To the south, the broad Colorado picks up speed as it squeezes into Marble Canyon. A few hundred yards north, across the Paria, the large parking lot is where **whitewater rafting** expeditions set off into the Grand Canyon – the first point where boats can get out again is at Diamond Creek, twelve days away by muscle power. From the far end of the lot, a trail leads within a couple of hundred yards to sturdy **Lees Ferry Fort**, erected in 1874 as defence against Navajo attacks that never materialized.

Lonely Dell Ranch

John Lee lived not at the ferry site, but in the much more congenial surroundings of the **Lonely Dell Ranch**, nestled in a fertile curve of the Paria River around half a mile up from the confluence. His original **log cabin** stands not far beyond a replanted approximation of his **orchards**, rich with apple, pear, plum and peach trees. For serious backpackers, this marks the end of an epic four- to six-day hike that traces the full length of **Paria Canyon**, starting at the White House trailhead off US-89 between Kanab and Page (see p.365).

The Vermilion Cliffs

West of Marble Canyon, US-89A curves beneath the southernmost section of the **Vermilion Cliffs**. These soaring sandstone walls glow a magnificent red at sunrise and sunset, but the road itself is featureless.

Once past the southernmost promontory of the cliffs, the highway runs straight as an arrow across the broad sagebrush desert. Just under forty miles from the river, it hits the Kaibab Mountains and climbs through thick forest for the final eleven miles to Jacob Lake.

Jacob Lake and DeMotte Park

Deep in the pine forest 44 miles north of the North Rim, the crossroads community of **JACOB LAKE** looks more like a Canadian logging camp than anything you'd expect to find in Arizona. In winter, when AZ-67 down to the Grand Canyon is closed by snow, Jacob Lake goes into hibernation; in summer, however, it makes a good living from the constant stream of tourists.

Jacob Lake is named for Jacob Hamblin, a Mormon missionary to the Paiute and Navajo. The Mormons made little use of the forests to the south, however, apart from grazing their cattle in large meadow-like clearings such as **DEMOTTE PARK**, 27 miles from Jacob Lake, along the road to the canyon. The park entrance is another five miles down the road, with visitor facilities nine miles beyond that.

ACCOMMODATION AND EATING

CAMERON

Cameron Trading Post 466 US-89, Cameron ☎ 928 679 2231 or ☎ 800 338 7385, ⦿ camerontradingpost .com. All the rooms in this large motel complex, surrounded by beautifully landscaped gardens, are smart, and those on the upper floors have large balconies that look out across the Little Colorado. A pleasant dining room with tin ceiling and large fireplace serves all meals, though the food itself is nothing special, with Navajo tacos at around $10 and steaks more like $20 (daily: summer 6am–10pm; otherwise 7am–9.30pm). RVs **$25**, rooms **$109**

MARBLE CANYON

Marble Canyon Lodge US-89A, not far west of Navajo Bridge, just past the turnoff for Lees Ferry ☎ 928 355 2225 or ☎ 800 726 1789, ⦿ marblecanyoncompany .com. More than fifty conventional motel-style rooms, with TVs but no phones, in low-slung buildings in a romantic desert-outpost setting at the foot of the cliffs. In the adequate but unexciting restaurant, open for all meals daily, main dishes cost $8–14, and a Navajo taco salad is $9. **$80**

VERMILION CLIFFS

Cliff Dweller's Lodge US-89A, 6 miles west of Lees Ferry Lodge ☎ 928 355 2261 or ☎ 800 962 9755, ⦿ cliffdwellerslodge.com. Built in 1890 as a mocked-up "ancient ruin", now run as a standard-issue Western motel, this little place is geared primarily towards river-runners, and also runs river fishing expeditions, so its restaurant – which has an attractive shady patio – makes a very early start (summer Mon–Thurs 5–10am & 4–10pm, Fri–Sun 5am–10pm; shorter hours in winter). **$80**

Lees Ferry Lodge US-89A, 3 miles west of Marble Canyon Lodge ☎ 928 355 2231, ⦿ vermilioncliffs.com.

Besides ten appealingly rustic guest cabins of varying sizes, in a very pretty location, this 1929 compound centres on a friendly little restaurant that serves good food, with main courses costing up to $20, washed down with an extraordinary range of bottled beers (daily: summer 6.30am–10pm; shorter hours in winter). **$80**

JACOB LAKE

Jacob Lake Campground US-89A, just west of intersection ☎ 928 643 7395, ⦿ fs.usda.gov/kaibab. Lovely wooded campground that caters to **tent campers** only, and is run by the Forest Service, which also has a visitor centre nearby. Closed mid-Oct to mid-May. **$17**

Jacob Lake Inn intersection of US-89A and AZ-67 ☎ 928 643 7232, ⦿ jacoblake.com. Sprawling but welcoming complex of timber-frame buildings at the road junction, open year round. Simple motel rooms and log cabins plus a gas station, a general store, an old-fashioned diner counter, and a restaurant where chicken, trout, or steak entrees cost well under $20. Cabins **$107**, rooms **$139**

DEMOTTE PARK

Kaibab Lodge AZ-67, 27 miles south of Jacob Lake ☎ 928 638 2389 in summer, ☎ 928 526 0924 in winter, or ☎ 800 525 0924, ⦿ kaibablodge.com. Three different kinds of cabin – cosy older ones with bare wooden floors, a few slightly more expensive ones with motel-style trimmings, and three larger family units with their own sitting rooms – set at the edge of an idyllic meadow. A simple restaurant that's open for all meals daily, from breakfast blueberry pancakes to $25 dinner steaks. mid-May to Oct only. Old cabins **$90**, newer cabins **$125**, family units **$170**

The North Rim

Higher, bleaker, and much more remote than the South Rim, the **North Rim** of the Grand Canyon is accessible to travellers for about half the year. Once **AZ-67**, the only road in, has been blocked by the first major snowfall of the winter, the area remains closed until the following spring. Although that first snow used to arrive toward the end of October, in several recent years the area has received a mere fraction of its official average annual snowfall of 140 inches, and the road has been known to close as late as December 19. The one accommodation option on the North Rim, *Grand Canyon Lodge*, continues to operate on a more rigid schedule, opening during the second week of May and closing on October 15. After it closes, the park itself remains open until the snow comes, but no food, gas, or lodging other than camping is available, and visitors must be prepared to leave at a moment's notice.

Even in peak season, the North Rim offers a sense of splendid isolation, and it receives less than a tenth as many visitors as the South Rim. You won't have the place to yourself, but you can still feel as though you're venturing into unexplored wilderness. The canyon itself is significantly different this side of the Colorado. Erosion is much more active: twice as much rain falls, and it freezes more often. As the Kaibab Plateau slopes south, the water flows toward the rim, which has cut twice as far back from the river, so the North Rim is far more indented with massive side canyons. The basic experience of visiting, however, is the same, with a cluster of venerable park-service buildings at **Bright Angel Point**, where the main highway reaches the canyon, and another rim-edge road where drivers can take their pick from additional lookouts.

Bright Angel Point

All visitor activity on the North Rim focuses on the glorified log cabin known as *Grand Canyon Lodge*. A short paved trail leads from its left side to the very tip of **Bright Angel Point**. In places, the trail fills the full width of the slender spit of land, with sheer drops to either side. After four hundred yards, you reach the sanctuary of a railed viewing area, backed by massive boulders that daredevils climb in search of solitude. Everyone understandably regards the prospect ahead as one of the great Grand Canyon panoramas, but strictly speaking the canyon itself is all but obscured by the long straight gorge of Bright Angel Canyon, cutting at an oblique angle across your entire field of vision.

Away to the right, you can just about see where it joins the Grand Canyon proper, but none of the Granite Gorge, let alone the Colorado River, is visible. You may hear the sound of rushing water, but it's coming from **Roaring Springs**, much closer to hand at almost 3500ft below, which supplies all the water used by the park on both rims.

Mentally extending the line of Bright Angel Canyon across to the far side reveals the fault continuing up to the South Rim, though it's hard to spot a sign of life at Grand Canyon Village, eleven miles away, until the sun goes down and the lights start to flicker. That simple turn of the head also traces the easiest trans-canyon hiking route – the **North Kaibab Trail**, which drops down to the Colorado on this side via Roaring Springs and Bright Angel canyons, and climbs up via the matching Bright Angel Trail across the river. On foot, that's a 24-mile one-way hike.

On a clear day, looking directly ahead, you can see far beyond the South Rim to the San Francisco Peaks near Flagstaff. The highest point on the horizon, Mount Humphreys, is 62 miles distant and 12,633ft high.

Cape Royal Road

Apart from Bright Angel Point, all the North Rim's **canyon overlooks** are ranged along the eastern edge of the **Walhalla Plateau**, a considerable drive east from *Grand Canyon Lodge*. This long, high headland is reached by turning east onto **Fuller Canyon**

6

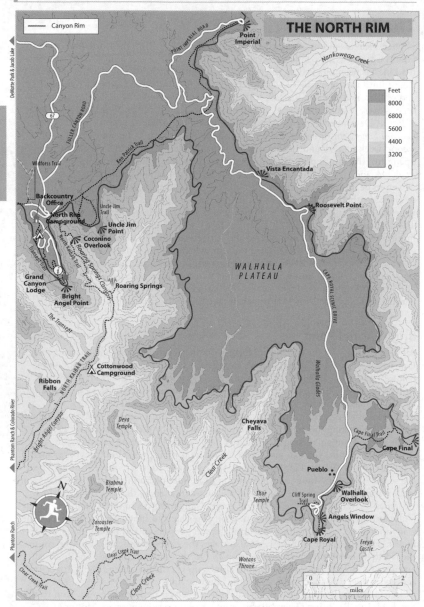

Road, three miles north of the *Lodge*. At a junction five miles along, **Point Imperial Road** branches off to the left, while **Cape Royal Road** winds into the cool dense woods to the right.

Even if your time is limited, it's well worth making your way right to **Cape Royal**, fifteen miles from the junction at the end of Cape Royal Road. From the unremarkable parking lot, an even, paved footpath leads first to **Angels Window**, a natural archway just below the top of a rocky spur. As you approach, you can look through it all the way down to the Colorado River. An extremely narrow railed pathway that detours off the main trail a little further along leads onto the top of the "window," for views across to the flatlands of the Navajo reservation. Two broad, green-trimmed stretches of river are visible from this point, including the foaming Unkar Creek Rapid.

Views from **Cape Royal** itself, a couple of hundred yards further along the main trail, extend much further west – virtually the full 360 degrees, though the intervening ridge immediately west obscures Bright Angel Point. This is the only Walhalla viewpoint from which you can see the central portion of the Grand Canyon, with major landmarks like Wotan's Throne and Vishnu Temple straight ahead, and Brahma and Zoroaster temples off to the right. The canyon is much narrower here, so flat-topped **Cedar Mountain** is very conspicuous, just above the South Rim.

Other possible halts along Cape Royal Road include **Walhalla Overlook**, a mile or so from the end, where a very short forest trail ends at the foundation walls of a small Ancestral Puebloan dwelling place. **Roosevelt Point**, halfway between Walhalla and Fuller Canyon Road, looks across Marble Canyon toward the Echo Cliffs.

Point Imperial

Turn left at the intersection of Fuller Canyon and Cape Royal roads for a gradual three-mile climb to **Point Imperial**. Although at 8803ft this is the highest spot along either rim of the entire canyon, the actual overlook lies just below the parking lot. A long red sandy ridge pokes out beneath your feet, with a stark butte at the end, while to the right is the thickly wooded ridge that ends at Cape Royal. Looking down, the landscape is as dry as dust, a labyrinth of spurs and buttes in which it's virtually impossible to guess which is the main gorge of the Colorado. The plateau of the Navajo reservation on the far side is almost three thousand feet lower, so it spreads for miles, pierced by further chasms and gorges. To the southeast, the Little Colorado emerges from its own canyon to join the main onward rush of the Colorado.

North Rim hikes

Hikers on the Grand Canyon's North Rim should take the same precautions – and be as aware of their capabilities – as their counterparts on the South Rim (see p.310). There tends to be less scope for getting into difficulties here, however, as almost all the North Rim trails suitable for day-hiking stay on top of the plateau. On the only route that descends into the canyon itself, the **North Kaibab Trail**, hiking to the river and back in a single day is completely out of the question – it's a 28-mile round-trip with a 6000ft change in elevation.

The North Kaibab Trail

Trailhead: 2 miles north of Grand Canyon Lodge • Day-hike to Supai Tunnel 4 miles round-trip, 3–5hr; day-hike to Roaring Springs 9.4 miles round-trip, 7–9hr; Phantom Ranch 14 miles one-way, with overnight stop at Cottonwood Campground 6.8 miles down

Some version of the **North Kaibab Trail**, following Bright Angel Creek down to the Colorado, has been in use for over a thousand years. Its current route, which starts by descending through Roaring Springs Canyon from a roadside trailhead, was established in the late 1920s. Parking at the trailhead is limited, but a limited, early-morning **hiker shuttle** service leaves *Grand Canyon Lodge* at 5.20am and 7.20am daily, costing $8 for the first person in each group, plus $5 per additional passenger.

Planning a day-hike on the North Kaibab, it's easy to be overambitious; the mileages may not sound that great, but the gradient is steep from the word go. Many people go no further than the **Coconino Overlook**, just 1.4 miles down through the fir forests, a high rocky vantage point from which you can see the junction of Roaring Springs and Bright Angel canyons. The gorgeous waterfalls at **Roaring Springs** come after another 3.6 miles, during which the trail burrows through the **Supai Tunnel**, crosses the suspended **Redwall Bridge**, and makes some spectacular cliffside traverses. Water from the springs is pumped up to the *Lodge* and also piped over to the South Rim, but there's enough left over to tend the "gardens" downstream that were originally planted by the Ancestral Puebloans.

The well-shaded **Cottonwood Campground**, 2.5 miles beyond the springs, is a major way-station for transcanyon hikers. The highlight of the final seven-mile segment to **Phantom Ranch** (see p.312) is lacy **Ribbon Falls**, reached via a short spur trail a mile past the campground.

Rim-edge trails

The ten-mile **Ken Patrick Trail**, the best canyon-edge trail near Bright Angel Point, alternates dramatic views with dense forest as it leads from the North Kaibab Trailhead all the way to Point Imperial. The four-mile **Uncle Jim Trail** branches off it half a mile along, to reach a viewpoint that overlooks the North Kaibab Trail, while the **Widforss Trail** heads the other way, west from the inland end of Bright Angel Point to the tip of the next headland along.

INFORMATION AND TOURS

THE NORTH RIM

Visitor centre At the entrance to *Grand Canyon Lodge* (mid-May to mid-Oct daily 8am–6pm; ☎928 638 7864, ⊛nps.gov/grca).

Tours No organized sightseeing tours are available at the North Rim, and there's no equivalent to the viewpoint shuttle buses that operate along the South Rim.

Transcanyon Shuttle The only public transportation to serve the North Rim (☎602 638 2820, ⊛trans-canyonshuttle.com). A van leaves from *Grand Canyon Lodge* at 7am daily, reaches the South Rim at 11.30am, then departs again at 1.30pm, and arrives back at the North Rim at 6pm. A one-way trip costs $85, and the round-trip $160; reservations required.

Mule rides A desk in the *Grand Canyon Lodge* lobby handles reservations for mule rides (☎435 679 8665, ⊛canyonrides.com). A one-hour rim-edge ride costs $40, while two half-day options – either along the rim to Uncle Jim Point or down the North Kaibab as far as the Supai Tunnel – cost $80. There are no full-day rides or overnight trips.

ACCOMMODATION AND EATING

Deli in the Pines Grand Canyon Lodge ☎928 638 2611. Little windowless cafeteria, serving very ordinary breakfasts, then deli sandwiches or salads for around $7 and pizza either by the slice or whole pie ($15–20). Daily 7am–9pm.

★ **Grand Canyon Lodge** ☎480 337 1320 or ☎877 386 4383, ⊛grandcanyonlodgenorth.com. Guest rooms are not in the main lodge building but in individual cabins and larger motel-style blocks. Most are ranged over the quiet, well-wooded hillside beside the approach road. Each of the well-appointed Western Cabins has a full-size bathroom and a porch and can sleep up to four people; just four stand close enough to the rim to offer canyon views; they cost $10 extra per night, which makes them fabulous value, but very difficult to reserve. The more spartan Frontier Cabins can accommodate three guests each and have smaller bathrooms, while the similar Pioneer Cabins have two separate bedrooms. In addition, a couple of two-storey blocks located furthest from the lodge hold twenty motel rooms apiece, each with a queen bed and private bathroom. Only the Frontier Cabins and the motel rooms have telephones. Reservations for all are available up to thirteen months in advance, and are absolutely essential. Cancellations are frequently available at short notice, so keep calling if you can't get a room or the precise kind of room you want. Motel rooms $124,

Pioneer & Frontier Cabins $129, Western Cabins $195

Lodge Dining Room Grand Canyon Lodge ☎928 638 2611, or ☎928 645 6865 out of season, ⊛grandcanyonlodgenorth.com. The room itself, with its soaring timber ceiling, is elegant and impressive, and if you get a window table (assigned at random), you'll enjoy awesome canyon views. The actual food is standard American resort cuisine, with mains such as blackened salmon or mushroom pasta costing around $20, and prime rib and steaks ranging up to $30. Lunch options, at around $10, centre on sandwiches, light grilled specials and salads, though there's also an all-you-can-eat buffet, while breakfast can either be a full buffet for $13.50 or à la carte. Service is friendly rather than formal, and the staff seem admirably keen to answer the same old canyon queries from every table. Reservations are accepted only for dinner, when they're essential; book your table as early in the season as possible, as trying to do so once you arrive is liable to be way too late. Daily 6.30–10am, 11.30am–2.30pm & 4.45–9.45pm.

★ **North Rim Campground** 1 mile north of Grand Canyon Lodge, reservations ☎877 444 6777 or ☎515 885 3639, ⊛recreation.gov. This very pleasant campground holds 87 car-camping sites spaced out through the forest, but no RV hook-ups. Although all vehicle sites are often reserved in advance, additional room is always available for backpackers, bicyclists, and others travelling without their own vehicles. Closed mid-Oct to mid-May. Tenters $5, vehicle sites $16

Rough Rider Saloon Grand Canyon Lodge

☎928 638 2611. This rough-hewn bar, stocked with a wide range of beers and liquor, has a separate early-morning incarnation as an espresso bar doling out coffee and pastries. Daily 5.30–10.30am & 11.30am–10.30pm.

DIRECTORY

Camping equipment Can be bought at the General Store, opposite *North Rim Campground*.

Camping permits The North Rim Backcountry Office, the place to request or pick up backcountry camping permits (see p.314), is just over a mile up the highway from *Grand Canyon Lodge*, not far north of the campground. Daily 8am–noon & 1–5pm; ☎928 638 7868.

Gas Near *North Rim Campground* (daily 8am–5pm).

Laundromat and showers Near *North Rim Campground*. Showers $1.50. Daily 7am–10pm.

Medical help There is no health clinic on the North Rim. Call ☎911 for emergencies.

Post office In *Grand Canyon Lodge* (Mon–Fri 8am–5pm).

The Arizona Strip

By any logic, you'd expect the **Arizona Strip** – the anomalous area sandwiched between the North Rim of the Grand Canyon and the Utah state line – to belong to Utah rather than Arizona. In 1864, Mormon leader Brigham Young called on Congress to grant the Mormons all territory that lay within two degrees of latitude of either side of the Colorado; the boundary was drawn instead along the 37th parallel, and that remains the Utah–Arizona border. Repeated attempts to incorporate the Strip into Utah failed, largely because this remote region became a stronghold of renegade Mormons who didn't accept their church's abandonment of multiple marriage (see p.474). Effective isolation from the state authorities of both Utah and Arizona suited these die-hard polygamists just fine.

Virtually no roads cross the Strip, and those that do hold just a few tiny, secretive, and often semi-derelict hamlets. Although you have to pass this way in order to complete a full tour around the Grand Canyon, the majority of visitors tend to be racing between the Grand Canyon and the national parks of southern Utah. Few are aware that they're missing perhaps the most spectacular section of Grand Canyon National Park: the **Tuweep** district, home to two stunning overlooks at **Toroweap Point** that provide a rare opportunity to see the canyon's innermost core.

Le Fevre Overlook
Between mile markers 590 and 591 on US-89A

At the point where Hwy-67 north of Jacob Lake drops off the edge of the Kaibab Plateau, the roadside **Le Fevre Overlook** offers tremendous views across southern Utah. Tier upon tier of cliffs rise one behind the other into the distance, making it abundantly clear why geologists call the entire region the **Grand Staircase**. First comes the red sandstone of the Vermilion Cliffs, the formation pierced by Zion Canyon (see p.350); next are the White Cliffs, which form the Kolob Canyons district of Zion National Park; and beyond them, forty miles away, stand the softer Pink Cliffs, sculpted into the hoodoos of Bryce Canyon (see p.367).

Fredonia

The largest town on the Arizona Strip, **FREDONIA** stands thirty miles northwest of Jacob Lake on US-89A. With the bigger and much more interesting community of **Kanab** a mere seven miles north, across the Utah border (see p.362), it's hard to see why anyone would choose to spend the night here, but Fredonia does hold a few small motels. A helpful **welcome centre**, near the state line at the north end of town

(☎928 643 7241; Tues–Sat 9am–5pm), can advise on the Strip's backcountry routes, and sells the necessary maps.

Pipe Spring National Monument

Just off AZ-389, 13 miles west of Fredonia • Daily: June–Aug 7am–5pm; Sept–May 8am–5pm • $5 • ☎928 643 7105, ⓦ nps.gov/pisp

Pipe Spring National Monument marks the site of one of the very few water sources on the Arizona Strip. Ownership of this precious spring has been much contested; Mormon rancher Dr James Whitmore, who appropriated it from the Paiute in 1863, was killed three years later by Paiute and Navajo raiders. The Mormons subsequently enclosed the spring in a fort, known as **Winsor Castle**. They retained control until it was declared a national monument in the 1920s, as much because it stood halfway between the Grand Canyon and Zion national parks as for any intrinsic interest.

Pipe Spring is now surrounded by, but distinct from the **Kaibab Paiute Indian reservation**. The buildings remain in good condition and serve as a rather unenthralling museum of early ranching life, of most appeal to students of Mormon history.

Colorado City

AZ-389 continues northwest from Pipe Spring, making it the most direct route from the North Rim to the I-15 interstate between Las Vegas and Salt Lake City. A mile or so before it reaches Utah, a spur road to the right runs up to the staunchly traditional Mormon community of **COLORADO CITY**. Set beneath the towering bluffs of the Vermilion Cliffs, this is a surreal-looking place, laid out with a small grid of extremely broad streets that see very few cars but plenty of gingham pinafores.

Massive homes built to house multiple marriages and even more multiple families stand on every corner, and with much of the male population currently in jail, on the

---

THE EXTRAORDINARY SAGA OF COLORADO CITY

In the first few years of the twenty-first century, exposé after exposé revealed that despite continuing to benefit hugely from state and federal funding, Colorado City was the virtual fiefdom of a small group of **Mormon polygamists**. The Fundamentalist Church of Latter Day Saints was run by the self-styled "Prophet" **Rulon Jeffs**. Not only did he assign the town's young women, often in their early teens, as brides to his middle-aged and already multiply-married cronies – and conduct the wedding ceremonies himself – but he also presided over a system in which as many as four hundred of its young men, their own children, were run out of town as they came of age so they could not become rival bridegrooms. Many ended up as homeless addicts in neighbouring towns.

After Rulon's death in 2002, his son **Warren Jeffs** succeeded him as Prophet, and within a week married all but two of his father's nineteen wives (though not his own mother). After a federal warrant for Warren's arrest was issued in 2005, on charges of sexual conduct with a minor and conspiracy to commit sexual conduct with a minor, he spent fifteen months on the run, on the FBI's "Ten Most Wanted" list.

Along with many of the town's menfolk, Jeffs spent time in a linked polygamist community in Eldorado, Texas, which became notorious following federal raids in 2008. Jeffs himself was however arrested in Nevada in 2006, and found guilty in St George in 2007 of two charges of first-degree rape for authorizing the marriage of a fourteen-year-old girl to her nineteen-year-old cousin. His Utah conviction was overturned in 2010 on the basis of erroneous instructions to the jury, but he was then extradited to Texas, where he was sentenced to **life imprisonment** in 2011 on two charges of sexual assault of a minor.

Meanwhile Colorado City is in complete chaos. Evidence of widespread financial fraud resulted in the dismantling of the church's property holdings, but its inhabitants and law enforcement officials continue to refuse to implement or respect court decisions, and it's widely believed that Jeffs' influence over the town remains as strong as ever.

run or hounded out of town, you're only likely to see female faces. As young women are forbidden to cut their hair before marriage, most are surmounted by extraordinary swept-back quiffs. Everyone will assume you're a magazine journalist hoping to write a sensational article about polygamy, and there's no encouragement to linger.

Toroweap

61 miles southwest of AZ-389 via BLM road 109, the Sunshine Route or 90 miles southeast St George, Utah, on the Main Street Route

The Arizona Strip holds one tremendous prize for visitors prepared to venture off the paved highways: **Toroweap Point**, the only place where you can drive to the very lip of the canyon's Granite Gorge and peer down sheer 3000ft cliffs to the Colorado River. As the crow flies, it's slightly under sixty miles west of Bright Angel Point, but by road it's almost 150 miles, and even a fleeting visit requires at least six hours of laborious driving on gravel roads.

There are two main routes: the eastern **Sunshine Route**, which starts by following **BLM road 109** south from AZ 389 seven miles west of **Fredonia** and then runs for 61 miles southwest, and remains open all year, and the more scenic but longer western **Main Street Route**, which takes a total of ninety miles from **St George**, Utah, but is closed by snow in winter. Both roads are generally passable in ordinary vehicles; if 4WD is necessary at all, it will be for the last few miles only. Be sure to enquire locally about driving conditions before you set off; carry plenty of food, water, and gas, and pack a spare tyre and emergency repair kit.

Both routes eventually converge to enter the **Tuweep Area** of Grand Canyon National Park. Five very rough miles on, a free **primitive campground** holds nine first-come, first-served sites, for which you have to have a backcountry camping permit (see p.314).

Toroweap Overlook

1 mile beyond the Tuweep Area campground

What doesn't quite sink in until you reach the end of the road at Toroweap is that this is an utterly unique segment of the Grand Canyon. Everywhere else, there are effectively two canyons in one, consisting of a towering rim, separated by mighty cliffs and, as a rule, a broad plateau, from the deep, narrow chasm that holds the Colorado River. Here, that high outer rim is absent on the north side of the river, and the road extends right to the brink of the Granite Gorge.

This wide, rocky hilltop, a mile beyond the campground, is the **Toroweap Overlook**, which at 4600ft is the lowest viewpoint within the national park. The view may lack the usual buttes and pyramids or labyrinthine spurs and mesas, but tiptoe to the southern edge of the parking lot, and the ground suddenly drops 3000ft from your feet. Though you can see the river approaching from the east and flowing away to the west, it's so directly below that you may have to lie full length and peep over the edge to see it right here.

Lava Falls Overlook

5 minutes' hike west from Toroweap Overlook

The stupendous west-facing **Lava Falls Overlook** stands five minutes' hike west of Toroweap Overlook. The view of the river here, turning from green to blue as it recedes toward the horizon, and interspersed with mighty white rapids, is so spellbinding that you may not at first notice the most awesome feature of the landscape. Straight ahead, a colossal black **lava cascade** spills over the North Rim and pours down to within a few feet of the Colorado. On at least eight separate occasions, volcanic eruptions here have filled the Grand Canyon to a depth of as much as 2330ft, and thus blocked the Colorado. The largest flow, around 1.2 million years ago, created the long-vanished Prospect Dam, which backed the river up to form a lake that stretched all the way east to Lees Ferry. It took an estimated 23 years to fill to the brim; then the Colorado burst over the top and, eventually, wore the dam entirely away.

Southern Utah

344 The southwest corridor

349 Zion National Park

362 East from Zion: US-89

367 Bryce Canyon National Park

371 East of Bryce Canyon

373 Grand Staircase–Escalante National Monument

383 North to Capitol Reef

384 Capitol Reef National Park

391 Lake Powell

400 Between Capitol Reef and Canyonlands

404 Canyonlands National Park

415 Arches National Park

421 Moab

426 Around Moab

428 Southeast Utah

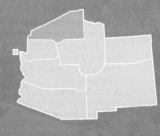

ANGELS LANDING, ZION NATIONAL PARK

Southern Utah

Southern Utah is a peculiar combination of the mind-boggling and the mundane. Its scenery is stupendous, a stunning geological freak show where the earth is ripped bare to expose cliffs and canyons of every imaginable colour; unseen rivers gouge mighty furrows into endless desert plateaus; and strange sandstone towers thrust from the sagebrush. The tiny Mormon towns scattered across this epic landscape, on the other hand, are almost without exception boring in the extreme. Each has its cluster of characterless motels and dull-as-ditchwater diners; they're not unfriendly places, but finding ways to while away your evenings can truly tax the imagination.

7

Most visitors therefore spend as much time as possible **outdoors**. Southern Utah has the greatest concentration of **national parks** in the US; in fact there have been serious proposals for the entire area to become one vast national park. The five parks that currently exist are not necessarily the most beautiful or spectacular spots in the state – their boundaries, the result of devious behind-the-scenes wrangling, exclude lands prized by the ranching and mining conglomerates. Taken together, however, they make an ideal focus for a first tour of Utah, each with its own well-maintained infrastructure of hiking trails and scenic overlooks.

In southwest Utah, **Zion National Park** centres on an awe-inspiring and richly fertile canyon, backed by barren highlands of sun-scorched white sandstone, while **Bryce Canyon** is a roaring inferno of flame-like orange pinnacles. Over to the east, **Arches** holds an eroded desertscape of graceful red-rock fins and spurs, all on a more manageable scale than the astonishing hundred-mile vistas of neighbouring **Canyonlands**. Both lie within easy reach of **Moab**, a dishevelled former mining town that's now Utah's hippest destination. The fifth park, **Capitol Reef**, stretches down the massive rainbow-tinted Waterpocket Fold in the middle of the region, pierced by slender, ravishing canyons.

Lesser-known but equally dramatic wildernesses include **Dead Horse Point** and **Muley Point**, on the eastern side of the state, and vast **Grand Staircase–Escalante National Monument** to the west. The most spellbinding wonder of all, **Glen Canyon**, has been drowned since the 1960s beneath **Lake Powell**, an elongated reservoir whose turquoise waters, lapping desultorily against the red desert rocks, are a playground for houseboaters and jet-skiers.

The defining topographical feature of southwest Utah is the **Grand Staircase**. Named by pioneer river-runner John Wesley Powell, it consists of a series of plateaus, stacked

Travelling among the Mormons p.345
A history of Zion Canyon p.351
Zion hiking permits p.354
Hiking the Zion Narrows p.356
Permits for Coyote Buttes and Paria Canyon p.365
A monumental affair p.376
The Hole-in-the-Rock Expedition p.378
The geology of Capitol Reef p.386
Lake Powell: controversy and compromise p.392
Renting a houseboat p.395
The Lake Powell Ferry p.397
John Wesley Powell p.401
The Green River p.402
Backcountry permits in Canyonlands p.404
The geology of Canyonlands p.405
The rock art of Horseshoe Canyon p.410
Charlie Steen: the Uranium King p.420
Adventure travel in Moab p.424

MULEY POINT

Highlights

❶ Zion Canyon Whether you admire it from the roadside, or hike up its soaring walls, Zion is pure magic. **See p.350**

❷ Bryce Canyon Towering incandescent sandstone hoodoos make this one of the most extraordinary-looking places on earth. **See p.367**

❸ Calf Creek Falls An easy trail leads to a magnificent waterfall that's the gem of Grand Staircase-Escalante National Monument. See p.381

❹ The Great Gallery Eerie ancient pictographs, hidden deep in a remote section of Canyonlands National Park. **See p.410**

❺ Delicate Arch The hike up to this free-standing natural arch is the crowning glory of a visit to Arches National Park. **See p.418**

❻ Rafting in Canyonlands Penetrate the mysterious wilderness at the heart of Utah on float trips down the Green or Colorado rivers. See p.424

❼ Muley Point Though not in a national park, this seldom visited viewpoint is perhaps the finest in all of Utah. **See p.432**

❽ Goosenecks State Park The convolutions of the San Juan River near Monument Valley have to be seen to be believed. **See p.433**

HIGHLIGHTS ARE MARKED ON THE MAP ON PP.342–343

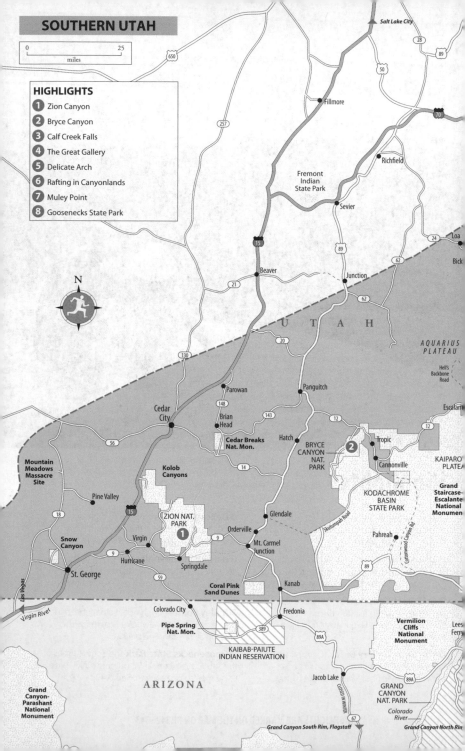

SOUTHERN UTAH

0 _____ 25
miles

HIGHLIGHTS

1. Zion Canyon
2. Bryce Canyon
3. Calf Creek Falls
4. The Great Gallery
5. Delicate Arch
6. Rafting in Canyonlands
7. Muley Point
8. Goosenecks State Park

N

Salt Lake City

Fillmore

Richfield

Fremont
Indian
State Park

Sevier

Loa

Bick

Beaver

Junction

U T A H

AQUARIUS
PLATEAU

Hell's
Backbone
Road

Parowan

Panguitch

Escalan

Cedar
City

Brian
Head

Hatch

BRYCE
CANYON
NAT.
PARK

Tropic

KAIPARO
PLATE

Cedar Breaks
Nat. Mon.

Cannonville

Mountain
Meadows
Massacre
Site

Kolob
Canyons

KODACHROME
BASIN
STATE PARK

Grand
Staircase-
Escalante
National
Monumen

Pine Valley

Pahreah

Glendale

Snow
Canyon

ZION NAT.
PARK

Orderville

Virgin

Mt. Carmel
Junction

Hurricane

Springdale

St. George

Kanab

Coral Pink
Sand Dunes

Vermilion
Cliffs
National
Monument

Colorado City

Fredonia

Lees
Ferry

Pipe Spring
Nat. Mon.

KAIBAB-PAIUTE
INDIAN RESERVATION

A R I Z O N A

Jacob Lake

GRAND
CANYON
NAT. PARK

Grand
Canyon-
Parashant
National
Monument

CLOSED IN WINTER

Colorado
River

Virgin River

Las Vegas

Grand Canyon South Rim, Flagstaff

Grand Canyon North Rim

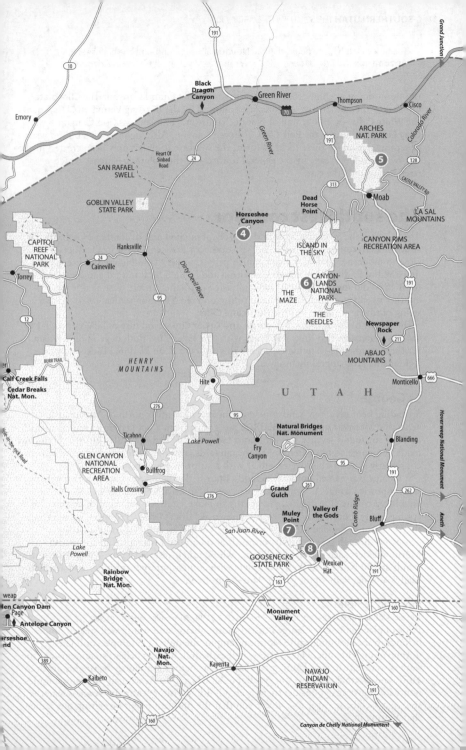

> The time in **Utah** is one hour later than **Nevada** all year round, and one hour later than **Arizona** from April to October; from November to March, it's the same as **Arizona**.

tier upon tier, that climb from the North Rim of the Grand Canyon. The **Chocolate Cliffs**, near the border with Arizona, are followed by the dazzling **Vermilion Cliffs**, then the **White Cliffs** – a 2000ft wall of Navajo Sandstone, best seen at Zion Canyon – the **Grey Cliffs**, and finally the **Pink Cliffs** of Bryce Canyon. Although it took a billion years of sedimentation for these rocks to form, the staircase itself has only been created in the last twelve million years, by the general upthrust of the **Colorado Plateau**, which stretches away to the east.

The southwest corridor

Though now the most accessible and densely populated area of southern Utah, the far **southwestern corner** was a forbidding prospect for early explorers. In October 1776, close to modern Cedar City, two Spanish priests, fathers Domínguez and Escalante, despaired of finding their way to California and headed back toward Santa Fe. Not until 1830 did the **Old Spanish Trail** establish a permanent route west, and it was another twenty years before Brigham Young ordered Mormon settlers to establish a string of towns at the foot of the **Hurricane Cliffs**.

The largest of those towns, **St George** and **Cedar City**, stand fifty miles apart on I-15, the busy interstate that links Las Vegas with Salt Lake City. Both depend on tourism for their livelihood – catering especially to visitors to Zion National Park – despite lacking any great appeal themselves.

St George

Spreading beneath a long sandstone escarpment, nine miles north of Arizona, the venerable Mormon town of **ST GEORGE** has grown from a population of ten thousand in 1970 to around seventy-five thousand today. While this influx, largely of retirees, has made St George cosmopolitan by Utah standards, anywhere else it would seem like a conservative country backwater, albeit with a surprising number of motels.

St George was named not for England's dragon-slaying patron but for a Latter-Day saint, Apostle George A. Smith, who was sent here with 309 families in 1861 to establish a colony. The original plan being to make Utah self-sufficient in **cotton**, this appropriately southern region became known as "Utah's Dixie." However, cotton from the Deep South flooded the market after the Civil War, and St George quietly prospered through growing other crops. It also became a winter refuge for ageing Mormon elders such as Brigham Young, whose much-restored adobe **Winter Home** still stands at 200 North 100 West, complete with contemporary furnishings and artefacts (daily: summer 9am–8pm, winter 9am–5pm; free).

Mormon Temple

440 South 300 East · **Visitor centre** Daily 9am–9pm · Free · ☎ 435 673 5181, ⓦ ldschurchtemples.com/stgeorge

Pride of place among St George's broad thoroughfares and sturdy well-spaced homes belongs to the gleaming white **Mormon Temple**, the only LDS temple completed during Young's lifetime. Half fortress, half cathedral, it was a defiant statement that the settlers were here to stay. Young presided over its dedication shortly before his death in 1877, and it remains a powerful symbol to all Mormons. As with all Mormon temples, non-Mormons can't go inside; there is an adjoining **visitor centre**, however, where the staff may well be so eager to convert you that the problem might be getting out rather than getting in.

TRAVELLING AMONG THE MORMONS

For many visitors, a trip to Utah serves as their first encounter with the much-misunderstood **Mormon** Church (see p.473), which claims something over sixty percent of the state's two million residents, and twelve million adherents worldwide. The word "Mormon" is no more than a widely accepted nickname for members of the **Church of Jesus Christ of Latter-Day Saints** (hence the adjectival abbreviation **LDS**), taken from their main work of scripture, the Book of Mormon.

The two most obvious ways in which Utah's Mormon heritage impacts upon travellers are in its notoriously arcane **alcohol laws** and its ponderous if logical system of **addresses**. Although tourists in small-town Utah can still find it hard to get a drink, regulations regarding the sale of alcohol have been relaxed in recent years. In most towns, at least one **restaurant** is licensed to sell beer, wine and mixed drinks to diners, and it may also be licensed to sell beer in its bar or lounge. However, you won't be shown a cocktail menu, or even offered a drink, unless you specifically ask. With the exception of low-strength beer, sold in supermarkets and grocery stores, take-out bottled drinks can only be purchased in State Liquor Stores and Package Agencies. For full details, see ⓦabc.utah.gov/laws.

Most Mormon towns are laid out on a **grid**, usually centred on the intersection of Main and Center streets. Streets north and south of that point are named "100 North," "200 South," and so on, and similarly to east and west. The **address** "165 North 300 West" pinpoints a spot on 300 West, between 100 North and 200 North.

7

ARRIVAL AND DEPARTURE   ST GEORGE

By bus Greyhound buses between Las Vegas and Salt Lake City stop outside *McDonald's* at 1235 S Bluff St (☎435 673 2933), while the St George Shuttle connects with Las Vegas nine times daily (☎435 628 8320 or ☎800 933 8320, ⓦstgshuttle.com; $36).

INFORMATION AND TOURS

St George Welcome Center 1835 Convention Center Blvd, near I 15 exit 8 (Mon–Sat 10am–6pm; ☎435 634 5747 or ☎800 869 6635, ⓦutahstgeorge.com).

Bus tours Red Rock Shuttle (☎435 635 9104, ⓦredrockshuttle.com) offers one-day **bus tours** and shuttle trips to Zion ($100) and Bryce ($150).

ACCOMMODATION AND EATING

Virtually all St George's commercial life takes place along the main drag, **St George Boulevard**. With forty-plus **motels**, finding a room is usually easy, though summer weekends get busy. **Dining out** tends to be a question of which highway steakhouse or fast-food outlet catches your eye; there's plenty of choice, but not much excitement.

Best Western Coral Hills 125 E St George Blvd ☎435 673 4844 or ☎800 542 7733, ⓦcoralhills.com. Centrally located chain motel, a veteran of the local scene but kept nicely up to date, with sizeable rooms and indoor and outdoor pools. Rates include a good breakfast. **$79**

Dixie Palm 185 E St George Blvd ☎435 673 3531 or ☎866 651 3997. St George's best-value budget motel, a simple family-run place with 15 freshly remodelled rooms. **$40**

The Pizza Factory 2 W St George Blvd ☎435 628 1234, ⓦstgeorgepizzafactory.com. The pick of assorted lively restaurants in the central Ancestor Square development, offering a full menu of pizzas and calzones; opt for one of their specials, like garlic chicken, or pick your own toppings. Typically costing $15 or so per person, it's relatively expensive for pizza, but the ambience makes it worth it. Mon–Sat 11am–9.30pm.

Snow Canyon State Park

Hwy-18, 7 miles north of downtown St George • Daily 6am–10pm • $6 per vehicle • ☎435 628 2255 or ☎800 322 3770, ⓦstateparks .utah.gov/parks/snow-canyon

One of Utah's most attractive state parks lies within ten minutes' drive of St George. Don't expect to see snow in **SNOW CANYON STATE PARK**; it's a classic red-rock canyon, where the most distinctive feature is the layer of jet-black lava that flakes off the tops of its sun-baked sandstone pinnacles, left by a volcanic eruption 10,000 years ago.

The park's six-mile **scenic drive** drops left from Hwy-18, winding down past overlooks and rounded monoliths to reach the **park headquarters** after a couple of miles, where you pay the entrance fee.

Hidden Pinyon Trail and the dunes

An excellent hour-long (1.5-mile) round-trip hike, the **Hidden Pinyon Trail**, starts a hundred yards further on. After cutting between the craggy outcrops into a peaceful meadow, it zigzags up and over a ridge to enter a heavily eroded landscape reminiscent of Canyonlands' Needles District (see p.412).

If it's too hot to hike, pull off another two miles on instead, where a cluster of lurid **red sand dunes** threatens to drift across the road. Kids especially will enjoy sliding down the slopes, which doubled for central Asia in Howard Hughes' movie *The Conqueror*, which starred John Wayne as Genghis Khan. When it was filmed in 1954, the Nevada Test Site, just ninety miles west, was at its busiest; Wayne, Hughes and three-quarters of the cast are thought to have died from cancers caused by fall-out from the nuclear explosions.

7

ACCOMMODATION	SNOW CANYON STATE PARK
Shivwits campground Alongside park headquarters ☎ 800 322 3770, ⓦ stateparks.utah.gov/reservations. Reservations for this pleasant, shaded 36-space	campground are recommended in spring and fall, but things get quieter during the hottest months. Without hook-ups **$16**, with water and electricity **$20**

Cedar City

CEDAR CITY, 53 miles northeast of St George on I-15 – and twenty miles north of the Kolob Canyons section of Zion National Park (see p.361) – is now half the size of its upstart rival. Like St George ten years later, it too was founded in Mormon Utah's precarious early years, as the church bid for self-sufficiency. The Mormons urgently needed **iron**, so when scouting parties discovered iron ore in southern Utah, the **Iron Mission** was dispatched to establish Cedar City in November 1851. Most of its first inhabitants were British miners; they soon succeeded in smelting iron from the hills to the west, but the venture ultimately failed, and ore mined locally has been shipped out for processing ever since.

Frontier Homestead State Park Museum

585 N Main St • Daily: June to early Sept 9am–6pm; early Sept to May 9am–5pm; closed Sun Nov–Feb • $3 • ☎ 435 586 9290, ⓦ utah.com/stateparks/iron_mission.htm

Historical markers dotted around Cedar City detail the former locations of its social hall, hospital, brick yard and flour mill, but the only place that offers much insight into local history is the **Frontier Homestead State Park Museum** (formerly known as Iron Mission State Park). Apart from rusty nuggets, this warehouse-like museum is filled with nineteenth-century horse-drawn vehicles, including wagons, sleighs and hearses.

Utah Shakespeare Festival

Southern Utah State University, 351 W Center St • $23–68 • ☎ 435 586 7878 or ☎ 800 752 9849, ⓦ bard.org

Cedar City's major tourist attraction is the summer-long **Utah Shakespeare Festival**, a semi-professional event held on the campus of the Southern Utah State University since 1962. Running from late June to the end of October each year, it usually features nine or so productions, with three or four Shakespeare plays among assorted others.

INFORMATION	CEDAR CITY
Visitor centre 581 N Main St (summer Mon–Fri 8am–7pm, Sat 9am–1pm; winter Mon–Fri 8am–5pm;	☎ 435 586 5124 or ☎ 800 354 4849, ⓦ scenic southernutah.com).

ACCOMMODATION AND EATING

Abbey Inn 940 West 200 North ☏ 435 586 9966 or ☏ 800 325 5411, ⓦ abbeyinncedar.com. Very well equipped new motel, just off the interstate at exit 59, with almost a hundred good-value rooms and an indoor pool. $93

Best Western Town and Country Inn 189 N Main St ☏ 435 586 9900, ⓦ bwtowncountry.com. Smart chain motel, north of the centre, charging reasonable rates for spacious rooms in separate wings either side of 200 West St. Heated indoor pool and good breakfasts. $110

The Grind Coffee House 19 N Main St ☏ 435 867 5333. Busy, very central local rendezvous, serving pastries and sandwiches for under $10 as well as coffee, and putting on regular live music. Mon–Sat 7am–6pm, Sun 8am–2pm.

Cedar Breaks National Monument

Visitor centre Late May to mid-Oct daily 9am–6pm • $4 per person • ☏ 435 586 0787, ⓦ nps.gov/cebr

The most direct route to Bryce Canyon from Cedar City, **Hwy-14**, climbs steadily onto a densely wooded plateau via a narrow gorge east of town. While Cedar City itself stands at an elevation of 5800ft, the plateau rises a further five thousand feet. The scenery along Hwy-14 is therefore spectacular, with views that stretch south to encompass all of Zion National Park.

Fifteen miles along, shortly after the highway enters the **Dixie National Forest**, the pink, white and orange rocks of **CEDAR BREAKS NATIONAL MONUMENT** stand immediately below the forest that tops the high ridge to your left. Cedar Breaks is a sort of pocket version of Bryce Canyon (see p.367), where erosive forces have scooped a natural amphitheatre into the hillside and filled it with brilliantly coloured limestone formations. While it lacks Bryce's opportunities for hiking, it's well worth seeing if you're in the area.

Cedar Breaks viewpoints

The road through Cedar Breaks, **Hwy-148**, branches north from Hwy-14 nineteen miles out of Cedar City. When it's clear – it's usually snowbound between late October and mid-May – you can choose between four similar cliff-edge viewpoints. The southernmost, **Point Supreme**, is the best, with pinnacles rising from the orange canyon floor at your feet and sweeping views to the south and west.

You can hike for short distances along the rim at both Point Supreme and **Chessmen Ridge**, a mile or so north, but no trails descend into the formations.

The road to Zion

The main road to Zion National Park, **Hwy-9**, a lovely thirty-mile drive, heads east from the I-15 interstate seven miles northeast of St George (see p.344). None of the pioneer villages along the way is especially exciting, but the scenery is great, with the cottonwood-fringed Virgin River to the south and gigantic sandstone cliffs to the north. Be warned that you have to pay the admission fee to Zion if you want to continue east beyond the park on Hwy-9.

Hurricane

The westernmost town along Hwy-9 is **HURRICANE**, ten miles east of the interstate at the junction with Hwy-59. While not actually on the Virgin River, it's connected to it by a seven-mile canal, conceived in 1863 but not completed until 1906. Only then was the town site settled, and it's still much the same agricultural community a hundred years on.

Southeast from Hurricane, Hwy-59 takes twenty miles to reach the Arizona border, marked by the polygamist community of **Colorado City** (see p.336). The **North Rim** of the Grand Canyon is a hundred miles beyond (see p.331).

Virgin, Rockville and Grafton

You'll probably barely notice **VIRGIN**, seven miles east of Hurricane – close to the foot of the **Kolob Terrace Road** north into the Zion backcountry (see p.361), and notorious

7

for having introduced a law making gun ownership compulsory. The same goes for **ROCKVILLE**, ten miles beyond Virgin. In fact, it's hard to keep your eyes on the road at all as you come closer to the wonders of Zion. Rockville is nevertheless a pretty little town, with several small-scale B&Bs along its tree-lined central avenue.

South across the river from Rockville, turn right off Bridge Road onto an unpaved track, to reach the photogenic little ghost town of **GRAFTON**. Mormon farmers abandoned the struggle against floods and Indians around 1900, but Rockville residents have kept an eye on it ever since. It's also been touched up by Hollywood crews shooting movies like *Butch Cassidy and the Sundance Kid*; this is where Paul Newman rode a bicycle to the tune of "Raindrops Keep Fallin' On My Head."

Just beyond Rockville, Hwy-9 veers north at the confluence of the North and East forks of the Virgin River, and heads for the maw of Zion Canyon.

Springdale

7

SPRINGDALE, the last town before Zion, spreads along a leafy three-mile stretch of the Virgin River just south of the park entrance. Rounding the final corner into town gives you your first stupendous view of Zion Canyon itself. Settled at the same time as the canyon, in the early 1860s, Springdale is now devoted almost exclusively to pampering tourists.

With its clashing and totally discordant architecture, Springdale is a classic national-park gateway community, but it's still somehow very appealing. Here and there green fields nestle right up to the highway – some even hold grazing cattle – while the occasional imposing private home punctuates the motels, inns and restaurants. The whole ensemble is dwarfed into insignificance by the magnificent canyon walls that loom on either side of the river. By the time you've driven up and down the only road, Zion Park Boulevard, a couple of times, you'll have seen everything Springdale has to offer, but this lively, friendly community makes by far the nicest base in southwest Utah, and spending three or four nights here is no hardship whatsoever.

ACCOMMODATION   SPRINGDALE

As Zion Park Boulevard runs straight between the burgeoning canyon walls toward the park, all the **motels** and **B&Bs** along the way offer the same attractive views. A couple of new properties tend to appear each year, so although Springdale remains busy between late April and late October, only in high summer is it liable to sell out completely. Compared to the rest of southern Utah, standards are generally very high. It's also possible to stay in the park itself, at *Zion Lodge* (see p.360) or two campsites (see p.360).

Best Western Zion Park Inn 1215 Zion Park Blvd ☎ 435 772 3200 or ☎ 800 934 7275, ⓦ zionparkinn .com. Modern convention-style hotel at Springdale's southern end, refurbished in 2013 and offering spacious rooms with panoramic windows, plus a heated swimming pool. $149

Cliffrose Lodge & Gardens 281 Zion Park Blvd ☎ 435 772 3234 or ☎ 800 243 8824, ⓦ cliffroselodge.com. The closest motel to the park makes a pretty place to stay, with separate units spreading down the hillside to the cottonwoods that line the Virgin River. It also has its own pool and wild gardens. $179

★ **Desert Pearl Inn** 707 Zion Park Blvd ☎ 435 772 8888 or ☎ 888 828 0898, ⓦ desertpearl.com. Absolutely gorgeous hotel, ranged alongside the Virgin River just outside the park, with superb views. From the parking areas it may look like a regular motel, but the actual rooms are extremely stylish, with high ceilings, wooden floors, huge windows and balconies, and face a lovely turquoise pool with hot tubs. $168

Harvest House 29 Canyon View Drive ☎ 435 772 3880, ⓦ harvesthouse.net. Classy, non-smoking B&B in a modern home, tucked beneath the sandstone cliffs. Four en-suite rooms, an outdoor hot tub, and gourmet breakfasts. $130

Terrace Brook Lodge 990 Zion Park Blvd ☎ 435 772 3932 or ☎ 800 342 6779. There's no point staying in Springdale's one remaining budget motel if you're looking for luxury; it simply offers rundown but acceptable motel rooms with no redeeming features other than price and a convenient central location. If you plan to spend all day in the park anyway, that's not a bad deal. Rates fluctuate day by day, according to demand, and drop below $50 in low season. $120

Zion Canyon Campground 479 Zion Park Blvd ☏ 435 772 3237, ⓦ zioncamp.com. Set beside the river half a mile outside the park, this commercial campground shares both a site, and facilities like its laundry, pool and pizzeria, with a *Quality Inn* motel. Very much dominated by RVs, it makes a poor alternative for tent campers. Tent sites $30, RVs $39

EATING

Bit & Spur Restaurant & Saloon 1212 Zion Park Blvd ☏ 435 772 3498, ⓦ bitandspur.com. Hectic dinner-only Mexican restaurant and bar, facing the red-rock cliffs across from *Zion Park Inn* at the south end of town, where the food has a creative edge, and the margaritas are top-notch. Chilli-rubbed steak costs $26, the Zuni lamb-and-corn stew $18, and a *chile relleno* (stuffed chilli) just $14. From the outdoor patio, you can watch the moon rise over the mountains. Daily 5–10pm.

Spotted Dog Cafe Flanigan's Inn, 428 Zion Park Blvd ☏ 435 772 3244, ⓦ flanigans.com. Reasonably priced restaurant, attached to a motel at the park end of town, that's much larger than it looks – the open-air patio is just the tip of the iceberg. Dinner entrees such as braised lamb shank ($22) or trout ($18) have a zesty, continental feel, and they also offer a substantial breakfast buffet. Daily 7–11am & 5–10pm.

Whiptail Grill 445 Zion Park Blvd ☏ 435 772 0283. Small central diner in a former gas station, with a few outdoor tables, which serves surprisingly good meals for $10 or less, ranging from pizza to tacos, with organic and wheat-free options. Daily noon–9pm.

7

Zion National Park

Zion National Park is divided into two main sections: Zion Canyon (see p.350) and Kolob Canyons (see p.361) • $25 per vehicle, $12 for motorcyclists, cyclists, and pedestrians; valid for 7 days • ☏ 435 772 3256, ⓦ nps.gov/zion

With its soaring cliffs, riverine forests, and cascading waterfalls, **ZION NATIONAL PARK** is Utah's most conventionally beautiful park. On first glance it's also the least "Southwestern", in that its centrepiece, **Zion Canyon**, is a lush oasis that feels far removed from the otherworldly desolation of Canyonlands or the downright weirdness of Bryce. Like California's Yosemite Valley, it's a spectacular gorge, squeezed between mighty walls of rock and echoing to the sound of running water. Also like Yosemite, it's prone to be crowded in summer, though an efficient seasonal shuttle-bus system alleviates traffic problems.

Too many visitors see Zion Canyon as a quick half-day detour off the interstate, as they race between Las Vegas and Salt Lake City. Beautiful though the **Scenic Drive** through the canyon may be, Zion deserves much more of your time than that. Even the shortest **hiking trail** within the canyon can help you escape the crowds, while a day-hike will take you away from the deceptive verdure of the valley and up onto the high-desert tablelands beyond. In addition, two less-used roads – **Kolob Canyons Road** and the **Kolob Terrace Road** – lead into remoter sections of the park.

With elevations varying from under 4000ft at the visitor centre to almost 9000ft at Kolob Peak, Zion is home to a bewildering array of **flora and fauna**. Its vegetation ranges from the cottonwoods and box elders along the Virgin River to the ponderosa pines and stunted *piñons* that cling to the high sandstone mesas. Desert flowers and cactuses provide unexpected flashes of colour in the uplands, as do darting hummingbirds. Resident animals include the bank beaver (so named because it doesn't build dams) and the generally retiring Western rattlesnake.

Summer is by far the busiest season. That's despite temperatures in excess of 100°F, and the violent thunderstorms, concentrated in August and a week or so to either side, that bring most of Zion's scant fifteen inches of annual rainfall. If you can, come in April or May to see the spring flowers bloom – though the mosquitoes are also at their peak – or in September and October, to enjoy the fall colours along the river. The park remains open throughout the winter, but daytime highs drop below 40°F in January, while the nights tend to be freezing from November to March.

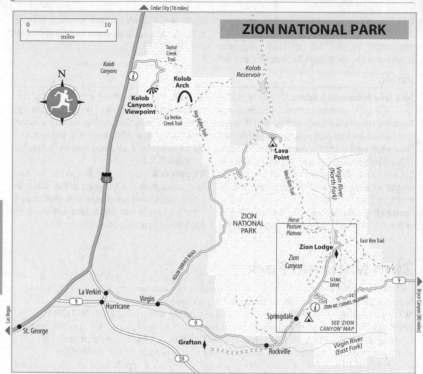

Zion Canyon

The North Fork of the **Virgin River** has taken thirteen million years to carve **Zion Canyon** into the southern edge of the Markagunt Plateau. For most of the year, the Virgin meanders placidly along the valley floor, en route to the Colorado. After summer thunderstorms, however, run-off from the mesa-tops is channelled down into the canyon, turning it into a torrent that carries as much as 600,000 cubic yards of rock and sand – a good-sized city block – in a single day. Each winter, the canyon walls grow further apart, as water that seeps through the porous sandstone turns to ice and shears mighty chunks off the cliffs.

As you approach from the south on Hwy-9, 30 miles east of I-15, it's abundantly clear that the **Markagunt Plateau** – named for a Paiute word meaning "highland of trees", it's one of the seven high plateaus that make up the Colorado Plateau in southern Utah – constitutes the next rung of the **Grand Staircase** (see p.335). Zion Canyon serves as a handy cross-section to display the different layers of rock. At the lowest level, around the South Entrance, the thick red **Vermilion Cliffs** rise from a barely discernible bed of the even older and darker Moenave and Kayenta strata, deposited at the bottom of swampy seas 200 million years ago. The 2000ft walls of the canyon itself are composed of rusty **Navajo Sandstone**, once a mass of drifting sand dunes.

The first of the colossal peaks that crown the chasm look down from either side of the South Entrance. The **West Temple** is one of two similar mountains here whose summits consist of neat little box-shaped mesas crowned with pine trees, while the **Watchman** stands guard to the east. At this point, the walls are well over a mile apart; officially the canyon doesn't begin for another few miles, but within just ten miles north it dwindles to a mere twenty feet wide.

Whether you access Zion Canyon using the park shuttle buses, or visit in winter when you're free to use your own vehicle, your first impressions are going to be garnered from the highway. The main road – **Hwy-9**, which becomes the **Zion–Mt Carmel Highway** – passes plenty of dramatic formations as it climbs east toward Bryce, but Zion's most memorable monoliths are ranged on either side of the dead-end **Scenic Drive**, which runs for six miles north alongside the Virgin River.

Zion Canyon visitor centre
Immediately inside the South Entrance • Daily: late April to late May & early Sept to mid-Oct 8am–6pm; late May to early Sept 8am–7.30pm; mid-Oct to late April 8am–5pm • Free • ☎ 435 772 3256, ⓦ nps.gov/zion

As well as providing detailed information on all aspects of Zion, the park's spacious and partly open-air **visitor centre** is the base for its two **shuttle bus** routes (see p.360), and thus an essential stop for all visitors. The parking lot alongside the visitor centre often fills up by 9am in summer, in which case you'll have to park in Springdale and take a shuttle from there. Free handouts include the park newspaper and maps; the bookstore stocks detailed guides; permanent displays explain the park's geology and history; and there's a full timetable of talks, slide shows and guided hikes.

Zion Human History Museum
Left of Hwy-9, not far north of visitor centre • Daily: late April to late May & early Sept to mid-Oct 10am–6pm; late May to early Sept 9am–7pm; mid-Oct to late April 10am–5pm • Free • ☎ 435 772 3256, ⓦ nps.gov/zion • Served by Canyon Shuttle bus route

A HISTORY OF ZION CANYON

Zion Canyon may seem like an oasis, but it has never held much of a **human** population. Its earliest inhabitants were probably semi-nomadic hunter-gatherers, who from 500 AD onwards grew crops beside the Virgin River. Known to archeologists as the **Virgin Anasazi**, they are regarded as less sophisticated cousins of the Ancestral Puebloan groups to the east; living in small bands, they never built "cliff palaces" or pueblos. By 1250 AD, drought had driven them out of Zion, leaving isolated pictographs on the canyon walls as their only monument.

During the ensuing centuries, **Paiute Indians** migrated seasonally throughout southern Utah, harvesting the few resources the desert could offer. They saw Zion, however, as the abode of Wai-no-Pits, the evil one, who cursed them with disease, and Kainesava, the God of Fire, whose lightning blazed from its high peaks. When **Mormon missionary** Nephi Johnson arrived in 1858 to explore the Upper Virgin River, the Paiute would lead him no further than Oak Creek, at the canyon entrance.

Isaac Behunin, who set up a log cabin in 1862 where *Zion Lodge* now stands, dubbed the canyon **"Little Zion"** in the hope it would serve as a place of refuge for beleaguered Mormons. Some of his fellow farmers were soon taking things too easy; Brigham Young thundered that their indulgence in tobacco and wine made the name **"Not Zion"** more appropriate. In the long run, Zion Canyon proved too narrow to support farming, and its main commercial role was simply as a route through which timber sawn on the high mesas could be shipped out to the plains. Between 1900 and 1930, logs lowered from "Cable Mountain" built the fine homes of such towns as St George.

John Wesley Powell's second Colorado expedition in 1872 (see p.401) had brought the scenery of Zion to national attention, under the Paiute name of "Mukuntuweap Canyon." The canyon itself was set aside in 1909 as Mukuntuweap National Monument; a larger area became Zion National Park in 1919, and the Kolob Canyons district was added in 1956.

Although most visitors assume Mormon settlers gave Zion's pinnacles and promontories their portentous names – the **Court of the Patriarchs**, the **Great White Throne**, **Angels Landing**, and so on – they were coined by a visiting Methodist minister in 1916.

In its first full year, 1920, the park attracted fewer than four thousand visitors. Trails and campgrounds remain little changed since their construction during the 1930s, but visitor numbers have since climbed to almost three million per year.

7

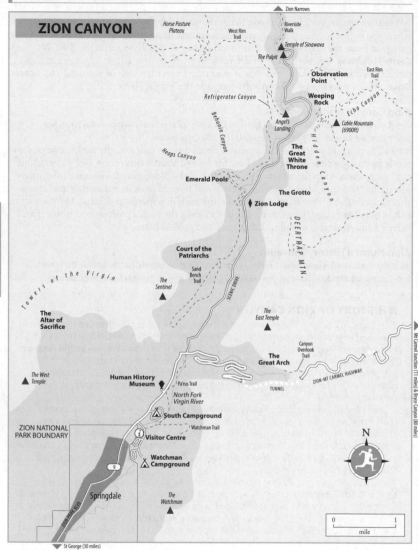

Mt Carmel Junction (11 miles) & Bryce Canyon (80 miles) ▶

Housed in a building that previously served as the park visitor centre, the **Zion Human History Museum** does not, despite the name, focus exclusively on people. The photo displays inside concentrate as much on plants and animals as they do on humans, and while it's not an essential stop, it does hold some interesting background material.

The Scenic Drive

Served by Canyon Shuttle bus route; accessible to private vehicles between November and March only, precise dates vary each year

It's possible simply to drive through the southern end of Zion Canyon and continue east towards Bryce. To see its full glory, however, it's essential to follow the **Scenic Drive** north beside the Virgin River for the full six miles until the canyon walls squeeze so tight together it can't continue any further. Only in winter is it possible to do so in your own vehicle; for most of the year, you're obliged to use the canyon **shuttle buses** instead (see p.360).

For half a mile north of the visitor centre, Hwy-9 parallels the west bank of the river. The highest of the peaks to the left, collectively known as the **Towers of the Virgin**, is the **Altar of Sacrifice**, named somewhat gruesomely for the blood-like streaks of rust that seem to flow from its flat crest.

The highway crosses the river just beyond its confluence with **Pine Creek**. Guarded by the **Sentinel** to the west and the **East Temple** to the east, this marks the start of Zion Canyon proper. It's also the site of the Canyon Junction shuttle stop, and the northern trailhead of the **Pa'rus Trail** (see p.355). The **Scenic Drive** branches left on the far side of the bridge, while Hwy-9 heads on east.

From here on north the canyon is so narrow, and the walls so steep, that there's barely room to squeeze in a road. Erosion continues as fast as ever, and the Scenic Drive has repeatedly to be rebuilt after landslides. The first major roadside pull-out comes after 1.7 miles, facing the **Court of the Patriarchs**, where peaks named for Abraham, Isaac and Joseph stand arrayed around a small canyon west of the river. A mile further on you reach the meadows of **Zion Lodge** (see p.360). In the height of summer, the crowds can be overwhelming, but for most of the year it's a pleasant, shady place to break the day, and it's also the trailhead for the popular **Emerald Pools Trail** (see p.355).

Zion Canyon's one designated picnic spot is the **Grotto**, less than a mile beyond the lodge near the foot of the **West Rim Trail** (see p.355). To one side stands **Red Arch Mountain**, named for a natural archway created in 1880 when a vast chunk of the mountain suddenly collapsed and obliterated a cornfield. To the other, the long western flank of the **Great White Throne** looks from this angle neither white nor especially dramatic.

During the next mile the road passes the trailhead for **Weeping Rock** (see p.357) and the **East Rim Trail** (see p.357), as well as a number of unnamed pull-outs where paths lead down to the river. The best views of all come just under five miles from the start of the Drive, as it completes its long curve around the river's "Big Bend." The lookout here faces the northern aspect of the Great White Throne, framed between the slender neck of **Angels Landing** (see p.355) to the right and the pipe-like formations of the **Organ** to the left. Glowing at sunset, the throne is utterly majestic.

A mile or so on, the Scenic Drive – and the shuttle-bus route – comes to an end at the large parking lot at the start of the mile-long **Riverside Walk** (see p.357) toward the Narrows. This general area is known as the **Temple of Sinawava**, after a wolfish deity of the Paiute Indians; the most prominent single rock is the **Pulpit**, standing alone near the west bank of the river.

The Zion–Mount Carmel Highway

Open all year • Visit ⓦ www.nps.gov/zion for current travel restrictions and/or fees for oversized vehicles – such as RVs – and cyclists

The side canyon formed by Pine Creek, half a mile north of the visitor centre, enables Hwy-9 to continue east, a route known as the **Zion–Mount Carmel Highway**. At first it heads straight for the **East Temple** – topped like its larger twin by a forested mesa – but it's soon forced to start tacking its way up the hillside. At the eastern end of each extravagant switchback comes a better view of the enormous **Great Arch** at the head of the canyon. Measuring 720ft wide by 580ft high, this is not in fact an arch at all, but simply a deep alcove, or what's known as a "blind arch."

Finally the highway burrows into the rock, entering the first and longer of two remarkable **tunnels** blasted through the canyon walls in the 1920s. Five "windows" punctuate its one-mile length to let in air and light, but you can't stop to admire the views. All the rubble from the excavation tumbled into Pine Creek far below; the river may seem innocuous, but it cleared the whole lot away in the space of a single year.

Easily seen on the enjoyable **Canyon Overlook Trail** (see p.358), the hot dry plateau beyond the eastern end of the main tunnel feels far removed from the lushness of Zion. These pale, smoothly undulating rocks, capped here and there by strange beehives and hoodoos, are the lithified remains of ancient sand dunes. One huge specimen, crisscrossed with stress lines from eons of erosion and resembling some long-abandoned pyramid, is known as the **Checkerboard Mesa**. It looms south of the highway at a clearly marked turn-off five miles beyond the second tunnel, a quarter of a mile short of the park's East Entrance.

Hiking in Zion Canyon

Every visitor to Zion Canyon should **hike** at least one of its many clearly marked and signposted trails. However, almost all trails except the short Riverside Walk require a stiff climb away from the canyon floor, and with summer temperatures in excess of 100°F and elevations of well over 6000ft, it's all too easy to overdo things. Carry plenty of food and drink, and don't simply assume that because you have no trouble walking five miles at home you can do it here, straight up a cliff. Water is available on most trails – although not until around five miles along the West or East Rim trails – but must be purified before use.

As for specific **routes**, avoid the sun by hiking the east side of the canyon in the morning and the west in the afternoon. If you're reasonably fit and have just one day, the best combination is probably an hour or two along the **Riverside Walk** and a longer climb either to **Angels Landing** on the West Rim Trail or **Hidden Canyon** on the East Rim Trail.

All the trails detailed on p.353 set off from either Hwy-9 or the Scenic Drive, but some of the longer ones leave the canyon altogether and end up on backcountry dirt roads. If you're planning a one-way hike, look at the **shuttle board** in the visitor centre, to see if you can swap vehicles with hikers coming in the opposite direction. Both *Zion Lodge* and the Zion Adventure Company (see p.360) also operate commercial **hiker shuttle services**.

Watchman Trail

Trailhead: Visitor centre • 2.7 miles round-trip; 2hr • Elevation change 368ft

Just inside the South Entrance, a right turning leads across the river to the *Watchman* campground (see p.360) and the start of the **Watchman Trail**. This steep mile-long climb switchbacks up a side canyon below Bridge Mountain, then heads back south to loop around a flat promontory below the Watchman itself. Thankfully, it doesn't go right to the top, but its views up the canyon, as well as across to the West Temple and back down to Springdale, tucked among the trees, are a good way to get your bearings when you first arrive. Until around 10am, the canyon walls keep most of the route in shade; later on, it's liable to be baking hot.

ZION HIKING PERMITS

Hiking permits are required for all **overnight** trips in Zion National Park, and all hikes that require technical equipment, most obviously the **Zion Narrows** (see p.356). **Permits** are issued for specific wilderness campsites and trails; they do not entitle you to go wherever you choose on the day. They cost $10 for one or two people, $15 for three to seven, and $20 for eight up to the group maximum of twelve. You can pick them up at any visitor centre the day before you hike, and reserve up to three months in advance via the park website, ⓦnps.gov /zion. At the very busiest periods, for the most popular routes, you may have to enter an online lottery to make a reservation, but around a third of all sites are kept free for walk-in visitors, and made available one day in advance.

Pa'rus Trail

Trailheads: Visitor centre and Canyon Junction • 1.8 miles one-way, 3.5 miles round-trip; 40min one-way, 1hr 20min round-trip • Elevation change 50ft

The gentle, paved **Pa'rus Trail**, also open to cyclists, is a level stroll of almost two miles that connects the two campgrounds either side of the visitor centre with the shuttle bus stop at Canyon Junction. Along the way, it repeatedly crisscrosses the Virgin River. While it lacks the glamour or rewarding destinations of other, more demanding trails in the park, it's a truly delightful walk, especially enjoyable around sunset at the end of a hard day.

Emerald Pools Trail

Trailhead: Zion Lodge **Lower pool** 1.2 miles round-trip; 1hr • Elevation change 69ft **Upper pool** 2.2 miles round-trip; 1hr 40min • Elevation change 200ft

The **Emerald Pools Trail**, which starts conveniently from *Zion Lodge*, is every bit as pretty as the name implies. It's also suitable for walkers of all levels, as the lowest of the three pools can be seen on a gentle round-trip stroll of little more than a mile, while the highest makes a good objective for a more energetic hike.

On the far side of the footbridge that crosses the Virgin River from the lodge, the pink-paved trail to the right is the direct route to the **lower pool**. After an easy climb through the forest, with views straight up the main canyon, it cuts left into Heaps Canyon, and soon reaches a huge overhang of red rock, streaked black by a broad cascade of water. The almost constant flow collects in pools that tend to be muddy red rather than emerald green; the overhang is deep enough for the trail to circle inside them, running behind the waterfall.

From this point, the trail becomes confusing, with countless possible routes made by lost or blundering hikers. If you're pressed for time, head back the way you came; alternatively, continue straight ahead, along the shelf on the canyon wall, and in just over half a mile you'll drop back to cross the river at the Grotto picnic area, half a mile north of *Zion Lodge*.

Most hikers head instead for the **upper pool**, by following a narrow path through a cleft in the gigantic split boulder to the left. Having first doubled back to the top of the waterfall, where the stream bubbles out of the woods to spill across a lip of slickrock, take the spur trail to the right on the far side.

A hot, hard climb of not much more than five minutes is rewarded by a delightfully cool seep-fed pool at the foot of the monumental outer walls of the canyon. Climbing any higher is out of the question, but this is a good place to linger, with a small sandy "beach" and plenty of shade.

Note that the separate trail that used to connect *Zion Lodge* with the so-called middle pool here, and made it possible to return to the lodge via a different route, was closed by a rockslide in 2011, and remained so when this book went to press.

Angels Landing and the West Rim Trail

Trailhead: The Grotto **Angels Landing** 5.4 miles round-trip; 4hr • Elevation change 1488ft **Horse Pasture Plateau** 11 miles round-trip; 10hr • Elevation change 2813ft

Serious hikers and backpackers rate the **West Rim Trail** as Zion's most compelling challenge. Even if you have nothing to prove, its views and variety make it well worth attempting, but it's not to be undertaken lightly. The first couple of miles involve a gruelling 1500ft climb out of Zion Canyon, while to reach the obvious day-hike destination, **Angels Landing** – a five-mile round-trip from the valley floor – you have to brave a terrifying knife-edge ridge.

The trail starts across the river from the Grotto picnic area, half a mile north of the lodge. As it winds ever more steeply toward the sheer canyon wall, it seems no onward route could possibly exist, but in the end it switchbacks several times and cuts back into a crack in the rock. Unless you've made a very early start, you'll have been out in the sun for a long time by now, and the cool shade of this narrow crevice – **Refrigerator Canyon** – comes as a merciful relief.

However, things soon get worse; beyond the brief flat stretch of the canyon you're confronted by a severe set of switchbacks known as **Walter's Wiggles**. Constructed during the 1920s, these serve as a ladder up an otherwise impassable cliff. At the top lies **Scout Lookout**, a tranquil patch of sand with views up and down Zion Canyon and a population of scavenging chipmunks that feast on the remains of countless well-earned picnics.

Daredevil day-hikers are invariably drawn to the spur trail from Scout Lookout to **Angels Landing**. What you're letting yourself in for is obvious from the outset; the trail sets off along the top of the steep promontory straight ahead, with awesome drop-offs to either side, and only token stretches of metal chain offer the illusion of security. If you think you're the brave one, take a look to see if there are any climbers scaling the sheer rock face on your left. Your goal is a knee-shaking half-mile on, with a

HIKING THE ZION NARROWS

Hiking the **Zion Narrows** – the slender gorge through which the Virgin River enters Zion Canyon from the north – has acquired the reputation of being *the* thing every Zion visitor simply must do. Don't believe the hype. It's a very demanding **wilderness experience**, much more suitable for devotees of extreme sports than for casual hikers.

A ravishing "slot canyon" squeezed between mighty sandstone cliffs and interspersed with fertile grottoes, the Narrows is undeniably spectacular. However, you can only trek its full length by following the river downstream from a remote trailhead which as a rule is only accessible in a four-wheel-drive vehicle. For at least ten of the sixteen miles of hiking from there, you can expect to be wading thigh- or even shoulder-deep in **cold**, **fast-flowing water**, struggling with every step to find a foothold on the slippery rounded boulders of the streambed. While it's just possible to complete the whole hike in a single, gruelling day – the average hiking time is **twelve hours** – it's more realistic to plan to camp overnight along the way.

Specialist **equipment** is essential, in the form of waterproof, super-grip footwear, neoprene socks, and a walking stick or two, complemented between October and May by a drysuit. It's not a question of whether, but of how often, you'll fall over, so you'll also need zip-lock plastic bags for everything you carry, and since the water isn't drinkable, you'll have to lug that along too. Though it doesn't have the same kudos among the adventure-sports fraternity, you can also sample the Narrows as a **day-hike** by pushing your way upstream, against the current, from the end of the Riverside Walk, and turning back when you've had enough. However, you'll still need all the gear – don't even dream of setting off without it.

For anything beyond a short day-hike upstream, you have to have a **permit** (see p.354) to hike the Narrows. The park service issues a maximum of eighty such permits per day, of which around half can be reserved in advance, while the rest are available first-come, first-served the day before. Making a reservation does not necessarily mean you'll be allowed to hike; the Narrows is always liable to be closed due to flash floods or wildfires. In principle, the **best times to hike** are in June or from September until early October. July and August see frequent thunderstorms, so the risk of flash floods is at its highest. In addition, the road to the trailhead is often closed altogether between December and April.

The Narrows is just one among many wonderful hikes on offer in the park, most of which don't require nearly so much planning, expertise, or expense. According to park rangers, its current popularity is largely because it's so heavily promoted by commercial companies. As the Narrows lies inside the national park, local operators can't offer guided trips, but they do rent **equipment** and run **shuttle services** (see p.360).

If you have your own 4WD vehicle – or if rangers advise you that road conditions are suitable for ordinary vehicles – you can get there by turning left 1.7 miles east of the East Entrance (just east of milepost 46 on Hwy-9), and then following North Fork Road, which in due course becomes a rough dirt track, for around seventeen miles north. The total thirty-mile drive from Zion Canyon takes about ninety minutes.

quarter-mile drop to the canyon floor at your feet and the Great White Throne towering a further thousand feet above you on the far side of the river.

Beyond Scout Lookout, the West Rim Trail climbs steadily out of the canyon. After crossing an expanse of slickrock, perilously close to the rim, it descends into a spectacular high-country valley. This is another side of Zion altogether, rimmed with white cliffs, "checkerboarded" by cross-bed hatching, and scattered with rounded outcrops of layered sandstone. For a couple of miles, the trail picks its way gingerly across the valley and up the far side, twice crossing streambeds that nurture forest glades. Finally it runs into the monumental wall of red sandstone that marks the head of **Behunin Canyon**, a huge side canyon off Zion Canyon (itself by now way out of view). Doubling back, it clings to the cliff face on a long exposed switchback that comes out atop **Horse Pasture Plateau**.

Just to set foot on Horse Pasture Plateau is a stiff target for a day-hike from the floor of Zion Canyon. In the full heat of summer even that would be too much to take on, but the trail continues north for another ten miles, to **Lava Point** off the Kolob Terrace Road (see p.361), with plenty of optional scenic detours en route. This is Zion's most popular backpacking trip, usually done as a two-day expedition, starting from Lava Point and working down, and camping near the southern edge of Horse Pasture Plateau. As with any such overnight hike, a backcountry camping permit is required (see p.354).

7

Riverside Walk

Trailhead: Temple of Sinawava • 2.2 miles round-trip; 1hr 30min • Elevation change 57ft

Not least because it involves no climbing, the mile-long **Riverside Walk** at the end of the Scenic Drive is Zion's best-loved trail. Having watched the canyon walls converge ever closer, the urge to find out what happens beyond the end of the road is irresistible. You may well have more company than you'd prefer, but the views from the gentle paved footpath are too beautiful for that to matter. While it's easy enough to complete the round-trip in under an hour, you'll enjoy it more if you allow much longer.

Walls of deep red sandstone soar to either side of the river, which is flanked by shimmering cottonwoods that turn a rich gold in the fall. There are even patches of low-lying "desert swamp," where bullfrogs bellow in the rushes and willows thrust from the mud.

Riverside Walk ends where the Virgin emerges from **the Narrows**, overlooked by the mighty **Mountain of Mystery**. For eight miles upstream from this sandy little beach, the river fills the entire gorge, often less than twenty feet wide and channelled between vertical cliffs almost a thousand feet high. As explained in the box opposite, it's possible to wade upstream, against the current, to see the Narrows for yourself, while if you arrive towards sunset, you'll also doubtless encounter plenty of exhausted backpackers who have hiked here sixteen miles downstream, from Chamberlain's Ranch.

Weeping Rock

Trailhead: Weeping Rock • 0.4 miles round-trip; 30min • Elevation change 98ft

As one of Zion Canyon's easiest short walks, the paved, half-mile hike to and from **Weeping Rock** is prone to be overcrowded in summer. Eaten from the canyon wall by a perennial spring, this damp alcove is filled with ferns and tiny flowers; while it comes as a surprise in the desert, however, it's not as beautiful as you may be led to expect.

Hidden Canyon and the East Rim Trail

Trailhead: Weeping Rock **Observation Point** 8 miles round-trip; 6hr • Elevation change 2148ft **Hidden Canyon** 3.4 miles round-trip; 4hr • Elevation change 850ft

Rewarding hikes of almost any length can be enjoyed by taking the **East Rim Trail**, which sets off from the Weeping Rock trailhead. Only backpackers who camp overnight on the mesa-top attempt its full 10.5-mile length, and they normally prefer to start from the far end, near the park's East Entrance. However, the strenuous two-mile climb out of Zion Canyon is its most exhilarating segment, with the alternative options of continuing all the way up to **Observation Point** if you fancy a full day's hiking, or taking the separate trail into **Hidden Canyon** for a half-day excursion.

After half an hour of ascending along a cement pathway, enjoying ever-improving views of Weeping Rock itself, the East Rim Trail reaches a stiff set of switchbacks. By the time you reach the top of those, you've climbed about half a mile up the face of Cable Mountain, but you're still only halfway up to the mesa. A stone bench here makes a good place to ponder the decision whether to keep on going, or head instead for **Hidden Canyon**, a "hanging canyon" that has yet to cut its way down to the floor of Zion. To reach it, follow a spur trail for a further half-mile, beyond a brief stretch of forest and a hair-raising segment, clinging to a wall of rock, which is enough to deter many would-be canyoneers. The broad "lip" of the canyon, perched 700ft above Zion, turns into a waterfall after heavy rain, while the rounded holes scoured into the slickrock fill with water and life. Strictly speaking, the trail ends here; it's just about feasible to press on into the canyon, but only expert rock climbers have any hope of approaching its head.

If Hidden Canyon sounds too intimidating, you may prefer to keep on switchbacking up the East Rim Trail beyond the Hidden Canyon turn-off. A mile or so further on, deep in wafer-thin Echo Canyon – a "slot canyon" with beautiful walls that drop far below the trail as well as towering above it – the **East Mesa Trail** climbs steeply off to the left, while the East Rim Trail itself continues straight on. Reaching **Observation Point**, two miles along the East Mesa Trail, involves quite a bit more climbing, switchbacking up a mighty sandstone cliff face on a very narrow red-dirt path. Eventually you pick your way through the woods atop the plateau, to be rewarded with breathtaking views all the way down Zion Canyon. The massive cliffs of Cable Mountain and the Great White Throne stare you full in the face, while Angels Landing towers proudly on the far side.

Hikers who choose to stay on the **East Rim Trail** rather than heading for Observation Point also face another mile of climbing out of Echo Canyon, with the possibility of having to negotiate streams en route. Once on top of the mesa, walking becomes much easier, as the trails simply follow former logging roads. **Stave Spring**, the only perennial water source on the East Rim Trail, is roughly halfway between Zion Canyon, five miles west, and the East Entrance, slightly further southeast. Overnight campers can head southwest at this point, along a trail that soon forks to the summits of **Cable Mountain** – where you can take a closer look at the century-old workings that hauled timber down into Zion (see p.351) – or Deertrap Mountain. Either hike is a six-mile detour from Stave Spring.

Canyon Overlook Trail

Trailhead: Zion–Mt Carmel Highway • 1 mile round-trip, 1hr • Elevation change 163ft

At the eastern end of the long tunnel on the Zion–Mount Carmel highway, alongside the ranger station, steps cut into the rock mark the start of the **Canyon Overlook Trail**. So long as you don't mind edging along the brink of a precipice – at one point the trail consists of wooden planks braced against the cliff face – this offers a fascinating variety of terrain in the space of just half a mile. It's also the only trail described here for which you can access the trailhead in your own vehicle year-round – though with so little parking that may make little difference. The scenery en route ranges from fern-filled grottoes fed by seeping water to a bare slickrock mesa topped by tiny hoodoos.

The trail ends at a railed viewing area at the head of Pine Creek Canyon; though you can't see it, you're directly above the Great Arch. Only one of the tunnel's five "windows" is visible in the rock wall to your left, but the road emerges below to zigzag into the valley. Straight ahead is the west wall of Zion Canyon; a helpful sign labels the

peaks ranged along the far side of the river, from the ruddy tree-capped West Temple to the paler Sentinel.

ARRIVAL AND DEPARTURE

By car Hwy-9 follows the Virgin River for 30 miles east of I-15, and enters the park via the South Entrance, just north of Springdale (see p.348). Half a mile north, it

ZION CANYON

abandons the river and heads east, to tunnel its way out of the canyon (see p.353).

GETTING AROUND

Between April and October – precise dates vary – all visitors to Zion Canyon, other than guests staying at *Zion Lodge* (see p.360), have to leave their vehicles either in Springdale or at the main park visitor centre and use the park's network of shuttle buses. These run on two separate loops and are free, and you can get on and off as often as you like.

Zion Canyon Shuttle Active all year round, and compulsory between April and October, the in-park shuttle runs between the visitor centre and the end of the Scenic Drive, with nine stops including *Zion Lodge*. It operates between 6am and 10.15pm from late May until early

September, between 7am and 9.30pm in spring and fall, and from dawn until sometime after dusk in winter.

Springdale Loop Connects Springdale with the visitor centre, with nine stops en route, between 5.40am and 10.15pm in summer, and 6.40am and 9pm in spring and fall, but closes down in the winter. A short walk connects the different shuttle bus systems at the visitor centre; the Springdale buses stop just outside the park, so passengers have to pass through entrance gates on foot to reach the visitor centre and canyon shuttles.

TOURS AND ACTIVITIES

Canyon Trail Rides ☎435 679 8665, ⓦcanyonrides .com. Horseback rides, starting *from Zion Lodge* (March–Oct; daily 3hr rides at 9am & 1.30pm, $60, minimum age 10; daily four 1hr rides $40, minimum age 7).

Zion Adventure Company 36 Zion Park Blvd, Springfield ☎435 772 1001, ⓦzionadventures.com. Tubing on the Virgin River; guided biking, photography, climbing and canyoneering trips; Narrows equipment rental from $20 per day; and hiker shuttles, including to Chamberlain's Ranch for $35.

Zion Canyon Field Institute ☎435 772 3264 or ☎800 635 3959, ⓦzionpark.org. Hikes, excursions and lectures in the park, covering topics that range from reptiles to basketry, photography to solar energy, and costing from $25 up to $100 for a full-day class.

Zion Rock and Mountain Guides 1458 Zion Park Blvd, Springfield ☎435 772 3303, ⓦzionrockguides.com. Guided climbing, biking and canyoneering trips in the vicinity of the park; Narrows equipment rental for around $20 per day in summer, $35 in winter; and daily hiker shuttles, including to Chamberlain's Ranch for $35.

ACCOMMODATION AND EATING

Red Rock Grill Zion Lodge, Scenic Drive, Zion Canyon ☎435 772 7760, ⓦzionlodge.com. Whether or not you stay at the lodge, it's well worth stopping to eat in its bright, cool, upstairs **dining room**. The river views will probably linger longer in your mind than its standard breakfasts and lunches, both costing $8–12. Dinners are slightly more sophisticated, featuring entrees like steak or trout for $16–24. Daily: summer 6.30–10.30am, 11.30am–3pm & 5–10pm; winter 7–10am, 11am–2pm & 5.30–8pm.

Zion Lodge Scenic Drive, Zion Canyon. Advance reservations ☎303 297 2757 or ☎888 297 2757, same-day reservations and property phone ☎435 772 7700, ⓦzionlodge.com. This appealing if often overcrowded complex of low-slung wooden buildings, occupying pride of place on lush well-shaded lawns a couple of miles up the Scenic Drive, offers the only **food** and **lodging** within the canyon. Stay if you can in one of the forty en-suite cabins, which have gas fireplaces and private porches; the 72 motel rooms are plainer, but still have porches or balconies. Open

all year; reserve well in advance, especially in summer. Room $186, cabin $193

CAMPING

South Campground Zion Canyon ☎435 772 3256, ⓦnps.gov/zion. Located, despite the name, just north of the park visitor centre, alongside the river and the Pa'rus Trail, this first-come, first-served campground is open between early March and early Nov only. Arrive early in summer, when it tends to fill by noon daily. Flushing toilets and cold running water, but no showers. $16

Watchman Campground reservations ☎877 444 6777, ⓦrecreation.gov. Although it's open year round, this large campground, amid the cottonwoods south of the visitor centre, accepts reservations between March and early November only. Flushing toilets and cold running water, but no showers. 18 walk-in, tent-only sites; the rest can hold one RV or two ordinary cars. Basic site $16, with electric hook-up $18, riverside site $20

Kolob Terrace Road

The only road access to the central uplands of Zion National Park is along **Kolob Terrace Road**, which branches inconspicuously north from Hwy-9 at tiny **Virgin**, fifteen miles west of the park's South Entrance. Especially in its earlier stages, it's a dramatic drive, but unless you have a high-clearance 4WD vehicle, you won't manage the full 43 miles to meet I-15 just south of Cedar City. Ordinary cars have to turn back after just over twenty miles, so only long-distance hikers or tourists with a spare afternoon tend to come this way. In addition, the entire road is closed to all traffic in winter.

The road starts by climbing through a dry desert valley, heading for two pyramidal mountains that dwarf the cliffs on the horizon. It reaches Zion after just over seven miles, only to exit almost immediately, and then dips repeatedly in and out of the park. As it next re-enters the park, you get superb views north across **Hop Valley** to the russet and white pinnacle of **Burnt Mountain**. Keen backpackers can hike to Kolob Arch from here along the **Hop Valley Trail**, but it's not as easy as it looks; you have to plough through thick sand for most of the way, so the fifteen-mile hike is even more difficult than the route from Kolob Canyons (see p.361).

Soon after you leave the park yet again, twenty miles up from the highway, a dirt road to the right leads 1.7 miles to **Lava Point**, back within the park. As well as being the trailhead for the West Rim Trail, which takes fourteen miles to drop down into Zion Canyon (see p.357), this is a superb vantage point in its own right. Poised four thousand feet higher than the visitor centre, it overlooks a panorama that stretches north to Cedar Breaks and southeast to the Kaibab Mountains, with the monoliths of Zion Canyon mere incidental details in the foreground. There's a **picnic area** and a free, first-come, first-served, six-site primitive **campground** with no water nearby (June–Oct only).

7

Kolob Canyons

Just off I-15, 161 miles northeast of Las Vegas and 20 miles south of Cedar City · $25/vehicle, $12 for motorcyclists, cyclists and pedestrians; valid for 7 days · ☎ 435 586 9548, ⓦ nps.gov/zion

Despite being easier to reach than Zion Canyon, the **Kolob Canyons**, which have formed part of Zion National Park since 1956, receive far fewer visitors. In all honesty, they're less immediately impressive than Zion Canyon, and you'll only get the most out of the area if you can spare the time and energy to **hike**. If you stay in your car, you can drive to the end of the five-mile road, admire the view of the red-rock canyons, and be back on the interstate within the hour, wondering what the fuss is about.

Kolob Canyons Road twists alongside Taylor Creek and then up through Lee Pass, with countless trailheads and roadside viewpoints en route. Its final parking lot faces across the riverbed to a succession of narrow, red-walled **"finger" canyons** cut into the west rim of the Markagunt Plateau. Each was carved by a separate tiny stream; one, Hanging Valley, is interrupted by a sheer 1500ft cliff, stranding an isolated patch of thick forest far above the valley floor. In the distance, you may just be able to make out the West Temple, above Zion Canyon.

Footpaths on the far side of the lot lead to a picnic spot in the woods. From here, the half-mile **Timber Creek Overlook** trail runs through low trees along the top of the ridge, to end at a rocky promontory with views over the endless rolling forests.

Taylor Creek Trail

Trailhead: Kolob Canyons Rd, 2 miles from visitor centre · 5 miles round-trip; 4hr · Elevation change 450ft

The **Taylor Creek Trail** follows the Middle Fork of Taylor Creek on a five-mile round-trip to **Double Arch Alcove**, passing long-abandoned cabins built by early homesteaders. The trail grows progressively less distinct before it culminates by climbing into the lush hollow in the canyon wall that lies beneath the Double Arch itself.

Kolob Arch Trail

Trailhead: Lee Pass Trailhead, Kolob Canyons Rd, 3.5 miles from visitor centre • 14 miles round-trip; 8hr • Elevation change 1037ft

Among Zion's very finest trails, the **Kolob Arch Trail** leads down from Lees Pass along the drainage of Timber Creek. At fourteen miles for the round-trip, it only makes an appropriate day-hike for confident, experienced desert hikers. It can be muddy going, but at least there's usually plenty of water en route (which must be purified before drinking). The first couple of miles, heading south, feature superb close-up views of the finger canyons; you then veer east to meet **La Verkin Creek** just above a waterfall.

Kolob Arch itself, seven miles along, may or may not be the world's longest natural rock span. Like Landscape Arch, in Arches National Park (see p.419), it's approximately 300ft across; no one agrees how to measure arches any more precisely than that, so they're generally considered equals. Camping somewhere nearby (by prior arrangement at the visitor centre) makes for a less gruelling hike and gives you the option of exploring the remote regions that lie farther along La Verkin Creek.

7

INFORMATION   KOLOB CANYONS

Visitor centre Exit 40, I-15 (daily: late April to late May and Sept to mid-Oct 8am–5pm; late May to Aug 8am–6pm; mid-Oct to late April 8am–4.30pm; ☎ 435 586 9548). As well as providing free hiking advice, rangers also allot 24 numbered backcountry campsites ($5). No gas or food is available.

East from Zion: US-89

As soon as you leave Zion National Park via its eastern entrance (see p.354), you're out in flat, open ranching country. Eleven nondescript miles further on, Hwy-9 meets **US-89** at Mount Carmel Junction. Turn **north** here if you're heading towards Bryce Canyon, to follow the broad **Long Valley** cut by the **Sevier River**. The only real point in heading **south** on US-89 is to reach Arizona, with the North Rim of the Grand Canyon (see p.331) almost exactly a hundred miles away. A century ago, when Mormons from Arizona would come this way to be married in the temple at St George, this route was known as the **Honeymoon Trail**. The largest town along the highway, **Kanab**, retains a strong Mormon identity, but it also has a back-of-beyond frontier feel to it and makes a good overnight stop.

Mount Carmel Junction

The eastward progress of Hwy-9 stops when a north–south wall of red cliffs rears up on the far side of the Virgin River. **MOUNT CARMEL JUNCTION** here, at the junction of Hwy-9 and US-89, is a bucolic spot, with cottonwoods lining the river and horses grazing in the meadows to the north. Unless you're ready to stop for the night in one of its two **motels**, however, there's little reason to get out of the car.

ACCOMMODATION   MOUNT CARMEL JUNCTION

Best Western East Zion Thunderbird Lodge Hwy-9 & US-89 ☎ 435 648 2203 or ☎ 888 848 6358, ⓦ zionnational-park.com. The larger and more upscale of the pair of motels at this isolated road junction, with large rooms plus a pool, spa, and even half a golf course. $106

Golden Hills Hwy-9 & US-89 ☎ 435 648 2268 or ☎ 800 648 2268, ⓦ goldenhillsmotel.com. Plain, low-slung little motel, where some rooms are right beside the river, and they also have a basic diner that's open for all meals, with lunchtime sandwiches well under $10, and dinner entrees for $10–20, as well as an internet cafe. $57

Coral Pink Sand Dunes State Park

15 miles south of Mount Carmel Junction • Daily dawn–dusk • $6 per vehicle • ☎ 435 648 2800, ⓦ stateparks.utah.gov/parks/coral-pink • Access roads leave US-89 4 and 9 miles southeast of Mount Carmel Junction, to meet just before the park itself

Few areas in the Southwest conform so exactly to the popular notion of a desert – graceful dunes of fine sand, their parallel crests sweeping toward the horizon – as **CORAL PINK SAND DUNES STATE PARK**. This pseudo-Saharan landscape, a dozen miles south of Mount Carmel Junction, can be reached via two separate paved roads off US-89.

The only dune field in the Colorado Plateau lies at the foot of a seven-mile bluff of the Vermilion Cliffs, which here unusually face the northwest. Its sand grains are eroded from Navajo sandstone, itself originally deposited in the form of dunes.

Hikers who launch themselves from the boardwalk near the park visitor centre usually find that a few minutes of wading knee-deep in sand sates their *Lawrence of Arabia* fantasies. However, in marked contrast to Utah's federal parks, **off-road vehicles** are positively encouraged. The park was created in response to campaigns by local off-road enthusiasts, and plays host to countless formal and informal **dune buggy races**, most notably each July 4.

ACCOMMODATION   CORAL PINK SAND DUNES STATE PARK

Campground Alongside the visitor centre ☎ 800 322 3770, ⓦ stateparks.utah.gov/reservations. The well-shaded campground remains open all year, though it only has water in summer. Spending a night here offers the

enticing prospect of seeing not only tiny kangaroo rats, named for their squatting postures, but, more to the point, the snakes that prey on them, which are not a danger to humans. $16

Kanab

Until new roads were pushed through the region in the 1950s, **KANAB**, seventeen miles southeast of Mount Carmel Junction and just two miles north of the Arizona state line, was renowned as the most inaccessible town in the US. Now it's a significant tourist rest-stop simply because it lies halfway between the Grand Canyon, eighty miles southeast, and Bryce Canyon, 83 miles northeast.

Kanab started life in 1864 as **Fort Kanab**, a frontier outpost so prone to Indian attacks that it was abandoned after just two years. Jacob Hamblin founded the town itself in 1870 as a God-fearing ranching community with a sideline in harbouring Mormons who fell afoul of the federal government, among them several perpetrators of the Mountain Meadows Massacre. Pulp novelist Zane Grey later cultivated that lawless image, setting many of his Westerns nearby. Kanab's rugged surroundings also drew Western film greats, from Tom Mix, who filmed *Deadwood Coach* here in 1924, to Clint Eastwood, who swept into town with *The Outlaw Josey Wales* in 1976. The town soon earned the nickname "Utah's Little Hollywood."

With ranching in decline, and the prospect of large-scale coal mining on the **Kaiparowits Plateau** to the northeast having been thwarted by the establishment of Grand Staircase–Escalante National Monument in 1996, Kanab now survives by catering to tourists. US-89 is lined with an above-par assortment of motels and restaurants, with the greatest concentration where it briefly doglegs to run east–west along **Center Street**. A few blocks south, US-89 proper branches off east toward Page, while US-89A continues south towards **Fredonia** in Arizona.

Apart from shopping in its Western-themed souvenir stores, there's almost nothing to do in Kanab, though hikers may enjoy the views from the **Squaw Trail**, which climbs the escarpment just north of town. It takes six miles – a hike of up to four hours – to loop back to Kanab, but if time is short you can simply turn around when you've had enough.

INFORMATION   KANAB

BLM field office 669 S US-89A (mid-March to mid-Nov daily 8am–4.30pm; mid-Nov to mid-March Mon–Fri 8am–4.30pm; ☎ 435 644 4600, ⓦ blm.gov/ut). Information on nearby public lands and current driving conditions.

Visitor centre 78 S 100 East (March–Oct Mon–Fri 9am–7pm, Sat 10am–6pm, Sun 9am–4pm; Nov–Feb Mon–Fri 9am–5pm; ☎ 435 644 5033 or ☎ 800 733 5263, ⓦ kaneutah.com).

ACCOMMODATION

Aiken's Lodge 74 W Center St ☎435 644 2625 or ☎877 644 2105, ⓦaikenslodge.com. This low-slung and not desperately pretty option is nonetheless the ideal budget motel: crisp and clean, right in the heart of town, and with its own pool. **$62**

Kanab Comfort Inn 815 E US-89 ☎435 644 8888, ⓦcomfortinn.com/hotel-kanab-utah-UT109. Large motel, isolated atop a bluff on the eastern edge of town, but with the best rooms in Kanab, plus a free breakfast bar. **$110**

Parry Lodge 89 E Center St ☎435 644 2601 or ☎888 289 1722, ⓦparrylodge.com. Opened in 1931, Kanab's oldest motel has an undeniable air of romance. Photos of celebrity guests festoon the lobby and restaurant, while nameplates identify the rooms in which they slept; you can even bathe in John Wayne's extra-large bathtub. *Parry's* isn't *that* great, though, and some of the newer rooms can be dingy and noisy. **$70**

EATING

Linda Lea's 4 E Center St ☎435 644 8191. Good central bakery, with sidewalk patio seating to enjoy its fine breads, pastries and coffee. Mon–Sat 6am–2pm.

Nedra's Too 310 S 100 East ☎435 644 2030, ⓦnedrascafe.com. Informal local hangout at the junction of US-89 and US-89A on the south side of town, with a sister restaurant in Fredonia (see p.335). The unifying factor of the Mexican/American menu is the fryer; even the ice cream comes deep-fried. Mexican dishes cost around $11, steak and seafood more like $20. Daily 7am–9pm.

Parry Lodge 89 E Center St ☎435 644 2601, ⓦparrylodge.com. Attractive dining room where the menu occasionally hints at the healthy, in the form of dishes like poached salmon. Unlike most places in Kanab, it has a licence to sell alcohol. The breakfast buffet costs $6, for guests only, while typical dinner entrees cost $13–20. Mid-June to mid-Sept daily 6–10am, 11.30am–2pm & 5.30–9.30pm; closed Nov–March, plus lunch in spring and fall.

Rocking V Café 97 W Center St ☎435 644 8001, ⓦrockingvcafe.com. This valiant and largely successful bid to improve Kanab's culinary reputation is housed in a former bank, one of the town's oldest buildings. Burgers, sandwiches and daily "taste of the Planet" specials like Thursday's chana masala vegetarian stew, for around $12 at lunch; dinner entrees like salmon Creole cost $23. Daily 11.30am–10pm.

East of Kanab: US-89 and Paria Canyon

US-89, which heads due east out of central Kanab, curves northwards into the southern reaches of Grand Staircase-Escalante National Monument (see p.373) as it makes its spectacular 73-mile run to **Page**, Arizona (see p.393). Though not as popular with visitors as the broadly parallel US-89A further south, which allows access to the North Rim of the Grand Canyon, it's still a dramatic drive and has its own potential diversions in the shape of the hikes into **Coyote Buttes** and **Paria Canyon**.

Exploring these or any other off-highway areas requires you to drive down dirt roads that become very treacherous in bad weather, while even the shortest hike leads swiftly into remote backcountry. It is therefore essential to pick up detailed, current advice on conditions, either at the BLM office in Kanab or at the BLM's **Paria Contact Station**, 43 miles east.

Coyote Buttes

A conspicuous but unmarked dirt road leads south from US-89, between mile posts 25 and 26, along a high ridge, toward the **Coyote Buttes** area. Since 2000, this has formed part of **Vermilion Cliffs National Monument**, but despite that enhanced status it remains relatively untrampled by human feet. Its guardians, the BLM, are so determined to keep it that way that hiking is rigidly controlled, by permit only (see p.365).

What everyone is so eager to see is a rock formation known as **The Wave**, an extraordinary, disorienting ripple of sculpted sandstone atop a hard-to-find prominence known as **Top Rock**, just south of the Arizona–Utah state line in the north section of the buttes. As there's no fixed trail, you'll need good advice to complete the seven-mile round-trip hike in a single day. The BLM requests that specific instructions not be published, in order to discourage unauthorized or poorly equipped hikers; if you're

PERMITS FOR COYOTE BUTTES AND PARIA CANYON

Day-hikers who stay within the upper reaches of Wire Pass, Buckskin Gulch, and Paria Canyon do not require **permits**, though they still must pay $5 per person per day at the trailheads. For overnight stays in those areas, and for day-hikes as well as overnight backpacking trips further afield, including to Coyote Buttes, permits are essential. With just twenty issued per day for Coyote Buttes North ($7 per person) and another twenty for Coyote Buttes South ($5), they're very hard to come by.

Only half of these places can be booked **online**, at Ⓦ blm.gov/az/paria. On the first day of each month, **reservations** become available for the fourth month ahead; thus March 1 is the date on which June permits are first sold. For Coyote Buttes North, you suggest three possible dates, and are entered into a lottery, typically with a ten percent chance of success; for Coyote Buttes South, you name a specific day, with a good chance of getting a permit if you apply on the first possible date. The remaining permits are allocated to **walk-ins** who arrive at a BLM office in the area and request a permit for some day in the coming week.

7

lucky enough to get the necessary reservation, they'll provide you with a detailed map. Both the Coyote Buttes and Buckskin Gulch routes start from the **Wire Pass Trailhead**, reached by leaving US-89 between mile markers 25 and 26 and just over eight miles south into the wilderness.

INFORMATION   COYOTE BUTTES

BLM field office The closest BLM office, the Paria Contact Station (daily 8.30am–4.15pm; ☎ 435 644 4628), is four miles east of the highway turn-off; if you're approaching from Page, remember it's an hour later here in Utah than it is in Arizona.

Paria Canyon

The same restrictions on backpacker permits as for Coyote Buttes (see p.365) also apply to hikers intending to make the four- to six-day trek down **Paria Canyon**, which ends at the start of the Grand Canyon at Lees Ferry, Arizona (see p.329). While it's possible to access the route by first hiking down Buckskin Gulch from the Wire Pass Trailhead mentioned above, most hikers start at the **White House Trailhead**, two miles south of US-89 just east of the Paria Contact Station. A basic **campground** near the trailhead charges $5 per night.

The road to Bryce Canyon

Drivers heading from Zion National Park to Bryce Canyon National Park should turn **north** on US-89 from Mount Carmel (see p.362), rather than heading south to Kanab. For just over forty pretty but uneventful miles, punctuated by the occasional Mormon hamlet, the road remains within **Long Valley**, with the Markagunt and Paunsaugunt plateaus rising to either side. Then you're faced with the choice of either continuing north toward Salt Lake City, or veering east toward Bryce Canyon and Utah's other national parks.

Orderville and Glendale

Tiny **ORDERVILLE** stands four miles north of Mount Carmel on US-89. Despite its historical significance as the longest-lasting of several experiments in communitarian living organized by the **United Order**, a nineteenth-century Mormon group that believed all property should be held in common, modern Orderville is not worth an extended stay. Aside from two gas stations and a couple of shabby motels it has little to attract passing tourists. The almost equally insignificant hamlet of **GLENDALE**, however, nestled amid a cluster of apple orchards five miles further north of Orderville, makes a pleasant lunch or even overnight stop.

Hatch

Long Valley steadily dries out north of Glendale, so travellers from Cedar City who pick up US-89 at the east end of Hwy-14 (see p.347) encounter further upland forests rather than farmland. At 7000ft up, little **HATCH**, 25 miles on, makes a cool overnight stop in summer, but that's the only time its handful of motels are at all busy.

Red Canyon

The only road in a hundred miles that manages to climb through the wild country east of US-89 is **Hwy-12**, which was blasted into the rocks ten miles north of Hatch to provide a route to **Bryce Canyon** and beyond. It starts by climbing through **Red Canyon**, a small-scale precursor of the joys ahead. Four miles along on the left, the short Pink Ledges **hiking trail** sets off from a parking lot that also holds a Dixie National Forest **visitor centre** (summer daily 9am–5pm; ☎435 676 2676); longer trails leave from the first-come, first-served *Red Canyon* **campground** ($12, no showers), half a mile further on. Immediately beyond that, the highway tunnels through two artificial red-rock arches, before topping out on top of the Paunsaugunt Plateau, with another ten miles to go before Bryce.

7

Panguitch

The spruce, squeaky-clean and oddly endearing Mormon town of **PANGUITCH** – 24 miles from Bryce, seven miles north of the intersection of Hwy-12 and US-89, and fifty from Mount Carmel Junction – was established in 1864 and named for no good reason after the Paiute term for "Big Fish." After an uncertain start, Panguitch became, and remains, the largest town along the Upper Sevier Valley. That was originally due in part to the brick factory responsible for the distinguished brick homes that still adorn its streets, but Panguitch today depends heavily on tourism for its bread and butter. It's a bit too chilly to linger in the off-season, but in summer, the pumps at the eight local gas stations rarely stop spinning, and twenty-odd budget motels and restaurants are kept busy.

INFORMATION

THE ROAD TO BRYCE CANYON

PANGUITCH
Visitor centre 55 S Main St (daily May–Oct 9am–5pm; ☎435 676 1160 or ☎800 444 6869, ⓦbrycecanyoncountry.com). They can provide a walking tour of the town's historic homes, but you'd have to be more than a little weird to spend your morning doing that rather than setting off into the wondrous deserts.

ACCOMMODATION AND EATING

GLENDALE
Buffalo Bistro 305 N Main St ☎435 648 2778, ⓦbuffalobistro.net. An unexpected find for such a tiny community, this Western-themed little restaurant serves well-prepared steaks (around $20) as well as burgers and even rattlesnake sausages (under $10), with fresh vegetables and great desserts, plus live music (and outdoor seating) on summer evenings. Thurs–Sun 4–9pm.
Smith Hotel 295 N Main St ☎435 648 2156 or 800 528 3558, ⓦhistoricsmithhotel.com. This white clapboard house, complete with a large upstairs veranda, looks much like the rest of Glendale's homes, but it's actually a welcoming wayside inn, with seven bright and very pleasant en-suite B&B rooms. $74

HATCH
Riverside Resort & RV Park 594 N Hwy-89

☎435 735 4223 or ☎800 824 5651, ⓦriversideresort-utah.com. Don't let the word "resort" raise your hopes too high, but if you're happy to get an ordinary motel room for half what you'd pay nearer the parks, or to park an RV or set up a tent in a field near the river, this complex a mile north of Hatch should suit you fine. Tents $15, RVs $30, rooms $67.50

PANGUITCH
Cowboy's Smokehouse Bar-B-Q 95 N Main St ☎435 676 8030, ⓦcowboyssmokehousecafe.com. This Victorian-era saloon is much the best of Panguitch's half-dozen humdrum **restaurants**, with moderately priced barbecued meats (half a rack of ribs for under $20) and huge fruit pies, plus regular live music. Mon–Sat 7am–9pm.
Harold's Place Intersection of US-89 and Hwy-12, 7 miles south of Panguitch ☎435 676 2350 or ☎676 8886, ⓦharoldsplace.net. Twenty log cabins lined

up side by side, of which two sleep six people, plus 32 motel rooms in a separate inn. Closed Nov to April. $89

Purple Sage Motel 132 E Center St ☎ 435 676 2659 or

☎ 800 241 6889, ⓦ purplesagemotel.biz/wordpress. Great value, well-run little budget motel a block from the town centre. $85

Bryce Canyon National Park

Hwy-63, 3 miles south of US-89, 86 miles northeast of Zion Canyon (2hr drive), or 120 miles southwest of Capitol Reef (over 3hr drive) · $25/vehicle, $12 for motorcyclists, cyclists and pedestrians; valid for 7 days · ☎ 435 834 5322, ⓦ nps.gov/brca

Few more freakish landscapes can exist than those confined within **BRYCE CANYON NATIONAL PARK**. From the safety of the park's rim road, visitors gaze down upon a throng of red, yellow and orange pinnacles of rock, eating like the flames of a forest fire into the thickly wooded plateau. Braver souls can hike down into the inferno and thread their way between the top-heavy towers, to explore a barren desert that's aglow with almost psychedelic colours.

Paiute Indians, who hunted in the vicinity, had an elegantly precise word for the landscape: *Unkatimpe-wa-Wince-Pockich*, "red rocks standing like men in a bowl-shaped recess." The current name comes from the Mormon settler **Ebenezer Bryce**, who established a short-lived homestead nearby in 1874 and memorably declared this was "a helluva place to lose a cow." In fact, however, "Bryce's Canyon" is not a canyon at all but a row of crescent-shaped amphitheatres, hollowed into a twenty-mile stretch along the eastern edge of the **Paunsaugunt Plateau**. At up to 9000ft above sea level, this marks the final and most spectacular rung of the Grand Staircase's ascent of southern Utah (see p.335). Between sixty and forty million years ago, the **Pink Cliffs** were deposited in layers of varying thickness and strength on the beds of shallow lakes. Some are limestone, some siltstone; all were dyed and stained with combinations of red, white, orange, blue or yellow by different concentrations of minerals, especially iron.

Conditions at Bryce are perfect for rapid erosion, with ice forming overnight and thawing in the morning over two hundred times per year. Water seeps into cracks in the ground, then expands as it freezes, to wedge the cracks ever wider. Spurs emerge from the cliff face as it recedes, then dwindle to slender fins and eventually break into separate standing columns. When the topmost rock of a column is hard enough, lower levels erode away beneath it at a much faster rate. A mighty boulder left precariously perched on a tall, narrow pillar is known as a **hoodoo**. At Bryce, thousands upon thousands of hoodoos are crammed into each successive amphitheatre, to form a menagerie of multihued, contorted stone shapes. The best known, and most precarious, is **Thor's Hammer**, near Sunset Point.

Since it became a national park in the 1920s – with irregular boundaries designed to minimize the impact on local ranchers – Bryce Canyon has deservedly ranked as a must-see attraction for any visitor to Utah. If you're at all stretched for time, however, this is one park that you can realistically hope to see in a single day, or even an afternoon. Just be sure that you do at least get out of your car and **hike** into the technicolour ravines – far more vivid than the Grand Canyon, as well as much more human in scale. Most visitors pass through between June and August, but the park is, if anything, even more inspiring in the stillness of winter, when the hoodoos rear their heads from a blanket of **snow**.

Visitor centre

Hwy-63, 1.5 miles beyond park entrance station · Daily: May–Sept 8am–8pm; April & Oct 8am–6pm; Nov March 8am–4.30pm · Free · ☎ 435 834 5322, ⓦ nps.gov/brca

Although Hwy-12 runs within the northern boundaries of the national park on its way across southwest Utah, you won't see Bryce's rock formations unless you turn south onto Hwy-63 thirteen miles east of US-89, or eight miles northwest of Tropic (see p.372).

7

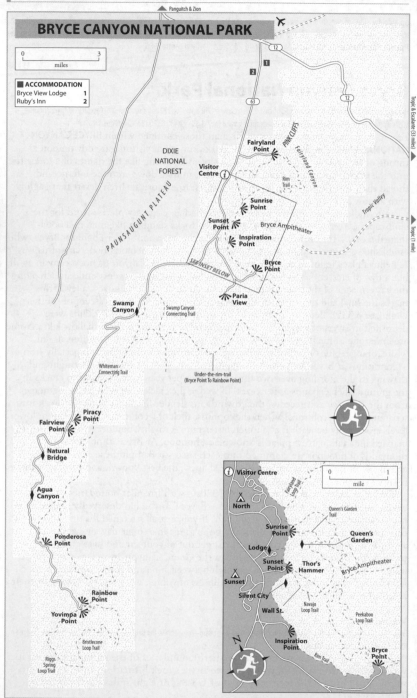

BRYCE CANYON NATIONAL PARK

Panguitch & Zion

0 — 3
miles

■ ACCOMMODATION
Bryce View Lodge **1**
Ruby's Inn **2**

12

1

2

63

12

7

DIXIE
NATIONAL
FOREST

PINK CLIFFS

Fairland
Point

Fairland Canyon

Tropic & Escalante (33 miles)

Visitor
Centre

Rim
Trail

Sunrise
Point

Tropic Valley

Sunset
Point

Bryce Ampitheater

Tropic (1 mile)

Inspiration
Point

PAUNSAUGUNT PLATEAU

Bryce
Point

SEE INSET BELOW

Paria
View

Swamp
Canyon

Swamp Canyon
Connecting Trail

Whiteman
Connecting Trail

Under-the-rim-trail
(Bryce Point To Rainbow Point)

N

Piracy
Point

Fairview
Point

Natural
Bridge

Agua
Canyon

Ponderosa
Point

Rainbow
Point

Yovimpa
Point

Bristlecone
Loop Trail

Riggs
Spring
Loop Trail

i Visitor Centre

0 — 1
mile

Fairland Loop Trail

Queen's Garden
Trail

North

Sunrise
Point

Queen's
Garden

Lodge

Thor's
Hammer

Bryce Ampitheater

Sunset
Point

Sunset

Silent City

Wall St.

Navajo
Loop Trail

Peekaboo
Loop Trail

Inspiration
Point

Rim Trail

Bryce
Point

N

For drivers and shuttle passengers alike, the park **visitor centre** makes a logical first stop, even though it's not within view of the canyon itself. A valuable source of information on current weather and hiking conditions, it's also the place to pick up $5 **permits** if you plan to camp in Bryce's **backcountry**. All the various designated sites are south of Bryce Point below the rim, well away from the main trails.

Bryce Amphitheater

Most visitor activity at Bryce is concentrated around **Bryce Amphitheater**, the largest and most accessible of the indentations in the Pink Cliffs. Whether you park your own car off the loop road that leaves Hwy-63 half a mile south of the visitor centre, or get dropped off by the shuttle bus, a brief walk will bring you to the brink of the crescent-shaped depression, which is paralleled for its full length by the paved Rim Trail. En route, you'll probably also drop in at the *Lodge at Bryce Canyon*, where the main lobby holds a fascinating large-scale relief model of the park, and there are several souvenir stores and snack bars as well as a restaurant (see p.371) and hotel accommodation (see p.371).

Where along the Rim Trail you get your first blast of the incandescent rocks makes little difference. Of the two official overlooks, around five hundred yards apart, **Sunrise Point** to the north attracts fewer of the tour-bus crowds than **Sunset Point** to the south. Neither name is particularly appropriate; both face east, so you won't see the sun set, while the best place to catch the dawn is **Bryce Point**, a mile or so further south. Here at the southernmost tip of the amphitheatre, you can look back west as the first rays of the sun strike the toy soldiers below. Although dawn and dusk are the prime times to **take photos** at Bryce, the views to the east and north are astonishing at any time of day, ranging as much as a hundred miles to encompass the Aquarius Plateau and the Henry Mountains.

Scenic Drive

Beyond Bryce Amphitheater, **Hwy-63** – also known as the **Scenic Drive** – meanders south along the rim of the Paunsaugunt Plateau for another fifteen miles. It's a slow drive, passing a succession of substantially similar viewpoints; no one stops at them all, though each has its merits. Look out in particular for the huge **Natural Bridge**, which spans a steep gully approximately halfway along the route, very close to the eponymous lookout. Suspended far above the forest, it doesn't cross running water, so technically it's not a bridge but an 85ft arch.

Hwy-63 steadily climbs another thousand feet higher as it continues south, until finally the ridge it's following narrows to a slender neck, and the road is forced to end at the highest viewpoint of all, **Rainbow Point** (9115ft). While that faces east, nearby **Yovimpa Point** commands sweeping views south, to Navajo Mountain and the Kaibab forest that fringes the Grand Canyon.

As you leave the park, bear in mind that **Fairyland Point**, reached via a separate turn-off a mile or so north of the visitor centre, is one of Bryce's quietest yet most scenic viewpoints

Hiking in Bryce Canyon

The **Rim Trail** follows the lip of the plateau for just over five miles, skirting Bryce Amphitheater between Sunrise and Sunset points, and extending both north and south. Die-hard backpackers can continue beyond its southern limit, at Bryce Point, all the way to Rainbow Point, 22.6 miles on, along the **Under-the-Rim Trail** (which has designated camping spots). By far the most popular trails in the park, however, are those that drop into Bryce Amphitheater itself. With several alternative routes to the bottom, and a choice of connections once you're there, you can tailor a hike to suit whatever time you have, from a couple of hours to a full day.

7

The basic experience is much the same whichever trail you take. The rock stratum that has eroded to form the hoodoos, just below the rim, averages from 300 to 500ft thick, so hiking consists of descending between them until you reach the flatter pine forest beyond, walking through the woods, and then climbing back up again. At an elevation of almost two miles, even a brief hike involves considerable effort; you'll need good footwear and plenty of water.

Navajo Loop Trail

Navajo Loop Trailhead: Sunset Point • 1.3 miles round-trip; 1–2hr • Elevation change 550ft • **Navajo/Queen's Garden combination** 2.9 miles round-trip; 2–3hr • 600ft

For a concentrated burst of Bryce at its best, the **Navajo Loop Trail** is ideal. The shortest and busiest trail of all, it plummets abruptly from Sunset Point into formations known as the **Silent City**, then circles back up to complete a hike of 1.3 miles. Allow plenty of time to enjoy the whole roundtrip without exhausting yourself. Taking the trail's steeper right-hand branch as you set off makes for an easier hike, and also brings you, by way of precipitous switchbacks, straight into the cool crevice of **Wall Street**. In places, this awe-inspiring gulf of orange rock is less than twenty feet wide, but it's too deep for the 800-year-old Douglas firs that grow from its sandy floor to poke their heads above the cliffs.

Beyond Wall Street, you swiftly reach a small sandy wash. The return leg of the Navajo Loop Trail starts a short way to the left and follows a slightly gentler incline back to Sunset Point, passing **Thor's Hammer** and other humongous hoodoos en route. Alternatively, continue northwards on the level footpath just above the wash, pausing perhaps to rest in the shade of the pines and junipers. The basin known as the **Queen's Garden** is somewhere over a mile along. Named for an almost translucent fin that's topped by a rocky pile bearing a vague resemblance to Queen Victoria, it's connected by a mile-long trail up the hillside to **Sunrise Point**. During its climb, the path cuts repeatedly through limestone fins and spurs, with each tunnel framing yet another irresistible photograph. Most of the horseback expeditions in the park pass this way. Dwarfed beneath the ludicrous, multicoloured spires and turrets, the horses make an especially surreal spectacle.

ARRIVAL   BRYCE CANYON NATIONAL PARK

By plane Charter and sight-seeing flights from elsewhere in the Southwest land at Bryce Canyon Airport on Hwy-12, to no fixed schedule (🖰 brycecanyonairport.com). Oddly enough, this is one of the oldest airports in the US,

with pine-log hangars built by the WPA in the 1930s.

On foot Keen hikers should note that it's possible to avoid the crowds by walking into the park from Tropic (see p.372).

GETTING AROUND AND TOURS

Shuttle buses Although visitors can drive to all the scenic overlooks year round, the park runs **free shuttle buses** to reduce traffic congestion (daily: first half of May & second half of Sept 8am–6.50pm; mid-May to mid-Sept 8am–7.50pm, first week of Oct 8am–6.50pm). The bus route connects the *Ruby's Inn* complex, just south of the intersection of Hwy-12 and Hwy-63, with the overlooks in Bryce Amphitheater. If that's as far as you want to go – and for most people, even enthusiastic hikers, it's entirely sufficient – then there's no reason to use your own car. The shuttles don't go as far south as Rainbow Point, but it's normally served by two bus tours each day from the visitor centre (☎ 435 834 5322 for reservations).

Horseriding Canyon Trail Rides, contactable via the desk at the *Lodge At Bryce Canyon* (☎ 435 679 8665, 🖰 canyonrides.com), arranges horseback rides into the canyon (2hr rides starting at 9am & 2pm, minimum age 7, $60; half-day rides at 8am & 1pm, minimum age 10, $80). Ruby's Horseback Adventures, based at *Ruby's*

(☎ 866 782 0002, 🖰 brycecanyonhorseback.com), offers a wider range of rides, at broadly similar prices.

Flight-seeing tours Bryce Canyon Airlines & Helicopters, based at *Ruby's* (☎ 435 834 8060), offer flights over Bryce Canyon and further afield, with rates starting at around $100 for a seventeen-minute flight.

ACCOMMODATION AND EATING

INSIDE THE PARK

Lodge at Bryce Canyon 100 yards from the rim between Sunrise and Sunset points ☎435 834 8700 or ☎877 386 4383, ⊛brycecanyonforever.com. The only accommodation option within the park itself, this venerable stone-and-timber lodge is open in summer only. Furnished in its original 1920s style, it consists of a handful of luxurious suites, a row or two of rough-hewn but very comfortable individual cabins, and about seventy relatively ordinary motel rooms. All have en-suite bathrooms but no TVs, and tend to be reserved several months in advance. Closed mid-Nov to March. Rooms $\overline{\$175}$, cabins $\overline{\$203}$, suites $\overline{\$244}$

North Campground Bryce Canyon Walking distance from the visitor centre ☎877 444 6777, ⊛recreation .gov (reservations) & ⊛nps.gov/brca, (information). This year-round park-service campground, stretching alongside the Rim Trail a short walk from the visitor centre, accepts reservations for 13 of its 99 sites only, between early May and September only. It's usually fully occupied by early afternoon. RVs can stay, but there are no hookups or showers; sites hold up to ten people, in two vehicles. $\overline{\$15}$

Restaurant Lodge at Bryce Canyon ☎435 834 5361, ⊛brycecanyonforever.com. This high-ceilinged and reasonably high-quality **dining room** is open to the public for all meals. Lunchtime salads and sandwiches are typically priced at around $12, though there are more expensive daily specials, and richer dinner entrees like slow-cooked short ribs or marinated pork tenderloin cost up to $30. Reservations can be made for dinner only, and only on the same day. Daily 7–10.30am, 11.30am–3pm & 5.30–10pm.

Sunset Campground Bryce Canyon Across from the Lodge at Bryce Canyon ☎877 444 6777, ⊛recreation .gov (reservations) & ⊛nps.gov/brca, (information). Seasonal campground, across the highway from the *Lodge at Bryce Canyon*, near Sunset Point. Only twenty of its 100 sites can be reserved in advance; all hold up to ten people, in two vehicles, and are available first-come, first-served, which means all tend to be taken by early afternoon. RVs can stay, but there are no hook-ups; the closest showers are by the General Store in the *Lodge* complex. Closed mid-Oct to April. $\overline{\$15}$

NEAR THE PARK

Half a dozen accommodation options loiter just outside the park along highways 12 and 63; the cluster at the intersection used to be known as Pink Cliffs Village, and they've now taken to calling it Bryce Canyon City, though there's no village to speak of, let alone city. All remain open year-round, with considerably reduced rates in winter, and have their own unenthralling restaurants. Otherwise, the nearby towns of Panguitch (see p.366) and Tropic (p.372) both offer motels.

Best Western Plus Bryce Canyon Grand Hotel 30 N 100 E, Bryce Canyon City ☎435 834 5700 or ☎800 780 7234, ⊛bestwesternutah.com. Large new chain motel, just off Hwy-63 a mile short of the park, with good comfortable rooms and an outdoor pool and hot tub. $\overline{\$160}$

Bryce Canyon Pines Hwy-12 milepost 10 ☎435 834 5441 or ☎800 892 7923, ⊛brycecanyonmotel.com. Reasonable if anonymous motel, three miles west off the road junction on Hwy-12, with a strangely shallow swimming pool in a separate shed. They also have an RV park and campground in the woods alongside. Tents $\overline{\$20}$, RVs $\overline{\$30}$, rooms $\overline{\$130}$

Ruby's Inn 26 S Main St, Bryce Canyon City ☎435 834 5341 or ☎866 866 6616, ⊛rubysinn.com. Large, unattractive motel complex on Hwy-63, a mile or so outside the park. Fifty of the 368 rooms feature whirlpool baths, and there's a heated indoor swimming pool. Paying extra to be housed in the main lodge, rather than one of the outlying sections, only makes sense in the depths of winter. The food in the dining room (open daily for all meals) is consistently atrocious. $\overline{\$117}$

Ruby's Inn Campground 26 S Main St, Bryce Canyon City ☎435 834 5341 or ☎866 878 9373, ⊛brycecanyoncampgrounds.com. The nearest commercial campground to the park, in the woods adjoining *Ruby's Inn*. As well as tent sites and RV hook-ups, they also have basic cabins, each holding two double beds, and tipis that sleep 6–8 guests, although the prices shown here are for two. Closed Nov–March. Tents $\overline{\$29}$, tipis $\overline{\$39}$, RVs $\overline{\$40}$, cabins $\overline{\$63}$

East of Bryce Canyon

By continuing east from Bryce Canyon, you're leaving civilisation firmly behind. This central region of southern Utah is almost entirely given over to wilderness, and there's barely time to draw breath after Bryce before you plunge into Grand Staircase–Escalante National Monument. A few tiny communities cling to the fringes, however, and **Tropic** offers a few creature comforts as you brace yourself for what lies ahead.

Tropic

The first community east of Bryce along Hwy-12, **TROPIC**, stands eight miles from the Bryce Canyon National Park turn-off. Among the migrants from Panguitch who settled this tiny hamlet in the 1880s – naming it for its allegedly superior climate – was Ebenezer Bryce himself (see p.367). His restored log cabin is now the centrepiece of the *Pioneer Village* motel.

Tropic may turn its back on the flamboyance of Bryce Canyon, ranged along the ridge above it, but it has little appeal of its own; the main street consists of a row of motels and fast-food joints, and strolling around the centre is unrewarding. However, the unmarked road that leads west from Bryce's log cabin reaches the park boundary in a couple of miles, from where it's a further two-mile hike up to the main formations.

ACCOMMODATION AND EATING   TROPIC

You don't gain much by staying in Tropic rather than the motels closer to the park, but it does have a reasonable range of **accommodation**. However, few of the motels have facilities – for example pools – that might entice you to hang around during the day. As for the limited array of **restaurants**, no one would make a special trip to eat in Tropic, but once you're here it's not worth driving anywhere else either.

Bryce Canyon Inn 21 N Main St ☎ 435 679 8502 or ☎ 800 592 1468, ⓦ brycecanyoninn.com. Standard motel rooms, plus 18 large, newer log cabins, available in summer only. Rates include continental breakfast. Room $70, cabin $99

Bryce Point B&B 61 North 400 West ☎ 435 679 8629 or ☎ 888 200 4211, ⓦ brycecanyonbedbreakfast.com. Cheerful family-run B&B attached to a private house. All of the five large rooms have picture windows facing Bryce Canyon, plus their own baths and TVs, and there's also a shared deck with a hot tub. $90

Buffalo Sage B&B 980 N Hwy-12 ☎ 435 679 8443 or ☎ 866 232 5711, ⓦ buffalosage.com. Modern, purpose-built B&B perched on a bluff at the northwest end of town, enjoying great views from a wraparound deck and offering four comfortable en-suite rooms. $80

Grand Staircase Inn 105 N Kodachrome Drive, Cannonville ☎ 435 679 8400 or ☎ 877 472 6346, ⓦ grandstaircaseinn.com. Simple but adequate highway motel five miles south of Tropic, attached to a grocery store and gas station. $69

Kodachrome Basin State Park

Cottonwood Canyon Road, 13 miles south of Tropic • Daily 6am–10pm • $6/vehicle • ☎ 435 679 8562, ⓦ stateparks.utah.gov/parks /kodachrome

At the village of Cannonville, five miles south of Tropic, Hwy-12 veers east across the Paria River. If you choose to continue south along Paria Valley instead, on Cottonwood Canyon Road, the pavement runs out after eight more miles at **KODACHROME BASIN STATE PARK**. This assortment of contorted rocky columns, tucked beneath the cliffs that climb to Kaiparowits Peak, was named by a *National Geographic* photographer in 1948 in honour of the latest Kodak film; he felt the area's existing name of Thorny Pasture was too prosaic.

By the standards of Utah's national parks, however, Kodachrome Basin is not especially worth making an effort to see. Its main focus is a unique geological phenomenon, not found anywhere else on earth: its 67 **sand pipes**. Each of these misshapen pillars was formed as an underground geyser, created by an earthquake, which was then blocked with tough calcite sediment. When the softer rock that surrounded them eroded away, they were left towering as high as 150ft above the scrubby plain.

After paying the **fee** at the park entrance station, follow the road for a couple of miles to the left to reach the park's attractive **campground** ($16 tents, $25 RV hook-ups). Various trailheads along the way mark the start of short hikes among the formations. Alternatively, the unpaved road that forks right from the entrance station ends after a little over a mile at the trailhead for **Shakespeare Arch**. A pleasant quarter-mile walk brings you to a small high natural arch, from where you can get good views across the valley to the Pink Cliffs of Bryce Canyon.

Grand Staircase–Escalante National Monument

No admission fee or opening hours • Ⓦ ut.blm.gov/monument

Created by presidential decree in 1996, **GRAND STAIRCASE-ESCALANTE NATIONAL MONUMENT** is, at 1.9 million acres, the largest US national monument outside Alaska. Though its staggering landscape unquestionably merits such recognition, it's not so much a homogenous entity as the final piece in a jigsaw puzzle, placing the leftover lands between Bryce, Capitol Reef, the Dixie National Forest and the Glen Canyon NRA under federal control. From the Aquarius Plateau in the north (as the highest segment of the Colorado Plateau, the top rung of the "staircase") to Lake Powell in the south, only the farming valleys around towns such as Tropic, Escalante, and Boulder remain in private ownership.

Although **Hwy-12** dips in and out of its northern flanks, **US-89** runs briefly through its southern extremities, and the rudimentary **Burr Trail** leads into Capitol Reef from its eastern end (see p.388), no paved roads cross this magnificent wilderness. True, dirt tracks provide limited access to the backcountry, but even they don't begin to penetrate the extraordinary canyon country at its heart, and all are in any case rendered impassable by poor weather. What's more, there's only one maintained hiking trail in the whole huge expanse.

Created to "maintain the unspoiled nature" of the region, rather than "develop" it for tourism, Grand Staircase–Escalante was the first national park or monument to be administered not by the National Park Service but by the Bureau of Land Management. No new paved roads have been built, and all facilities are located in existing towns, primarily **Escalante** itself.

Most of the million visitors who pass this way each year arrive with little idea of what to do other than simply drive the hundred-mile stretch of **Hwy-12** between Bryce Canyon and Capitol Reef. Only completed in 1980, thanks to the difficulty of the terrain and the lack of towns en route, this is indisputably the most scenic of southern Utah's fifteen or so designated "Scenic Byways." Although no driver could fail to be awed by the highway's ever-changing panoply of red-rock canyons, crystal-clear rivers, and shimmering oases, it's well worth taking the time to get out of your car and explore at least a little on foot.

The **Escalante River**, which drains this whole region, was the last river to be named, let alone explored, in the continental US, and to this day most maps show the area as a vast blank. However, the back roads and trails now bustle with venturesome tourists, who tend to stay two or three nights rather than just one, spending perhaps one day exploring the remarkable **slot canyons** along rugged **Hole-in-the-Rock Road**, and another in and around delightful **Calf Creek**. For backpackers, the options are all but infinite, though the sandstone bridges and arches on the lower reaches of **Coyote Gulch** and the Escalante River itself are the prime attraction.

Skutumpah and Cottonwood Canyon roads

Two long, lonely, mostly dirt roads cut north–south trajectories through the western end of Grand Staircase–Escalante, branching off from the paved road to Kodachrome Basin (see p.372). In principle, both can be travelled in ordinary, two-wheel-drive vehicles, but check current conditions with rangers before setting off. Even slightly adverse weather can make the going impossible, while in winter the roads will almost certainly be not only impassable, but potential death-traps. Unless you have 4WD, don't base your itinerary on the assumption you'll be able to get through.

7

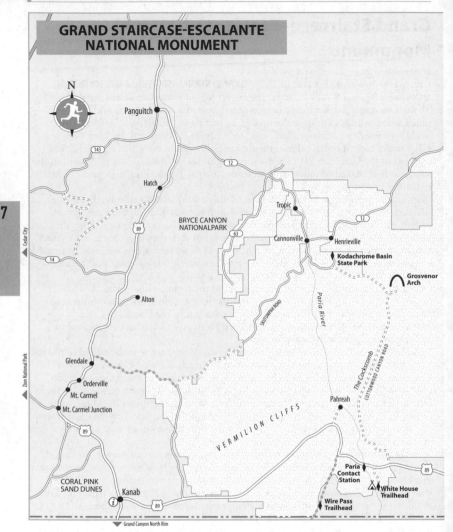

GRAND STAIRCASE-ESCALANTE NATIONAL MONUMENT

Skutumpah Road

Skutumpah Road, the better maintained of the two north–south roads through Grand Staircase–Escalante, starts three miles south of Cannonville and takes 52 miles to reach US-89, nine miles east of Kanab. Both the first sixteen and the last sixteen of those miles are paved (the latter part as Johnson Canyon Road), but that still leaves twenty difficult unpaved miles, as the road picks its way across **Bull Valley Gorge** and through the **White Cliffs**. One of the best hikes comes early on, before the terrain becomes difficult: the five-mile round-trip stroll though the narrows of **Willis Creek**. From the **trailhead**, six miles down Skutumpah Road, it only takes a few minutes' walking before canyon walls begin to climb to either side of the wash, and they swiftly close in to stand just a few feet apart.

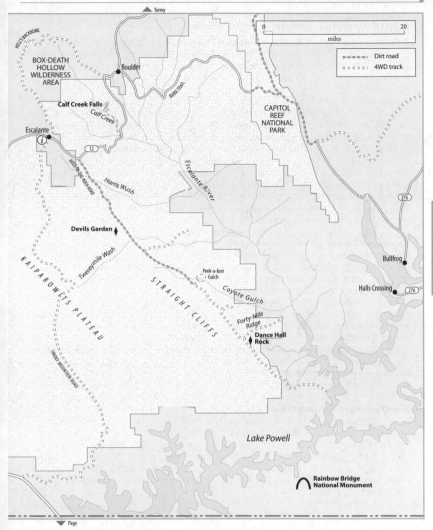

Cottonwood Canyon Road

Much of **Cottonwood Canyon Road**, which heads east from Kodachrome Basin, runs across bare **slickrock**. Its graded gravel surface becomes extremely dangerous after rain, but during drier periods, it's well worth continuing for ten miles beyond the park to see the intricate double **Grosvenor Arch**. At that point, the road turns south, to meet **US-89** thirty miles on, roughly halfway between Kanab and Page. En route it threads its way between the dark pyramidal fins of the **Cockscomb**, a bizarre geological oddity, resembling the armour-plated back of a stegosaurus, which forms the boundary between the Grand Staircase and the Kaiparowits Plateau.

A MONUMENTAL AFFAIR

The first proposal to create **Escalante National Monument** was submitted to Franklin Roosevelt in 1940. Its boundaries would have enclosed 4.5 million acres, stretching from Lees Ferry as far as Moab and Green River, and taken in 280 miles of the Colorado River, 150 miles of the Green River, and 70 miles of the San Juan. That vast area was then crossed by just one road, and no bridge spanned the Colorado. Although Roosevelt saw himself as an environmentalist, the greenery of the Hudson River Valley was far more to his taste than the red rocks of the West. In the face of vociferous Mormon opposition in Utah, the idea was quietly dropped.

When Canyonlands National Park was created in the 1960s (see p.405), it included only a small proportion of that suggested tract. Glen Canyon on the Colorado River was by now submerged beneath Lake Powell (see p.392), while the **Kaiparowits Plateau**, which stretches south of Escalante all the way to the lake, remained outside federal protection. That was thanks to southern Utah's business community, acutely aware that the so-called Fifty-Mile Mountain stands atop the world's largest known deposits of **coal**.

Rumours surrounded plans to mine the Kaiparowits Plateau for well over fifty years. The closest any came to fruition was in the 1970s, when the Southern California Edison Company announced its intention to open a 6000-acre mine, complete with new roads and an on-site electricity generating plant. Controversy over the scheme pitted its supporters, the so-called **Sagebrush Rebels** – an informal grouping of Utah's Mormon-dominated business elite, plus the workers whose livelihoods were at stake – against environmentalists from across the nation. Although its abandonment in 1976 was largely due to slackening demand for electricity, communities such as Kanab, desperate for jobs, took out their anger by burning effigies of green activists in the streets.

In 1980, a study commissioned by Congress showed that almost 400,000 acres on the Kaiparowits Plateau had already been logged to clear the way for mines. Much of that timber was processed at a mill in Escalante, and when green opposition resulted in a moratorium on tree-felling, Escalante too witnessed its own share of public "hangings."

Hopes that mining money might revitalize Escalante rose once more in the mid-1990s, with the news that a Dutch conglomerate was considering strip-mining the Kaiparowits. By now, however, the pro-mining lobby had become merely a vociferous minority, and President Clinton decided that delighting environmentalists in every state was more important than appeasing the business community in Utah. In 1996 he therefore declared the creation of the **Grand Staircase–Escalante National Monument**.

Utah legislators promptly condemned it as "the mother of all land grabs," and the ropes came out once again, this time to "hang" both Clinton and his Interior Secretary Bruce Babbitt. However, the move was welcomed in the rest of the nation, and now that the die has been cast, even Escalante has accepted it. After years of insisting that they'd rather be farming, logging and mining than running motels, the predominantly Mormon local population has at least been guaranteed a secure economic future, even if it's not the one it anticipated.

Escalante

Hwy-12 climbs northeast from Cannonville, passing through the speck that is **Henrieville** and then ascending the clay cliffs known as "The Blues." Once atop the cliffs you're confronted by the unexpected sight of the high but fertile **Upper Valley**, kept well watered by snowmelt from the Aquarius Plateau.

Mormon militiamen who pursued Indian raiders through the Upper Valley in 1866 noted the rich meadowland beyond, and dubbed the region "Potato Valley" in honour of its abundant wild sweet potatoes. Within ten years, several returned to establish a ranching and farming community. They called it **ESCALANTE**, despite the fact that the Spanish explorer-priest Fray Silvestre de Escalante (see p.470) never came within a hundred miles of here.

Life was harsh during Escalante's early years; the pioneers spent their first winter huddled in primitive dugouts. Then came a period of deceptive ease, as their sheep and cattle multiplied on the open range. By 1910, however, the native grasses on which they grazed were gone forever. The land has never recovered, and Escalante has remained frozen at much the same size and appearance ever since.

Escalante is a neat enough little town, with its main street gently sloping down from west to east and a couple of blocks of four-square brick and timber homes to either side. It's also a screamingly dull place to spend the night, though the wilderness that stretches away in every direction more than makes up for that.

INFORMATION
ESCALANTE

Multi-Agency visitor centre 755 W Main St (mid-March to mid-Nov daily 7.30am–5.30pm; mid-Nov to mid-March Mon–Fri 8am–4.30pm; ☎ 435 826 5499, ⓦ ut.blm.gov /monument). Up-to-date information on hiking, and mountain-biking in the public lands in and around Grand Staircase–Escalante National Monument, plus free permits for backcountry camping.

ACCOMMODATION

Canyons Bed & Breakfast 15 South 100 East ☎ 435 826 4747 or ☎ 866 526 5667, ⓦ canyonsbnb.com. Behind this ordinary townhouse you'll find four attractive en-suite guest rooms, each with its own little patio. Rates include a high-quality organic breakfast. **$135**

Circle D Motel 475 W Main St ☎ 435 826 4297, ⓦ escalantecircledmotel.com. Basic old-style motel, perched at the west end of town, with assorted rooms arrayed a long wooden veranda; ask for one of the newer ones. **$74**

Escalante's Grand Staircase B&B 280 W Main St ☎ 435 826 4890, ⓦ escalantebnb.com. B&B-cum-motel, with eight spacious, bright and cheerfully decorated rooms. No children under 12. **$145**

Escalante Outfitters 310 W Main St ☎ 435 826 4266 or ☎ 866 455 0041, ⓦ www.escalanteoutfitters.com. Hikers' and campers' supply store where each of the seven attractive little log cabins out back has heating but no phone or TV. They share use of a bathhouse. There's also tent camping. Closed Nov to mid-March. Tent **$16**, cabin **$45**

Prospector Inn 380 W Main St ☎ 435 826 4653, ⓦ prospectorinn.com. Escalante's largest and most modern motel offers spacious, comfortable and good-value twin-bedded rooms. **$125**

EATING

As **restaurants** struggle to survive in Escalante, it holds just a handful of nondescript diners, where it's hard to stretch a night on the town much beyond twelve and a half minutes.

Circle D Eatery 425 W Main St ☎ 435 826 4297, ⓦ escalantecircledeatery.com. Faux-adobe diner/steakhouse, specializing in home-smoked, locally raised meats like beef brisket ($14) and pork ribs (full slab $19). Lunchtime burgers and sandwiches cost well under $10. Summer daily 7am–9.30pm.

Esca-Latte Escalante Outfitters 310 W Main St ☎ 435 826 4266, ⓦ escalanteoutfitters.com. Small-scale espresso bar in outfitters' store, which serves light snacks, $8–12 salads and $10–15 pizzas as well as coffee, smoothies and beer. Service is brusque in the extreme, but it's still the best lunch spot around. Summer daily 8am–10pm; winter Tues–Sat 8am–6pm.

Hell's Backbone

While Hwy-12 is by far the quickest route between Escalante and Boulder, summer thrill-seekers can choose instead to take a two-hour, forty-mile trip across the top of the Aquarius Plateau, along the old "Upper Road." Turn north on the 300 East block in Escalante, and the paved **Forest Road 153** heads up Pine Creek Canyon, to reach the appealing mountain-set **Posey Lake** fourteen miles on.

Turn east at the lake, onto Hell's Backbone Road, and the fun begins. Having crawled up the flanks of the 10,000ft Roger Peak, this dirt track teeters along the slender ridge known as **Hell's Backbone**, with sheer drops down to Sand Creek on one side and Death Hollow on the other. The best views come at the hair-raising bridge halfway along. The bizarrely named **Box-Death Hollow Wilderness** far below can only be penetrated on foot and is southern Utah's most difficult hiking region. Tracing its full length necessitates eighteen miles of wading in ice-cold water and takes between four and seven days; don't even consider setting off without talking to the rangers at the visitor centre in Escalante.

7

THE HOLE-IN-THE-ROCK EXPEDITION

These days, **Hole-in-the-Rock Road** is emphatically a dead end, its progress blocked by tumbled boulders high above the waters of Lake Powell. When it was created, however, this was intended to become the most direct route across southern Utah.

In November 1879, the 230 Mormon pioneers of the **San Juan Mission** gathered outside Escalante. Intent on reaching their new home, almost two hundred miles east, they were convinced they'd find a shortcut along the uncharted east flank of the Kaiparowits Plateau and across the Colorado. Even when confronted with the abyss of Glen Canyon, their faith saw them through. In the space of six weeks, they dynamited a narrow slit in a fifty-foot cliff – the **Hole-in-the-Rock** itself – until it was wide enough to squeeze through. Despite snow and ice, they then used ropes to lower 83 wagons down a precipitous "road" that descended 1800ft to the river. Once there, they ferried the whole lot across the Colorado on makeshift rafts, then repeated the entire process to escape the canyon on the far side. A mere hundred more miles of desert brought them to **Bluff** (see p.433), which they established on April 6, 1880. All 230 members of the party lived through the trek, joined by three babies born en route.

For the last ten miles, as it descends through the woods to Boulder, Hell's Backbone Road is paved, but the backcountry section is usually closed by snow between October and late May.

Hole-in-the-Rock Road

The most popular route into Grand Staircase–Escalante National Monument, **Hole-in-the-Rock Road**, turns south from Hwy-12 five miles east of Escalante. Following a route established by Mormon pioneers, it continues for more than fifty hard miles to stop just before Lake Powell. While it has never been paved, its first forty miles are passable for ordinary vehicles for most of the year. It's a long, slow drive, however – allow three hours to get as far as Dance Hall Rock and back, and carry water and emergency supplies – and despite the build-up it's not nearly as dramatic as Hwy-12. The **hiking trails** that branch away from it do make the effort worthwhile though; the best of which for day-trippers is the loop down to the Peek-A-Boo and Spooky **slot canyons**. Staff at the visitor centre in Escalante (see p.377) can provide leaflets and simple maps, but if you're planning anything substantial, buy a proper topographical map.

Devils Garden

12 miles south of Hwy-12 on Hole-in-the-Rock Road • Free

For its first five miles, Hole-in-the-Rock Road crosses mundane, level ranching country. It then climbs to reveal a first glimpse of the red rocks of Escalante Canyon away to the east, and the surface changes from gravel to mud. As you continue across a sagebrush-strewn plateau, there's no incentive to get out of your car before **Devils Garden**, twelve miles along. The one official picnic area en route, this small valley, below the highway to the west, is scattered with rounded, clay-ish hoodoos and arches, reminiscent of Goblin Valley (see p.400). Countless trails and footpaths weave among the excrescences; none leads anywhere in particular, but it's a great place to play hide-and-seek.

In winter, after the snow has set in – usually some time in December – Hole-in-the-Rock Road is normally blocked beyond Devils Garden.

The slot canyons of Dry Fork

1 mile along Dry Fork Road, which starts 26 miles south of Hwy-12 on Hole-in-the-Rock Road • Free

Apart from crossing the occasional bouncy, sandy wash, Hole-in-the-Rock Road remains uneventful as you continue beyond Devils Garden. Now and then, vistas of the colour country open up, and 24 miles along you begin to see rounded slickrock domes perched above the canyon. Just as the thought of what lies to the east is becoming seriously frustrating, however, you finally get the chance to see what's down there.

Head east on **Dry Fork Road**, a couple of miles along Hole-in-the-Rock Road – something over 45 minutes' driving from the highway – and after five hair-raising minutes you'll come to a makeshift parking lot on the edge of a shallow canyon. A steep, sandy, and rather hard-to-follow trail takes roughly twenty minutes to switchback down from here into the Dry Fork of Coyote Gulch, where you'll find a couple of Utah's most accessible **slot canyons**, **Peek-a-Boo Gulch** and **Spooky Gulch**. Scoured by fierce desert storms, these kind of impossibly slender and delicate canyons have become hugely popular tourist destinations in the last few years, mainly because they look so utterly gorgeous in photographs. In real life, they're breathtaking, but they're also very dangerous. If there's the slightest threat of rain anywhere nearby, don't go in – and as if that weren't enough, they're also home to midget rattlesnakes.

Peek-a-Boo Gulch

Although **Peek-a-Boo Gulch**, the first slot canyon you come to on the Dry Fork of Coyote Gulch, is facing you as soon you reach the canyon floor, you might not recognize it. It's *not* the sandy-bottomed canyon heading off to your left, which may be narrow but isn't quite narrow enough to count as a "slot." Peek-A-Boo instead is on the far side, with its mouth at first glance appearing to be blocked by a "chimney" of slickrock. Just to enter it, you have to haul yourself up a couple of chest-high ledges, which serve as a foretaste of several more to come. Exploring is irresistible, however, as each twist and turn reveals some new arch, bridge, or tunnel to scramble through or over. The walls to either side are never all that high, and it doesn't take long to get all the way through, but the elegant swirls and patterns in the storm-gouged rock make it a constant delight.

Spooky Gulch

Spooky Gulch, fifteen minutes' walk down Dry Fork beyond Peek-A-Boo Gulch, is by contrast downright intimidating. It starts narrow and just keeps on getting narrower and darker. To keep going at all, you have to crawl early on beneath a big fallen boulder, and after that it becomes a very tight squeeze indeed. Soon it's only possible to walk sideways, with serious pressure on your rib cage and back, and a sandpaper-like rasping at your clothes.

Coyote Gulch

Hurricane Wash, 33.5 miles south of Hwy-12 on Hole-in-the-Rock Road • Free

Beyond Dry Fork, the surface of Hole-in-the-Rock Road becomes sandier and more uneven, and progress is that much slower. A mile or so after the solitary finger of **Chimney Rock** appears on the edge of the mesa, a parking lot on the right signals your arrival at **Hurricane Wash**. This is the starting point for the monument's most popular **backpacking** route, the three- to four-day round-trip hike down through **Coyote Gulch** to the Escalante River. If you plan to attempt it, ask someone at the monument visitor centre in Escalante to talk you through the route before you set off.

Strictly speaking, the trail proper begins a quarter-mile down a dirt track to the left of Hole-in-the-Rock Road, but even if your vehicle can get that far, there probably won't be space to park. From there, it's five miles' walk along the sandy but ever-narrowing bed of Hurricane Wash before you reach Coyote Gulch, and then a further eight miles until that meets the Escalante in turn.

Coyote Gulch itself is a spellbinding creek, cutting through a slickrock canyon that's lined with gorgeous sandstone bridges and arches, and punctuated by dramatic waterfalls. Most of it actually lies within the Glen Canyon NRA, but this is the only way to reach it on land. When Lake Powell is at its maximum high-water level, the lake extends all the way up the canyon of the Escalante to its confluence with Coyote Gulch, which means there's no scope for hikers to see, let alone explore, the Escalante

River itself. However, in recent years, the lake waters have tended to remain considerably lower than that. When this book went to press in 2013, for example, the surface of the lake was a little above 3600 feet, and around eight miles of the Escalante River were exposed below the Coyote Gulch confluence, making it possible to hike to long-submerged side canyons as well as beside the river.

The day-hike from Forty-Mile Ridge

Starting from Hurricane Wash, there isn't time to hike to any significant features of Coyote Gulch and back within a single day. However, it is possible to snatch a glimpse on a **day-hike** from the end of **Forty-Mile Ridge**, an almost pure-sand "road" that leaves Hole-in-the-Rock Road another couple of miles further on. The first snag is that if you don't have 4WD, you'll probably only be able to drive the first five miles of Forty-Mile Ridge, and thus face an extra two-mile hike to reach the trailhead at its far end. The second snag is that the trail itself enters Coyote Gulch, two miles along, through the **Crack in the Wall**, an incredibly tight squeeze between sandstone boulders perched above a towering cliff that is every bit as alarming as its name suggests. And the final snag: it's much more difficult coming back the other way, so never climb down unless you're certain you can climb up again.

Assuming you can cope with these obstacles, the rewards are tremendous. Before you drop down into the gulch, you cross some fabulous slickrock slopes with colossal views out over the wilderness. Once there, Cliff Arch, Coyote Natural Bridge and the huge Jacob Hamblin Arch all lie within reach.

Dance Hall Rock
36 miles south of Hwy-12 on Hole-in-the-Rock Road • Free

Under normal conditions, two-wheel-drive vehicles should go no further along Hole-in-the-Rock Road than **Dance Hall Rock**, a mile beyond Forty-Mile Ridge. The 1879 Mormon party (see p.378) camped alongside this superb natural amphitheatre while they worked out how to get across the Colorado, creating evening entertainment to keep up their spirits. An easy walk from the roadway enables you to tread the same stage, and it's also worth exploring the rolling slickrock hills immediately behind. In a couple of places, natural tanks have been scooped deep into the rock, each sheltering a solitary tree on its sandy floor.

The Hole-in-the-Rock
51 miles south of Hwy-12 on Hole-in-the-Rock Road • Free

Beyond Dance Hall Rock, the gravel surface gives way to bare slickrock, only negotiable in high-clearance vehicles. The original **Hole-in-the-Rock** lies just past the last parking lot, fifteen miles on. Keen hikers can scramble over the rocks that block it and pick their way down to the lake, which depending on its current level, obliterates some or all of the lowermost thousand feet of the pioneers' primitive pathway.

The Upper Escalante River

While driving Hole-in-the-Rock Road certainly offers the thrill of venturing into the back of beyond, several wonderful hikes start right alongside Hwy-12. If your time is at all limited and you'd rather spend it on the trails than behind the wheel, there's a lot to be said for staying on the main road until it reaches the **Escalante River**.

The first sighting of the Escalante system comes from a roadside lookout at an extravagant curve five miles on from the Hole-in-the-Rock turn-off. From here, the highway takes five more miles to drop down to the river itself, which it crosses very close to its confluence with Calf Creek, on a low bridge that's designed to allow floodwaters to flow harmlessly over. Immediately on the far side, a parking lot serves as the trailhead for exhilarating hikes both up- and downstream.

While this can be the starting point for major **backpacking** trips in either direction – Escalante town is two days' walk upstream, while Lake Powell lies at least ten days' hike downstream – intriguing natural features much closer at hand serve as obvious **day-hike** destinations. Whichever way you go, trailside notices announce "Yup, You Gotta Get Wet;" be prepared to ford the river several times. If you're just going a short distance there's no great need to keep pulling your boots on and off – the riverbank is sandy enough to walk barefoot. That said, the whole concept loses its appeal in winter, when the river can freeze right over.

Upstream: Escalante Natural Bridge

Trailhead: Escalante River bridge, Hwy-12, 13.3 miles east of Escalante or 14.6 miles south of Boulder City • 3.2 miles round-trip; 2hr

The shorter of the two potential day-hikes from Hwy-12 heads **upstream** as far as **Escalante Natural Bridge**. Having started by following the river away from the highway bridge, you're soon obliged to wade over to its south bank. The canyon here is broad and open, and the trail gentle. Once you've crossed the river four times, so you're now back on its northern side, you'll see the bridge open up on its southern wall. Although it's 100ft wide and 130ft high, it spans a mere trickle, dribbling down from a little side canyon.

Downstream: Maverick Bridge and Phipps Arch

Trailhead: Escalante River bridge, Hwy-12, 13.3 miles east of Escalante or 14.6 miles south of Boulder City • 6.6 miles round-trip; 5hr

Heading **downstream** from Hwy-12 – the trail is accessed by walking beneath the road bridge then crossing a footbridge over Calf Creek – is slightly heavier going than heading upstream. Much of the valley floor belongs to private farmers, so you have to scramble and dodge to stay outside their fences, but it's still a lovely walk.

The best day-hike in this direction is twice as long as its upstream equivalent, at nearly seven miles for the round trip. The route leaves the Escalante 1.6 miles along, heading south into sandy **Phipps Wash**. There are no signs or marked trail, so look for footprints and carry a good map. After another half mile, you'll see two prominent knobs of Navajo sandstone atop the canyon wall to your right. A hundred yards before you reach the larger of the two, head right again, up a sandy slope into a side canyon. One hundred yards along, pick your way onto a ledge on your left to avoid a deep sink hole; another hundred yards after that, you'll come to **Maverick Bridge**, spanning the wash in front of another round cavity.

Back on Phipps Wash, keep going south for half a mile until another side canyon opens up to your left. Now things get difficult; to reach the stark, mesa-top **Phipps Arch**, you have to scramble up a steep slickrock ledge, and there's no way of knowing whether you've got the right one until you're up there. The views are so good it doesn't really matter in the end, but make sure you keep track of how to get down again.

ACCOMMODATION & EATING	THE UPPER ESCALANTE RIVER

★ **Kiva Koffeehouse** Mile 73.86, Hwy-12 ☎ 435 826 4550, ⓦ kivakoffeehouse.com. Solitary little cafe in as spectacular a setting as it's possible to imagine, perched on a rocky eminence immediately below the Escalante River lookout. Through panoramic windows or from the flowery patio, you can enjoy fabulous views along the river while enjoying simple snacks such as granola, sandwiches, or enchiladas. A separate cottage nearby holds two very comfortable guest rooms, named Sunset and Sunrise for obvious reasons. Closed Nov–March. Café April–Oct daily except Tues 8.30am–4.30pm. $170

Calf Creek Falls

The two most enjoyable hiking trails along Hwy-12 lead from separate trailheads to two entirely distinct but similar waterfalls on **Calf Creek**, the tributary stream that meets the Escalante River alongside the highway bridge. The trail to **Lower Calf Creek Falls** is more popular, but if your time is limited, the hike to the smaller **Upper Calf Creek Falls** makes a quicker, if more physically challenging, alternative.

Lower Calf Creek Falls

Trailhead: Calf Creek Recreation Area, milepost 75 on Hwy-12, 1.1 miles north of Escalante River bridge • Day-use fee $2 • 6.2 miles round-trip; 3–4hr

The magnificent six-mile round-trip walk to the 125ft **Lower Calf Creek Falls** is one of the very best **day-hikes** Utah has to offer. To reach the trailhead, look out for the parking lot for the **Calf Creek Recreation Area** on Hwy-12. There's a nice little **campground** right here, with minimal facilities ($7 per night), but most visitors simply come to hike. Summer sun and deep sand can make it more effort than you might expect, but this would be a lovely canyon walk even if it didn't culminate with the falls.

The clearly marked trail heads upstream between the high red walls of Calf Creek Canyon, following a perennial creek, interrupted by beaver ponds, that feeds a lush riparian environment. Fremont pictographs testify to a long-standing human presence. It takes around ninety minutes to reach the falls themselves, which are absolutely stupendous. Spilling over the pouting lip of a crevice in the centre of a vast sandstone amphitheatre, they spread over a mossy slope of golden stone, iridescent with permanent rainbows. The (utterly freezing) water that collects in the pool below is fringed by a shaded beach where you can rest before you hike back out again.

Upper Calf Creek Falls

Trailhead: Between mileposts 80 and 81 on Hwy-12, 22.4 miles northeast of Escalante or 5.5 miles south of Boulder City • 2 miles round-trip; 1hr 30min • Elevation change 600ft

The **Upper Calf Creek Falls**, a photogenic pocket version of the better known Lower falls, cannot be accessed from Calf Creek Recreation Area. Instead, the trail starts just off Hwy-12 six miles north – watch out for a white-painted roadside boulder, which marks the start of a short and bumpy 100-yard dirt road to the parking lot. From here, you have to make your way for a mile across exposed open slickrock, following a trail that's steep and not clearly marked. The slope can seem intimidating, but with good boots it's not too hard, and the views are amazing. As you descend, fix a landmark back on the rim in your mind, so you'll have a target to aim for when you return.

When you get low enough to sense the location of the stream bed, don't head straight there, but keep going to your right. Eventually, the trail forks; one strand goes to the top of the 50ft falls, the other to the bottom, where once again a lovely pool awaits.

Given a choice, it's preferable to do the hike in the late afternoon, when the light hits the falls at the optimum angle, and the climb back to the trailhead is cooler.

Boulder

BOULDER, thirty miles beyond Escalante, is not so much a town as a group of farms scattered across a pleasant high-mountain valley. Cattle ranching in this remote spot started in 1889, and in the fifty years it took for it to be connected by road with the outside world, it acquired a reputation as Utah's own little Shangri-La. Now that it's just another stop on the highway, what magic it may once have had has largely gone.

As the western terminus of the **Burr Trail** – see p.388 – Boulder makes an ideal launching point for explorations into the backcountry of Capitol Reef, but few visitors spend much time in the valley itself.

Anasazi State Park

460 N Hwy-12 • Daily: March–Oct 8am–6pm; Nov–Feb 9am–5pm • $5 • ☎ 435 335 7308, ⊛ stateparks.utah.gov/parks/anasazi

On a shallow knoll beside Hwy-12 in the heart of Boulder, the small **Anasazi State Park** holds the excavated remains of an ancient pueblo. Its 83 rooms were occupied by the Kayenta Anasazi, an Ancestral Puebloan subgroup, from 1129 AD until

1169, when the complex was destroyed by fire; charred stumps still poke from the ruins. A good little museum, and a six-room replica at the start of the short ruins trail, do a good job of illustrating their daily life, farming along Boulder Creek – and the fact that modern farms still stand alongside helps make the site particularly evocative.

ACCOMMODATION & EATING   BOULDER

★ **Boulder Mesa Restaurant** 153 E Burr Trail Rd ☎ 435 335 7447, ⊚ bouldermesa.com. This spruce, spotless, timber-built restaurant is the best place to eat in Boulder, just off the highway on the Burr Trail. Everything from cooked breakfasts to sandwiches, burgers and fried chicken is meticulously prepared and presented; pork tamales or chilli costs around $12, steaks up to $18. Summer daily 8am–9pm; winter Mon–Fri 11am–7pm, Sat & Sun 8am–7pm.

Boulder Mountain Lodge 20 N Hwy-12 ☎ 435 335 7460 or ☎ 800 556 3446, ⊚ boulder-utah.com. Twenty

comfortable rooms, including some with kitchenettes and some two-room suites, plus a pretty good grill restaurant, at the point where Hwy-12 meets the Burr Trail. Rooms $135, suites $205

Pole's Place 465 N Hwy-12 ☎ 435 335 7422 or ☎ 800 730 7422, ⊚ boulderutah.com/polesplace. Simple, friendly family-run motel, opposite the state park, with its own café and store. It's by no means luxurious – the least expensive rooms don't have a bathroom but access to a locked bathroom cabin outdoors. Closed Dec–Feb. $75

INFORMATION   GRAND STAIRCASE-ESCALANTE NATIONAL MONUMENT

As well as the visitor centre in Escalante (see p.377), two additional information centres serve the national monument.

CANNONVILLE
Information centre 10 Center St (☎ 435 826 5640).

KANAB
Information centre 745 E US-89 (☎ 435 644 4680).

North to Capitol Reef

Although Hwy-12 leaves Grand Staircase–Escalante for good as it heads north of Boulder, the scenery remains every bit as sublime. The 35-mile link between Boulder and Torrey, across the eastern segment of the Aquarius Plateau, also known as **Boulder Mountain**, takes around an hour to drive. Once Hwy-12 has climbed out of Boulder Valley, successive roadside lookouts face fabulous vistas to the east, across a sea of gold and red sandstone outcrops to the Waterpocket Fold and beyond.

Torrey

Poised at the intersection of highways 12 and 24, eleven miles west of Capitol Reef National Park, **TORREY** has thrown its lot in firmly with the tourist trade. Quietly prospering while so many of its neighbours have faltered, it still consists of little more than one tree-lined central avenue – measuring well over a mile north to south, so a little too far to walk, and surrounded by golden meadows grazed by contented cows – plus a handful of slightly stark brick motels on a ridge to the west. However, for visitors who see their evenings as opportunities to meet other travellers, Torrey is the most exciting prospect for at least a hundred miles.

ACCOMMODATION   TORREY

Austin's Chuck Wagon Motel 12 W Main St ☎ 435 425 3335 or ☎ 800 863 3288, ⊚ www.austinschuckwagonmotel.com. Well-kept two-storey motel, beside a tiny church in the town centre, with conventional motel rooms plus newer two-room log cabins. Closed Dec–Feb. Rooms $94, cabins $155

Best Western Capitol Reef Resort 2600 E Hwy-24

☎ 435 425 3761 or ☎ 800 780 7234, ⊚ bestwestern.com/capitolreefresort. Well-equipped modern motel-style hotel, three miles east of Torrey, with great views and a good pool. $130

Capitol Reef Inn & Cafe 360 W Main St ☎ 435 425 3271, ⊚ capitolreefinn.com. Long-established but crisply maintained little motel, just off the highway in the heart of town, looking south to Boulder Mountain. On-site restaurant and small bookstore. **$65**

Rim Rock Inn 2523 E Hwy-24 ☎ 435 425 3398 or ☎ 877 342 6099, ⓦ therimrock.net. Modern, wood-built hotel, across the highway from the *Best Western* three miles east of Torrey, and offering cheaper rooms and two restaurants. **$64**

Skyridge B&B 950 E Hwy-24 ☎ 435 425 3222 or ☎ 877 824 1508, ⓦ skyridgeinn.com. Six non-smoking en-suite B&B rooms – three of which have hot tubs – in tasteful, imaginatively furnished modern home with expansive grounds. It's on the way toward central Torrey from the intersection of highways 12 and 24. **$119**

EATING

Whether it's the pressure of competition or just a little local pride, the **restaurants** and **diners** of Torrey make more effort to please than you may have come to expect of southern Utah.

★ **Café Diablo** 599 W Main St ☎ 435 425 3070, ⓦ cafediablo.net. Inventive modern restaurant, offering a slight Southwestern twist to meats and fish, with marinated lamb loin at $29, pumpkin trout for $24, and even "free-range rattlesnake patties", served with aioli, for $9. The food is good without being incredible, but that's enough to keep it packed out every night in summer; they're very efficient at coping with the crowds, but it's advisable to reserve ahead. Mid-April to Oct, daily 11.30am–10pm.

Capitol Reef Inn & Cafe 360 W Main St ☎ 435 425 3271. Bright café that serves some of Torrey's best food, using fresh ingredients like just-caught local trout. Full pork ($18) or chicken ($13) barbecue dinners, while the amazing ten-vegetable salad ($4.50 or $9) can form part of a real vegetarian feast, with sumptuous banana pies to follow. Avoid the coffee, though. April–Oct, daily 7am–9pm.

Rim Rock Restaurant Rim Rock Inn, 2523 E Hwy-24 ☎ 435 425 3398, ⓦ therimrock.net. This hotel restaurant serves better food than its rustic log-cabin decor might suggest. The $18 turkey *molé* is recommended, while the menu also roams the wilds of "Spaghetti Western " dishes like "Lee Van Cleef spaghetti and meat boulders" for $18. Daily noon–10pm.

Robbers Roost 185 W Main St ☎ 435 425 3265, ⓦ robbersroostbooks.com. Rustic central bookstore, complete with hammocks and a wooden deck, that's an invaluable resource for information on the parklands, and also serves great coffee, pastries and breads. Mon & Wed–Sun 8am–5pm.

Capitol Reef National Park

Hwy-24, 11 miles east of Torrey, 120 miles northeast of Bryce Canyon, and 100 miles southwest of Green River • $5/vehicle • ☎ 435 425 3791, ⓦ nps.gov/care

CAPITOL REEF NATIONAL PARK, the second largest of Utah's five national parks, is also the least visited. Life might be different if it bore the name originally proposed by locals – **Wayne Wonderland**, this being Wayne County. As it is, that word "reef" seems to confuse visitors. It refers to the fact that the hundred-mile rock wall thrust up by the **Waterpocket Fold** presented an almost impenetrable obstacle to nineteenth-century travellers, who therefore likened it to a reef on the ocean. Add the resemblance of the rounded "knobs" of white sandstone that top its central section to the US Capitol in Washington and you have "Capitol Reef."

Capitol Reef is very much of a piece with the Southwest's other national parks. Within its 378 square miles lie hidden canyons, verdant valleys, and strange rock formations whose colours are drawn from an extravagant palette of golds and greens, reds and whites. Despite stretching for over a hundred miles north to south, the park is often less than ten miles wide. The one east–west highway, **Hwy-24**, crosses it in under twenty miles, following the gorge of the Fremont River. It's an impressive drive, but that's nothing rare in southern Utah, and unless you time your arrival from the west to coincide with the daily magnificent sunset, you could easily pass straight through Capitol Reef without feeling any great urge to stop. Only if you take the time to explore will you get a sense of the magic of the place, and why it fully deserves its national park status.

Even a couple of hours is enough to admire the western cliffs from the dead-end **Scenic Drive**, south of the park headquarters at **Fruita**. Given half a day or more, you

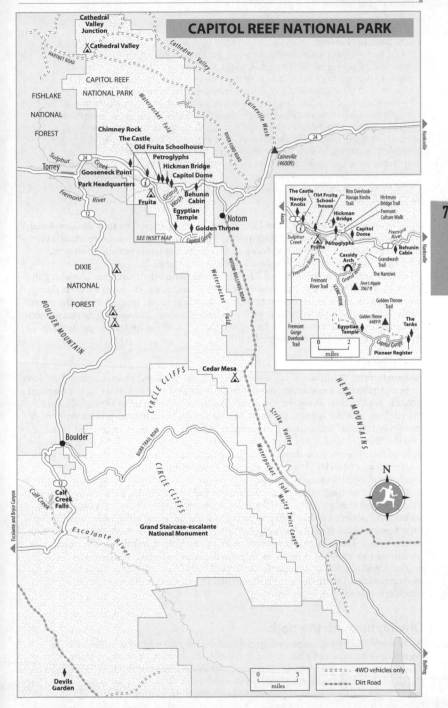

CAPITOL REEF NATIONAL PARK

THE GEOLOGY OF CAPITOL REEF

The **Waterpocket Fold**, which slopes from north to south for the full hundred-mile length of Capitol Reef National Park, is what geologists call a **monocline**, created when layers of sedimentary rock buckled under pressure sixty million years ago. Within the last ten million years, it has in turn been lifted a mile or so above sea level by the general raising of the Colorado Plateau. Most of the original fold has long since eroded away; the reef itself is just the rump. Its western face consists of a long, jagged cliff of hard rock; it rises more gently from the east, in multicoloured waves of sandstone that the Navajo called the "Land of the Sleeping Rainbow".

Here and there, the fold is pierced right through by deeply incised **canyons**. Often hundreds of feet deep but less than twenty feet wide, these slender gorges were mostly blocked by fallen rocks until Mormon pioneers cleared a way through. After summer thunderstorms, rainwater can cascade through the canyons in fearsome flash floods. At other times, it collects in depressions worn into the rock – the "**waterpockets**" for which the whole mighty edifice is named.

---

could venture all the way south to Lake Powell on the unpaved **Notom–Bullfrog Road**, tracing the eastern flank of the Waterpocket Fold, or loop back westward via the **Burr Trail**, halfway along. With **hiking trails** of all lengths and levels setting off into the wilderness, it would be easy to spend a week in this one park.

The best **seasons** to visit Capitol Reef are spring, when the fruit trees blossom and the wild flowers bloom, or fall, when the crowds have gone, the cottonwoods change colour, and hiking conditions are at their peak. Midsummer temperatures can reach 100°F, and August in particular is prone to flash-flooding, but so long as you set your sights appropriately low – say, to lazing on your back in the orchards, eating fresh fruit – a summer visit is not such a bad idea.

Brief history

Although traces of human occupation date back ten thousand years, Capitol Reef's first known inhabitants were an Ancestral Puebloan subgroup, now known as the **Fremont Anasazi**, who farmed along the Fremont River from 700 AD until climate changes forced them to move on around 1300 AD. Archeologists distinguish them from their more sophisticated cousins to the southeast by the fact that they lived in pit houses dug into the hillsides, and didn't keep domesticated dogs or turkeys. The most enduring signs of their presence are the intriguing **petroglyphs** still visible on the canyon walls.

After many centuries when only the occasional Paiute hunter passed this way, a small group of Mormons established a permanent settlement beside the Fremont in 1878. The orchards they planted transformed the landscape, and when the post office insisted they gave their community a proper name, a few years later, **Fruita** seemed the perfect choice. The population of the fledgling town never rose above fifty, however, and it was soon suggested that the region had more future as a park than a home. The immediate vicinity of Fruita became Capitol Reef National Monument in 1937, and that was upgraded to national park status when it was enlarged to include the entire Waterpocket Fold in 1971. Former Fruita townspeople and their heirs are still entitled to graze cattle within the park, but ranching is slowly being phased out.

Driving through the park

At its simplest, driving through Capitol Reef on **Hwy-24** takes well under half an hour. However much of a hurry you may be in, pause once or twice en route. Rather than a token pit stop at the visitor centre, try taking a five-minute hike from one of the clearly marked trailheads. Only if you turn south of Hwy-24 onto the Scenic Drive (see opposite) do you have to pay the $5 per vehicle park entrance fee.

Gooseneck Point

Capitol Reef's westernmost scenic viewpoint lies a short distance south of Hwy-24, roughly three-quarters of the way from Torrey to the visitor centre. The brief climb to **Gooseneck Point** is rewarded with a 500ft view down into the canyon of Sulphur Creek, an "entrenched meander" that once curved across a flat floodplain but has been etched deep into solid rock by the uplifting of the Colorado Plateau. Reached by walking ten minutes along a different trail from the same parking lot, **Sunset Point** is as you'd expect a fabulous vantage point to watch the cliffs glow gold and red as the sun goes down.

Visitor centre

52 Scenic Drive, 11 miles east of Torrey • Daily: summer 8am–6pm; spring & fall 8am–5pm; winter 8am–4.30pm • ☎ 435 425 3791, ⓦ nps.gov/care

The point where the park's Scenic Drive branches south from Hwy-24 is overshadowed by a huge, fluted red-rock butte known as the **Castle** on the highway's north side. Across the road to the south, the **visitor centre** holds displays on the park and its history, stocks all sorts of free handouts, and can advise on current driving and hiking conditions.

Fruita

The defunct village of **FRUITA** ranges for a mile or so around the confluence of Sulphur Creek and the **Fremont River**, at the heart of Capitol Reef National Park. Spreading alongside both Hwy-24 and the Scenic Drive, eleven miles east of Torrey, its **orchards** are Capitol Reef's crowning glory. A waxy, luxuriant green against the towering red cliffs, they hold almost three thousand trees planted by the pioneers. The cherries and peaches **blossom** in the first half of April, the apples slightly later, while the **harvest** lasts from the second half of June until well into October. So long as you stay in the orchards, you can eat as much fruit as you like; you only pay for what you take away.

Fruita's former **schoolhouse**, just north of Hwy-24 where the rivers meet, was built in 1896, and hasn't had a pupil since 1941; park rangers, not a Mormon schoolmarm, keep it spick-and-span.

A short distance down the highway beyond the schoolhouse, the **Fremont Culture Walk** is an easy boardwalk amble beside a canyon wall crammed with ancient **petroglyphs**. As well as stylized representations of goats and Bighorn sheep, some show how the Fremont people may have seen themselves – unless of course these strange helmeted figures, with triangular bodies and massive shields, really did come from other planets.

East of Fruita

Hwy-24 crosses the Fremont two miles east of the visitor centre, near the start of the **Hickman Bridge Trail** (see p.390). Only beyond this point does **Capitol Dome**, high above the north bank another half-mile ahead, resolve itself into a dome; so far you've seen it from the side, as a slender fin. By now Fremont Canyon is at its deepest, and it's joined within the next couple of miles by **Chimney Rock Canyon** from the north and **Grand Wash** from the south (see p.389). A mile past Grand Wash stands the sandstone cabin of one of Fruita's earliest settlers, **Elijah Behunin**, with the eastern boundary of the park another 2.5 miles down the road.

The Scenic Drive

Other than Hwy-24, the only paved road in Capitol Reef is the **Scenic Drive**, which parallels the golden cliffs of the Waterpocket Fold for eight miles south from the visitor centre. The first couple of miles lead through Fruita, where a cluster of restored barns and houses serve as homes for park employees, while overnight visitors camp out in the orchards.

Beyond the village and fee station, the road undulates through the desert, dipping into dry sandy washes and then climbing scrubby rolling hillocks. Successive individual pinnacles, such as **Fern's Nipple** and the **Egyptian Temple**, line the crest of the red-rock battlements to the east. Until Hwy-24 was pushed through Fremont Canyon in 1962, this unlikely route was southern Utah's main east–west thoroughfare. It now ends at a large parking lot, facing a crack in the cliffs that marks the start of **Capitol Gorge**. For a century, traffic squeezed its way between the narrow walls beyond, but now the gravel continuation known as the Capitol Gorge Road peters out just over two miles in. Hikers however can keep going on foot, to see the Pioneer Register where early wagon-drivers carved their names (see p.390).

The Notom–Bullfrog Road

If you'd rather survey the Waterpocket Fold from the comfort of your car than sweat it out on foot, the long drive south along the **Notom–Bullfrog Road** is Capitol Reef's best option. Just be sure to stock up on gas and water; you'll have to drive at least seventy miles to find any facilities.

The road leaves Hwy-24 nine miles east of the visitor centre, not far outside the park. Only its first eleven miles – which include the tiny but well-irrigated settlement of **NOTOM**, now home to half a dozen ranchers, four miles along – are paved. Thereafter, its rough surface repeatedly ripples into a "washboard" as it follows a dry-as-dust bench above Sandy Creek, with the eerie badlands of the Waterpocket Fold to the west and the volcanic **Henry Mountains** to the east.

Ordinary vehicles should have no problem negotiating the full length of the Notom–Bullfrog Road, which re-enters the park twenty miles along and then leaves it again in the southeast corner fifteen miles on. Seventy miles from the highway, after a final 25-mile segment where you find yourself constantly stopping to swoon at the turquoise expanse of Lake Powell on the southern horizon, you come to the marina at **Bullfrog** (see p.397).

The Burr Trail

Most drivers who set off south on the Notom–Bullfrog Road don't make it to Bullfrog but complete a loop around the Waterpocket Fold by branching onto the **Burr Trail**. The only road actually to cross the fold, rather than slice through it, it does so via a fearsome set of switchbacks that climb west from the Notom–Bullfrog Road, 29 miles south of Hwy-24 – roughly halfway to Lake Powell.

The Burr Trail began life as a rutted wagon trail, which was upgraded by uranium prospectors in the 1940s and 1950s. The four miles within the national park are still unpaved, but the remaining thirty, running west to Boulder on Hwy-24, were paved during the late 1980s. Wilderness advocates argued that increased road use would irreparably damage one of Utah's least-spoiled regions; Garfield County authorities, keen to grab a piece of the Capitol Reef action from their Wayne County neighbours, went ahead anyway. From their point of view, they were just in time; the area now belongs to Grand Staircase–Escalante National Monument, so there'll be no further road construction.

If all that leaves you feeling too guilty to take the Burr Trail, you're missing out. The panorama that unfolds as you ascend the switchbacks and head west is out of this world. Looking back across the Notom–Bullfrog Road, you see the top of Swap Mesa and the stark Henry Mountains. Just past the topmost ridge, the Upper and Lower sections of **Muley Twist Canyon** stretch to north and south through the heart of the Fold. Both make excellent multi-day backpacking expeditions, starting from near the highway. As you leave the park and enter the national monument (where the pavement begins), an extraordinary procession of reefs marches south, with the white canyons of the Waterpocket Fold in the foreground and four or five craggy red cliff-faces beyond, leading on to Lake Powell.

The oval plain just west of the park, ringed by the Circle Cliffs, was described by the nineteenth-century geologist Clarence Dutton as "a spot which is about as desolate as any on earth." The Burr Trail leaves it by way of the deep **Long Canyon**, then struggles on to reach Hwy-24 immediately south of Boulder (see p.382).

Cathedral Valley

Capitol Reef's least accessible section is **Cathedral Valley**, north of Hwy-24. Like the Notom–Bullfrog Road, it parallels the eastern side of the Waterpocket Fold, but the territory here is much more forbidding than the sagebrush plain to the south. In among the heavily eroded red, blue and grey hills lie deep canyons and primeval gardens, populated by strange stone monoliths. Unless you have your own 4WD or high-clearance vehicle, you'll only see it by joining a guided 4WD tour (see p.390).

Two roads run north into the backcountry from Hwy-24, 11.5 and 18.6 miles east of the visitor centre. The first, **River Ford Road**, traverses the Fremont River by means of a crude ford a few hundred yards along. If you're planning a loop drive, come this way first – it's not safe to cross when the water's more than a couple of feet deep, and you wouldn't want to find that out at the end of a sixty-mile drive. The second route, the **Caineville Wash Road**, meets the first – by now Hartnet Road – at the far end of Cathedral Valley. Several more dirt roads leave the park at this northern extremity, connecting with I-70 to the north or joining Hwy-72 above Loa to the west.

Hiking in Capitol Reef

You probably won't drive far in Capitol Reef before you feel the backcountry beckoning. Choosing which of the many, mostly short, **trails** to hike is largely a matter of whether you feel up to climbing; only a few, such as the walks through the Capitol Gorge or Grand Wash, remain on level ground, while the rest demand mountain-goat-style scrambling up the slickrock.

If you do choose to stick to the canyon floors, bear in mind the danger of **flash floods** after rain, and don't pause where there's no clear escape route.

Grand Wash Trail

Trailheads: 4 miles southeast of visitor centre at end of unpaved Grand Wash Road, and 4 miles east of visitor centre on Hwy-24 • 2.5 miles each way; 1hr

The busiest Capitol Reef trail connects the Scenic Drive with Hwy-24, along the gravelly bed of the **Grand Wash**. The western trailhead is at the end of the unpaved Grand Wash Road, which leaves the Scenic Drive a mile past Fruita, while its eastern end is on the south bank of Hwy-24 a mile or two beyond Capitol Dome.

As a one-way walk, the **Grand Wash trail** takes around an hour, but unless you arrange a pick-up at the far end you'll have to double back. In the half-mile stretch known as **The Narrows**, the vertiginous 800ft canyon walls close in to a mere sixteen feet apart. **Butch Cassidy** and his gang are said to have used the tangle of side canyons that lead off Grand Wash as hideouts, but there's no evidence that Butch ever saw **Cassidy Arch**, reached by a short steep climb from near the southeast end of the trail.

Capitol Gorge Trail

Trailhead: end of Capitol Gorge Road, 2 miles beyond end of Scenic Drive • 2.5 miles round-trip; 1hr

The **Capitol Gorge trail**, reached by driving the full length of the Scenic Drive, is every bit as claustrophobic as the Grand Wash. It's a short and easy walk, providing you spare yourself an extra 4.6-mile round-trip by parking not at the foot of the Scenic Drive but at the end of the gravel road beyond.

In the space of a mile, the trail inches all the way through a crack in the Waterpocket Fold, though hikers have to turn back when they reach the private land on the far side. From 1871 onwards, this "**Blue Dugway**" was a major trans-Utah thoroughfare, as the painstaking inscriptions on the **Pioneer Register**, carved into the canyon wall halfway along, will testify.

A couple of twists of the canyon past the Register, side canyons start to open up to both left and right. Not far along, after two or so sets, a sign on the left reads "Tanks 0.2." Climb up the cairned trail here and within a few hundred yards you'll reach a succession of circular clifftop "tanks." Early travellers would break off from the laborious haul through the gorge, in the hope of finding fresh water in such clifftop "**waterpockets**."

Golden Throne Trail

Trailhead: end of Capitol Gorge Road, 2 miles beyond end of Scenic Drive • 4 miles round-trip; 2hr 30min • Elevation change 730ft

The strenuous but exhilarating **Golden Throne Trail** launches itself north from the Capitol Gorge trailhead, straight up the side of the canyon. It then threads its way west, parallel to the dirt road below and climbing consistently all the way back to the mouth of the gorge. En route, it weaves in and out of countless side canyons before finally emerging on the slickrock flatlands that cap the Waterpocket Fold, and command huge views to Boulder Mountain in the west. The dominant feature up here, however, is the towering yellow Navajo-sandstone butte known as the **Golden Throne**, beneath which the trail peters out.

Hickman Bridge Trail

Trailhead: Hwy-24, 2 miles east of visitor centre • 2 miles round-trip; 2hr • Elevation change 400ft

While not the easiest of Hwy-24's roadside trails, the **Hickman Bridge Trail** makes a supremely rewarding hike. Setting off along the north bank of the Fremont River, it meanders briefly through the cottonwoods before climbing a brisk stairway out of the canyon to the shadeless heights up top.

Once you've marvelled at Capitol Dome, off to the east, fork left at the junction ahead. Pockmarked black boulders strewn on all sides, incongruous against the red, pink and cream sandstone, testify to ancient lava flows. Three-quarters of a mile along, the path loops around and through the arching span of **Hickman Bridge**. A hundred feet high, a hundred feet wide, it's a genuine natural bridge, worn through the rock by a side channel eager to reach the Fremont below. The rocky chaos beneath somehow complements the grace of the bridge itself.

ACTIVITIES AND TOURS

Hondoo Rivers & Trails Torrey ☎ 435 425 3519 or ☎ 800 332 2696, ⊛ hondoo.com. Jeep tours of the park, starting from your motel – half-day $90 per person, full day $150 – plus guided hiking trips, and a wide range of longer tours, including **horseback** adventures.

Redrock Adventure Guides Torrey ☎ 435 425 3339, ⊛ redrockadventureguides.com. Guided hikes in the park, at $200 all-in for groups of up to four; canyoneering classes, with a half-day intro for $100; and backpacking trips.

CAMPING

There are no motels or lodges inside the park; the closest **accommodation** is in Torrey (see p.383). In addition to the three **campgrounds** listed below, it's possible to camp in Capitol Reef's backcountry, with a free permit from the visitor centre (see p.387).

Cathedral Valley Cathedral Valley ⊛ nps.gov/care. Six-site primitive campground, 25 miles north of Hwy-24 along either the Hartnet Road (which requires you to ford the Fremont River) or the Caineville Wash Road. Picnic tables and pit toilets but no water. First-come, first-served. <u>Free</u>

Cedar Mesa Notom–Bullfrog Road ⊛ nps.gov/care. Five-site primitive campground, 22.5 miles south of Hwy-24, with picnic tables and pit toilets but no water. First-come, first-served. <u>Free</u>

Fruita Campground Scenic Drive ⓦ nps.gov/care. The park's only developed campground is available on a first-come, first-served basis only, with no reservations. Set amid the orchards, a mile south of the visitor centre, it makes a good overnight stop even if you never see the rest of the park. All its 71 RV/tent sites are usually taken by early afternoon in spring and fall. No hook-ups or showers. While it remains open all year, in winter can be without water altogether. $10

Lake Powell

Until the early 1960s, it was all but impossible to travel between southwest and southeast Utah. In the unseen heart of the endless desert, the mighty Colorado River churned its way toward the Pacific through a succession of yawning canyons. Here and there boatmen might ferry the occasional passenger across, and a few adventurous souls even rafted down the river itself, but there was no highway for two hundred miles north of Arizona.

Now the Colorado has gone, submerged beneath the huge, docile **Lake Powell**. For many people – especially those who knew the sublime **Glen Canyon** that it destroyed – the lake is a loathsome abomination. Many more see it as a thing of beauty, and Lake Powell has become Utah's number-one tourist attraction, drawing four million visitors per year – by tradition, over half a million on Labor Day alone – and matched in popularity in the Southwest only by the Grand Canyon. It is, undeniably, an extraordinary spectacle, its turquoise waters rippling against its stark red-rock rim and cradling islands that once were buttes and mesas. No one could ever mistake this for a natural landscape, however, and you don't have to be an out-and-out environmentalist to be disturbed by the transformation of America's last great wilderness into a playground. The concessionaires of the **Glen Canyon National Recreational Area** invite you to "think of Lake Powell as a 160,000-acre bathtub and consider our boats, floats, boards, and tubes as your toys." Beyond the unappealing rhetoric, there's some truth in what they say; granted that the lake exists, if you're going to come here at all, the best way to enjoy your visit is to get out on the water.

Five of Lake Powell's six **marinas** are accessible by road. Two are south of the state line in Arizona: the largest, **Wahweap**, lies just west of the dam itself and the purpose-built town of **Page**, while the newest, **Antelope Point**, is on Navajo land immediately east of Page. The remaining four are in Utah. **Bullfrog** and **Hall's Crossing**, two-thirds of the way northeast up the lake from the dam, are connected by a ferry service that makes it possible to drive between Capitol Reef National Park and Natural Bridges National Monument. **Hite** is in theory at the northeast limit of the lake, though low water levels have left it stranded high and dry, and it's not currently in operation. The sixth and final marina, **Dangling Rope**, is a refuelling station that can only be reached by boat.

There's surprisingly little accommodation on land; it's assumed you'll want to join the armada out on the water, either in your own vessel or in a rented **houseboat**. For a quick taste, you can join a **guided tour** at either Wahweap or Bullfrog – the trips to **Rainbow Bridge** are by far the most popular – or take the **ferry** between Bullfrog and Hall's Crossing.

Brief history

Lake Powell's success as a wet'n'wild theme park has been a surprise spin-off from its real purpose. Glen Canyon Dam was constructed to regulate the flow of water along the Colorado River. Half is kept back to irrigate the deserts of the plateau, while the rest gushes through its turbines, generating electricity as it makes for Arizona and California. Demand is so precisely monitored that the level of the lake fluctuates according to whether it's dinnertime in Phoenix. Hence its closest resemblance to a bathtub – the scummy dirty-bath tidemark that sullies the sandstone around its edge.

LAKE POWELL: CONTROVERSY AND COMPROMISE

The western half of the United States would sustain a population greater than that of our whole country today if the waters that now run to waste were saved and used for irrigation.

President Theodore Roosevelt, State of the Union address, 1901

The twentieth-century growth of the American West was largely the story of the "taming" of the **Colorado River**. If the Colorado were to run dry, Los Angeles, Las Vegas and Phoenix would die, and the exodus from the Southwest would dwarf anything from the Dustbowl era.

In terms of volume, the Colorado does not rank among the top 25 rivers in the US. However, the sheer aggression with which it hurtles from 13,000ft up in the Rockies makes it the fastest and fiercest of them all. That's why it's responsible for so many magnificent canyons; and that's also why civil engineers can't bear to leave it alone. They yearn to harness its energy with hydroelectric dams, and divert its flow to irrigate the desert.

Early in the twentieth century, the sparsely populated southwestern states began to fear that southern California's ever-increasing thirst might drain them dry. 1922's **Colorado River Compact** divided the river between an **Upper Basin**, consisting of Utah, Wyoming, Colorado and New Mexico, and a **Lower Basin** – Arizona, Nevada and California. Each basin was to receive 7.5 million acre-feet of the estimated annual flow of 16.8 million, with the dregs left over for Mexico. This was the first of fifteen such agreements in fifty years, largely because the estimates were wrong; the long-term average is thought to be more like 13.9 million acre-feet.

The task of distributing the water fell to a new federal agency, the **Bureau of Reclamation**. Its engineers saw their mission as being to "reclaim" the West to the way it ought to be; the main tool at their disposal was the **dam**. They began in 1935, by damming Black Canyon, on the doorstep of California, with the **Hoover Dam** (see p.457). That project inspired a dam-building spree, in the US and all over the world. The Bureau's subsequent plans for the Colorado Plateau were clear from the subtitle of one report: *A Natural Menace Becomes A Natural Resource*. Proposals included damming the Green River in northwest Colorado, the San Juan in New Mexico, and the Colorado itself in both Bridge Canyon in Arizona and Utah's Glen Canyon.

Almost a century earlier, in 1869, John Wesley Powell had been entranced by the idyllic canyon that stretched southwest from the confluence of the Green and Colorado rivers: "A curious ensemble of wonderful features – carved walls, royal arches, glens, alcove gulches, mounds, and monuments … We decide to call it **Glen Canyon**." Those few river-runners who had seen it since knew it as a cool, tranquil haven, bursting with luxuriant vegetation and desert wildlife, and a far cry from the cataract-filled canyons both up- and downstream. Theirs were lone voices in the wilderness, however; too little known to receive federal protection, Glen Canyon's remoteness was to work against it.

The environmental movement was in its infancy in the 1950s, and its strategy concentrated on defending national parks. The Green River dam-site being within Dinosaur National Monument, **David Brower**, the executive director of the Sierra Club, told Congress that damming Glen Canyon was a far better idea – in fact, he originally endorsed construction of a dam in the

The whole vast system cost \$300 million to build. When full, Lake Powell is 550ft deep at the dam and holds enough water to cover all of Arizona five inches deep. It stretches back up 186 miles of the Colorado River and 72 miles of the San Juan River, as well as inundating 96 side canyons formed by rivers such as the Escalante and the Dirty Devil. The total shoreline of 1960 miles is longer than the entire US Pacific coast. Despite the searing sun, the lake is officially claimed to lose a mere 2.5 percent of its volume each year to evaporation.

The fullest the lake has ever been was in 1983, when water flowed over the top of the dam, and an emergency release had to be instigated. As recently as 1999, the level was just four feet below the maximum, but drought set in from 2000 onwards, and by 2005 the waters had dropped 146 feet, with the reservoir a mere one-third full. That was enough for Glen Canyon to begin to reappear, and backpackers flocked to marvel at such long-submerged wonders as the Cathedral in the Desert. The lower reaches of

Grand Canyon *on condition* that a dam was built in Glen Canyon as well. Conservationists prided themselves on a job well done when it was decided to dam the Green River outside Dinosaur, at Flaming Gorge to the northwest, and to go ahead with damming Glen Canyon. The one concession to "the abominable nature lovers," as one Utah senator termed them, was that water would not be allowed to encroach upon Rainbow Bridge National Monument.

President Eisenhower triggered the first blast at the dam-site in September 1956. Meanwhile, with Glen Canyon doomed but not yet drowned, archeologists, artists and photographers set out to chronicle its disappearing treasures. These included the glowing, fern-dripping alcove known as the **Cathedral in the Desert**, and the **Crossing of the Fathers**, where the Spanish priests Domínguez and Escalante forded the river in 1776.

On January 21, 1963, the same day that the Colorado River was brought to a halt, President Kennedy's Secretary of the Interior, Stewart Udall – great-grandson of John D. Lee, of Lees Ferry (see p.329) – announced plans to build two further dams within the Grand Canyon. By now, the Sierra Club had realized its mistake; and it promptly made another. This time it argued for building coal-burning power stations instead of hydroelectric dams. The Navajo, thinking nuclear power might soon render its mineral resources worthless, decided to cash in by permitting the strip-mining of Black Mesa (see p.54), and the hideously polluting Navajo Generating Station was constructed outside Page.

It took seventeen more years for Lake Powell to fill to the brim, on June 22, 1980. By now, David Brower, who left the Sierra Club to found Friends of the Earth in 1969, was describing his support for Glen Canyon Dam as "the greatest sin I have ever committed." Shortly before his death, in 2000, the 87-year-old "Archdruid" hosted a "Day of Action Against Dams" at the dam site, and called for Lake Powell to be drained so the canyon could regenerate. One original argument for the dam had been that the Colorado would otherwise fill **Lake Mead**, behind the Hoover Dam, with silt within a few years; Brower argued that the floodgates at Glen Canyon should remain open until that really does happen, perhaps two hundred years from now. Other activists went further. In *The Monkey-Wrench Gang*, Edward Abbey fantasized about dynamiting the dam, and he was among the demonstrators who in 1981 signalled the birth of the **Earth First!** movement by suspending a 300ft strip of plastic down its face to simulate an almighty crack. To some extent, the argument has been won; no major dam has been built since the 1960s, and the general consensus is that Glen Canyon Dam will be the last.

The debate over the future of Lake Powell was given an extra spin by the **droughts** of the early twenty-first century (see p.392), which threatened to restore Glen Canyon by default, and demonstrated how rapidly flora and fauna could re-establish themselves. Some argued that the lake would never refill, others that this latest dry spell was typical of long-term weather patterns, and showed precisely why the dam was necessary. In any case, though drought may be a natural phenomenon, the level of the lake is dictated by political decisions, and specifically the amount of water released to the Lower Basin states. A five-year "trial agreement" between the US and Mexico, signed in 2012, has finally guaranteed Mexico 1.5 million acre-feet of water per year; it's hoped that it may enable the Colorado to flow all the way to the sea once more.

the Escalante River sprang back to life; the banks were host once more to 25-foot trees, while the thick layer of sediment deposited on the lake bed steadily washed away. Recent years have seen levels rise somewhat, but as this book went to press in 2013, the lake was only half-full, still almost 100 feet down.

Page

Home to almost ten thousand people, **PAGE** – which is actually just south of the state line in Arizona, but is the only town of any size on the periphery of Lake Powell – is now the largest community in a 720-mile stretch of the Colorado River. Before Glen Canyon Dam was constructed four miles west, this all but barren mesa belonged to the Navajo Nation. Thanks to a small spring, however, it made the best site to house the dam's workforce. The Navajo agreed to swap it for a similar-sized chunk of desert between Bluff and Hatch in southeast Utah, a new road was blasted through the Echo Cliffs, and the town was born on Thanksgiving Day 1958.

At first, Page seemed destined to wither away once the dam was completed. Ironically, it gained a new lease of life when Congress decided that instead of building more dams, the Southwest could meet its power needs by burning coal instead. The **Navajo Generating Station**, which creates electricity using coal from Black Mesa and pumps water from Lake Powell to Phoenix, went up four miles southeast of town, and has kept Page in work ever since.

The view as you descend toward Page is utterly surreal. The three power plant chimneys stand silhouetted amid sandstone outcrops, while lines of pylons march off across the desert and the misty hump of Navajo Mountain rises in the distance. As you approach, the waters of Lake Powell emerge from the haze, with drowned buttes poking their heads here and there above the surface. Page itself, on the other hand, resembles a dull suburban mall writ large; if it has a redeeming feature, you'll have a hard time finding it.

Powell Memorial Museum

6 N Lake Powell Blvd • April–Oct Mon–Sat 9am–5pm, Nov–March Mon–Fri 9am–5pm • $5 • ☎ 928 645 9496, Ⓦ powellmuseum.org

The only sight of any interest in Page is the **John Wesley Powell Memorial Museum**. As well as charting the exploits of the first man to raft down the Colorado (see p.401), the museum celebrates later river-runners and recounts Page's own brief history. It also holds a locally excavated plesiosaur fossil and an amazing collection of fluorescent rocks.

Antelope Canyon

Mile marker 299, AZ-98, 2 miles southeast of Page • Visitable on guided tours only; $36–48 for 1hr 30min, $81 for 2hr 30min with recommended operator Antelope Slot Canyon Tours (☎ 928 645 5594, Ⓦ antelopeslotcanyon.com); mid-March to Oct daily 8am–5pm, Nov to mid-March daily 9am–3pm • ☎ 928 698 2808, Ⓦ navajonationparks.org/htm/antelopecanyon.htm

Antelope Canyon, a couple of miles southeast of Page, is Arizona's most famous, and irresistibly, astonishingly beautiful, **slot canyon**. The canyon actually comprises two separate sections, on either side of AZ-98, both of which are on Navajo land. The closest to the highway, **Lower Antelope Canyon** immediately north, achieved worldwide notoriety in 1997, when the tragic deaths of eleven hikers in a flash flood proved just how dangerous such places can be.

In the last few years, the Navajo have realized what an invaluable tourism asset Antelope Canyon represents; they now control all access and were constructing a new visitor centre as this book went to press. All visits are by guided tour only; the official website lists several operators.

Much the most popular destination for tours is **Upper Antelope Canyon**, a two-mile dirt-road drive down from the highway. Shuttle buses deposit visitors just outside a slender, unprepossessing crack in a red sandstone wall. Stepping inside is like entering both a cathedral, in that you find yourself in a majestic chamber adorned with delicate glowing colours, and a pinball machine, in that you can just imagine that any second some mighty and unavoidable boulder will come thundering down the narrow passageway. Walking the full length of the canyon and back takes barely twenty minutes, even with frequent pauses to admire the interlacing fins of multihued rock that swirl overhead, in places to a height of 120ft. A flash flood is capable of filling the slot to the brim with water and spilling over the top; once such a flood recedes, on the other hand, it leaves the canyon floor scrubbed bare of its usual eight-foot layer of fine soft sand.

Be warned that while Antelope Canyon is every bit as beautiful as photos suggest, it offers little of the wilderness feel of other desert highlights. It's both short and narrow enough to feel *very* crowded at busy times, and as the main priority for all visitors is to take photographs, it can feel like a working set rather than a place to contemplate beauty.

Horseshoe Bend

Just south of mile marker 545 on US-89, 3 miles south of Page • Daily dawn–dusk • Free

An easy self-guided hike not far south of Page leads to an amazing view of **Horseshoe Bend**, where the Colorado River makes an extravagant 180-degree turn in the depths of Marble Canyon, roughly halfway through its short course between Glen Canyon Dam and the official start of the Grand Canyon at Lees Ferry.

To reach the overlook, turn west off US-89, exactly 2.6 miles south of the Wal-Mart in Page, onto a dirt road that leads to a parking lot at the foot of a small sandy hill. Climb the railed path to the top of that hill, then down another 0.4 mile to the lip of the gorge. The river itself is only visible from the very edge, which is unrailed, windy, and pretty hair-raising. The huge curving sweep far below barely fits into the widest-angled lens. Be sure to carry water, and allow about an hour for the exposed round trip hike.

INFORMATION

Visitor centre 608 Elm St (April–June Mon–Sat 8am–6pm; July–Oct 7am–7pm; Nov–March Mon–Fri 8am–5pm; ☎928 645 2741 or ☎888 261 7243, Ⓦ visitpagearizona.com). Several other offices that purport to be information centres are in fact tour operators offering trips to Antelope Canyon (see p.394).

ACCOMMODATION

Courtyard by Marriott 600 Clubhouse Drive ☎928 645 5000 or ☎877 905 4495, Ⓦ courtyard.com/pgacy. Page's most incongruous splash of luxury – a 153-room resort, complete with golf course – is below the mesa in view of the dam. **$249**

Lake Powell Motel 750 S Navajo Drive ☎928 645 3919. Page's best-value budget motel; the huge, well maintained rooms are more like apartments than standard hotel offerings, complete with kitchenettes and living rooms. Closed Nov–Feb. **$65**

LuLu's Sleep Ezze Motel 208 N Lake Powell Blvd ☎928 608 0273 or ☎800 553 6211, Ⓦ lulussleepezzemotel.com. Tiny, very welcoming little motel in central Page, with simple but nice rooms. **$95**

EATING

Beans Gourmet Coffee House Dam Plaza 644 N Navajo Drive ☎928 645 6858. Espressos and light snacks, plus picnic lunches to go. Daily 7am–6pm.

Bonkers 810 N Navajo Drive ☎928 645 2706, Ⓦ bonkerspageaz.com. Something for everyone, with a full menu of Italian specialities – seafood Alfredo and veal parmesan both cost $21 – plus burgers and sandwiches.

Mon–Sat 4–9.30pm.

Dam Bar & Grille Dam Plaza 644 N Navajo Drive ☎928 645 2161. Themed diner and bar, appealingly designed to echo the days when Page was populated solely by dam-building hard-hats. Steak and pasta entrees for around $20. Daily 11am–10pm.

Glen Canyon Dam

US-89, 2 miles northwest of Page • **Hayden Visitor Center** Daily: March–April & Oct 8am–5pm; May–Sept 8am–6pm; Nov–Feb 8.30am–4.30pm • Dam tours $5 • ☎928 608 6404, Ⓦ nps.gov/glca

Glen Canyon Dam plugs **Marble Canyon** (see p.329) not at its narrowest point, but at its northern end, just downstream from Wahweap Creek. As US-89 crosses Glen Canyon

---

RENTING A HOUSEBOAT

To rent a **houseboat** on Lake Powell, contact Lake Powell Resorts and Marinas (☎928 645 2433 or ☎888 896 3829, Ⓦ lakepowell.com) in Wahweap. The smallest Expedition houseboat, capable of sleeping six, costs $2160 for three days in summer, while the luxury twelve-berth Odyssey class of boat costs $15,000 per week.

Any number of **package deals**, offering different combinations of time spent on houseboats, in the marina lodges and on guided tours, are also available. Many houseboat users like to **camp** overnight onshore; National Recreation Area (NRA) regulations insist that anyone who camps within a mile of the lake must carry and use portable toilets.

Bridge outside Page, the vast curve of the dam is to the north, while Marble Canyon drops 700ft below you.

You can't stop on the bridge, so if you want a better look, call in at the **Carl Hayden Visitor Center** on the west bank, which doubles as the main source of information on the **Glen Canyon National Recreational Area**. Guided **tours** of the actual dam take 45 minutes to drop via two elevators first to the walkway along the top, and then a further 500ft to the generating station at the bottom. Beneath the roar of the 1.3-million kilowatt turbines, a digital counter steadily ticks off the billions of dollars earned thus far by the sale of power.

Just before the bridge, a spur road on the east bank tunnels down through the cliffs to the river; rafters use it as an access point for the gloriously lazy fifteen-mile **float trip** down to Lees Ferry (see p.329). There's no whitewater along the way, and strictly speaking you never enter the Grand Canyon, but it's still a very pleasant drift between imposing high-canyon cliffs.

Wahweap

Unlike Page, **WAHWEAP**, a couple of miles west of Glen Canyon Dam, has never become a town. Lake Powell's principal **marina** has, however, grown steadily since it was established in 1963, coordinating most of the boat rental and tour business and also offering several hundred motel rooms.

To the fury of the federal authorities, the first man to appreciate Wahweap's potential did so long before the dam was ever built. Art Greene, the owner of the *Marble Canyon Lodge* (see p.330), ran boat trips upriver to Rainbow Bridge from the 1940s onwards; when he got wind of plans to dam Glen Canyon, he shrewdly leased the land at the mouth of Wahweap Creek at a knockdown rate. Knowing it made the perfect site for a marina, Greene refused to budge, and wound up making a killing as official concessionaire.

BOAT TOURS
WAHWEAP

Boat tours In addition to Rainbow Bridge trips (p.396), Lake Powell Resorts and Marinas (☎928 645 2433 or ☎888 896 3829, ⌨lakepowell.com) runs boat tours that range from ninety-minute water-only Antelope Canyon excursions ($42 adults, $28 under-13s) to a dinner cruise (daily June–Oct; $75/$35).

ACCOMMODATION AND EATING

Lake Powell Resort Wahweap Marina ☎928 645 2433 or ☎888 896 3829, ⌨lakepowell.com. Only half the rooms in this very plush resort actually overlook Lake Powell. Its *Rainbow Room* restaurant, however, provides huge lakeside windows and serves good food daily for all meals, priced to suit the many tour groups that pass through. Breakfast buffets cost $10 or $15, and you can get a full dinner for $20 (seared chicken breast) to $32 (strip steak). The same management also operates the adjacent first-come, first-served campground, and an RV park. Tents $26, RVs $48, rooms $230

Rainbow Bridge National Monument

Accessible by boat, on 100-mile round-trip tours from Wahweap • April–Oct daily 7.30am, Nov–March Sat 9am • $117, under-13s $84 • ☎928 645 2433 or ☎888 896 3829, ⌨lakepowell.com

Millions of tourists have Lake Powell to thank for providing access to the world's largest natural bridge, the magnificent **RAINBOW BRIDGE NATIONAL MONUMENT**. The Navajo, seeing this formerly sacred site swarming with visitors, are far less enthusiastic, though at least the height of Glen Canyon Dam, and thus the level of the lake, was mandated to ensure that Rainbow Bridge was not drowned – unlike the nearby and equally revered confluence of the Colorado and San Juan rivers.

Both the Navajo and the Paiute knew of Rainbow Bridge long before the first university-sponsored expedition reached it in 1909. Within a year, it was declared a national monument, but it remained far off any beaten track until the construction of Lake Powell made it accessible by **boat**. The bridge now lies a couple of miles down **Forbidding Canyon**, a side canyon located around fifty miles by water from Glen Canyon Dam.

Tours from Wahweap operate year-round. Schedules are open to considerable variation, however, as the length of the trip depends on the level of the lake. What used to be a half-day excursion has become an eight-hour one in recent years because certain deep-water channels are no longer navigable. It's possible that the waters may rise again sufficiently for the tour boats to make two round-trips in a single day. For much of the year, the tours are booked well in advance, so reserve your boat trip before you finalize your accommodation.

Even with the water low, Lake Powell remains a broad expanse, spread beneath a huge sky. When you reach Forbidding Canyon, on the other hand, you enter another world; it's a beautiful high-walled slot canyon that twists mysteriously away from the lake proper. Eventually, the tour boats moor at a floating jetty, the precise location of which varies. A walk from here that's currently over a mile leads to the astonishing sandstone gateway of the bridge, climbing nearly 300ft high. It's also almost 300ft wide, with Navajo Mountain visible through its superbly smooth curve. The upper section, including the forty-foot-thick span, is composed of Navajo sandstone, while the base belongs to the harder Kayenta formation, not so easily cut by flowing water. When the lake is full, the bridge spans open water, but these days the former streambed is usually dry. What were once waterfalls nearby have also been exposed; what a spot this must have been. The Park Service asks visitors to consider not walking right up to, or beneath, the bridge itself, out of respect for Navajo spiritual traditions. Almost everyone goes anyway.

Hiking to Rainbow Bridge

Hiking permits from Navajo Nation Parks & Recreation $5, plus $5/person/night • ☎ 928 968 2808, ⓦ navajonationparks.org • Route information on ⓦ glencanyonnha.org

With a great deal more difficulty, Rainbow Bridge can be reached **on foot** as well as by boat. Two fourteen-mile trails start respectively 38 and 42 miles up Arrowhead Hwy-16, which runs north from Hwy-98 from a junction 57 miles southeast of Page. They loop to either side of Navajo Mountain, then join for the last half-mile. Only experienced canyoneers should attempt this hike, having obtained the compulsory permits from Navajo Nation Parks & Recreation.

Bullfrog

The marina at **BULLFROG** is slapped atop the slickrock on the west side of Lake Powell, seventy miles upstream from Wahweap, or seventy miles southeast of Capitol Reef National Park on the Notom–Bullfrog Road (see p.388). It's the focus of a small community that now proudly boasts its own high school, as well as a Glen Canyon NRA **visitor centre**.

THE LAKE POWELL FERRY

Schedules for the 25-minute **ferry crossing** between Bullfrog and Hall's Crossing have become too irregular in the last few years to make it appropriate to publish a detailed timetable. If frequency continues at its current level, expect up to four sailings per day in each direction in summer, diminishing to a complete suspension of service between late September and early April. The one-way fare for ordinary cars is $25.

Contact Glen Canyon visitor centres for current information (☎ 435 634 3088 or ⓦ nps.gov/glca).

Visitor centre At the Bullfrog marina (May–Oct   ☎ 435 684 7423, ⊛ nps.gov/glca).
daily 8am–5pm, Nov–March Thurs–Sun 9am–1pm;

ACCOMMODATION

Defiance House Lodge Bullfrog Marina ☎ 435 684   itself is indifferent. The park concessionaires also have
3000 or ☎ 800 528 6154, ⊛ lakepowell.com. While this   some fully furnished but deeply unatmospheric three-
pricey mesa-top motel, marked by a houseboat on stilts   bedroom "family units" (similar to trailers) for rent, and
above the road, holds some very comfortable rooms, the   there's a year-round first-come, first-served RV park too.
best place to enjoy the big lake views from is its *Anasazi*   RVs $50, rooms $158, family units $327
restaurant (open daily for all meals), even though the food

Hall's Crossing

HALL'S CROSSING, on the east shore of Lake Powell, now plays second fiddle to its larger neighbour Bullfrog to the west. As the name suggests, it was the base of a river ferry operator long before the lake existed. **Charles Hall** started out by building his own boat at Hole-in-the-Rock, 35 miles downstream (see p.380), in 1870. Business there was so bad that he moved here in 1881, only to give up altogether when the transcontinental railroad rendered his service redundant. Hall charged $5 per wagon and 75¢ per passenger; the going rate for a family car on the **Lake Powell Ferry** these days is $25.

When they finally get around to colonizing Mars, the first settlement should look much like the airstrip on top of the bare red mesa that rises above Hall's Crossing. Hwy-276 to the east makes an exhilarating drive, dropping down the **Clay Cliffs** with views across the red plains to Monument Valley, and running for forty empty miles to meet Hwy-95 near Natural Bridges (see p.431).

Accommodation possibilities are limited to family units in a glorified trailer park, while if you're looking for a meal, you can either take your pick from a small assortment of Twinkies on sale at the local gas station, or a marginally wider range of groceries at the marina store. There's nothing at all at the ferry ramp, just over a mile beyond the marina.

Hite

Lake Powell's northernmost marina, at **HITE**, is reached via **Hwy-95**, which branches off Hwy-24 halfway between Capitol Reef and I-70 to run for 122 miles southeast to Blanding. The only highway to cross the Colorado between the Glen Canyon Dam and Moab, Hwy-95's most dramatic segment is the twenty-mile stretch as it approaches the river from the west, rattling along beside the North Wash.

At the mouth of the North Wash canyon, the highway climbs to the windswept hilltop that holds **Hite Overlook**. You'll almost certainly be confronted here by the fact that while Hite remains accessible by road, it's no longer on the lake. An ongoing drought let Lake Powell recede out of sight several years ago; it's just possible the waters will have returned by the time you read this, but don't bet on it.

Hite has always felt like something of a God-forsaken spot, and even more so these days that it's lake-forsaken as well. Beyond the overlook, Hwy-95 loops north to cross first the Dirty Devil River and then the Colorado. Reaching the ramshackle **Hite Marina** itself involves a detour of a couple of miles on the far side. At the time of writing, no boats could reach Hite, so all the marina facilities were shut. There's still a small gas station and a grocery store (open 11am–2pm only), and it's even possible to rent a "family unit" like those at Bullfrog (see p.398), though that would be a seriously bad idea.

OPPOSITE UPPER ANTELOPE CANYON, P.394>

Between Capitol Reef and Canyonlands

No direct route crosses the tract of craggy sandstone and eroded clay that stretches for a hundred miles **east of Capitol Reef**. Travellers making the circuit of Utah's parks are obliged to make a giant detour to the north or south, either crossing Lake Powell at Hite or taking **Hwy-24** up to meet I-70, and then looping back down to Moab – a total drive of around 150 miles.

The scenery along Hwy-24 is consistently awesome, beginning with the **badlands** twenty miles beyond Capitol Reef, where the 1500ft **Factory Butte** rises above corrugated humps of greyish-blue clay reminiscent of Arizona's Painted Desert (see p.252). Only small sections of the backcountry are at all accessible, however, and the town of **Green River** on the interstate is the only town of any size the whole way to Moab.

Hanksville

Forty miles east of the Capitol Reef visitor centre, Hwy-24 turns sharply north toward the interstate, while Hwy-95 runs south toward Lake Powell. The tiny farming community of **HANKSVILLE** stands at the intersection, a few miles south of the confluence where the Fremont and Muddy rivers join to form the Dirty Devil.

Hanksville is only a dot on the map, but with the next dot a good fifty miles away in any direction, it draws in enough weary drivers to keep it ticking.

ACCOMMODATION AND EATING   HANKSVILLE

Blondie's Eatery 3 N Hwy-95 ☎ 435 542 3255. Poised on a low bluff close to the intersection, with an expansive veranda, this cheerful diner is better than it looks, serving burgers for $5–8, ham and eggs or fried chicken for $9, and steak and eggs for $11. Daily 8am–9pm.

Luna Mesa Oasis Milepost 101, Hwy-24 ☎ 435 456 9122. Inexpensive but dependably good Mexican restaurant, in the middle of nowhere 16 miles west of Hanksville. Feb–Oct Mon–Sat 8am–9pm.

Rodeway Inn at Caineville Cove 25 E Hwy-24

☎ 435 456 9900, ⊚ cainevilleinn.com. Small, comfortable and gloriously isolated motel with an outdoor swimming pool, out in the badlands facing a spectacular butte at milepost 99 on Hwy-24, around 18 miles west of Hanksville. $80

Whispering Sands Motel 90 S Hwy-95 ☎ 435 542 3238, ⊚ whisperingsandsmotel.com. This clean and welcoming family-run motel at Hanksville's main intersection, across from *Blondie's*, fills quickly each evening as the sun goes down. $89

Goblin Valley State Park

Temple Mountain Rd, 32 miles north of Hanksville, 48 miles southwest of Green River • Daily 6am–10pm • $7/vehicle • ☎ 435 275 4584, ⊚ stateparks.utah.gov/parks/goblin-valley • Branch west from Hwy-24 near mile post 137, drive 5 miles on Temple Mountain Road, then 7 miles south on a paved spur road

Utah's quirkiest park, **GOBLIN VALLEY STATE PARK**, nestles at the foot of the San Rafael Reef, twelve miles west of Hwy-24 around halfway between Hanksville and the interstate. This small patch of barren desert became a park for the simple reason that its clay-like rock formations are **funny**. The man who first noticed them, in the 1940s, called it Mushroom Valley, but "goblin" is as good a name as any. In the 1999 movie *Galaxy Quest*, Goblin Valley doubles believably as an alien planet, with its rocks coming to life in one fabulous sequence.

Past the entrance kiosk, the road ends beside a sheltered overlook, poised above a slim valley whose sandy floor is completely devoid of vegetation. It's filled instead with parallel fins of pale Entrada sandstone, each topped by a ridge that's indented with weird eroded figures. Some hoodoos also stand alone, while larger buttes and columns loom around the periphery.

A couple of formal trails lead down into the valley, but no one bothers to follow them, preferring to slither at random from one misshapen masterpiece to the next.

Once you're on the valley floor, a typical monster in the maze will rise a few feet over your head; some really do look like goblins, complete with eyes and ears.

ACCOMMODATION

Goblin Valley Campground Goblin Valley State Park ☎ 800 322 3770, ⓦ utahstateparks.reserveamerica .com. Away from the main valley, but still engulfed by stunted sandstone sprites, the park's well-equipped campground has running water, toilets and showers, and also a couple of yurts, with bunk beds that sleep up to five but are not equipped with bed linens. Open year-round. Tents $\overline{\$16}$, yurts $\overline{\$60}$

The San Rafael Swell

Fronted by the "reef" that soars immediately northwest of Goblin Valley, the **San Rafael Swell** is one of southern Utah's least known but most tantalizing wilderness areas. With so many mapped and tamed parklands in the region, offering such instant and

---

7

JOHN WESLEY POWELL

Until **John Wesley Powell** led the first expedition to float down the full length of the Green and Colorado rivers, the Colorado Plateau was a vast blank at the heart of maps of the American West. No one knew how the mountains and waterways of the region fitted together, or whether falls larger than Niagara might prevent river traffic completely.

Born in Ohio in 1834, the son of a travelling preacher, Powell spent his youth making solo forays along the Ohio, Mississippi and Illinois rivers. He lost his right arm fighting for the Union at Shiloh, where he formed a lasting friendship with future president Ulysses Grant. Once the Civil War was over, the veteran major headed west to explore the Colorado Plateau.

Powell, his brother Walter, and a volunteer crew of eight frontier types set off in four flat-bottomed wooden boats from Green River, Wyoming, on **May 24, 1869**. Powell was lashed to an upright wooden chair in the leading vessel. Not long after entering the Uintah Mountains, by way of **Flaming Gorge**, one boat was smashed to smithereens in Lodore Canyon. They then whisked through Green River, Utah, and plunged into the desert, encountering their biggest challenge so far in the shape of **Cataract Canyon**, soon after the Green met the Grand to form the Colorado. Wherever possible, they carried their boats around the fiercest rapids, and with prodigious energy Powell repeatedly climbed out of the canyon to get his bearings. After several terrifying days, they burst out of the gorge, for an idyllic period of respite in **Glen Canyon**.

Three members of the party became demoralized in the depths of the **Grand Canyon**, when the blackness of the walls to either side seemed to presage further ferocious rapids ahead. They decided to hike their way out, only to be murdered mysteriously – some say by suspicious Mormons, others by Shivwits Indians. Powell, however, made it through the remainder of the canyon with unexpected ease; it took him merely one more day to reach the **Grand Wash Cliffs**, at the confluence of the Colorado and Virgin rivers (now beneath Lake Mead) on August 30. Two of his crew continued all the way to the Pacific, but Powell and his brother left the river, after almost a hundred days afloat.

Now a national celebrity, Powell returned for a better-funded and more leisurely trip two years later. Starting this time from Green River, Utah, he documented his experiences in much greater detail, and used them as the basis of a bestselling book. During the voyage, he left the canyon at every opportunity, and even returned to Washington DC for the winter, while his crew holed up in Kanab.

In later years, Powell became director of the Smithsonian Institution's **Bureau of Ethnology** in Washington, DC, and of the **US Geologic Survey**. His forceful opinions as to how the federal government should administer the limited resources of the West – and especially its water – are now regarded as prophetic. Refusing to accept the then-current adage that "rain follows the plow," he argued that state boundaries should be drawn along natural watersheds, to prevent water issues from bedevilling the region's political future. His advocacy of federally funded water projects led the bureaucrats to name **Lake Powell** in his honour, but one can't help imagining that Powell himself would prefer Glen Canyon as it was in the beginning.

abundant rewards, few out-of-state visitors add this difficult, mountainous terrain to their itineraries. A glimpse of it from I-70, as the interstate plunges east down its craggy foothills toward Green River, usually suffices.

In the past, most of the swell was only safely accessible in 4WD vehicles. Now a significant number of dirt roads have been upgraded, and local tourist authorities have produced lavish booklets and maps of possible driving tours. If you're driving an ordinary two-wheel-drive vehicle, it's still essential to enquire locally, in Green River or Goblin Valley, before attempting to explore on your own. Conditions vary month to month; many roads become impassable every winter, and are only fit for conventional use in early summer, when the latest winter's damage has been repaired.

A couple of highlights are detailed below; others, for which you're more likely to need 4WD, include **Little Wild Horse Canyon**, a slot canyon that cuts into the reef roughly seven sandy miles west of Goblin Valley, and the swell's highest point, the **San Rafael Knob**, a four-hour round-trip hike from the end of Copper Globe Road, which heads south from I-70 at exit 114.

Black Dragon Canyon
Milepost 147 I-70, 3 miles west of junction of Hwy-24, and 17 miles west of Green River • Free

The most accessible part of the San Rafael Swell, spectacular **Black Dragon Canyon**, immediately north of I-70, can only be approached from the interstate's westbound lane. Pull directly off the highway just past milepost 147, and go through the gate, closing it behind you. Drive straight ahead for a mile on a dirt road, ignoring a possible west turn, then follow the sign west, and park when the road surface deteriorates. From there, a short walk leads into the towering, golden-walled canyon itself. The prime goal is a group of dramatic Barrier Canyon-style **pictographs** (see p.410), on the north side a quarter-mile along. If that's all you have time for, you can easily be back on the interstate within an hour of leaving it.

Alternatively, with a good map, you can make a day of it by hiking the full length of the canyon, which is barely two miles long, then climbing north over a pass and back down again to meet the San Rafael River, which will lead you back to where you left your car. That demanding fifteen-mile loop will take at least seven hours to complete.

THE GREEN RIVER

But for political shenanigans in the 1920s, the **Green River** might rank among the world's most famous rivers. It starts by flowing north to loop around the Wind River Mountains of central Wyoming, then heads south into Utah, briefly ducks into the northwest corner of Colorado, and then crosses Utah to meet the **Colorado River** after a 730-mile journey.

The Green River was first identified by Fray Alonzo de Posada in 1686 as the boundary between the territories of the Ute and the Comanche. Until 1859, when Captain J.N. Mancomb discovered the confluence deep in the heart of the canyonlands, no one knew that it flowed into the Colorado. The **Colorado River** had been named by the Spanish founder of New Mexico, Juan de Oñate, in 1606, while French trappers in what's now Colorado stumbled across what they named the **Grand River** a century later.

The trouble is, at the confluence the Colorado has flowed a mere 430 miles from the Rockies of central Colorado. As geographical convention dictates that the principal course of a river is its longest, the Green River should be regarded as the main course of the Colorado River, and their entire combined course should bear the same name. Either the Green should become the Colorado, or the Colorado below the confluence should become the Green – in which case the Grand Canyon should arguably be called the Green Canyon, which doesn't bear thinking about.

The news that the "Colorado River" did not originate in Colorado, as had always been assumed, mortified Colorado's legislators. In the 1920s, they simply defied convention and renamed the Grand the Colorado, which fortunately dovetailed with a vote in conservative Utah against changing the name of the Green River.

Heart of Sinbad Road

The 24-mile **Heart of Sinbad Road** runs from the end of Temple Mountain Road – the spur road off Hwy-24 that leads to Goblin Valley (see p.400) – up to exit 131 off I-70, 33 miles west of Green River. Unpaved, but usually good enough for ordinary vehicles, it provides access to many remote and fascinating areas of the San Rafael Swell. There's no room here to describe them all; pick up a brochure in Green River and choose for yourself.

Green River

Hwy-24 joins I-70 44 miles north of Hanksville, just as the interstate completes a dramatic descent from the uplands of the San Rafael Swell to slope gently east through a landscape of soaring buttes. Within a few miles, a ribbon of green vegetation becomes visible ahead, cutting through the desert at the bottom of a long broad valley – the line of the **Green River**. To the north stand the forbidding **Uintah Mountains**, while to the south the stream burrows into a labyrinth of twisting canyons, so this is the best place to ford the river for hundreds of miles.

The town of **GREEN RIVER** has long straddled crucial cross-country routes. For east–west travellers, it remains the major way-station between Colorado and Utah, while river-runners from John Wesley Powell onwards have launched themselves south from here toward the Colorado.

While Green River is a welcome oasis, however – fertile enough to be the "melon-growing capital of east Utah" – it still amounts to little more than a strip of motels, gas stations and fast-food outlets. Given a sensible reluctance to erect permanent structures too close to the river, there's a gap where you might expect downtown to be; most of the built-up strip lies to the west.

John Wesley Powell River History Museum

1765 E Main St • Daily: April–Oct 8am–7pm; Nov–March 9am–5pm • $6 • ☎ 435 564 3427, ⊕ jwprhm.com

The well laid-out **John Wesley Powell River History Museum**, on the east bank of the river in the heart of Green River, recounts the epic journeys of the Canyonlands region's first true explorer, whose second voyage started here on May 22, 1871. Powell made that trip partly because he lost the notes from his first, so the second time around he ensured his every movement was fully recorded, in photos that now make marvellously evocative viewing. A multimedia show and several rooms of exhibits cover later developments in river navigation, ranging from steamers – none managed more than a handful of voyages – up to the army-surplus rubber inflatables that triggered the postwar boom in whitewater rafting. Glance out of the panoramic windows, and you'll see that the river here is not green at all, but a dark muddy brown.

ARRIVAL AND DEPARTURE   GREEN RIVER

By train Amtrak's *California Zephyr* calls at the train station at 250 S Broadway daily, heading east toward Denver at 7.59am and west toward Salt Lake City at 5.58pm.

By bus Greyhound buses between Denver and points west stop at the *Rodeway Inn*, 525 E Main St (☎ 435 564 3421).

INFORMATION AND TOURS

Visitor centre In the Powell museum, 1765 E Main St (Daily: April–Oct 8am–7pm; Nov–March 9am–5pm; ☎ 435 564 3427, ⊕ greenriverutah.com).

Boat trips Companies running rafting trips from Green River include Moki Mac River Expeditions (☎ 435 564 3361 or ☎ 800 284 7280, ⊕ mokimac.com) and Holiday

River Expeditions (☎ 435 564 3273 or ☎ 800 624 6323, ⊕ bikeraft.com). Every Memorial Day, hundreds of boats set out on weekend-long convoy trips that cruise down to the Colorado confluence and then chug back upriver to Moab.

7

ACCOMMODATION

Although Green River is not much of a destination in its own right, it has around five hundred **motel** rooms. They tend to fill by early evening in summer, partly with the overspill from Moab and partly with long-distance interstate travellers.

Green River State Park Just south of Main Street ☎435 564 3633, reservations, ☎800 322 3770, ⓦutahstateparks.reserveamerica.com. This attractive waterfront campground, on the river's west bank south of Main Street, offers the best camping in town. It stays open year-round, but there's no water Dec–Feb. $16

Holiday Inn Express 1845 E Main St ☎435 564 4439 or ☎800 465 4329, ⓦihg.com. Crisp, clean chain motel, next door to the museum and visitor centre, with an indoor pool, laundry, and free breakfast. $115

River Terrace Inn 1740 E Main St ☎435 564 3401 or ☎877 564 3401, ⓦriver-terrace.com. High-quality motel, often filled by tour groups, with a pool, river views, and adjacent restaurant. $100

Super 8 1248 E Main St ☎435 564 8888 or ☎800 800 8000, ⓦsuper8.com. Reliable budget motel, perched on a slight elevation at the east end of town. $68

EATING

Green River Coffee Co 25 E Main St ☎435 564 3411. Lively local coffee bar-cum-antique store, just south of the main drag a mile or so west of the river. Mon–Thurs 6am–2pm, Fri–Sun 6am–5pm.

Tamarisk Restaurant 870 E Main St ☎435 564 8109.

Brisk, busy restaurant, overlooking the river opposite the museum. The menu is wide-ranging and cheap, with most full dinners costing under $10, but the salad bar is atrocious. Daily 7am–9.30pm.

Canyonlands National Park

Canyonlands National Park is divided into four sections: the Island In The Sky district (see p.406), Horseshoe Canyon (see p.409), the Maze district (see p.411) and the Needles district (see p.412) • $10 per vehicle, $5 for motorcyclists, cyclists and pedestrians; valid for 7 days • ☎435 719 2100, ⓦnps.gov/cany

CANYONLANDS NATIONAL PARK, the largest and most magnificent of Utah's national parks, is as hard to define as it is to map. Its closest equivalent, the Grand Canyon, is simply an almighty crack in an otherwise relatively flat plain; the Canyonlands area is a bewildering tangle of canyons, plateaus, fissures and faults, scattered with buttes and monoliths, pierced by arches and caverns, and penetrated only by a paltry handful of dead-end roads.

The 527 square miles of the park are just the core of a much larger wilderness that stretches the horizon in every direction. To nineteenth-century explorers, this was

BACKCOUNTRY PERMITS IN CANYONLANDS

Only limited numbers of visitors are allowed to spend a night or more in the **backcountry** of Canyonlands National Park, and all such groups are required to have permits. **Backpacking permits**, covering a maximum party of seven persons in the Needles and Island In The Sky districts, or five persons in the Maze, cost $30. Permits for **four-wheel-drive** or **mountain biking** expeditions that involve backcountry camping, issued for groups of up to three vehicles with a total of fifteen people in the Island In The Sky, ten in the Needles, or nine in the Maze, are $30. **Day-use** permits, costing $10, are also required for bikes and 4WD vehicles that enter Horse or Lavender canyons in the Needles district.

Though not compulsory, **reservations** are essential for the most popular areas, especially in spring and fall. They must be purchased at least two weeks in advance, and are issued for dates throughout each calendar year from the second Monday of July in the previous year. Permits must be picked up in person – with every member of the group present – from the appropriate park visitor centre, at least one hour before it closes.

Reservations can only be made by mail or fax (NPS Reservations Office, 2282 S West Resource Blvd, Moab UT 84532-8000, ☎435 259 4285). For more information call ☎435 259 4351 (Mon–Fri 8am–noon); contact a park visitor centre; or see the park website ⓦnps.gov/cany.

THE GEOLOGY OF CANYONLANDS

In a land with so little water, the sheer *effort* that went into creating the splendour of **Canyonlands** is almost impossible to conceive. As you look out from the park's highest point, atop the Island In The Sky, the cliffs drop away a thousand feet, with the rivers a thousand feet below that. For a hundred miles south, successive plateaus, benches and tablelands diminish into the distance, studded with the occasional butte. And yet twelve million years ago, this entire landscape was one vast plain, level with where you're standing. Bit by bit, at the rate of two inches every thousand years, the topsoil has crumbled to silt and been carried away by the rivers. Most was deposited at the edge of the Pacific, but now it's gradually filling up Lake Powell instead.

Canyonlands was not literally carved by the rivers, however. Both the Green and the Colorado began life as gentle streams. In the last twelve million years, as the Colorado Plateau pushed up, they have remained in their original courses, ever more deeply entrenched into the earth. Meanwhile, ice produced in a ceaseless cycle of freezes and thaws has chiselled away at the rocks that surround them, tumbling boulders into the water to be swept away.

Canyonlands is unique in that it rests on a mile-thick bed of **salt**, deposited on the bottom of an ancient sea three hundred million years ago. That salt was covered by subsequent layers of sediment, themselves interspersed with further deposits of salt. Under the pressure of thousands of feet of harder rock, the salt layers are squeezed like toothpaste until they flow far underground, then bubble up toward the surface. As they do so, they push up fins and spurs of rock that crack and split to create phenomena such as the Needles, or they may hit ground water and dissolve, leaving gaping caverns behind.

7

the epitome of useless desolation; only since uranium prospectors blazed crude trails across the trackless wastes in the 1950s has it become at all widely known. Even after Canyonlands park was created in 1964, it took a couple of decades before tourists arrived in appreciable numbers.

Canyonlands focuses upon the Y-shaped confluence of the Green and Colorado rivers, buried deep in the desert forty miles southwest of Moab. There's only one spot from which you can see the rivers meet, however, and that's a five-mile hike from the nearest road. With no way to get down to the rivers, let alone cross them, the park therefore splits into three major sections. The **Needles**, east of the Colorado, is a red-rock wonderland of sandstone pinnacles and hidden meadows that's a favourite with hardy hikers and 4WD enthusiasts, while the **Maze**, west of both the Colorado and the Green, is a virtually inaccessible labyrinth of tortuous, waterless canyons that presents a stiff challenge even to expert climbers and backpackers. In the wedge of the "Y" between the two, the high, dry mesa of the **Island In The Sky** commands astonishing views across the whole park and beyond, seen from overlooks that can easily be toured by car. Getting from any one of these sections to the others involves a drive of at least a hundred miles. The Needles and the Island In The Sky are reached via long approach roads that leave US-191 north and south of Moab respectively; the Maze is an endless jolting ride on dirt tracks from either Hwy-24 or the town of Green River.

A fourth subsection of the park, **Horseshoe Canyon** in the west, was added in 1971 to preserve the Southwest's finest collection of ancient **rock art**.

The **rivers** themselves count as Canyonlands' final major component. A **rafting** expedition from Moab (see p.424), is the best way to experience the eerie stillness of the deep canyons, at once exhilarating and supremely restful. However, since there's no way out before Lake Powell, you'll need to set aside several days, and several hundred dollars – and be prepared to face the intense whitewater rapids of **Cataract Canyon**, just beyond the confluence.

With no lodging and little camping in the park, you'll probably need to make repeated visits on successive days, while as there's no loop road to whisk you through it, it takes a full day to have even a cursory look at a single segment. If you're among the many visitors who find the conditions too gruelling to spend much time out of your car – summer temperatures regularly exceed 100°F, and most trails have no water and little shade – then the Island In The Sky is the most immediately rewarding option. On the other hand, if you fancy a long day-hike you'd do better to set off into the Needles.

The Island In The Sky

It's not obvious from most maps, but like the Colorado River confluence over which it looms, the mesa known as the **Island In The Sky** is itself shaped like a "Y." After a steady climb of around 25 miles, **Hwy-313**, which heads southwest from US-191 eight miles north of Moab, enters the park across the slender **Neck** that forms the right-hand fork of the Y. It then branches to the northwest, to run as far as the crater of **Upheaval Dome**, and to the south, where it ends at the overwhelming **Grand View Point**.

Most Island In The Sky visitors simply drive from one overlook to the next. Some also walk one or two of the short, easy trails that cross its thin capping of Kayenta sandstone, to gaze over the brink of the sheer Wingate cliffs that hold it up. It is also possible, however – either in a sturdy 4WD vehicle, or by some very strenuous hiking – to make your way down to the pale plateau of the **White Rim**, prominent a thousand feet below.

By the middle of each day, the entire landscape takes on a hazy pallor; for the best **photographs**, you'd ideally be at the national park overlooks early in the morning, and the overlooks of the nearby **Dead Horse Point State Park** at sunset.

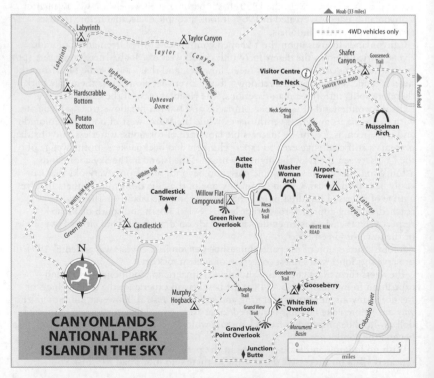

Dead Horse Point State Park

Drive 10 miles north from Moab on US-191, 20 miles southwest on Hwy-313, then 7 miles southeast to the point itself • $10 per vehicle, National Parks passes not valid • ☎ 435 259 2614, ⊛ stateparks.utah.gov/parks/dead-horse

Just before the boundary of Canyonlands National Park, a turning to the east leads in four miles to the smaller but equally breathtaking **Dead Horse Point State Park**. This miniature version of the Island In The Sky stands at the tip of a narrow mesa, poised two thousand feet above a stupendous "gooseneck" loop in the Colorado, which here is much more visible, receding into the distance, than from the national park. Off to the east, the turquoise ponds of Moab's potash plant (see p.426) make a garish contrast with the red rocks, while the Anticline Overlook (see p.427) stands guard above the far side of Meander Canyon. A mile or so of easy paved trails lead to assorted alternative overlooks, and there's plent of picnic space scattered about.

The visitor centre

3 miles before Dead Horse Point overlook • Daily: summer 8am–6pm; winter 8am–5pm • ☎ 435 259 2614

Dead Horse Point's **visitor centre** is located three miles short of the main overlook. In summer, a trailer outside sells coffee and snacks, while inside you'll find a **Desert Museum** of human and natural history. Displays here explain the park's name: nineteenth-century cowboys used the mesa as a corral, herding wild horses behind the piñon fence that blocked its ninety-foot neck. One band of horses was too scared to cross the gap even when the gate was left open, and perished of thirst. For that matter, Dead Horse Point remains a death trap for unwary pet **dogs**; the current record is three drop-offs in a month.

ACCOMMODATION   DEAD HORSE POINT STATE PARK

Kayenta Campground Dead Horse Point State Park ☎ 435 259 2614, reservations ☎ 800 322 3770, ⊛ utahstateparks.reserveamerica.com. The park campground makes an excellent alternative if there's no room in Canyonlands, though it doesn't offer showers. **$20**

Island In The Sky visitor centre

Drive 10 miles north from Moab on US-191, then 22 miles southwest on Hwy-313 • Daily: March–Oct 8am–6pm; Nov–Feb 9am–4pm • Free • ☎ 435 259 4712, ⊛ nps.gov/cany

A couple of miles south of the turn-off to Dead Horse Point, and a mile or so in from the entrance to Canyonlands National Park, the **Island In The Sky visitor centre** stands to the right of the highway. Rangers can provide details on road and trail conditions as well as campsite availability.

Mesa Arch Trail

Trailhead: 4 miles beyond visitor centre • 0.5 miles round-trip; 30min

The best short hike in the Island In The Sky, the **Mesa Arch Trail**, starts from a small parking lot just before the fork in the road. It's more of a walkway than a trail really, cemented for some of its length and running across bare slickrock elsewhere, equipped with occasional stairways. During a half-mile loop around the mesa-top hillocks, it runs to the very rim of the abyss, where long, shallow **Mesa Arch** frames an extraordinary view of the La Sal Mountains, 35 miles northeast. Admiring Washer Woman Arch and Monster Tower, closer at hand, it would be easy to stumble right through the gap – there's no barrier.

Grand View Point Overlook

Grand View Point Overlook, at the southern end of the road, is the Island In The Sky's definitive vantage point, and an agoraphobe's nightmare. It commands a hundred-mile prospect of layer upon layer of naked sandstone, here stacked thousands of feet high, there fractured into bottomless canyons.

The most conspicuous feature is the plateau formed by the **White Rim** layer, a thousand feet below, whose faint smattering of grass is crisscrossed by abandoned mining trails and ends at the White Rim itself. That peters out in the mass of white-capped red-rock pillars known as **Monument Basin**, amid which the **Totem Pole** may look the size of a pencil but is actually 305ft tall. Neither river can be seen; the Colorado River is tucked out of sight another thousand feet down, while the equivalent canyon of the Green River is hidden by the twin buttes to the west. Everything is mirrored by an identical chaos on the far side, however, rising toward the snow-capped peaks of the **Abajo Mountains**, forty miles south.

Grand View Trail

Trailhead: Grand View Point Overlook • 2 miles round-trip; 1hr

The **Grand View Trail**, which sets off across a lovely level shelf just below and to the right of Grand View Point Overlook, enables you to contemplate the whole jigsaw puzzle from countless additional angles. Every now and then, you may spot the silhouette of the Needles, far to the south. Keep going beyond the end of the shelf, and you'll eventually reach the very tip of the promontory, where you can clamber atop various rocky eminences for wonderful views to the north as well.

Green River Overlook

A couple of hundred yards north of the fork in the park road, a paved 1.2-mile spur road leads to a parking lot a few short steps away from the **Green River Overlook**. The expanse of the White Rim that spreads below – clearer and flatter than at Grand View Point – is pierced by the green-trimmed meandering course of the river itself, as it flows through placid **Stillwater Canyon**. At this very spot, in the 1965 Biblical epic *The Greatest Story Ever Told*, Max von Sydow (aka Jesus) delivered the Sermon on the Mount to an audience of Moab Rotarians bedecked in false beards and tea towels.

Upheaval Dome

The park road ends five miles north of the fork at the geological oddity of **Upheaval Dome**. This jagged 1500ft-deep crater is a highlight of air tours (see p.424), but from close up, at the end of the steep ten-minute climb from the parking lot, it's a disappointment. Elaborate theories that explained the prongs of pale stone bursting from its darkest depths as the product of undulating subterranean salt have recently been abandoned in favour of the simpler notion of a sixty-million-year-old **meteor strike**.

Over the Edge: the White Rim Road

The reason the Island In The Sky is accessible at all, and that crude dirt tracks strike off into the wilderness everywhere you look, is that this region was a prime target for freelance **uranium prospectors** in the 1950s (see p.420). They knew uranium is often found in the grey-green rocks of the **Chinle formation**, which here forms the talus slopes at the bottom of the Wingate-sandstone cliffs, not far above the White Rim.

The rough-and-ready hundred-mile **White Rim Road**, scraped by would-be miners at the base of the cliffs, is now most often explored on three- or four-day **4WD expeditions**, with overnight stops at primitive campgrounds en route by permit only (see p.404). Only the hair-raising **Shafer Trail Road**, which drops just south of the visitor centre, connects the mesa-top with the White Rim; otherwise drivers join the White Rim Road by means of the **Potash Road** from Moab (see p.426), or along **Mineral Bottom Road**, which runs west from Hwy-313 a couple of miles north of the Dead Horse Point turn-off. None of these routes should be attempted in ordinary vehicles.

Hikers can, however, clamber between the Island In The Sky and the White Rim along various trails. All are too demanding for a round-trip day-hike down to the White Rim – let alone to either river – to be a good idea. Register with the Park Service before you set off on a multi-day trip. Options include the **Lathrop Trail**, an utterly exhausting nine-mile route all the way to the Colorado, passing close to abandoned but potentially toxic uranium mines; the **Upheaval Canyon Trail**, which drops down to the Green River from the far side of Upheaval Dome; and the **Shafer Trail Road** itself.

ACCOMMODATION	ISLAND IN THE SKY
Willow Flat Campground Green River Overlook ☎ 435 259 4712, ⓦ nps.gov/cany. The Island In The Sky's only developed campground, just back from the overlook, has	twelve basic sites, with vault toilets but no water. Available first-come, first-served only, it's usually full in spring and autumn. $10

Horseshoe Canyon

Remote **Horseshoe Canyon**, a detached chunk of Canyonlands National Park located northwest of its main body and 42 miles by dirt road southeast of Green River, is home to the most extraordinary **rock art** in North America. No one now knows the meaning of the mysterious, haunting figures that line the sandstone walls of the **Great Gallery**. Although to the modern eye they suggest an astonishing sophistication, they are among the **oldest** such images to survive.

The San Rafael Desert: the road to Horseshoe Canyon and the Maze

Unless the weather has been dreadful – check at the Green River visitor centre (see p.403) – ordinary vehicles should have no problem driving to Horseshoe Canyon. Of the two alternative routes, the one that starts from **Green River** is more convenient if you want to sleep in a motel the night before, but it's marginally more likely to be impassable. Assuming it's clear, follow signs for the airport from the town centre until you cross the railroad tracks. Once the surface has turned to gravel, fork left at a BLM sign pointing toward the San Rafael River.

After an initial flat section, the road from Green River pushes through painted-desert badlands formed by the fossil-rich Morrison Formation, then winds down to a glorious panorama of Monument Valley-style buttes. It crosses the **San Rafael River** on a rickety wooden bridge after nineteen miles, then climbs again to offer views that stretch west to the Henry Mountains and east to the La Sals.

Just over forty miles south of Green River, beyond **Antelope Valley** – home to one of Utah's few surviving herds of pronghorn antelope – an easily missed spur road branches off east. The **Horseshoe Canyon trailhead** is at its far end, at the edge of the plateau two miles along.

As the road veers west, a junction 5.5 miles past the Horseshoe Canyon turn-off marks the start of the 21-mile drive south to **Hans Flat Ranger Station**, the main point of access for the Maze (see p.411). Keep going west, and a total of 32 miles from Horseshoe Canyon – at best, around an hour's driving – you'll finally meet **Hwy-24**, just south of Goblin Valley (see p.400). This last stretch crosses Sweetwater Reef before dropping into the **San Rafael Desert**, where it insinuates itself between two impressive buttes known as Little Flat Top and Big Flat Top.

Note that if you're heading east from Capitol Reef, it's much quicker to reverse the route described above; just be sure you have enough gas.

Horseshoe Canyon Trail

Trailhead: 42 miles by dirt road southeast of Green River • 7 miles round-trip, 5hr, elevation change 750ft • Ranger-led guided hikes Sat 9am in spring and fall • ☎ 435 259 2652, ⓦ nps.gov/cany

Even if you're not a rock-art enthusiast, the **Horseshoe Canyon Trail** down to the Great Gallery – there's no road access – ranks among the most beautiful hikes in Utah. With

7

THE ROCK ART OF HORSESHOE CANYON

At the time it was first studied, Horseshoe Canyon was called **Barrier Canyon**, and that name still defines the style of art for which it's famous. Such art is characterized by anthropomorphic figures, roughly life-sized but weirdly elongated, and often lacking both arms and legs. Those that have eyes have large round ones, or simply empty sockets, and many seem draped in stylized robes; for most visitors to this lonely desert backwater, the cumulative effect is to suggest **ghosts** or spirits from another, different time.

While spear points found in Horseshoe Canyon date back twelve thousand years, archeologists believe the pictographs were produced by people of the **Archaic** culture, which flourished between 7500 BC and 500 AD. At the start of that period, the climate was much wetter, and the canyon held lakes, ponds and plentiful game. When conditions dried out, it was briefly abandoned, but then reoccupied.

Life was now far more difficult, and **shamanistic rituals** attempted to ensure successful hunting. These involved the creation first of clay statuettes, from 5000 BC onwards, and later of figurines made from split willow-twigs. Many represent what seem to be deities or shamans as well as animals, and the Great Gallery pictographs are thought to depict those same entities.

As for **technique**, the Great Gallery is very literally rock art. To produce the paint, different coloured rocks were ground up, dissolved in water, and bonded with saliva produced by chewing seeds. The red is hematite, heavy with rust; the white is gypsum or chalk; even the blue comes from a local stratum. Some figures were produced with brushes, others by blowing or flicking paint at a stencil. Digital manipulation of photos of the images reveals not only faded colours but even different layers, so archeologists can see how specific figures were changed and redrawn over the centuries.

Experts estimate the gallery to be between 1600 and 6000 years old. Certain sites seem to have been rendered inaccessible by rockfalls that occurred a very long time ago indeed. All that's certain is that none dates from later than 400 AD, when the Archaic people acquired the bow and arrow – not shown in any Great Gallery images – and began to transform into the **Fremont** culture. Fremont art, as seen elsewhere in Utah as well as here in Horseshoe Canyon, has its own very distinct style.

either forty miles of dirt road to negotiate south of Green River, or 32 miles southeast from Hwy-24, before you even reach the trailhead, few visitors come this way, so you may well get the gorgeous red-rock canyon, rustling with wildlife, to yourself. It's a long, exposed hike though, so carry all the provisions you might conceivably need, and either start early, or sit out the midday sun down in the canyon. It was from the Horseshoe Canyon trailhead, incidentally, that **Aron Ralston** set off on the 2003 hike to Blue John Canyon, beyond Horseshoe Canyon, which culminated in his having to cut off his right arm, as immortalized in the film **127 Hours**.

The route picks its way down from the trailhead, marked by cairns as it crosses patches of deep sand alternating with slickrock. Once you reach the bottom, after perhaps half an hour, follow the sandy wash to your right. Stay initially on its left bank, and within ten minutes you should spot the first rock-art site, the **High Gallery**, above the talus on the canyon's left wall. It's not easy to see detail here, though, so you'll soon be ready to press on.

All the remaining sites lie across the wash on the right wall. The first, the **Horseshoe Shelter**, nestles beneath an overhanging cliff a hundred yards further on. When Harvard archeologists excavated this site in 1930, it held several rooms; all that remains is a vivid band of **pictographs** in the palest stratum of the rock, which was above the roofs of the shelters and is thus now out of reach. The animals, squiggles, and triangular figures – many with strange protuberances on their heads – date from the Fremont era, but the scattering of ghostly footless figures are in the earlier Barrier Canyon style.

Another twenty minutes' walk on, beyond several twists and turns in the canyon walls, climb up into a massive pale sandstone alcove, where a red-and-white band of rock holds another small collection of pictographs.

Eventually, after twenty more minutes, you round the final bend to be confronted by the **Great Gallery**, suddenly apparent beneath a lesser overhang. It's a breathtaking moment. Framed between the cottonwoods, a long row of dark, hollow-eyed, otherworldly entities stands stark against the pale rock. Though the details grow clearer the closer you get, somehow a sense of vast, alien distance remains.

Apart from a couple of well-shaded stone benches, and pit toilets nearby, there are no facilities for visitors. Look out, however, for two army-issue metal boxes, marked PLEASE OPEN ME: one holds a set of powerful binoculars, the other copies of relevant academic papers.

ACCOMMODATION	HORSESHOE CANYON
Horseshoe Canyon Trailhead campsite No camping is permitted in Horseshoe Canyon itself, but there's a basic	site with no services beside the parking lot at the Horseshoe Canyon Trail trailhead. **Free**

The Maze

The name of Canyonlands' **Maze** district is no exaggeration. This brainteaser of convoluted canyons and barren desert washes, west of the Green and Colorado rivers, must be the least explored region of the US. If you're determined to get away from it all, the Maze is the place for you; getting back to it all when you've finished is more of a problem.

Somewhere in the heart of the Maze is the legendary **Robbers Roost**, a canyon fastness used as a hideout by nineteenth-century cattle rustlers and bandits like **Butch Cassidy** and his Wild Bunch. They'd escape the long arm of the law by riding the Outlaw Trail up from the Green River near Mineral Bottom; lacking their familiarity with the terrain, pursuing posses had to turn back defeated. No roads entered the region until uranium prospectors bulldozed their way in during the 1950s.

Even today, you'll need a high-clearance 4WD vehicle to get any further than **Hans Flat Ranger Station**, also referred to as the **Maze Visitor Centre**, which stands 21 miles south of the road through the San Rafael Desert to Horseshoe Canyon, described on p.409. Though technically the ranger station is in Glen Canyon NRA, it's the main source of information for hikers and drivers setting off into the Maze.

The **jeep roads** beyond Hans Flat take another twenty or thirty miles to jostle and switchback into the actual Maze. One route in ends at the **Maze Overlook**, another at **Doll House Butte**, which marks the far end of the **Land of Standing Rocks**, above the west bank of Cataract Canyon and straight across from the Needles.

Having come this far, most backpackers launch themselves into the wilderness for days or weeks at a time. There are few formal trails, but favoured destinations include **Pictograph Canyon**, not far beneath the Maze Overlook, where Barrier Canyon-style pictographs (see opposite) seem to record the moment when the Archaic people first acquired agriculture. However, unless you're extremely self-sufficient, a workhorse when it comes to carrying vast quantities of water, and a fearless, fully equipped rock-climber, you're never going to see them.

INFORMATION	THE MAZE
Hans Flat Ranger Station 46 miles east of Hwy-24, 66 miles south of Green River Daily 8am–4.30pm	☎ 435 259 2652, ⓦ nps.gov/cany.

7

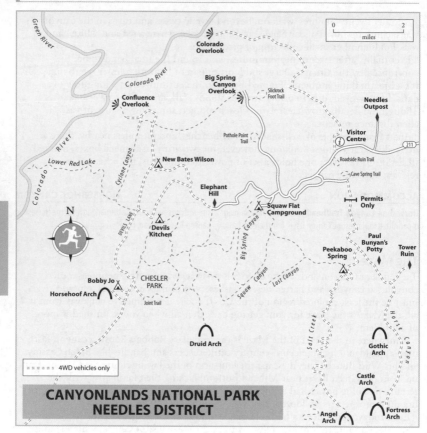

Green River

Colorado River

Colorado River

Lower Red Lake

Cyclone Canyon

DEVILS LANE

0   miles   2

Colorado Overlook

Confluence Overlook

Big Spring Canyon Overlook

Slickrock Foot Trail

Needles Outpost

Pothole Point Trail

Visitor Centre

211

Roadside Ruin Trail

Cave Spring Trail

New Bates Wilson

Elephant Hill

Squaw Flat Campground

Permits Only

N

Devils Kitchen

Big Spring Canyon

Paul Bunyan's Potty

Peekaboo Spring

Tower Ruin

Bobby Jo

Horsehoof Arch

CHESLER PARK

Joint Trail

Squaw Canyon

Lost Canyon

Salt Creek

Horse Canyon

Druid Arch

Gothic Arch

= = = = = 4WD vehicles only

Castle Arch

Angel Arch

Fortress Arch

CANYONLANDS NATIONAL PARK NEEDLES DISTRICT

The Needles

Thanks to its intricate tracery of backcountry trails, which offer the chance to engage with the landscape as opposed to merely marvelling from a distance, the **Needles** district is Canyonlands National Park's most satisfying segment for hikers, bikers and 4WD drivers. While it has its share of long-range vistas – including the park's only **Confluence Overlook** – the Needles is noted primarily for its namesake thickets of candy-striped **sandstone pillars**. Clustered on scrubby rock outcrops, concealing pockets of incongruous grassland, these intriguing formations can be explored on brief forays or multi-day backpacking expeditions.

The **Needles** area is a very long way from civilization, at the far end of the stunning **Hwy-211**, a total of 75 miles from Moab and fifty from Monticello. If you're planning a number of successive day-hikes, it makes sense to camp overnight, so reserve a spot at *Squaw Flat* or in a backcountry site as soon as you know you're coming (see p.413). Note incidentally that, confusingly enough, the **Needles Overlook** is not in the national park at all, but in the BLM's Canyon Rims area (see p.427).

Ordinary mortals, as opposed to obsessive canyoneers, should also be warned that even casual **hiking** in the Needles may be the hardest thing you've ever done. Carry a good map and at least four pints of water per person, stick to the trails, and above all be very careful how far you climb – it's much easier to go up than it is to come down, and you run the risk of getting "rim-rocked."

The road to the Needles: Squaw Flats Scenic Byway

The 35-mile **Hwy-211** – also known as the **Squaw Flats Scenic Byway** – heads west of US-191 forty miles south of Moab. You can't miss the turning; it's marked by a colossal butte immediately opposite, which, if you happen to be hungry, may well seem to resemble a giant brioche.

As it winds lazily into the park, between cottonwood-lined **Indian Creek** stream and canyon walls of rich red sandstone, and overlooked by the twin castellated **Sixshooter Peaks**, the byway seems to carry you back a century, into the unspoiled Wild West. Much of the route lies through open grazing country, making this one of the few spots in the Southwest where you're still likely to see genuine **cowboys** riding the range. The Dugout Ranch, halfway along, was established in 1885, and later amalgamated with its neighbours to form the Indian Creek Cattle Company, Utah's largest cattle outfit.

Newspaper Rock

Hwy-211, 12 miles west of US-191 • Daily 24hr • Free

Newspaper Rock Recreation Site, alongside Hwy-211, preserves a panel of black desert varnish that's inscribed, like some prehistoric newspaper, with literally hundreds of **petroglyphs**. For ancient peoples, this made a perfect site to create conspicuous and enduring images, sheltered by a protective rock lintel beneath a hillock at a narrow bend in the valley immediately north of the Abajo Mountains. Besides abstract designs, images include helmeted human figures, buffalo and bighorn sheep, plus lots of six-toed footprints and what look like bear pawprints. Some are probably symbols left by clans who performed particular ceremonies here, or simply passed by. With the obvious exception of recent graffiti, it's hard to say when they were executed, but you have to suspect that most are not in fact all that old; nineteenth-century Ute are thought to be responsible for the mounted riders, shown hunting with bows and arrows.

The riverside woods across the road from the rock hold a lovely if basic **campground**, free but waterless. A short way further west, Hwy-211 meets the mountain road from Monticello (see p.428).

Needles Visitor Center

35 miles west on Hwy-211 from US-191, a total of 75 miles from Moab or 49 miles from Monticello • March–Oct daily 8am–5pm; Nov & second half of Feb daily 9am–4 pm; closed Dec to mid-Feb • Free • ☎ 435 259 4711, ⓦ nps.gov/cany

Rangers at the **Needles Visitor Center**, a mile inside the park boundary, can provide up-to-date hiking information. They issue 34 **backpacking permits** per night, each for a group of up to seven people; in high season, if you don't have a reservation (see p.404) the chances are none will be available. Day-hikers don't need permits.

Three miles beyond the visitor centre, the road forks at the Squaw Flats campground (see p.415). Keep on its main paved section for another four miles to reach the **Big Spring Canyon Overlook,** confronting an array of mushroom-shaped hoodoos, or turn left onto an uneven dirt road and you'll come to **Elephant Hill** in three miles.

Short hikes in the Needles

The best hiking in the Needles is unquestionably on the Chesler Park and Confluence Overlook trails. If you're pressed for time, however, several shorter trails set off from close to the main park road. A mile south of the visitor centre, the **Cave Spring Trail** is an enjoyable 25-minute hike that begins by leading under a group of overhangs. One holds a remarkably preserved old cowboy camp, another shelters assorted petroglyphs. Two short ladders then climb to the top of a low mesa, where you walk back to your car across the slickrock.

Another two miles west, the half-mile **Pothole Point Trail** is an easy stroll to the top of the roadside ridge. Half a mile on from there, the 2.5-mile, two-hour **Slickrock Trail** is much more challenging. While the trail itself is not technically difficult, if you're on it at all that's probably because you didn't get here early enough to tackle anything longer, in which case you'll be exposed to the full heat of the midday sun. Its shadeless route nonetheless provides a tremendous orientation to the region, following cairns from one sandstone knoll to the next in a lasso shape, with an initial straight section leading to a longer loop. Four separate spur trails along the way lead to successive overlooks, each with its own distinct long-distance mountain-and-mesa views.

The Chesler Park Loop Trail

Trailheads: Elephant Hill or Squaw Flat • From Elephant Hill 11 miles round-trip, 7hr, elevation change 500ft; From Squaw Flat 15 miles round-trip, 10hr, elevation change 500ft

Chesler Park, the high grassy meadow whose stubby sandstone pinnacles gave the Needles its name, makes a great destination for a long day-hike. Simply to reach it requires a six-mile round-trip trek from Elephant Hill, or a ten-mile one from Squaw Flat campground, while looping around the "park" itself adds another five miles.

As you climb across the cairned stretches of slickrock that rise from both Elephant Hill and Squaw Flat, look north for sweeping views to the Island In The Sky, with the White Rim etched beneath it. The two trails meet half an hour up from Elephant Hill, then dip west to cross the wash that runs through **Elephant Canyon** – it may look dry, but there's usually water flowing beneath the sand – before the final ascent to Chesler Park.

For the most part, the **Chesler Park Loop Trail** undulates around the edge of the 600-acre clearing, on the slopes below the red-and-white barber-pole Needles. On the eastern flank, however, it runs straight across the lavender-tinted grassland, while in the far southwestern corner it disappears into an extraordinary mini-canyon whose blackened walls are seldom even three feet apart. This claustrophobic segment, the mile-long **Joint Trail**, is the highlight of the trip. A ledge perched above its eastern end, a 500ft detour off the main trail, provides a superb overview of Chesler Park. Through a gap to the west, the gigantic Doll House Butte (see p.411), across the Colorado, can also be glimpsed. If you have a 4WD vehicle, you can join the Chesler Park Loop near the Joint Trail, and walk the loop alone as a five-mile hike.

As an alternative to circling Chesler Park, consider following the spur trail that branches south along Elephant Canyon. It takes just over three miles of steady climbing to reach **Druid Arch**, named for its resemblance to the rough-hewn monuments of Stonehenge.

Several more trails connect Chesler Park and Elephant Canyon with Squaw Flat, including routes through **Squaw Canyon** and the upper reaches of **Big Spring Canyon**. Backcountry **camping** is only allowed at specific sites along the jeep road that runs west and north of Chesler Park, of which the closest to the main trails is at Devils Kitchen Camp – and you'd be lucky to get a permit (see p.404).

The Confluence Overlook Trail

Trailhead: Big Spring Canyon Overlook • 11 miles round-trip, 7hr, elevation change 20ft

According to writer Edward Abbey, the local business community only agreed to the creation of Canyonlands park in 1964 on the understanding that its different parts would be linked by a loop drive, of which the focus would be the **Confluence Overlook**. It was even anticipated that this would be the site of a Junction Dam, which would create an even larger lake than Lake Powell. In the absence of either road or dam, the demanding but utterly magnificent eleven-mile round-trip hike from **Big Spring Canyon Overlook** remains the only way to see the spot where the Green River meets the Colorado.

The trail starts with a steep drop down into Big Spring Canyon, then laboriously climbs out again. After twenty exhausting minutes you emerge through a natural portal between two huge nodules to be greeted by long-distance views of the red-rock wilderness ahead – and cool shade closer at hand. A short metal ladder brings you out onto a level plateau, but you're soon descending again into **Elephant Canyon**, at this point several miles north of, and considerably broader than, the segment near Chesler Park (see p.414). Each time you climb back onto the slickrock mesa-top, new views open up, either south to the Needles or north to Junction Butte beneath the Island In The Sky.

Clambering from rock to rock beyond Elephant Canyon, you pass through several lifeless valleys known as **grabens**, from the German for "ditches." These were created 55,000 years ago, when shifting underground salt beds caused landslides. At times, the scrambling is hard going, and you have to haul yourself up onto head-high ledges, but it always stops short of actual rock climbing. Finally, after a half-mile section of jeep road – 4WD drivers can get this far via a nine-mile drive from Elephant Hill – you teeter out to the edge of the plateau and see the confluence for the first time.

A thousand feet below the **Confluence Overlook**, the Green River flows in from the west, and the Colorado from the northeast. They're never the same colour. Sometimes the Green really is a pale green, and the Colorado almost red, tinted with dissolved red sandstone; at other times the Green is more of a yellow, and the Colorado a muddy chocolate. In any case, the two hues remain distinct for the first mile or two after the rivers combine, intermeshing like a zipper as they flow parallel but separate toward fearsome Cataract Canyon.

ACCOMMODATION   THE NEEDLES

Needles Outpost Hwy-211 ☎435 979 4007, ⓦcanyonlandsneedlesoutpost.com. This privately owned, summer-only grocery store and gas station, up a short spur road just outside the park boundary, serves simple inexpensive meals (March–Nov daily, store 8am–7pm, dinner 8.30am–4.30pm), and has its own small campground, with flush toilets and drinking water. Showers cost $3 extra, or $7 if you're not staying overnight. Closed Dec–Feb. $20

Squaw Flat Campground Needles District ☎435 259 4711, ⓦnps.gov/cany. Space at this first-come, first-served campground, roughly three miles west of the visitor centre, is at an absolute premium in spring and fall. Bathrooms and water year round. $15

Arches National Park

US-191, 5 miles northwest of central Moab • $10 per vehicle, $5 for motorcyclists, cyclists, and pedestrians; valid for 7 days • ☎435 719 2299, ⓦnps.gov/arch

ARCHES NATIONAL PARK seems to have become the national park for people who aren't quite sure whether they like national parks. It's not too hard to get to, just five miles north of Moab; it's not too big, with just twenty miles of paved roads; and it has a catchy name, to tell you what to expect. Nearly a million visitors a year drive in, tick off however many arches they feel they have time for, and drive on to their next destination.

Thanks to *Desert Solitaire*, **Edward Abbey**'s lyrical evocation of his year as an Arches ranger, the park is also dear to environmentalists and wilderness enthusiasts. The irony is that when Abbey was here, during the 1950s, there was no road into the body of the park, and the only way to explore it was to blaze your own trails. Now you can cruise round in a couple of hours, and barely step out of your vehicle.

For all that, Arches remains very much worth visiting. The **Colorado River** here is literally peripheral, running unseen along the park's southern boundary. The emphasis instead is on the stark, strangely disjointed **sandstone scenery** of the higher ground to the north. As at Canyonlands, these rocks rest on an unstable layer of salt. Salt Valley, which slopes down across the park toward the Colorado, was formed by the collapse of an underground salt dome. That massive subsidence left high ridges to either side, which cracked along vertical fault lines to create long parallel "fins" of orange-pink Entrada sandstone.

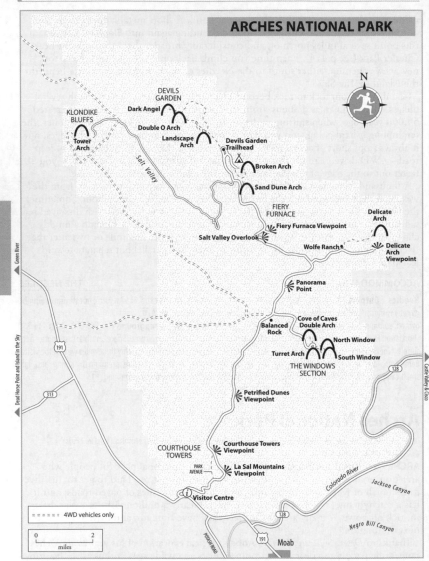

7

Over the eons, water collects in pores in the fins and scours them into potholes; piece by piece, the stone flakes away, until a hole is worn right through. Estimates of how many such "**arches**" the park holds vary from the eighty or so named on maps to the official count of over two thousand. No one has bothered to define whether a "window" is a type of arch or just another word for one, but it's agreed that an arch or window has to be at least three feet wide. Both are distinct from "bridges," which span running water.

To Abbey, the arches themselves were a "small and inessential" feature of the landscape. Unless you're a real obsessive, the appeal of hunting down arch after arch soon palls. The park's short, straightforward **hiking trails** are enjoyable in their own

right, however, so you're bound to see a good number of arches along the way.
Delicate Arch is by far the most impressive, in that it's a free-standing crescent of rock.
Most of the rest are just holes, though **Landscape Arch** is such a big one it would be a
shame not to see it.

Apart from one solitary cabin, testament to a failed attempt at cattle ranching, very
few traces of human occupation remain in this forbidding desert. It became a national
monument after the Klondike Bluffs area was found by a wandering prospector in the
1920s, and was enlarged into a national park in 1971.

Most visitors now arrive in **midsummer**, despite blazing temperatures that can reach
110°F. Hiking conditions are much more bearable in spring – when the wild flowers
blossom – or fall.

Visitor centre

US-191, 2.4 miles northwest of Colorado River, 5 miles northwest of central Moab • Daily: early March to Oct 7.30am–6.30pm; mid-Nov to
early March 8am–4.30pm • Free ☎ 435 719 2299, ⓦ nps.gov/arch

The fancy **visitor centre** for Arches National Park, alongside the only entrance to the
park, stands at the base of a long, tall escarpment that conceals the bulk of the park
from the highway. While it's bursting with the latest technology, its huge model
arches are much more show than tell, and there's little information of any substance
to be found.

Rangers also provide hiking advice, and issue free backcountry camping permits.
Although you're allowed to camp anywhere that's out of sight of roads, trails and
named arches, Arches actually sees very little overnight backpacking, as most visitors
do all the hiking they want within a day.

Immediately beyond the visitor centre, the park road begins its eighteen-mile journey
north to Devil's Garden with a steep climb up the cliffs, offering views across to Moab.
Note that each **parking lot** along the road is designed to hold a specific number of
vehicles, to limit hiker numbers on any one trail. Park illegally, and there's a $25
on-the-spot fine. No vehicles, or bikes, are allowed on the trails.

Park Avenue

Trailheads: Park Avenue Viewpoint and Courthouse Towers Viewpoint • 2 miles round-trip; 1hr • Elevation change 320ft

The first parking lot you come to in the park proper, a mile up from the visitor centre,
marks the start of **Park Avenue**. Visitors keen to reach the big-name trails and
attractions tend to ignore this straightforward one-mile walk, and in truth if you've
only time for one hike this isn't the one to choose, but it's still an enjoyable stroll. The
best views of the "avenue", named for the "skyscrapers" that top the high ridges to
either side of a dry wash, come from the trailhead itself.

The main elevation change on the hike is right at the start, as you drop down to the
rocky bed of the wash via a neatly maintained staircase. Once there, you keep going
straight ahead, with slickrock and boulders alternating with thick sand underfoot. The
long dramatic orange fin to your right peters well before the far end of the trail, which
leads to a group of chunky monoliths known as the **Courthouse Towers**. Any arches
there may once have been have long since fallen.

Unless you arrange to be met at the northern trailheads, you'll have to walk Park
Avenue as a two-mile round-trip. The road in between the two passes the **La Sal
Mountains Viewpoint**, which offers the first glimpse of the peaks to the east.

The Windows Section

In the heart of the park, almost ten miles up from the visitor centre, the fifty-foot
Balanced Rock rests precariously on its slanted pedestal. Immediately beyond, a spur

road to the right leads in three miles to the **Windows Section**. Several fine arches can be admired from the parking lot at the end, the largest in the park, which is also the starting point for a couple of very popular short trails.

North and South Windows
Trailhead: Windows parking lot • 1 mile round-trip; 30min

The busy loop trail to the North and South Windows ambles gently upwards for a couple of hundred yards toward **North Window**, the only one of the pair visible from the road. Take the steeper spur trail that leads right up to it, gaze through, and you'll appreciate why the word "window" is so appropriate. So far the gaping aperture has framed only blue sky, but now a magnificent desert panorama comes into view.

    South Window is just a few yards away, though you have to rejoin the main trail and round one last pinnacle to see it properly. You can't climb right up to it, though a much rougher trail continues around the back and leads eventually back to the parking lot. Alternatively, you'll have noticed by now that the lone fin across the main trail is pierced by **Turret Arch**. Wander over there, then look back for a shot of the two windows side by side – a pair of dazzling blue eyes, separated by a bulbous snub nose.

Double Arch
Trailhead: Windows parking lot • 0.5 mile round-trip; 15min

A separate half-mile trail leads from the Windows parking lot to **Double Arch**, where the roof of a wedge-shaped arch has fallen in to create either a skylight, or two distinct arches, depending on your point of view. On the far side, the **Cove of Caves** is packed with incipient future arches, burrowing into the cliffs.

Delicate Arch

As befits the state's single most remarkable natural phenomenon, **Delicate Arch** has become a symbol of Utah. Oddly enough, its sturdy bow-legged form is not in fact all that delicate. It was originally called "Landscape Arch," for the view of the La Sal Mountains it so neatly frames, and only swapped names with what is now Landscape Arch (see p.419) due to a mapmaker's mistake.

    A side road toward Delicate Arch leaves the park road shortly beyond **Panorama Point**. The arch itself can only be reached via the gruelling **Delicate Arch Trail**. If you lack the time or energy for that, you can see it from afar from the **Delicate Arch Viewpoint**, at the end of a level hundred-yard trail that begins a mile further on. For **photographs**, Delicate Arch Viewpoint is best in the early morning, while the Delicate Arch Trail is better in the afternoon.

The Delicate Arch Trail
Trailhead: Wolfe Ranch parking lot • 3 miles round-trip; 2–3hr • Elevation change 480ft

The **Delicate Arch Trail** may be just 1.5 miles long, but the round-trip to the arch and back involves a steep climb across bare slickrock that can take the wind out of the hardiest hiker's sails. The trail starts just short of **Wolfe Ranch**, 1.2 miles along the spur road, where Civil War veteran John Wolfe built a cabin in 1906, using cedar and cottonwood logs hauled seven miles from the Colorado. His cattle had by then been denuding the nearby slopes for almost twenty years; when sheep-farmers began to graze their animals on this impoverished soil as well, Wolfe gave up and moved back to Ohio.

    Beyond the cabin, a footbridge crosses the shallow perennial **Salt Wash**, and the trail begins its determined ascent. Considering that fewer than ten inches of rain fall here each year, the terrain is surprisingly varied, from the scrubby riverbanks, choked with tamarisk, by way of a small-scale piñon-juniper forest, up to the naked rock three-quarters of a mile up. An alcove off to the left, just below the hilltop, cherishes "**hanging gardens**" of rushes and even orchids, fed by a spring that stains the rocks.

It's easy to lose the sparsely cairned trail at the top of the mesa; the trick is to follow a narrow ledge in the rock that leads around the back of a high fin. Suddenly, from a viewing area neatly fenced off by a natural rock parapet, you're confronted by the full glory of **Delicate Arch**. Standing in superb isolation on the high lip of a canyon, it looks taller than its 45 feet. Quite how much closer you dare to approach depends on your confidence walking across the steeply inclined slickrock. There's no physical reason to stop you from standing right under it; lots of people do.

Delicate Arch is deservedly the most popular place in the park from which to see the **sunset**. Be sure to arrive at the trailhead at least an hour before the sun is due to go down, and longer in busy periods, when parking is at a premium. The sumptuous red glow of the arch deepens right until the final moment, so it's worth staying up there as long as you can – which means you'll be glad of a **flashlight** or torch for the hike back down again.

The Fiery Furnace

Guided hikes daily: Late Feb to mid-June & mid-Sept to Nov 10am & 2pm, mid-June to mid-Sept 9am & 4pm • $10, ages 5–12 $5 • Reserve at least 4 days in advance on ⓦ recreation.gov

An uninspiring overlook three miles on from the Wolfe Ranch turn-off gives little idea of the labyrinthine complexity of the **Fiery Furnace**. Named not for any exceptional heat but for its golden late-afternoon glow, this warren of high-walled dead-end gullies and parallel fins is so disorientating, and so fragile, that you're strongly advised to enter it on a ranger-led **guided hike**. The hikes are fascinating, but don't involve walking all that far; most of the time is spent standing still, while the ranger explains the rock formations and signs of life along the way. Only in February and November is it usually possible to get a same-day reservation for the hikes from the visitor centre; for the rest of year, reserve in advance.

Even if you hike into the Furnace without a guide, you need to register at the visitor centre, and pay $1. No backcountry camping is permitted.

Devil's Garden

Trailhead: Devil's Garden • **Landscape Arch** 1.6 miles round-trip; 1hr **Double O Arch** 4 miles round-trip; 2–3hr

The park's largest concentration of arches is found in the **Devil's Garden**, beyond the far end of the road eighteen miles up from the visitor centre. The prime target here is the 300ft **Landscape Arch**, reached within a mile by a gravelled, reasonably level trail. This slender span is so frail that hikers are not allowed up to or through the arch itself. A sixty-foot-long slab dropped off it in 1991, and lesser rockfalls happen all the time, such as the one that destroyed nearby **Wall Arch** in 2008. Arch aficionados will probably still be debating whether Landscape Arch or Kolob Arch in Zion National Park (see p.362) is the world's longest arch when it finally disintegrates. Landscape Arch is much harder to photograph than Delicate Arch, especially when the sun is behind it in the afternoon; try to come as early in the day as you can.

If your appetite for high-desert hiking has been whetted, press on beyond Landscape Arch on a trail that immediately becomes far cruder. After another mile – during which one hundred-yard section obliges you to totter along the top of a narrow sandstone fin – you round a corner to see **Double O Arch** on the skyline. At first, only its large upper oval is visible; as you approach, you'll see the much smaller ring beneath it as well. The pallid alkali wastelands that stretch away to the east were once prime uranium territory, and one heavily polluted section is still known as the "**Poison Strip.**"

The four-mile round-trip hike to Double O Arch also leads past half a dozen other named arches and assorted minor pinpricks and peepholes. Real gluttons for

7

CHARLIE STEEN: THE URANIUM KING

In the early 1950s, as the Cold War gathered steam and nuclear power stations seemed to hold infinite promise, the US government offered a $10,000 reward to anyone who discovered a mineable domestic uranium deposit – even on public land – and guaranteed to buy whatever it produced for the next ten years.

Freelance prospectors converged on the Colorado Plateau, where uranium had been found and mined as early as 1912. Their war-surplus jeeps piled with provisions, they set off into Utah's uncharted backcountry, waving their Geiger counters at any likely-looking rocks. Most knew which strata offered the best odds, and searched for places along the cliffs and canyon walls where they might be exposed.

Charlie Steen, a geologist from Texas, was mocked for insisting that he could find uranium by **drilling**. Projecting the angle of the canyonlands' crazily tilted slopes deep underground, he'd calculate where the precious mineral might have accumulated atop layers of harder rock. Concentrating on the **Lisbon Valley**, thirty miles southeast of Moab, he staked out countless claims and gave each a Spanish name.

In July 1952, the 31-year-old Steen broke his last drill bit in a 200ft bore on the **Mi Vida** ("my life") claim. Driving back to his trailer home in despair, he pulled into a gas station in Cisco, Utah. The attendant offered to test the final plug of rock on Steen's pick-up; his Geiger counter went straight off the scale.

Following his $60-million strike, Steen opened a processing mill in Moab that became Grand County's largest employer. As the "**Uranium King**," he built himself a hilltop mansion above town and threw a lavish annual party for all its citizens. He'd circle above Moab at night in his own plane, since TV reception was better at that altitude, and was even a celebrity guest on/ *Love Lucy*. In quick succession, he was elected to the Utah senate, then resigned after failing to change the state's liquor laws. Selling Mi Vida, he moved to Nevada, only to fritter his entire fortune away, losing $250,000, for example, on a pickle factory.

By the early 1970s, Steen was back in Utah, once more searching the canyon country as a penniless prospector. This time he travelled in disguise under a false name, in order both to avoid media attention and to protect any discoveries he might make. Success eluded him, however, and he eventually conceded defeat and moved to Colorado, where he died in 2006.

punishment can turn it into a seven-mile loop, by circling back on the Primitive Loop Trail, but that route is every bit as demanding as its name implies.

Klondike Bluffs

Trailhead: Klondike Bluffs • **Tower Arch** 2 miles round-trip; 2hr

For hikers keen to escape the crowds, the park's most readily rewarding destination is the **Klondike Bluffs** area, reached by a narrow but good-condition road that branches west from the main road a mile or so south of Devil's Garden. After seven miles, take the second of two all but adjacent left turns, and park at the end another mile along. The wonderful **Tower Arch Trail** sets off straight up the steep bluff ahead of you. The arch itself, at the far end, is totally stupendous, an enormous graceful arc topped by a giant hoodoo, but the high-desert landscape en route, overlooked by the so-called **Marching Men**, orange monoliths reminiscent of Canyonlands' Needles district, is equally enjoyable.

ACCOMMODATION   **ARCHES NATIONAL PARK**

Devil's Garden Campground Devil's Garden ☎ 518 885 3639 or ☎ 877 444 6777, ✆ recreation.gov. Rangers at the visitor centre will know whether there's room at Arches' only campground, 18 miles north at the far end of the road. The campground remains open all year; all its 50 sites, which hold up to ten people each, can be reserved between March and October; between November and February, 24 of them are first-come, first-served. No showers. <u>$20</u>

Moab

Boom-and-bust cycles are a recurring theme in Western history, but few communities have experienced such a rollercoaster ride as **MOAB**. Within the last seventy years, it has gone from an insignificant backwater in the 1940s to being celebrated as "The Richest Town in the USA" during the 1950s, before slumping into depression in the 1980s only to re-emerge, almost against its will, as the Southwest's number-one adventure-vacation destination.

Through it all, Moab has never been a large town – its population remains little more than five thousand – and neither is it, in itself, a particularly attractive one. The **setting** is what matters. With two national parks on its doorstep, plus millions more acres of public land, Moab is an ideal base for **outdoors enthusiasts**. The first to turn up were **jeep** drivers, taking advantage of the remote dirt roads cleared by the uranium prospectors. Then the **whitewater rafting** companies moved in, and the town swiftly started to lure in **mountain bikers**, too. These days, Moab is almost literally bursting, all year, with lycra-clad holidaymakers from all over the world.

Main Street, the broad five-mile section of **US-191** that sweeps through the heart of Moab, is lined with gas stations, diners, motels and other businesses. For two blocks north and south of **Center Street**, window-shopping pedestrians stroll the sidewalk and browse the menus. Elsewhere, everybody drives or cycles. Squeezed between Swiss Cheese Ridge to the east and the Moab Rim to the west, the town has little room to expand, but you can still see a few pioneer homes, and the occasional apple orchard, if you venture down the side streets.

Perhaps the main reason Moab has grown so fast is that out-of-state visitors tend to find the rest of Utah's rural communities so irredeemably boring. As soon as Moab emerged from the pack, it became a beacon in the desert, attracting tourists ecstatic to find the only southern Utah town that stays up after dark.

7

Brief history

Moab stands just south of the Colorado River, at the north end of a long valley created by the collapse of an underground salt dome. A similar valley slopes down to the river on its northern side, making this the best place to cross the Colorado in all Utah. Though Ute Indians passed this way for generations, the site was first recorded by Juan de Rivera in 1765, and a ferry service later helped travellers on the **Old Spanish Trail**. Mormon pioneers named the farming settlement they established here in the 1870s for the biblical wilderness of Moab, at the edge of Zion.

Until Charlie Steen discovered **uranium** in 1952, the biggest thing to hit Moab was when **Butch Cassidy** hijacked the Colorado ferry on his way home from a bank job. The uranium boom lasted well into the 1970s, but as it dwindled, the local political scene turned very sour. Moab was a major focus of the **Sagebrush Rebellion** (see p.376), which pitted mine-owners and Utah businessmen, together with their fearful workforce, against the burgeoning national coalition of **environmentalists** and the federal government. Grand County commissioners repeatedly defied federal legislation by smashing bulldozers into protected wilderness areas, hoping to open them for mineral exploitation.

While they may have won the bitter **Bulldozer Wars** – Ronald Reagan came to power proclaiming that he too was a "Sagebrush Rebel" – Utah's conservatives were no match for the world economy. When the uranium market crashed in 1980, and the bottom also fell out of oil, coal and potash, unemployment in Moab rocketed, and the population dwindled.

The wilderness devotees who saw the region's future as resting with **tourism** seized their opportunity. Out of nowhere, Moab became the West's hottest new destination, the desert equivalent of chic mountain hideaways like Aspen in Colorado.

Sadly, almost everyone agrees that things have now gone too far. Most of the old-timers have left, driven out by rising real-estate prices and reluctant to swap mining

7

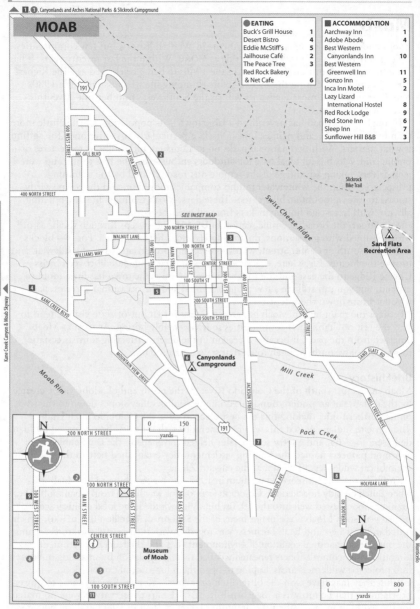

▲ 🅱️,🅾️, Canyonlands and Arches National Parks & Slickrock Campground

MOAB

●EATING	
Buck's Grill House	1
Desert Bistro	4
Eddie McStiff's	5
Jailhouse Café	2
The Peace Tree	3
Red Rock Bakery & Net Cafe	6

■ ACCOMMODATION	
Aarchway Inn	1
Adobe Abode	4
Best Western Canyonlands Inn	10
Best Western Greenwell Inn	11
Gonzo Inn	5
Inca Inn Motel	2
Lazy Lizard International Hostel	8
Red Rock Lodge	9
Red Stone Inn	6
Sleep Inn	7
Sunflower Hill B&B	3

for motel clerking at a third of the wages. Low-impact ecotourism seemed a real possibility when only the select few had even heard of Moab, but the canyonlands are taking as hard a battering from the fat-tyre brigade as they ever did from the mining conglomerates. Just to make matters worse, the price of uranium is rising once again. Amid rumours that Utah is about to experience another uranium boom, a handful of mines have already reopened, and nearby Green River has even announced plans to build a nuclear power station.

Museum of Moab

118 E Center St • March–Oct Mon–Fri 10am–5pm, Sat noon–5pm; Nov–Feb Mon–Sat noon–5pm • $5 • ☎ 435 259 7985, ⓦ moabmuseum.org

Local history is enjoyably recalled at the **Museum of Moab**, also known as the Dan O'Laurie Museum. Displays start with a mammoth tusk dredged from the Colorado and a replica petroglyph claimed to show the "Moab mastodon." The usual small-town assortment follows, ranging from an Ancestral Puebloan basket to Moab's first telephone switchboard, plus souvenirs from the uranium days.

ARRIVAL AND DEPARTURE   MOAB

By bus Moab Luxury Coach (☎ 435 940 4212, ⓦ moabluxurycoach.com) runs **shuttle services** to Moab from Salt Lake City (1 daily, continues to Bluff; $159 one-way per person; rate diminishes for groups of 3 or more) and the Amtrak station at Grand Junction, CO

(2 daily; $180 per vehicle).
By air Great Lakes Airlines offers scheduled flights to Moab Airport, on US-191 16 miles northwest of town, from Denver, CO, and, strangely, Prescott, AZ (from $94.50 one-way; ⓦ flygreatlakes.com).

INFORMATION AND GETTING AROUND

Moab Information Center Center and Main (daily: Mid-March to Oct Mon–Sat 8am–7pm, Sun 9am–6pm; Nov to mid-March Mon & Thurs–Sun 9am–5pm, Tues 1–5pm, Wed 9am–2pm; ☎ 435 259 8825 or ☎ 800 635 6622, ⓦ discovermoab.com). Brochures and maps for the nearby parks and public lands, plus free wi-fi. The website has a

full calendar of local events and festivals.
Taxis and shuttles Taxis in town, including shuttle services for bikers, rafters, and hikers, are operated by Coyote Shuttle (☎ 435 260 2097, ⓦ coyoteshuttle .com) and Roadrunner Shuttle (☎ 435 259 9402, ⓦ roadrunnershuttle.com).

ACCOMMODATION

If you've already been in Utah for a while when you reach Moab, its glittering neon **motel** signs may well come as a surprise. On many nights between mid-March and October, all the 1500-plus rooms in the town's thirty-plus motels are taken, so **reservations** are strongly recommended. **Room rates** can drop as low as $40 per night in winter, but you'd be lucky to find anything much below $90 in high season.

HOTELS, MOTELS AND HOSTELS

Aarchway Inn 1551 N Hwy-191 ☎ 435 259 2599 or ☎ 800 341 9359, ⓦ aarchwayinn.com. Large, well-equipped motel with a nice heated pool and a basketball court, not far from the Colorado River at the north end of town. $192

Best Western Canyonlands Inn 16 S Main St ☎ 435 259 2300 or ☎ 800 649 5191, ⓦ canyonlandsinn.com. Dependable upscale *Best Western*, in walking distance of restaurants across from the visitor centre, with a fitness centre, large pool and its own bicycle storage and repair room. $229

Best Western Greenwell Inn 105 S Main St ☎ 435 259 6151, ⓦ bestwesternmoab.com. Central, modern hotel that offers spacious good-value rooms with tasteful furnishings and fittings. $140

Gonzo Inn 100 W 200 South ☎ 435 259 2515 or ☎ 800 791 4044, ⓦ gonzoinn.com. Luxurious if rather self-consciously hipper-than-thou 43-room inn – or "funky place to crash," if you prefer – complete with kitsch-retro furnishings, quirky artworks, and an espresso bar. $169

Inca Inn Motel 570 N Main St ☎ 435 259 7261 or ☎ 866 462 2466, ⓦ incainn.com. Clean, minimally equipped but adequate budget motel, with pool and free basic breakfast. You may balk at paying these prices for

such a small, unfancy room, but you're unlikely to find better rates in Moab. $85

Lazy Lizard International Hostel 1213 S Hwy-191 ☎ 435 259 6057, ⓦ lazylizardhostel.com. This laid-back independent hostel, a mile south of the centre, is really nothing special, but backpackers appreciate its six-person dorms, and private rooms and cabins, and it also has a hot tub, kitchen, and wi-fi. Dorms $10, rooms $30, cabins $34

Pack Creek Ranch La Sal Mountain Loop Road ☎ 435 259 5505 or ☎ 800 879 6622, ⓦ packcreekranch.com. Large guest ranch, 20 miles southeast of town, just off the lower reaches of the La Sal Mountain Loop Road (see p.426). Eight individual cabins and cottages capable of holding from two to twelve guests, plus assorted pools and tubs. Two-night minimum stay. $175

Red Cliffs Lodge Mile 14, Hwy-128 ☎ 435 259 2002 or ☎ 866 812 2002, ⓦ redcliffslodge.com. Luxury resort occupying a beautifully verdant location beside the Colorado sixteen miles northeast of town. As well as seventy Western-themed suites, it holds spacious riverfront cabins, plus two restaurants, stables, a large pool, and even a winery. Suites $240, cabins $340

★ **Red Rock Lodge** 51 North 100 West ☎ 435 259 5431 or ☎ 877 253 5431, ⓦ red-rocklodge.com. Though

7

7

ADVENTURE TRAVEL IN MOAB

As southern Utah's main centre for wilderness activities, Moab is filled with companies that specialize in guiding and equipping adventurous travellers. The visitor centre supplies free route maps for bikers and 4WD drivers, plus lists of tour operators and rental outlets, online at ⓦdiscovermoab.com/tour.htm. The National Park Service keeps a similar list at ⓦnps.gov /cany/planyourvisit/guidedtrips.htm.

COLORADO RIVER TRIPS

Virtually everyone who goes **rafting** on the Colorado River does so with one of Moab's **river-running operators**. Motorized half- and one-day Colorado River trips start at around $45; multi-day expeditions, and day-trip combinations such as jeep-and-raft or horse-and-raft, are also available. **Shorter** trips start northwest of Moab, near Fisher Towers, and arrive near town in the afternoon; many companies give passengers the chance to float quieter stretches in two-person kayaks. While there are enough stretches of small-scale whitewater to whet the appetites of first-timers, a little romance is lost by the fact that the road runs alongside the river for much of the way. **Longer** (2–7 day) trips head through **Cataract Canyon** and other wild Canyonlands spots. **Oar-powered rafts** are slower but much quieter, and less expensive. Expect to pay from around $1000 for a five-day trip, depending on whether you're prepared to lift a finger to help.

Adrift Adventures ☎435 259 8594 or ☎800 874 4483, ⓦadrift.net
Tag-a-Long Expeditions ☎435 259 8946 or ☎800 453 3292, ⓦtagalong.com
Worldwide River Expeditions ☎435 259 7515 or ☎800 231 2769, ⓦworldwideriver.com

MOUNTAIN BIKING

While the Moab area is ideally suited to **mountain biking**, only experienced riders should attempt its most famous route, the **Slickrock Bike Trail**, in the **Sand Flats Recreation Area**. Laid out as a motorbike trail in 1969, this challenging ten-mile loop explores the sandstone knobs east of Moab, skirting the rim of Negro Bill Canyon. Following the white dotted line around this exposed expanse of lithified red dunes, up steep inclines and along narrow ledges, takes at least four hours. Be sure to allow enough daylight, and carry two gallons of water – far more than you can take in bike bottles alone.

To reach the trail, climb Salt Flats Road up from Millcreek Drive, which branches off 400 East Street four blocks south of Center Street. There's a fee of $5 per vehicle or $2 per person. Several Moab companies, including Roadrunner Shuttle (☎435 259 9402, ⓦroadrunnershuttle .com), offer a shuttle service to carry cyclists up to this and other trails. If you're looking for an easier ride, try the red-rock side canyons east and west of Moab, such as **Kane Creek**.

The following Moab **bike shops** offer daily rental and guided tours, including trips into Canyonlands National Park:

Rim Tours ☎435 259 5223 or ☎800 626 7335, ⓦrimtours.com
Poison Spider ☎435 259 7882 or ☎800 635 1792, ⓦpoisonspiderbicycles.com

JEEP TOURS AND RENTALS

Most of the thousands of miles of **jeep trails** around Moab were built by miners and haven't been maintained since; collect a free map and guide at the visitor centre.

Canyonlands Jeep Adventures 225 S Main St ☎435 259 4413 or ☎866 892 5337, ⓦmoab-utah .com/canyonlandsjeep. Rent a four-wheel-drive jeep or pickup truck for around $150 per day.
Tag-a-Long Expeditions ☎435 259 8946 or ☎800 453 3292, ⓦtagalong.com. Guided jeep tours from $80.

SCENIC FLIGHTS

Redtail Aviation ☎435 259 7421 or ☎800 842 9251, ⓦredtailaviation.com. Unforgettable flights over the Canyonlands area, starting at around $175 per person for one hour. Moab Airport, 16 miles northwest of Moab on US-91.

entirely lacking the flair of Moab's fancier inns, this simple traditional motel offers clean rooms in a quiet but supremely central location. **$70**

Red Stone Inn 535 S Main St ☎435 259 3500 or ☎800 772 1972, ⓦmoabredstone.com. Modern motel, a few blocks south of the centre, where the plain good-value rooms have kitchenettes, and guests can use a nearby pool. **$105**

Sleep Inn 1051 S Main St ☎435 259 4655, ⓦmoab -utah.com/sleepinn. Comfortable chain motel, with a pool and an indoor spa, whose location a mile south of downtown means it offers competitive rates. **$119**

B&BS

Adobe Abode 778 W Kane Creek Blvd ☎435 259 7716 or ☎970 424 6815, ⓦadobeabodemoab.com. Attractive, low-slung, Pueblo-style home, which despite being a few hundred yards from downtown Moab feels like it's way out in the desert. All its six B&B rooms are comfortable and tastefully furnished, and the breakfasts are superb. **£139**

Castle Valley Inn 424 Amber Lane, Castle Valley ☎435 259 6012, ⓦcastlevalleyinn.com. Large, beautifully furnished B&B, set in spacious grounds in magnificent Castle Valley, 20 miles east of town (see p.426). Five en-suite rooms and three separate bungalows. Rooms **$105**, bungalows **$185**

Sunflower Hill B&B 185 North 300 East ☎435 259 2974 or ☎800 662 2786, ⓦsunflowerhill.com. Antique-furnished former farmhouse, now a twelve-room B&B, away from the bustle on a dead-end side street. All units are en suite, some are in separate cottages, and there's a pool. **$175**

CAMPING

Canyonlands Campground 555 S Main St ☎435 259 6848 or ☎800 522 6848, ⓦcanyonlandsrv.com. Large, well shaded year-round site in the heart of town, catering mainly to RVs but also equipped with tent sites and small bunk-bedded cabins that sleep up to six. Tents **$26**, RVs **$40**, cabins **$60**

Sand Flats Recreation Area 1924 S Roadrunner Hill ☎435 259 2444, ⓦsandflats.org. Barely developed BLM campground, intended primarily for mountain bikers, along the top of the mesa to the east of town near the Slickrock Bike Trail. **$10**

Slickrock Campground 1301 N Hwy-191 ☎435 259 7660 or ☎800 448 8873, ⓦslickrockcampground .com. Moab's largest site, a mile north of town, is a pleasant spot, with plenty of trees and grass. As well as its tent sites and a row of 14 cabins, each sleeping 3–4 people, it offers a pool and hot tub, plus a store. Tents **$26**, RVs **$33**, cabins **$53**

EATING

Moab offers by far the greatest choice of **restaurants** in southern Utah, and for once most places make a serious effort to cater to **vegetarians**. Full menus appear in the *Moab Menu Guide*, available free at local motels (ⓦmoabhappenings .com/menuguide.htm). There's also no problem getting a **drink** – Moab even has two pubs and its own winery. Several bike shops have espresso counters for early-morning customers.

★ **Buck's Grill House** 1394 N Hwy-191 ☎435 259 5201, ⓦbucksgrillhouse.com. Belying its stockade-like exterior, this "American Western Food" joint is actually a sophisticated affair, serving rich, classy Southwestern food, such as artichoke ceviche or duck tamales, at reasonable prices. Most entrees cost $16–19, though steaks and chops range up to $30. Mon–Sat 11.30am–9.30pm, Sun 10am–9.30pm.

★ **Desert Bistro** 36 South 100 West ☎435 259 0756, ⓦdesertbistro.com. Top-notch dinner-only restaurant, set in a former 1892 home with outdoor seating at both front and back. On the modern Mediterranean-influenced bistro menu, entrees like or smoked rabbit *agnolotti* or buffalo mignon cost up to $44. Tues–Sun 5.30–10pm.

Eddie McStiff's 57 S Main St ☎435 259 2337, ⓦeddiemcstiffs.com. Central pub, next to the visitor centre, where interesting beers include raspberry and blueberry. The restaurant serves a varied menu, with inexpensive salads, fancy Southwestern pizzas (with

toppings like sundried tomatoes and jalapeño peppers) from $13, plus pasta and steak dinners, but the service can leave a lot to be desired. Daily 11.30am–10.30pm.

Jailhouse Café 101 N Main St ☎435 260 9961. Very popular central café, open for breakfast only. Indoor and outdoor seating year-round, and great specials like ginger pancakes and eggs Benedict, for around $12. Mon & Wed–Sun 7am–noon.

The Peace Tree 20 S Main St ☎435 259 0101. Very central café-restaurant that besides delicious smoothies serves full cooked breakfasts, like huevos rancheros for $9; good sandwiches and wraps for $8–9; and dinner entrees like lasagne or scampi for up to $19, all of which are best enjoyed on the large outdoor patio. Daily 7am–9pm.

Red Rock Bakery & Net Cafe 74 S Main St ☎435 259 5941. Small café-bakery opposite the visitor centre, with good coffee, breads and pastries, plus free wi-fi. Mon–Thurs 7am–4pm, Fri & Sat 7am–9pm, Sun 7am–3pm.

7

Around Moab

Although most visitors head straight for the national parks, several lesser-known areas in the Moab region are well worth exploring. Both upstream and downstream, minor roads run alongside the **Colorado River**, while the **La Sal Mountains** to the east make a snowy contrast to the aridity of the desert.

The Potash Road

The dead-end **Potash Road**, Hwy-279, which doubles back southwest along the Colorado's west bank from just north of the bridge on US-191, passes several intriguing **rock art** sites and provides a great close-up view of the river. In this stretch the Colorado is broad and lazy, tinted the same reddish brown as the Navajo sandstone cliffs, often busy with **rock climbers**, that tower above it.

Seven miles down the road, you reach a group of **petroglyphs** a dozen feet up on the canyon wall to the right. Scraped into the dark "desert varnish" by Fremont Indians, between 700 and 1300 AD, they depict animals and anthropomorphic figures, including a chain of linked humans resembling paper dolls.

A mile further on, two mounted metal tubes tucked among the roadside bushes point to a group of barely discernible **dinosaur tracks**. More petroglyphs can also be seen, this time higher on the cliffs.

Just beyond the frankly unremarkable **Jug Handle Arch**, seven miles on and seventeen miles from US-191, the valley floor widens. The road officially ends here, at the ugly green plant where Moab Salt produces salt and **potash** (potassium carbonate), accompanied by billowing clouds of white smoke. How much further you choose to drive will probably depend on whether you own the vehicle you're driving. The surface is paved for another 1.3 miles, while 1.7 bumpy miles beyond that you get your first glimpse of the 23 vinyl-lined **evaporation ponds** where the potash is prepared. Dyed a lurid bluish-turquoise to speed evaporation, they're a real eyesore, clearly visible from Dead Horse Point far above (see p.407).

Only **4WD** vehicles can continue past the ponds and the nearby boat-launch ramp. *Thelma and Louise* freeze-framed their way into the final credits from the mesa-top a few miles further up, and in due course the Potash Road meets up with the White Rim Road in Canyonlands (see p.408).

Castle Valley and the La Sal Mountains

Turning northeast off US-191 just south of the Colorado river bridge takes you onto **Hwy-128**, which follows the Colorado's east bank for 35 miles, then crosses the river to meet **I-70** ten miles further up. In summer, this superbly scenic section of the river is busy with one-day rafting trips. Roughly twenty miles along, the three-pronged red butte of **Fisher Towers** rises to the right of the road. These were originally "Fissure Towers"; there was no "Fisher."

For an excellent sixty-mile **loop trip** back to Moab – which takes something over two hours to complete in summer, and is usually closed by snow between November and April – turn right, southeast, fifteen miles along the river road, onto Castle Valley Road. **Castle Valley** is a verdant cleft that boasts some quintessentially Western scenery, with red sandstone walls and buttes such as the **Priest and Nuns** to the east and high dark hills to the west. At its far southern end, eleven miles along, another right turn sets you climbing up the volcanic 10,000ft **La Sal Mountains**. A handful of narrow squeezes and hairpins later, you reach a vantage point commanding views across the Colorado to Arches and Canyonlands. Beyond that, the road runs through the high mountain landscape of the **Manti–La Sal National Forest**, a feast of colour in late fall. A few campgrounds are tucked into the woods, but you won't see another building before the road eventually drops back toward Moab Valley.

It's equally easy to drive this loop in the opposite direction – for morning starts, drive south from Moab to keep the sun behind you for most of the way.

Hole N" The Rock
11037 S US-191, 15 miles south of Moab • Daily 9am–5pm • $6 • ☎ 435 686 2250, ⓦ theholeintherock.com

The peculiarly punctuated **Hole N" The Rock** is a classic piece of 1950s Americana. Having started out with a roadside diner at the foot of a cliff, Albert Christensen and his wife Gladys ended up hollowing an entire home deep into the red sandstone. Albert was a dreadful taxidermist – his unfortunate donkey Henry has to be seen to be believed – and painter – cross-eyed Christs a speciality – but his cool, well-lit house is a masterpiece. He died in 1957, without completing the spiral staircase that was planned to lead 65ft up to a roof-top patio. In the fine tradition of the jewellery that Gladys made from broken beer bottles, the gift store is stocked with home-spun souvenirs.

Don't confuse the Hole N" The Rock with the Hole-in-the-Rock pioneer river crossing near Escalante, incidentally (see p.380).

7

Canyon Rims Recreation Area
The vast and almost completely empty mesa, west of US-191, that separates Moab from the Needles district of Canyonlands National Park (see p.412), is largely taken up by the BLM-run **Canyon Rims Recreation Area**. Not much recreation goes on up here, although it has the usual 4WD-only roads, a couple of basic year-round campgrounds, and a scattering of hiking trails.

Only consider visiting the two main overlooks if you have a lot of time to spare – it involves a two-and-a-half-hour detour from the highway – or if you're not going to the Needles district, in which case the **Needles Overlook** provides a (relatively) quick overview as dramatic as any in Canyonlands itself.

The Needles Overlook
The paved road into Canyon Rims leaves US-191 32 miles south of Moab. Its dreary 22-mile course westwards comes to an abrupt halt at the windswept **Needles Overlook**, where a short railed footpath gives eagle's-eye views across the canyonlands. Specific landmarks are hard to pick out amid the orange sandstone ledges that spread below, but looking south you should spot the twin **Sixshooter Peaks** and Hwy-211 winding alongside Indian Creek toward the Needles district (see p.413). Further west, the Needles themselves poke from the hillocks, while the Colorado loops from the north toward its confluence with the Green River.

The Anticline Overlook
Fifteen miles in from US-191, or seven miles short of the Needles Overlook, forking right onto an even, broad gravel road commits you to the 25-minute drive across the tumbleweed-strewn sagebrush desert to the **Anticline Overlook**. You probably won't pass another vehicle before the final parking lot, from which a five-minute walk leads to a high promontory that faces the potash ponds and **Dead Horse Point** across the Colorado.

Some people call this the Anti-climax Overlook, disappointed to realize that they've driven almost all the way back to Moab. As you'll see if you follow the fence around the headland, only **Kane Creek Canyon** – where the creek is a tiny green sliver in the red wasteland – intervenes. You'll almost certainly hear motorbikes scrambling across the slickrock of the Moab Rim on the far side. To the northeast, silhouetted above a brief stretch of the Colorado, you also get a remarkable view of the fins of **Arches National Park**, where the line of sight passes straight through the South Window.

Southeast Utah

While it may lack big-name national parks, Utah's **southeast corner** is every bit as scenic as the neighbouring regions. The desert here is so unforgiving that only a handful of widely separated settlements cling to life, and large tracts remain entirely without roads.

Culturally as well as geographically, southeast Utah has much in common with the Four Corners area. The **Ancestral Puebloans** were here in force, as countless abandoned pueblos testify. They moved off to the south and east around 1250 AD, but even now almost half the population of **San Juan County**, which covers the bulk of the region and is larger than several states, is Native American. A few are Ute, but most are **Navajo**, many of them descended from families who hid here during the 1860s to escape the Long Walk (see p.481).

The first **Mormons** to reach this far-flung corner were the Hole-in-the-Rock pioneers (see p.378), who established **Bluff** in 1880 and went on to found **Blanding** and **Monticello** as well. All those towns make viable bases, but the real attraction, as ever, is the landscape, with hikers heading for **Natural Bridges National Monument**, more ambitious backpackers for **Grand Gulch**, and drivers rattling across the desert to the unbelievable **Muley Point**, **Goosenecks State Reserve** and the **Valley of the Gods**.

Monticello

The first fifty miles of US-191 south of Moab are so desolate that it comes as a major shock, on climbing some straggling foothills, to find yourself confronted by ploughed green fields. To Mormon pioneers, this terrain resembled Thomas Jefferson's country home in Virginia – hence the name of **MONTICELLO** (pronounced "monti-sello"), six miles further on. Farming has never been all that easy here, however, and the economy has only recently been steadied by tourism.

To the east of Monticello, US-491 (previously infamous as US-666) heads off to Colorado through what looks like a segment of the Great Plains that has wandered astray, complete with grain silos and fields of wheat and beans.

ARRIVAL AND INFORMATION   MONTICELLO

By bus Moab Luxury Coach runs shuttle services from Bluff to Moab and Salt Lake City (1 daily; $159 one-way per person; ☎ 435 940 4212, ⊛ moabluxurycoach.com).

Visitor centre 232 S Main St (daily except Tues 9am–6pm; ☎ 435 587 3235 or ☎ 800 574 4386, ⊛ utahscanyoncountry .com). Also holds a small museum of frontier life.

ACCOMMODATION AND EATING

Canyonlands Motor Inn 197 N Main St ☎ 435 587 2266, ⊛ canyonlandsutah.com. Run-of-the-mill roadside motel, on the north side of town; adequate rooms at reasonable rates. $55

Inn at the Canyons 533 N Main St ☎ 435 587 2458, ⊛ monticellocanyonlandsinn.com. Monticello's newest motel, opposite the *Peach Tree* on the brow of the hill at the north end of town, with clean, simple, well priced rooms,

plus an indoor pool and hot tub and free breakfasts. $79

MD Ranch Cookhouse 380 S Main St ☎ 435 587 3299. Attractive timber-built restaurant, with wooden furniture and a gift store, that's a bright oasis in such a quiet town. Grilled breakfasts and sandwich lunches, but the real *raison d'être* is big steak dinners, like the $22 rib-eye steak. They also have fish, shrimp, barbecued ribs, and veggie burgers – but no alcohol. Mon–Sat 11am–9pm, Sun 4–9pm.

The Abajo Mountains

The normal route from Monticello to Canyonlands' Needles District, fifty miles northwest, is to take Hwy-211 west from US-191, 22 miles north of town. In summer, however, it's also possible to take a very different approach, through the volcanic **Abajo Mountains**, which rise west of Monticello to over 11,000ft. The straightforward road up, reached by turning left onto Abajo Drive from the west end of 200 South, passes through some lovely quasi-Alpine meadows where you may spot browsing deer. You then veer north and drop down a much rougher track, to meet Hwy-211 near Newspaper Rock (see p.413).

Blanding

BLANDING, just over twenty miles southwest of Monticello, was established as "Grayson" in 1905, when a new irrigation channel brought water to this site from the Abajo Mountains. In 1915, **Thomas Bicknell**, an East Coast millionaire, offered to give a library to any Utah town that would change its name to his own. Two jumped in; Thurber, near Torrey, became Bicknell, while Grayson took his wife's maiden name, Blanding. Each got a new library, though it's said they didn't get as many books as they'd expected.

Having skirted the Abajos, US-191 runs due west as it enters Blanding, and at the four-way stop in the centre of town, makes a sharp dogleg turn south. That brief pause is as much time as most travellers give Blanding, whose broad avenues seldom display much sign of life.

7

Edge of the Cedars State Park

660 West 400 North • Mon–Sat 9am–5pm • $5 • ☎ 435 678 2238, ⓦ stateparks.utah.gov/parks/edge-of-the-cedars

The interesting **Edge of the Cedars State Park**, on the western fringes of Blanding, preserves a pueblo that was occupied between 700 and 1220 AD. In the only excavated section, visitors can climb down a ladder into a musty, haunting *kiva*.

Displays in the park's excellent museum range from the Ancestral Puebloans to the Anglos. In a town with a notorious reputation for illegal pot-hunting by profit-seeking amateurs – or "Moki poachers" – it emphasizes the importance of proper archeology. Some of the Ancestral Puebloan artefacts are truly remarkable, including pots and pendants, stylish wooden plates, and a complete loom dated to 1150 AD.

ARRIVAL AND INFORMATION
BLANDING

Visitor centre 12 N Grayson Parkway (Mon–Sat 8am–7pm, restrooms daily 24hr; ☎ 435 678 3662, ⓦ blandingutah.org). Also holds a good little museum, with some fascinating material on the local Ute.

ACCOMMODATION AND EATING

Abajo Haven Guest Cabins 5440 N Cedar Edge Lane ☎ 435 979 3126, ⓦ abajohaven.com. Comfortable, wonderfully rural rental cabins, six miles north of Blanding, each with one double and two single beds, and heated by solar power. Barbecue dinners available, at $28 for two. **$79**

Four Corners Inn 131 E Center St ☎ 435 678 3257 or ☎ 800 574 3150, ⓦ fourcornersinn.com. Large, modern, two-storey motel, just after the highway doglegs to the right, with some kitchenettes and free continental breakfasts. **$72**

Homestead Steak House 121 E Center St ☎ 435 678 3456. Friendly small-town diner, serving ribs, burgers, chicken and steaks for lunch and dinner in the throbbing epicentre of downtown Blanding. Daily 11.30am–8.30pm.

★ **Stone Lizard Lodging** 88 W Center St ☎ 435 678 3323, ⓦ stonelizardlodging.com. Nicely spruced up by new owners, this very central budget motel offers surprisingly comfortable rooms at excellent rates. **$59**

West of Blanding

A mile or so south of Blanding, at a junction marked only by a solitary gas station, **Hwy-95** heads west from US-191, to embark on a magnificent 120-mile trans-Utah journey to Hanksville. Until it was completed in 1976 – hence its other name, the **Bicentennial Highway** – east–west travel was effectively barred by the massive monocline of **Comb Ridge**, ten miles west of Blanding. To the Navajo, this thousand-foot wall of red rock, stretching eighty miles from north to south, was the backbone of the earth, as well as one of four "arrowheads" protecting their homeland. To Mormon pioneers, it was a definitive "reef" (see p.384). To the modern highway builders, it was an obstacle they simply had to blast their way through.

No towns interrupt Hwy-95 apart from the speck that is **Hite**, 87 miles along at Lake Powell (see p.398). Several side canyons off Hwy-95 bear traces of an Ancestral Puebloan presence, while the cattle ranchers who tried their hands here a century ago were succeeded by uranium miners in the 1950s.

Butler Wash Ruins

Trailhead: roadside parking lot, 10.5 miles west along Hwy-95 from US-191 • 1 mile round-trip; 30min

Butler Wash Ruins, a stimulating Ancestral Puebloan site located on BLM land, can be reached by a simple ten-minute hike from Hwy-95. The trail heads gently but consistently upwards from the parking lot, crossing bare slickrock for its latter half, to reach an overlook facing a side canyon just short of the crest of Comb Ridge. The ruins are in the topmost of three natural rock alcoves; a long stone ledge to the left leads down to the fertile wash where the inhabitants farmed. The complex includes one Kayenta-style square *kiva* and three Mesa Verde-style round *kivas*. Invisible from the overlook, but close at hand to the right, a waterfall ends at a natural stone bridge.

Comb Ridge

Eleven miles west of its intersection with US-191, immediately beyond Butler Wash, Hwy-95 picks its way down the intense red wall of **Comb Ridge** to a cottonwood-rich valley, watered by **Comb Wash**. Confronted by this ridge on their endless journey east, the Hole-in-the-Rock party decided to head south at this point, which explains why they ended up at Bluff (see p.433). Don't copy them, however; a tempting dirt road does branch south from the highway beside the stream, with a nice little campground a short way along, but it soon succumbs to deep drifts of sand no ordinary vehicle could hope to overcome.

Mule Canyon

Atop the plateau seven miles west of Comb Wash, a dirt road signed for Texas Flat leads north from Hwy-95 to two separate trailheads for **Mule Canyon**. The northern sides of each of this shallow canyon's two forks hold several small, well-preserved Ancestral Puebloan **cliff dwellings**. Both forks are around six miles long, but the most interesting ruins are roughly one mile and three miles along the South Fork, so a six-mile day-hike is enough for most visitors. In itself, it's not a difficult walk, but as few hikers pass this way it's important to be prepared for all eventualities. Ask for advice at Kane Gulch Ranger Station (see p.432).

A separate paved turnoff, half a mile along from the Texas Flat road, leads in a few yards to **Mule Canyon Ruin**, a partly restored Ancestral Puebloan pueblo dating from 1000 AD. This small site, a bit too near the highway to be very evocative, is similar to Boulder's Anasazi State Park (see p.382). Its most conspicuous features – a round *kiva* now roofed over for preservation, and a two-storey masonry tower – are connected by an underground tunnel, perhaps used for surprise appearances during religious ceremonies.

Through the Bear's Ears

Before Hwy-95 was constructed, the main road west of Blanding – and the principal access to Natural Bridges (see p.431) – was a dirt track that climbed across the southern fringes of the Abajo Mountains. In reasonable weather, ordinary vehicles can still follow this attractive route, by turning north from Hwy-95 seven miles from the intersection. The 32-mile detour takes well over an hour.

After a cool, pleasant drive through mountain-top woodlands, the road crosses a razorback ridge above Arch Canyon to descend between two rounded outcrops known as the **Bear's Ears**. This prominent landmark is regarded by the Navajo as the embodiment of a bear, guarding the northern limits of their territory. The road eventually switchbacks down a sheer red cliff to join the approach road into Natural Bridges.

Natural Bridges National Monument

4 miles north of Hwy-95, a total of 44 miles west of Blanding · Daily: dawn–dusk · $6 per vehicle · ☎ 435 692 1234, ⓦ nps.gov/nabr

Three of the world's largest natural bridges span the streambeds of the small, unspectacular White and Armstrong canyons, which cut through the white sandstone of **Cedar Mesa** southwest of the Abajo Mountains. **NATURAL BRIDGES NATIONAL MONUMENT** was the loneliest of spots when prospector Cass Hite stumbled across it in the 1880s, and remained all but inaccessible when it became Utah's first federal park in 1908. It's now easily accessed by a four-mile spur road off Hwy-95.

Originally dubbed Edwin, Augusta, and Caroline, the bridges were given Hopi names when it was realized that much of the rock art on the canyon walls represented Hopi clan symbols. This was one of the many places that the Ancestral Puebloan ancestors of the Hopi passed through during their migrations, departing around 1270 AD after a stay of perhaps six hundred years.

Each bridge can be seen from overlooks along the one-way, nine-mile **Bridge View Drive** that loops through the monument. With considerably more effort, you can clamber down into the canyons for closer inspection, and also follow the stream from one to the next for a potential hike of up to nine miles.

Visitor centre

Daily: April & Oct 8am–5pm, May–Sept 8am–6pm, Nov–March 9am–5pm · ☎ 435 692 1234, ⓦ nps.gov/nabr

Excellent displays in Natural Bridges' **visitor centre** explain how the bridges were formed, and you can pick up free trail guides and other background material. It's also the only source of water for the first-come, first-served, 13-site **campground** nearby ($10).

Sipapu Bridge

The first and largest bridge in Natural Bridges National Monument, **Sipapu Bridge**, was named for the "hole" through which the Hopi emerged into this world. Standing at 220ft high by 268ft wide, it is surpassed only by Rainbow Bridge (see p.396). Although the roadside overlook provides a good straight-on view as it thrusts from a tangle of rocks, you'll only really appreciate Sipapu's size if you hike down from the trailhead half a mile further on. The monument's most difficult trail involves three short ladders, two metal staircases, and a couple of stretches of slickrock with steep drop-offs. A ledge halfway down offers the best photos; by the time you're amid the trees directly beneath it, it's too big for most lenses to squeeze it in.

A roadside parking lot just beyond Sipapu marks the start of a half-mile mesa-top trail that leads to a vantage point above **Horsecollar Ruin**. This small Ancestral Puebloan site, tucked into an alcove low on the canyon walls, is not visible from below.

Kachina Bridge

Kachina Bridge is much thicker than Sipapu, being more of a tunnel beneath a broad span of desert-varnish-stained sandstone. Seen from the overlook, it's far less distinct, with rocks rather than sunlight visible through the gap. On the trail down, railings guide you across the slickrock, and there's a crude staircase made from sandstone slabs. The stream at the bottom is lined by splendid cottonwoods, while pictographs near the base of the bridge resemble the *kachinas* of Hopi religion (see p.67).

Owachomo

Natural bridges are short-lived phenomena. Even the oldest in the monument – **Owachomo**, two miles beyond Kachina by road – is a mere five thousand years old, and it's unlikely to last much longer. Though 180ft across, it tapers to just nine feet thick. It now stands slightly to one side of the streambed of Armstrong Canyon, reached by an easy half-mile round-trip hike down from the overlook.

The Streambed Trail
Trailhead: Sipapu Bridge • 8.6 miles; 5hr

In addition to taking the short trails that connect each overlook with the relevant bridge, it's also possible to hike the **Streambed Trail** that connects all three. Meandering along the sandy wash beneath the trees makes a delightful walk, but unless you double back, returning to your starting point involves a long hike across the mesa top, which is not as flat as you'd imagine and offers very little shade. One idea would be to start from Owachomo or Kachina and hike back toward Sipapu, hoping you'll meet up with someone who can give you a ride back to your vehicle.

7 Grand Gulch Primitive Area
March to mid-June, plus Sept & Oct, daily 8am–noon

If you share a passion for archeology with the stamina for long-distance hiking, an expedition into the **GRAND GULCH PRIMITIVE AREA**, south of Natural Bridges, can make you feel like a real-life Indiana Jones. Every twist and turn of this deep, dramatic gorge seems to be filled with relics of its thousand-year occupation by the Ancestral Puebloans, although they abandoned the canyon six centuries before it was named by the Hole-in-the-Rock pioneers.

Grand Gulch gouges across Cedar Mesa for just over fifty miles, dropping 2700ft to meet the San Juan River. There's no access for vehicles; the only path in starts from **Kane Gulch Ranger Station,** on Hwy-261 four miles south of Hwy-95. Typical backpacking expeditions last as long as a week, and you can only camp overnight in the gulch with a permit, which can be obtained between two and ninety days in advance from BLM office, 365 N Main St, Monticello (☎435 587 1510, ⊚blm.gov/ut). So long as your group consists of fewer than eight people, you should be able to pick up a permit at the ranger station on the day you set off. In any case, register there before you set off, even if you're just day-hiking, for which a fee of $2 is levied.

Hiking in Grand Gulch
The trail into Grand Gulch begins by dropping steadily down Kane Gulch, a side canyon that deepens as it goes, and joins Grand Gulch proper four miles along. **Junction Ruin** here, the largest ruin in the canyon system, makes a popular day-hike destination, though **Turkey Pen Ruin**, at 4.7 miles, and **Stimper Arch** just beyond, are also within round-trip reach. If you're making a longer trip, it's possible to leave Grand Gulch via **Bullet Canyon** to the east – in which case a total hike of 23 miles brings you back to Hwy-261 roughly seven miles south of the ranger station – or **Collins Canyon** to the west further along – a 38-mile hike that ends at a dirt road south of Hwy-276. For either route, you'll need a car shuttle to get back to your vehicle, but that's probably easier to arrange than fixing for someone to meet you by boat on the San Juan, the only way out if you hike all the way to the end of Grand Gulch. Most visitors find it simpler just to double back at some point en route.

Kane Gulch Ranger Station can also provide details on day-hikes that head **east** from Hwy-261, into remote side canyons on Cedar Mesa. Road conditions are often treacherous, so don't set off without up-to-the-minute advice.

Muley Point
South of Kane Gulch, Hwy-261 crosses Cedar Mesa for its remaining seventeen miles. Before you take the plunge on the **Moki Dugway**, **MULEY POINT**, exactly five miles west

of its top along a red-dirt road, is an absolute must-see. Note that the turn-off is signposted, but the sign is only conspicuous if you're coming from the north, and that the lesser viewpoint 3.9 miles along is *not* Muley Point.

When they finally get around to declaring all of southern Utah to be one vast national park, Muley Point will surely be the centrepiece. Quite simply, these are among the most stupendous views in the world (though they're at their finest in the morning, when the sun is behind you). You're now at the southernmost tip of Cedar Mesa and the eastern extremity of Glen Canyon NRA. Far below, the San Juan River goosenecks its way west, while the Navajo Nation stretches off on the far side. Features on the horizon include Monument Valley in all its glory, the Sleeping Ute in Colorado, Navajo Mountain, and the cliffs above the west shore of Lake Powell.

The Moki Dugway

Hwy-261 doesn't stand on ceremony when it needs to get down off Cedar Mesa; it just plummets over the edge. The **MOKI DUGWAY**, which drops 1100ft in little more than two miles, is an exhilarating switchback ride, much of it still on a "washboard" strip of gravel, although it feels a whole lot safer now that most of its many hairpin bends are paved. This ancient trail was originally improved by mining companies during the 1950s; you'll just have to hope you don't meet a truck-load of uranium coming the other way. If you have the nerve, the pullouts for vehicles to pass make great viewpoints, but it's best to do all your sightseeing at the top.

Soon after the pavement resumes at the bottom of the Moki Dugway, another dirt road marks the western end of the **Valley of the Gods** (see p.434).

Goosenecks State Park

3.5 miles southwest of Hwy-261 on Hwy-316, a total drive of 8 miles west of Mexican Hat • Daily 24hr • Free

To reach the extraordinary **GOOSENECKS STATE PARK,** look out for inconspicuous **Hwy-316**, which branches away west from Hwy-261 shortly before it meets US-163. Although the railed viewing area at the overlook stands a thousand feet below Cedar Mesa, the **San Juan River** is still another thousand feet down – and it's an amazing sight, looping between huge pyramidal buttes in a textbook example of what geologists call an "entrenched meander." Its serpentine coils – once meanders on a muddy plain, later fixed in stone by the uplifting of the Colorado Plateau – are so extravagant that it flows six miles while advancing little more than one mile west. Above the distant sliver of riverbank greenery, alternate layers of grey limestone and red sandstone stripe the cliffs, while Monument Valley stands out on the skyline.

Bluff

BLUFF, a pretty little riverside settlement whose somewhat humdrum existence belies the extraordinary efforts its founders made to get here, lies 23 miles south of Blanding on US-191. The 230 **Hole-in-the-Rock** pioneers who reached this site on April 6, 1880, had trekked right across the heart of Utah, literally blasting their way through the canyons of the Colorado (see p.378).

Once they arrived, they settled down to a life of ranching and agriculture, made difficult by the San Juan River's propensity to flood. The back streets still hold a dozen or so of their original sturdy homes, making Bluff the region's least spoiled, most authentic town. Its setting is consistently stunning, from the red-rock pinnacles known as the **Navajo Twins**, which mark the mouth of the narrow **Cow Canyon** gorge through which US-191 drops in from the north, to the cottonwoods that line the

7

San Juan River, glinting against the sheer red bluff that rises on the far side. **Ancestral Puebloan** remains abound, including petroglyphs along Hwy-163 to the east, and the unexcavated mound, thought to conceal a buried pueblo, beside the town cemetery on a hillock just north of the centre.

Bluff is very much at the edge of the desert; driving west you soon descend the southern end of **Comb Ridge** (see p.430) into vintage red-rock badlands, with the buttes of Monument Valley silhouetted above the horizon.

TOURS AND ACTIVITIES   BLUFF

Far Out Expeditions (☎435 672 2294, ⓦfaroutexpeditions.net). Customized hiking tours, ranging from half-day jaunts to archeological sites to extended backpacking expeditions.

Wild Rivers Expeditions (☎435 672 2365 or

☎800 422 7654, ⓦriversandruins.com). Bluff is a centre for river-running on the San Juan; rafts put in at Sand Island Recreation Area, 3 miles west. The chief local operator, Wild Rivers runs one-day float trips to Mexican Hat (adults $175, under-13s $133), plus assorted multi-day voyages.

ACCOMMODATION

Bluff may not be the fanciest place in the world, but its **genuine small-town feel** makes it a nicer prospect than any of its neighbours. It's also a handy overnight stop for Hovenweep National Monument, forty miles northeast.

★ **Desert Rose Inn** 701 W Main St ☎435 672 2303 or ☎888 475 7673, ⓦdesertroseinn.com. Modern timber-built motel at the west end of town, holding thirty attractively designed and well-furnished rooms, plus individual cabins of similar standard. $119

Far Out Guest House 700 East & Mulberry ☎435 672 2294, ⓦfaroutexpeditions.net. This historic home holds two guestrooms, each of which has six beds and can be rented by groups of up to six people at progressively increasing rates. Most visitors are here to take one of Far

Out's tours (see p.434). $95

Kokopelli Inn 161 E Main St ☎435 672 2322, ⓦkokoinn.com. Friendly, quiet roadside motel, adjoining a gas station and grocery with a deli counter. $82

Recapture Lodge PO Box 309, Main St ☎435 672 2281, ⓦrecapturelodge.com. Pleasantly rural wooden motel, reaching back toward the river, with a pool; also a few rooms in two old pioneer homes. The owners also offer a shuttle service, including to Monument Valley. $85

EATING

Comb Ridge Coffee 680 W Main St ☎435 672 9931, ⓦcombridgecoffee.com. Espressos and pastries in a buzzy gallery setting, opposite the *Desert Rose* at the southwest end of town; breakfast granola, or a nutty avocado sandwich at lunchtime, cost around $6. Tues–Sun 7am–5pm.

★ **Cottonwood Steakhouse** 409 W Main St ☎435 672 2282, ⓦcottonwoodsteakhouse.com. Open-air barbecue at the west end of town, with wooden tables arranged around a giant cottonwood. A great place to enjoy beer and steaks (priced at up to $25) beneath

the stars – though the menu's a bit short if you're not a beef-eater. One corner of the pseudo-Western stockade serves as Fort Crapper. April, May & Oct 5–9pm, June–Sept 6–10pm.

Twin Rocks Cafe 913 E Navajo Twins Drive ☎435 672 2341, ⓦtwinrockscafe.com. Glass-fronted diner, set against the rocks north of town, just west of US-191. Breakfast bagels and muffins, then salads and sandwiches, and chicken or fajita dinners for $12–15. The adjoining *Trading Post* is well worth exploring. Summer daily 7am–10pm; winter Mon–Sat 8am–9pm.

Valley of the Gods

Dirt road meets US-163 beside Lime Creek, 9 miles northeast of Mexican Hat, and Hwy-261, 10.6 miles northwest of Mexican Hat • Daily dawn-dusk • Free

Visitors to southeast Utah whose appetites have been whetted by Monument Valley can tour similar, smaller-scale monoliths, with no admission fees, in the **VALLEY OF THE GODS**. This "garden" of isolated sandstone columns – said by the Navajo to be petrified warriors – holds no fixed hiking trails. Drivers can see it all from a winding **seventeen-mile dirt road** that connects US-163, west of Bluff, with Hwy-261 near the foot of the Moki Dugway (see p.433).

It's a rough road, which becomes impassable when wet, but if you don't mind a few bangs on the bottom as you cross dry stony washes you should be able to make it in a rental car. The east side holds the best "monuments," and the most difficult terrain, but there's something to be said for driving in from the west, which offers great views all the way along.

ACCOMMODATION   **VALLEY OF THE GODS**

Valley of the Gods B&B Valley of the Gods dirt road, half a mile east of Hwy-261 ☎970 749 1164, ⓦzippitydodah.com/vog. The only building in the valley, squatting in superb isolation, with a superb sunset-view veranda. All of its four rooms have baths, dinner is served by prior arrangement, and the owners can also fix backcountry tours. No internet access. $140

Mexican Hat

MEXICAN HAT, the last stop in southeastern Utah before the start of the Navajo Indian reservation across the San Juan River – and thus the last place you can get a beer – is an appealingly dusty outpost that has never amounted to a town. Having sprung into being in 1901, following false reports that gold had been discovered nearby, it was kept going by a genuine oil strike in 1908 and the uranium boom of the 1950s. It now makes a convenient base for **Monument Valley**, twenty miles south (see p.54).

Mexican Hat Rock, the sandstone sombrero for which the settlement was named, looks down on the San Juan a mile north. The highway passes a few hundred yards west, but a gravel road permits closer inspection. It's at its best in the afternoon, when the sun strikes the amazing zigzag striations of the grey and white cliffs across the river. This pattern, known as the **Navajo Blanket**, is said to show the skin markings of a giant bullsnake that lives in the river below, and carved out the "goosenecks" to the west (see p.433).

7

ACCOMMODATION   **MEXICAN HAT**

All Mexican Hat's four **motels**, except the budget *Canyonlands*, have their own inexpensive restaurants and stores and are substantially the same. There are virtually no other buildings around.

Canyonlands Motel US-163 ☎435 683 2230. Very basic, no-frills ten-room motel, on the higher side of the highway next to the Texaco gas station, and open in summer only. $45

Hat Rock Inn US-163 ☎435 683 2221, ⓦhatrockinn .com. Modern, timber-built motel, 100 yards up from the river, and run by the same family as the nearby *Lodge*. Good quality rooms, an "infinity pool" overlooking the river, and its own Mexican restaurant, the *Hat Rock Café*. Trail rides and jeep tours available. Closed Nov–Feb. $139

★ **Mexican Hat Lodge** US-163 ☎435 683 2222, ⓦwww.mexicanhat.net. Mexican Hat's northernmost motel – a former dance hall – with thirteen rooms of differing sizes. Its open-air *Swingin Steak* restaurant (daily 6–9pm) is everything you could wish for from a cowboy steakhouse, grilling huge perfect steaks over a fire of sweet-smelling wood, at $21 for an 8-oz steak, $36 for an 18-oz. Closed Nov–Jan. $84

San Juan Inn US-163 ☎435 535 2210 or ☎800 447 2022, ⓦsanjuaninn.net. Solid, long-established motel perched fifty feet above the north bank of the San Juan, beside the highway bridge. The *Olde Bridge Grill* serves all meals (daily 7am–9pm), ranging from $9.50 Navajo tacos to $25 steaks, plus cold beers. $94

Las Vegas

442 The Strip

447 Downtown

457 Around Las Vegas

NEW YORK–NEW YORK

Las Vegas

Little emphasis is placed on the gambling clubs and divorce facilities – though they are attractions to many visitors – and much is being done to build up the cultural attractions. No cheap and easily parodied slogans have been adopted to publicize the city, no attempt has been made to introduce pseudo-romantic architectural themes or to give artificial glamour or gaiety. Las Vegas is itself – natural and therefore very appealing to people with a wide variety of interests.   WPA Guidebook to Nevada, 1940

Shimmering from the desert haze of Nevada like a latter-day El Dorado, **LAS VEGAS** is the most dynamic, spectacular city on earth. At the start of the twentieth century, it didn't even exist; now it's home to two million people. Boasting twenty of the world's twenty-seven largest hotels, it's a monument to architectural exuberance, whose flamboyant, no-expense-spared **casinos** lure in forty million tourists each year.

Las Vegas has been stockpiling superlatives since the 1950s, but never rests on its laurels for a moment. Many first-time visitors expect the city to be kitsch, but the casino owners are far too canny to be sentimental about the old days. Yes, there are a few Elvis impersonators around, but what characterizes the city far more is its endless quest for **novelty**. Long before they lose their sparkle, yesterday's showpieces are blasted into rubble, to make way for ever more extravagant replacements. Twenty-five years ago, when the fashion was for fantasy, Arthurian castles and Egyptian pyramids mushroomed along the legendary Strip; next came a craze for constructing entire replica cities, like New York, Paris, Monte Carlo, and Venice; and the current trend is for high-end properties that attempt to straddle the line between screaming ostentation and "elegant" sophistication.

While Las Vegas has cleaned up its act since the early days of Mob domination, there's little truth in the persistent notion that it's become a **family** destination. Neither is it as consistently **cheap** as it used to be. It's still possible to find good, inexpensive rooms, and the all-you-can-eat buffets offer decent value, but the casino owners have long since discovered that high-rollers happy to lose hundreds of dollars per night don't mind paying premium prices to eat at top-quality restaurants, and the newest properties charge room rates closer to $300 than $30 per night.

Although its metropolitan sprawl measures fifteen miles wide by fifteen miles long, few tourists see any more of Las Vegas than the six-mile stretch of **Las Vegas Boulevard** that includes both the **downtown** area, slightly southeast of the intersection of I-15 and US-95, and the **Strip**, home to the major casinos. Your first hours in the city are like entering another world, where the religion is luck, the language is money, and time is measured by revolutions of a roulette wheel. Once you're acclimatized, the whole spectacle can be absolutely exhilarating – assuming you haven't pinned your hopes, and your savings, on the pursuit of a fortune. Even so, while Las Vegas is an unmissable destination, it's also one that palls for most visitors after a couple of (hectic) days.

If you've come solely to gamble, there's not much to say beyond the fact that all the casinos are free and open 24 hours per day, with acres of floor space packed with ways to lose money: **million-dollar slots**, video **poker**, **blackjack**, **craps**, **roulette** wheels, and much, much more. The casinos will just love it if you try to play a system; with the odds stacked against you, your best hope of a large win is to bet your entire stake on one single play, and then stop, win or lose.

Getting married in Las Vegas p.442   **All you can eat** p.452

GONDOLA ON THE VENETIAN'S GRAND CANAL

Highlights

❶ Luxor Festooned in Egyptian motifs, stuffed with corpses and even a chunk of the Titanic, this smoked-glass pyramid epitomizes Las Vegas's postmodern pot-pourri. **See p.443**

❷ New York–New York A loving recreation of the Big Apple in the heart of the Big Cheese. See p.443

❸ The Conservatory The seasonally changing, tongue-in-cheek displays of plants, flowers and assorted oddities at Bellagio's Conservatory are guaranteed to serve up a riot of colour. **See p.445**

❹ Grand Canal Flowing through the heart of the Venetian, the irresistibly absurd Grand Canal is populated by stately, opera-singing gondoliers. **See p.446**

❺ SkyJump In the city's craziest thrill ride, you simply jump from the top of the 1000-foot Stratosphere. **See p.447**

❻ Le Village Buffet Celebrating the varied splendours of French cuisine, the buffet at Paris is perhaps the most imaginative and enjoyable in the city. **See p.452**

❼ Cirque du Soleil With Love, O, Mystère, and KÀ, plus plenty more besides, the exhilarating Canadian troupe dominates Las Vegas' entertainment scene. **See p.455**

❽ Jubilee A throwback to the great days of ostrich feathers and showgirls galore, this gloriously kitsch spectacular is truly something to savour. **See p.466**

HIGHLIGHTS ARE MARKED ON THE MAP ON P.440

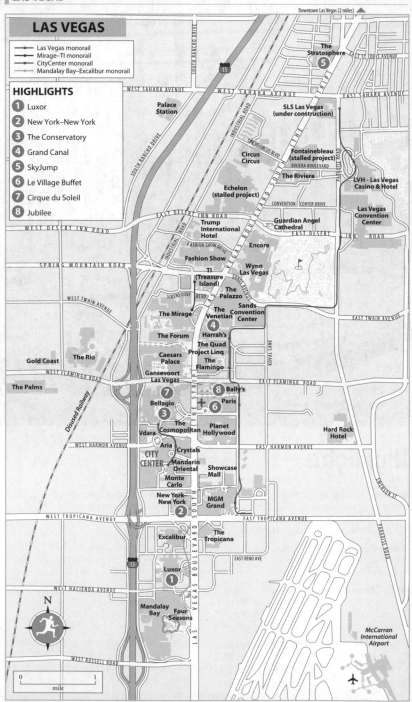

Downtown Las Vegas (2 miles) ▲

LAS VEGAS

- ●━━● Las Vegas monorail
- ●━━● Mirage–TI monorail
- ●━━● CityCenter monorail
- ●━━● Mandalay Bay–Excalibur monorail

HIGHLIGHTS

1 Luxor
2 New York–New York
3 The Conservatory
4 Grand Canal
5 SkyJump
6 Le Village Buffet
7 Cirque du Soleil
8 Jubilee

The Stratosphere 5

EAST ST LOUIS AVENUE

WEST SAHARA AVENUE — WEST SAHARA AVENUE — EAST SAHARA AVENUE

SOUTH RANCHO DRIVE

SOUTH RANCHO DRIVE

INDUSTRIAL ROAD

THE STRIP

LAS VEGAS BOULEVARD SOUTH

Palace Station

SLS Las Vegas (under construction)

Circus Circus

CIRCUS CIRCUS BLVD

Fontainebleau (stalled project)

RIVIERA BOULEVARD

The Riviera

LVH - Las Vegas Casino & Hotel

Echelon (stalled project)

CONVENTION CENTER DRIVE

Las Vegas Convention Center

EAST DESERT INN ROAD

Trump International Hotel

Guardian Angel Cathedral

WEST DESERT INN ROAD

EAST DESERT INN ROAD

FASHION SHOW DRIVE

Encore

Fashion Show

SPRING MOUNTAIN ROAD

TI (Treasure Island)

SIRENS COVE BLVD

Wynn Las Vegas

WEST TWAIN AVENUE

The Palazzo

SANDS AVENUE

EAST TWAIN AVENUE

The Mirage

The Venetian

Sands Convention Center

8

The Forum

Harrah's

4

Gold Coast

The Rio

Caesars Palace

The Quad

Project Linq

KOVAL LANE

The Palms

Gansevoort Las Vegas

The Flamingo

WEST FLAMINGO ROAD

EAST FLAMINGO ROAD

Disused Railway

7

Bellagio

8 Bally's

+ 6 Paris

3

The Cosmopolitan

Planet Hollywood

Hard Rock Hotel

Vdara

WEST HARMON AVENUE

Aria

Crystals

EAST HARMON AVENUE

CITY CENTER

Mandarin Oriental

Showcase Mall

Monte Carlo

New York–New York

2

MGM Grand

WEST TROPICANA AVENUE

EAST TROPICANA AVENUE

PARADISE ROAD

SWENSON ST

Excalibur

The Tropicana

EAST RENO AVE

I-15

Luxor 1

WEST HACIENDA AVENUE

N

Mandalay Bay

Four Seasons

McCarran International Airport

WEST RUSSELL ROAD

0   1
          mile

Brief history

Las Vegas has a shorter history than almost any other city in the world. The only US city founded in the twentieth century to boast over a million inhabitants, it's also the only one that has consistently prioritized the need to attract visitors over the quality of life of its own residents.

The name *Las Vegas* – Spanish for "the meadows" – originally applied to natural springs where from 1829 onwards travellers on the Old Spanish Trail would halt. For the rest of the nineteenth century, the Paiute Indians shared the region with Mormon ranchers, and the valley had a population of just thirty in 1900. Things changed in 1905, with the completion of the now-defunct rail link between Salt Lake City and Los Angeles. Las Vegas itself was founded on May 15 that year, when the railroads auctioned off lots around what's now Fremont Street.

The growth of gambling

Ironically, Nevada was the first state to outlaw gambling, in 1909. It was made legal once more in 1931, however, and the workers who built the nearby **Hoover Dam** flocked to Las Vegas to bet away their pay-packets. Providing cheap electricity and water, the dam amounted to a massive federal subsidy for the infant city. Hotel-casinos such as the daring 65-room **El Rancho** began to appear in the early 1940s, but the Midwest Mafia were the first to appreciate the potential for profit. Mobster **Bugsy Siegel** raised $7 million to open the **Flamingo** in December 1946; early losses soon forced him to close again, and although he swiftly managed to reopen, his erstwhile partners were dissatisfied enough with their returns to have him murdered in LA in June 1947.

By the 1950s, Las Vegas was booming. The military had arrived – mushroom clouds from **A-bomb tests** in the deserts were visible from the city, and visitors would drive out with picnics to get a better view – and so too had big guns like **Frank Sinatra**, who debuted at the *Desert Inn* in 1951, and **Liberace**, paid $50,000 to open the *Riviera* in 1955. As the stars gravitated toward the Vegas honeypot, nightclubs across America went out of business, and the city became the nation's undisputed live-entertainment capital.

Las Vegas reinvented

The beginning of the end for Mob rule came in 1966, after reclusive tycoon **Howard Hughes** sold Trans World Airlines for $500 million and moved into the *Desert Inn*. When the owners tired of his non-gambling ways, he simply bought the hotel, and his clean-cut image encouraged other entrepreneurs to follow suit. **Elvis** arrived a little later, starting a triumphant five-year stint as a karate-kicking lounge lizard at the *International* in 1969.

Endless federal swoops and stings drove the Mob out of sight by the 1980s, in time for Vegas to reinvent itself on a surge of junk-bond megadollars. The success of Steve Wynn's **Mirage** in enticing a new generation of visitors, from 1989 onward, spawned a host of imitators. *Excalibur* and the *MGM Grand* were followed by *Luxor* and *New York–New York* and then, as the millennium approached, by the opulent quartet of **Bellagio**, *Mandalay Bay*, the *Venetian*, and *Paris*. Although the 21st century started with shockwaves, when Steve Wynn was forced to sell *Bellagio* and the *Mirage* to the MGM group, and 9/11 triggered a major downturn, Las Vegas bounced back. The **Venetian** has gone from strength to strength as the flagship for all that the city does best; Wynn himself opened his biggest casino yet, **Wynn Las Vegas**; and MGM Resorts saw the colossal **CityCenter** development through to completion, even as the storm clouds of recession were appearing on the horizon.

GETTING MARRIED IN LAS VEGAS

Second only to making your fortune as a reason to visit Las Vegas is the prospect of **getting married**. Over 120,000 weddings are performed here each year, many so informal that bride and groom just wind down the window of their car during the ceremony. Though a Vegas wedding has become a byword for tongue-in-cheek chic, however, most marriages are deeply formal affairs, and casinos and independent chapels alike compete to offer elaborate ceremonies with all the trimmings.

Assuming you're at least 18 years old and carrying picture ID, you don't have to be a local resident or take a blood test. Simply turn up at the **Clark County Marriage Licence Bureau**, downtown at 201 E Clark Ave (daily 8am–midnight; ☎ 702 671 0600, ⓦ clarkcountynv.gov), and buy a marriage licence for $60 cash. You can then walk over to the office of the **Commissioner for Civil Marriages**, at 330 S Third St (Mon–Thurs & Sun 2–6pm, Fri 10am–9pm, Sat 12.30–9pm; ☎ 702 671 0577), and pay another $50 cash to have the ceremony itself performed.

Reckon on paying at least $200 for the most basic service in a wedding chapel, which is liable to be as romantic a process as checking in at a hotel, and to take about as long. The full deluxe service ranges up to whatever you can afford.

WEDDING CHAPELS

Graceland Wedding Chapel 619 S Las Vegas Blvd ☎ 702 382 0091, ⓦ gracelandchapel.com. Home of the King – Elvis will act as best man, give the bride away, or serenade you, but unfortunately he can't perform the service. Daily 9am–11pm.

Little Church of the West S 4617 Las Vegas Blvd S ☎ 702 739 7971, ⓦ littlechurchlv.com. This fifty-year-old chapel has moved progressively down the Strip to its current site south of *Mandalay Bay*. Among the quieter places to exchange Vegas vows. Daily 8am–11pm.

Little White Chapel 1301 Las Vegas Blvd S ☎ 702 382 5943, ⓦ alittlewhitechapel.com. The chapel (indeed, little and white) where Bruce Willis and Demi Moore married each other, and Michael Jordan and Joan Collins married other people. For those in a major hurry, they offer drive-through ceremonies in the "Tunnel of Love". Daily 8am–midnight.

The Strip

For its razor-edge finesse in harnessing sheer, magnificent excess to the deadly serious business of making money, there's no place like the **Las Vegas Strip**. It's hard to imagine that Las Vegas was once an ordinary city, and Las Vegas Boulevard a dusty thoroughfare scattered with the usual edge-of-town motels. After almost seven decades of capitalism run riot, with each new casino-hotel setting out to surpass anything its neighbours ever dreamed of, the Strip remains locked into a hyperactive drive for thrills and glamour, forever discarding its latest toy in its frenzy for the next jackpot.

Each casino is a self-contained fantasyland of high camp and genuine excitement, where the action keeps going day and night, and you rapidly lose track of which is which. Until recently, the casinos deliberately made it difficult to find your way back out onto the streets. Now that much of the Strip is owned by just two giant corporations – MGM Resorts and Caesars Entertainment – they're much happier to let you stroll from each to the next, and there's plenty of action outdoors as well as in. In summer, though, the scorching heat of day is often too much to take; night is the best time to venture out, when the neon's blazing at its brightest.

Mandalay Bay

3950 Las Vegas Blvd S • ☎ 702 632 7777, ⓦ mandalaybay.com • **Shark Reef** Daily 10am–10pm • $18, under-13s $12 • ☎ 702 632 4555, ⓦ sharkreef.com

Glowing like beacons as their gilded windows commandeer the sunset, the twin forty-storey sentinels of **Mandalay Bay** soar above the southern limits of the Strip. Financed through the profits from its neighbours, *Luxor* and *Excalibur, Mandalay Bay* opened in 1999 and is more upmarket than either, kept lively at night by its excellent restaurants, bars, clubs and shows.

During the day, all it has to offer the casual sightseer is the **Shark Reef** aquarium, a long walk from the Strip at the back of the property. The emphasis here is more on eye-catching monsters than education, with the basic premise that you're exploring a steamy, half-submerged temple complex, encountering yellow crocodiles, Komodo Dragons and (of course) sharks. Despite the substantial price, it's nowhere near the scale of a major aquarium; many visitors scoot through in around twenty minutes.

Luxor

3900 Las Vegas Blvd S · ☎ 702 262 4444, ⓦ luxor.com · **Bodies** Daily 10am–10pm, last admission 9pm · $32, under-14s $23 · ☎ 702 262 4400, ⓦ bodiestheexhibition.com · **Titanic** Daily 10am–10pm · $32, over-64s $30, ages 4–12 $24 · ☎ 702 492 3960, ⓦ rmstitanic.net

Guarded by an impassive Sphinx, the 350-foot black-glass pyramid of **Luxor** stands a block north of *Mandalay Bay*. While it remains an astonishing building, it has been stripped of most of its original ancient Egyptian trappings, and rebranded as the sort of "hip," upscale casino resort that now dominates the Strip. Its upstairs Atrium Level houses two intriguing permanent exhibitions: **Bodies**, an eye-catching but ultimately sobering collection of genuine but "plastinated" human corpses, and **Titanic**, featuring not just artefacts and reconstructions but the huge "Big Piece" of the doomed liner, complete with portholes, recovered from two miles down in the Atlantic Ocean.

Excalibur

3850 Las Vegas Blvd S · ☎ 702 597 7777, ⓦ excalibur.com

Luxor's architect, Veldon Simpson, had previously designed **Excalibur**, immediately to the north of *Luxor*. A less-sophisticated mock-up of a medieval castle, complete with drawbridge, crenellated towers, and a basement stuffed with fairground-style sideshows for the kids, it's usually packed out with low-budget tour groups.

MGM Grand

3799 Las Vegas Blvd S · ☎ 702 891 7777, ⓦ mgmgrand.com · **CSI: The Experience** Daily 9am–9pm, last admission 7.30pm · $28, ages 4–11 $21 · ☎ 702 891 7006, ⓦ csiexhibit.com

Considering that it was built as the world's largest hotel and is still growing, the **MGM Grand** presents a remarkably small frontage to the Strip. Instead its colossal size only becomes apparent once you're inside, perhaps after you've been walking for twenty minutes and are still nowhere near where you want to go. Created by Veldon Simpson, responsible for both *Luxor* and *Excalibur*, it's bigger than the two combined. Despite its fine array of restaurants and shows, it holds few attractions for sightseers other than the enjoyable, self-paced **CSI: The Experience**, in which participants attempt to solve a murder mystery by inspecting the crime scene and then undertaking detailed lab work.

New York–New York

3790 Las Vegas Blvd S · ☎ 702 740 6969, ⓦ newyorknewyork.com · **Roller Coaster** Mon–Thurs & Sun 11am–11pm, Fri & Sat 10.30am–midnight · $14 first ride, $25 for an all-day pass

The intersection of Las Vegas Boulevard and Tropicana Avenue is said to be the busiest traffic junction in the US. Its northwest corner, diagonally opposite the veteran *Tropicana*, is occupied by an exuberantly meticulous recreation of the Big Apple, **New York–New York**. This miniature Manhattan – built vertically, like the original, in response to space limitations – boasts a skyline featuring twelve separate skyscrapers and is fronted, of course, by the Statue of Liberty.

8

Unusually, the interior too is carefully realized, with some nice Art Deco flourishes and entertaining nightlife options in its Greenwich Village area. In one respect, it even surpasses New York itself: you can swoop around the whole thing at 65mph, inside and out, in the little yellow cabs of its hair-raising **Roller Coaster**.

CityCenter

The enormous **CityCenter** complex was unveiled in 2009 between the *Monte Carlo* and *Bellagio*, as a bold attempt by MGM Resorts to reshape Las Vegas' urban landscape. The exciting new theme here is that there is no theme: CityCenter is supposedly the kind of project that might be built in any city. Focussing on the **Aria** casino, set back from the Strip, and the Strip-front **Crystals** shopping mall, it's intended to mark the moment that Las Vegas stops thinking in straight lines, and steps away from building an endless progression of casinos, marching down the Strip, in favour of branching out to create new multi-purpose districts. To many people's surprise, it has quietly prospered so far, though the jury's still out as to whether it will prove that Las Vegas has finally come of age, or ultimately crash in the face of recession.

The most striking aspect of CityCenter for visitors is its abundant contemporary artworks, and especially **sculpture**. Big names include Claes Oldenburg, represented by the outsized steel-and-fibreglass typewriter eraser beside the *Mandarin Oriental*; Henry Moore, whose abstract Reclining Connected Forms (1969–74) fills the "pocket park" between *Aria* and Crystals; and Maya Lin, responsible for the gleaming 84ft Colorado River, cast in reclaimed silver, above *Aria*'s check-in desks.

Aria
3730 Las Vegas Blvd S • ☎ 702 590 7111, ⓦ arialasvegas.com

CityCenter's centrepiece, the 4004-room **Aria**, flaunts a new modernist aesthetic that makes its plush marble-clad predecessors seem suddenly old and tired. And yet there's only so far you can take minimalism when you also have a casino to run, filled with slot machines, gaming tables, and glamorous trappings. Approaching from the Strip, your first impression will be of several curving glass skyscrapers, which turn out to be connected to form a single structure, and fronted by a fountain that spurts multi-coloured pulses of water. Once inside, you're plunged into much the same artificially lit gloom that characterizes most Las Vegas casinos.

The Cosmopolitan
3708 Las Vegas Blvd S • ☎ 702 698 7000, ⓦ cosmopolitanlasvegas.com

The glittering **Cosmopolitan** casino, which from the Strip sidewalk looks like it must surely be the main entrance to CityCenter, is actually nothing of the sort – it's an entirely separate, independent entity. With irresistible chutzpah, its owners bought up a former parking lot that had somehow escaped MGM's clutches, squeezed a brand-new modern casino on top of it, and packed it with lively clubs and bars and top-notch restaurants. Completed in 2010, it's almost the only property on the Strip that still follows the old fly-trap principle – once you're in it, it can be almost impossible to find your way out again.

Bellagio
3600 Las Vegas Blvd S • ☎ 702 693 7111, ⓦ bellagio.com

In 1998, Steve Wynn unveiled **Bellagio** as his attempt to build the best hotel in world history. It is undeniably a breathtaking achievement, striving to be somehow more authentic than the original town on Lake Como. The trouble is that *Bellagio* is not in Italy; it's in Las Vegas, and stuffed full of slot machines. The main hotel block, a stately curve of blue and cream pastels, stands aloof from the Strip behind an eight-acre artificial lake in which hundreds of submerged fountains erupt from two to four times each hour after dark in Busby-Berkeley water-ballets, choreographed with booming music and coloured lights.

Otherwise, *Bellagio*'s proudest boasts are the **Via Bellagio**, a covered mall of impossibly glamorous designer boutiques, and its opulent **Conservatory**, where a network of flowerbeds beneath a Belle Epoque canopy of copper-framed glass is replanted every few weeks with ornate seasonal displays.

Planet Hollywood

3667 Las Vegas Blvd S · ☎ 702 785 5555, ⓦ planethollywoodresort.com

Planet Hollywood is a remodelled version of the former *Aladdin*, which hit the rocks in 2004. In keeping with the latest generation of casinos, it's all geared towards a young crowd, with a screaming loud decor it calls "Hollywood Hip." The mile-long **Miracle Mile Shops**, wrapped in a figure-eight around the casino and its theatre, is among the Strip's more affordable shopping malls, but short on decent eating options.

Paris

3655 Las Vegas Blvd S · ☎ 877 603 4386, ⓦ parislasvegas.com · **Eiffel Tower** Daily 9.30am–12.30am · $10.50 daytime, $15.50 evening

Paris was the 1999 handiwork of the same designers as *New York–New York*. With a half-size **Eiffel Tower** straddling the Arc de Triomphe and the Opera, it all feels a little compressed, but the attention to detail is a joy. There's also a fine assortment of top-notch French restaurants. Elevators soar through the roof of the casino and up to the summit of the Eiffel Tower – cheekily positioned to enjoy a perfect prospect of *Bellagio* – for stunning views of the city, at their best after dark.

Caesars Palace

3570 Las Vegas Blvd S · ☎ 866 227 5938, ⓦ caesarspalace.com

Across Flamingo Road from *Bellagio* – this is the intersection where Tupac Shakur was gunned down in 1996 – **Caesars Palace** still encapsulates Las Vegas at its best, almost fifty years since it opened. Outside, ever more bars and restaurants fill extensive open-air patios, while the interior is filled with grand marble staircases that lead nowhere, and full-size replicas of Michelangelo's *David*, into a vast labyrinth of slots and green baize, peopled by strutting half-naked Roman centurions and Cleopatra-cropped waitresses. Above the stores and restaurants of the **Forum**, the blue-domed ceiling dims and glows as it endlessly cycles from dawn to dusk and back again. The mall itself is now three storeys tall, but you may have to hurry to see the gloriously kitsch "living statues" who inhabit its various fountains; they seem to be disappearing into the netherworld at an alarming rate.

Project Linq

The stretch of the Strip immediately across from *Caesars Palace* has long been home to a row of veteran casinos that include the **Flamingo** and **Harrah's**. All belong these days to Caesars Entertainment, which set about transforming the area from 2012 onwards. Work on the so-called **Project Linq** was still underway as this book went to press, but so far the Asian-themed *Imperial Palace* had been "re-skinned" and rebranded as **The Quad**, while the much smaller *Bill's Gamblin' Hall* was closed, and scheduled to reopen as **Gansevoort Las Vegas**, focussing on a new rooftop nightclub. The centrepiece of the whole development will be a 550-ft big wheel, the **Las Vegas High Roller**, which although set well back from the Strip is promised to offer superb views.

The Mirage

3400 Las Vegas Blvd S · ☎ 702 791 7111, ⓦ mirage.com · **Secret Garden & Dolphin Habitat** Daily 10am–7pm · $20, ages 4–12 $15

Night-time crowds jostle for space on the sidewalk outside the glittering **Mirage**, beyond *Caesars*, to watch the volcano that erupts every fifteen minutes, spewing water and fire into the lagoon below. Although veteran magicians Siegfried and Roy were finally driven into retirement by Roy's near-fatal accident in 2003, their trademark white tigers can still be seen in the *Mirage*'s spacious **Secret Garden & Dolphin Habitat**.

TI (Treasure Island)

3300 Las Vegas Blvd S · ☎ 702 894 7111, ⓦ treasureisland.com · **Sirens of TI** Every 90min after dark · Free

The casino known as both **TI** and **Treasure Island** epitomizes the changing face of Las Vegas. When Steve Wynn built it in 1993, using the first profits from the *Mirage* next door, the city was in thrall to the notion that it was about to become a child-friendly destination. Its entire lower facade was sculpted into a novelty attraction – an intricate, pastel-pretty seafront village straight out of *Pirates of the Caribbean*. The pirate galleon and British frigate moored outside still do noisy battle every night; ludicrously enough the sailors these days are no longer gnarled buccaneers but the scantily clad **Sirens of TI**. *Treasure Island* was sold off to raise funds to build CityCenter, and with its lovingly crafted fripperies stripped away, it has now turned into an incongruous blue-collar resort, all country honky-tonks and party bars.

8

The Venetian

3355 Las Vegas Blvd S · ☎ 702 414 1000, ⓦ venetian.com · **Madame Tussaud's** Mon–Thurs & Sun 10am–9.30pm, Fri & Sat 10am–10.30pm · $26, ages 7–12 $16 · ☎ 866 841 3739, ⓦ mtvegas.com

Across the Strip from TI, the facade of the **Venetian** includes loving facsimiles of six major Venice buildings, as well as the Rialto Bridge and the Bridge of Sighs. The main emphasis in the casino itself is on the **Grand Canal Shoppes**, reached via a stairwell topped by vivid frescoes copied from yet more Venice originals. The ludicrous recreation of the **Grand Canal** at the top, complete with gondolas and singing gondoliers ($16 a ride), is quintessential Las Vegas, and as such utterly irresistible – it's *upstairs*, for God's sake.

When the Venetian first opened, it held two much-publicized outposts of the Guggenheim Museum. Both, sadly, have now closed, leaving just a ridiculously expensive branch of **Madame Tussaud's** waxwork museum where the main attraction is the opportunity to have your photo taken with President Obama in a replica Oval Office.

The adjoining **Palazzo** can be entered either via the Grand Canal Shoppes or directly from the Strip. Officially, it's regarded as being a resort in its own right, but it's remarkably devoid of any identity, and just feels like a big, bland mall.

Wynn Las Vegas

3131 Las Vegas Blvd S · ☎ 702 770 7000, ⓦ wynnlasvegas.com

Wynn Las Vegas was built by Steve Wynn on the site of the vanished *Desert Inn*, using all the fortune he accrued by building and selling the *Mirage* and *Bellagio*. In a nutshell, it's *Bellagio* re-imagined for a younger, hipper and even richer crowd, with a shift away from European elegance in favour of contemporary Asian design. The resort is partly obscured behind an artificial tree-covered mountain; once you find your way inside, you find that's the backdrop for the enormous **Lake of Dreams**, an "environmental theatre" in which ethereal sculpted figures emerge from a large expanse of water, in front of a massive waterfall that continually changes colour.

The interior of *Wynn Las Vegas* is a riot of colour, with spectacular patterns and motifs sprawling all over carpets, mosaics and tiles and a central atrium filled with sparkling trees and dazzling flowers. It has all proved profitable enough for the original hotel tower to be joined by a second, taller tower, dubbed **Encore** and clad in the same glossy "Wynn Bronze."

Circus Circus

2880 Las Vegas Blvd S · ☎ 702 734 0410, ⓦ circuscircus.com · **Adventuredome** Mon–Thurs 11am–6pm, Fri & Sat 10am–midnight, Sun 10am–9pm; daily 10am–midnight in school hols; $5–8 individual attractions, $28 all-day wristband, children under 4ft $17 · ☎ 702 734 0410, ⓦ adventuredome.com · **Chuck Jones Experience** Daily 10am–10pm · $20, ages 5–17 $15 · ☎ 702 224 2580, ⓦ chuckjonesexperience.com

A rare constant in the ever-changing world of Las Vegas, **Circus Circus** has remained true to itself for nigh-on fifty years. Back in the 1960s, combining children's entertainment with casino gambling under a single roof was a radical concept. Later on, that idea was embraced as a surefire money-spinning formula. When it subsequently became a discredited cliché, *Circus Circus* carried on regardless. Since the recession hit, and the stalwarts along this portion of the Strip were destroyed to build replacements that never materialized, pedestrian traffic hereabouts has plummeted, and *Circus Circus* finally seems to be running into the rails.

For kids, though, *Circus Circus* still holds a couple of enjoyable distractions – the indoor **Adventuredome** theme park, sheltered beneath a huge bubble of pink glass, and the **Chuck Jones Experience**, an interactive celebration of the great animator and his creations, including Bugs Bunny and Daffy Duck.

8

The Stratosphere

2000 Las Vegas Blvd S · ☎ 702 380 7777, ⓦ stratospherehotel.com · **Tower** Mon–Thurs & Sun 10am–1am, Fri & Sat 10am–2am · $18, discounts for guests · **Thrill rides** Mon–Thurs & Sun 11am–1am, Fri & Sat 11am–2am · X-Scream, Big Shot & Insanity $15 each, $34 for an all-day package; SkyJump $110, minimum age 14

At 1149ft, the **Stratosphere** is the tallest building west of the Mississippi. The outdoor deck near its summit offers amazing panoramas across the city, while assorted wonderfully demented **thrill rides** can take you even closer to heaven. Insanity and X-Scream dangle riders over the edge, strapped into individual seats and in a precarious gondola respectively; and the terrifying Big Shot is an open-air couch that shunts to the top of an additional 160-foot spire, then free-falls down again. As for the **SkyJump** – a "controlled free-fall", more like a zip line than a bungee jump – you simply jump off the top and plummet 855ft.

Downtown

As the Strip has evolved from strength to strength, **downtown** Las Vegas, the city's original core, has been neglected. Long known as "Glitter Gulch," it never really was a "downtown" in the conventional sense, having never held many stores or businesses apart from its few compact blocks of lower-key casinos. It is, however, forever attempting to recast itself as a genuine rival to the Strip. In the **Fremont Street Experience**, five entire blocks of its central street have been roofed over to form a "Celestial Vault", studded with over twelve million LED nodules to create a screen that's illuminated in dazzling nightly displays (hourly, sunset–midnight; free). The casinos here are lower-key than on the Strip, and much more devoted to the serious business of gambling; the only one that comes even close to matching the Strip giants is the **Golden Nugget**.

Slotzilla

Unveiled in 2013, **Slotzilla** is an extraordinary two-tier **zipline** that centres on what's claimed – at 120 feet tall – to be the world's biggest slot machine. This huge contraption ejects four riders at a time on each level, who zoom east–west along the full length of Fremont Street, to land at Main Street. Riders on the upper level hang prone, enabling them to fly like Superman, and pass through holes cut into the canopy of the Fremont Street Experience.

The Mob Museum

300 Stewart Ave · Sun–Thurs 10am–7pm, Fri & Sat 10am–8pm · $18, ages 5–17 $12 · ☎ 702 229 2734, ⓦ themobmuseum.org

The latest bid by former Mayor Oscar Goodman – himself a lawyer who defended Mob-linked figures in court – to bring tourists downtown, the intriguing **Mob Museum** opened in 2012. Filling three storeys of a former courthouse, it explores the ongoing fear and fascination of the underworld figures who once dominated the city, with plenty of gory detail amid its high-minded displays.

INFORMATION   LAS VEGAS

Visitor centre 3150 Paradise Rd, east of the Strip, but not worth visiting (Mon–Fri 8am–5pm; ☎ 877 847 4858).
Websites Useful sources of information include the city's official website, ⓦ visitlasvegas.com, and sites such as ⓦ lasvegascitylife.com, ⓦ lasvegassun.com, ⓦ lasvegasweekly.com, and ⓦ lvol.com.

ARRIVAL AND DEPARTURE

By plane McCarran International Airport is a mile east of the southern end of the Strip, and four miles from downtown. Some hotels run free shuttle buses for guests, while Bell Trans (☎ 702 739 7990, ⓦ bell-trans.com) runs minibuses to the Strip ($7.50) and downtown ($10). Taxi fares from the airport can vary enormously; broadly speaking, expect to pay around $20 to reach casinos at the southern end of the Strip, $30 or more for casinos further north or downtown.
By bus Long-distance Greyhound buses arrive at 200 S Main St downtown.

GETTING AROUND

Traffic is so bad in Las Vegas that if you've just come to explore the Strip, it's not worth renting a car. Be warned, though, that on summer days it's **too hot to walk** more than a couple of blocks along the Strip.

By bus Both the most useful routes on the RTC network (ⓦ catride.com) – the Deuce on the Strip (daily 24hr) and the faster Strip & Downtown Express or SDX (daily 9am–12.30am) – run the full length of the Strip and connect with downtown. Buy tickets before you board; 2hr pass $5, 24hr pass $7, 3-day pass $20.
By monorail The overpriced and less-than-convenient Las Vegas Monorail runs along the eastern side of the Strip from the *MGM Grand* to the defunct *Sahara* (Mon–Thurs 7am–2am, Fri–Sun 7am–3am; single trip $5, 1-day pass $12; ⓦ lvmonorail.com), but doesn't go to the airport or downtown. Separate, free monorail systems also link *Mandalay Bay* with *Excalibur* via *Luxor*, the *Monte Carlo* with *Bellagio* via *CityCenter*, and the *Mirage* with *TI*.

ACCOMMODATION

Although Las Vegas has well over 160,000 motel and hotel rooms, it's best to book **accommodation** ahead if you're on a tight budget, or arriving on Friday or Saturday; upwards of two hundred thousand people descend on the city every weekend. Even if you stay in the same room for several days, you'll be charged a different rate for each day, depending on the day of the week, and what's going on in town. The only sure-fire way to get a cut-price room is to **visit during the week** rather than on the weekend. Rates rise enormously on Friday or Saturday, by at least $50 extra in a lower-end property, well over $100 in the big-name casinos. On top of that, many hotels won't accept Saturday arrivals. **Room taxes** add an additional thirteen percent downtown, twelve percent elsewhere. Almost all hotels also add so-called **resort fees** of $15–25 per day.

THE STRIP

Aria 3730 Las Vegas Blvd S ☎866 359 7757 or ☎702 590 7111, ⓦarialasvegas.com. The chocolate-brown and gold-toned guest rooms feel subdued and somewhat anonymous by Las Vegas standards, but with their high-end amenities, *Aria* can be a real bargain on weekdays, especially if you have the time – and weather – to enjoy the superb pool complex. Resort fee $25. Mon–Thurs & Sun $169, Fri & Sat $259

Bellagio 3600 Las Vegas Blvd S ☎888 987 6667 or ☎702 693 7111, ⓦbellagio.com. No longer state-of-the-art, but still at the top end of the Vegas spectrum. Plush European furnishings and marble bathrooms now give *Bellagio*'s luxurious rooms a slightly retro feel; some face the fountains at the front, others the superb pool complex. Resort fee $25. Mon–Thurs & Sun $199, Fri & Sat $269

Caesars Palace 3570 Las Vegas Blvd S ☎866 227 5938, ⓦcaesarspalace.com. The older rooms in this epitome of 1960s luxury still burst with pseudo-Roman splendour, while those in the newer towers are more conventionally elegant. Resort fee $25. Mon–Thurs & Sun $209, Fri & Sat $299

Circus Circus 2880 Las Vegas Blvd S ☎800 634 3450 or ☎702 734 0410, ⓦcircuscircus.com. Venerable hotel, popular with budget tour groups. Kids love the theme park and (almost) non-stop circus acts, adults love the low room rates. Rooms in the motel-like Manor section at the back are pretty grim; pay a little more to stay in one of the Towers instead. Resort fee $9. Mon–Thurs & Sun $29, Fri & Sat $94

★ **The Cosmopolitan** 3708 Las Vegas Blvd S ☎702 698 7000, ⓦcosmopolitanlasvegas.com. While it's far from cheap, this very central new casino is for once on a manageable scale, and offers smart modern rooms in the very thick of things, plus great restaurants and nightlife. Resort fee $25. Mon–Thurs & Sun $180, Fri & Sat $270

Encore Las Vegas 3121 Las Vegas Blvd S ☎888 320 7125 or ☎702 770 8000, ⓦencorelasvegas.com. Setting Las Vegas' current standard for high-end luxury, *Encore* ever-so-slightly raised the bar above its adjoining older sister *Wynn*. Rooms are plush and colourful, though not quite as red as the public areas downstairs, and the pool (sorry, "Beach Club") is the best in town. Resort fee $25. Mon–Thurs & Sun $209, Fri & Sat $399

★ **Excalibur** 3850 Las Vegas Blvd S ☎877 750 5464 or ☎702 597 7777, ⓦexcalibur.com. While the 4000 rooms in this garish fake castle can be very ordinary indeed, the much nicer modernized "wide-screen rooms", typically costing $10 extra, are excellent value. Thanks to an endless stream of tour groups and families, the whole place is often uncomfortably crowded. Resort fee $15. Mon–Thurs & Sun $36, Fri & Sat $120

The Flamingo 3555 Las Vegas Blvd S ☎888 902 9929 or ☎702 733 3111, ⓦflamingolasvegas.com. Bugsy Siegel's oft-renovated *Flamingo* has dropped well below the premier league. The tropical-themed pool complex is great, but the actual rooms vary enormously; some have real flair, but the standard ones can be very shabby indeed. Resort fee $18. Mon–Thurs & Sun $85, Fri & Sat $175

★ **Luxor Las Vegas** 3900 Las Vegas Blvd S ☎877 386 4658 or ☎702 262 4444, ⓦluxor.com. All two thousand rooms in this vast smoked-glass pyramid have tremendous views – and they're much larger than usual. Unlike the extra two thousand rooms in the newer tower next door, however, most have showers, not baths. Resort fee $18. Mon–Thurs & Sun $65, Fri & Sat $125

Mandalay Bay 3950 Las Vegas Blvd S ☎877 632 7800 or ☎702 632 7777, ⓦmandalaybay.com. This upscale, young-adult playground is a long way south of the central Strip, but all of its luxurious rooms have both bath and walk-in shower, and there's a special wave pool. Resort fee $25. Mon–Thurs & Sun $90, Fri & Sat $160

MGM Grand 3799 Las Vegas Blvd S ☎877 880 0880 or ☎891 7777, ⓦmgmgrand.com. Waiting for any kind of service, especially check-in, in this behemoth – 5044 rooms and counting – can be horrendous, and now that the rooms have lost their former movie theming, they've become rather anonymous. Resort fee $25. Mon–Thurs & Sun $89, Fri & Sat $179

The Mirage 3400 Las Vegas Blvd S ☎800 374 9000 or ☎702 791 7111, ⓦmirage.com. The glitzy *Mirage* is not the market leader it used to be, and its smallish rooms are complemented by even smaller bathrooms. Even so, the public areas downstairs remain impressive, the pool complex is nicely laid out, and the entertainment and nightlife options are among the best in town. Resort fee $25. Mon–Thurs & Sun $125, Fri & Sat $240

★ **New York–New York** 3790 Las Vegas Blvd S ☎866 815 4365 or ☎702 740 6969, ⓦnewyorknewyork.com. Thanks to sheer attention to detail, this is among the most exuberantly enjoyable places to stay on the Strip – and it's small enough that you're not always shuffling down endless corridors. The rooms are very nice, if a bit cramped, and filled with Art Deco flourishes. Resort fee $18. Mon–Thurs & Sun $85, Fri & Sat $170

★ **Paris–Las Vegas** 3655 Las Vegas Blvd S ☎877 796 2096 or ☎702 946 7000, ⓦparislasvegas.com. If not the absolute pinnacle of luxury, rooms and services at the flamboyant French-themed *Paris* are still pretty good, and for location, views, and for ambience it more than holds its own. Resort fee $20. Mon–Thurs & Sun $93, Fri & Sat $201

Planet Hollywood 3667 Las Vegas Blvd S ☎866 919 7472 or ☎702 785 5555, ⓦplanethollywoodresort .com. Some of the nicest mid-rate rooms in town, remodelled with movie memorabilia and upgraded with contemporary furnishings. They're an awful long way from the self-park garage though. Resort fee $20. Mon–Thurs & Sun $79, Fri & Sat $159

The Stratosphere 2000 Las Vegas Blvd S ☎ 800 998 6937 or ☎ 702 380 7777, ⓦ stratospherehotel.com. Despite its unfashionable location, the *Stratosphere* has survived thanks to rock-bottom rates and a steady flow of tour groups. Don't expect amazing views – the large, plain rooms aren't in the tower itself – but they're good-value, and often have last-minute availability. Resort fee $7.50. Mon–Thurs & Sun $\underline{$39}$, Fri & Sat $\underline{$99}$

TI (Treasure Island) 3300 Las Vegas Blvd S ☎ 800 288 7206 or ☎ 702 894 7111, ⓦ treasureisland.com. Though no longer geared toward families, *TI* remains a fun and convenient place to stay, though the rooms themselves are relatively small. Resort fee $25. Mon–Thurs & Sun $\underline{$79}$, Fri & Sat $\underline{$149}$

The Venetian 3355 Las Vegas Blvd S ☎ 866 659 9643 or ☎ 702 414 1000, ⓦ venetian.com. Even the standard rooms at this upscale Strip behemoth are split-level suites, with antique-style canopied beds atop raised platforms, plus spacious living rooms, marble bathrooms with walk-in showers, and a mind-blowing array of shops and restaurants at hand. Resort fee $20. Daily $\underline{$209}$

Wynn Las Vegas 3131 Las Vegas Blvd S ☎ 877 321 9966 or ☎ 702 770 7000, ⓦ wynnlasvegas.com. Since the 1980s, Steve Wynn has repeatedly redefined Las Vegas' highest standard of luxury. The exceptionally large guest rooms boast wonderful beds with fabulous linens, and super-sized tubs in the bathrooms. Resort fee $25. Mon–Thurs & Sun $\underline{$259}$, Fri & Sat $\underline{$399}$

DOWNTOWN AND OFF THE STRIP

The D 301 E Fremont St ☎ 702 388 2400, ⓦ thed.com. Formerly known as *Fitzgerald's*, this is now one of downtown's best bargains, with comfortable renovated rooms and a decent array of bars and restaurants. No resort fee. Sun–Thurs $\underline{$39}$, Fri & Sat $\underline{$99}$

El Cortez 600 E Fremont St ☎ 800 634 6703 or ☎ 702 385 5200, ⓦ ecvegas.com. Veteran downtown casino, refreshed by a recent facelift, with cut-price rooms in the main building, and great-value mini-suites in a newer tower. No resort fee. Mon–Thurs & Sun $\underline{$28}$, Fri & Sat $\underline{$68}$

Golden Gate Hotel and Casino 1 E Fremont St ☎ 800 426 1906 or ☎ 702 385 1906, ⓦ goldengatecasino.com. Downtown's oldest joint dates from 1906, when Las Vegas was just a year old. Now rebranded as a "boutique hotel", it holds a hundred tiny retro-furnished rooms. No resort fee. Mon–Thurs & Sun $\underline{$39}$, Fri & Sat $\underline{$69}$

The Golden Nugget 129 E Fremont St ☎ 800 846 5336 or ☎ 702 385 7111, ⓦ goldennugget.com. The only downtown casino to make a serious bid for the luxury end of the market is undeniably glittery, with a stunning pool complex and opulent rooms. No resort fee. Mon–Thurs & Sun $\underline{$69}$, Fri & Sat $\underline{$129}$

Hard Rock Hotel 4455 Paradise Rd ☎ 800 473 7625, ⓦ hardrockhotel.com. Over a mile east of the Strip, "the world's only rock'n'roll casino" can't match Las Vegas' showcase giants for size or splendour. Instead, it's a relatively intimate and even chic alternative, with above-average rooms, high-class restaurants, a fabulous pool, and the odd big-name rock gig. Resort fee $22. Mon–Thurs & Sun $\underline{$62}$, Fri & Sat $\underline{$249}$

Las Vegas Hostel 1322 E Fremont St ☎ 800 550 8958 or ☎ 702 385 1150, ⓦ lasvegashostel.net. Price-wise, there's little point staying in a hostel in Las Vegas these days, and this former motel is in an inconvenient, somewhat forbidding neighbourhood ten blocks east of downtown. Rates for its basic 4- to 8-bed dorms include free breakfast. There's also a heated pool, and the friendly staff arrange city tours, plus a weekly clubbing night. Dorms $\underline{$13–17}$, private doubles $\underline{$36}$

The Plaza 1 Main St ☎ 800 634 6575 or ☎ 702 386 2110, ⓦ plazahotelcasino.com. Since the management cleverly managed to shoehorn the unused furnishings from the never-opened *Fontainebleau* into the fading *Plaza*, its thousand rooms are looking great, and offer some of downtown's best rates. Resort fee $10. Mon–Thurs & Sun $\underline{$40}$, Fri & Sat $\underline{$79}$

EATING

The **restaurant** scene in Las Vegas ranks among the most varied and vibrant in the US, with each major casino holding as many as ten high-class restaurants. Not that **fine dining** comes cheap in Las Vegas; it's just that most of the big-name restaurants are **less expensive** – and less snooty – than they are in their home cities. The choice on the **Strip** is overwhelming, and you'll almost certainly find a good restaurant to suit your tastes and budget in your own hotel. For that reason, the places reviewed here tend toward the higher end of the spectrum; they're the exceptional ones worth making a special effort to reach.

BUFFETS

Buffet Bellagio Bellagio, 3600 Las Vegas Blvd S ☎ 702 791 7111, ⓦ bellagio.com. Las Vegas' first gourmet buffet set a standard that subsequent competitors have now surpassed. While it has cut a few corners, there's still a lot to like. Around eight hundred items are prepared fresh in small quantities, and the sheer range is impressive.

Breakfast costs $17, while lunch (Mon–Fri $20), brunch (Sat & Sun $25) and dinner (Mon–Thurs & Sun $30, Fri & Sat $37) can include sushi, cold cuts, dim sum, green curry duck, *coq au vin*, roasted salmon and roast lamb with mint sauce, plus fresh-baked focaccia, tasty fruit tarts, and fancy desserts. The large dining area is not especially attractive, but offers spacious seating. Breakfast Mon–Fri 7–11am;

8

ALL YOU CAN EAT

In time-honoured Las Vegas fashion, almost every casino offers an **all-you-can-eat buffet**. While standards (and prices) are highest at casinos like *Wynn*, *Bellagio* and *Paris*, most buffets remain locked in the cheaper, more traditional approach; much like a food court in an upmarket mall, you'll get good fast food, but not great cooking. The best of this latter kind are neither on the Strip nor downtown, but in casinos like the *Rio* and the *Stations* chain that depend on locals as well as tourists. By contrast, those at the largest Strip casinos, like *Excalibur* and the *MGM Grand*, are often poor value.

lunch Mon–Fri 11am–4pm; brunch Sat & Sun 7am–4pm; dinner daily 4–10pm.

★ **The Buffet at Wynn** Wynn Las Vegas, 3131 Las Vegas Blvd S ☎ 702 770 7000, ⓦ wynnlasvegas.com. *Wynn's* plush Belle-Époque buffet remains the best in town. While each dish is labelled as though on a gourmet menu – marinated snapper with edamame, five distinct kinds of ceviche, and so on –it's the sheer variety that makes it exceptional, with buffet staples like Alaskan crab legs and peeled shrimp prepared to perfection – diners grab phenomenal amounts from the bottomless trays – and daily specials like baba ganoush or clams in black bean sauce. It can't quite match a top restaurant, but it's still a definitive Las Vegas experience. On weekdays, breakfast costs $20 and lunch $23; weekend brunch is $32; and dinner is $37, rising to $40 on Fri & Sat. Breakfast Mon–Fri 8am–11pm; lunch Mon–Fri 11am–3.30pm; brunch Sat & Sun 8am–3.30pm; dinner Mon–Thurs & Sun 3.30–10pm, Fri & Sat 3.30–10.30pm.

Golden Nugget Buffet Golden Nugget, 129 E Fremont St ☎ 702 385 7111, ⓦ goldennugget.com/lasvegas. Downtown's best buffet occupies a plain but bright and spacious room on the *Golden Nugget's* second floor, overlooking the pool complex, and charges relatively down-to-earth prices, with breakfast $11, weekday lunch $13, and weekday dinners and the weekend brunch both $19. The food is wider-ranging than you'll find elsewhere on Fremont Street, especially on the weekend "seafood and more" dinners (Fri–Sun $22). Meat entrees like roast beef or Chinese orange chicken are relatively ordinary, but more interesting offerings include entire roasted heads of garlic or tasty baked catfish. Breakfast Mon–Fri 7–10.30am; lunch Mon–Fri 10.30am–3.30pm; champagne brunch Sat & Sun 8am–3.30pm; dinner daily 3.30–10pm.

★ **Le Village Buffet** Paris, 3655 Las Vegas Blvd S ☎ 702 946 7000, ⓦ parislasvegas.com. Rather than incorporating every conceivable cuisine, *Paris'* buffet showcases only delicious French dishes, and does so extremely well. The meat offerings tend to be best, with roast chicken fricasseed, as *coq au vin*, or with mustard, along with duck à l'orange and a creamy pork and beef cassoulet, but there's plenty of seafood, from scallops, shrimp and crab to Dover sole and rich bouillabaisse. Vegetables such as baby squash and creamed spinach are super-fresh; and there's even a full French cheese board. The setting is a little cramped, squeezed into a very Disney-esque French village, but the food is *magnifique*. Breakfast costs $19 on weekdays, $22 at weekends; weekday lunch is also $22; and both the weekend champagne, and dinner daily, cost $31. Breakfast Mon–Fri 7–11am, Sat & Sun 7–10am; lunch Mon–Fri 11am–3.30pm; brunch Sat & Sun 10am–3.30pm; dinner daily 3.30–10pm.

Wicked Spoon Cosmopolitan, 3708 Las Vegas Blvd S ☎ 702 698 7000, ⓦ cosmopolitanlasvegas.com. Despite being hidden away upstairs at the back of the property, the *Cosmopolitan's* buffet has quickly proved a big hit with locals and visitors alike, thanks to its extensive array of international cuisines. Unusually, each specific item is set out on an individual portion-sized plate, so everything looks good, and has more of the feel of dining in a restaurant. There's no dividing line between breakfast and lunch (both Mon–Fri $22, Sat & Sun $29), while dinner is priced at $35 all week. Mon–Thurs 8am–2pm & 5–9pm, Fri 8am–2pm & 5–10pm, Sat 8am–3pm & 5–10pm, Sun 8am–3pm & 5–9pm.

RESTAURANTS
THE STRIP

★ **Beijing Noodle No. 9** Caesars Palace, 3570 Las Vegas Blvd S ☎ 877 346 4642, ⓦ caesarspalace.com. This casual noodle shop has perhaps the most delightful decor of any Las Vegas restaurant. Entered via an avenue comprising six large tanks of Japanese goldfish, it's a lovely space, dazzling white, with tracery screens that create the feeling of being in an aquarium. The food, like the Imperial Seafood Dumplings, each of which contains seafood in a hot chicken broth; the salt and pepper shrimp; and the tender beef chow fun with flat noodles, is delicious. With entrees approaching $20 it's more expensive than you'd pay for noodles elsewhere, but "single" portions are very substantial; one each and you've got a good meal. Daily 11am–10.30pm.

★ **Bouchon** Level 10, Venezia Tower, The Venetian, 3355 Las Vegas Blvd S ☎ 702 414 6200, ⓦ bouchonbistro.com. Despite its sky-high reputation and exclusive setting, Thomas Keller's spacious recreation of a classic French bistro is friendly and affordable. Breakfast is a Francophile's dream of croissants, pastries, yogurt and coffee, while brunch is the best value, with sandwiches or quiche for under $20; dinner mains like steak frites or sole marinière cost $37. Sitting outside on the huge piazza is a real joy. Mon–Fri 7am–1pm & 5–10pm, Sat & Sun 8am–2pm & 5–10pm.

Estiatorio Milos Cosmopolitan, 3708 Las Vegas Blvd S ☎ 877 893 2003, ⓦ milos.ca/restaurants/las-vegas. The $20 lunch menu at this gorgeous Greek seafood restaurant, adorned with replica antiquities, is a real bargain. In the evening, it's very much a place for a romantic treat; your pick from an array of succulent Mediterranean fish, freshly arrived from the Athens fish market, will cost $50-plus per person. Mon–Thurs 5.30–11.30pm, Fri 5.30pm–midnight, Sat noon–2.30pm & 5.30pm–midnight, Sun noon–2.30pm & 5.30–11pm.

Fat Burger 3763 Las Vegas Blvd S ☎ 702 736 4733, ⓦ fatburger.com. There's no more to this gleaming, all-American burger joint than meets the eye. Quite simply, you can walk or drive in from the Strip at any time, and get a perfect burger, fries, and shake. Daily 24 hours.

Gordon Ramsay Steak Paris, 3655 Las Vegas Blvd S ☎ 702 946 7000, ⓦ parislasvegas.com. Britain's favourite loudmouth chef has moved into Las Vegas in a big way. This very fancy steakhouse, all but beneath the Eiffel Tower and supposedly designed to resemble the Channel Tunnel, offers prime slabs of beef and veal in all shapes and one size – big. Choose your own from the trolley, and for upwards of $50 it'll soon be slapped down in front of you, cooked to perfection. Daily 5–10.30pm.

Jean Phillippe Patisserie Bellagio, 3600 Las Vegas Blvd S ⓦ jpchocolates.com. The perfect way to start or finish an indulgent Las Vegas day – spectacle, excess and gluttony. Cakes, pastries, pancakes, chocolate and coffee, all served within the warm, swirling embrace of the world's largest chocolate fountain. No reservations. Mon–Thurs 7am–11pm, Fri–Sun 7am–midnight.

Julian Serrano Aria, 3730 Las Vegas Blvd S ☎ 877 230 2742, ⓦ arialasvegas.com. Almost everything in this superbly stylish tapas restaurant comes from different regions of Spain, including the glassware and armchairs as well as ingredients like pata negra ham from Extremadura and olive oil from Jaén. It sounds inexpensive, at $8–15 per plate, but you can quickly eat $100 worth. In general, the more elaborate the dish, the better; they're unusual without being merely gimmicky. The little balls of cocoa butter filled with chilled gazpacho are out of this world, while the avocado cannelone with Scottish salmon and seaweed is exquisite. There are also a few larger entrees, including lamb chops at $30 and paellas, designed to share, at $40 and up, plus a $39 pre-theatre menu. Mon–Thurs & Sun 11.30am–11pm, Fri & Sat 11.30am–11.30pm.

★ **Mon Ami Gabi** Paris, 3655 Las Vegas Blvd S ☎ 702 944 4224, ⓦ monamigabi.com. The first and the finest

casino restaurant to offer open-air seating right on the Strip has the feel of a proper French pavement bistro. At lunch, try the gloriously authentic onion soup ($10), the mussels ($12 or $24), or the thin-cut steak frites ($25). Dinner features more expensive steak cuts and fish entrees. Mon–Thurs & Sun 7am–11pm, Fri & Sat 7am–midnight.

Olives Bellagio, 3600 Las Vegas Blvd S ☎ 702 693 8865, ⓦ bellagio.com. *Bellagio's* best-value gourmet restaurant has a lovely terrace setting, facing the Eiffel Tower across the lake. Even if it is the kind of place that calls a $18 pizza an "individual oven-baked flatbread," and your food is more likely to be arranged vertically than horizontally, the largely Mediterranean menu is uniformly fresh and superb. It's a great spot for lunch, with $13–18 appetizers like beef carpaccio, pasta dishes like butternut squash tortelli ($17), and specials such as a jumbo lump crab cake sandwich ($25). Dinner entrees are pricier, at up to $50. Daily 11am–2.45pm & 5–10.30pm.

Phô at the Coffee Shop TI (Treasure Island), 3300 Las Vegas Blvd S ☎ 702 894 7111, ⓦ treasureisland.com. If you're looking for a simple, cheap and tasty meal that's a little out of the ordinary, there's no faulting the Strip's only Vietnamese restaurant, which takes over half the space of the *Coffee Shop* at *TI*. The speciality here is hearty bowls of *phô* soup, available in chicken, beef or vegetable flavours for around $12.50; rice or vermicelli noodle dishes cost much the same. Mon–Thurs & Sun 11am–11.30pm, Fri & Sat 11am–2.30am.

★ **Scarpetta** Level 3, Cosmopolitan, 3708 Las Vegas Blvd S ☎ 877 893 2003, ⓦ cosmopolitanlasvegas.com. This wonderful, inventive "new Italian" restaurant enjoys one of Las Vegas's very best views, looking out across the fountains of Bellagio. Open for dinner only, until late, just like in Italy, the menu is divided between primi piatti such as roasted scallops ($23); pasta, with even the simplest spaghetti sauce at $24; and consistently delicious main courses, like fennel spiced black cod for $32 or Colorado lamb loin for $40. There's also a $110 tasting menu. Daily 6–11pm.

'wichcraft MGM Grand, 3799 Las Vegas Blvd S ☎ 702 891 3166, ⓦ mgmgrand.com. Set near the back of the enormous *MGM Grand*, the Las Vegas outpost of Tom Colicchio's gourmet New York sandwich bar is a perfect stop-off for on-the-go visitors in need of a quick snack but unwilling to compromise on quality. Whether hot (eg roasted pork ciabatta) or cold (shrimp salad), typical sandwiches cost under $10. Daily 10am–5pm.

DOWNTOWN AND OFF THE STRIP

Mr Lucky's 24/7 Hard Rock Hotel, 4455 Paradise Rd ☎ 702 693 5000, ⓦ hardrockhotel.com. The *Hard Rock's* 24hr coffee shop is a very stylish joint, and the food is well above average too. As well as all the usual breakfast items, it serves burgers, sandwiches, pizzas, and pasta dishes for

8

$10–17, a strip steak for $26, and milkshakes or microbrews for $6. Daily 24hr.

★ **Oscar's Steakhouse** The Plaza, 1 Main St ☎702 386 7227, ⓦplazahotelcasino.com. An absolute only-in-Las-Vegas experience, set in a spherical see-through ball at the west end of Fremont Street, this dinner-only steakhouse belongs to former mayor Oscar Goodman, who's often to be seen dining here with his wife, current mayor Carolyn Goodman. The food is unimaginative but pretty good, at $40-plus for steak, $25 for roast chicken. Mon–Thurs & Sun 5–10pm, Fri & Sat 4.30pm–midnight.

Paymon's Mediterranean Café and Market 4147 S Maryland Parkway at Flamingo ☎702 731 6030, ⓦpaymons.com. This simple but highly recommended Middle Eastern restaurant – much easier to reach heading south rather than north on Maryland – is Las Vegas' best vegetarian option. The Cretan murals are attractive, the food tasty and substantial, and the service friendly. Salads and pita sandwiches cost $8–10, and spinach pie $12, while dips such as hummus or the eggplant-based baba ganoush are $6. If you can't make up your mind, a mountainous best-of-everything combination plate is just $13. Mon–Thurs 11am–1am, Fri & Sat 11am–3am, Sun 11am–3pm.

★ **Ping Pang Pong** Gold Coast, 4000 W Flamingo Rd ☎702 367 7111, ⓦgoldcoastcasino.com. Las Vegas' best Chinese restaurant is in the closest casino to the small local Chinatown, a mile or so west of *Treasure Island*. Packed with Chinese customers around the clock, with a great selection of inexpensive dim sum on the lunchtime trolleys – try the $9 soft-shell crab, wrapped in rice paper– and a full menu of rice, noodle and meat entrees, few of which cost over $13. Daily 10am–3pm & 5pm–3am.

Roy's 620 E Flamingo Rd ☎702 691 2053, ⓦroysrestaurant.com. Thanks to its off-Strip location – rare indeed for a big national name – Roy's sees fewer tourists than locals, but it's every bit the match of the top casino restaurants, with significantly lower prices to boot. The Asian-inspired fusion cuisine has an emphasis on fish. A melt-in-your-mouth miso butterfish appetizer costs $14, while entrees featuring Hawaiian species ($22–32) include lemongrass *opah* and the irresistible whole *moi* or threadfish. Meat-eaters can get steak, veal or lamb for similar prices, while a set three-course meal goes for $37. Mon–Thurs 5.30–9.30pm, Fri 5.30–10pm, Sat 5–10pm, Sun 5–9.30pm.

DRINKING AND NIGHTLIFE

As the perfect fuel to turn a dithering gawker into a diehard gambler, alcohol is very easy to come by in Las Vegas. If you want a drink in a casino, there's no need to look for a bar; instead, a tray-toting waitress will come and find you. All the casinos have actual **bars** as well, but they're just a small part of the picture. The old-fashioned **Las Vegas lounge** has returned in force, whether knowingly retro-styled for 20-something rockers, glammed up as an "ultra-lounge," or lovingly recreated for older visitors looking to recapture the decadent flavour of the Rat-Pack era. Las Vegas has also become an international **clubbing** capital. No longer are clubbers considered a breed apart from tourists; instead, all the major casinos have opened their own clubs, often with spectacular results.

BARS AND LOUNGES

Chandelier Cosmopolitan, 3708 Las Vegas Blvd S ☎702 698 7000, ⓦcosmopolitanlasvegas.com. Festooned in the dangling tentacles of a colossal chandelier, this three-level bar is the epicentre of the glamorous Cosmopolitan. Kickstart your night with a cocktail, or spend the whole evening in its enclosed DJ section. Casino level open 24hr, other levels hours vary.

Chicago Brewing Co Four Queens, 202 E Fremont St ☎702 924 5222, ⓦfourqueens.com. Downtown's liveliest bar has something of the feel of a pub, especially once you've sampled a massive 64-oz flagon of beer ($14), brewed on site. Mon–Fri 11.30am–1.30am, Sat & Sun 10am–1.30am.

Minus5 Ice Lounge Mandalay Bay, 3930 Las Vegas Blvd S ☎702 740 5800, ⓦminus5experience.com. There's nothing tricksy about the name here; it's minus 5, and it's an ice lounge. What's an ice lounge? It's a lounge where everything – the seats, the bar, the walls and even the glasses – is made of ice. Customers are kitted out in Eskimo-style parkas and furry hoods, the better to savour

frozen margaritas and the like. Mon–Thurs & Sun 11am–2am, Fri & Sat 11am–3am. Cover varies, typically $25 including 1 drink.

Nine Fine Irishmen New York–New York, 3790 Las Vegas Blvd S ☎702 740 6463, ⓦninefineirishmen.com. The affinity between New York and all things Irish finds expression in this wood-panelled pub, shipped from Ireland and featuring Irish musicians, singers and dancers nightly. Daily 11am–2.45am. Cover $5 Wed & Thurs, $10 Fri & Sat.

Parasol Up, Parasol Down Wynn Las Vegas, 3131 Las Vegas Blvd S ☎702 770 7000. Matching pair of see-and-be-seen bars, decked out in *Wynn's* signature psychedic palette and facing the Lake of Dreams; *Up* is at the top of the central staircase, while *Down*, at the bottom, offers additional outdoor seating that's very much in demand. Mon–Thurs & Sun 11am–4am, Fri & Sat 11am–5am.

Revolution Lounge The *Mirage*, 3400 Las Vegas Blvd S ☎702 693 8300, ⓦmirage.com. Once you get past the somewhat silly claim that this ultra-lounge truly reflects an artistic collaboration between the Beatles and the Cirque du Soleil, you can enjoy the psychedelic lightshow and fab 1960s decor. DJ sets most nights, plus occasional live bands. Bar daily noon–4am, free; lounge Thurs–Sun 10pm–4am, cover varies.

V Bar The Venetian, 3355 Las Vegas Blvd S ☎702 740 6433. The minimalist Oriental styling in this upscale, understated, grown-up bar is tempered with warm auspicious reds, and glamorous waitresses glide around dressed in slinky slips. An espresso martini kicks off the evening nicely. Mon–Wed & Sun 5pm–2am, Thurs & Sat 5pm–3am. Cover from $10, after 10pm.

CLUBS AND MUSIC VENUES

Encore Beach Club Encore, 3121 Las Vegas Blvd S ☎702 521 4005, ⓦencorebeachclub.com. Las Vegas' premier "dayclub" even before Prince Harry's 2012 escapade made it world-famous, this extraordinarily lavish labyrinth of pools, bars and patios makes the perfect venue for a no-expense-spared lost weekend or two. Late April to Oct Fri noon–7pm Sat & Sun 11am–7pm. Cover $20–60.

House of Blues Mandalay Bay, 3950 Las Vegas Blvd S ☎702 632 7600, ⓦhob.com. The voodoo-tinged, folk-art-decorated *House of Blues* has a definite but not exclusive emphasis toward blues, R&B, and the like. Typical prices range from around $35 for B-list names up to $100 for stars like Aretha Franklin. Mon–Thurs & Sun 8am–11pm, Fri & Sat 8am–midnight.

The Joint Hard Rock Hotel, 4455 Paradise Rd ☎702 693 5066, ⓦthejointlasvegas.com. The venue of choice for big-name touring rock acts is now capable of holding 4000-plus audiences. Tickets to see the Rolling Stones here cost $505 and $1005, but more typically admission for performers such as Elvis Costello ranges between $75 and $125. See website for schedule and prices.

Krave Massive Neonopolis, 450 Fremont St ☎702 836 0830, ⓦkravelasvegas.com. What's claimed to be the world's largest gay nightclub moved downtown early in 2013, to occupy several floors of the under-used Neonopolis mall. With four dance floors and three bars, you're bound to find a niche that takes your fancy. Daily from 10.30pm. Cover varies.

★ **Marquee** Cosmopolitan, 3708 Las Vegas Blvd S ☎702 333 9000, ⓦmarqueelasvegas.com. This indoor-outdoor club, artfully put together by the clubbing masterminds of the TAO group, features top DJs day and night, but also holds lower-key bars and lounges. Expect to pay heavily to enjoy its full amenities. Nightclub Mon & Thurs–Sat 10pm–4am; Dayclub daily 10am–7pm; cover varies $20–80.

Piranha 4633 Paradise Rd ☎702 791 0100, ⓦpiranhavegas.com. This extravagant gay club, half of a complex that's also home to *8-½ Ultra Lounge*, is in the so-called "Fruit Loop", the focus of Las Vegas' off-Strip gay scene. Beyond either a flaming waterfall or a wrap-around piranha-filled aquarium, you'll find the frenetic dance floor, with a plush bar alongside and an exclusive VIP section, featuring private "skyboxes", upstairs. There's also a fabulous outdoor patio, with individual fireplaces. Daily 10pm–5am. Cover varies, typically $20.

Pure Caesars Palace, 3570 Las Vegas Blvd S ☎702 731 7873, ⓦpurethenightclub.com. Ordinary clubbers can wait three hours or more to get into the massively popular *Pure*, but with three separate clubbing areas, each with its own DJs and dance floor, there's usually enough space inside not to feel crowded. Be sure to ride the glass elevator to the top level, for a drink on the huge open-air Strip-view terrace. Tues & Thurs–Sun 10pm–4am. Cover $20–50.

Tao The Venetian, 3355 Las Vegas Blvd S ☎702 388 8588, ⓦtaolasvegas.com. The decor at *Tao* is extremely opulent, and very Asian-influenced, with lots of glowing golden Buddhas, and it attracts very big names indeed. The rooftop, poolside *Tao Beach* opens in summer only. Nightclub Thurs–Sat 10pm–5am; Tao Beach Mon–Thurs 10am–sunset, Fri–Sun 10am–5am. Cover Thurs & Fri $20, Sat $40; weekend wristband $100.

ENTERTAINMENT

Live entertainment remains a crucial component of the Las Vegas package, and it's nothing like as cheesy and kitsch as first-time visitors might imagine. One by one, the cheesy, feathers-and-tassels revues have closed down, to be replaced by surprisingly stimulating, postmodern shows by the likes of the now-ubiquitous **Cirque du Soleil** and the **Blue Man Group**. More generally, individual performers, like comedians, magicians and singer-impressionists, tend to have been supplanted by ensemble pieces such as Broadway shows. There's still a place for the old-fashioned **headliner**, though – Celine Dion paved the way for a new generation in the 4000-seat Colosseum at *Caesars Palace*, and she's been followed by the likes of Elton John, Rod Stewart and Shania Twain.

★ **Big Elvis** Harrah's, 3475 Las Vegas Blvd S ☎702 369 5000, ⓦharrahslasvegas.com. No Las Vegas trip would be complete without an audience with the King. The lounge at *Harrah's* is always packed for the undeniably sizeable Pete Vallee's good-natured, full-throated, sweat'n'sequins Elvis tribute show. Mon, Tues & Thurs–Sun 2–6pm. Free.

Blue Man Group Monte Carlo, 3770 Las Vegas Blvd S ☎800 258 3626, ⓦblueman.com. Blue Man Group have become long-term fixtures on the Strip, where so many other shows – shows with stars, plots, and even words – have failed within months. How? By the synchronized munching of breakfast cereal; by performing live endoscopies on audience members; by catching marshmallows in their mouths. Their deadpan humour is complemented by exhilarating music, including lots of meaty drumming, and some truly stunning special effects. Mon, Tues & Sun 7pm, Wed–Sat 7pm & 10pm; $65–149.

★ **Human Nature** The Venetian, 3355 Las Vegas Blvd S ☎702 414 1000, ⓦhumannaturelive.com. When this vocal quartet bounds on stage to perform their "Ultimate Celebration Of The Motown Sound", they acknowledge upfront that four fresh-faced, clean-cut, and above all white Australians singing Motown in Vegas makes a pretty odd fit. And then, quite simply, they blow your socks off, with good old-fashioned panache and hard work, plus the aid of a hot six-piece band. From fierce stompers to sweet acappella numbers, it's much more than pastiche, and the audience laps it up. Mon & Thurs–Sun 7pm; $73–117.

Jersey Boys Paris, 3655 Las Vegas Blvd S ☎702 777 7776, ⓦjerseyboysvegas.com. While Broadway shows are normally truncated to suit restless Las Vegas audiences, this hugely enjoyable romp lasts the full 2hr 20min – there's simply so much material to cover, in what's a genuine emotional narrative rather than simply a vehicle for the songs of Frankie Valli and the Four Seasons. Expect its quick-fire repartee, lightning-fast staging, and above all, irresistible music. Tues 6.30pm & 9.30pm, Wed–Fri & Sun 7pm, Sat 5pm & 8.15pm; $53–185.

★ **Jubilee** Bally's, 3645 Las Vegas Blvd S ☎800 237 7469, ⓦballyslasvegas.com. If you've never been to a Las Vegas show, Jubilee is probably what you think they're all like. In fact, it's the sole survivor of the old tits'n'tassels tradition, a lumbering great thing that after its first few jaw-dropping moments can't help but grow on you. The music may be abominable, but if you're finally tiring of cutting-edge postmodernism, nothing beats the sheer camp of leather-clad Roman soldiers cavorting with Arabian-Nights maidens, and dancing showgirls tottering beneath huge ostrich-feather headdresses. Mon–Thurs, Sat & Sun 7.30pm & 10.30pm (topless); $58–118.

★ **KÀ** MGM Grand, 3799 Las Vegas Blvd S ☎702 531 3826, ⓦka.com. With so many superb Cirque du Soleil productions running in Las Vegas, it's all too easy to overlook KÀ. In fact, it's an absolute must-see, boasting a quite extraordinary set; the stage floor not only rises, but can swivel and pivot in every direction. One moment it's a steep cliff-face, to which the performers cling for dear life; the next, they simply fall, mid-battle, into the abyss below. KÀ is much more plot-driven than other Cirque shows, allowing more scope for darkness and emotional impact during the succession of truly breathtaking set-pieces.

★ **Love** The Mirage, 3400 Las Vegas Blvd S ☎702 792 7777, ⓦcirquedusoleil.com. In which the Cirque du Soleil do their stuff to a remixed Beatles soundtrack. Sometimes intimate, sometimes exuberantly all-embracing, Love is a beautifully judged and profoundly moving show. Nostalgic and visionary, it celebrates the Beatles' achievement while skilfully avoiding anything too literal – the actors don't play specific Beatles, for example. The costumes, lighting and staging are all magnificent, and some of the set-pieces are astonishing. When all's said and done, it's a dance show, but if that might normally put you off, don't let it in – it's an irresistible evening. Mon & Thurs–Sun 7pm & 9.30pm; $79–180.

Mac King Harrah's, 3475 Las Vegas Blvd S ☎702 369 5222, ⓦmackingshow.com. This afternoon magic show is one of Las Vegas' best entertainment bargains. Mac King's an endearing innocent in a plaid suit who specializes in good old close-up magic, using ropes, cards, torn-up $20 bills and the like. His corny patter leaves plenty of room for good-natured improvised gags. Tues–Sat 1pm & 3pm; $33.

★ **Mystère** TI, 3300 Las Vegas Blvd S ☎702 894 7722, ⓦcirquedusoleil.com. The Cirque du Soleil's original Las Vegas show is such a visual feast that it barely matters whether you see its dreamscape symbolism as profound and meaningful or laboured and empty. Seen at first as being too "way-out" for Las Vegas, its success redefined the city's approach to entertainment. Above all, it's a showcase of fabulous circus skills, with tumblers, acrobats, trapeze artists, pole climbers, clowns, and strong men, but no animals apart from fantastic costumed apparitions. Sat–Wed 7pm & 9.30pm; $69–119.

★ **O** Bellagio, 3600 Las Vegas Blvd S ☎702 693 8866, ⓦcirquedusoleil.com. Another Cirque du Soleil triumph, in which any part of the stage at any time may be submerged to any depth. From the synchronized swimmers onwards, the Cirque display their magnificent skills to maximum advantage. Highlights include a colossal trapeze frame draped like a pirate ship and crewed by fearless acrobats and divers, and footmen flying through the air in swirls of velvet drapery. Wed–Sun 7.30pm & 10pm; $98.50–155.

Terry Fator Mirage, 3400 Las Vegas Blvd S ☎702 792 7777, ⓦmirage.com. If you saw Terry Fator win America's Got Talent, you'll know why this amazing ventriloquist-impressionist so quickly become a major Las Vegas headliner. The man is quite extraordinary; while manipulating animal puppets, he delivers note-perfect imitations of anyone from Marvin Gaye and Roy Orbison to Gary Numan and Gnarls Barkley – without moving his lips. Even if his humour is hardly cutting-edge, it is at least funny. Tues–Sat 7.30pm; $66–143.

Around Las Vegas

Spend more than a day or two in Las Vegas and you'll soon find yourself gasping for a blast of sunlight and fresh air away from the casinos. You'll have to cross an expanse of empty desert before you reach anywhere interesting, but exhilarating day-trip destinations do exist, including **Red Rock Canyon** and the **Hoover Dam**. A more distant day outing is the **Grand Canyon**, or more precisely, the so-called Grand Canyon West, the nearest part of the canyon; see p.326.

Red Rock Canyon

17 miles west of the Strip • **Visitor Centre** Daily 8am–4.30pm • ☎ 702 515 5350, ⓦ redrockcanyonlv.org • **Scenic Drive** Daily: March 7am–7pm, April–Sept 6am–8pm, Oct 6am–7pm, Nov–Feb 6am–5pm • $7 per vehicle

For a taste of Southwestern canyon scenery, head west along Charleston Boulevard to **Red Rock Canyon National Conservation Area**, a cactus-strewn desert basin that's surrounded by stark red cliffs and pierced repeatedly by narrow canyons. The **Scenic Drive**, a thirteen-mile loop road, provides access to the cool, slender **Ice Box Canyon** (a 2.5-mile round-trip hike), and the three-mile **Pine Creek Trail**, which follows a flower-lined creek beyond a ruined homesite toward a towering, red-capped monolith.

Lake Mead

30 miles southeast of the Strip • **Visitor centre** US-93, 4 miles northeast of Boulder City • Daily 8.30am–4.30pm • ☎ 702 293 8990, ⓦ nps.gov/lake

Many Las Vegas visitors make the pilgrimage to **LAKE MEAD**, the vast reservoir that straddles the border between Nevada and Arizona, behind the Hoover Dam. As with the similarly incongruous Lake Powell (see p.391) it makes a bizarre spectacle – the blue waters a vivid counterpoint to the surrounding desert – but it can get excruciatingly crowded. The best views along its five-hundred-mile shoreline come from the Nevada side; call in at the **visitor centre** to enjoy a sweeping prospect of the whole thing.

Hoover Dam

30 miles southeast of the Strip • ☎ 702 494 2517, ⓦ usbr.gov/lc/hooverdam • **Parking** Daily 8am–6.15pm • $7 • **Visitor Center** Daily: April–Sept 9am–6pm, Oct–March 9am–5pm • $8 **Powerplant Tour** April–Sept 9.25am–4.55pm, Oct–March 9.25am–3.55pm; $11, seniors & ages 4–16 $9 • **Dam Tour** April–Sept Mon–Thurs 9.30am–4pm, Fri & Sat 9.30am–4.30pm; Oct–March daily 9.30am–3.45pm • $30, no reductions, minimum age 8

Beyond Boulder City, across the rocky ridges of the Black Mountains, US-93 reaches the **Hoover Dam** itself. Completed in 1935, and designed to block the Colorado River and provide low-cost electricity for the cities of the Southwest, it's among the tallest dams ever built (760ft high), and is made of enough concrete to build a two-lane highway from the West Coast to New York. Three levels of visit are possible. You can simply explore the **Visitor Center** on the Nevada side of the river; take the half-hour **Powerplant Tour**, in which you ride an elevator to the base of the dam; or join the hour-long **Dam Tour**, which involves an additional mile or so of walking in the damp dark tunnels deep inside the dam.

8

NAVAJO IN CANYON DE CHELLY, EARLY 20TH CENTURY

Contexts

459 History

476 The Hopi

480 The Navajo and the Apache

486 Books

489 Glossary

History

What is now the Southwest USA has been home to Native Americans for about twelve thousand years. Around four hundred years ago, a small group of Hispanic colonists claimed the region for Spain as New Mexico, while two centuries later it passed briefly into the hands of the newly independent nation of Mexico, before being taken over by the United States.

Throughout that long history, the Southwest has been either controlled, or at least heavily influenced, by distant powers. Its best-known ancient peoples, the Ancestral Puebloans and the Hohokam, drew their cultural inspiration from Mexico; the settlers of Santa Fe looked to Madrid and Mexico City for financial and spiritual support; and even today the region owes much to federal funding from Washington.

What makes the Southwest so fascinating is that so many of the different peoples who have migrated into the region are still there, and still interacting with each other. In the words of an anthropologist from Zuni Pueblo, "the Anasazi are alive and well and living in the Rio Grande valley." The Navajo, relative latecomers, form the majority population in the Four Corners; Santa Fe remains a visibly Hispanic, Catholic city; Utah remains over sixty percent Mormon; and Phoenix and Las Vegas typify the Anglo impact.

The Paleo Indians

No trace of human beings in the Americas has been dated any earlier than 15,000 BC, around which time the true pioneers of North America, nomadic hunter-gatherers from Siberia, first reached Alaska. Thanks to the last ice age, when sea levels were three hundred feet lower than the modern Bering Strait, a **"land-bridge"** – actually a vast plain, measuring six hundred miles north to south – connected Eurasia to America.

Separated by impenetrable glacier fields from Canada, Alaska was then effectively part of Asia rather than North America. Much like an air lock, the region "opened" in different directions at different times; migrants reaching it from the west, oblivious to the fact they were leaving Asia, found their way blocked to the east. Several generations might pass, and the connection back to Asia be severed, before an eastward passage appeared. This migration was almost certainly spurred by the pursuit of large mammal species, especially the mammoth, that were already extinct throughout almost all of Eurasia. Imagine therefore the glee of the so-called **Paleo Indians** when they finally encountered America's own indigenous "megafauna," such as mammoths, mastodons, giant ground sloths and long-horned bison, all of which had evolved without fear of human predation.

The original group of human settlers may have been every small. A band of a hundred individuals, advancing eight miles deeper into the virgin continent each year, with an annual population growth of 1.1 percent, could have filled North and South America with ten million people within a thousand years.

15,000 BC	11,000 BC	10,000–8000 BC
First nomadic peoples from Asia reach Alaska	Almost all North America's large mammals, from mammoths to horses, become extinct, possibly due to over-hunting	Clovis culture present in New Mexico

Between 10,000 BC and 8000 BC, the Southwest was dominated by the so-called **Clovis** culture, whose distinctive flaked-stone spear-points were first identified at Clovis, New Mexico. Living in small groups, constantly on the move, Clovis hunters pursued their prey across large distances. Their weapons have been found poking from the ribs of mammoths, and they seem to have been such successful killers that they drove the indigenous fauna – which included horses – to extinction.

The Archaic culture

As the large animals died out, early Southwesterners adapted to become **hunter-gatherers**. Learning where and when particular plants ripened, the people of the **Archaic** or **Desert culture** would migrate seasonally within limited areas, such as between canyons and nearby hillsides. Hunting for small mammals such as rabbit and deer remained important. Clay statuettes and split-twig figurines, found in remote locations in the Grand Canyon and elsewhere and depicting deities as well as animals, show that shamanistic rituals evolved. The most remarkable manifestation of Archaic culture was the mysterious rock art of the **Great Gallery** in Canyonlands National Park (see p.410); they also constructed giant earthworks in the deserts of southwest Arizona. Few traces of actual homes survive, however; it's thought these people lived in caves wherever possible.

The arrival of **agriculture** from Mexico played a crucial role in ending the Archaic era. **Corn** – as tiny fingers of maize, much smaller than today's strains – may have been cultivated in the highlands of southern Mexico as early as 5000 BC. The skill of growing it then spread northwards from group to group, accompanied by the prayers and rituals necessary to ensure a good harvest, and may have reached southern New Mexico around 1500 BC. Like hunter-gatherers the world over, notoriously reluctant to give up a lifestyle that offers food in return for comparatively little effort, Southwesterners at first simply used a low level of farming – more like gardening – to supplement their traditional diet. Communities only made the transition to intensive agriculture once population levels increased.

The Basketmakers

Southwestern peoples embarked on the large-scale cultivation of crops – corn, together with a more recent arrival, **squash** – from around 100 BC onwards. The first such society was named **Basketmaker II** by early archeologists, who assumed that more primitive "Basketmaker I" sites waited to be found. The Basketmakers lived in extended family groups, in shallow **pithouses** – rectangular pits two to six feet deep, with earth-covered roofs that rose above ground level. They hunted using the *atlatl*, a lever-like spear-throwing device. Cooking entailed dropping hot rocks into waterproof yucca-leaf baskets lined with pitch. By now they had also domesticated **dogs**, for hunting, and **turkeys**, for feathers rather than food.

Pottery too spread from Mexico during the first few centuries AD. All pots were made by women, hand-coiling successive strips of rolled clay one atop the next, then smoothing them together. The use of fragile ceramic vessels presupposes a sedentary society, but brings great benefits: **beans** are much easier to boil in a pot than a basket, so the Southwest acquired its third great staple food, and basketmaking declined.

4000 BC onwards	1500 BC	100 BC
Archaic artists create Great Gallery in Canyonlands	Agriculture reaches the Southwest from Mexico	The first Basketmakers start to live in pithouses, growing corn and squash

Around 500 AD, the so-called **Basketmaker III** culture emerged. As well as corn, squash and beans, they grew another Mexican import, **cotton** – originally cultivated mainly for its oil-rich edible seeds – and used **bows and arrows**. Sizeable **villages** (what the Spanish later called **pueblos**) started to appear.

Each village soon focused around one specific, extra-large pithouse, probably set aside for public or ritual use. Such buildings are recognizable as the first **kivas** – the ceremonial underground chambers that remain at the heart of Pueblo religion. Each *kiva* was entered from above, via an opening that also served as a smokehole. A bench ran around its circumference, and niches were set into the walls, perhaps to hold ritual objects. A small depression in the floor in front of the central firepit, known as the **sipapu**, symbolized the hole through which human beings emerged onto this earth.

The Ancestral Puebloans

By 700 AD, much of the Southwest was populated by the forerunners of modern Pueblo Indians. Archeologists and Pueblo Indians alike now call these people "**Ancestral Puebloans**" instead of the previously common term "**Anasazi**." The Hopi especially object to that name, which comes from a Navajo word meaning "enemy ancestors," preferring to use either their own word for "ancestors," **Hisatsinom**, or the more generally applicable "Ancestral Puebloans."

Between 700 AD and 1300 AD, Ancestral Puebloan civilization spread beyond the **Four Corners** to cover most of what's now northern Arizona and New Mexico, as well as southern Utah and Colorado, and into southern Nevada. Besides the initial increase in the size and sophistication of villages came a crucial change. Individuals stopped living in pithouses, and instead built surface structures of mud plastered onto a brushwood framework – a style known as wattle-and-daub. However, they continued to dig large subterranean *kivas* for communal or ceremonial use. Many such *kivas* could now also be accessed via concealed tunnels, thus enabling costumed priests or dancers to make surprise appearances during rituals.

The Ancestral Puebloans were the first North Americans to use looms to **weave** cotton. In addition to cotton clothes, they made blankets and even socks from yucca leaves interwoven with turkey feathers, and wore yucca sandals. For a time, they flattened and broadened their skulls by binding infants' heads against cradleboards. Women averaged around five feet in height, men a few inches more, and life expectancy was thirty or less, although perhaps one in ten reached the age of fifty. Adults were plagued by arthritis and loss of teeth, which were worn away by grit, the result of grinding corn between a hand-tool or *mano* and a flat slab known as a *metate*, both made from sandstone. They also had some medical expertise, using cottonwood bark, which contains the main ingredient of aspirin, as a painkiller, and piñon sap as an all-purpose antiseptic.

By the time the Ancestral Puebloans reached their cultural peak in the Four Corners, during the eleventh century, three main subgroups had emerged, centred on Chaco Canyon in what's now northwest New Mexico, Mesa Verde in southwest Colorado, and the Kayenta region of northeast Arizona.

The **Chacoans** seem to have been the most sophisticated of all, as witnessed not only by the architectural complexity of the multistorey pueblos of Chaco Canyon (see p.91), but by the fact that the canyon was so unsuited for large-scale occupation that they must

350 AD	500	700–900
Hohokam civilization constructs canals and ballcourts in Phoenix Basin	Pottery and cotton become established, and the first pueblos appear	The Hohokam establish their largest settlement, Snaketown

have survived by extracting tribute from surrounding regions. Their wealth demonstrates that by 1050 AD the Southwest was crisscrossed by extensive **trading routes**. In the absence of pack animals, most trade was in lightweight ritual or ornamental objects. In exchange for **turquoise**, which passed from group to group all the way down to the Aztecs, the Ancestral Puebloans received silver and copper goods from Mexico, sea-shells from the Pacific, and the most prized ceremonial objects of all – live **macaws**.

During the first half of the twelfth century, the decline of Chaco was mirrored by a general decline in the Ancestral Puebloan population. Following a period of instability and mass migrations, however, Ancestral Puebloan civilization had a majestic final flourish in the Four Corners during the thirteenth century. Major **towns** were constructed, including eight large pueblo complexes in Colorado's Montezuma Valley that held over a thousand people each. The nearby "**cliff dwellings**", squeezed into alcoves on the canyon walls of **Mesa Verde** National Park (see p.74) were home to a smaller, probably peripheral group; though compellingly beautiful to modern eyes, they represent a relatively minor aspect of Ancestral Puebloan life.

The disappearance of the Ancestral Puebloans

Although the "**disappearance**" of the Ancestral Puebloans from the entire Four Corners region between 1275 and 1300 AD is still widely presented as a great mystery, modern Pueblo peoples are so self-evidently their descendants that it's clear the Ancestral Puebloans migrated away rather than simply dying out. *Why* they did so is harder to explain. Traditional accounts say that a sustained **drought** forced them to leave, but such droughts were not uncommon, and the region remained capable of producing enough food.

It seems more likely that the drought coincided with a period of cultural upheaval and violent conflict. Recent proof of cannibalism has shattered notions of Ancestral Puebloan society as being utterly peaceful, and isolated groups appear to have banded together in larger settlements for mutual defence.

The influence of the blood-drenched civilizations of ancient Mexico was also at its height. Centring on supernatural entities that, at this formative stage, closely paralleled the warring deities of the Aztecs, the **kachina** religion spread rapidly across the Southwest; some archeologists controversially argue that it was introduced by cannibalistic warrior refugees from the south. In any case, over time, religious emphasis shifted away from blood and sacrifice toward ceremonies designed to bring rain, and thus corn. The drought of the late thirteenth century may have been the first crucial test of, or judgment upon, those rainmaking powers; possibly charismatic religious leaders persuaded their followers that the failure of the harvest was a signal to move on.

The Ancestral Puebloans had also severely depleted their **environment**, stripping the landscape around their settlements bare; the pueblos of Chaco Canyon, for example, used over 200,000 large wooden beams. It may be no coincidence that the Four Corners remained all but deserted until the arrival of the Navajo during the sixteenth century; it may have taken that long to recover from overexploitation.

A separate history of the **Hopi** tribe appears on p.476, and of the **Navajo** and **Apache** peoples on p.480.

1050	1100	1250–1300
Ancestral Puebloan culture reaches its peak at Chaco Canyon in the Four Corners	The Mimbres people of southern New Mexico produce exquisite ceramics	The ancestors of today's Navajo and Apache migrate into the Southwest

The Hohokam

While the Basketmakers and Ancestral Puebloans held sway further north, the deserts of southern Arizona and northern Mexico were home to the equally sophisticated **Hohokam** civilization. This region was not then so barren as it appears today – much of it was covered with grass until it was overgrazed by Spanish cattle – and the Hohokam were primarily **farmers**. They lived in what the Spanish later called **rancherías** – sprawling farming communities, where each homestead consisted of a framework of timber, brush-coated with mud. Thousands of such villages were scattered across the desert, interspersed with larger "towns" that were probably ceremonial and trading centres rather than residential districts. The population was most heavily concentrated in the **Phoenix Basin**, where inhabitants compensated for the lack of rainfall by digging over three hundred miles of irrigation **canals**. Constructed without the use of metal tools, and requiring constant maintenance, these enabled the Hohokam to reap two separate harvests each year, with corn, beans and squash as their staple crops.

Whether the Hohokam arrived from central Mexico around 300 BC, as some archeologists believe, or simply evolved from indigenous desert peoples, they were clearly heavily influenced by Mexican culture. Each major town had at least one Mexican-style **ballcourt**, where a ritual game was played with a rubber ball, and a raised-earth **platform mound** used for religious ceremonies. Like the Ancestral Puebloans, with whom they had little direct contact, the Hohokam traded commodities like cotton and salt for treasured ritual items from the south, such as copper bells, onyx, parrots and macaws.

During the eleventh century, the Hohokam trading complex known as **Snaketown**, at the confluence of the Gila and Salt rivers, rivalled Chaco as the Southwest's largest settlement. Though Snaketown then declined, the Phoenix Basin became one of the most densely populated areas in North America, with perhaps eighty thousand inhabitants in the thirteenth century. However, the Hohokam **disappeared** at much the same time as the Ancestral Puebloans, around 1350 AD. The very word "Hohokam" means "all used up" in the language of the later **O'odham** people of southern Arizona. So extensively did they drain every possible drop of sustenance from the land that their descendants were reduced to an impoverished subsistence lifestyle. In addition, by the end of the seventeenth century the arrival of European **diseases** such as smallpox, measles and typhus reduced the population of the Phoenix Basin to less than five thousand.

While no modern Native American group claims direct descent from the Hohokam, certain cultural traits endure. The *ranchería* style of dwelling persisted until recently among tribes like the Yavapai, Havasupai and O'odham. Those peoples' individualistic system of belief – lacking *kachinas* or *kivas*, and depending on shamans rather than priests – also matches what little is known about Hohokam religion.

The Mogollon

Archeologists distinguish a third significant group among the pre-Columbian peoples of the Southwest – the **Mogollon**. Contemporaneous with the Ancestral Puebloans and the Hohokam, and sharing elements of both cultures, the Mogollon occupied what's now west-central New Mexico and east-central Arizona. The Mogollon people lived on the cool plateau above the **Mogollon Rim**, a 200-mile long escarpment that marks the

1275	1300	1350
The three "Hopi Mesas" in northern Arizona are home to 35 villages, including Oraibi, the oldest	Shortly after constructing the cliff dwellings of Mesa Verde, the Ancestral Puebloans leave the Four Corners	Hohokam people disappear from southern Arizona

southern limit of the Colorado Plateau, farming the upland meadows and hunting in the mountains.

Being so close to Mexico, the Mogollon heartland, which focused on the valleys of the **Gila** and **Mimbres** rivers, was probably the first area of the Southwest to acquire agriculture and pottery. The Mogollon only stopped building pithouses around the eleventh century, and the few pueblos they constructed, such as the one now preserved as Gila Cliff Dwellings (see p.198), were on a small scale. In one respect, however, Mogollon culture was unsurpassed – the extraordinary **pottery** produced by the **Classic Mimbres** people (see p.198).

Much like the Four Corners, the entire Mogollon region became **depopulated** during the fourteenth century. As the Mogollon peoples had probably introduced the *kachina* religion to the Southwest, their descendants presumably helped to create modern Pueblo culture. Specific Mogollon-descended pueblos may well have been the hardest hit by the arrival of both the Spaniards and the Apache, however, and if their inhabitants survived at all, they probably fled north as refugees.

The Pueblo world and the Spanish invasion

Although the Ancestral Puebloan era ended with their departure from the Four Corners, their immediate descendants created the Southwest's largest pre-Hispanic communities of all. The city of **Casas Grandes**, which flourished between 1300 and 1400 AD in what's now northern Mexico, consisted of over two thousand rooms and served as a major macaw-breeding centre.

However, the most enduring legacy of the Ancestral Puebloans was the emergence of **Pueblo** communities throughout what had previously been under-populated areas of northern New Mexico. Most Mesa Verdeans migrated to the northern reaches of the **Rio Grande** valley, where they founded Taos Pueblo among others; their language, known as Tanoan, evolved into today's Tiwa and Tewa languages. The Chacoans, on the other hand, who spoke the language that became Keresan, moved further south to establish pueblos like Cochiti and Kewa, as well as Ácoma and Zuni to the west.

By the time the Spanish arrived, the Southwest may have held a hundred separate pueblos, with a total population approaching one hundred thousand. New forms of social organization had emerged, and individual pueblos consisted of alliances of either **clans** – each with its own religious or military responsibilities – or **moieties** – societies in which half the pueblo might belong to a *kiva* associated with winter ceremonies, and the other half to one connected to summer. However, pueblos did not have chiefs or leaders in the European sense, and neither was there any tradition of alliances between pueblos. That lack of political unity seriously weakened their ability to resist the Spanish invaders, who turned their attention northwards after completing the conquest of Mexico.

The coming of the Spaniards

The first Spanish expedition to reach what's now the US, led by **Ponce de León**, sailed up the Atlantic coast in 1513 and named **Florida**. The next Spanish voyage, in 1528, ended in shipwreck, but a junior officer, **Alvar Núñez Cabeza de Vaca**, survived. Together with three shipmates, he spent eight years on an extraordinary

1521	1528	1539
Hernán Cortés and his conquistadores seize control of the Aztec capital of Tenochtitlán	A Spanish expedition is shipwrecked in Florida; Cabeza de Vaca and three survivors, including Esteban, a black African, take eight years to walk to Mexico City	Esteban, now serving as the advance party for Fray Marcos de Niza's expedition from Mexico, is killed at Zuni

transcontinental odyssey. Living with various Native American groups – initially held as slaves, later revered as seers – they made their way across Texas, following the Pecos River and the Rio Grande. While they never reached modern New Mexico or Arizona, they heard tales in the Rio Grande pueblo of the Jumano tribe that larger pueblos lay further north, and they were given emeralds in northern Mexico that had been purchased with parrot feathers from a people who lived to the north.

The first entrada: Esteban and Fray Marcos de Niza

After Cabeza de Vaca's sensational arrival in Mexico City in 1536, the Viceroy of New Spain resolved to investigate his tales of golden cities deep in the desert. After all, it was still less than twenty years since the Spanish had conquered the inconceivably wealthy Aztecs. One of Cabeza de Vaca's companions, a black African ex-slave from Morocco called **Esteban de Dorantes**, volunteered to map the route for a new expedition led by the Franciscan friar **Fray Marcos de Niza**. He set off in 1539, following a long-established native trading route north across the Rio San Pedro into what's now Arizona.

A giant of a man, dressed like a shaman in jewellery and feathers and accompanied by two colossal greyhounds, he amazed the native peoples he encountered, and soon acquired a large entourage. Having arranged to send a signal back to Fray Marcos if he discovered anything to rival the marvels of Mexico, he duly did so as he approached the pueblo of **Zuni**. A major trading centre, Zuni nonetheless simply consisted of adobe houses clustered into small villages. Esteban's demands for tribute appearing incompatible with his claims to be a medicine man, the Zuni punished his sacrilegious behaviour by killing him, cutting him into strips, and distributing his flesh among their neighbours.

Hearing of Esteban's death, Fray Marcos fled back to Mexico. Although he had probably not even reached Arizona, he announced "this land … is the greatest and best of all that have been discovered." Calling the six Zuni villages the **Seven Cities of Cíbola**, he identified them with the legendary Seven Cities of Antillia, prosperous Christian communities long sought by Spanish explorers.

The Coronado Expedition

On February 22, 1540, a second Spanish expedition, led by **Francisco Vásquez de Coronado**, set off into the Southwest from Compostela in northern Mexico. More than three hundred Spanish soldiers, along with hundreds of Indian "allies" and servants and several thousand horses and cattle, marched through Arizona to reach Zuni on July 7. In front of the town of Hawikku, the Zuni drew a line of sacred cornmeal along the ground, and forbade the Spaniards to cross. During the pitched **battle** that ensued – the first ever fought between Europeans and Native Americans – Coronado himself was knocked unconscious, but Spanish weapons prevailed. When the town was taken, its storehouses revealed not gold, but something by now equally precious – food.

Within two weeks, news of the fall of Zuni spread throughout the Southwest. Coronado made his headquarters in the conquered pueblo and dispatched exploratory parties in all directions. One such, under Pedro de Tovar, forced the "warlike" Hopi pueblos to surrender (see p.477) and reached as far as the **Grand Canyon**; another, commanded by Melchor Díaz, crossed the Colorado further south, and thus penetrated modern **California**. A detachment led by Hernando de Alvarado headed east to the pueblos of the Rio Grande.

1540–42	1598	1610
Coronado Expedition reaches the Grand Canyon and devastates many New Mexican pueblos before losing its way on the Great Plains and returning to Mexico empty-handed	Don Juan de Oñate establishes the colony of New Mexico	Founding of Santa Fe

Meanwhile, emissaries from the Pueblo world were travelling to Zuni. Peaceful overtures from two men known to the Spaniards as **Cacique** ("Governor") and **Bigotes** ("Whiskers") persuaded Coronado to move his expedition east. Camping for the winter beside the Rio Grande, in a region they called **Tigüex**, they commandeered an entire pueblo for a base. Relations soon degenerated into full-scale war, and in a bloody succession of sieges and massacres, all the Tigüex pueblos were destroyed.

Coronado remained convinced that gold lay somewhere to be found. In the spring of 1541, he decamped northeast to prosperous **Cicuyé** (see p.118), where Pueblo peoples traded with nomads from the Plains. In what may well have been a deliberate plot, Cacique and Bigotes introduced him to "**the Turk**", a Pawnee captive, who knew of a city far to the east, **Quivira**, that was rich in gold. Details of the story suggest the Turk was familiar with the culture of the Mississippi Indians; the leaders of Cicuyé probably hoped he'd lead the Spaniards into oblivion on the endless Plains.

In the event, the expedition wandered for three fruitless months across what they called "the domain of the cows," in honour of its vast buffalo herds. From the Llano Estacado or "Staked Plains" of **Texas**, where they drove wooden stakes into the ground to avoid losing their way, they veered northeast into **Kansas**. They did indeed reach a land known as Quivira, but its inhabitants were nomadic, gold-free buffalo-hunters. At that point, Coronado lost patience; the Turk was garrotted and the Spaniards returned to the Rio Grande.

Remarkably, at their furthest east Coronado's party may have come within a hundred miles of Hernando de Soto's even more rapacious military expedition, which having marched up from Florida was then exploring west of the Mississippi. Legend has it that one unfortunate Indian band fleeing Coronado's advance blundered into the de Soto group.

After another beleaguered winter in Tigüex, the Coronado expedition embarked on the long journey back to Mexico, leaving behind a handful of (swiftly martyred) missionaries and many of their Mexican-Indian allies.

The colony of New Mexico

During the fifty years after Coronado's departure, unauthorized Spanish adventurers made occasional forays into the Southwest. Not until 1598, however, was **Don Juan de Oñate** granted royal permission to establish a permanent **colony**. His expedition, consisting of 130 families and two hundred single men, crossed the Rio Grande near modern El Paso on May 1 and took possession of the land as **New Mexico**. Broadly speaking, the colony's as-yet-unspecified boundaries extended from the Colorado River in the west to the Pecos River in the east; as well as what's now New Mexico, it included all of Arizona, plus parts of Utah, Colorado, Nevada and California. The name "Mexico" then referred only to Mexico City, so "New Mexico" was named in the hope that it would match the riches of the Aztecs.

Each pueblo Oñate's party reached as they travelled north had been hurriedly deserted by its inhabitants, fearful of being captured as slaves. Eventually, at the confluence of the Rio Grande and the Chama River near modern Española, the settlers took over the pueblo of Ohkey Owingeh, renamed it San Juan, and made it their **capital**. Like Coronado before him, Oñate despatched soldiers in every direction in search of gold; and like Coronado he soon found himself at war. After a group

1626	1640	1680
First Spanish mention of "de Nabajú", the people who became the Navajo and the Apache	Thanks to horses, newly acquired from the Spaniards, the Navajo are by now regularly raiding Pueblo settlements	New Mexico's Native American population join forces to drive out the Spaniars in the Pueblo Revolt

commanded by Oñate's nephew was all but wiped out, he launched a full-scale artillery onslaught on Ácoma Pueblo. Over eight hundred Acomans were killed, and eighty male prisoners had their feet chopped off in the pueblos of the Rio Grande.

By the time Oñate returned to his capital, most of the colonists had given up and returned to Mexico. Oñate himself was recalled to Mexico City in disgrace once Franciscan missionaries reported his cruelty. Meanwhile, however, Captain Pérez de Villagrá had trumpeted his "achievements" in an epic poem, *Historia de Nueva México*. Villagrá's insistence that New Mexico could become the greatest kingdom in the Spanish empire was sufficiently believed for Madrid to launch another attempt at colonization. **Don Pedro de Peralta** was therefore sent to New Mexico to found a new capital, and the city of **Santa Fe** was duly laid out in 1610.

New Mexico in the seventeenth century

New Mexico's first Spanish colonists dreamed of emulating their predecessors in Mexico, who had accumulated land and wealth in prodigious quantities. However, it soon became clear that New Mexico was the end of the road, with no access to the ocean and no rich neighbours to either trade with or plunder. Santa Fe never grew into a mighty city, but remained a remote military outpost of crude adobe buildings. Enterprising colonists therefore dispersed up and down the Rio Grande valley, appropriating Pueblo farmlands – and often enslaving Pueblo peoples – to create **ranches** to raise sheep and corn and grow peaches, plums and cherries. **Wheat** was the most significant new crop. Unlike corn, beans and squash, which must be grown in spring and summer, wheat can be planted in December for harvest in June.

At the same time, **Franciscan missionaries** set out to convert the Pueblo Indians to Catholicism. One or two friars would attach themselves to a pueblo, recruit Indian labour to build adobe mission churches, and set about persuading the Pueblos that their *kachina* cults and corn ceremonies were wicked. The Spanish civil and religious authorities found themselves at perpetual loggerheads. While deploring violence against the Pueblos, the church demanded the eradication of their beliefs; the military governors preferred not to antagonize the Indians unnecessarily, but felt their authority ultimately rested on the sword.

Quite apart from any specific actions, the very presence of the Spaniards utterly disrupted the region. Settled communities like the Rio Grande villages were especially vulnerable to **epidemic diseases** such as smallpox, measles and typhus, unknown before the arrival of the Europeans. By 1640, the Pueblo population had dropped from a hundred thousand to around thirty thousand, and more than half of all pueblos had been abandoned. Existing patterns of **trade** were shattered, and the Rio Grande valley became a prime target for raiders who coveted Spanish arms and, above all, **horses**. Tribes such as the Navajo and the Apache turned from wandering nomads into fearsome mounted warriors, and all too often the Pueblo peoples bore the brunt of their attacks.

The Pueblo Revolt

In 1675, aware that traditional Pueblo beliefs still endured beneath a veneer of Catholicism, the Spanish arrested 47 Pueblo religious leaders. Three were condemned as "witchdoctors" and hanged at Santa Fe; the rest were publicly horsewhipped. One of

1696	1693–1750	1720
Don Diego de Vargas completes the Reconquest of New Mexico	Living alongside Pueblo refugees in the remote Pueblitos of Dinétah, the Navajo acquire Pueblo skills such as weaving and sheep farming	A joint force of French and Pawnee defeats a Spanish-Pueblo incursion into Nebraska

these, a man called **Po'pay** from Ohkey Owingeh, made his way to Taos Pueblo and turned a *kiva* into the centre of a campaign of resistance. A date was set for a concerted uprising against the Spanish, and knotted strings were sent out to all the pueblos, with the instruction to untie one knot each night until the last signalled the arrival of the great day. Somehow, the plot was betrayed, so the **Pueblo Revolt** began a day early, on August 9, 1680.

For the first and only time in their history, the Pueblos of the northern Rio Grande, plus their cousins in Acoma, Zuni and the Hopi mesas, combined in unison; they were even joined by the Navajo and the Apache. Their anger fell especially upon the missionaries; 21 out of New Mexico's 33 priests were murdered, as were 375 men, women and children out of a total of 2350 Spanish colonists.

After a ten-day **siege of Santa Fe**, the governor, the garrison and one thousand citizens were allowed to retreat south. They were joined en route by the Christianized majority from Isleta Pueblo – the only modern pueblo not to join the attack – and all the Pueblo peoples who lived south of Albuquerque. For the next thirteen years, the refugees remained together at what's now Ciudad Juarez, across the Rio Grande from El Paso.

Back in Santa Fe, the doors and windows of the Palace of the Governors had been sealed and the building turned into a multistorey pueblo. Po'pay was nominally in control, but the concept of a central political administration was alien to the Pueblos, and the alliance soon fragmented.

Reconquest

In 1692, the Spanish crown appointed a new governor of New Mexico, **Don Diego de Vargas**. His exploratory expedition encountered no opposition when it returned to Santa Fe that September. He set off again with a party of colonists the following year; this time they had to fight before they could re-enter the city, in December 1693. The return of the Spanish triggered mass migrations throughout the region. Modern Navajo culture originated from the intermingling of the ancestral Navajo with Pueblo refugees during this period. Further minor insurrections followed, but the **Reconquest** was completed by 1696.

The eighteenth century

Although Hispanic settlers continued to dominate New Mexico for 150 years after the Pueblo Revolt, it was always a peripheral part of the Spanish empire. Cut off by vast tracts of empty desert, the colonists were obliged to be self-sufficient, and found themselves thrown into alliance with the Pueblo peoples to resist the threat of Ute and Comanche attack. The Spaniards and the Pueblos had much in common; the New Mexican landscape was similar to that of Andalucia in Spain, as indeed were its adobe hamlets or *pueblos*. The Pueblos had long been subsistence farmers who traded for rare luxuries with far-off civilizations to the south, and the Hispanic ranchers slotted into the same pattern. Although there was little intermarriage, Pueblo communities acquired sizeable populations of *genízaros*, the bastard offspring of captured Plains Indians and their Spanish masters.

When the **French** established their own colony to the east, **Louisiana**, early in the eighteenth century, the Spanish responded by setting up missions among the Indians of

1776	1821
Spanish colonists establish Tucson; Father Garcés visits the Havasupai Indians; and fathers Domínguez and Escalante explore Utah	Mexico achieves independence, with New Mexico as part of its territory

what now became a separate province of New Spain, **Texas**. As the French and Spanish zones of influence expanded, there were armed clashes; thus a combined force of Spaniards and Pueblos was defeated by a French–Pawnee alliance near North Platte, Nebraska, in 1720.

In general, the French coexisted more amicably with Native Americans than did the Spanish; predominantly traders, eager to acquire beaver and other furs, they were less interested in converting Indians to Christianity. Unlike the Spanish, they were also prepared to supply Indians with **guns**. As a result, the Comanche, Ute and Apache, equipped with European firearms, consistently raided along the Rio Grande at harvest time, seizing crops and livestock, while the Hispanic villagers, inadequately supplied from Mexico, could only offer minimal resistance with their bows and arrows. The colonists financed the occasional retaliatory expedition by selling Indian captives to work as slaves in the silver mines of Mexico, thereby incurring ever greater Indian hostility.

Louisiana ultimately proved no more profitable to France than was New Mexico to Spain, so Louis XV of France simply gave it to Spain in 1762. The Mississippi River now formed the Spanish frontier in North America. Determined to resist encroachment by the infant United States, King Carlos III placed the entire region under direct control from Spain in 1776. However, too few Hispanic settlers moved in to make any difference, and in 1802, as the Spanish empire weakened, he handed Louisiana back to Napoleon. Carlos' hope that the French would serve as a buffer against the Yankees was misplaced; Napoleon sold his American territories to the US the next year, in the **Louisiana Purchase**.

At the end of the century, Santa Fe was home to around two thousand Hispanic citizens, while the Pueblo population had dwindled to perhaps nine thousand, in a mere nineteen pueblos.

The settlement of Arizona

Before the Pueblo Revolt, the Spanish presence in New Mexico was confined to the valley of the Rio Grande and the scattered pueblos to the west. Under the names of **Pimería Alta** and **Papaguería**, what's now southern Arizona was left to peoples the Spaniards called the **Pima** and the **Papago**, known today as the **O'odham**.

Around 1700, however, **Jesuit** missionaries conceived the notion of erecting a chain of missions from New Spain to California, and built churches in a couple of O'odham villages. Hispanic ranchers and prospectors also drifted in. In 1736, a Yaqui Indian created a silver-mining camp, a few miles southwest of modern Nogales, called **Arizonac**. The name came either from the O'odham *ali shonak*, meaning "small springs", or from the Basque language of Spain, in which *arritza onac* means "valuable rocky places", and *aritz onac* means "good oaks."

After an O'odham rebellion killed several Jesuits, the Spanish installed a military *presidio* (fort) at **Tubac** in 1752, relocated forty miles north to San Agustín de **Tucson** in 1776. Another Indian revolt in 1781, in which 150 settlers were wiped out during mass at **Yuma**, dashed Spanish hopes of establishing a permanent trail to California, and Tucson, like Santa Fe, came to be seen as an insignificant dead-end town. In 1804, when around a thousand Spanish colonists lived in the vicinity, its commander reported, "we have no gold, silver, lead, tin, quicksilver, copper mines, or marble quarries ... the only public work here that is truly worthy of this report is the church at **San Xavier del Bac**" (see p.230).

1830	1847
Joseph Smith establishes the Mormon Church in upstate New York	Mormon settlers found Salt Lake City; then, following the Mexican War, the US acquires Texas, California and New Mexico north of the Gila River

The end of the Hispanic era

The decline in New Mexico's importance to its Spanish rulers was mirrored by increasing contacts with the rest of North America. In the closing years of the eighteenth century, permanent trails were established both west to California – in the form of the **Old Spanish Trail**, painstakingly mapped across Utah by Franciscan friars **Domínguez** and **Escalante** in 1776 – and east to St Louis, along the **Santa Fe Trail** blazed by French explorer Pedro Vial in 1792. After the Louisiana Purchase, official US expeditions also crossed the Plains, such as **Lewis and Clark**'s trek to the Northwest in 1804 and **Lt. Zebulon Pike**'s incursion into New Mexico in 1807.

Within a few years, the Spanish grip on the New World finally loosened; Mexico became an independent nation following a **revolution** in 1821. Although their governors swiftly transferred allegiance to Mexico City, neither New Mexico nor California saw any advantage in their new status as Mexican territories. As the flow of resources from the south – including the handouts that were keeping the Apache relatively docile – dwindled, the effect on the New Mexican economy was crippling.

For the authorities in Santa Fe, the only answer seemed to be to increase trade with the US. Traffic along the Santa Fe Trail swiftly turned New Mexico into an entrepôt through which American goods were shipped south into Mexico. No Americans were permitted to live in New Mexico, but freebooting Anglos made their way across the Plains to seek their fortunes in the West. Fur-trapping "**mountain men**" such as **Bill Williams** and **Kit Carson** made extended forays along the region's rivers in pursuit of beavers (or "hairy banknotes"). **Taos** became renowned for its annual rendezvous, at which Anglo, Hispanic and Native American traders gathered far from the authority of any government.

Meanwhile, enough Yankee newcomers had flocked into **Texas** to outnumber its loyal Mexican subjects. In 1836, after Texas fought to gain independence from Mexico and then voted for annexation by the US, the president of Mexico attempted to hold onto New Mexico by closing down the Santa Fe Trail. It was too late. The doctrine that it was the United States' "**Manifest Destiny**" to extend across the whole continent led the US government first to try to **buy** New Mexico and California, and then, when negotiations failed, to declare **war** on Mexico in 1846. American economic might was neatly illustrated when the US Army of the West took Santa Fe without a fight, in August 1846; the Mexican governor was simply paid $50,000 to leave, together with his garrison.

Territorial days: New Mexico and Arizona

Under the **Treaty of Guadalupe-Hidalgo**, signed in September 1847 after US soldiers had captured Mexico City, the United States paid $18.25 million to take formal possession of New Mexico, Texas and California – seen as the real prize. New Mexico, which consisted of all those parts of modern New Mexico and Arizona that lie north of the Gila River, plus areas of Nevada and Utah, was generally regarded as an arid, worthless wasteland.

Ironically, only the discovery of **gold** in California in 1847 gave New Mexico any great value to the US – as a route west. Surveyors mapping possible courses for a southern transcontinental railroad soon realized that the best routes lay on the Mexican side of the border. The Mexican government accepted the least extensive of five suggested land deals, and in June 1854, the $10 million **Gadsden Purchase** gave the US what's now southern Arizona, including Tucson, Tubac and Tumacácori.

1854	1864	1869
The $10 million Gadsden Purchase buys southern Arizona for the US	The Navajo are rounded up and sent on the Long Walk to the Bosque Redondo reservation in New Mexico, from which they return in 1868	An expedition led by John Wesley Powell explores the canyons of the Green and Colorado rivers for the first time

Another 25 years passed before the railroad reached the Southwest, but prospectors trekking to and from California soon began to investigate the region more thoroughly. After gold was found near the confluence of the Gila and Colorado rivers, **miners** fanned out across central Arizona, and reports of rich silver and copper lodes lured ever more migrants in.

Feeling little in common with the Hispanic farming communities of the Rio Grande, the new arrivals argued that the territory was too large to govern as a single unit and should be split in two. Many came originally from the South, and seized upon the start of the **Civil War** in 1861 to declare the formation of the Confederate Territory of **Arizona**, consisting of all the Gadsden Purchase lands. Its capital was Mesilla, in what's now New Mexico. The Confederate cause in the Southwest was short-lived: a Confederate army was turned back by Union forces outside Santa Fe in March 1862. The federal government recognized the existence of Arizona in 1863, but to avoid giving it a built-in Confederate majority drew a north–south boundary rather than an east–west one, and thereby delineated the two modern states.

The Indian wars

In the early years of the Civil War, US Army outposts throughout the Southwest were abandoned when the troops were sent east. That spurred a new era of raiding by the **Apache** and **Navajo**, and the Anglo and Hispanic settlements of southern Arizona in particular became depopulated. By late 1861, only two significant non-native settlements survived in Arizona; two hundred citizens remained in Tucson, while a band of miners held out at Patagonia.

However, the Army soon returned in greater strength than ever, resolved to eradicate the Indian "menace" once and for all. Brigadier General James Carleton and Kit Carson drove the **Navajo** into exile in New Mexico in 1864 – they were soon back in Arizona, but never again posed a military threat – while a long cycle of treaties, betrayals and guerrilla campaigns wore down **Apache** resistance by 1886.

Towards statehood

The increasing subjugation of the region's Native American population opened the way for an influx of Anglo settlers. During the 1860s, ancient Hohokam canals in the Salt River Valley were cleared to irrigate the new city of **Phoenix**, which swiftly became the capital of Arizona. Mining camps in the mountains, such as **Silver City** in New Mexico and **Tombstone** and **Jerome** in Arizona, turned into fully fledged towns, while massive cattle ranches spread across the open desert.

At first, the Anglo newcomers were almost exclusively male and married into Hispanic families. Spanish remained the lingua franca, Catholicism the dominant religion, and silver Mexican pesos the common currency. With the coming of the **railroad**, however, around 1880, things began to change, and north–south links were replaced by commerce oriented to east and west. The Southwestern economy became increasingly **extractive**, digging up minerals and depleting natural resources for shipment to distant cities. Where Native Americans and Hispanics had farmed for self-sufficiency, the Anglos sought profit. During the 1880s, huge herds of sheep and cattle were introduced to marginal grasslands that swiftly proved incapable of supporting them.

1880	July 14, 1881	October 26, 1881
New Mexico governor Lew Wallace publishes the novel Ben Hur	Sheriff Pat Garrett kills Billy the Kid in Fort Sumner, New Mexico	Wyatt Earp and "Doc" Holliday emerge victorious in a shoot-out at OK Corral, in Tombstone, Arizona

Toward the end of the nineteenth century, tensions pitted both the large-scale mining and cattle-raising concerns, backed by wealthy eastern corporations and the federal government, against individual prospectors and cowboys. These swiftly became so acute, and so recurrent, that some historians speak of a **Western Civil War of Incorporation**. Many legendary Wild West incidents, like the **Gunfight at the OK Corral** in Tombstone, Arizona and the **Lincoln County War** in New Mexico, stemmed more from behind-the-scenes political manoeuvring than from the whims of trigger-happy outlaws.

Besides luring cowboys, miners and other adventurers to the Southwest, the railroads also created new industries. Communities like Flagstaff and Williams sprang up to exploit the vast ponderosa forests of northern Arizona, while the increased accessibility of the Grand Canyon, publicized by the voyages of John Wesley Powell (see p.401), meant that the first **tourists** began to arrive.

Meanwhile, in New Mexico, Hispanic villagers looked on helplessly as their lands were parcelled out to newly arrived Anglo ranchers. New Mexicans had traditionally owned small plots for individual use, with grazing lands shared in common, but American courts refused to recognize communal land rights.

To a considerable degree, it was anti-Hispanic Anglo racism that delayed **statehood** for both Arizona and New Mexico. For many years, Republicans in Washington clung to the idea that they should be reunited and admitted as a single state, in the hope that Arizona's larger Anglo population would help to "temper" the Hispanic majority in New Mexico. Arizonans overwhelmingly defeated that proposal in a referendum in 1906 (which passed in New Mexico), and both were finally admitted in 1912 – **New Mexico** in January as the **47th state**, **Arizona** in February as the **48th**, the last of what are now known as the "**Lower 48**."

Utah in the nineteenth century

Until the nineteenth century, the history of what's now the state of Utah forms a minor adjunct to that of the Southwest as a whole. Its main Ancestral Puebloan groups, the Virgin and the more nomadic Fremont peoples, abandoned southern Utah around the same time their Four Corners brethren moved away. By the time Spanish explorers began to pass through, searching for a route to California, it was the domain of Ute and Paiute Indians. Twelve to thirty thousand were present in 1850; most had traditionally been farmers, but they had recently acquired horses and were starting to raid travellers on the newly created Old Spanish Trail, which linked Santa Fe to Los Angeles.

The reports of men like the fur trapper **Jedediah Smith**, who named the Virgin River, and **John C. Frémont**, who mapped much of southwest Utah in the early 1840s, attracted the region's first permanent white settlers. By far the most important of these were the massed ranks of the Church of Jesus Christ of Latter-Day Saints, known to the outside world as the **Mormons**.

The coming of the Mormons

Although it was widely assumed that the Mormon Church would disintegrate after the death of Joseph Smith – and one of his sons decamped to Missouri with his own monogamous splinter group – his successor, **Brigham Young**, held the flock together. Promising the governor of Illinois in 1845 that the Mormons would abandon Nauvoo,

1886	1896	1905
Geronimo is tricked into surrendering in southern Arizona, thus ending Apache resistance to the US Army	The Mormon church having renounced polygamy, Utah becomes a state	The city of Las Vegas is founded, following the arrival of the railroad

JOSEPH SMITH AND THE MORMON CHURCH

The founder of the Mormon church, **Joseph Smith**, was born to a family of itinerant farmers in Sharon, Vermont, on December 23, 1805. Smith was a farmhand in Palmyra, New York, when he had his first vision of the **Angel Moroni** in 1823. On his third annual visit, Moroni led him to a set of golden plates hidden in a nearby hillside. Only Smith ever saw them; concealed behind a curtain, he translated them from the "reformed Egyptian" with the aid of two mysterious devices (the Urim and the Thummim), and thus dictated the **Book of Mormon**. Described by Mark Twain as "chloroform in print," this revealed that two Israelite families fled Jerusalem around 600 BC, and sailed east from the Red Sea to the "Promised Land," led by a man named Lehi. His sons later quarrelled; Nephi remained loyal and was rewarded by a visit from the risen Christ, while Laman and Lemuel led the dissident, cursed Lamanites, the ancestors of the Native Americans. After a thousand years of conflict, the Lamanites finally defeated the Nephites in a great battle at the hill of Cumorah. The one Nephite survivor – Moroni, son of Mormon – buried the plates close by.

Smith proclaimed his new church on April 6, 1830. He was not unique among frontier prophets in attracting thousands of followers. Rooted in the economic uncertainty of his own life, his vision of an ordered, communalistic society struck a deep chord with his peers. To their "**Gentile**" neighbours, on the other hand, leadership by divine revelation smacked of Catholicism, and the Mormons were suspected of owing loyalty to their church not their country. Their most controversial trait was **polygamy**, or "celestial marriage." Smith denied this to outsiders, pointing to a passage in the Book of Mormon that called polygamy "abominable". In private, however, he declared his disciples to have a sacred duty to marry and produce children, thereby freeing disembodied spirits from limbo by giving them bodily form. Preaching that the dead could be baptized by proxy, he argued that Mormon marriage was different to the "until death do us part" Christian sacrament. Church elders had a duty to establish polygamous, patriarchal families that would endure into the afterlife. Smith also became a Mason, and many of his church's rituals were inspired by Masonic practices.

In the face of constant harassment, Smith moved his family to Kirtland, **Ohio** – where they built their first temple – and then on to **Missouri** in 1838. After bloody clashes between slave-holding Gentiles and the Mormon militia, the Sons of Dan, he was captured and sentenced to death, then allowed to escape by sympathetic guards. The Mormons were next given sanctuary by the governor of **Illinois**, who saw them as hard-working potential citizens, and their new settlement of **Nauvoo** swiftly became the largest city in that state, with a population of 25,000.

In 1844, when Joseph Smith announced that he was running for president, the Latter-Day Saints were being attacked not only by their neighbours but also from within. When a group of anti-polygamy dissenters attempted to establish a rival church in Nauvoo and set up their own newspaper, Smith ordered that its presses be destroyed. Together with his brother Hyrum, Smith was arrested and imprisoned in nearby Carthage. A "blackface" mob attacked the jail, and both men were shot.

Young set about organizing a mass **westward migration**. In the winter of 1846, ten thousand Saints camped near modern Omaha, Nebraska, while Young scouted ahead. Descending the western flank of the Rockies, he declared "This is the place," and in 1847 his followers founded **Salt Lake City**.

At that time, the all but empty wilderness claimed by the Mormons as **Deseret** (a Mormon word meaning "honeybee," to denote industry), or the **Great Basin Kingdom**,

1908	1912	1935
President Theodore Roosevelt creates Grand Canyon National Monument, which becomes a National Park in 1919	Arizona and New Mexico achieve statehood	The Hoover Dam blocks the Colorado River near Las Vegas

still belonged to Mexico. As well as what's now Utah, its putative boundaries included almost all of modern Nevada, most of Arizona and southern California, and sizeable chunks of four other present-day states. Mormon dreams of establishing an independent theocracy, outside the United States, were dashed within a year, when the US government annexed the entire region and the Gold Rush wagon trains began to roll west. The Saints therefore petitioned Congress for Deseret to be granted statehood. Suspicious of its religious underpinnings, Congress instead recognized a smaller area as the **Territory of Utah** in 1850, and appointed Brigham Young as its first governor.

Embarking on a vast communal effort to irrigate the desert, the Mormons were joined over the next decade by converts recruited throughout America and Europe, to reach a total by 1860 of over fifty thousand. Fifteen thousand arrived from England alone, of whom three thousand literally walked across America, pushing their belongings in handcarts ahead of them.

During the 1850s, and especially once Young, who felt no further need for diplomacy, had publicly acknowledged the existence of polygamy in 1852, the federal government came to see the Mormons as a significant threat to the Union. The newly formed Republican party railed against slavery and polygamy in equal measure, as "twin relics of barbarism." Congress decided to appoint a new non-Mormon governor of Utah, and sent him west with a detachment of 2500 soldiers, representing one sixth of the US army. Salt Lake City was temporarily abandoned, but thanks to the secession of the Confederacy, the anticipated Mormon War never quite happened.

When the **Civil War** in the East cut off supplies of commodities such as cotton, Brigham Young redoubled his commitment to making the Mormons **self-sufficient**. Pioneer parties created "missions" throughout the Southwest, but while many such farming communities still survive – including **Cedar City** and **St George** in southern Utah – they did little to diminish Utah's economic interdependence with the rest of the US. The advent of the railroads and the arrival in Utah of ever-increasing numbers of non-Mormons – especially miners – exacerbated the situation.

As the Mormons set out to "tame" the wilderness, the **Ute** fought back. After the **Black Hawk War**, waged between 1865 and 1867, the Ute were confined to reservations in the territory that by now bore their name, and the Mormons spread throughout southern Utah. The "**Hole in the Rock**" party (see p.378), for example, trekked across the central deserts in the winter of 1879–80 to establish **Bluff** in the east. Little now survives from simultaneous Mormon attempts to settle in **northern Arizona**, apart from a few tiny settlements along the **Arizona Strip**.

Meanwhile the federal authorities renewed their attacks on polygamy. When the Supreme Court subjected polygamists to disenfranchisement and the confiscation of their property in 1878, Utah retaliated by giving women the vote, so Mormon women could consolidate the Church's hold on State power. The **Edmonds-Tucker Act** of 1887 hit back, dissolving the Church and confiscating its assets, and once more disenfranchising women.

Brigham Young had died in 1877, and new Mormon leaders sensed they'd do better to drop polygamy on their own terms before being forced to do so. Polygamy was therefore formally renounced in 1890, clearing the way for Utah to become a **state** in **1896**.

1938	1945	1947
John Ford films Stagecoach in Monument Valley	Developed in secrecy at Los Alamos, the first atomic bomb is exploded at the Trinity Site in central New Mexico	After crash-landing near Roswell, New Mexico, "alien invaders" begin to seize control of Earth

The modern Southwest

Arizona, New Mexico and Utah spent most of their first century of statehood battling to secure ever greater quantities of **water**. In the early years, the main objective was to prevent California from grabbing the lion's share of the flow of the Colorado River. Later on, cities like Phoenix fought for federal funds to build grandiose water-diversion schemes. With the completion of the **Central Arizona Project** in 1991, John Wesley Powell's nineteenth-century prediction that "All the waters of all the arid lands will eventually be taken from their natural channels" has now all but come true.

While New Mexico at the start of the twentieth century remained as a cluster of farming towns along the Rio Grande Valley, Arizona was prospering on the large-scale exploitation of its mineral wealth. **World War I** saw copper prices leap, and in alliance with state politicians mine-owners easily quashed labour disputes. Arizona employers could also take cynical advantage of the vast pool of potential workers just across the border to the south. After the Wall Street Crash of 1929, for example – by which time the state was responsible for half of all US copper production – over 500,000 Mexican labourers, now surplus to requirements, were deported.

Though the **Depression** hit hard across the Southwest, the region also benefited from a massive injection of federal cash, in the form of make-work public projects such as dam- and road-building. **World War II** not only renewed demand for copper and other metals but kick-started **urbanization** throughout the Southwest. Partly to make them less vulnerable to attack, defence installations were relocated away from the coasts, presenting **Albuquerque** and **Phoenix** in particular with their first major industrial plants, as well as greatly increased numbers of consumers. A former school in **Los Alamos**, New Mexico, was transformed into the laboratory that developed the atomic bomb – hence, some say, the alien crash-landing at **Roswell** in 1947.

After the war, the defence and other industries stayed on, and the ensuing period of mass migration to the Southwest resulted in an extraordinary population boom. Arizona and New Mexico were home to around 500,000 people each in 1940; Arizona's population has now topped six million, with half that number in the metropolitan Phoenix area alone, while New Mexico holds over two million. Even more striking is the fact that whereas Arizona was 84 percent rural at the start of the twentieth century, around 90 percent of the population were city-dwellers by the end. **Las Vegas**, Nevada, did not even exist until 1905; it now boasts well over a million inhabitants.

Meanwhile, **southern Utah** has remained sparsely inhabited. Attempts at large-scale ranching in the late 1800s resulted in destructive overgrazing, and the region relied on subsistence farming until the discovery of **uranium** in 1952 (see p.420) triggered a **mining bonanza** that sent prospectors scurrying into every nook and cranny of the wilderness. Local Mormon businessmen of southern Utah lobbied hard for mine and dam projects in the face of growing environmental opposition. Calling themselves the "**Sagebrush Rebels**," they attracted support from then-President Ronald Reagan, but were ultimately defeated as much by the realities of world commodity markets as by the "tree-huggers" they despised. Since the collapse of mining in the early 1980s, **tourism** has finally been appreciated as a major industry, and towns like **Moab** have developed facilities for travellers smitten by the lure of the desert.

1963	1967	1996
Stopping the flow of the Colorado River into the Grand Canyon, the Glen Canyon Dam creates Lake Powell	Elvis Presley films Stay Away Joe in Sedona, Arizona	President Clinton creates Grand Staircase–Escalante National Monument, in southern Utah

The Hopi

Nowhere in the Southwest is the continuity between the pre-Hispanic past and the present more apparent than on the three Hopi mesas, on the southern edge of Arizona's Black Mesa (p.66). The Hopi have lived here for at least one thousand years, preserving their culture despite repeated incursions from outsiders.

The origin of the Hopi

According to Hopi mythology, this, the **Fourth World**, is inhabited by the righteous people who escaped the destruction of the Third World by climbing a reed through the dome of the sky. They emerged in the depths of the Grand Canyon, through a hole beside the Little Colorado River known as the *sipapu*. There they were greeted by the terrifying but kindly disposed deity **Maasaw**, who explained the rules of life in this world and despatched them on migratory journeys to the four points of the compass. Their wanderings ended with a return to the **Sacred Circle** and the establishment of the villages on what are now the Hopi mesas.

Both myth and history depict the Hopi as a peripatetic people who became ever more sedentary as they learned agriculture and pottery. Archeologists and Hopi alike recognize their cultural continuity with the ancient peoples of the Southwest. There's no doubt that the earliest occupants of the Hopi mesas migrated from nearby Kayenta Anasazi and Sinagua settlements, but whether they had previously wandered into central America, where the language and beliefs of the **Aztecs** show clear parallels to the Hopi, remains unproven.

Though the Hopi mesas were probably inhabited by around 700 AD, what the Hopi call the "**gathering of the clans**" peaked between 1100 and 1300 AD, and thus coincided with the Ancestral Puebloans' abandonment of the Four Corners. One by one, small groups of refugees arrived at the mesas and petitioned for land and the right to settle. Each was required to demonstrate what it had to offer, with the crucial factor being the ceremonial power to produce rain. Once allowed to stay, each group – most were no more than individual families – was regarded as a separate **clan**.

The Bear clan, said to have come from Mesa Verde, was the first to arrive, and thus retains precedence to this day. It established Maseeba as the Second Mesa's "mother village" at the foot of the mesa, which changed its name to **Shungopavi** when it relocated to the mesa-top several centuries later. Similarly, **Walpi** on First Mesa, when founded by the Snake clan from Hovenweep, stood several hundred yards below its present, highly defensible mesa-top site. **Oraibi**, the "mother village" of Third Mesa, is generally regarded as the oldest Hopi village because it has occupied the same spot since its foundation; beams have been dated to 1260 AD, but some dwellings may be a century or more older.

By 1275 AD, the three mesas held 35 villages. The Fire, Water and Coyote clans had come from the cliff dwellings of Keet Seel and Betatakin, now in Navajo National Monument; the Flute clan from Canyon de Chelly; the Rabbit clan from the south, perhaps Casas Grandes in Mexico; and others had streamed in from Chaco Canyon and the Sinagua sites of Wupatki and Walnut Canyon. While each village remained autonomous, this disparate community forged a common culture, adopting its own variation of the **kachina** religion as it spread throughout the Southwest (see p.67).

The coming of the Spaniards

Hopi prophecies have long predicted the return of *Pahaana*, the "True White Brother" separated from the Hopi at an early stage of their migrations. Assuming that he finds the Hopi living in purity and righteousness, he will help solve any problems they face and lead them into the Fifth World.

If the Hopi saw *Pahaana* in the first **Spanish** explorers to reach the mesas, their illusions were soon shattered. Exactly what happened when a detachment of Coronado's expedition, led by Lieutenant Pedro de Tovar, arrived in 1540, is uncertain. Alerted by the Zuni, the Hopi greeted the party in the fields, signalling them not to cross a line of sacred cornmeal sprinkled on the earth. According to the official Spanish report, a Franciscan friar, exasperated by the rigmarole, commented, "To tell the truth, I do not know why we came here" – and that was enough to trigger a Spanish onslaught. By the next sentence, the two sides are at peace, and Hopi guides went on to lead a group of Spaniards to the Grand Canyon.

During that and subsequent sixteenth-century Spanish incursions, the Hopi took care to make their lands – which the Spanish called **Tusayan** – appear valueless. As a result, the Spanish never bothered to leave either a garrison or any settlers. Franciscan **missionaries** did, however, return in 1629 to build churches in Awatovi, Shungopavi and Oraibi. The one at Awatovi was on a similar scale to the mission that still survives at Ácoma, and required a similar amount of forced Indian labour; others involved filling in and "rededicating" existing *kivas*. The missionaries also introduced sheep and cattle, making the Hopi the first people to raise livestock in Arizona.

The Hopi were enthusiastic participants in the **Pueblo Revolt** of 1680, sacking the churches and killing four priests. Fearing a Spanish return, they welcomed Tewa-speaking Pueblo refugees from the Rio Grande, who founded the First Mesa village of Hano. By now, the **Navajo** – said by the Hopi to bash in their captives' skulls with a rock, and thus called *Tasavuh* or "head pounders" – had entered the picture. They too joined the Pueblo Revolt, but were also starting to crowd the Hopi away from their summer farming and grazing lands, and to raid for animals. During this unsettled period, the villages of Walpi, Shungopavi and Mishongnovi moved to fortified positions on the mesa tops.

After the Spanish reconquered New Mexico, those Hopi who still regarded themselves as Christians gathered in **Awatovi**. When the other Hopi villages realized the people of Awatovi were willing to invite the missionaries back, they determined to eradicate the Christian menace once and for all. At the end of 1700, the men of Awatovi were betrayed by their headman, who called a predawn meeting in the *kiva*. Warriors from all the other villages pulled up the ladder, rained arrows down on the trapped men, and then set light to the *kiva*; surviving women and children were shared out as booty.

That brutal act probably spared the Hopi both internal dissent and missionary interference for the rest of the Spanish and Mexican era. The mesas were, however, increasingly beleaguered by mounted Navajo and Ute war parties and slave raiders from the south.

The Hopi under the United States

By the time the Southwest was acquired by the United States, during the 1840s, the Hopi were desperate for protection from the marauding Navajo. Hopi scouts eagerly participated in General Carleton's 1864 round-up which forced the Navajo on the Long Walk to Bosque Redondo (see p.481).

Within a few years, the Navajo were back, reasserting control over their former territory and raiding to replenish their herds. Called to define who "owned" what land, the US government was inadequate to the task. The very concept of a "tribe" was a federal invention; neither Navajo nor Hopi recognized any authority above clan or village level. Moreover, the idea of a reservation only worked if one group or other had exclusive use of an area. Only villages and fields counted as the "possession" of land; hunting grounds were regarded as unoccupied. Because the San Francisco Peaks are sacred to, and used by, both the Navajo and the Hopi, they belong to neither.

Until the 1920s, the Hopi were generally known by a name coined by the people of Ácoma: Moki, or Moqui. Because that sounded too much like a Hopic word meaning "to have died," they then changed to Hopi, which means "well-behaved." The **Moqui Indian reservation**, established in 1882 as a rectangle measuring 70 by 55 miles, did not even include all the Hopi villages. The hundred Hopi at Moenkopi were excluded, while three hundred Navajo lived within the boundaries. As was standard, the decree creating the reservation states that it was intended not only for the Hopi but for "such other Indians as the Secretary of the Interior shall settle thereon." The resultant disputes have simmered ever since.

Outsiders now appeared on the mesas in ever-increasing numbers. Mormon and Mennonite **missionaries** came and went, and **anthropologists** stuck their oars in; Jesse Walter Fewkes called the Hopi "the most primitive aborigines of the United States" in 1891. **Tourists** too came by bus and railroad, with two-thousand-plus turning up for the annual Snake Dances. Century-old images of Hopi ceremonies make it clear why photography was soon barred altogether; crowds and cumbersome equipment made it all but impossible to move. Above all, the federal agents of the **Bureau of Indian Affairs** caused the most grief, ordering haircuts for all Hopi men, for whom long hair is a sign of initiation, and kidnapping Hopi children to attend distant boarding schools, from 1887 onwards. Nineteen elders who protested against compulsory Christian education were imprisoned on Alcatraz in 1894.

The modern era

At the start of the twentieth century, the Hopi were divided between what outsiders perceived as the "**Friendlies**," who if not well disposed toward the federal government at least felt resistance was futile, and the "**Hostiles**," who sought to defend and preserve the old ways. Their differences in fact stemmed largely from tensions between clans, and a breakdown in the allocation of resources and land. The split became explicit at **Oraibi**, where the two factions declared themselves unable to coexist any longer. On September 8, 1906, each lined up behind its leader, with each man's hands on the shoulders of the next, for a "pushing contest." Literally pushed out, the "Hostiles" established their own village of **Hotevilla** nearby.

The dispute at Oraibi politicized the role of each village's ceremonial priest, known as the **kikmongwi**. When the Hopi were obliged to adopt a Tribal Constitution in 1936, the *kikmongwis* were automatically appointed as governors of their village. Part of their function was to endorse members elected to the new **Hopi Tribal Council**. Ever since then, however, many *kikmongwis* have refused to recognize the authority of the tribal council and aligned themselves instead with the **Traditionalists**, the heirs of the "Hostiles."

Paradoxically, the Traditionalists, who regard themselves as the guardians of all that is truly Hopi, have raised awareness of the Hopi throughout the world. Rather than waiting for their saviour *Pahaana* to appear, they have embarked on a search for him. The movement started immediately after World War II, when certain Hopi elders announced that following the use of the atomic bomb it was time to reveal teachings and prophecies that were supposed to remain secret until "a gourd of ashes fell from the sky." Since 1948, the Traditionalists have written to every US president, and addressed the United Nations, with a message stressing Hopi sovereignty and religious integrity and the importance of respecting the environment. Among their successes was the recognition of Hopi religion as a "peace religion," which excluded Hopi from military service.

In practical terms, the Traditionalist movement has been a focus for opposition to **mineral leasing**. After the Hopi Constitution's definition of the role of the tribal council as being to *prevent* leasing was illegally overruled by the Secretary of the Interior in 1961, strip mining by the Peabody Company devastated much of Black Mesa (see p.54). Almost all the income the leases earned during the 1960s was invested in an unsuccessful bra factory near Winslow. In the 1980s, the leases were renegotiated on much more favourable terms, including environmental stipulations, and mining became more acceptable to many Hopi. However, Traditionalists resistant to becoming dependent on external agencies continued to strive through the courts to have the mines closed down, and although they didn't succeed, Black Mesa Mine did indeed cease operations in 2006.

Meanwhile, the **Navajo–Hopi land dispute** has raged on. By 1958, the Navajo living on Hopi lands outnumbered the Hopi by more than two to one, and the Navajo reservation had completely surrounded the Hopi mesas. Much of the impetus to resolve the problem came from the federal authorities and the mineral companies, who could not start mining until definite title to the land was established. Public sympathies, and court rulings, swayed back and forth for decades. A **Joint Use Area** was established in 1958, to be shared equally between the Hopi and the Navajo, but it soon became evident that 98 percent of it was being used by the Navajo alone. In the 1970s, therefore, separate Hopi and Navajo **Partitioned Lands** were defined, stipulating that Hopi living on the Navajo side of the line relocate, and vice versa. More Navajo than Hopi were affected, and the plight of the **Big Mountain** Navajo in particular, who were given five years to move in 1981, made them a national *cause célèbre*.

The **Navajo–Hopi Land Dispute Settlement Act**, authored by John McCain, was signed by President Clinton in 1996. It allowed Navajo residents of Hopi land to sign 75-year leases, after which ownership will revert to the Hopi. Dissident Navajo argue that the problem has simply been postponed for another generation.

The Navajo and the Apache

Thanks largely to their fierce resistance against the US Army in the nineteenth century, the Navajo and the Apache are the best-known Native American peoples in the Southwest. Now largely concentrated in Arizona, both also occupy parts of New Mexico, and the Navajo Nation extends into southern Utah as well. Both are also relative newcomers, having moved into their current territories around the time that the Spaniards arrived, and with just as devastating an impact.

Although the Navajo and the Apache are now distinct peoples, their languages are, with patience, mutually comprehensible. Their paths only diverged within the last five hundred years. Both are descended from **Athabascan** peoples, whose Asian ancestors crossed into Alaska seven or eight thousand years ago, long after the New World's first migrants. Other Athabascans remained in the north, becoming the **Dene** peoples of Alaska and northwest Canada, and the **Na** of the northwest US, who included the Haid and Tlingit. At some point, however, the ancestral Navajo and Apache migrated south, hauling their possessions on dog-sleds as they pursued bison down the eastern flanks of the Rockies.

Estimates of when they first arrived in the Southwest – somewhere on the edge of the Plains, east of the Rio Grande – range between 575 and 1525 AD, with the most likely date being 1250 to 1300 AD. Like nomads the world over, they traded the fruits of their hunting and gathering, especially buffalo hides, for the agricultural produce of more settled communities like the Rio Grande pueblos. Chroniclers travelling with Coronado in 1540 drew no distinction between the Navajo and the Apache, referring to both as *Querecho*. However, by the time the Spanish returned at the end of the century, the Navajo, who called themselves the *Diné*, had separated from the Apache, or *Ndee*.

The Navajo

It used to be thought that it was the arrival of the warlike Navajo in the Four Corners that forced the Ancestral Puebloans to leave at the end of the thirteenth century (see p.462). In fact, however, the Navajo only moved west to occupy the now-empty San Juan Basin after the Ancestral Puebloans had gone. Some even suggest that when the Ancestral Puebloans headed east to establish pueblos along the Rio Grande, they displaced the ancestors of today's Navajo from their riverside homes.

During the late sixteenth century, a region centred on Largo Canyon, east of modern Farmington – still the core of Navajo territory – became known as the **Dinétah**, meaning "Among the People." The *Diné* defined their new realm as lying between four **sacred mountains**: Blanca Peak, or *Sis Naajini*, away to the east in Colorado; Hesperus Peak (*Dibé Nitsaa*), further north in Colorado, near modern Durango; Mount Taylor (*Tsoodzil*), further south in New Mexico; and the San Francisco Peaks (*Dook'o'oosliid*) near what is now Flagstaff, Arizona. Legends grew up detailing how First Man and First Woman lived near **Huerfano Mountain**. They found a baby on **Gobernador Knob** whom they named Changing Woman, who in turn gave birth to the Navajo Twins, Monster Slayer and Child Born for Water.

The Lords of the World

By the 1580s, the Navajo were impinging upon the pueblos of Ácoma, Zuni and Hopi. Their expansion was given a huge boost when a permanent Spanish presence enabled them to acquire **horses**. From 1606 onwards, the Navajo embarked on a cycle of raiding Hispanic and Pueblo settlements along the Rio Grande, seizing livestock, new crops and metal goods. In the Tewa language, spoken in many pueblos, *apache* means "strangers" or "enemies," and *nabajú* means "big planted fields." The first Spanish mention of the "**Apaches de Nabajú**" appeared in 1626, and the name was soon truncated to "Navajo."

The Navajo and Pueblo peoples were not always at war, however. Some Navajo joined the 1680 **Pueblo Revolt**, and when the Spanish reconquered the region a dozen years later, many Pueblo peoples escaped their revenge by retreating to live with the Navajo. A hybrid of Athabascan and Pueblo elements, modern Navajo culture was forged in the remote "**Pueblitos of Dinétah**," in Largo and Gobernador canyons (see p.90).

By the eighteenth century, the Navajo had acquired such Pueblo skills as pottery and weaving, as well as Pueblo-influenced social and religious structures. Obtaining horses vastly increased their mobility, while their large flocks of **sheep** enabled them to live well on what had previously been marginal lands. They therefore expanded westwards to cover a much greater area, occupying most of northeast Arizona and encircling the Hopi.

To contemporary Spaniards, the Navajo were **Los Dueños del Mundo**, the "Lords of the World" – feared horsemen with a solid economic base in their own lands who still plundered the pueblos at will. For most of the eighteenth century, however, the Navajo and the Hispanic settlers of New Mexico were nominally at peace, united in resisting incursions by the **Ute** and **Comanche** of the north. Then the Navajo realized that the Spanish were tacitly encouraging **Ute** and **Comanche** raiders, and buying their Navajo captives as slaves. After 1786, when the Spanish signed a formal treaty with the Comanche, they were at constant war with the Navajo.

With conversion to Christianity as an excuse, Navajo women and children were shipped into slavery in Mexico; the Navajo replenished their numbers by carrying off Pueblo villagers. Certain mission settlements had to be abandoned in the face of Navajo attacks. By and large, the Navajo heartlands remained impregnable, although **Lieutenant Narbona**'s party of 1805 penetrated the Canyon de Chelly and massacred over a hundred Navajo (see p.60).

War with the United States

Mexican independence in 1821 did nothing to diminish the conflict, and the Navajo and the Hispanic settlers of New Mexico were still at loggerheads when the US Army took control of the Southwest in 1846. To Navajo amazement, the American invaders expected them to make peace with their old enemies, on the basis that the New Mexicans were now themselves Americans.

A major factor in the American failure to sign and keep treaties with the Navajo was the fact that the Navajo did not have "chiefs", let alone a single paramount chief. No Navajo could speak for much more than his immediate family, or felt bound by a pact signed by another. Even so, the Navajo remained broadly at peace with the Americans until a widely respected elder – who, confusingly, had taken the name **Narbona** – was murdered and scalped by US soldiers, under a flag of truce, in 1849. For the next fifteen years, Narbona's son-in-law, **Manuelito**, fought a running war with the US cavalry.

In 1863, **General James Carleton** resolved that the Navajo should be removed from their lands altogether, partly so that they might "become an agricultural people and cease to be nomads" and partly to allow New Mexicans to expand beyond the Rio Grande valley. A scorched-earth campaign led by veteran scout **Kit Carson** culminated in 1864 with the destruction of the *hogans*, fields and peach orchards of Canyon de Chelly. As the starving Navajo surrendered, they were sent to "Fair Carletonia," the **Bosque Redondo reservation** at Fort Sumner in eastern New Mexico.

Nine thousand Navajo made the **Long Walk** of 370 miles to Bosque Redondo, where three thousand of them died. The reservation was utterly unsuitable for agriculture; far from being self-supporting, it became a burden on the federal government. Carleton

NAVAJO CLANS

The **basis of Navajo society** and family life is the **clan** system. Each Navajo child is born "to" its mother's clan, and "for" its father's clan. Navajo identify themselves to each other by the clans of their parents; no one is supposed to marry a member of either their mother's or father's clan. Traditionally, all clan members were responsible for each other's crimes or debts.

Originally, there were just four clans, each descended from one of the four pairs of men and women created in the west by Changing Woman. New clans arise when a woman from another tribe or place marries into the Navajo, however, so now there are more like sixty. While certain clan names identify the descendants of Zuni, Mescalero, Mexican, Ute and Jemez newcomers, most hark back to specific locations on the reservation, mythical incidents, or other attributes – the Turning Mountain Clan, Salt Clan, the People That Have Fits Clan, the Rock-Extends-into-Water Clan and so on.

was dismissed, and in 1868, after four years, twelve Navajo leaders – including **Barboncito**, who pleaded "I hope to God you will not ask me to go to any other country except my own" – signed a treaty that allowed them to return home.

The Navajo Nation

The 1868 treaty (or "Old Paper") formed the basis of the Navajo Indian reservation – or **Navajo Nation** – as it endures to this day. The original reservation of 1868 was, however, just a small rectangle of northeast Arizona and northwest New Mexico, which included Canyon de Chelly and Shiprock but not Window Rock. Here the survivors of Fort Sumner rejoined those Navajo who had evaded capture in the backcountry; some had hidden near **Navajo Mountain**, and now regarded it too as a sacred peak.

During the twentieth century, the Navajo **population** grew at a phenomenal rate, from twenty thousand in 1900 to approaching 350,000 today. Similarly, the reservation expanded from six thousand to 27,000 square miles. A formal Navajo **government** was only established in 1923, when the major oil companies needed someone to sign leases so they could exploit the reservation's newly discovered oil reserves. The **chapter** system of local administration was set up soon afterwards, and Window Rock became tribal headquarters in 1927.

In 1933, insisting that over-grazing was washing silt into the Colorado and threatening the new Hoover Dam, the federal authorities killed off a million sheep and goats and reduced the total Navajo herd to half a million animals. That traumatic **stock reduction** had the effect of forcing a change away from pastoralism toward wage labour.

Since World War II, the Navajo Nation has continued to modernize, acquiring its first paved road in 1947 and the first college ever built on an Indian reservation, Tsaile's Navajo Community College, in 1969. While many families still manage to live a traditional Navajo lifestyle, the exploitation of **mineral** resources has brought the greatest change. Mines and generating stations have appeared across the region, often just outside the reservation but still dependent on Indian labour. Many projects have been deeply controversial. The **Four Corners power plant** near Farmington has been described as the single worst source of pollution in the US – the three oldest of its five generating units finally shut down in 2012 – while the Peabody Company's strip-mining of **Black Mesa** to feed the **Navajo Generating Station** at Page is widely regarded as an environmental tragedy. In 1979, **Church Rock**, northeast of Gallup, was the scene of the worst contamination in US nuclear history, when a dam burst at the United Nuclear Corporation mill and released almost a hundred million gallons of radioactive water and a thousand tons of radioactive mud.

In 1975, Tribal Chairman **Peter MacDonald** (subsequently jailed for corruption) helped set up the Council of Energy Resource Tribes, which he described as a "domestic OPEC." While the mineral leases of the 1950s and 1960s paid pitifully low returns, more lucrative agreements have now strengthened the Navajo economy.

Navajo opposition to the principle of mineral exploitation has also grown however, as its long-term effects become apparent. Many feel that the long-running **Navajo–Hopi land dispute** (see p.479) has been manipulated by federal politicians and mineral companies for their own ends.

The Apache

Around 1600 AD, as the Navajo began to incorporate Pueblo elements and become an entirely distinct people, the **Apache** fragmented into several separate groups. The **Western** Apache occupied the mountains of central Arizona; the **Jicarilla**, regions of northwest New Mexico between the Chama Valley and the Four Corners; and the **Lipan** moved east onto the plains of west Texas. At the same time, in southern New Mexico, the **Mescalero** started to range east of the Rio Grande, while the **Chiricahua** spread west as far as what's now southern Arizona.

These groups were not the "tribes" outsiders like to imagine. Apache lived in nomadic, clan-based societies of between thirty and two hundred people, each with its own "chief." A chief's primary responsibility was to ensure his band got enough food; his authority collapsed in the event of failure. Most groups raised a few seasonal crops, but supported themselves above all by **raiding**, against not only settled Pueblo communities, but the Navajo, and even each other.

The coming of the Spaniards gave the Apache **horses** for the first time. At first, they stole them solely to eat, but once they learned to ride they swiftly adapted to a calendar of raiding the Rio Grande villages at harvest time, while allowing them to continue unmolested for the rest of the year. It was beneath Apache dignity to breed their own horses, let alone sheep like the Navajo; they simply stole livestock as they needed it.

The colonists of New Mexico, who throughout Spanish and Mexican rule remained confined to a fragile ribbon of riverside land, called the vast Apache-dominated territories that surrounded them **Apachería**. Since the Apache never united to engage in formal warfare – no Apache war party in history exceeded two hundred warriors – it was impossible to take concerted action against them. In the first half of the eighteenth century, the Apache were nonetheless forced to consolidate into smaller and more mountainous areas, as even more aggressive mounted **Comanche** warriors swept in across the Plains with ever-increasing regularity.

Later in the eighteenth century, the Spaniards managed to pacify the Apache by establishing *presidios* or forts that supplied them with food, alcohol and even guns (adequate for hunting but not war). When Mexico became independent, however, in 1821, the new administration could no longer afford such subsidies. Instead it placed a bounty of $100 on each Apache scalp – male or female, young or old – brought into the *presidios*.

The Apache Wars

To the US government, which took over New Mexico in the 1840s, the Apache way of life was anathema. As a group of Mescalero Apache acknowledged to a US Army quartermaster in 1850, "We must steal from somebody ... if you will not permit us to rob the Mexicans, we must steal from you or fight you." In total, the Southwest held between six and eight thousand Apache. By far the strongest resistance came from a group of just over a thousand, the **Chiricahua**, led by a chief known as **Cochise**, or "Oak."

Conflict between the US Army and the Apache flared into war in 1861, when Cochise agreed to meet Lt. George Bascom in southeast Arizona, and found himself falsely accused of kidnapping a child. Although Cochise managed to escape into the Dragoon Mountains, his brother and two nephews were hanged. Cochise then rampaged across Arizona, killing miners, prospectors, stagecoach passengers and soldiers. As Anglos packed up and fled the territory, he imagined he had driven them out forever. Little did he realize that his campaign had coincided with the start of the Civil War, so all US forces had been withdrawn east.

Within a year, the Union army was back, led by General James Carleton. His Apache policy, directed at first against the Mescalero rather than the Chiricahua, was simple: "All Indian men of that tribe are to be killed whenever and wherever you can find them." During the winter of 1862–63, the Mescaleros were rounded onto the **Bosque Redondo** reservation in eastern New Mexico, where they were soon joined by the Navajo.

In 1862, Cochise's group had linked up with another Chiricahua band, the **Warm Springs** Apache of New Mexico, under the veteran **Mangas Coloradas**. The treacherous murder of Mangas Coloradas the following year, after US soldiers invited him to peace negotiations at Pinos Altos, hardened Chiricahua resolve. Over the next ten years, the US Army spent $38 million on campaigns that killed a total of a hundred Apache; the Apache meanwhile accounted for over a thousand Americans.

During this period, the name of **Geronimo** became widely feared. He was born around 1823 into the Bedonkohe subgroup of the Chiricahua Apache, near New Mexico's Gila cliff dwellings. Named Goyahkla, "One Who Yawns," he reached adulthood without seeing a white American. After his mother, wife and three children were killed by Mexican soldiers at Janos in northern Mexico, in 1851, he sought revenge in repeated raids on Mexico. Somehow, the Mexican battle-cry to St Jerome, "Geronimo," became the name he used for the rest of his life. Although he became a respected healer and medicine man, he was never, strictly speaking, a "chief."

In the **Camp Grant Massacre** of 1871, a Tucson-based alliance of Tohono O'odham Indians, Hispanics and Anglos massacred 144 Apache – of whom no more than eight were men – supposedly under the protection of the US Army in Aravaipa Canyon, Arizona. A public outcry back East led President Grant to adopt a new policy toward the Apache, under which the **White Mountain** and **San Carlos** reservations were established in 1872.

Any Apache who failed to present themselves at the reservations were deemed renegades. **General George Crook**, ordered to hunt them down, adopted the scorched-earth strategy of "total war," developed during the Civil War. Employing White Mountain Apache scouts, he "overhauled" the Tonto Basin during the winter of 1872–73, killing five hundred Apache.

Following an uneasy truce, the Chiricahua were granted their own reservation, a fifty-mile square centred on what's now Chiricahua National Monument. Within three years, however, renewed cross-border raiding after the 1874 death of Cochise caused the reservation to be disbanded. The Chiricahua were moved onto the San Carlos reservation.

In 1877, another Chiricahua leader, **Victorio**, assembled a five-hundred-strong band of Apache from the many different groups who hated life at San Carlos. A lengthy guerrilla campaign across New Mexico and West Texas resulted in a thousand more Anglo deaths before the Chiricahua were driven into Mexico and killed in Chihuahua in October 1880. The few survivors were sold into slavery.

Geronimo, who had not joined Victorio, now became the focus for dissident Apache. During the 1880s, he repeatedly burst out of the reservation and onto the warpath, each time with a dwindling band of followers. The first time was in 1881, when he passed within a few miles of Tombstone and was pursued by Wyatt Earp and his brothers. In 1883, General Crook tracked him down in the Sierra Madre in northern Mexico, and was briefly captured by the Apache before Geronimo chose instead to surrender to him.

Geronimo fled the reservation again in 1885 and surrendered to Crook once more in Mexico in 1886, on the understanding that he'd be exiled to the eastern United States for not more than two years. Before Crook could get him back to San Carlos, Geronimo got drunk and escaped yet again. Crook resigned his command, to be replaced by **General Nelson Miles**.

The Chiricahua's final five-month guerrilla campaign, in the summer of 1886, pitted 37 Apache, of whom eighteen were warriors, against five thousand soldiers, a quarter of the entire US Army. General Miles eventually managed to contact Geronimo in Mexico, and falsely told him that all the Chiricahua who remained on the reservation had been shipped to **Florida**. In despair, Geronimo **surrendered** for the fourth and final time in Skeleton Canyon, Arizona on September 3, 1886. The general's lie now became the truth. Geronimo and five hundred Chiricahua – along with the Apache scouts who had fought alongside the US Army – were indeed sent to Florida. Men and women were segregated in separate camps. In time, the Chiricahua were reunited on reservations in first Alabama, and then Oklahoma, but Geronimo never returned to the Southwest. Among many public appearances in his later years, he rode at the head of Teddy Roosevelt's inaugural procession in 1905; he died in 1909.

In 1913, the 261 surviving Chiricahua were allowed to choose between remaining in Oklahoma or joining the Mescalero Apache in New Mexico; around two-thirds made the trip. It's thought that the Army never did round up perhaps ten Chiricahua, who stayed hidden in Mexico; free Apache were reported still to be fighting in the Sierra Madre as late as the 1930s.

The Apache today

Around twenty thousand Apache now live in the Southwest. Their largest two reservations are in Arizona: the **Fort Apache** Reservation (see p.259), which has the third highest population of all Native American reservations in the US, and the neighbouring **San Carlos** Reservation (see p.218). The **Jicarilla** still live in northwest New Mexico, concentrated around Dulce (see p.158).

Visitors are most likely to come into contact with the **Mescalero Apache**, who share their lands with the descendants of the last Chiricahua in the mountains of southeast New Mexico. Among ventures here that have brought them a rare degree of economic security are the Ski Apache **ski resort** (see p.182), which the tribe bought for $1.5 million in 1962 and features the luxurious *Inn of the Mountain Gods* hotel/casino.

Books

The following books proved useful, interesting or entertaining during the research for this guide.

HISTORY AND ARCHEOLOGY

Donald A Barclay, James H Maguire and Peter Wild (eds) *Into the Wilderness Dream*. Gripping collection of Western exploration narratives written between 1500 and 1800. Thanks to numerous little-known gems, the best of many such anthologies.

★ **Pedro de Castañeda** *The Journey of Coronado*. The eyewitness journals of a Spaniard who accompanied Coronado into the Southwest in 1540, and an invaluable historic document.

Richard Flint *No Settlement, No Conquest*. A satisfying and accessible overview of current knowledge about Coronado's epochal expedition, from an author who's written and edited several more academic volumes.

Jack D. Forbes *Apache, Navajo, and Spaniard*. An unsettling but thoroughly documented account of seventeenth-century frontier conflicts, which challenges much received wisdom by suggesting, for example, that the Ancestral Puebloans violently displaced the Navajo along the Rio Grande.

Pat Garrett *The Authentic Life of Billy, the Kid*. "I have known the Kid personally since and during the continuance of what was known as the Lincoln County War, up to the moment of his death, of which I was the unfortunate instrument" – irresistible Western history, straight from the horse's mouth.

Robert Goodwin *Crossing The Continent*. A valiant and always stimulating attempt to chronicle the life of Esteban, the black African ex-slave who in 1539 became the first explorer ever to penetrate the Southwest.

Paul Horgan *Great River: The Rio Grande in North American History*. Horgan's monumental study of New Mexican history makes weighty reading; his more accessible *The Centuries of Santa Fe* is a lightly fictionalized

set of biographies drawn from different periods of history.

John D Lee *Mormonism Unveiled*. In his "Life and Confession," John Lee, of Lees Ferry fame, doesn't quite tell all he knows – like where he buried the gold – but there's a lot of eye-opening material in here.

Stephen Plog *Ancient Peoples of the Southwest*. Much the best single-volume history of the pre-Hispanic Southwest, packed with diagrams and colour photographs.

Carroll L. Riley *The Kachina and the Cross*. A history of the early relations between Pueblo peoples and Hispanic colonists, highlighting how they grudgingly came to share the land of New Mexico. The same author's *Rio del Norte* traces the story of the upper Rio Grande valley from prehistoric times to the Pueblo Revolt, while his *Becoming Aztlan* explores links between the ancient Southwest and Mexico.

Joe S. Sando and Herman Agoyo (eds) *Po'pay: Leader of the First American Revolution*. A remarkable collection of essays by Pueblo Indians on the history of the Pueblo Revolt and its charismatic leader.

Thomas E. Sheridan *Arizona – A History*. Stimulating reassessment of 11,000 years of Arizona history.

Alex Shoumatoff *Legends of the American Desert*. Anecdotal and entertaining first-person survey of several centuries of Southwestern history.

Hampton Sides *Blood And Thunder*. Hugely readable retelling of the exploits of Kit Carson and his role in the campaigns against the Navajo.

★ **Richard White** *It's Your Misfortune and None of My Own*. Dense, authoritative and all-embracing history of the American West, which debunks romanticization of the rugged pioneer by stressing the role of the federal government.

NATIVE AMERICANS

★ *Between Sacred Mountains*. Superb overview of Navajo history, culture and politics, written by Navajo teachers and parents as a sourcebook for Navajo students.

Nancy Yaw Davis *The Zuni Enigma*. An intriguing if ultimately unconvincing elaboration of the author's theory that a wandering group of Japanese pilgrims joined the Zuni tribe during the thirteenth century.

Angie Debo *Geronimo*. Gripping full-length biography of the Apache medicine man who led the last Native American uprising against the US Army.

Paula Richardson Fleming and Judith Lynn Luskey

The Shadow Catchers. A history of nineteenth-century photographers of Native Americans, with some stunning images of the Hopi and Navajo.

Robert H. Keller and Michael F. Turek *American Indians and National Parks*. What happens when the federal park system appropriates land from its former indigenous inhabitants; Mesa Verde, Rainbow Bridge and the Grand Canyon are among examples considered in detail.

Raymond Friday Locke *The Book of the Navajo*. Comprehensive history of the Navajo, from their mythic origins to the present day.

Robert S. McPherson *Sacred Land Sacred View*. Intriguing anthropological account of how the Navajo perceive the Four Corners region.

★ **David Roberts** *Once They Moved Like The Wind*. Excellent, fast-moving history of the Apache.

Polly Schaafsma (ed) *Kachinas in the Pueblo World*. Well-illustrated survey of the *kachina* cult in the Southwest (see p.67).

Stephen Trimble *The People*. Superb introduction to all the Native American groups of the Southwest, bringing the history up to the late twentieth century via contemporary interviews.

Frank Waters *The Book of the Hopi*. As authoritative an account of Hopi religion as it's possible to find, though it's said that Waters' informants were not themselves initiated into all the secrets of the *kiva*.

TRAVEL

Edward Dolnick *Down The Great Unknown*. Deft retelling of the saga of John Wesley Powell's first Grand Canyon voyage that takes great pains to make it all intelligible to modern readers, with the analogies flowing thick and fast.

Colin Fletcher *The Man Who Walked Through Time*. Enjoyable account by the first man to hike the full length of the Grand Canyon.

Susan Shelby Magoffin *Down the Santa Fe Trail and into Mexico*. Absorbing first-person account by a trader's wife who reached Santa Fe in August 1846 in time to witness the Yankee takeover of New Mexico.

John Wesley Powell *The Exploration of the Colorado River and Its Canyons*. Powell adjusted the details of his first epic journey down the Colorado – see p.401 – for public consumption, but his journals still make exhilarating reading.

Douglas Preston *Cities of Gold*. Long but very readable account of a horseback journey in the steps of Coronado, which throws a lot of light on history both ancient and modern.

David Roberts *In Search of the Old Ones*. An engaging chronicle of one man's obsession with Southwestern archeology.

★ **Mark Twain** *Roughing It*. This rollicking account of Twain's peregrinations across the nineteenth-century West may well be the greatest story ever told, though only his account of the Mormons is of much relevance here.

Ted J. Warner (ed) *The Domínguez-Escalante Journal*. The extraordinary diary of the two Franciscan friars who crossed Utah in 1776 in search of a new route to California, and came back via the Grand Canyon.

THE CONTEMPORARY SOUTHWEST

Christina Brinkley *Winner Takes All*. The inside story of how billionaires Steve Wynn and Kirk Kerkorian battled to shape twenty first-century Las Vegas.

Alan Hess *Viva Las Vegas*. A beautifully illustrated survey of Las Vegas' architectural history, throwing fascinating sidelights on the development of the city.

Shawn Levy *Rat Pack Confidential*. Enjoyable hymn to the "last great showbiz party," when Las Vegas prostrated itself at the feet of Frank Sinatra and the boys.

Scott Norris (ed) *Discovered Country*. Essays on the impact of tourism on the Southwest, with some interesting material on the repackaging of Native American culture for Anglo consumption.

Hal K. Rothman *Devil's Bargains: Tourism in the Twentieth-Century American West*. Thought-provoking

assessment of how tourism has shaped the modern West, which overturns many a cozy historical myth about places such as Santa Fe and Las Vegas.

Jim Stiles *Brave New World*. An idiosyncratic Moab writer lays out how tourism, though supposedly environmentally aware, has served southeast Utah no better than did mining and ranching.

Hunter S. Thompson *Fear and Loathing in Las Vegas*. Classic account of a drug-crazed journalist's lost weekend in early-1970s Vegas; what's really striking is how much further over the top Las Vegas has gone since then.

Chris Wilson *The Myth of Santa Fe*. Eye-opening and very detailed account of how the Santa Fe known to tourists today is largely a twentieth-century concoction.

ENVIRONMENT AND NATURAL HISTORY

Edward Abbey *Desert Solitaire*. Abbey's classic evocation of his year as a ranger at Arches National Park was the first of his many volumes championing the wildernesses of the Southwest.

Philip L. Fradkin *A River No More*. The story of the Colorado River, from John Wesley Powell to the water-management issues of today.

Michael P. Ghiglieri and Thomas M. Myers *Over The Edge: Death in Grand Canyon*. In their bid to account for the

demise of every single person known to have died within the Grand Canyon, the authors transcend the merely morbid to throw fascinating light on every aspect of the canyon's history, and provide masses of useful advice on how to avoid becoming another fatality. The morbid stuff's good, too.

Russel Martin *A Story That Stands Like A Dam*. Meticulously chronicled indictment of the West's last great dam, which inundated Glen Canyon in the 1960s.

Lisa Michaels *Grand Ambition*. Gripping novelistic

reconstruction of a true-life romantic mystery; just what did happen to honeymooners Glen and Bessie Hyde in the winter of 1928, when they tried to row down the Grand Canyon?

Barbara J. Morehouse *A Place Called Grand Canyon*. Fascinating academic analysis of how the Grand Canyon has been defined and exploited.

John A. Murray *Cinema Southwest*. A critical, well illustrated overview of the long history of movies filmed in the Southwest, with plenty of location information.

★ **Marc Reisner** *Cadillac Desert*. The damning saga of the twentieth-century damming of the West.

★ **Jeremy Schmidt** *Grand Canyon National Park – A Natural History Guide*. A superb single-volume account of the Grand Canyon's environment, ecology and geological origins.

Bette L. Stanton *Where God Put The West*. Photo-packed history of moviemaking in Monument Valley and Moab.

FICTION

Edward Abbey *The Monkey Wrench Gang*. Classic wishful thinking from the wilderness advocate, this fast-paced novel centres on plans by environmental saboteurs to destroy the Glen Canyon dam.

★ **Willa Cather** *Death Comes for the Archbishop*. Not as sensational as the title implies, but a magnificent evocation of the landscapes and cultures of nineteenth-century New Mexico. Cather's *The Professor's House* features an extended account of the discovery of Ancestral Puebloan remains on a remote New Mexican mesa.

Zane Grey *Riders of the Purple Sage*. Gloriously purple prose, first published in 1912, from the doyen of Western writers.

Tony Hillerman *A Thief of Time, The Dark Wind* and several others. The late Tony Hillerman wrote around a dozen entertaining, intricately plotted detective novels set on and around the Navajo Nation, all packed with fascinating detail about Navajo, Hopi and Zuni culture and beliefs.

★ **Barbara Kingsolver** *Pigs in Heaven*. A magnificent evocation of tensions and realities in the contemporary Southwest, by a Tucson-based writer who ranks among America's finest prose stylists.

Cormac McCarthy *Blood Meridian*. A disturbing portrayal of the West in all its bloody reality – the scenes at Yuma Crossing are horrendous – if a tad macho for some tastes.

N. Scott Momaday *House Made of Dawn Time*. Pulitzer Prize-winning novel, written by a Kiowa Indian, about the spiritual crisis of a young Pueblo Indian.

John Nichols *The Milagro Beanfield War*. Thanks to the Robert Redford movie, this entertaining saga of a water-rights rebellion by dispossessed Hispanic villagers in northern New Mexico is the best known of Nichols' *New Mexico* trilogy (the others are *The Magic Journey* and *The Nirvana Blues*).

★ **Michael Ondaatje** *The Collected Works of Billy the Kid*. Slim volume of poetry and contemporary accounts which add up to an evocative picture of New Mexico's most famous tearaway.

Simon J. Ortiz *Men on the Moon*. Evocative contemporary short stories by an Ácoma Indian poet.

Leslie Marmon Silko *Almanac of the Dead*. Epic novel, by a Laguna Pueblo Indian, of a Native American mother searching for her lost child on the fringes of the Tucson underworld; look out also for Silko's *Ceremony*.

Glossary

adobe Construction material, consisting of bricks of mud, sand and grass or straw; by extension, a building itself (see p.109).

Anasazi Term formerly used for the ancient people of the Four Corners region (see p.461).

anticline Geological term for a dome or ridge shoved upwards by subterranean bulging.

arroyo Flat, often dry desert streambed.

atlatl Spear-throwing device – a sort of detachable, lever-like handle that gave extra power and accuracy – used by ancient Native Americans.

backcountry Term used particularly in national parks to signify wilderness areas that cannot be reached by road (as opposed, occasionally, to frontcountry).

bulto or **santo bulto** Carved wooden statue of a saint, characteristic of Hispanic New Mexico.

butte A flat-topped outcrop of rock that's taller than it is wide, usually formed by the erosion of a larger mesa.

casita Cottage, now applied mainly to individual guest accommodation in upmarket B&Bs.

cuesta Long sloping mesa terminated by an abrupt bluff.

desert varnish A natural veneer, caused by leaching minerals, that accretes on exposed rock faces and makes an ideal surface on which to etch petroglyphs.

genízaros In colonial New Mexico, the mixed-race offspring of captured Plains Indians and their Spanish masters.

graben Narrow valleys created by the erosion of underground salt beds, from the German for "ditches".

Grand Staircase Topographical feature of southwest Utah, stretching from the Grand Canyon to Bryce Canyon (see p.335).

Great House Archeological term for a defensively oriented, multistorey ancient pueblo with hundreds of rooms, as seen at Chaco Canyon (see p.91).

Great Kiva Archeological term for a *kiva* that was used by an entire community rather than an individual clan or family.

heishi Necklace of threaded disks, usually cut from seashells, as made originally by Ancestral Puebloans and now by Kewa Pueblo.

Hisatsinom The Hopi name for their Ancestral Puebloan forebears.

hogan Navajo dwelling (see p.62).

Hohokam Ancient people of southern Arizona (see p.463).

hoodoo Natural sandstone formation in which a boulder is left balanced on a slender pillar, as at Bryce Canyon.

kachina (also spelled katsina) "Spirit messengers," central to the religions of the Hopi and other Pueblo Indians (see p.67).

kiva Chamber used for religious ceremonies by Pueblo Indians, usually located underground.

latilla Light pole used in the roof construction of adobe buildings.

LDS Abbreviation to denote the Latter-Day Saints, or Mormons.

mano Handheld stone traditionally used to grind and crush seeds.

mesa From the Spanish for "table;" a large, broad flat-topped outcrop of rock.

metate Stone slab or trough, used with a *mano* for grinding seeds.

Mimbres Ancient people of southern New Mexico, renowned for their pottery (see p.198).

Moki or **Moqui** The former name for the Hopi people of northern Arizona.

monocline An abrupt irregularity in the usual stratification of rocks, often resulting in a dramatic cliff.

Penitentes Catholic sect in nineteenth-century New Mexico (see p.143).

petroglyph Ancient rock-art image carved or pecked into stone.

pictograph Ancient rock-art image painted into stone.

Presidio Spanish term for a fortress built during the colonial period.

Pueblo Spanish word meaning "village;" applied to ancient Native American dwellings and also to modern Indian communities and peoples.

reef Word applied by early Anglo settlers to such vast natural barriers to their progress across the desert (usually created by monoclines) as Utah's Capitol Reef (see p.384).

reredos Painted altarpiece, as seen in Hispanic churches at Chimayó (see p.144) and elsewhere.

retablo A kind of Hispanic religious folk art, painted on tin or wood.

ristra Garland of chile peppers, sold as souvenirs in New Mexico.

santo In Hispanic folk art, an image or holy object.

Sinagua Ancient people of central Arizona.

sipapu In Pueblo religion, the hole through which humans reached this earth.

slickrock Pioneer term for smooth, undulating stretches of sandstone, as a rule only slick after rain.

syncline The opposite of an anticline, a syncline is a rock formation created by an underground collapse.

talus Fallen rock debris which accumulates to form slopes at the bases of cliffs and canyon walls.

viga A broad beam of ponderosa or fir, as used by the Ancestral Puebloans in roof construction, and prominent in adobe architecture today.

Small print and index

491 Small print

492 About the author

493 Index

501 Map symbols

A ROUGH GUIDE TO ROUGH GUIDES

Published in 1982, the first Rough Guide – to Greece – was a student scheme that became a publishing phenomenon. Mark Ellingham, a recent graduate in English from Bristol University, had been travelling in Greece the previous summer and couldn't find the right guidebook. With a small group of friends he wrote his own guide, combining a highly contemporary, journalistic style with a thoroughly practical approach to travellers' needs.

The immediate success of the book spawned a series that rapidly covered dozens of destinations. And, in addition to impecunious backpackers, Rough Guides soon acquired a much broader readership that relished the guides' wit and inquisitiveness as much as their enthusiastic, critical approach and value-for-money ethos.

These days, Rough Guides include recommendations from budget to luxury and cover more than 200 destinations around the globe, as well as producing an ever-growing range of eBooks and apps.

Visit **roughguides.com** to see our latest publications.

Rough Guide credits

Editor: Steven Horak
Layout: Jessica Subramanian
Cartography: Deshpal Dabas
Picture editor: Raffaella Morini
Proofreader: Stewart Wild
Managing editor: Mani Ramaswamy
Assistant editor: Dipika Dasgupta
Production: Charlotte Cade
Cover design: Nicole Newman, Wilf Matos, Jessica Subramanian

Editorial assistant: Olivia Rawes
Senior pre-press designer: Dan May
Design director: Jason Mitchell
Travel publisher: Joanna Kirby
Digital travel publisher: Peter Buckley
Operations coordinator: Helen Blount
Publishing director (Travel): Clare Currie
Commercial manager: Gino Magnotta
Managing director: John Duhigg

Publishing information

This sixth edition published October 2013 by
Rough Guides Ltd,
80 Strand, London WC2R 0RL
11, Community Centre, Panchsheel Park,
New Delhi 110017, India
Distributed by the Penguin Group
Penguin Books Ltd,
80 Strand, London WC2R 0RL
Penguin Group (USA)
345 Hudson Street, NY 10014, USA
Penguin Group (Australia)
250 Camberwell Road, Camberwell,
Victoria 3124, Australia
Penguin Group (NZ)
67 Apollo Drive, Mairangi Bay, Auckland 1310,
New Zealand
Penguin Group (South Africa)
Block D, Rosebank Office Park, 181 Jan Smuts Avenue,
Parktown North, Gauteng, South Africa 2193
Rough Guides is represented in Canada by Tourmaline
Editions Inc. 662 King Street West, Suite 304, Toronto,
Ontario M5V 1M7
Printed in Singapore by Toppan Security Printing Pte. Ltd.

504pp includes index
A catalogue record for this book is available from the
British Library
ISBN: 978-1-40936-267-8

MIX
Paper from
responsible sources
FSC
www.fsc.org   FSC™ C018179

Help us update

We've gone to a lot of effort to ensure that the sixth
edition of **The Rough Guide to Southwest USA** is
accurate and up-to-date. However, things change – places
get "discovered", opening hours are notoriously fickle,
restaurants and rooms raise prices or lower standards. If
you feel we've got it wrong or left something out, we'd like
to know, and if you can remember the address, the price,
the hours, the phone number, so much the better.

Please send your comments with the subject line
"Rough Guide Southwest USA Update" to ⊚mail
@uk.roughguides.com. We'll credit all contributions and
send a copy of the next edition (or any other Rough Guide
if you prefer) for the very best emails.

Find more travel information, connect with fellow
travellers and plan your trip on Ⓦroughguides.com.

ABOUT THE AUTHOR

Greg Ward has been writing about the Southwest for more than twenty years. As well as all five previous editions of this book, he's the author of separate Rough Guides to Las Vegas and the Grand Canyon. He has also written many other Rough Guides, including those to the USA, the *Titanic*, Hawaii, Brittany & Normandy, Provence, Spain, Blues CDs and US History; edited many more; and written books on travel and music for several other publishers. For more information, visit ⓦgregward.info.

Acknowledgements

Greg Ward: Thanks once again to my wonderful wife Sam, for sharing the whole thing and making it all possible, and to Steven Horak, my editor at Rough Guides, for his painstaking work and local expertise. Thanks too to everyone who helped me along the way, especially Ann Klein and Linda Illsley in Durango; Steve Lewis and Kyra Lausmann in Santa Fe; Kimberley Diller and David Gonzalez in Las Vegas; Joanne Hudson and Richard Svendsen in Flagstaff; and Jessica Stephens and Jim and Marion Hook in Tucson. Lastly, thanks to those in Delhi and London who made this edition possible, in particular Jessica Subramanian, Raffaella Morini, Deshpal Dabas and Alison Roberts.

Photo credits

All photos © Rough Guides except the following:
(Key: b-below/bottom; c-centre; l-left; r-right; t-top)

p.1 Corbis/George H.H. Huey
p.2 AWL Images/Michele Falzone
p.4 Getty Images/Panoramic
p.5 Getty Images/Sapna Reddy Photography
p.9 Corbis/Alan Copson/JAI (br); Chris Cheadle/All Canada Photos (tl); Blaine Harrington III (bl); Getty Images/Harald Sund (tr)
p.10 Corbis/Steven Vidler/Eurasia Press
p.11 Corbis/Dave G. Houser (b); George H.H. Huey (t); Getty Images/John P. Kelly (c)
p.12 Corbis/Marilyn Angel Wynn/Nativestock Pictures
p.13 Getty Images/Yuko Smith photography
p.14 Corbis/A. Geh/F1 Online
p.15 Alamy /ZUMA Wire Service (c); Getty Images/Danita Delimont (t); Rozanne Hakala (b)
p.16 Corbis/Doug Meek (cr); Nik Wheeler (t, b)
p.17 Corbis/Konrad Wothe/Minden Pictures (c); Neale Clark/Robert Harding World Imagery (b); Getty Images/L. Geoffroy (t)
p.18 Corbis/John Frumm/Hemis (t); Getty Images/Robert Alexander (b); Daniel Lutzick, *La Posada Hotel* (c)
p.19 Corbis/Blaine Harrington III (b); Dave G. Houser (tl); Getty Images/Sam Diephuis (tr)
p.20 Corbis/Robert Wagenhoffer (t)
p.21 Corbis/Keith Kapple/SuperStock (b); Mark Skalny/Visuals Unlimited (cl); Getty Images/John Wang (t); Markos Berndt (cr)
p.22 Cirque du Soleil Inc./Mystère image by Matt Beard © Cirque du Soleil (b); Getty Images/Danita Delimont (t)
p.23 Corbis/Michael DeYoung/Blend Images (br); Whit Richardson/Aurora Photos (bl); Getty Images/Gary Koutsoubis (tr); Michele Falzone (tl)
p.24 Getty Images/Bob Stefko
p.26 Corbis/SuperStock
pp.44–45 Getty Images/Sapna Reddy Photography
p.47 Corbis/George H.H. Huey
p.65 Corbis/George H.H. Huey (br); Richard T. Nowitz (t); Getty Images/Robyn Beck/AFP (bl)

p.87 Getty Images/Larry Gerbrandt (b)
pp.102–103 Corbis/Myles McGuinness/Aurora Open
p.105 Corbis/Arnold Drapkin/ZUMA Press
p.127 Corbis/Arnold Drapkin/ZUMA Press (br); Blaine Harrington III (bl)
p.155 Corbis/Jay Syverson (b); Paul Seheult/Eye Ubiquitous (c)
pp.162–163 Corbis/G. Brad Lewis/Science Faction
p.165 Getty Images/Robin Wilson Photography
p.187 Corbis/Richard Cummins (t); Tom Bean (bl); Getty Images/Nativestock.com/Marilyn Angel Wynn (br)
pp.200–201 Corbis/Richard Cummins
p.203 Getty Images/Hisham Ibrahim
p.215 Corbis/Richard Cummins (b); Getty Images/Walter Bibikow (t)
p.231 Corbis/David Kadlubowski (bl); James Hager/Robert Harding World Imagery (t); Richard Cummins (br)
pp.250–251 Getty Images/Marco Brivio
p.253 Corbis/Nik Wheeler
p.279 Corbis/David Kadlubowski (b); Ocean (t)
pp.292–293 Getty Images/Don Smith
p.295 Corbis/Tim Fitzharris/Minden Pictures
p.311 Getty Images/Matt Dil
pp.338–339 Getty Images/J. Martin Paige III
p.341 Getty Images/Keiji Iwai
p.359 Getty Images/Ropelato Photography; EarthScapes (t)
p.399 Getty Images/Slow Images (b)
p.458 Corbis

Front cover Cactuses, Saguaro National Park © Corbis/George H.H. Huey

Back cover Sunset over Sedona © Getty Images/Jeffrey Murray (t); Las Vegas Strip at twilight © Getty Images/Stuart Dee (bl); Delicate Arch of Arches National Park, Utah © Corbis/Tetra Images (br)

Index

Maps are marked in grey

A

Abajo Mountains, UT 428
Abiquiu, NM 140
Abó, NM 178
accommodation..............33
Ácoma Pueblo, NM 99
Acomita, NM..............100
adobe..............109
adventure travel..............38, 424
Agua Prieta, Mexico..............242
airlines serving the Southwest
..............27
airports in the Southwest..............27
Ajo, AZ..............245
Alamogordo, NM..............183
ALBUQUERQUE, NM.... 164–175
Albuquerque area..............168
Albuquerque, Old Town and
    Downtown..............170
  ABQ BioPark..............169
  accommodation..............174
  Albuquerque Museum of Art and
    History..............169
  arrival..............173
  Balloon Fiesta..............167
  Downtown..............171
  eating..............174
  getting around..............173
  Indian Pueblo Cultural Center.....171
  information..............173
  National Hispanic Culutral Center
..............171
  National Museum of Nuclear
    Science and History..............172
  New Mexico Museum of Natural
    History and Science..............169
  nightlife..............175
  Old Town..............167
  Petroglyph National Monument
..............172
  Rail Runner..............173
  Sandia Mountains, the..............172
  tours..............173
**Albuquerque and southern
    New Mexico..............162–199**
Albuquerque and southern
    New Mexico..............166
Albuquerque International
    Balloon Fiesta..............167
Alcalde, NM..............141
alcohol..............35
Algodones, NM..............125
All-American Futurity..............182
Alpine, AZ..............259
Amerind Foundation Museum,
    AZ..............236

Amtrak..............28
Anasazi, the..............461
Anasazi Heritage Center, CO ...73
Anasazi State Park, UT..............382
Ancestral Puebloans, the.......461
Angel Fire, NM..............159
Antelope Canyon, AZ..............394
Anticline Overlook, UT..............427
Antonito, CO..............158
Anzac, NM..............100
Apache, the..............483
Apache history..............483
Apache Pass, AZ..............243
Apache Trail, AZ..............216
Apache-Sitgreaves National
    Forest, AZ..............259
Aravaipa Canyon, AZ..............218
Archaic Culture, the..............460
Arches National Park, UT
..............415–420
Arches National Park..............416
Arcosanti, AZ..............281
Arizona, central..............254
Arizona, southeast..............236
Arizona, southern..............204
Arizona Snowbowl, AZ..............268
Arizona Strip, the AZ..............335
Arizona-Sonora Desert Museum,
    AZ..............225
Ash Fork, AZ..............287
ATMs..............40
A'ts'ina Ruins, NM..............97
automobile rental..............29
Aztec, NM..............89
Aztec Ruins National
    Monument, NM..............89

B

B&Bs..............34
backpacking..............37
balloons..............167
Bandelier National Monument,
    NM..............132
Basketmakers, the..............460
Bear, Smokey..............179
Bear's Ears, UT..............430
Beaver Falls, AZ..............325
bed and breakfasts..............34
Benson, AZ..............235
Bernalillo, NM..............125
Besh-Ba-Gowah, AZ..............217
Betatakin, AZ..............53

bibliography..............486
bikes..............31
biking..............424
Billy the Kid.....177, 179, 180, 196
Biosphere 2, AZ..............219
Bisbee, AZ..............240
Black Dragon Canyon, UT.......402
Black Hawk War..............474
Black Mesa, AZ..............54
Blanding, UT..............429
Bloomfield, NM..............91
Blue Hole, NM..............176
Bluff, UT..............433
books..............486
Bosque del Apache Wildlife
    Refuge, NM..............191
Bosque Redondo, NM..............177
Boulder, UT..............382
Boulder Mountain, UT..............383
Box-Death Hollow Wilderness,
    UT..............377
Boyce Thompson Arboretum,
    AZ..............218
Brazos Cliffs, NM..............157
Brigham City, AZ..............261
Broken Saddle, NM..............129
Brower, David..............88, 392
**Bryce Canyon National Park, UT
..............367–371**
Bryce Canyon National Park
..............368
Buckskin Gulch, UT..............365
Bullfrog, UT..............397
Bullhead City, AZ..............289
Burr Trail, UT..............388
buses..............29, 31
Butler Wash Ruins, UT..............430

C

Cabeza de Vaca, Alvar Núñez
..............464
Calf Creek Falls, UT..............381
camels..............247, 249
Cameron, AZ..............328
Camp Grant Massacre..............218
camping..............37
**Canyon de Chelly National
    Monument, AZ..............58–63**
Canyon de Chelly..............61
Canyon Lake, AZ..............216
Canyon Rims Recreation Area,
    UT..............427

CANYONLANDS NATIONAL PARK, UT **404–415**
Island in the Sky **406**
Needles, the **412**
 camping 404, 409, 415
 Chesler Park 414
 Confluence Overlook.................414
 fees and permits 404
 geology 405
 Grand View Point Overlook.........407
 Great Gallery.................................410
 Green River Overlook.................408
 Horseshoe Canyon 409
 Island in the Sky 406
 Maze, the.......................................411
 Mesa Arch Trail............................407
 Needles, the.................................412
 Upheaval Dome............................408
 White Rim Road............................408
Canyons of the Ancients
 National Monument, CO....... 73
Capitan, NM...............................178
Capitol Reef National Park, UT
384
Capitol Reef National Park
 .... **385**
Capulin Volcano National
 Monument, NM......................161
car rental.................................. 29
Carlsbad, NM...........................186
Carlsbad Caverns National Park,
 NM...188
Carrizozo, NM..........................178
Carson, Kit 149, 471
Casa Grande Ruins National
 Monument, AZ 219
Casa Malpais, AZ.....................258
cash 40
Castle Valley, UT 426
Cathedral Valley, UT................389
Cather, Willa............................113
Cedar Breaks National
 Monument, UT.......................347
Cedar City, UT 346
Cedar Crest, NM 129
ceramics..................................... 39
Cerbat, AZ.................................289
Cerrillos, NM............................128
Chaco Canyon, NM 91
Chama, NM...............................157
Chetro Ketl, NM........................ 93
chicken scratch.........................245
Chimayó, NM............................142
Chinle, AZ.................................. 63
Chiricahua National Monument,
 AZ..242
Chloride, AZ..............................289
Cimarron, NM...........................159
Clarkdale, AZ............................277
Claypool, AZ.............................217
Cliff Palace, CO......................... 78
climate chart.............................. 13

Cloudcroft, NM........................182
Cochise......................................483
Cochiti Pueblo, NM 124
Cockscomb, the, UT................375
Colorado City, AZ....................336
Colorado River Indian
 Reservation, AZ 249
Colter, Mary Jane 261, 299, 308
Columbus, NM.........................196
Comb Ridge, UT.......................430
condors......................................304
Coral Pink Sand Dunes State
 Park, UT....................................362
Coronado, Francisco Vásquez de
 .... 96, 237, 259, 465
Coronado National Memorial,
 AZ..237
Coronado State Monument, NM
125
Coronado Trail Scenic Road, AZ
259
Cortez, CO 72
Cosanti Foundation, AZ 210
costs and money 40
Cottonwood, AZ 276
Cottonwood Canyon Road, UT
375
Coyote Buttes, UT....................364
Coyote Gulch, UT.....................379
crafts.. 38
credit cards 40
crime and personal safety........ 40
Crow Canyon Archeological
 Center, CO 74
Crownpoint, NM 94
Cumbres & Toltec Scenic
 Railroad, NM 157
Cumbres Pass, NM...................158
cummings, e e 57
CVBs 43
cycling 31

D

Dance Hall Rock, UT 380
Datil, NM...................................191
Dead Horse Point State Park, UT
407
Death Carts...............................143
Delicate Arch, UT.....................418
Deming, NM 195
DeMotte Park, AZ.....................330
Deseret.......................................473
desert driving 30
desert survival 31
Devils Garden, UT....................378
dinosaur tracks.......................... 51

Dolores, CO............................... 73
Domínguez, Fray......................470
Douglas, AZ 241
drinking..................................... 35
drinking in Mormon Utah 345
driving 29
driving in the desert.................30
Dry Fork, UT..............................378
Dulce, NM.................................158
Durango, CO **80–83**
Durango 82
Durango & Silverton Railroad,
 CO.. 80

E

Eagar, AZ...................................258
Eagle Nest, NM 159
Earp, Wyatt...............................238
Edge of the Cedars State Park,
 UT..429
El Camino Real International
 Heritage Center, NM............191
El Malpais National Monument,
 NM... 98
El Morro National Monument,
 NM... 97
electricity................................... 41
Embudo, NM 142
Enchanted Circle, NM.............158
entry requirements for foreign
 travellers 41
Escalante, Fray..........................470
Escalante, UT............................376
Escalante Natural Bridge, UT
381
Escalante River, Upper, UT......380
Española, NM 140
Esteban................................96, 465
Eureka, CO................................. 83

F

Farmington, NM........................ 88
feast days, Pueblo 139
festivals 35
Fiery Furnace, UT 419
First Mesa, AZ........................... 68
Fisher Towers, UT 426
Flagstaff, AZ.................. **262–267**
Flagstaff, around 267
Flagstaff, downtown 263
Flagstaff and central Arizona
 .... **250–291**
Flagstaff and central Arizona
 .... **254**

flora and fauna 37
Florence, AZ 219
flying to the Southwest 27
food and drink 34
Ford, John 57
Fort Apache, AZ 259
Fort Apache Indian Reservation,
  AZ 259
Fort Bowie, AZ 243
Fort Selden State Monument,
  NM 193
Fort Sumner, NM 177
Four Corners, the 44–101
Four Corners, the 48–49
Four Corners Monument 70
Four Corners Power Plant, NM
  86
Fredonia, AZ 335
Frijoles Canyon, NM 132
Fruita, UT 387

G

Gadsden Purchase, the 470
Gallup, NM 94
Ganado, AZ 64
Garrett, Pat 177, 180
gay and lesbian travellers 41
Georgia O'Keeffe Museum,
  Santa Fe, NM 113
Geronimo 484
getting around 29
getting there 27
  from Australia, New Zealand and
    South Africa 28
  from North America 27
  from the UK and Ireland 27
Ghost Ranch, NM 141
giardia 32
Gila Bend, AZ 246
Gila Cliff Dwellings National
  Monument, NM 198
Glen Canyon, UT 392
Glen Canyon Dam, AZ 395
Glendale, UT 365
Globe, AZ 217
Glorieta Pass, NM 118
glossary 489
Gobernador Canyon, NM 90
Goblin Valley State Park, UT
  400
Golden, NM 129
Goldfield Ghost Town, AZ 216
Goosenecks State Park, UT 433
Goulding's Lodge, UT 58
Grafton, UT 348
Gran Quivira, NM 178
GRAND CANYON, THE
  292–337

Grand Canyon, the 297
**Central Canyon Overlooks and
  Trails 308**
Corridor Trails 313
Grand Canyon Village 303
North Rim 332
  admission fee 297
  backcountry camping 314
  Bright Angel Lodge 317
  Bright Angel Point 331
  Bright Angel Trail 310
  bus tours 300
  buses between the rims 334
  camping 314, 318, 334
  Cape Royal 332
  cycling 317
  Desert View 307
  Desert View Drive 305
  El Tovar Hotel 317
  flight-seeing tours 301
  geology 298
  getting around 316
  getting there 315
  Grand Canyon Field Institute 300
  Grand Canyon Lodge 334
  Grand Canyon Railway 315
  Grand Canyon Village 301
  Grand Canyon West 326
  Grandview Point 307
  Grandview Trail 314
  Havasupai Indian reservation, the
    320
  helicopters 301
  Hermit Road 304
  Hermit Trail 314
  Hermit's Rest 305
  hiking (North Rim) 333
  hiking (South Rim) 309
  hiking advice 310
  history 297
  Hopi Point 305
  horseriding 300
  Hualapai Indian reservation, the
    326
  information 316, 334
  Lava Falls Overlook 337
  Maricopa Point 305
  Mather Point 302
  mule rides (North Rim) 334
  mule rides (South Rim) 300
  North Kaibab Trail 333
  North Rim, the 331
  North Rim accommodation 334
  Phantom Ranch 312, 318
  Plateau Point 312
  Point Imperial 332
  Powell Point 305
  rafting 301
  Shoshone Point 306
  shuttle buses 316
  South Kaibab Trail 313
  South Rim, the 299
  South Rim accommodation 317
  South Rim buses 316
  South Rim camping 318
  South Rim eating and drinking
    319
  South Rim information 316

  South Rim tours 300
  sunset and sunrise 306
  Toroweap Overlook 337
  tours to Grand Canyon 315
  Transcanyon Shuttle 334
  Tusayan accommodation 318
  Tusayan Ruin 307
  Tuweep 337
  West Rim, the 326
  Yaki Point 306
  Yavapai Point 302
Grand Canyon West, AZ 326
Grand Gulch Primitive Area, UT
  432
Grand Staircase, the 335
**Grand Staircase-Escalante
  National Monument, UT
    .... 373–383**
**Grand Staircase-Escalante
  National Monument 374**
Grants, NM 98
Great Gallery, UT 410
great outdoors, the 36
Green River, the 402
Green River, UT 403
Greyhound 29, 31
Grosvenor Arch, UT 375

H

Hall's Crossing, UT 398
Hanksville, UT 400
Hano, AZ 68
Hatch, NM 193
Hatch, UT 366
Havasu Falls, AZ 324
Havasupai, the 322
**Havasupai Indian Reservation,
  AZ 320–326**
Havasupai Reservation 321
Hawikku, NM 97
health 31
Heard Museum, Phoenix, AZ
  208
Heart of Sinbad Road, UT 403
Hell's Backbone, UT 377
Henrieville, UT 376
Hickman Bridge, UT 390
High Road, the, NM 142
hiking trails, top five 37
Hillsboro, NM 192
history of the Southwest 459
Hite, UT 398
hogans 62
Hohokam, the 463
Holbrook, AZ 257
Hole-in-the-Rock, the, UT 380
Hole-in-the-Rock Road, UT 378
Hole N"The Rock, UT 427

holidays, public 42
Holliday, Doc 238
Homolovi Ruins State Park, AZ
....261
Hoover Dam, NV 457
Hopi, the 476
Hopi Cultural Center, AZ...........69
Hopi Indian reservation, AZ 66
Hopi Mesas, the, AZ 66
Horseshoe Bend, AZ.................395
Horseshoe Canyon, UT 409
hostels 34
hotels and motels 33
houseboats on Lake Powell...395
Hovenweep National
    Monument, UT 71
Hualapai Hilltop, AZ 320
Hualapai Indian Reservation,
    AZ.......................................326
Hubbard Museum of the
    American West, Ruidoso, NM
   181
Hubbell Trading Post, AZ.........64
Humphreys, Mount, AZ...........268
Hurricane, UT 347
Hyatt Regency Tamaya Resort &
    Spa, NM 135

I

Indian country, travelling in 38
Indian Market, Santa Fe 107
Indian Pueblo Cultural Center,
    Albuquerque, NM...............171
information...............................43
Inscription Rock, NM 97
insects.......................................32
insurance...................................41
internet access...........................41
Inter-Tribal Indian Ceremonial,
    Gallup NM 95
Iron Mission State Park, UT....346
Island in the Sky, UT 406
Island in the Sky, UT 406
Isleta Pueblo, NM....................173
itineraries.................................24

J

Jacob Lake, AZ..........................330
Jemez Pueblo, NM....................134
Jemez Springs, NM 134
Jemez State Monument, NM
   134
Jerome, AZ................................277
jewellery 39

Jicarilla Apache Indian
    Reservation, NM...................158
Jornada del Muerto, NM.........190
Joshua Forest Parkway, AZ.....284

K

kachinas 67
Kaiparowits Plateau, UT 376
Kanab, UT 362
Kartchner Caverns, AZ 235
Kasha-Katuwe Tent Rocks
    National Monument, NM....125
Kayenta, AZ................................54
Keet Seel, AZ..............................53
Kewa Pueblo, NM 125
Kingman, AZ..............................287
Kodachrome Basin State Park,
    UT.......................................372
Kokopelli....................................114
Kolob Canyons, UT...................361
Krazy Kat.....................................57
Kuaua, NM.................................126

L

La Bajada, NM 124
La Fonda, Santa Fe, NM...........120
La Posada, Winslow, AZ...........261
La Sal Mountains, UT...............426
Laguna Pueblo, NM 101
Lake Havasu City, AZ...............290
Lake Mead, NV.........................457
Lake Powell, UT 391
Lake Powell Ferry.....................397
Lamy, Archbishop Jean Baptiste
    ....113, 143
Lamy, NM..................................119
Largo Canyon, NM 90
Las Cruces, NM.........................193
Las Palomas, Mexico................196
Las Trampas, NM......................145
Las Vegas, NM..........................160
LAS VEGAS, NV 436–457
Las Vegas...................... 440
    accommodation...................448
    bars and lounges 454
    buffets.................................451
    clubs and music venues.........455
    Downtown............................447
    eating.................................451
    entertainment.....................455
    getting around 448
    history.................................441
    information..........................448
    Mob Museum, the................448
    Strip, the..............................442

weddings..........................442
Laughlin, NV.............................289
Lawrence, D H.........148, 150, 158
Lawrence Ranch, the, NM.......158
Le Fevre Overlook, AZ.............335
Lee, John D 329
Lees Ferry, AZ...........................329
lesbian and gay travellers 41
licensing laws in Utah.............345
Lincoln, NM...............................179
London Bridge, AZ....................290
Lonely Dell Ranch, AZ.............329
Long Walk, the..........................481
Lordsburg, NM..........................199
Los Alamos, NM........................130
Los Ojos, NM.............................157
Lost Dutchman Mine, AZ.........216
Lowell Observatory, Flagstaff,
    AZ.......................................262
Lowry Pueblo, CO.......................74

M

Madrid, NM...............................129
Magdalena, NM.........................191
mail..41
Mancos, CO.................................74
Manhattan Project, the 131
Manti-La Sal National Forest,
    UT.......................................426
maps..41
Marble Canyon, AZ...................329
Martinez, Maria........................137
Maverick Bridge, UT.................381
Maze, the, UT............................411
McCartys, NM............................100
Mesa, AZ...................................210
Mesa, eating.............................214
Mesa Arch Trail, UT..................407
Mesa Verde National Park,
    CO...............................74–80
Mesa Verde............................ 75
Mescalero Apache Indian
    reservation, NM...................182
Mesilla, NM...............................193
Meteor Crater, AZ.....................261
Mexican Hat, UT.......................435
Miami, AZ..................................217
Millicent Rogers Museum, Taos,
    NM.....................................150
Mimbres, the............................198
Mineral Park, AZ.......................289
Mishongnovi, AZ 69
Mission Trail, the, AZ 230
Moab, UT 421–425
Moab............................. 422
Moenkopi, AZ.............................51
Mogollon, the 198, 463

Mogollon Rim, AZ 258
Moki Dugway, UT 433
money...40
Montezuma Castle National
    Monument, AZ 280
Montezuma Valley, CO..............73
Monticello, UT...........................428
Monument Valley, AZ/UT 54
Monument Valley 56
Mooney Falls, AZ 325
Mormons 345, 473
mosquitoes.................................32
Mount Carmel Junction, UT
   362
mountain biking.........................424
Mountainair, NM.......................178
Mule Canyon, UT 430
mule rides, Grand Canyon.....300,
    334
Muley Point, UT.........................432
Museum of Northern Arizona,
    Flagstaff, AZ 262

N

Nageezi, NM 94
Nambé Pueblo, NM...................137
Narrows, the, UT.......................356
National Museum of Nuclear
    Science and History,
    Albuquerque, NM.................172
national park passes................. 36
national parks............................ 36
Native American crafts 38
Native Americans .... see names
    of individual tribes
Natural Bridges National
    Monument, UT 431
Navajo, the.................................480
Navajo Bridge, AZ.....................329
Navajo clans...............................482
Navajo fairs 50
Navajo Generating Station, AZ
   394
Navajo history............................480
Navajo Indian Reservation.......50
Navajo Mine, NM 86
Navajo Nation 50
Navajo Nation Museum and Zoo
    64
Navajo National Monument, AZ
    52
Navajo Rug Auction................... 94
Needles, the, UT.......................412
Needles, the, UT 412
Needles Overlook, UT.............427
New Mexico, northern....... 106
New Mexico, southern....... 166

New Mexico Museum of Space
    History, Alamogordo, NM...183
New Navajo Falls, AZ.................324
Newspaper Rock, AZ.................257
Newspaper Rock, UT 413
Nogales, AZ................................233
North Rim, Grand Canyon......331
Nothing, AZ................................284
Notom, UT..................................388

O

O'Keeffe, Georgia............ 113, 141,
    148, 152, 158
Oak Creek Canyon, AZ.............271
Oatman, AZ................................290
Ohkay Owingeh, NM...............141
OK Corral, AZ............................238
Oñate, Don Juan de..................466
O'odham, the.............................245
opening hours...........................42
Oppenheimer, J Robert...........131
Oracle, AZ..................................219
Oraibi, AZ.................................... 69
Orderville, UT............................365
Organ Pipe Cactus National
    Monument, AZ 245
Orilla Verde Recreation Area,
    NM.......................................142
Ouray, CO.................................. 84
outdoors 36

P

package tours
    from Australia, New Zealand and
        South Africa............................. 28
    from the UK and Ireland................. 29
Page, AZ.....................................393
Painted Desert, AZ...................252
Pajarito Plateau, NM 130
Palace of the Governors, Santa
    Fe, NM..................................110
Paleo Indians.............................459
Pancho Villa State Park, NM
   196
Panguitch, UT............................366
Paria Canyon, AZ.......................329
Paria Canyon, UT.......................365
Parker, AZ..................................249
parks, national......................... 36
passes, national park................ 36
Patagonia, AZ............................234
Patagonia-Sonoita Creek
    Sanctuary, AZ......................234
Paunsaugunt Plateau, UT 367

Payson, AZ..................................259
Peach Springs, AZ......................328
Pecos National Historical Park,
    NM.......................................118
Peek-A-Boo Gulch, UT..............379
Penitentes, the..........................143
**Petrified Forest National Park,
    AZ 252–257**
**Petrified Forest National Park
    .... 256**
Petroglyph National Monument,
    NM.......................................172
Phipps Arch, UT.........................381
PHOENIX, AZ................ 202–214
Phoenix, downtown 208
Phoenix, metropolitan 206
    accommodation..............................211
    arrival...211
    Arizona Science Center................207
    Central Phoenix............................205
    eating 212
    Heard Museum.............................208
    nightlife.......................................214
    Phoenix Art Museum....................208
**Phoenix and southern Arizona
    .... 200–249**
**Phoenix and southern Arizona
    .... 204**
phones 42
Picuris Pueblo, NM 145
Pilar, NM....................................142
Pima Air & Space Museum, AZ
   225
Pinos Altos, NM 197
Pipe Spring National Monument,
    AZ..336
Po'pay.............................. 141, 468
Poeh Museum, NM 137
poison oak 32
Pojoaque Pueblo, NM 136
Polacca, AZ................................ 68
polygamy....................................336
Potash Road, UT 426
pottery......................................39
Powell, John Wesley 392, 394,
    401, 403
Prescott, AZ 281
Prescott 282
Presley, Elvis...............................272
prices...40
public holidays...........................42
public lands............................... 37
public transport.........................29
Pueblitos of Dinétah, NM 90
Pueblo Bonito, NM...................92
Pueblo feast days 139
Pueblo Indians...........................464
Pueblo Revolt, the...................467
Pueblos, visiting........................138
**Pueblos and the High Road,
    the....................................... 136**

Pueblos of New Mexico, the 138
Puyé Cliff Dwellings, NM.........140

Q

Quarai, NM.................................178
Quartzsite, AZ............................248
Questa, NM.................................159
Quijotoa, AZ...............................245

R

Radium Springs, NM.................193
rafting...............301,403, 424, 434
Rail Runner, NM..............118, 173
rail services....................... 28, 31
railroads, historic
Cumbres and Toltec Scenic Railroad
....157
Durango & Silverton Railroad.......80
Grand Canyon Railway.................315
Santa Fe Scenic Railway...............119
Verde Canyon Railroad.................277
Rainbow Bridge National
Monument, AZ.......................396
Ralston, Aron.............................410
Ramsey Canyon Preserve, AZ
....237
Rancho de las Golondrinas,
NM...117
Ranchos de Taos, NM...............152
Raton, NM...................................161
Red Canyon, UT.........................366
Red Mountain Pass, CO.............84
Red River, NM............................159
Red Rock Canyon, NV..............457
Red Rock State Park, AZ..........274
Redford, Robert.........................145
rental cars.....................................29
Ridgway, CO..................................84
Río Grande del Norte National
Monument, NM......................142
Rio Grande Gorge Bridge, NM
....156
Rio Rancho, NM.........................126
Robbers Roost, UT.....................411
rock art.............. 12, 387, 402, 410,
411, 413
Rockville, UT..............................348
Roosevelt Dam, AZ....................216
Roswell, NM...............................185
Route 66..............................10, 24
Route 666.....................................88
rugs.......................................39, 94
Ruidoso, NM...............................181
RVs...30

S

Sagebrush Rebellion, the......376,
421
saguaro cactuses.......................226
Saguaro National Park, AZ.....225
St George, UT.............................344
sales tax...40
Salinas National Monument,
NM...178
Salmon Ruins, NM......................91
San Carlos, AZ............................218
San Carlos Indian Reservation,
AZ...218
San Felipe Pueblo, NM.............125
San Francisco de Asis, NM......152
San Francisco Peaks, AZ..........268
San Ildefonso Pueblo, NM......137
San Juan Pueblo, NM...............141
San Juan Skyway, CO.................83
San Rafael Desert, UT..............409
San Rafael Swell, UT.................401
San Xavier del Bac, AZ............230
Sand Canyon Pueblo, CO..........74
Sandia Crest, NM......................129
Sandia Mountains, NM............172
Sandia Pueblo, NM....................126
Santa Ana Pueblo, NM............135
Santa Clara Pueblo, NM..........140
Santa Domingo Pueblo, NM
....125
SANTA FE, NM...............104–124
Santa Fe area.......................... 108
Santa Fe, downtown........... 110
accommodation...............................120
airport..118
arrival and departure....................118
camping...121
Canyon Road.......................... 115, 123
eating...121
festivals and markets....................107
Georgia O'Keeffe Museum..........113
getting around................................119
getting to Santa Fe.........................118
Guadalupe District.........................115
hiking...119
history...107
horseback riding.............................119
Indian Market..................................107
information.......................................119
Loretto Chapel.................................114
Museum of Contemporary Native
Arts..113
Museum of Fine Arts.....................112
Museum of Indian Arts and Culture
....116
Museum of International Folk Art
....116
Museum of Spanish Colonial Art
....117
New Mexico History Museum.....112
nightlife and entertainment........123
opera..123
Palace of the Governors................110
plaza...109
Rail Runner.......................................118
Railyard..115
Rancho de las Golondrinas..........117
St Francis Cathedral.......................113
San Miguel Mission........................114
Santa Fe Scenic Railway...............119
Santa Fe ski area.............................118
Santuario de Guadalupe...............115
shopping...123
Spanish Market...............................107
Ten Thousand Waves.....................119
walking tours...................................119
Wheelwright Museum of the
American Indian.........................117
**Santa Fe and northern New
Mexico 102–161**
**Santa Fe and northern New
Mexico 106**
Santa Rosa, NM..........................176
Santuario de Chimayó, NM
....144
SCOTTSDALE, AZ................... 209
Scottsdale, central 210
accommodation...............................212
Cosanti Foundation........................210
Desert Botanical Garden..............210
eating...213
Taliesin West...................................209
Second Mesa, AZ.........................69
Sedona, AZ..................................271
Sedona................................. 272
Seligman, AZ..............................287
Sells, AZ......................................245
senior travellers..........................42
Seven Lakes, NM..........................94
Shakespeare, NM.......................199
Shakespeare Festival, Utah
....346
Shiprock, NM................................88
Show Low, AZ.............................259
Shungopavi, AZ............................69
Sichomovi, AZ..............................68
Sierra Vista, AZ..........................237
silver...39
Silver City, NM...........................196
Silverton, CO................................83
Sipapu, NM.................................145
Sipaulovi, AZ................................69
Ski Apache, NM.........................182
Skutumpah Road, UT...............374
Sky City, NM...............................100
Skywalk, the...............................326
Slickrock Bike Trail, UT...........424
Slide Rock State Park, AZ........271
slot canyons............... 11, 378, 394
Smith, Joseph.............................473
Smokey Bear...............................179
snakes...32
Snow Canyon State Park, UT
....345

Socorro, NM 191
Sonoita, AZ 234
South Rim, Grand Canyon 299
SOUTHERN UTAH 338–435
Southern Utah 342–343
southwest Colorado 70
space flights 192
Spaceport America, NM 192
Spanish invasion, the 464
spectator sports 42
Spence Hot Spring, NM 134
Spooky Gulch, UT 379
Springdale, UT 348
Springerville, AZ 258
Squaw Flats Scenic Byway, UT
....413
state tourist offices 43
Steen, Charlie 420
study and work programmes
....42
Sunset Crater National
   Monument, AZ 268
Supai, AZ 323
Superior, AZ 218
Superstition Mountains, AZ
....216

T

Taliesin West, AZ 209
Tamaya Resort & Spa, NM 135
TAOS, NM 146–156
Taos area 147
Taos, downtown 148
   accommodation 153
   balloon flights 153
   D. H. Lawrence Forbidden Art 150
   eating 154
   Ernest L. Blumenschein Home and
      Museum 150
   Fechin Home 149
   Governor Bent House and Museum
     149
   Hacienda Martinez 152
   Harwood Museum of Art 150
   information 153
   Kit Carson Home and Museum
     149
   Millicent Rogers Museum 150
   Rafting 153
   Ranchos de Taos 152
   San Francisco de Asis 152
   shopping 156
   Taos Art Museum 149
   Taos Pueblo 151
   Taos Ski Valley 153
   tours 153
tax 40
telephones 42
Telluride, CO 84
TEMPE, AZ 210

   accommodation 212
   eating 214
temperature chart 13
Tent Rocks National Monument,
   NM 125
Tesuque Pueblo, NM 136
Third Mesa, AZ 69
Thoreau, NM 94
Tierra Amarilla, NM 157
Tigüex, NM 126
Tijerina, Reies López 157
time zones 43
tipping 40
Titan Missile Museum, AZ 232
Tohono O'odham Indian
   Reservation, AZ 245
Tombstone, AZ 237–240
Tombstone 239
Tonto National Monument, AZ
....217
Tonto Natural Bridge, AZ 260
Toroweap, AZ 337
Torrey, UT 383
Tortilla Flat, AZ 216
tour operators in the UK and
   Ireland 29
tourist offices 43
Towaoc, CO 70
trading posts 11, 39, 64, 328
trains 28, 31
travel insurance 41
travellers with disabilities 43
travellers' cheques 40
travelling in Indian country 38
travelling with children 43
Trinity Site, NM 184
Tropic, UT 372
Truchas, NM 144
Truth or Consequences, NM
....192
Tsaile, AZ 63
Tsankawi, NM 133
Tuba City, AZ 51
Tubac, AZ 232
TUCSON, AZ 220–230
Tucson, downtown 223
Tucson, metropolitan 221
   accommodation 227
   arrival and departure 227
   Arizona–Sonora Desert Museum
     225
   Arizona State Museum 224
   Barrio Historico 223
   Downtown 222
   eating 228
   information 227
   Mount Lemmon 224
   Nightlife 229
   Pima Air & Space Museum ...225
   Sabino Canyon 224
   Saguaro National Park 225
   Tucson Museum of Art 223

University district, the 222
Tucumcari, NM 176
Tumacácori National Historical
   Park, AZ 233
turquoise 39, 169, 192
Turquoise Trail, NM 128
Tusayan, AZ 318
Tuweep, AZ 337
Tuzigoot National Monument,
   AZ 277

U

Utah, southern 342–343
Utah Shakespeare Festival 346
Ute Mountain Tribal Park, CO
....71

V

Valle Grande, NM 133
Valles Caldera National Preserve,
   NM 133
Valley of Fires Recreation Area,
   NM 178
Valley of the Gods, UT 434
Verde Canyon Railroad, AZ 277
Vermilion Cliffs, AZ 329
Very Large Array (VLA), NM
....191
Virgin, UT 347
visa waiver scheme 41
visas 41
visitor centres 43
Vulture Mine, AZ 284

W

Wahweap, AZ 396
Wallace, Lew 180
Walnut Canyon National
   Monument, AZ 270
Walpi, AZ 68
water 32
Wave, the, UT 364
Wayne, John 57, 84, 346
weaving 39
websites for the Southwest 43
when to go 10
White House, the, AZ 62
White Mountains, AZ 258
White Sands Missile Range
   Museum, NM 185

White Sands National
  Monument, NM......................184
White's City, NM 190
Whiteriver, AZ 259
Why, AZ 245
Wickenburg, AZ...........................283
wi-fi.. 41
Wildcat Trail, Monument Valley
 57
Willcox, AZ 244
Williams, AZ 285
Window Rock, AZ 64
Winslow, AZ..................................261
Wright, Frank Lloyd...................209
Wupatki National Monument,
  AZ..269

Y

Yavapai, the 322
Young, Brigham 473
Yuma, AZ 246

Z

Zia Pueblo, NM..........................135
Zion Canyon 350–360
Zion Canyon 352
ZION NATIONAL PARK, UT
  349–362

Zion National Park............. 350
  accommodation...................348, 360
  Angels Landing...............................355
  camping...360
  getting to Zion Canyon...............360
  hiking 354
  history 351
  information 351, 362
  Kolob Arch.......................................362
  Kolob Canyons...............................361
  Kolob Terrace Road 361
  Scenic Drive, the............................352
  shuttle buses 360
  visitor centre..................................351
  Zion Canyon 350
  Zion Narrows 356
Zuni Pueblo 95

Map symbols

The symbols below are used on maps throughout the book

⊠	Post office	⋏	Campsite	⋀⋀	Spring	✈	Airport
ⓘ	Tourist office	⌂	Ranger station	⋎⋎	Viewpoint/overlook	Ⓜ	Metro
Ⓟ	Parking	⌂	Lodge	⌃⌃	Mountains	•-•	Cable car
✚	Hospital/clinic	■	Pueblo	▲	Peak	⊞	Church
◆	General point of interest	⊠-⊠	Gate	⌇	Gorge/canyon/cliffs	▢	Building
⌣	Bridge/pass	⚲	Ski area	◗	Cave	▭	Park/monument
♣	Museum	≋	Rapids	∩	Arch	⊞	Cemetery
∴	Ruin	⚱	Waterfall	⛰	Butte	▧	Indian reservation

Listings key

- ■ Accommodation
- ● Eating
- ■ Drinking and Nightlife
- ● Shop

A ROUGH GUIDE TO
ROUGH GUIDES

Published in 1982, the first Rough Guide – to Greece – was a student scheme that became a publishing phenomenon. Mark Ellingham, a recent graduate in English from Bristol University, had been travelling in Greece the previous summer and couldn't find the right guidebook. With a small group of friends he wrote his own guide, combining a highly contemporary, journalistic style with a thoroughly practical approach to travellers' needs.

The immediate success of the book spawned a series that rapidly covered dozens of destinations. And, in addition to impecunious backpackers, Rough Guides soon acquired a much broader and older readership that relished the guides' wit and inquisitiveness as much as their enthusiastic, critical approach and value-for-money ethos.

These days, Rough Guides feature recommendations from shoestring to luxury and cover more than 200 destinations around the globe. Our ever-growing team of authors and photographers is spread all over the world, particularly in Europe, the US and Australia.

Rough Guides now number around 200 titles, including Pocket city guides, inspirational coffee-table books and comprehensive country and regional titles, plus technology guides from iPods to Android. As well as print books, we publish groundbreaking apps and eBooks for every major digital device.

Visit ⓦ roughguides.com to see our latest publications.

Rough Guide travel images are available for commercial licensing at ⓦ roughguidespictures.com.

ROUGH
GUIDES

SO NOW WE'VE TOLD YOU
HOW TO MAKE THE MOST
OF YOUR TIME, WE WANT
YOU TO STAY SAFE AND
COVERED WITH OUR
FAVOURITE TRAVEL INSURER

WorldNomads.com
keep travelling safely

GET AN ONLINE QUOTE
roughguides.com/travel-insurance

MAKE THE MOST OF YOUR TIME ON EARTH™